1 : 30

SFFO
Engine 12

MARKETING RESEARCH

David J. Luck

Southern Illinois University

Hugh G. Wales

Louisiana Tech University
University of Illinois
(Emeritus)

Donald A. Taylor

Michigan State University

Ronald S. Rubin

University of Central Florida

Marketing Research

FIFTH EDITION

PRENTICE-HALL, INC., ENGLEWOOD CLIFFS, NEW JERSEY 07632

Library of Congress Cataloging in Publication Data

Main entry under title:
Marketing research.

    Second-4th ed. by D. J. Luck, H. G. Wales, and D. A.
Taylor.
    Bibliography: p.
    Includes index.
    1. Marketing research.   I. Luck, David Johnston.
Marketing research.
HF5415.2.L8–1978   658.8′3   77-17170
ISBN   0-13-557637-7

Marketing Research, *Fifth Edition*
Luck, Wales, Taylor, and Rubin

Printed in the United States of America

10 9 8 7 6 5 4 3 2

PRENTICE-HALL INTERNATIONAL, INC., *London*
PRENTICE-HALL OF AUSTRALIA PTY. LIMITED, *Sydney*
PRENTICE-HALL OF CANADA, LTD., *Toronto*
PRENTICE-HALL OF INDIA PRIVATE LIMITED, *New Delhi*
PRENTICE-HALL OF JAPAN, INC., *Tokyo*
PRENTICE-HALL OF SOUTHEAST ASIA PTE. LTD., *Singapore*
WHITEHALL BOOKS LIMITED, *Wellington, New Zealand*

Dedicated to: Adele K. Luck
Mary F. Wales
Shirley M. Taylor
Cynthia B. Rubin

Contents

vii

viii

ix

Epilogue   484

Appendixes   493

Selected Bibliography   503

Name Index   509

Subject Index   513

Preface

When a book has passed its quarter-century milestone, its authors must feel grateful to the many friends and adopters who have made that possible. These emotions are mixed with those of anticipation as a fifth edition enters the marketplace with new features that may add to the book's effectiveness and attractiveness. We earnestly hope that we have retained those features that have contributed to its popularity while also introducing new ones that remedy its past shortcomings.

Our basic policy is unchanged: to offer an intelligible and accurate learning instrument that contributes to students' preparation for the actual world of marketing. We stress contemporary and useful concepts from the field of application and seek to avoid the esoteric and novel developments that have little or no application—although they may create an aura of rigor and mystique. Our aim is clear communication rather than to present unnecessary difficulties to the reader.

Again we wish to accommodate the predominant technique of students experiencing research by conducting projects. After orientation in the first chapter we now proceed directly into the research and problem-solving process, and so a class project can begin to "grow" by the second week of a term. Our unfolding of the research process is intended to parallel the evolving of an actual class project. We still accommodate, however, those who wish to utilize a case teaching approach wholly or to blend this with projects (which we prefer). Selected cases both fortify understanding of a particular subject and broaden appreciation of the variety of research situations beyond the confines of one actual project.

You will find numerous new features herein. We have expanded the quantitative aspects, particularly with an additional chapter on analytical methods and some new treatment of all methods. Sampling has been reorganized in format and enhanced with new examples. Skill in written expression, so demanded in the business world and lacking among students, is treated with expanded material on report preparation and an innovative section on writing research proposals. We now devote an entire chapter to research designs, to which is added simulations. Preparatory phases in problem identification and resolution and the interface between decision-makers and researchers has new and extended treatment. Project evaluation and scheduling are other early phases on which we have new and (we hope) practical material. Nor have we neglected cases. Although more than half the cases are new ones, many of the popular cases from past editions have been logically retained.

Two application chapters, which rarely could be squeezed into a course, are deleted, but that on market analysis and forecasting is retained. These subjects are universal among all enterprises and also afford student projects that can be accomplished with library data.

Teachers are entitled to a full explanation of the objectives and intended usage of each phase of the book. Such detail would be inappropriate here but is set forth in the Teacher's Manual together with various teaching aids. It is indispensible for administering the cases.

We are indebted to many fellow teachers and students, many times the number that we can mention. Professors who contributed greatly as reviewers are Odies C. Ferrell and Jim L. Grim of Illinois State University, Richard A. Hamilton of the University of Missouri at Kansas City, Milton M. Pressley of the University of North Carolina at Greensboro, Ronald E. Frank of the University of Pennsylvania, and Fred S. Zufryden of the University of Southern California. Among colleagues on our own faculties we must mention James Benjamin and Henry Siegle of Southern Illinois University and Donald F. Fuller of Florida Technological University.

From the practical world of marketing research and business, we particularly thank Raymond Suh of the Coca-Cola Company, Norman Krandall of the Ford Motor Company, Robert Lavidge of Elrick & Lavidge, Thomas E. Hatch of Miles Laboratories, and David Hardin of Market Facts. Some of the material that appears on page 415 is used with permission of Minnesota Mining and Manufacturing Company.

Much credit should be given to various persons at Prentice-Hall including thanks to the whole field force of the college division. We would single out Judith L. Rothman, the marketing editor, for invaluable assistance at every turn, and Ann Marie McCarthy, our production editor. And also we have depended on Delores Kohler, Rebecca Swengrosh, Joyce Waring, and Martha Tyler for secretarial assistance.

May our adopters and readers find this a satisfactory volume. Still there are bound to be faults and errors, so suggestions are cordially invited.

DAVID J. LUCK   DONALD A. TAYLOR
HUGH G. WALES   RONALD S. RUBIN

To The Student

It is fitting to write a message particularly to you because our book is intended primarily for students. It tells you what we basically designed the book to do, which should facilitate your use of it.

Two qualities have been foremost in our desires for this book. One is practicality, which makes it suitable to be put into practice. Beginning with the second chapter, we lead you through the successive phases of a marketing research project and present to you at each stage the alternative methods from which you might choose. This progression is highlighted with tables that display the questions faced and steps to take as a project is carried out. Further, you are directed to the key subjects in each chapter by means of the main questions that are addressed in it. If you utilize these learning aids that precede each phase of discussion, you will keep oriented to the thread of development and interrelate the various phases as parts of a single project.

The other chief desire has been one of realism. Your authors have enjoyed wide and continuous experience in applied marketing research, so these writings incorporate what is actual and feasible in current applications. Therefore, we not only describe examples of each concept or technique but also utilize actual events as illustrations. Realism is also found in the cases, as is obvious among those for which the research sponsor or agency has been willing to let us use its actual name. If your teacher does not assign cases, for which time may be lacking, may we suggest that you read them anyway in order to learn more about the variety of applications and problems in the real world.

Earlier editions of this book have been used by many teachers, and their suggestions have led to important improvements in readability and content. Some ideas have come directly from students, and if you have some, will you kindly write to one of us? We earnestly hope that you find practical information in this book and that, when your course is over, you will wish to keep it for your future library.

DAVID J. LUCK   DONALD A. TAYLOR
HUGH G. WALES   RONALD S. RUBIN

MARKETING RESEARCH

PART **One**

AS THIS BOOK'S TITLE implies, it is concerned primarily with marketing research techniques. Pure technicians rarely succeed in worldly affairs, though, when they lack understanding of the environment in which they operate, especially its human aspects. Since your interests are probably those of a practical doer or user, you will be most interested in the position of this research field within the economic and human environment. Here is that foundation, on which we will later build an understanding of the techniques and decisions of marketing researchers.

The plan of Part I may be described by analogy with a camera. First we stand distant from our subject and picture it within the broad view of science. Then we focus more closely and bring out the general details: the nature of the field, the problems to which it is applied, and an orientation to organizations and their management systems. Next, we zoom in for more detailed shots, of which the first brings you into the picture so that you can see how the field relates to you. Then we take individual pictures of the decision maker who uses its services, and of the researcher, who offers them. Finally, we bring all the views together so that we can examine their relationships and the joint decisions that underlie the management of effective marketing research.

1 Science and Its Marketing Applications

Chapter 1 opens with the broadest viewpoint, of science, and concludes with the specific viewpoint of a student reader. Some major questions that it addresses are these:

What is marketing research, not only abstractly but also in terms of the particular things it does?

Is it really a science? And what would qualify it as a science?

How are businesses and other organizations actually using it?

How has it grown — in speed and magnitude?

Is marketing research important to me? In what concrete ways?

What lies ahead in this book?

WE BEGIN, as a textbook should, by reaching some basic understandings. First there is the matter of agreeing on a definition of our major subject. Then we are going to consider the nature of science and how that affects marketing research. Then we shall deal with the essential function of this field, after which it will be described more fully. To this foundation is added a preview of the book's content, with the rationale for its sequencing.

1.1 Nature of Marketing Research

When you refer to a dictionary to determine what constitutes "research," you may find a statement that it is a study or investigation in a field of knowledge that is "careful, systematic, patient. . . ." Those three adjectives are significant, and one is included in the American Marketing Association's official definition of marketing research:

 The systematic gathering, recording, and analyzing of data about problems relating to the marketing of goods and services.[1]

That is a useful statement, but two comments are needed:

1. The functions of marketing research go beyond "gathering, recording, and analyzing of data" in ways that will become apparent as we proceed.
2. The full scope of "marketing" might suggest that some types of research are included in marketing research which are not. We refer particularly to some aspects of physical distribution, which normally is defined within marketing. In the large field of transportation, as a prime example, there are many engineering problems whose research calls for physical or engineering scientists. Marketing research is a different sort of specialization, not qualified to solve such problems but rather those connected with the marketplace.

Examples can make the meaning of marketing research concrete. As a starter, we list below nine groups of questions addressed in various research projects conducted by one research agency during 1975.[2]

1. What size cars will people buy in 1980? How will car owners satisfy their needs for space and their concern for economy?
2. Is the growth of Citizens' Band radio sales a trend or a fad? Is it a speed-limit device limited to truck drivers? Or a new party-line trend? Or a major growth industry?

---

[1] Committee on Definitions, *Marketing Definitions, A Glossary of Marketing Terms* (Chicago: American Marketing Association, 1960), p. 17.
[2] *1975 Annual Report of Market Facts, Inc.* (Chicago: Market Facts, Inc., 1976), pp. 3–4.

4

3. How can we have a better Army? Navy? Air Force? What can the current services do to improve the competence and commitment of the persons who are likely to enlist?
4. How much need is there for safer consumer appliances?
5. How does a national fast-food chain expand its share of the market?
6. Where should a company spend its advertising dollars?
7. Should a food company change its trade figure, one that the company has been using as its spokesman for a number of years?
8. Should a drug company pay attention to dentists? Are dentists becoming important drug prescribers in areas such as antibiotics and tranquilizers?
9. What do city planners have to do to get people to use their buses? And their subways? And NOT their cars?

In these examples, note that each study was problem-oriented, to answer a specific decision faced by an organization. This, then, is *applied* research. Another realm is *basic* research, which is devoted to uncovering facts and principles for fundamental learning rather than to solve any particular problem. Without basic research there could not be fruitful applied research, but we emphasize marketing research practice, the applied realm. Although our discussion is so oriented, the described techniques would be applicable to basic studies.

Notice also that two examples were for nonbusiness sponsors (the Armed Forces and urban planners), which signifies that marketing research should not be considered as solely a "business" activity, as it serves other kinds of organizations. Another characteristic of each of these studies was its aim to *predict* something lying in the future. Prediction is inherent in all problem-solving studies, and that brings us to the next subject.

1.2 Science in a Disorderly Environment

Some of the fields of knowledge, or disciplines, are true sciences. Many others are ambitious to become scientific but still have little of that quality, and one is marketing. Some questions about science need to be examined, if we are to understand what marketing research is all about. This section deals with the following questions.

1. What are the characteristics and benefits of a science?
2. What are the obstacles to marketing becoming a science?
3. Why is creating a science so important?
4. In that endeavor, what is the place of marketing research? And what scientific qualities are needed in that research?

A relatively few sciences are, like physics, *exact* sciences. These are characterized by the possibility of making precise statements which are susceptible of some sort of check or proof. . . . (They) are in general characterized by the possibility of exact measurement.[3]

Those sciences also have a suitable method of describing their subject matter, which, as expressed by the source just quoted, "must be capable of responding or recalling the subject matter with precision and uniqueness." When a new problem arises—or in dealing with the frontiers of knowledge—a physicist is armed with such a precise classification scheme and methods of exact measurement. This scientist thus can check a speculation about how things may work by making repeated measurements. And if these lead to uniform results, this confirms the speculations to be dependable principles on which the world may rely and make confident predictions. This can happen, though, only in an orderly environment on whose regularity we can depend.

Sciences are not always infallible, as we all know from weather forecasts. Meteorology is a science, but its experts face vagaries in the atmosphere, which is somewhat a "disorderly environment." If the weather forecaster knew exactly what conditions would prevail during the period being forecasted, the predictions could be very accurate.

A decision maker in marketing would envy the meteorologists for achieving such a high and growing percentage of accurate weather prognostications. Marketing executives and most people responsible for managing some phase of human affairs face a much more disorderly environment. Their decision tasks are more difficult than weather forecasting because they need to foretell not only (1) what the environment is going to be during a future period, but also (2) which of the alternative actions available will have the best effect in terms of the objectives sought.

There is a distant hope for the marketing executive that there may be created a true *marketing science*, which was well defined in this way:

A classified and systematized body of knowledge, organized around one or more central theories and a number of general principles . . . usually expressible in quantitative terms . . . which permits the prediction (and under some circumstances, the control) of future events . . . as applied in the planning and direction of marketing.[4]

To have such ability to predict and control is indeed a great vision for management, but very serious obstacles in the nature of marketing must be contended with:

○ The *intangibility* of human and economic forces involved, rendering measurement difficult and inexact.

---

[3] *McGraw-Hill Encyclopedia of Science and Technology*, Vol. 12 (New York: McGraw-Hill, Inc., 1971), p. 102.

[4] Robert D. Buzzell, "Is Marketing a Science?" *Harvard Business Review*, January/February, 1963, pp. 32–40, 166–170.

②The *dynamics* of markets and marketing forces that may obsolete yesterday's measurements before they are applied tomorrow.

③The *diffusion* and *heterogeneity* of marketing and of buyers, which makes measurement costly and classification difficult.

④The *immaturity* of marketing as a field of scientific study, whose theorems and implements are yet inadequate for the challenge.

All that is compounded by today's typical marketing manager being poorly trained or informed in decision and forecasting methods, too little aware of the tools of science, and too accustomed to making intuitive or crude decisions.

Perhaps an example would serve to explain what the marketing executive faces.

> One of the successful liquor distilling firms is the Brown & Foreman Company. They closely watch changing demands for liquor and observed several years ago that there was a drift toward light whiskeys (in contrast with a heavy whiskey like bourbon). To serve this apparent demand, they developed a new whiskey that was so light that it was almost colorless. They gave it the brand name "Frost 8/80."

> Brown & Foreman also made consumer studies to discover how typical drinkers would react to the new product. Responses were quite favorable, although what they measured was hardly the same thing as actually buying their brand. It seemed important to beat competition, so the product was rapidly launched on the market. Sales results were only a fraction of what was expected or needed to earn a profit, and a product failure ensued.[5]

Why did Frost 8/80 fail? We do not know this, but dissecting the decision that Brown & Foreman had to make reveals a number of aspects in which they may have erred. One was in their interpretation of what whiskey buyers really wanted — or in their forecast of whether such a trend would continue and offer an ample demand. Various other forecasts concerned the specific formulation of the new whiskey, its brand name, its label, how it was advertised and priced, or other factors in the Frost 8/80 marketing mix. Brown & Foreman unavoidably faced a number of risky decisions, in this as in many other situations confronted in their marketing. Fortunately, they have more often made right than wrong decisions, leading to their prosperity. As they are locked into a continuous competitive struggle with other distillers, though, there is a great urgency to lessen risks and to make more decisions correctly.

How can this be accomplished? Partly, as is later explained, through timely problem recognition and accurately defining what is to be decided. Equally important is having adequate knowledge on which to base the decisions, which can sharply reduce risks. The latter is the major purpose of marketing research: *risk reduction.* More deliberate and thorough research might have prevented the costly mistake in Frost 8/80, for

---

[5] Based on Frederick C. Klein, "How a New Product Was Brought to Market Only to Flop Miserably," *Wall Street Journal,* January 5, 1973, pp. 1,11.

example, either through indications that the product ought not to be placed on the market or through better guidance in planning marketing.

Another vital benefit from marketing research, which is more positive, is that of *opportunity discovery*. Opportunities found in new tastes or needs of buyers, in changing marketing channels, or in more effective marketing technology are suggestive of what may be learned through communication and interpretation of market behavior and developments.

Another example, in which there was ample use of marketing research, was in the launching of L'Eggs hosiery by the Hanes organization. Some impression of the scope and sharpness of their studies underlying the L'Eggs venture is given by this quotation:

> Initially L'Eggs spent $400,000 on market research. The company found that women were not especially impressed by strong price promotion of hosiery in supermarkets, and were often disgusted by poor hosiery quality. One pair would sag and bag, while another pair would fit too tightly for comfort."[6]

Taking advantage of this knowledge, Hanes created a new type of hosiery that overcame these consumer problems and also an innovative distribution system and effective advertising. The results are now history: the most dramatic success in the hosiery industry, a new brand and product that swiftly conquered over 35 percent of the market in food and drug stores. Thus marketing research can pay off enormously.

If marketing research is to provide correct guidance, obviously the research itself must be conducted by methods that will yield correct evidence and answers. That is, the research must employ *scientific methods*. With what criteria can we judge whether or not research is scientific? There are these five that characterize acceptable research in the exact sciences:

1. The research should be an orderly investigation of a defined problem.
2. Adequate and representative evidence should be gathered and should be given exact and correct measurement.
3. Logical reasoning, uncolored with bias, should be used in placing meaning on the evidence and then drawing conclusions relevant to the problem.
4. The researcher should be able to demonstrate or prove the validity of the findings through repeated or replicated investigation.
5. To be scientifically fruitful, the accumulated results of research in a given area should lead to finding principles that may be applied confidently in the future, under similar circumstances.

In summary, these criteria call for research to be (1) systematic, (2) impartial, and (3) reproducible.

Unfortunately, marketing research can rarely fulfill all these criteria,

---

[6] "How to Keep Your Market in Motion," *Textile World*, May, 1974, p. 179.

primarily for the same reasons as those we listed above as obstacles to creating a true marketing science. Again, this is a problem that will be explained as we go along, but it is important that researchers attempt to achieve the scientific criteria, in their methods, as well as they practically can. At a minimum, marketing research should be systematic and impartial. The fourth and fifth criteria stated above are typically more of a hope than an actuality, but there is some progress.

1.3 Applications of Marketing Research

In this disorderly world of marketing, in which research may provide more orderliness and guidance, there are abundant problems. As our attention is to be concentrated on facilitating action-oriented decisions, we are going to emphasize research methods best suited to applied research, not basic (as earlier distinguished). And our discussion will be structured in terms of various techniques—without attempting to relate them to the particular problem areas in which they are most applicable. Therefore, you should comprehend these application areas for two reasons: (1) when we discuss the various research techniques, you can consider the particular types of marketing problems in which they would be appropriate, and (2) you will recognize our discussion's relation to the practical world and to problems that you are likely to encounter.

The classification scheme of marketing research applications used below is that of the American Marketing Association. This enables us to relate the applications to data on their usage that will be shown in Figure 1–1, but we have added another category for nonbusiness applications. Some actual studies are given as examples of each category, and most of them were conducted by one marketing research service.[7]

1. *Sales and market research*. Studies in this classification are mainly to identify markets, determine buyer behavior and attitudes, measure market potentials, analyze sales data and a firm's market share, and to study various problems in connection with selling activities and distribution channels.
    a. Definition of teenage market for medicated complexion products, including usage, brand preferences, and switching patterns.
    b. Air travel habits and information about persons flying from Philadelphia International Airport.
    c. Market for variable-speed centrifugal pumps in the food-processing industry.
    d. Determine student reasons for selecting a certain correspondence school.
    e. Analysis of sales territories, compensation of salesman, and forecasts for a jewelry manufacturer.

---

[7] *Types of Studies Conducted by Chilton Research Services* (Marketing Release No. 808) (Radnor, Pa.: Chilton Research Services undated).

f. Determine retailers' experience in selling certain brands of toys.
g. Determine location feasibility of a new branch bank.

2. *Business economics and corporate research.* Under this heading are the vital studies of business trends and their projection as both short- and long-range forecasts, company-wide planning of product mix and diversification, and other problems normally the responsibility of the corporate staff.
   a. Usage and future plans for nuclear power generation.
   b. Evaluation of alternative investment opportunities for a broadcasting company that is accumulating profits but is barred from further mergers in the broadcasting fields.
   c. Image and awareness of an engineering company among executives in the top 500 companies.
   d. Attitude of stockholders toward a specific company.
   e. Ideal location for egg-processing plants of the leading regional egg producers' cooperative.

3. *Product research.* This encompasses all research that deals with products and their packaging relative to improving that is presently offered and to planning and developing new products and services.
   a. Consumer brand purchase history and quality opinions of competing brands of food wrapping.
   b. Usage of moisture-barrier compounds on packages of crackers, potato chips, and snacks.
   c. Attitudes and opinions of consumers toward various types of beer containers and tops.
   d. Testing the sales volume and acceptance of a new cooking oil made of sunflower oil, in the St. Louis and Dallas–Fort Worth markets, to decide whether to market nationally.
   e. Estimating the sales volume and profitability of a new decongestant, annually for its first five years on the market, if introduced on a national basis next October.

4. *Advertising research.* This covers studies dealing with the selection of advertising themes, creation of copy and commercials, and planning media and expenditures.
   a. Recall of recruitment advertising in a campus newspaper.
   b. Learning how dentists interpret a new advertising phrase that a competing company is using as one of its main product claims.
   c. Readership of selected news publications by top management in business and industry.
   d. Determining which, among several TV advertising jingles under consideration, would create the most favorable response for a popular cola beverage.
   e. Attitudes and opinions of visitors to a metals exhibit.

5. *Corporate responsibility research.* This includes studies made of subjects outside the commercial aspects of marketing of goods and services. It deals with business firms' responsibilities to other publics, often with matters outside marketing, yet appropriate for marketing researchers' special competencies.
   a. Determine public knowledge about the "Truth-in-Lending" Law as well as interest in credit and borrowing practices.

b. Consumer demand, knowledge, and misunderstanding of U.S. Grades for selected food products.

c. Test the adequacy of insurance rating schedules for consumer buyers.

d. On-the-street observation of seat-belt usage with telephone interview follow-up.

e. Public's image and knowledge of an electric power company's ecological program.

6. *Nonbusiness research*. This covers the many sorts of problems faced by government, social, political, and other organizations that are of marketing natures or best served with marketing research techniques.

a. Measure the impact of policewomen on a metropolitan police department.

b. Determine possible mail usage under various-priced postal plans.

c. Determine opinions and attitudes toward the United Fund, together with reasons for giving.

d. Public preference for future individual transportation in the United States, to guide highway and urban mass-transit planning.

e. Measure popularity of various political figures, in light of their potential candidacy for certain offices.

Those brief topical descriptions may make marketing research projects sound much simpler than the reality. Frequently, they have sophisticated designs and typically deal with a complex of subjects.

Our listing omits the many purely *descriptive* marketing studies that are made, not to serve a particular decision, but to obtain information for possible future uses. The greatest example is the U.S. Census. Its original enumeration of population was applied to serve decisions in allocating votes in the Electoral College and seats in the House of Representatives. However, the vast array of data now collected by the Bureau of the Census is not oriented toward a particular purpose. On the contrary, it creates a wealth of facts useful for many people and organizations in a variety of decisions that will arise in the future. Similarly, many data gathered within organizations and by outside agencies are purely descriptive, to chart changing conditions or to be available when problems arise.

Now we are going to portray the subjects of commercial marketing research in terms of their frequency. The American Marketing Association has conducted a survey of research practice at five-year intervals beginning in 1958. Its most recent information regarding the proportions of firms that do each type of research is presented in Table 1-1.

The "all reporting companies" column of Table 1-1 includes retailers, advertising agencies, and publications, which are not comparable with producers of goods and services, and so we show the latter separately in the two right-hand columns. The greatest activity is found in studying markets and sales performance, in several ways. However, forecasting and product research are nearly as prevalent. Nearly all the listed re-

TABLE 1-1. Research Activities of Companies in 1973.

Subject of Studies	Percentage of Reporting Companies Doing Easy Type of Research		
	All Reporting Companies	Consumer Product Companies	Industrial Product Companies
1. Sales and market research			
Market potential measurement	68	79	75
Market characteristics	68	78	74
Market-share analysis	68	80	75
Sales analysis	65	80	75
Establishing sales quotas and territories	57	79	73
Distribution-channel studies	48	71	67
Sales-compensation studies	45	66	64
Promotional studies	39	64	31
Test markets, sales audits	38	73	33
2. Business economics and corporate research			
Short-range forecasting	63	77	75
Long-range forecasting (over one year)	61	76	73
Business-trends analysis	61	69	73
Pricing studies	56	70	68
Acquisition studies	53	67	69
Product-mix studies	51	66	65
Plant and warehouse location	47	66	63
3. Product research			
Competitive product studies	64	79	73
New product acceptance and potential	63	79	73
Testing existing products	57	77	68
Packaging research	44	67	53
4. Advertising research			
Ad-effectiveness studies	49	64	47
Media research	44	51	43
Copy research	37	54	32
Motivation research	33	53	24
5. Corporate responsibility research			
Legal constraints on advertising and promotion studies	38	52	42
Ecological-impact studies	27	35	34
Social values and policies	25	29	24
Consumers' "right-to-know" studies	18	30	14

Data reported by 1,322 companies to the American Marketing Association.

Source: Adapted from Dik W. Twedt (ed.), 1973 Survey of Marketing Research (Chicago: American Marketing Association, 1973), pp. 41, 43.

search subjects are rather prevalent, with more than half of the companies doing them. (We deleted the less-frequent categories in the American Marketing Association study.) Several categories under "corporate responsibility research" are listed so that you may see the breadth of modern application.

We have found some interesting changes from the comparable data reported in the AMA survey of five years earlier. There is no change in the ranking of the four top items under "sales and market research" but considerable change in other categories. The 1973 survey shows the most extensive frequency gains in diversification studies and forecasting and business-trends analyses. Product research has moved moderately closer to the top subjects, and advertising research had gained slightly in frequency. Another large increase is in the corporate responsibility category, which was not even listed in 1968 and seems to reflect a great change in the business climate and related need for marketing research assistance on these new key decisions.

1.4 Development of Marketing Research

Your background will be completed with a sketch of how marketing research evolved historically and its situation today. We shall also briefly sketch the composition of this field.

There is no written record of the beginning of marketing research, but it evidently was of modern origin. In the Middle Ages, it is said, "the merchant families of Fugger and Rothschild prospered in part because their far-flung organizations enabled them to get information before their competitors did."[8] These were only loose intelligence networks rather than systematic research. Nor were marketers any better served by research, apparently, until the present century. Organized marketing research seems to have been pioneered by Charles C. Parlin, who started a marketing research department around 1910 in the Curtis Publishing Company, then the world's largest. His novel idea was that advertising space could be sold more effectively by presenting organized market data to prospective advertising buyers.

Nevertheless, development was very slow, with only a few firms having marketing research specialists, until 1929. Two signal events then took place: the first Census of Distribution and the first extension distribution studies, conducted by the U.S. Department of Commerce. Then followed the shock of the Great Depression, when many businessmen became aware of marketing's enormous wastes and their great shortage of information about these problems.

Since that awakening, this research field has grown quite fast. Figure 1–1 charts this growth in terms of the number of new marketing research departments founded during five-year intervals since 1918. After moderate growth during the 1930s depression, it started sharp growth

[8] L. C. Lockley, "Notes on the History of Marketing Research," *Journal of Marketing*, April, 1950, p. 733.

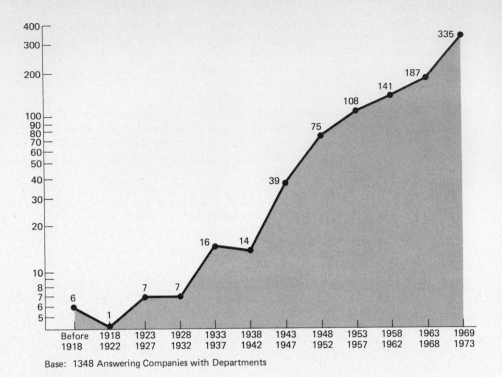

FIGURE 1–1. Number of New Marketing Research Departments Formed in Successive Five-Year Periods

Data are not cumulative.

Source: Dik W. Twedt (ed.), 1973 Survey of Marketing Research *(Chicago: American Marketing Association, 1973), p. 21.*

after World War II. A consistent rate of increase was sustained, around 7 percent per year, until 1968. Then the addition of more marketing research departments spurted again at a 16 percent rate during the five years to 1973. By this measure, the field of marketing research should be considered to be "a growth industry."

This evidence of rapid expansion is paralled by other indicators. The sales of the A. C. Nielsen Company, largest of marketing research services, grew during the five years ending in 1976 by 105 percent—more than doubling. The number of firms listed under "Marketing Research and Analysis" in the Manhattan (New York City) classified telephone directory reached 327 in 1976, an indication of the large size of this industry. Meanwhile, the membership of the American Marketing Association, which is composed primarily of marketing research professionals, passed 14,000 in 1976, another impressive magnitude.

This continued growth has been taking place despite a period of serious recession at the time of writing. The reason for this growth during economic adversity clearly is this: marketing research pays off. Here is a bit of testimony on its value, significant enough that an outstanding life insurance company quoted it in its annual message to policyholders:

One reason why our advertising results have been so good since 1972 is because of our unusually strong dedication to research. Every advertising move we have made has been based on research with policyowners and prospects. We discuss with consumers their needs, their satisfactions, their dissatisfactions, their perceptions of life insurance and their perceptions of us.[9]

While speaking of the field or industry of marketing research, it is logical to tell you something about its makeup. It is a complex field, and so only the major groupings of firms or agencies will be described here. In Chapter 2 we shall begin to explain relationships between these groups.

1. *Users.* Here we place those who primarily use research findings in making decisions, setting policies, evaluating performance, and the like. They usually do some stages of studies or complete studies, but they have much work done by outside agencies. Corporations comprise most of this category, but nonbusiness users are of growing frequency.

2. *Users and doers.* These are firms that exist primarily to serve other firms with services, and they perform marketing research that—either directly or indirectly—is relayed on to their clients. Additionally, however, these firms utilize their own research and have substantial dependence on outside agencies to perform research or supply data to them. Advertising agencies and media and consulting firms are in this classification. Governmental agencies, when viewed in the aggregate, also are placed here.

3. *Doers.* Here we place firms and other organizations that perform marketing research primarily for others (who fall in the two above categories). In the main, they generate data or conduct studies for others and only incidentally depend on outside sources. Here are the research firms and data services. Also, university and foundation research is obviously intended wholly as a service to others.

4. *Specialized services.* A number of firms and agencies are specialized in certain functions, wherewith they enable others to conduct marketing research. Their availability to conduct certain stages is vital to those in the first three categories. Firms specializing in interviewing and in data-processing services are the most numerous types.

This completes your introduction to the subject and field of marketing research, but more is needed to introduce you to this book.

1.5 Relevance of Marketing Research

You logically may inquire how the subject of marketing research can relate practically to your future success, especially in advancing your ca-

---

[9] *Report on 1976 Policyowners' Meeting* (Milwaukee, Wis.: Northwestern Mutual Life Insurance Company, 1976), p. 2.

reer. "What can this course and book teach me that will be useful?" In response to this proper challenge, we are going to point out some benefits that others have been gaining from competency in this subject, in various roles in marketing. If you visualize yourself in these future roles, then our subject is quite relevant to you.

Possibly you may specialize in marketing research, and then everything in this book will prove to be relevant but only a fraction of what you eventually would need to know. In fact, this book has been used as a training manual. Your chances of entering that specialty are slight, though, for it is a small field. For most readers, justification must be found in other possibilities.

Solving complicated and dynamic problems is a very frequent responsibility of any type of marketing executive. More and more corporations are conducting or sponsoring research projects for solving marketing problems, as Figure 1–1 showed, and far more are utilizing data from projects sponsored by others. If you reach executive capacity in a corporation (or often in large nonbusiness agencies), you are likely to be faced with two involvements with marketing research:

1. You may initiate the request for research or participate in deciding what sort of study, if any, is needed. Thus you would be a *specifier* of research needs with the ability to communicate with research experts and to judge the merits of what they propose. This calls for practical competence in research design and in value analysis of such proposals, which are two subjects that we shall emphasize. You really would need to show intelligence in all phases of the planned work.
2. As a consumer or *user* of the data, you would be faced with applying it to your problem and with interpreting it. If you have the ability to make a critical assessment of a completed study (that is, ask the right questions about it) and to find useful meaning in it, you will be marked as a really sharp person and will achieve a higher rate of correct decisions.

All executives frequently are in those situations. At lower supervisory levels, one is likely to get involved at least as a user of data. In staff positions involving planning work, almost everyone uses marketing research results.

Supposing that you work for a smaller concern, not large enough to afford a marketing research specialist. Would you have little need of marketing research knowledge? In our experience, you would have a greater need. As a college graduate who is expected to have such know-how, you would be a likely person to conduct or arrange for any marketing research that is done. In many small firms unaccustomed to having any research, you might be the instigator of its first research work.

The occasions mentioned above may seem distant now, so let us think about two other career stages. Take your entry job. If you start in a management trainee program, rotating among various functions, you are likely to find yourself handed a difficult problem to study and asked to submit a report. Whether that actually is in a marketing aspect or not, your ability to approach and study the problem and to write an effective report would be quite related to subjects in this book. In a sales position it might prove to be as valuable as the following actual case:

> A pharmaceutical manufacturer placed a new sales representative ("detail man") in its central Wisconsin territory, based in Madison. This representative began to have some misgivings about the routing and sales-potential data provided by the central office, perceiving some interesting recent changes. Therefore, he spent a few Saturdays in the university and state libraries amassing some area data, analyzed them, and sent his conclusions and some new ideas to the general sales manager. The latter was so impressed that within months he transferred this representative to the home office. Subsequently, this man rose to become the company's executive vice-president.

Of course, that might not happen to you—but your voluntarily doing some useful and needed research could make you stand out in the crowd.

In finding a desirable job you may find your first use of marketing research. The diligent job seeker makes a careful analysis of identifying growth industries and firms, to narrow the objectives. Then for the selected firms where interviews have been secured, that job seeker makes careful study of its markets and the position and trends of its product lines—among other data about each company. The display of such knowledge and insight during a job interview cannot fail to make a fine impression.

If you can identify yourself with any of the foregoing future situations, you will perceive marketing research as relevant to your personal success. If you cannot, your aims do not lie in marketing or perhaps in any administration area.

1.6 Preview

From the general aspects with which this chapter has dealt, we now proceed into specific ones. The understanding from this preview should orient you as we move along. The book is divided into four parts, as follows.

Part I is, of course, our present location. It has only one more chapter, which will be an adequate foundation. It will tie together the roles of decision makers and researchers and will equip you with rational concepts for judging the scope and desirability of research on marketing problems.

Part II deals with the early stages of a project. Crucially the problem itself must be crystallized and developed into a researchable statement, which leads to specifying data needs appropriate for the desired precision. That comprises Chapter 3. Then Chapter 4 discusses the project design task and offers you alternative types of designs that might be used. This chapter is capped with the decision on research design. This section culminates in the tasks of detailed planning and decisions on who conducts the work. Then a too-often-overlooked step is discussed: preparing and presenting the proposal to do the work to the executives whose approval is required.

Part III is longer, with five chapters. The first, Chapter 6, concerns the careful assessment of the data to be gathered and their source. If collection of fresh data is involved, the project moves into gathering it. This requires first (Chapters 7 and 8) a sampling plan and then (Chapter 9) preparation of questionnaires or other instruments. Those steps completed, the project moves into actual collection of the data, with which Chapter 10 deals.

Part IV will bring us to the culminating tasks of getting the meaning out of the gathered data. In Chapter 11 are explained the decisions and the alternatives in arranging the data processing, together with some techniques. When processed, the work of analysis begins, to which Chapters 12 and 13 are devoted. The analyses enable interpretations and reaching conclusions, which in turn must be communicated effectively to the decision makers. These are the subjects of Chapter 14. Then the application of marketing research is described in two related areas of its use, market analysis and forecasting, in Chapter 15.

Finally the Epilogue is mentioned separately because it does not continue the concept development of the preceding chapters but, instead, peers into the future on a number of issues that may vitally affect marketing research in the future. Since the future is where you will be living, you should find that interesting.

This chapter has covered a lot of ground, which should acquaint you with the whys and wherefores of marketing research, and orient you personally with the subject. Our attention will now be focused on the immediate situation for research and its two main characters, the decision maker and the researcher.

2 Integrating Research with Decisions

In Chapter 2 we place marketing research within a business organization and then examine relationships and decisions of the two principal parties: those who make decisions on marketing problems and those who do research on them. We deal with such questions as these:

Why are the findings of research often not used?

How does marketing research function in an information system?

Where is it usually placed within a business organization?

What are the needs and viewpoints of executives relating to marketing research? What are those of the researchers?

What do executives and researchers need to tell one another if the research is to be efficient and appropriate?

How would they approach the question of whether or not to do research?

Must report decisions w/decision maker

RESEARCH FINDINGS that are not put to use, in the analogy of one experienced colleague, "are like medicine that is left in the bottle." In our term "applied research" we assume its reaching application, and when it does not, the work has been futile. Nevertheless, many studies that were technically competent have failed to be considered useful by the problem solvers for whom they were undertaken.

In modern organization, researchers and executives (decision makers) are separate persons with their individual specializations. There are justifiable reasons why a decision maker may reject or ignore the findings of research:

Reasons for rejecting research findings:

1. *Invalidity* of research methods. If the decision maker suspects the accuracy or appropriateness of the methods for the problem faced, lack of confidence would lead to rejection.
2. *Faulty communication,* so that the findings are difficult to comprehend and utilize — or unconvincing.
3. *Irrelevance* of the findings to the perceived problems, in the view of the decision maker.

The first two of these causes will be dealt with in later chapters. Here we are dealing with the danger of irrelevance, a failure of the decision maker and the researcher to share a mutual view of the problem(s) and of the decision methods. To achieve such a coordination and efficient use of marketing research demands accurate appreciation of the role and placement of that function in the organization, which is our first subject.

2.1 Research in the Marketing Information System

Information may be considered to be the life blood of planning, directing, and controlling any enterprise. Data circulate, like blood, through channels of the organization. In loosely managed enterprises that circulation is casual, but in modern ones it is planned for efficiency. The simple chart of data flows in a manufacturing organization (Figure 2–1) includes only major arteries among functional departments and outside environments. It excludes data flows to and from top management, which coordinates the whole. You may envision that in a third dimension. In Figure 2–1 all tiers of the system adjust to the information inflows at the basic level of marketing, thus realizing the "marketing concept" of attuning the whole organization with the market environments.

We want to emphasize the vital function that marketing research performs in those organizations that progressively seek to fulfill the marketing concept, of which a good definition is:

The *marketing concept* is a management orientation that holds that the key task of the organization is to determine the needs, wants, and values of a target market and to adapt the organization to delivering the desired satisfactions more effectively and efficiently than its competitors.[1]

To accomplish that fulfillment, it is imperative to "determine the needs ... (etc.)" and also to measure whether or not the organization is "delivering the desired satisfactions." These essentials are provided through the marketing information inflows shown in Figure 2–1.

We are interested in the Marketing Information System (MIS), which comprises the flows below the box labeled "marketing" in this diagram. A necessary component of modern marketing management an MIS has been defined as:

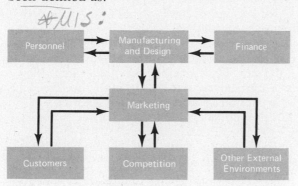

FIGURE 2–1. Major Business Functions in a Management Information System

Source: R. G. Murdick and J. E. Ross, Information Systems for Modern Management *(Englewood Cliffs, N.J.: Prentice-Hall, Inc., 1971), p. 135. Reprinted with permission.*

A structured, interacting complex of persons, machines, and procedures designed to generate an orderly flow of pertinent information, collected from both intra- and extra-firm sources, for use as bases for decision-making in specified responsibility areas of marketing management.[2]

Let us consider what kinds of information are utilized by management before examining the structure of an MIS. Kotler has used striking terms in distinguishing information used by executives in two categories: (1) *results* data, which show what has taken place and current situations, and (2) *happenings* data, which report on current events and developments that foreshadow significant future changes.[3] These two terms, "results" and "happenings," may not suffice to cover all management data but will serve our purpose here.

---

[1] Philip Kotler, *Marketing Management,* 3rd ed. (Englewood Cliffs, N.J.: Prentice-Hall, Inc., 1976), p. 14.

[2] S. V. Smith, R. H. Brien, and J. E. Stafford, *Readings in Marketing Information Systems* (Boston: Houghton Mifflin Company, 1968), p. 7.

[3] Kotler, *Marketing Management,* 3rd ed., p. 423.

An MIS should provide data on both results and happenings, but much information is received by other means. A firm's internal accounting system is an equally important source of results data, which are reported in balance sheets and various operating statements. Happenings data may be chiefly reported casually or "through the grapevine" instead of through the orderly flow of the information system. Executives learn much about current and relevant events through reading, observation, and conversations, while the field sales representatives are acting as the market "eyes and ears" of the organization. Although the MIS may not provide as much data as obtained through the accounting department or casual intelligence, its data inputs to marketing decisions tend to be more significant because of being deliberately gathered for them and because of their richness and reliability.

In a total view of marketing management, the MIS is one of its four subsystems, which are diagrammed in Figure 2–2. In that flow, the MIS is acting as the link between the internal organization and the outside environments, particularly markets, where the effects of the firm's outputs and those of competitors are being exerted. The four subsystems are acting in this sequence:

1. *Planning* decides the objectives, policies, and strategies and then plans marketing programs for action.
2. *Operations* executes the marketing actions that have been planned by delegating and supervising the work. *Implement policies.*
3. The *MIS* connects the outside environment with the firm, feeding in data on markets, competitors, and other external factors. These data are inputs to the control function (below) and to the planning function that is seeking new opportunities and new marketing programs.
4. *Controlling* monitors the operations and their results. If feedback indicates that the system's results are deviating from plans, it either adapts the operations to changing conditions or modifies the standards (that is, the objectives) to reflect environmental changes.

MIS is one of 4 subsystems :

We have been looking at the entire MIS, of which marketing research is a major component. Data flowing through the MIS partially are *rou-*

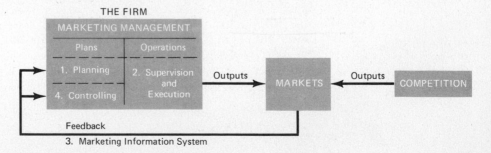

FIGURE 2–2. Marketing Management System

tine, reported at regular intervals in a standard format. An example would be sales representatives' reports on inventories held by distributors. Another would be television audience data provided by an external research service. Such routine and standard data are useful to executives in the form received without any refinement or analysis by marketing researchers. In Figure 2–3 we indicate this with the line bypassing the Marketing Research department. Another solid line passes through that department, however, because it may analyze and interpret some of those routine data to assist the executives. The dashed line, for specific studies, is our main interest. The specific or ad hoc studies are designed to obtain the data and findings relative to particular opportunities or problems. Typically they are "one-time" studies and are tailored to very specific data needs (in contrast to routine or repetitive data that are of more general usefulness). Specific studies are the main activity of marketing researchers and will receive our greater attention.

2.2 Placement in the Organization Structure *responsibilities of staff people*

As a staff activity, marketing research should report to that executive whom it actually serves the most. The most recent information on this shows that most commonly marketing research reports to the top marketing executive (who may be titled "Vice-President Marketing," "General Sales Manager," "Director of Marketing," and similar designations).[4] That includes, though, only half of the corporations, and in 40 percent of the cases this function reports above the marketing level, mainly to the top executive. Reporting at a high level is desirable, both because the marketing situation of the firm is of great importance to top executives

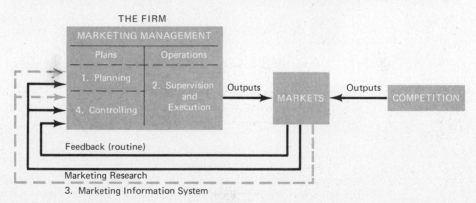

FIGURE 2–3. Marketing Research in the Marketing Information System

The dashed lines indicate the irregular timing of specific marketing studies. The solid lines are regular data flows, in the MIS.

---

[4] *1973 Survey of Marketing Research* (Chicago: American Marketing Association, 1973), p. 25.

and because it removes this function from possible pressures at lower levels that might distort or suppress unfavorable findings.

The organizational relationships of one marketing research department is described in Figure 2–4. In this instance, the head of marketing research is responsible to the Vice-President in charge of the division. That important individual is, however, only one of the executives served by that department. Managers of five functions within the Vice-President's domain are utilizing marketing research services, too. Under the Marketing Director are various product managers who represent a form of organization in which each plans and coordinates assigned products.[5] With their concentration on a few products, these managers can study them intensively and become the outstanding users of the research department.

With a "director" and the many interfaces shown in Figure 2–5, obviously there are several persons in marketing research. Smaller companies may have a single person or part-time assignment to do this work. The survey to which we referred above shows that manufacturing firms of under $25,000,000 annual sale volume tend to have a single researcher (or none full-time).[6] Large manufacturers (with over a half-billion dollars

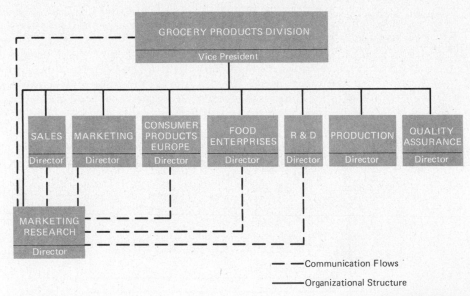

FIGURE 2–4. Principal Internal Flows of Communication to and from the Marketing Research Director in the Grocery Products Division of Ralston Purina Company in 1977.

Source: Ralston Purina Company.

---

[5] An Association of National Advertisers' study found that 93 percent of its packaged-goods members with advertising expenditures over $10 million utilized the product-manager form of organization. Quoted by Robert Donovan in *Product Management*, November, 1976, p. 29.

[6] Dik W. Twedt (ed.), *1973 Survey of Marketing Research* (Chicago: American Marketing Association, 1973), p. 18.

25

Grocery Products Division

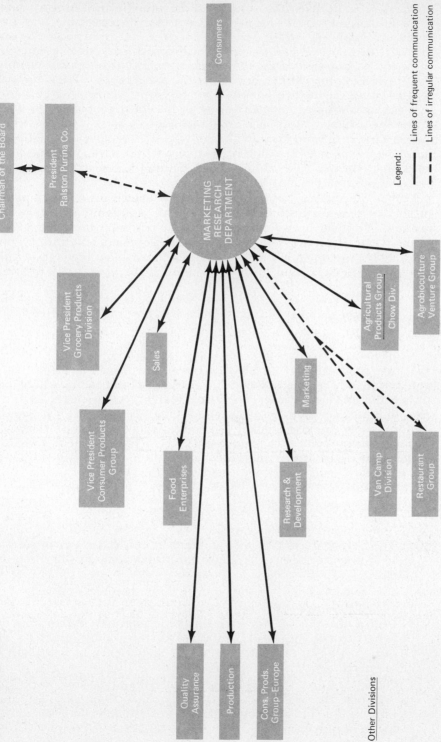

Other Divisions

FIGURE 2–5. Interfaces of the Marketing Research Department in the Consumer Products Group of Ralston Purina Company.

Various other departments both within its division and in other divisions and the outside public are shown. The distances that they are placed from the Marketing Research Department indicates the degree to which the department is involved with them.

Source: Adapted from information supplied by Ralston Purina Company.

in sales) typically have from 10 to 20 persons in marketing research, while the largest advertising and broadcasting organizations may have double this number.

Where there are several or more persons in a marketing research department, its manager begins to take on administrative tasks in planning and supervising the work. Simultaneously, some people under the manager take on expanded responsibilities and specializations. A logical form of specialization is for the analytical or professional people in this group to become assigned to serving certain decision makers or other departments. Thus in Ralston Purina Company the sales department might have sufficient and peculiar research needs that justify assigning one person in marketing research to work with them. Pairing a research analyst with one or two product managers is common practice, also.

Very large corporations often decentralize marketing research among various divisions, as does General Foods Corporation among its several divisions. This may be essential where the divisions are far apart (for example, General Electric's lamp division in Cleveland and major appliances in Louisville), but a single centralized department tends to be most efficient where there is not such separation.

2.3 Utilizing External Services

We have been speaking of internal research activities or departments, and you may have inferred that the marketing studies are wholly conducted there. There also are various research agencies external to the firm that uses research, as we mentioned in Chapter 1. Such agencies are commonly employed, either to conduct entire studies or to provide certain services to the client's marketing research department. Organizational relationships differ when they are involved, which is just one reason why one should be well informed about them.

Use of outside agencies is sometimes undesirable, for it can entail the following possible disadvantages:

1. The outside agency may be unfamiliar with the client firm, especially if it has not engaged in work for that client during the recent past.
2. The outside agency is more or less inaccessible, seriously hampering communication.
3. Unless the same agency is retained for repeated studies and permitted to become closely informed of the client's problems and plans, the lack of continuity causes inefficiency and inability to serve well.
4. Outside agencies' costs often are higher than the same work when done by the client's internal researchers, especially for small projects, due to fixed costs, contingency cushions, and profits that figure in their prices.

disadvantages of outside research agencies (external)

The first three disadvantages, above, can hamper a good integration be-tween decisions and research, our main topic in this chapter.

Nevertheless, the extensive use of outside agencies implies that their advantages often outweigh disadvantages. The 1973 survey that we have quoted found the following percentages of companies' marketing re-search budgets paid to outside agencies:[7]

Consumer product manufacturers	46
Industrial product manufacturers	24
Advertising agencies	40
Publishers and broadcasters	37

The survey also reported an increase in these percentages spent on out-side agencies over the comparable 1968 survey.

An outside research agency may offer some weighty advantages, among them:

1. Its independent viewpoint, unaffected by biases in the client orga-nization.
2. The varied experience that it may bring to its work, so that it may offer better techniques and information obtained for other clients and situations. (Confidential information, however, would never be divulged to another client by reliable firms.)
3. Special skills of the agency's staff that the client's internal depart-ment lacks.
4. Larger staffs are offered by the outside agency, particularly for field work, than a client could afford to maintain.
5. Flexible usage of such agencies, which can be retained only as needed.

Many corporations have no internal marketing researchers or no capa-bility for some rare and complex studies, and so it would be logical to hire an outside research firm to carry out the entire project. There is an evident tendency among large corporations, on the contrary, to plan a project internally and then farm out its data-collection phases to an agency. The internal researchers also would complete the study with in-terpretations of data and presenting findings to management.

Marketing research practice is a complex of many sorts of agencies, some offering a complete service but a majority concentrated in certain specializations. The user or client organizations, whose executives' deci-sions are the ultimate use of research data, may use a number of these when appropriate. To give you some appreciation of when and how these outside agencies or sources may be employed, a hypothetical ex-ample is described below. The network of research suppliers involved is sketched in Figure 2–6.

In Company A, an important consumer item is Brand Y. Company A sub-scribes to the retail store sales audits of a syndicated data service, which

---

[7] Ibid., p. 38.

sells such data in standardized form—shown as flow 1. A great new advertising campaign for that brand seems to be singularly unsuccessful in the Southwest region, according to retail sales data from that source. These data are purchased by Company A's marketing research unit, which distributes those of interest to the executives shown at the far left.

Asked by executives to learn whether the problem may be market conditions in the Southwest, the marketing researchers obtain data from government bureaus (flow 2) that are regional economic indicators. These signify firm demand in the Southwest, despite Brand Y's poor showing.

Now Company A's advertising agency is brought into the act, when the client relates its troubles in the Southwest and the agency decides to make a specific study of Brand Y by its own research department. As the agency does not have its own field interviewers, it hires an agency in Dallas whose specialty is interviewing in that region. Its results come to the advertising agency (flow 3). After that firm has decided whether the advertising is at fault and its recommendations, it presents its data to the client company (flow 4). Notice that the agency is using these data for its own decisions as well as being a "doer" of research.

The executives in Company A, aided by interpretations of its own researchers, decide that there are deeper problems faced by Brand Y in the Southwest, into which the agency did not probe. They have the marketing research department select an outside research agency to make an adequate study. That agency draws many of its data from government sources (flow 5) but otherwise gathers its own. The research firm's findings are reported to the client company (flow 6).

As you understand what is involved in conducting research, later in our book, you will appreciate the value of these outside sources and services. Their use presents additional functions and problems for the person in charge of marketing research—in the client organizations. This person now must serve as a bridge between the executives who use the results and the firms utilized outside. Negotiating with outside agencies, selecting them, and keeping informed on the quality of their work—these are expansions of the inside manager's job.

2.4 Decision Makers

In the foregoing discussion a number of individuals have been taking some role in both the reaching of decisions and the conduct of marketing research. That is the reality for major decisions in large organizations, but for clarity's sake we must simplify the situation to a one-on-one relationship: one decision maker dealing with one researcher. In examining what should happen to integrate research with decisions, we begin on the decision side.

Decisions are made by you, me, and everyone. Our attention, though, is only on those who direct an enterprise, whether it be a business firm or in some noncommercial area of the world's work. They might be called executives or administrators, but we will call them simply "decision makers," since it is this aspect that we are considering. We are going to

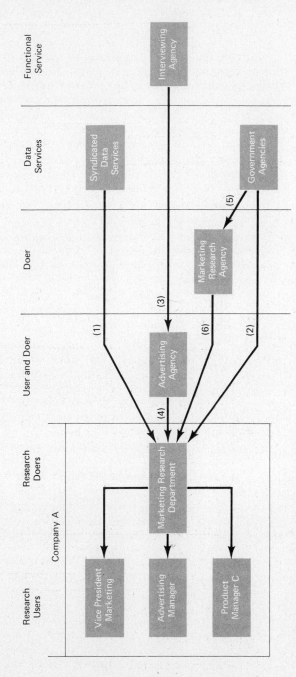

FIGURE 2–6. Network of Research Suppliers

The inputs of various research organizations or data sources relative to problem of hypothetical Brand Y of Company A. The lines represent data flows. Their numbering is explained in this example in the text.

sketch their needs and tasks, how research may (and may not) benefit them, and how to identify them.

2.4.1 Tasks and Needs

[handwritten margin note: decision making]

One might describe the total task or mission of such a decision maker as that of optimizing his or her profit contribution to the enterprise—but we will not. Profit is an elusive term and only the top executive can be held clearly responsible for the "bottom line" of profit. A more generally pertinent overall task, for any decision maker, is the dual one of (1) optimizing goal attainment with (2) efficient use of resources. Research is desirable that actually promotes the accomplishment of this dual task.

Any major problem requires not just a single decision but rather a series of decisions that culminate in the conclusive one that selects or approves the course of action to be taken. If we are to understand what is faced, we need to note the types of decisions in this series.

[handwritten margin note: Types of decisions]

1. One necessary determination is whether or not a problem is of major or minor proportions. The degree of gravity of a problem would lead to placing it in one of these three categories of problem solving:
   a. Routine decisions, minor or repetitive problems that may safely be made on the basis of precedent or some policy indicating what should be done in the given situation. No research whatever is justified.
   b. Limited problem solving. These may merit considerable thought and the study of information already on hand, but no substantial effort to seek new information. Researchers may serve such decisions by acquiring a reservoir of data in anticipation of them, including the providing of past relevant studies when a problem like this arises.
   c. Extensive problem solving. These are decisions of large magnitude, usually involving commitments over a rather long period or large financial involvements.

[handwritten note: major/minor problems]

It is the decisions falling under the last category, extensive problem solving, that need marketing research the most and are the major occupation of the researchers. Our discussions will deal largely with them.

2. Another vital determination is whether the relevant factors in a situation are controllable or uncontrollable. Most of the outside environment would be uncontrollable and needs to be taken as given, although research may be needed to measure those factors. The decision maker can accomplish anything solely with some controllable factors, which in turn can affect some external factor (such as consumers' brand preference) favorably.

[handwritten note: Controllable/uncontrollable]

Assuming that the preceding determinations will be made, there are seven aspects to be considered in every major problem, which are given below:

7 aspects to consider w/ every major problem

1. *Objectives* are essential to direct the enterprise and to set the types and levels of performance of those within it. Organizational objectives should be determined by top authorities for the whole enterprise (for example, by its directors and president). Going down through levels of authority, each then would be assigned his or her objectives, and then the manager or each unit of function needs to set its subobjectives in order for its results to satisfy responsibility to meet its assigned goal.

2. *Environments* need to be determined and interpreted, within which the actions will take place.

3. *Problems* that are encountered in reaching objectives or optimizing performance need to be recognized and defined.

4. *Priorities* need to be assigned to the identified problems, in term or urgency, levels of risk, difficulty of solution—leading to selection of those to be given extensive problem-solving and probably research.

5. *Alternative actions* or options need to be found or generated. Problem-solving success is closely tied to the relevance, originality, and potency of the alternatives that are taken into consideration.

6. *Resource allocations* need to be made to the various opportunities or problems in order to optimize the overall attainment of objectives.

7. *Conclusion* is the final decision on what to do, the decision to which the foregoing ones led.

Two conditions tend to handicap marketing executives in their efforts to reach accurate decisions:

hindrances in making accurate decisions:

1. *Obscurity.* It may be hard to discern and to measure what is going on among remote buying publics and the diffused operations of marketing. Thus problems may be obscure and hard to identify or describe. There also may be vagueness regarding the marketing actions taking place, especially competitors' actions, and their effects.

2. *Uncertainty.* Virtually all marketing decisions are made under some uncertainty. This handicap deserves some discussion at this point.

There are various degrees of uncertainty, which are categorized in three states:

1. *Certainty.* having *assurance* that something *will happen* and its effects. An example might be that an automatic order-picking machine is

under consideration for a warehouse, to replace the manual picking in which employees went about the warehouse and picked the items to fill an order. Dependable measurements have shown that with a specified and typical volume of orders, the new machine would cost $377 per day to operate as compared with $510 per day manually. A decision on installing the machine, at least in this respect, would be made under certainty.

2. *Risk.* having assurance of the relative *probability* with which an event would take place, although unable to forecast which among alternative events will take place. Actuaries, for instance, may have compiled experience tables on the mortality of outside sales personnel that indicate a 23 percent chance that our top sales representative will die before reaching the retirement age. True as that may be of all sales personnel of that age, we know only the tendency and not positively whether a certain person will survive until retirement age. Knowing the risk, however, we can plan staffing for that contingency.

3. *Uncertainty.* having no assurance or advance knowledge about what may happen or its probability of happening—ignorance about the future.

2.4.2   Benefits of Research = reduction of uncertainty

For the decision maker, faced with the decisions and doubts described above, what should be the benefits of having research conducted? The most universal and usually most vital is this: reduction of uncertainty. If research findings contribute any relevant knowledge of what exists, that the decision maker was ignorant of, or if it provides new clues to what is likely in the future, they should enable a more accurate conclusive decision to be reached.

> For example, a toy manufacturer in the United States (Company B) is considering exporting toys to Canada. With no experience up there whatever, any estimate of available market size would be a guess: let us say that the chance of predicting its size has only a 10 percent chance of coming within ± $1,000,000. If, instead, research is conducted into the toy-buying market there and into receptivity to this firm's type of toys, the market size can be predicted with a 50 percent chance of coming within ± $1,000,000.

Thus uncertainty cannot be wholly eliminated with relevant research, but it may be markedly reduced.

Research also may be of benefit in ways ordinarily thought of as uncertainty reduction: (1) problems may come to light that otherwise would not be known until they became very serious or even insoluble; (2) objectives may come under reevaluation when evidence indicates that (a) they may be too high to be feasible under expected conditions or (b) they should be higher due to overlooked opportunity; (3) better alternatives may be revealed or their conception stimulated; and (4) marketing research may be useful as evidence in legal matters:

A prominent manufacturer's laboratories developed a new design of a consumer product that has enormous demand, and a patent was sought. The "new" design actually was a combination of some existing designs that were not patentable, but the manufacturer claimed that creation of the new design should be. This was backed by evidence acquired by marketing research that demonstrated outstanding consumer benefits to consumers over the earlier designs. On these grounds, the patent was granted.

We would call attention to other benefits, such as the psychological one of making the decision maker feel more confident and willing to be decisive. Prejudice against new ideas may be overcome by evidence from the marketplace. Sociologically, research can keep the executives attuned to changing consumer needs and wants and to the impacts of consumerism. Less laudable are political motives for marketing research, like the executive who wants it to confirm some preconceived ideas and overcome rivals in the organization (but would suppress findings if they fail to confirm them).

2.4.3 Objections to Research

Do not assume that a cordial reception by decision makers always awaits the researcher. Some of the reasons are *without* merit except in the particular decision maker's viewpoint:

1. Threats may be anticipated in the findings. An insecure person may fear sharing personal doubts or decision methods with another person, the researcher. More common may be fear that the research will uncover poor performance on the part of this person or evidence that would lead higher authorities to replace him or her. While a research firm was planning a study of distributors for a farm equipment company, its top marketing executive showed much reluctance to contribute and sought to limit the study's scope. The reason: it was the company's President who asked for the study, and this other executive feared that the sales force (that he had built with great pride) might be shown in a bad light.
2. Conceit on the part of the decision makers may cause them to believe that they already know the answers—at least better than any research can determine. Being so self-assured, naturally they find any research on such a subject to be sheer waste.
3. Impatient and indolent persons also may oppose the time and effort that is entailed in research without regard for its merits.

On the other hand, there may be very sound reasons for opposing the conduct of research on some problem. We would include in these:

reasons for opposing research:

1. *Lack of time.* New research seldom can be completed in time for a decision that must be made quickly (for example, in two weeks). Projects tailored for specific decisions normally require at least a month's lead time, often more. Furthermore, both executives and

[handwritten: con't reasons for opposing research]

research personnel have limited available time to be rationed to most profitable uses. This objection to research, however, should not rule out consulting the research department to find what they could compile quickly.

2. *Questionable benefit.* There are problems of such novelty or relating to such an uncertain future that today's data are unlikely to be of much benefit. It is only fair to recognize that there are such problems.

3. *Adequate information.* The decision maker may feel that the information already in hand is sufficient. He or she has the authority to judge the risks. If comfortable with existing knowledge, it is that person's prerogative to decline research assistance.

2.5 Marketing Researchers

Let us now look at the individual on the research side who interfaces with the decision maker. This person may be backed up with others in analytical, interviewing, computing, and clerical work who will not be covered in our discussion.

2.5.1 Functions *[handwritten: of researchers: staff (aid & advise)]*

The researcher facilitates those who make decisions and take actions. The latter would include (1) executives at high levels, (2) managers of "line" marketing functions (for example, advertising, selling, physical distribution, and product planning), and (3) product or brand managers. Research jobs thus are *staff* ones, aiding and advising the general and line executives.

If a single person executes all the research tasks, they would be the following:

[handwritten: single person research task execution:]

1. Anticipate the routine or repetitive decisions for which information is needed from time to time, having it ready.

2. Upon requests from decision makers, determine the nature of their decisions, timing, and the decision methods to be used (a subject we shall discuss shortly).

3. Describe in writing each research study that is being proposed and submit it for approval by the researcher's superior.

4. Draw up plans for the research operation and supervise their implementation (if not doing the work personally).

5. Interpret the gathered evidence and direct data processing; then write and present a report of findings.

6. On trends and developments of significance to a decision maker, furnish current data.

7. Suggest research needs to the decision maker when they are perceived by the researcher and evidently have not been recognized.

It is important also to keep files of data gathered in the past for ready retrieval and to be abreast of what data are available, in order to be of maximum service. Too often this is neglected.

2.5.2 Needs

The researcher needs support from various decision makers, for this work can be considered a dispensable luxury unless those who would use it think it worthwhile. In order to create their acceptance of the research function and maintain a desire for more studies, the intelligent researcher keeps well posted on what is happening in the organization and the relevant power structure. Much needs to be known about the individual decision makers who would be served in order that research efforts may be efficient and appreciated.

The following are a number of vital questions that the researcher would need to answer about these individuals:

1. What are the payoffs or accomplishments that are sought in the decisions?
2. What are the key factors in the environment and the particular courses of action that are favored, in the decision maker's views?
3. What constraints or limitations would rule out some actions?
4. What is the decision maker's capacity or preference in complexity and analysis of the information? Is the preference to reach his or her own interpretations or for the researcher to digest the evidence before submitting it?
5. What is the specific format of presentation that is preferred?
6. How much time can be permitted for the research?
7. What is the decision maker's posture toward research expenses: liberal or thrifty? How would the amount spent be decided?
8. What problems or trends are concerning this individual, on which current data would be helpful?

Frequently a group, such as a committee or a venture team, is making a decision in which such information is needed about several clients.

2.6 The Dialogue

Decision and research within the firm should be treated as an integral matter involving a minimum of two persons, one or more decision makers and a researcher. In any interpersonal process, clear and ample communication is vital, and this is particularly true of marketing research. On the one hand, there is the person with a problem to solve. This problem solver should know what goals are to be reached, the difficulties or problems confronted, and the nature of the unknown factors that involve undue risk unless research can provide the needed knowledge. On the other hand, there is the person who is technically capable of conducting the research, provided that it is feasible. He or she would answer the questions, whose work may be less costly than the risks that would be avoided. Until communication is adequate, one cannot help the other.

Therefore, a dialogue needs to take place. The researcher needs to know what the decision maker hopes to accomplish, how he or she views the problem, what courses of action would be acceptable, when the decision must be made, and other things that will become evident when a decision is examined in Section 2.7. Some things, however, the decision maker may be unable or unwilling to relate: certain prejudices and patterns of thought, whether full details and qualified answers are wanted or simple and positive statements, and other hidden thoughts and emotions. The decision maker's thought should not be hidden in the "black box," as the executive's mind is sometimes called, for the researcher is not clairvoyant.

The researcher, on the other hand, must level with the decision maker. He or she should be candid regarding the limitations on what can be done and give honest and full revelation of the findings. In the preliminary stages an earnest dialogue is particularly valuable. Few executives are prone to explain their problems lucidly. When the researcher persists in a logical effort to pry out a clear statement of the problem, this should enhance executive thinking. As the researcher plays back his or her version of the problem, new aspects and additional possible solutions may be discovered.

The dialogue we describe is more ideal than is generally found today, but it is important to strive for this whenever possible.

Table 2–1 compares some aspects of two projects, undertaken by the same research agency with one of the authors' participation. Both companies were manufacturers with sales volumes in the hundreds of millions. At first glance, it probably appeared that the project with Company D should have been more successful because of the extensive communication; the reasons why it was unsuccessful are summarized below:

1. *In Company C*, the executive responsible for the decision had direct contact with the researchers and was so sharp in defining the problem and the several alternatives that designing an appropriate project was facilitated. The study involved extensive field work and a major policy decision, but its findings were directly applicable and lucidly explained in a concise report.

2. *In Company D*, the real decision maker was its president, who, for reasons that were never explained, refused to communicate with the researchers until the study's completion. He had delegated one of the vice-presidents to be his liaison but apparently never shared his views with this subordinate. The study therefore turned out to be an exploration for problems, covered much scope, and produced few answers acceptable to the president.

TABLE 2-1. Comparison of Client Research Agency Relationships

Characteristics of the Project	Company C's Project	Company D's Project
How it was initiated	Telephone call from client's Vice-President Sales.	Personal visit to research agency by Vice-President Marketing of Company D (for long discussions).
Communications as project was planned and conducted	By mail with Vice-President Sales.	Researchers' personal visits to offices of client; study of records, plants, field selling. Discussions included: vice-presidents of marketing, finance, and production; product managers; marketing research manager; controller; cost analysts and others.
Time spent in the study	Five weeks.	Over six months.
Method of reporting findings	Mailed a report of thirty pages.	Personal meeting, most of a day, with Company's president and vice-presidents. Thick two-volume report.
Cost of study	$15,000	$95,000
Value of findings	Excellent: "Tells us precisely what we need to know!"	Poor: Company president felt most of the data irrelevant to actual problems.

Summary of communications and results of studies sponsored by two manufacturing companies with same research agency.

The case of Company D, in which there was no dialogue between the real decision maker and the researcher, was an extreme situation, but it points up the dangers of faulty communication.

The dialogue should continue from time to time during any large project. As our ensuing discussion will relate, there may be a series of studies that provide guidance to the decision maker at several phases. Typically, though, there is a single research project, but one of major dimensions that would take months. In its course there may be developments that might change the decision maker's views of the problem or its alternative solutions. Or some considerable change in the study design or scope may seem desirable to the researcher. As its end approaches and unexpected findings may be emerging, again questions arise that could radically change the research work. Accessibility of the decision maker and researcher to one another can continue the dialogue about matters like these that add much efficiency to the problem-solving process.

2.7   Integrating Model

An adequate dialogue between the decision maker and the marketing researcher would involve a number of complexities. Solving a major problem is not accomplished with a single decision but rather with a series of decisions. The problem itself is situated amidst a number of past and current decisions that impinge on it. And the problem may be complicated also by involving a number of significant factors that somewhere need to be given due consideration in the problem's solution.

It may be apparent from this description that major decisions cannot be well made when the executive has only a fuzzy notion about these various aspects and how they should be dealt with in reaching a problem solution. Efficiency demands that explicit and lucid statements be reached regarding:

1. An accurate representation or model of how the problem is to be solved, including definition of decisions to be made.
2. Specific understanding of when and how additional information would contribute to those decisions.

If research is to be undertaken regarding those decisions, obviously the researcher needs to be fully informed of the problem-solving model in order to systematize the executive/researcher functioning.

2.7.1   Problem-Solving Model

You are probably quite familiar with the use of models in solving problems. The types of models, which are miniature or abstract representations of much larger entities under study, that might be useful for marketing problems are (1) conceptual or (2) mathematical. Only when we can define relationships and supply measurements to enable a mathematical solution can research fully qualify with scientific criteria. The mathematical form, though, is a stage beyond the conceptual model of the problem. Most marketing problems either are not or cannot be translated into useful mathematical models in the present state of the art, as earlier mentioned. For these reasons, our attention will be solely on developing a conceptual model of the problem solution. (Later, when we take up analytical methods, tools for mathematical models will be presented.)

We are interested in a model of how a decision is going to be made, which we hope the researcher obtained in discussion with the decision maker. A general model for decisions is described in Figure 2–7, which is an abstraction of the sequential stages in a decision. Specifics of any decision would have to be added to make this useful, as we shall do

38

Research steps!

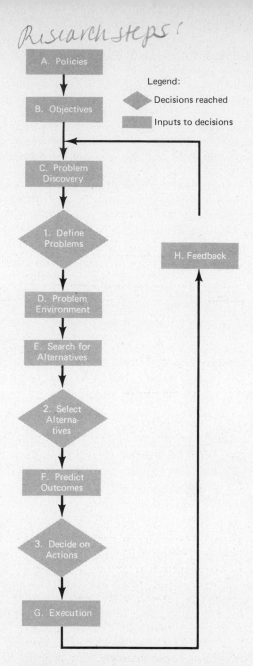

FIGURE 2-7. Sequence of Steps in Problem Solving

later. You should recognize that this is *only one* method of reaching a decision. One variant that often occurs is that the solution—or a possible solution—occurs first. For example, someone in package design happens onto a means of adding convenience to dispensing the contents from our package of a product. Beginning with that stage, a different route would be followed from the one depicted in Figure 2–7. For our discussion it suffices to show the one model.

Very briefly we shall describe the three decision stages and eight inputs into them that you find in Figure 2–7. Notice that none of these inputs is from research (which will be added next) and that we are assuming this decision to deal with the first action of this nature (for otherwise we would have to start with feedback from earlier actions, a practical complexity that will be brought up at the end of this sequence).

A. *Policies.* There are guidelines, limitations, customs, and constraints in most organizations that affect actions taken. They should be set forth in writing but may be only informal. They may importantly direct or circumscribe a decision.

B. *Objectives.* These indicate the state or accomplishment that the enterprise desires to be in, perhaps by some given time. When definitely stated, they should be determined in two respects: (1) a "value" to be sought, and (2) a level or quantitative goal to be reached. A value might be: "percent of industry sales" or "consumer preference over competitive product." Respective levels added to objectives would be: "20 percent of industry sales in the Los Angeles metropolitan area" or "preference for our package over competitors' by more than 50 percent of present buyers."

C. *Problem discovery.* There is no problem until some evidence indicates that there is an unsolved difficulty. A problem emerges when the objective may not be met. If our objectives or standard of performance seems certain to be achieved, happily we have no problem and have an automatic decision to continue the same action as at present. In the normal ongoing situation, there is information received that goal fulfillment is threatened, which raises the existence of a problem. That information may be feedback on actions that have been taking place (H).

1. *Define problem.* The first decision now is encountered, to answer distinctly and accurately: Exactly what sort of a problem is being faced? A sufficiently detailed statement of the problem will need to identify its parameters and dimensions. Possibly a number of problems may be suspected to exist. Notice that we are referring to the specific shortfalls and dangers in performance and meeting objectives, *not* the causes (which occur in decision 2).

D. *Problem environment.* For the problem(s) that have been discovered, probably there is incomplete or perhaps meager information about the situation. The decision maker must be adequately informed on these in order to proceed intelligently, to take into account all crucial variables.

E. *Search for alternatives.* This refers to alternative solutions to the problem which are related to the causes of the problem. Finding, recognizing, and developing alternatives is a task calling for strong perceptive and creative abilities. Probably the most demanding phase of decision making is conceiving of workable, appropriate, and potent solutions.

2. *Select alternatives*. The decision maker should have found a number of possible ways to solve the problem. If only one is found (beyond the method in current use), then that is optional to continuing the status quo—but any bright decision maker will find various options, including actions formerly taken or those in use by others.

F. *Predict outcomes*. Having two or more alternatives, the question of final selection should rest on which will best satisfy the objective. When the objective was determined as input B, its statement should have included the payoff being sought. Now the decision maker wants to compare the payoffs expected from each alternative. Another question is the risk associated with each option. Only those that are in accord with policy (input A) should be considered here.

3. *Decide on action*. This is the final decison, where one of the alternatives is chosen. Whoever is to do the work then is directed to take the chosen action.

G. *Execution*. The fact that the action is taken now becomes one input to future decisions. Obviously, any deviations from the chosen alternative should be one of the future decision inputs.

H. *Feedback*. What happened? As early as practical after the action takes place, information should be reported that indicates its effects. Also needed is information on whether the environment turned out to be significantly different from that anticipated in step D. *see if plan was really effective — or not. If not → change objectives → whole process again*

One decision cycle now has been completed, which feeds into future decisions on that aspect of the enterprise's operation. Recycling, the feedback (H) is compared with the objectives (B), which may have been modified. If the results fed back fall short of objectives in some important respect, a problem is perceived and the problem-solving cycle repeats.

2.7.2 Research Inputs into Decisions

In the cycle presented in Figure 2–7, the decisions were made without information contributed by research. The decision maker was informed about the preceding decisions and had such information as was available without conducting research. For the typical and routine marketing decisions, limited problem solving is adequate. From the researcher's viewpoint, those decisions are not of interest.

Any organization encounters decisions involving high risk and complexity, those that require extensive problem solving. Large and diversified organizations face many such problems constantly, for which research is profitable and virtually necessary. Research may make valuable inputs into complex problem solving at any of four intervals of the model shown in Figure 2–7. We have added those inputs, which are given on the left side of Figure 2–8. Each of these inputs differs in the way it advances the problem solution. It would be unusual to conduct a formal study for each of these inputs, although that is possible.

use for research projects:

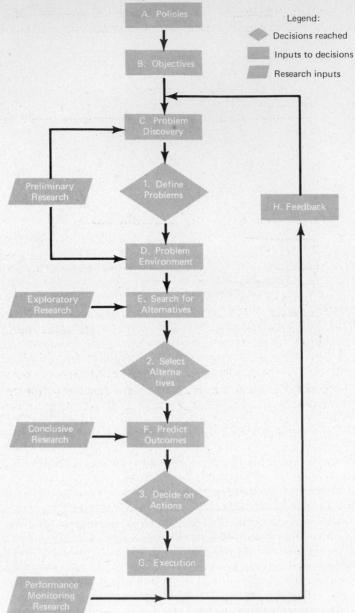

Legend:

◇ Decisions reached

▭ Inputs to decisions

▱ Research inputs

A. Policies

B. Objectives

C. Problem Discovery

Preliminary Research

1. Define Problems

H. Feedback

D. Problem Environment

Exploratory Research

E. Search for Alternatives

2. Select Alternatives

Conclusive Research

F. Predict Outcomes

3. Decide on Actions

G. Execution

Performance Monitoring Research

FIGURE 2–8. Sequence of Steps in Solving a Problem, with Research Inputs

The four types of research distinguished in Figure 2–8 tend to be quite different from one another. It is of the utmost importance for the researcher to be certain about the phase or phases in a major decision in which the findings are to be used so that he or she can select an appropriate research design. If the data are to be specified and later analyzed suitably, the desirable research inputs must be painstakingly spelled out.

1. *Preliminary research* has two purposes that are interrelated: (1) discovering and crystallizing the problems, and (b) describing the relevant situation or environment. A single preliminary study may serve both purposes, at least partially, for one almost inevitably learns more about a problem's environment while sharpening one's knowledge of its nature and location. If a preliminary study is aimed mainly at crystallizing the problem, it is diagnostic and stresses depth, whereas determination of the environment stresses breadth. Also, the former tends to zero in on evidence closely related to the suspected problem, while the situation analysis uses more superficial data. Nevertheless, we bracket the two aims together because they are practically inseparable.

2. *Exploratory research* looks about for hypothetical solutions or actions and describes them well enough for their consideration by the decision maker. Specific studies may be directed toward this aim, but they are unlikely to be very formal or precise, as their range of inquiry would be broad and exact methods of analysis inappropriate. Frequently, such a study does not involve a special effort to gather new data, but rather a surveillance over some period of data obtained in other studies and fed in by the marketing intelligence system. Of the four types of studies that we are distinguishing, this tends to be the least likely to be conducted as a specific project.

3. *Conclusive studies* are what the name implies—those that provide the evidence that enables the decision maker to determine what course of action to take. Therefore, they tend to be the studies on which the most care and effort would be expanded. One or more hypotheses are given serious consideration, and conclusive study validates or verifies (as clearly as feasible) the expected outcome of each hypothesis.

Perhaps the most common notion of research is that of conclusive research. This is the type in which the greatest volume and intensity of data are likely to be gathered. Ideally, experiments would be conducted to indicate with high degrees of certainty the outcome of adopting a hypothesis, but this ideal is usually impractical and recourse must often be made to less scientific methods. Very important decisions may have to be made hurriedly or have to contend with such intangible and unpredictable variables that the formal research studies could contribute little to reducing the decision maker's uncertainties. These conditions may obviate the use of conclusive research and force the decision maker to decide with largely intuitive judgment, but the rational executive would always prefer to have a conclusive research basis for his major decisions.

4. *Performance-monitoring research* follows up the action taken to determine what happened. It has dual concerns: (a) to report changes in operating results that seem attributable to the action, and (b) to as-

certain whether the conditions in which the action was taken have turned out significantly different from those anticipated when that action was chosen.

We shall give more details later on these four types of research inputs. Chapter 3 covers research procedures for three of them: performance monitoring, preliminary, and exploratory research. The extensive and more significant contributions of research to solving marketing problems is in the conclusive studies. Beginning with Chapter 4, we shall be concerned mainly with techniques used largely in conclusive studies.

At this point a specific example may aid your understanding of the flow of decisions in solving a major problem. We shall describe briefly what happened relative to a problem that arose in an automobile manufacturing company, whose car is given the hypothetical name of the Argus. This decision flow is keyed to Figure 2–8 with corresponding letters and numbers.

The Argus Motor Car Company (which was not its real name) had comprehensive objectives and policies and also detailed ones. One minor policy (A) was that consumers shopping in Argus dealer salesrooms should have demonstration rides to become convinced about Argus quality. An objective was to give demonstrations to more than half of them.

A periodic shopping survey, (H) that observed Argus dealer salesmen and trade-in offers, reported that only 21 percent of the salesmen were offering rides, which was lower than found in competitive dealerships. This revealed the problem as initially stated (C) as this: Determine how to stimulate salesmen to offer demonstration rides to at least half of their prospects, in a successful manner.

Preliminary study of the situation was conducted, which radically changed management's initial view. It found that both salesmen and dealers opposed giving demonstration rides and had strong arguments that would need to be disproven, if they were erroneous.

The decision (1) at that stage therefore was changed to the following: Determine when, how, and if demonstration rides are profitable.

Information from the preliminary study also was utilized to gain insights into the dealer operations and records and into automobile salesmen. This filled in details of the problem (D) and provided clues regarding types of data that might be obtained. It was apparent at this stage that a further exploratory study was needed.

The *exploratory study* focused on two kinds of hypotheses that were necessary elements in the decision: that specific kinds of buyers presumably were those who should be given demonstrations and that the profitability of such rides might take several forms. This study presented such alternatives to management.

Decision (2) was that of narrowing the market-segment categories and the types of possible payoffs from demonstration rides to those deemed worthy of serious consideration.

The *conclusive study* was a large one, taking place in eight cities in four states and obtained information from recent buyers of Argus and competing cars. Also, Argus dealer invoice data were obtained, with relevant information also from the particular salesmen and dealers. Findings predicted gross profits earned from demonstration rides under certain conditions, with certain market segments.

Argus executives made an ultimate decision (3) to conduct dealer sales training, in those above a given size, to inform salesmen on how to detect when a demonstration ride will pay off and how to capitalize on it. This program was then implemented (G) in the field sales organization. Later there were periodic measurements of demonstration rides to *monitor performance*. This yielded feedback to management (H) on the program's success.

The foregoing example, although based on fact, utilized an unusual number of studies. It does illustrate, if you read it carefully, how preliminary research can correct management's perceptions of a problem and guide the subsequent research. Also exploratory research obtained fruitful alternatives that the managers would not have perceived and narrowed the scope of the conclusive study.

We have suggested that research might or might not be conducted and have also indicated some kinds of inputs it might make. This is a question that keeps recurring: Is the cost and time of research justified or not? Our final section of Chapter 2 addresses this matter.

2.8 Value Analysis of Possible Research

We have not yet dealt with an inevitable question that arises in problem solving: Should research be conducted or not? Most problems that arise are minor or routine and obviously do not justify formal research. Many are faced, though, either currently or in looming difficulties that are too risky to decide without the aid of fact finding and analysis. Here is another important facet of the decision maker/researcher interface.

All research involves costs, which must be charged to someone's budget. In some corporations the procedure is to have each department head or key decision maker, who has been allocated funds, decide how much to spend for any marketing studies. The predominant method, instead, is to place the whole marketing research fund in the hands of that function's head, who then divides this among various studies that are adopted during the budgeted year. Under this method, the marketing research manager could arbitrarily allocate funds with his or her own preference. That would be folly, though, because close collaboration with each decision maker is essential to efficient spending decisions.

As a basis for reaching this joint decision, some of the inputs would already exist through the determinations in our decision-flow model (Figure 2–7). This would include the objectives and payoffs sought and, if it is conclusive study that is under consideration, the alternative solutions to be considered. Some essential questions would not yet have been answered, especially these:

What degree of confidence—or uncertainty—does this decision maker have in making the decision on the basis of the information now at hand?

What are the perceived risks? What possible costs or losses are faced in those contingencies? What is their apparent likelihood of occurring?

What additional information is obtainable that should improve the accuracy of the decision? What are the methods of research and on what scale would a study be made?

How reliable would that information probably be? To what degree would it reduce the risks involved in making the decision?

How much would alternative studies cost? When that is compared with the profitability that may be yielded by the increased accuracy of the decision, would the profit exceed the research cost sufficiently to proceed with the desired study?

The marketing researchers would like to assist every important marketing decision for which there is inadequate information. Practically always, though, demand for information far exceeds the resources available for the marketing research work. The most recent data available on companies' marketing research outlays indicate a typical budget of only $286,000 per year, in a sample of companies whose median sales volume was over $50,000,000 annually. We said "only" that amount for it averaged merely 0.3 percent of sales revenue in consumer goods companies and 0.1 percent in industrial goods manufacturers.[8] That represents large industry, in which many difficult marketing problems are likely to occur each year. Their marketing research departments would need to devote probably the majority of the $286,000 to fixed costs of internal staff and overhead and to purchasing various data services that are of general benefit but not related to specific problems. If the remainder would provide for, say, three to six substantial research studies a year, some hard choices would be necessary among the problems meriting extensive and specific conclusive studies.

The determination of whether or not to invest in research on any marketing problem may be called "value analysis." That term is used in industrial purchasing for a systematic assessment procedure whereby potential suppliers can be compared objectively, so that the buying firm maximizes the value obtained. Or we might apply the term "cost/benefit analysis" to such a determination. In this chapter we are merely describing the rudiments of such decisions, which cannot be resolved until the researcher has specified the design of alternative projects. Therefore, we will explain formal methods for determining whether or not to conduct research in Chapter 5, section 5.4.

What is involved in value analysis of possible studies may be grasped better through a hypothetical example. We return to the firm that was considering exporting its toys to Canada, which we call Company B. The

Value analysis

[8] Ibid., p. 27–28.

firm has ruled out options of making the toys in that country or of licensing a Canadian manufacturer, incidentally, so the question focuses on exporting.

When Company B's marketing director contemplates Canada, it literally is a foreign market to him, about which he has little information. The problem is predicting the probable volume of sales that Company B would obtain with its lines of toys, for unless there is sufficient certainty of a profitable volume, the venture would not be attempted.

This decision maker's present state of knowledge about Canada is this: (1) that its population is around 10 percent of that in the United States; (2) Canadians have a total consumer income about 9.6 percent of the United States figure; and (3) total Canadian toy sales amounted to about $190,000,000 last year. The Canadian data do not offer a relevant breakdown of industry segments, but the decision maker knows that in the United States the kinds of toys in which Company B competes comprise 35 percent of total toy sales. In this country, the company has a 15 percent share of the market. Putting all of this together, his estimate of probable Company B sales in Canada is $10,000,000.

The director already has had the cost analysts make estimates of costs of making and shipping toys to Canada at various volume levels, to which marketing costs were added as well as duties. The estimates are that a net profit of $500,000 would be earned at the $10,000,000 level. The break-even volume would be $8,000,000. Obviously not much error margin can be tolerated.

A key question faced by the marketing executive is his degree of confidence in two types of predictions: (1) the state of the environment, or size of the market, in Canada and (2) the degree to which Canadian consumers will favor purchasing Company B's toys versus the Canadian competitors. Both are fraught with risk.

The marketing researcher needs to bring to this continuing dialogue inputs such as these:

1. What types of information would be pertinent?
    (These would include sounder figures on actual toy sales there, comparative distribution channel practices and obstacles, consumer demands for types of toys, strength of brand insistence, reactions to Company B's toys, etc.)

2. How might such information be obtained?
    [Alternative studies might be: (a) Purchasing or gathering various other Canadian statistics; (b) inquiring among Canadian wholesalers and retailers about the market's size and peculiarities; (c) having representative children and parents consider a selection of Company B's toys in comparison with competitive toys; and (d) conducting an actual test market in a medium-sized Canadian city.]

3. How long would it take to make such studies?
    (Ranges from two weeks to six months.)

4. How much would they cost?
   (Would vary with the magnitude and range from $1,000 to $70,000.)

When the decision maker and the researcher confer on whether or not it will be "profitable" to conduct any research on the Canadian toy market, and what specific research, their decision methods may range from the quite crude to the very refined. We might place these methods in three broad categories:

decision methods on whether or not project will be profitable — 3

1. *The intuitive approach.* The executive, let us say, ponders the problem (with or without the researcher's inputs that we described just above) and comes out with this remark: "Well, I feel pretty good about our Canadian prospects with what I know about it. This one isn't going to need any research." The researcher may or may not feel the same way. However, neither of them can make any objective comparison of their views, because that conclusion was not reached by a deliberate process that either could explicate to the other. The "gut feeling" might be right, but there is no proof whatever.

2. *The judgmental approach.* This could be done with care, with both of the parties in lucid dialogue, possibly even writing pro's and con's on paper. Each factor that they consider relevant may be specified and listed. Weights could be conceived and applied to the factors, and then these mentally analyzed. This procedure could be skillful and fairly objective, and yet it would be only a matter of judgment. Its conclusions could be specific, for example, "I would say that my profit forecast would be improved by around $50,000 with the data you'd gather with your proposal (c), which would justify spending $20,000 on it." Such an approach seems to characterize the extent of value analysis normally found now in deciding whether to do marketing research.

3. *Probabilistic decision analysis approach.* This would apply modern decision theory to the making of decisions under uncertainty. It would reduce the decision maker's best assessments of the current uncertainties, the consequences of various contingencies, and their probabilities of occurrence. Simultaneously, the degree to which specified information would be reliable and, within those limitations, would improve the decision would be assessed. These are matters that can be expressed quantitatively, so that actual computation can take place rather than vague judgment. The probabilistic approach has apparent complexity, and so our discussion of it will continue in Chapter 5. *Collecting dat*

Quantitative approach

2.9 Summary

Chapter 2 has been concerned primarily with the fact that marketing research will not be applied and efficient unless it meets the needs of the decision makers who would use it. The benefit of integrating the decisions with the planning of the research (and its ultimate reporting to the executives) is obvious. We have noticed, though, a number of reasons why it tends to be difficult.

Our discussion began broadly by describing marketing information systems and then detailing the role of marketing research in them. Next we placed the reseachers within a normal marketing organization, to help identify the executives whom it would serve. That referred to departments within the organization that uses the research, and so next we observed the values and problems of external research agencies.

At that point we narrowed to individuals, so that there could be clear views of parties on the two sides: the decision makers and the researchers. We proceeded to consider the situations and roles of these two parties, in that order. After that, we spoke of their relationship as a continuing dialogue. That would evolve around the developing decisions, whose flow was shown as a model. Possible research inputs to that flow were next added, with an example described. Finally, we reached an essential question: Should research be conducted or not, in terms of the decision maker's information needs? Three general approaches were suggested, and we will return to the third and most objective one in Chapter 5. Although this ends our chapter on achieving decision/research integration, bear in mind that this should be continued while the planning and execution of the studies proceed.

CASE 1

MILES LABORATORIES, INC. (A)

The recently appointed New Products Manager of Miles Laboratories had been brought in from another manufacturer of proprietary health care products, where he occupied a similar position. Among the problems inherited from his predecessor was a chewable antacid tablet that had performed poorly in a market test, so its development had been stopped. Entering a successful new product in this category was very desirable, but this tablet's project had fallen into limbo under the preceding manager. It now seemed likely that a new marketing strategy might solve the problem, and so the New Products Manager revived the project.

Miles was one of the prominent firms in the proprietary drug field, in 1972. Its sales volume had expanded by 14 percent annually over the previous five years and reached $288,337,000 in 1971. Net profits had been steady around 6 percent of investment during this period. Their most famous product and largest seller was Alka-Seltzer, which dominated its product category in antacids. That category was effervescent tablets, which must be taken with water.

To describe the competitive scene, we should point out that there are two major sectors of the drug market: ethical (promoted to physicians for their prescription or endorsement and unadvertised to the public) and proprietary (advertised to consumers). The antacid category had brands of both types, and the proprietary portion comprised about two thirds of sales volume. These products were sold in two forms, liquid and tablet, and our interest is only in the latter. Annual sales volume in the tablet field was divided roughly like this:

Chewable tablets	$105,000,000
Effervescent tablets	65,000,000

Alka-Seltzer completely dominated the effervescent type, with some 90 percent of volume. More than 30 brands contended in the chewable category, but three were holding most of the market with approximately the following shares: Rolaids, 40 percent; Tums, 21 percent; and Di-Gel, with nearly 20 percent and the fastest growth rate. This was the rivalry that Miles would have to vanquish with a new chewable tablet, if marketed as a proprietary product.

When Miles's laboratory scientists had come up with the proposed chewable tablet, it appeared to be a very attractive innovation. It was markedly superior to existing tablets on two qualities: (1) It crumbled faster and thus was faster-acting, due to a new Miles compression process, and (2) it was more palatable, for they had discovered that the compound mannitol would make it sweeter and creamier. The product management at that time made two decisions about positioning the new product: (1) to stress the palatability feature and (2) to compete in the ethical sector, where competition was less intense. A marketing campaign was arranged and quantities were produced—packaged in a bottle instead of a box like the other ethical brands. Pilot quantities were produced and a marketing campaign launched in the test city. After six months, though, there appeared no likelihood of reaching a breakeven sales volume, so it was withdrawn from the test market and left on the shelf.

The incoming New Products Manager sought new marketing approaches that could achieve target profits and sales volume. He wanted research to underlie major decisions, following a seven phase procedure that he had utilized in the past. Reviving the chewable tablet project, he accomplished these first two phases in three months:

Phase 1: Concept Generation. This utilized a mathematical model known as PERCEPTOR for the analysis of a competitive market structure. Placing the product idea (of the new chewable tablet) into this model, a go/no go decision could be reached on the idea's competitive viability. It passed this decision.

Phase 2: Preliminary Screening and Concept Viability. This phase subjected a statement describing the concept to consumers. They were brought together in group interviews, where their attitudes toward antacids and their reactions to the new idea (versus existing brands) were obtained. The concept was refined through successive waves of interviews. The sample was large enough to be quantified. These data were inputs in another mathematical model, known as SPRINTER, which had been created by Glen L. Urban, who aided as consultant. This was used to reach another go/no go decision, which was favorable to proceeding with the product concept.

Two key decisions that had been reached in these two phases were (1) that the new product would compete in the proprietary, not ethical, sector; and (2) that its positioning would stress its crumbling feature, as consumers seemed to be most concerned about a pill's fast action. There were a number of equally crucial questions to be faced during remaining phases of the new product development process.

Discussion

1. What are the important marketing aspects or decisions that had not yet been dealt with in this product's development? *where market is no descript to consumer*
2. Which of these, in your judgment, ought to be given formal research? Among these, which two or three seem to be most serious? Why?

CASE 2

COCA-COLA USA (A)

The Coca-Cola Company was the largest manufacturer of soft drinks in the world and had prospered since its founding in 1886. Its major brand of Coca-Cola (also known as "Coke")[9] was made and marketed in the United States by a division titled Coca-Cola USA.

Although its sales volume continually outstripped rival firms in its industry, The Coca-Cola Company was constantly appraising its market situation and its proposed marketing programs. Its marketing organization had conducted some form of marketing studies since the early 1920s—a time of infancy for marketing research. Subsequently, marketing research had become one of the larger departments at the company's Atlanta headquarters in number of personnel. As the company became diversified and divisionalized, decentralized marketing research units were established, and marketing research was a vital operation within Coca-Cola USA at the time of our interest, 1975.

Organization Structure

Figure 1 describes the departmental arrangement of Coca-Cola USA's marketing research functions as it existed in March, 1975. As this is the usual type of chart that depicts lines of authority and responsibility, it should be largely self-explanatory.

The Marketing Research Department embraced five subdepartments,

---

[9] Registered trademarks of The Coca-Cola Company.

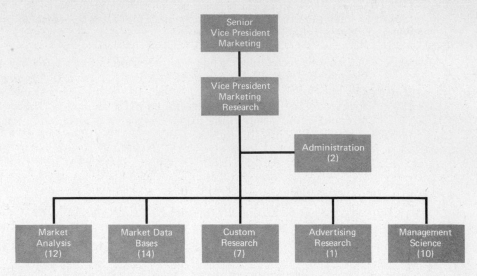

FIGURE 1. Structure of Marketing Research Organization of Coca-Cola USA in 1975

Figures in parentheses give the number of personnel in each section.

Source: The Coca-Cola Company.

which included all functions specialized in the analysis of business problems and served decision makers both inside and outside the marketing realm. This was particularly true of the Management Science group. The department was headed by a vice-president, who reported to the Senior Vice-President Marketing. The latter had responsibility, in addition to Marketing Research, for the Marketing Service, Marketing Planning, and Bottler Sales departments. This arrangement was appropriate for coordinating the marketing research department's plans and projects with those three functions.

Department Functions

Each of the five subdepartments in Marketing Research was assigned a fairly distinct area of research and analysis. We are going to summarize them for each of these units, as their titles may not be indicative to the reader of their work.

Market analysis. This staff gathered and analyzed data on the standing and potentials for Coke in every market area. This meant dealings with more than a thousand local bottlers of Coca-Cola around the nation who bought the syrup exclusively from The Coca-Cola Company. Bottler, fountain, and vending machine sales data were obtained in addition to data obtained from an outside service on competitive brand sales, enabling determination of market shares for Coke by area. Special analyses of sales, distribution, and competitive activities for market tests or when unusual conditions occurred also were made.

Market data bases. It was this group that consolidated and maintained all the market data on Coke. This included the local bottler audits mentioned above and also audits of the fountain and vending-machine channels, with which it performed liaison. It also obtained and analyzed data from the consumer level regarding brand preferences and consumption, thereby doing consumer tracking studies. With its wealth of historical data, it performed analyses and trend studies for various administrative functions.

Custom research. In contrast with the two previously described units that concentrated on repetitive analyses of markets, this group conducted ad hoc studies of various natures. The subjects researched included: consumer behavior, segmentation of markets, acceptance of proposed products and packages, and consumer brand images and attitudes. These projects were planned by this department and then farmed out to agencies that gathered the data under its general supervision.

Advertising research. The creation and execution of Coca-Cola advertising programs rested primarily with its advertising agency, McCann-Erickson. That agency also was responsible for the creative advertising research. This section in the company, in addition to that liaison, was responsible for testing of advertising results after publication or broadcasting.

Management science. This group was considerably different from the others. Its work largely was divided into two types, one of which was *operations research*. This was done by a technically specialized group of management scientists with strong mathematical orientation. They constructed computerized models of complex decisions, with which solutions were run for the advice of higher management. Some, like models of distribution systems, were in the marketing area, while others were on nonmarketing problems, such as plant locations. Earlier this group had been located in a corporate planning area of the parent company, but it was found advantageous for them to be under a research-oriented management and to have greater potential utilization and cross-fertilization when in proximity with other business research personnel.

Its other work was *forecasting*. Periodic forecasts of sales and related data were prepared and reported to management, throughout the top level. Outside business economists were retained to furnish basic inputs of independent forecasts. Also, executives of the Coca-Cola company who had unusual vantage points to examine future portents were polled for other inputs to the final forecasts.

Outside Services

The bulk of data utilized in marketing research was obtained from outside research services. The company alone could hardly have afforded the field staff and services maintained by those organizations. Its policy was to employ as few outside research firms as could conduct its work competently and to retain them rather permanently. Continuing series of measurements were considered to be more fruitful than unique studies that would not be repeated at intervals. Therefore, consulting firms were not engaged by this department, although occasionally they were retained by higher management and the sales department.

Two outside services constituted most of the data purchases:

1. A. C. Nielsen Company, of Chicago. The retail sales audit of this syndicated service was the main source of facts on product sales. The Coca-Cola Company had subscribed to the Nielsen index since the 1930s and had been a pioneer Nielsen client. The character of the data provided by Nielsen was similar to its standardized service for hundreds of other subscribers, but the Coca-Cola Company paid for special breakdowns in accordance with its sales branch districts and for special monthly frequency.

2. Audits and Surveys, Inc., of New York. The A & S field staff conducted the regular consumer surveys for the company. The Coca-Cola Company advised A & S on what was desired and approved questionnaires before they went to the field, and A & S handled the rest of the work and its supervision.

Two other research service vendors that were heavily utilized were the Majers agency, which monitored price promotions, and the Winona Interviewing Service, which conducted in-store sales tracking. Earlier the conduct of advertising research outside the company, through the McCann-Erickson advertising agency, was mentioned. That firm was a member company of the Interpublic Group, which had a subsidiary specializing in research and consulting, to which advertising research was largely delegated. Also outside were business economists who aided in forecasting.

Discussion

1. Did you find any research activities among the above-described departments that you had not expected? Were any missing that you consider important to marketing management?
2. Suppose that, as Vice-President Marketing Research, you were recommending annual budgets for the five research groups. Which would you want to support most generously? Why?
3. Would you recommend any changes in the organization, either for the sake of efficiency or for the ability to cope with change?

PART

Development

of a

Project

THE MOST FAR-REACHING DECISIONS in the course of a research study tend to occur at its beginning. The research begins its formation when the problem is identified or crystallized, for which a research project is later conducted.

This part of the book begins in Chapter 3 with the methods of finding and defining problems and the decisions to be made about them. It proceeds to the gathering of data to obtain background information and to explore for possible solutions that might be researched. These stages lead to determining whether or not to go ahead and plan a conclusive study.

That brings us to Chapter 4, in which we determine precisely the data that will be needed and the specific research designs we might use if conclusive research is conducted. Part of the researcher's expertise should be the ability to prescribe the appropriate research design, and we go extensively into this subject.

In Chapter 5 we begin to write down the formal project describing the research proposed and the plan of action. What kind of data do we need and how will we get it? Costs are specified and we evaluate whether research is likely to be profitable. If the decision is to go ahead, the work is scheduled and controls provided to meet the schedule.

3 Research Problem Identification and Development

Chapter 3 addresses the basic question of whether or not we have a problem calling for research. It develops answers to such questions as:

What is the distinction between symptoms and problems? What are the functions of symptoms?

How should one decide whether or not there is a significant problem?

What are the primary kinds of information feedback? From what sources are they obtained? What sorts of clues may they provide?

How should research contribute to the determination of the problem and its related decisions?

Why is a background study needed? An exploratory study? Of what dimensions? What methods are suggested for these?

At the end of these research phases, what should be decided?

EARLY IN CHAPTER 1 we explained that a major benefit of applied market research is *risk reduction*. Through the recognition of problems and the kind of decisions that must be made, managers can seek information that will aid in making those decisions more efficiently. Of no less importance is the need to provide for *opportunity assessment*. The monitoring of the environment about us may appear to be mundane and descriptive, but in the affairs of business, it may be a most important determinant of a company's survival.

In this chapter we shall explore some of the ways in which managers and researchers ferret out problems and the kind of decisions that must be made about them. Then we shall look at how problems may be defined for research purposes and finally the research decisions that must be made before we launch into a full-blown investigation.

In Chapter 2 the four types of research were identified as: preliminary, exploratory, conclusive, and performance monitoring. As a device to preview this chapter, Table 3–1 gives a synopsis of the questions the decision maker faces and the steps the researcher may take in the conduct of preliminary and exploratory research.

3.1 Problem Discovery

The ferreting out of problem situations that may be worthy of research to solve them is a part of the problem-solving process. It involves a search for causation among symptoms, problems, and decisions. A *symptom* is a condition that indicates the existence of a problem, and we must be careful not to confuse this with a problem. Symptoms occupy an essential place in the problem-solving process, for they signal the existence of problems and guide the search for the underlying problem. A *problem* exists whenever one faces a question whose answer—or a need whose fulfillment—involves doubt and uncertainty. If there is no answer or solution, there is no problem (although the consequences might be terrible); and if there is only a single possible answer or solution, there is no problem. A *decision* is a determination or resolution of a question. In the terms of a business executive, a decision is the determination of a course of action to be taken. Many routine or repetitive decisions face no appreciable uncertainty about the outcome of the selected action. Those decisions to which marketing research is applied often invoke a complex of problems, and considerable work is entailed in the choice of the best available course of action.

Business problems are not found by surprise or accidental circumstances. The persons who find problems are sensitized to be on the alert and are prepared to find them. Always there is evidence that the searching mind penetrates with insight. Our abilities can go beyond intuition or a sixth sense. Fortunately, there are means available to sharpen our capacities in problem discovery. First, an understanding of the different types of difficulties or symptoms which may call for decisions is useful. Second, provision of a marketing information system may often signify the existence of the problem to a decision maker.

58

TABLE 3–1. Preliminary and Exploratory Stages

Management Questions Faced	Research Steps To Take
1. What problem faces us? (What are the opportunities or obstacles to meeting objectives?)	1. Make a preliminary study of performance feedback information. Examine research conducted on other problems to obtain insights and indicate location and nature of information that points to new or unsolved problem(s).
2. What is the present environment of the problem?	2. Obtain background information on various factors that affect the problem and its solution.
3. What significant changes in the environment should be expected (by the time a solution is put into effect?)	3. Project the background data, with historical trends, to forecast the future situation.
4. What is the actual problem(s) faced?	4. Define the problem for research purposes.
5. What alternative courses of action might solve the problem and thereby reach the final objective?	5. Make an exploratory study: a. Seek and report likely ideas unearthed in past research and experience. b. Obtain clues and ideas from persons who would be in an advantageous position to provide them.
6. Which alternative courses of action merit final consideration?	6. Confer with the decision maker in weighing the worth of the results of research and its costs against the risk reduction that probably would be gained.
7. What uncertainties would be reduced, in the final choice of hypothetical situations, if formal research was conducted? Would such research be justified?	7. Decide on "go" or "no go" for planning conclusive research.

3.1.1 Symptomatic Situations

We can identify three categories of symptomatic situations:

1. *Overt difficulties.* When a difficulty openly manifests itself, this shows that a problem exists and a decision must be made to solve it. A firm is suffering from a lagging sales volume. This is a symptom,

not a problem. It is now necessary to search for a probable cause, develop a solution, and execute the solution.

2. *Latent difficulties.* These are difficulties that are not yet evident but will eventually become aggravated to the point where the difficulty would become overt. Let us suppose that the firm that began to suffer a lag in sales volume also experienced a decline in morale of the salesforce twelve months earlier. An unrecognized decline in morale triggered off an overt difficulty twelve months later. If that initial difficulty had been recognized, the factors causing the decline in morale identified as a problem, and a solution applied, it never would have emerged into a full-fledged, overt difficulty. Clearly, it is more efficient to recognize and tackle problems at earlier stages. As we shall see later, one of the purposes of a marketing information system is to identify difficulties that can be explored for problem identification. Likewise, formal research may reveal the existence of symptomatic-latent difficulties. The firm that found it was beginning to have a lagging growth of sales volume gathered evidence by quizzing its existing district sales managers about the performance and attitudes of sales personnel. This evidence revealed the worsening morale and also produced evidence that suggested that the "fixed salary" method of compensation was failing to stimulate effort. The firm then conducted a formal research study regarding the effects of compensation on the salespeople. The evidence produced in this study had an important byproduct, for it revealed that the salesforce was poorly allocated to sales territories and that it might not have a sufficient number of salespersons to meet competition. Both were further reasons for salesforce dissatisfaction and performance.

3. *Opportunity assessment.* Opportunities are a more subtle form of difficulty. Failure to capitalize on them can often be disastrous for the firm. The need to be constantly evaluating opportunities is very important in a competitive society in which innovation is continuously displacing old products, and changing consumer behavior patterns demand new adjustments on the part of the business firm. Heightened public interest in ecology and environment represents an opportunity for product adaptation and new products to meet society's new desires. So important has this area become that companies have established organizational units for dealing with it. Some have established departments of acquisitions and new ventures.

How does the decision maker become aware of these symptomatic situations? Information channels yield important evidence of value in problem identification. These channels include observations made by the decision maker and clues that he or she happens upon in reading of trade news and other literary sources. Fellow marketing managers and supervisors, salespersons, distributors, and customers often report significant facts and speculations. Such information deals with competitive activity, innovations, users' difficulties, troubles and gripes within the organization, and many other facts, views, and conditions. Irregular and unorganized as such information tends to be, it may be the chief basis of problem discovery. The mark of a brilliant manager is the capacity to filter these informal information flows and identify those areas that may impede the company's achievement of objectives.

Formal research studies that have been conducted for other recent decisions may also lead to problem discovery and assist in clarifying the source and nature of the problem. The example of the firm with a decline in morale of the salesforce is a case in point. Although research findings do not typically produce so much valuable "fallout" in revelation of other problems, as in the case described, such unplanned findings are possible in any marketing study. As each study is being conducted, a determined effort should be made to observe manifestations of other problems (hidden difficulties and new opportunities), which may point the way to timely decisions and continuing research. Simple familiarity with the kinds of situations that can require decisions in the future as well as continuous surveillance of information sources is helpful in training ourselves to be on the lookout for problems requiring solution.

2 types of feedback: Results + happenings

As explained in Chapter 2, marketing information systems provide information feedback of two types: results and happenings. _Results_ refer to the feedback of certain decisions' results. These are often called "performance analyses" and usually are statistical and standardized within the particular organization. Another type of feedback information are _happenings_, or continuous monitoring of the environment. This type of information feedback is relatively new in business circles and is designed to assess nonrecurring events such as the energy crises, shortages of basic raw materials, and so on, on the firm's market affairs as well as long-run legal, political, and value changes affecting business affairs. In this chapter we confine our treatment to results feedback found in performance analyses.

3.1.2 Information Feedback and Performance Analysis

describes major types of performance analysis

Performance analyses employ data largely gathered within the organization, but often are supplemented with available external data. Making internal data available promptly and classifying them suitably without being wasteful demands good liaison among the affected departments, such as accounting, marketing management, the field sales organization, and marketing research.

This section examines five main types of performance analyses: (1) sales analysis, (2) market-share analysis, (3) distribution analysis, (4) salesforce performance analysis, and (5) cost and profit analysis.

Types of Performance analyses:

1. Sales Analysis

Nearly all businesses analyze their sales figures, at least to some extent. True sales analysis calls for accurate determination, fine cross-classification, and tabulation that facilitate clear perception of superior and inferior areas of performance. Two questions must be answered if sales analyses are to signal overt difficulties or shed light on latent difficulties. They are: (1) how will sales be classified, and (2) what standards of comparison will be used?

Rarely is each individual transaction analyzed. Rather, sales of a similar type are grouped, and the aggregate of that group are analyzed. Some of the more common groupings are by market, product, geographical unit, and individual customers.

When sales are grouped by market, this usually means by class of customer, trade channel, or end user. The broadest classification would be to divide sales data into sales to industrial buyers or sales to ultimate consumers. Within the industrial buyer category, sales could be broken down again by industry or by size of purchase. If several channels of distribution are used, it is appropriate to monitor each channel separately and consequently to record sales through each channel.

In multiproduct firms one must know in addition to aggregate sales volume how each product is moving. Products vary with the seasons as to ease or difficulty of sales and in contribution to profits. The alert company wishes to know which ones are moving well and which are not; which ones the salesforce is favoring and which they are not. If products are a profit center in the organization, sales must be analyzed by product to complete the cost and profit analysis.

Practically all companies organize their sales effort on some geographical basis, usually the sales territory. Since marketing effort is applied through space, the company should know geographical variations in sales movement so that remedial action can be applied in the right locations. Further, responsibility for territorial management is often given to the salesperson in the territory or to a district manager of the territory. For purposes of evaluating the performance of this managerial unit, sales must be grouped on this basis.

In those cases in which a large proportion of sales are made to a few large customers, such as the automobile manufacturers in the industrial goods field or to large chains in the consumer goods field, it is wise to keep a close track of sales to these customers.

An interesting revelation was found in the food-processing industry when a larger and larger proportion of sales were being made to the institutional market—restaurants, schools, hospitals, in-plant feeding operations, and so on. This was in contrast to sales made into the retail sector, where food is destined for household consumption. Further research into this trend has forecast that by 1985 two out of every three meals will be eaten outside the home. This finding has caused a drastic change in management operation, investment allocation, and product specifications in this industry. Analysis of sales customer by customer may include speed of delivery (time between order and shipment) and detailed analysis about customers' product requirements.

Standards of comparison are needed to interpret any sort of data, as sales figures alone actually tell very little. Comparisons with similar data in previous years are helpful, although such a comparison does not single out a sales territory or product that has been weak year after year. Sales targets or quotas provide standards, but such targets are erroneous if they are based only on sales records. To reach conclusions useful for corrective actions, one must use indexes of market potential and information on competitive activity and other market conditions.

The amount of data needed for a complete sales analysis seems almost endless, yet all of it is available in the average company. With the advances made in electronic data processing, it is a relatively easy task to make these data available once a decision has been made on the sales information needs of the management.

perform share analysis #2. Market-Share Analysis

provides data on brand Rankings w/ competitors in sales volume

Among the deficiencies of sales analysis is the failure to measure the market share obtained by a particular organization's product lines, that is, its proportion of total industry sales in a market. As a result, one might draw misleading conclusions, for example, if total sales of a product were falling substantially and the particular company's fell only gradually. Another need not satisfied by sales analysis is that of providing data on how one's own brand ranks against competitive brands in sales volume. Market-share analysis meets these needs, among others.

Market-share analysis requires the gathering and interpretation of data on the sales of individual brands at the level of sale to the ultimate buyer. Obtaining such data is more difficult than getting data for sales analysis, because these data are normally external to the organization and must be gathered by a very broad sampling of the entire market. A market researcher might find the research required to monitor the competitive situation prohibitively costly if outside sources were not available.

For many companies, accurate data on industry sales are available from trade associations or trade publications. For others, such as automotive, liquor, and insurance companies, accurate data are available through compulsory registration or excise and consumption tax data.

determines brand positions

Several companies now offer retail store audit services, and these will be described in Chapter 6. Consumer purchase panels are used to measure the performance of specific products in the marketplace. The data collected are based upon consumers' diaries kept by a national panel of consumers. Many companies now offer this service. The special virtues of these data include showing sales related to many consumer characteristics, loyalty to, or switching among brands, and consumer buying practices. The store audit data have the advantage of measuring entire sales volumes of items through particular stores. Consumer panels, on the other hand, provide continuous histories of a family's purchases of many items, even though panel families may buy from many stores. These two approaches to market-share analysis are, therefore, somewhat complementary, although each in its buyer breakdowns provides measurements of competitive brand position and a basis for projecting total market size. The brand position analysis in this kind of performance data frequently triggers conclusive research to ascertain the reasons for changes in competitive position and possible solutions.

Subscribing to such syndicated data services may cost anywhere from $5,000 to (depending on type of service) $35,000 per year or more for a minimal service. Large marketers find this worthwhile, and many of them subscribe to one or more of these types of services. The vast number of marketers who cannot afford to subscribe may have little factual basis for determining their brand positions. They can, however, determine their market share if total industry figures are available. A growing number of industries combine sales data through their trade associations. This practice does not give brand breakdowns, but it does give each member the means of determining his share of the market and of examining trends in total sales volume. In the absence of trade association data, the marketers must rely upon whatever evidence their field representatives can pick up or on their own forecasts of market potential.

The following example describes the procedure used by one company:

> To determine total market demand for its share-of-market studies, a manufacturer of corrugators' tape had its sales personnel count the number of taping machines in operation at each customer location. Knowing that such machines are run constantly through the day, except for time needed to thread on new tapes, and the daily consumption of each such machine, the company can determine the amount of tape used by a customer or prospect. Comparing this figure with the tape purchases the customer has made from the company gives management a share-of-market figure.[1]

Standards of comparison for market-share analysis include data from past experience and norms established in relationship to competitors if brand position is known. Data indicating market fertility and facts on the plans and actions of the company and its competitors are used in interpreting market-share studies.

3   Distribution Analysis – *Reasons for poor performance are frequently found here.*

Sales and market-share analyses often highlight overt problems or symptoms of latent difficulties. The reasons for poor performance are frequently found in distribution analysis. To state the obvious, if goods are to sell, they must be available where consumers want to buy them. Therefore, the most common type of distribution analysis is the number and quality of the outlets in which the brand is distributed, relative to competition. Salespersons' reports indicate the extent of distribution only if they call on every possible outlet, which generally is not the case. On the other hand, outlets must be checked frequently or out-of-stock conditions may be missed, and this is a common means of losing brand patronage.

Retail stores' audit services record a wealth of facts at the retail level for a wide array of products. Not only do they record extent of distribution, but a number of quality variables, such as inventory levels, out-of-stock, and dealer support (display, local advertising, coupon redemption) are also recorded.

---

[1] "Sales Analysis," *Studies in Business Policy, No. 113* (New York: The National Industrial Conference Board, Inc., 1965), p. 43.

Many companies make detailed evaluations of their distributors and have organized reporting systems to do so. The evaluations of distributors are of two types: (1) current operating appraisals, and (2) overall performance reviews. The first type of evaluation is very similar to the kind of evaluations made by the company's own sales efforts. In fact, many companies consider the distribution organization as an extension of its own field organization. The data needed for continuous monitoring of operations are found in the company's records and usually are a part of its sales analysis program. Most distributor sales performance evaluations are based upon three types of comparisons:[2]

1. Comparison of the distributor's current sales with its sales attainments in prior periods (analyzing historical performance).
2. Comparisons of the performances of various distributor outlets (usually classified by outlet type or geographic region).
3. Comparisons of sales figures with predetermined quotas and other gauges of territorial potential.

Overall performance reviews are made less frequently and inquire into such activities as inventory maintenance, number of salespeople, technical knowledge and competence, attitudes, competition, general growth prospects, and financial status.

The demise of the traditional department store as the favored outlet for household appliances in the 1950s was revealed to some manufacturers by continuously monitoring the differing merchandising strategies of the different classes of outlets handling their products. Where those strategies were favorably viewed by consumers, those outlets continued to prosper, along with the suppliers using them. In a short period of time, the discount store surpassed the past outlet leader, the department store.

Integration of distribution and other performance analyses, together with other marketing plans and knowledge, bring into focus problems that deserve more costly forms of research.

Salesforce Performance Analysis

A principal focus of performance analysis is on members of the field selling force. This is hardly surprising since successful sale of the product nearly always depends, to a large degree, on the efforts of sales personnel, and since a major portion of the firm's competitive efforts and strategies are effected through the sales organization. Table 3–2 shows the basic items measured and the ways of measuring them. Most of the information needed for measuring sales results and nonselling activities is already available and has been described in the performance analyses already discussed. However, there are additional items of information not normally available from the sales analysis program. They are:

---

[2] "Selecting and Evaluating Distributors," *Studies in Business Policy, No. 116* (New York: The National Industrial Conference Board, Inc., 1965), p. 109.

add'l

*info not
avail. from
sales analysis*

1. New account development.
2. Investigation of complaints.
3. Sales service and engineering.
4. Sales promotion and merchandising.
5. Distributor assistance or training.
6. Check on distributor stocks.
7. Price checks.

Of course, the extent of the information collected will depend upon the nature of the particular selling job required. The information above, together with other information from sales analysis, must be collected in an orderly way so that the data will be comparable. Care must be exercised in designing forms so that they can be filled out quickly and easily by the salespersons. Care must also be exercised in interpreting the data. An item-by-item interpretation may give the wrong impression. For example, high expenses may result from traveling in sparse markets or areas of high travel costs. A salesperson may be below average on number of calls per day but above average on sales per call because he or she spends more time on thoroughly selling each customer. Further, the changes in competitive conditions may require emphasizing different facets of selling activities at different times. For these reasons data should be interpreted in an integrated way. Bear in mind that salesforce perfor-

TABLE 3-2. How Companies Assess the Performance of Their Salesforce

What Is Measured	*Common Ways of Measuring*
I. Sales results	I. Sales, expense, and/or profitability analyses:
A. Sales volume (total, or by product, account, etc.)	A. Sales analysis—determination of absolute unit or dollar sales figures for the period; comparison with performance of other salespeople or with salesperson's own past performance.
B. Quota attainment (unit or dollar sales total, or by product, account, etc.; profitability of sales; new accounts; etc.)	B. Sales analysis—comparison of actual achievement with predetermined quota(s) for the period; comparison of relative attainment of quota(s) with that of other salespeople.
C. Selling expenses	C. Expense analysis—determination of direct selling expenses for the period; computation of ratio of
D. Profitability of sales	
E. Product mix	

TABLE 3–2. (Cont.)

What Is Measured	*Common Ways of Measuring*
	direct selling expenses to total dollar sales; comparison with predetermined standards or norms, with performance of other salespeople or with salesperson's own past performance. D. Profitability analysis—determination of profits on sales for the period; determination of relative profit contribution and assignment of profitability weights to product classes sold; comparison with predetermined standards or norms, with performance of other salespeople or with salesperson's own past performance.

II. Sales-related and nonselling activities
  A. New account development
  B. Calls made (total, or by type customer, etc.)
  C. Matters discussed or handled during calls
  D. Investigation of complaints
  E. Sales service and engineering
  F. Sales promotion and merchandising
  G. Distributor assistance or training
  H. Check on distributor stocks
  I. Price checks
  J. Travel
  K. Filling of reports
  L. Time on job vs. time lost
  M. Time selling vs. time spent on other activities
	E. Sales analysis—determination of absolute unit or dollar sales figures by product for the period; determination of inclusion and/or relative importance of product classes in total sales; comparison with predetermined standards or norms, with performance of other salespeople or with salesperson's own past performance.
	II. Sales and similar analysis—determination of relevant numbers, time spent, or expense for given activity during the period; comparison with predetermined standards or norms, with performance of other salespeople or with salesperson's own past performance.

III. Personal qualities, aptitudes, and development	III. Personal observation by superior or other observer(s); self-evaluation; testing

Source: Courtesy of the National Industrial Conference Board.

67

mance analysis does not provide solutions to unhealthy situations. It does, however, indicate trouble spots that may require further study in depth and possible research to find accepted remedies.

SALES
PERFORMANCE
ANALYSIS.

5. Cost and Profit Analysis

A number of strong and weak spots in a marketing operation can be revealed through sales, market-share, distribution, and salesforce analyses. Yet a business may sustain losses though all these indicators look favorable; profits may be substantially lower than given sales performance ought to earn. The cost phase of performance analysis must be dealt with.

Financial data must be analyzed in specific ways, depending upon the purpose of the analysis. Cost analyses have been classified as (1) natural cost analysis, (2) functional cost analysis, (3) responsibility cost analysis, and (4) profit analysis.

Natural cost analysis is that used in the regular financial accounting system where the accounts identify the goods or services purchased, such as rent, advertising, freight, and so forth. Hardly any diagnosis is possible when these are merely lump totals, such as the total of all salesperson's salaries during a given period. Natural expenses give only a meager basis for management or research guidance because natural account classifications can be allocated to functions performed (selling, field sales, promotion) for only a few sizable direct expenses. Keeping a watch on whether natural expense data are in accordance with plans and budgets ought to be standard practice, but it does not reveal the payoff of marketing activities in profits.

Functional cost analysis records cost data in terms of the activity or tasks performed as a result of the expenditure. For example, costs are assigned to warehousing, advertising and sales promotion, credits and collection, transportation, direct selling, and so forth. The data in the accounting records charge each expense against its "natural" purpose, for instance, "telephone and telegraph." Telephone calls and telegrams are not marketing functions, although many of them and part of the switchboard service are used in marketing. As every other phase of the enterprise also is facilitated by the telephone and telegraph expense, it is a joint cost. Every concern has many joint overhead or administrative costs.

Whether costs are joint or separable, the natural account classifications do not permit much marketing cost analysis; hence a breakdown by costs of marketing functions is required. A functional classification may include expenses of direct selling, advertising and sales promotion, credit and collection, transportation, warehouse and handling, and general marketing.

Let us consider one of these, warehouse and handling expense. Many costs of warehouse and handling are chargeable directly to that function, particularly wages of employees in that department. Many others — such as property taxes, heat, light and power, and service departments whose benefit is jointly shared with other functions, marketing and nonmarketing — are not so chargeable. A logical basis for allocation to the benefit-

4
types
of
cost
analyses

1 —

2 —

ing function may be found for some costs, for example, by dividing heating costs on the basis of the space occupied. Frequently, however, the basis must be arbitrary.

3- In *responsibility cost analysis*, costs are assigned to those responsible for specific functions within the organization. Organization theory, today, favors making managerial units profit centers. For example, the territory is expected to generate a profit, and this is the responsibility of the territory manager—in some cases, the single salesperson in the territory. Responsibility for a single product or groups of products are the responsibility of product managers, and in some companies marketing activities are organized in terms of types of customers, or channels of distribution with a managerial unit in charge of sales to these groups.

4- *Profit analysis* matches costs with profits to determine profit. This type of analysis is generally confined to profits generated by responsibility centers, such as a territory, a branch, a product, a channel of distribution, or a class of customer.

An elementary form of profit performance analysis can be obtained through periodic data on gross profits, the amount that is left from sales after paying for the cost of goods sold (that is, production and materials cost in a manufacturing company). Generally, gross profit measures are made for products, for territories, or for any objective of the analysis. The resulting gross profit is considered to be a contribution to marketing and general expenses and profits. Often the gross profit is adjusted by deducting direct selling expense to arrive at an adjusted gross profit.

Gross profit analysis often reveals distinct differences between sales territories, between products, and between various channels of distribution. It may point toward the problems where more complex research may find causes of poor performance and means of restoring profit levels.

Net profit for products, territories, channels of distribution, or class of customer is the preferable measure. This, however, entails allocating every functional expenses classification to the responsibility center under analysis. In many instances, there is no sound basis for allocation. In a territory profit analysis, direct selling expenses can be allocated to a territory fairly easily because most of the expenses are incurred in the territory and recorded as such. On the other hand, it would be much more difficult to allocate the advertising and promotional expenses to a territory. First, these expenses cover the cost of communication through national media and can only be allocated to a territory on the basis of circulation in that territory. Second, it is not easy to determine what share of the advertising cost generated the revenues during the time period for which the analysis is made. Much of the advertising payoff may come in future periods. If the responsibility center happens to be a product or product group, it is relatively easier to allocate advertising cost to products because one knows what products were featured in the advertising program. This expense becomes a direct expense for this analysis. The direct selling expense, however, is an indirect expense in this case. Sales personnel usually sell many products in the line, and the only way of allocating expenses to each product or product group is through monitoring the time spent by each salesperson on each product. Occasionally, this information is available from salesforce performance analysis.

Even though reasonable bases for allocation are developed, many executives feel that it is unfair to judge a responsibility center on factors over which the manager of the center has no control. Because of the difficulty in allocation and the desire to judge responsibility centers fairly, most companies confine their profit analyses to adjusted gross profit, varying the number of expenses deducted from gross profit, depending upon the ease of allocation and control by the responsibility center manager.

In Table 3–3, the adjusted profit contribution made by three brands sold by a farm supply house is reviewed. Although market potentials for each brand are not known, there is some evidence of unbalanced selling effort. That is, the sales personnel are favoring Brand A, the brand with

TABLE 3–3. Profitability by Brands

	Brand		
	A	B	C
Sales (dollars)	100,000	84,000	45,000
Gross profit (dollars)	15,000	16,800	9,900
Gross profit (percent)	15	20	22
Direct costs (dollars)	8,000	12,600	7,200
Direct costs (percent)	8	15	16
Profit contribution (dollars)	7,000	4,200	2,700
Profit contribution (percent)	7	5	6

the lowest gross margin. Usually, the low gross margin brands are the easiest to sell and favored by sales personnel. The absolute dollar contribution on Brand A is higher than Brand C, but the opportunity for a higher volume and profit on Brand C may be overlooked.

Marketing cost analysis is rarely impossible: it is just difficult and burdensome. The benefits in highlighting areas of waste or low profitability (and outright loss) have brought striking increases in efficiency and profits to many organizations. Therefore, some program of marketing cost analyses ought to be included in any system of performance analysis.

An interesting series of opportunities, overt and latent difficulties, can be seen in Table 3–4. In this instance, the company conducted performance analysis of the types described above to ascertain its relative, competitive position. In each instance, the analysis revealed areas for action which in most cases would require further preliminary research to determine if conclusive research may be warranted.

TABLE 3–4. Simplified Competitive Analysis

Competitive Dimensions		Us	Competitors			Comments on Data
			A	B	C	
Salesforce performance analysis						
1. Overall marketing strength						
No. representatives	Line 1	5	10	15	15	A strongest and equal to us. B and C vulnerable to more intensive selling effort offered by us.
No. distributors	2	40	35	30	30	
No. salespersons	3	25	20	10	7	
2. Geographic strength						
No. salespersons and reps						
Territory E		9	7	7	6	We may be weak in district G and should consider adding salespeople; otherwise we are equal or superior to competition.
F		7	7	6	6	
G		5	8	7	6	
H		9	8	6	4	
Distribution analysis						
3. Distributor strength						
No. distributors						
Territory E		12	10	8	7	A approximately equal in strength. B and C weaker and definitely vulnerable.
F		10	9	7	8	
G		10	9	7	7	
H		8	7	6	6	
4. Delivery norm (weeks)						
Product 1		6	6	4	7	Delivery improvements necessary in 1, 2 to be competitive. Improvement beyond competitive levels will not gain share. Improvement in line 3 will gain advantage against A, B, and C according to salesforce survey.
2		6	3	4	4	
3		6	6	7	9	

TABLE 3–4. (Cont.)

Competitive Dimensions	Us	Competitors A	B	C	Comments on Data
Sales analysis					
5. Penetration by account size (%)					
$ Market—all products					We're weak in medium and small accounts, need program to improve penetration and coverage there.
40 Large	40	30	15	15	
15 Medium	15	30	25	30	
10 Small	10	30	20	40	
$65MM					

Market-share analysis

6. Product Position	Market Size (millions of dollars)	Growth per Year (percent)	Market Share (percent) Us	A	B	C	Comments on Data
Line 1	15	0	65	20	10	5	1. Not subject to share gain; manage for cash.
2	30	10	25	40	15	20	2. Subject to share gain; A most vulnerable, B, C less so.
3	20	15	10	25	30	35	3. Subject to share gain; A, B, C equally vulnerable. Substantial unfilled need for a new product.

Price analysis

7. Pricing strategy		Us	A	B	C	Comments on Data
H = price for margin	Line 1	C	C	C	H	B and C will be easiest to take share away from on price, and it will be least expensive to maintain share taken away. A is more competitive, will require larger price differentials to gain and maintain share, and it is therefore more costly to take share away.
C = price with market	2	C	L	C	C	
L = price leader or very aggressive	3	C	L	C	C	

TABLE 3–4. (Cont.)

Product analysis
8. New product policy
L = leader
F = follower

Line 1	L	L	F	F
2	F	L	L	F
3	L	L	L	F

Conclusions

9. Probable reaction to:

Lower price
A—Immediate retaliation, continued price reduction to gain share back.
B, C—Weaker response; will try to hold large accounts.

Expect new products first from *A*, monitor market carefully to identify what they're working on—expect *A* to imitate earliest any new products introduced.

Cost in taking share away from *A* on price will be high. *B* and *C* more vulnerable.

New product
A—Will immediately match new product offering.
C—May match immediately.
B—Eventually match.

B and to some extent *C* vulnerable to new product offering.

Increased sales coverage
A—Will match.
B, C—Some increase.

B and *C* vulnerable in some measure to sales coverage, particularly if a new product is launched.

Key Strategic Conclusions

1. *Product policy:* Focus on lines 2 and 3, where gain is possible by increased penetration and growth with the market and product modification for product 3.
2. *Competitive strategy:* Focus on taking share away from *B* and *C*, who are vulnerable to lower pricing and a new product innovation requested by sales personnel. Selectively take business away from competitor *A*—only up to the point where expensive price retaliation is expected.
3. *Marketing strategy:* Add three salespeople to territory G and one to F to build strength against key targets—*B* and *C.* Shift call pattern and develop marketing programs for medium to small accounts where penetration is poor. Develop distributor promotion program to capitalize on advantage over *B* and *C.*
4. *Service:* Invest in capacity to lower delivery time in product 2 to level competitive with *B* and *C.* Maintain competitive standards in other lines.

73

Source: *Adapted from C. Davis Fogg, "Planning Gains in Market Share," Journal of Marketing, July, 1974, p. 35. Reprinted by permission of the American Marketing Association.*

This section has described the major types of performance analyses. Such analyses are conducted primarily with data obtained within the corporation but also with syndicated or other external data. These analyses are the marketing information system of the company. They indicate those difficulties, overt or latent, that marketing research may investigate with more complex techniques. They do not, however, indicate those unnoticed opportunities that are so important to survival in today's environment of rapid change. These can only be assessed by continuous attention to economic, social, and political indexes of change as well as being alert to information flows and radically new ideas whatever may be their source.

3.2 Preliminary Research

You will recall from Chapter 2 that preliminary research involves (1) discovering and crystallizing the problem, and (2) describing the relevant situation or environment. The result is research-problem definition. In this section we examine each of these stages.

3.2.1 Discovering and Crystallizing Problems

Recognition of a problem is in itself fruitless until the vague concept of its existence is refined, which in turn enables the nature of the decision to be defined. Our sequencing of events at this point becomes complicated and a review of the process may help. We have suggested how we ferret out those symptoms that signify the existence of problems. The researcher and the decision maker must then informally probe the symptom to try to understand the cause. In the instance above regarding the salesforce, the researcher quizzed existing district managers about performance and attitudes of salespersons. This information revealed that the worsening of morale was related to the fixed-salary method of compensation. The objective of the decision maker is to increase sales volume through improved morale of the salesforce. This is the area for decision and it also represents the decision problem but not the research problem. Nevertheless, a clear definition of the decision is necessary to proceed to a definition of the problem for research purposes.

The way in which the researcher helps the decision maker at this point is to consider the ways in which morale may be improved, for there are any number of alternatives that could be used. The preliminary probe, however, suggested that compensation may be a major factor, and they have jointly agreed that the research-problem definition is "to determine the effect of compensation methods on salesmen's attitudes and performance."

Although this example is simple, this same process of reasoning from symptom, to cause, to decision alternatives and problems, to research problem can be used even in the most complicated of situations. A subtle example not based on feedback will serve to illustrate the series of events leading to a research problem definition. The Whirlpool Corporation, a major appliance manufacturer, continuously monitors retail developments and retail change through a series of monthly reports made available to management.[3] Because of the experience span of a number of Whirlpool executives, they were very much aware that in spite of a continuous flow of data there was no way to alert decision makers of the consequences of retail changes. In fact, a major shift in the retail appliance area took place in the early fifties with the march of the mass merchandiser into the appliance field. It was not until many years later that manufacturers and retailers alike recognized the importance of this event. For many it was too little too late, and the opportunity to recoup lost position had passed. Whirlpool management began to ask such questions as:

1. Is another change in the retailing of appliances around the corner?
2. Are mass merchandisers losing market position?
3. Will leasing become the most popular means of acquiring appliances?
4. Will developments in furniture retailing have an application in appliance retailing?

In a sense the management was exploring new opportunities, which were perceived as difficulties if they were to pass by unnoticed. After brainstorming the area of concern for several days, the problem faced by the decision makers was not really an evaluation of each new retailing change but something much broader: *what mix of retail outlets should the corporation service to attain and maintain a balanced retail distribution system in the future?* Since shifts in support of new retail outlets cannot be accomplished by a manufacturer in a short period of time, the loss of competitive position resulting from failure to cultivate (or even recognize) emerging retail leader types could be disastrous. The statement above represents the decision area and the decision problem. What, then, is the research problem? The excellent statement of the decision that some one will have to make gives little direction to the researcher if he or she is to be helpful in finding the answer. Unfortunately, an extensive search of available data on appliance purchasing revealed nothing.

3.2.2 Searching for Causation

At this point, a process of reasoning began in an attempt to understand the variables involved in finding an answer for the decision maker. Initially, the researchers thought it was necessary to document the existence of shifts in purchase volumes through different types of retail outlets by different groupings of consumers over time. A partial evaluation for the shifts could be inferred if distinctly different consumer groupings clustered in distinctly different classes of retail outlets. On the other hand, a

---

[3] This study was conducted under the direction of Sol Goldin, Director of Retail Marketing, Whirlpool Corporation, and is used with the permission of Whirlpool Corporation.

change in consumer behavior would be manifest in a change in the relative strengths of brand loyalty and store preference, as both are significant elements in the purchase decision. At this point, two different situations could be hypothesized. The stronger a consumer preference for a particular store or store type, relative to his loyalty to a particular brand, the greater the need for the manufacturer to pay close attention to his mix of retail outlets. Conversely, where consumers have a strong brand loyalty but weak store preference, the manufacturer can be highly selective about what stores handle his products and not be concerned about shifts in retail-store-type strengths. A tentative research problem, then, is the number of stores and brands shopped by different market segments. Before accepting this position, however, additional background information should be collected to provide familiarity with the environment of the problem.

3.2.3 Background Information

A competent decision maker needs abundant knowledge of the current environment about which he or she is going to make important decisions. As the decision is going to be executed in some future time, realistic projection of situation changes is also needed. The researcher tends to acquire part of the background while engaged in problem discovery and definition. Nevertheless, we distinguish this as a separate phase because background information is essential in assessing the risks and problems that will be encountered in conducting the research.

Need for Background Information

Two considerations would determine the need and size of the background study: (1) the nature and magnitude of the problem, and (2) the extent of the researcher's present knowledge about the situation. Usually, the collection of background information is less extensive where the area of inquiry has been focused by a particular difficulty. On the contrary, when dealing with underlying difficulties or unrecognized opportunities, the background study must be extensive since there is no way of pinpointing its scope.

A researcher who approaches a company, product, or phase of marketing with which he or she has had no previous experience has much to learn about the problem's environment. More typically, some of the background is familiar, and the background study can be brief.

Scope of Background Study

What type of information should be acquired in the background study? This must be decided in each case, but some essential aspects of any marketing situation should either be already known or be obtained in the background study. The possibility of overlooking these can be avoided with a checklist such as the following:

Research
Problem
Identification
and
Development

1. The industry
   a. Its various products and their relative volume and value
   b. The concerns comprising the industry, their size, financial power, and trends
   c. The geographical locations of the industry, importance of location for materials, costs, transportation, and markets
2. The company
   a. The age, size, and growth trends of the company
   b. Relations of the company to the industry in size, products, profits, location, financial ability, and facilities
   c. Type of legal organization and control arrangements
   d. Organization plan and its administration (especially in marketing departments)
3. Its products
   a. The products and their physical characteristics
   b. The manufacturing processes and production capacity
   c. The existence of substitute products and their relative merits
   d. The features of the product most vital to its marketability
   e. Whether the product is standardized or custom-made; variations in sizes, materials, models, flavors, etc.
4. Packaging and unit of sale
   a. Special packaging requirements of product
   b. Material and design of packages
   c. Color and other eye appeal of packages and importance of this
   d. Sizes of packages: consumer sizes and bulk sizes
5. The markets
   a. The uses made of products
   b. The persons or firms who consume or buy the products
   c. The locations of superior markets for the product
   d. The characteristics of superior markets and buyers within them
   e. The nature of demand: elastic or inelastic; constant, seasonal, cyclical
   f. Actual sales of the product as compared with competitors' and with the market characteristics
6. Distribution
   a. The channels of distribution used and trends in outlet importance
   b. The extent distributed: by area and by intensity of coverage
   c. Distribution policy: exclusive franchises, distributorships, and the like
   d. Extent to which buyers shop for this type of product
   e. Practices of the company in assisting dealers
7. Pricing and profits
   a. Current and past pricing by this company and by competitors
   b. Seasonal or special promotional price cuts
   c. Margins allowed to distributors and dealers
   d. Profits earned by types of product, territories, and so forth
   e. Profit margins of distributors and dealers
8. Promotional methods
   a. Costs and function of personal selling
   b. Character of sales personnel and their coverage of markets

c. Advertising media and expenses
d. Appeals used in sales and advertising campaigns
e. Sales promotion material provided for sales and dealer organizations
f. Promotional strategy and the timing and magnitude of campaigns
g. Public relations activity: extent and coordination with marketing efforts

---

The foregoing is only a suggested outline, but it indicates the broad nature of the background study. Although researchers may lack time for thorough background exploration, they should have more than a smattering of observations on each topic in the checklist.

Sources of Background Information

Where will the researcher find this information? Mostly from secondary sources, some of which are described in Chapter 6. On topics concerned with the company and its marketing, a great deal can be learned from its records and financial statements, in addition to valuable opinions and reports of experiences from many persons in the organization (executives, salespeople, product designers, engineers, credit managers, and others) and from its advertising agency. Information on the industry may also be obtained from trade association and government sources. To save time and expense, the background information should be limited largely to that readily available.

In our appliance study, the research team obtained extensive information on the problem area before proceeding to problem definition. Internal studies in the Whirlpool Corporation were reviewed to search for indications of shifting buying habits by different socioeconomic groups as well as brand and store preferences of potential customers. Data from a syndicated data service purchased by one of Whirlpool's largest customers every two weeks was studied for similar trends. A sample of retailers in a representative city was interviewed extensively to determine if they observed any changes in buyers' attitudes regarding store and brand preferences. Only after these additional forays for information was the research team prepared to define the research problem.

3.2.4 Research-Problem Definition

Both the decision maker and the researcher need a clear-cut definition of the problem as a starting point for a solution to it. Three specific reasons for needing problem definition are:

1. The problem definition orients the decision and research within the framework of classified marketing knowledge. This relates the problem to other marketing problems; it suggests sources of data and facilitates their interpretation.
2. Any business organization faces many marketing decisions. Some

are so complex that the most systematic decision methods are needed, and some of these may demand formal research. With clear definition of the many problems, one can determine which deserve priority and also which will require unusual pains.

3. When research is to be undertaken, lucid definition delineates the inquiry and enables the researcher to distinguish the data relevant to the problem.

Proper definition not only arrives at an operational statement that enables the action related to the decision to proceed, but it also uncovers the *basic problem* that underlies the symptoms which must be solved. We noticed this in the instance above regarding the salesforce. Although every problem situation is different, a clear and concise statement enables the decision model to be well conceived. Proper definition may also pinpoint gaps in knowledge that may call for formal research.

Referring once again to our appliance example, the problem was defined as: *a study of the number of stores shopped and number of brands shopped by socioeconomic groupings of recent purchasers of major appliances in a selected market.* It was further reasoned that if there were difference in brand preference and store preference by different socioeconomic groupings, the study would be repeated in other markets to check for consistency.

So important is the precise definition of the research problem that another example of problem definition follows. The executive in charge of marketing–planning in a large paper products company expressed concern to the marketing research manager about the relative location of paper departments in supermarkets, which seemed unfavorable in comparison to most other product locations in such stores. The executive further said that he felt that paper departments were losing ground to other types of supermarket merchandise lines and that retailers needed help in merchandising paper. He suggested that a formal project be directed to study this matter.

The researcher in this case observed that a problem situation had been identified, but the problem itself had been stated too vaguely to permit either sharp decision making or truly relevant research. She refined and elaborated what the executive had said into a three-part statement: (1) the paper company wished to influence supermarket managements to place paper departments in those locations that would maximize such departments' profits; (2) if that is the objective of supermarket managements and they can control locations of the various departments in stores, then the paper company needs to decide which locations to recommend to the merchants. She went on: (3) the paper company could make and support these recommendations only if research findings demonstrated that specified locations existed in which the paper departments' profits would increase. Since location in the store was only one factor that might influence the departments' profits, other factors were considered, such as product attributes, price, and so on. The research-problem definition finally settled upon was: *to study the content and intensity of product attributes and alternative store locations on paper department profitability.*

3.3 Exploratory Research

Now we will consider the second type of research relative to its phasing into the decision sequence: exploratory research. The main purpose of exploratory research is to learn of plausible solutions to the given problem.

3.3.1 Purpose

No matter how sharply we have defined our research problem, we shall need to state more specifically those facets of the problem that we wish to study. Referring again to the firm that conducted the study on the effect of compensation methods on salesmen's attitudes and performances, we might ask the following questions: What method of compensation: all possible alternatives or only specific methods? What attitudes are we interested in? What do we mean by performance? What aspects of performance are we concerned about? To study all methods and all attitudinal and performance responses would be excessively costly and of limited value. We must explore this area intensively to select those aspects of the problem that, if studied, would provide some insight into what actions might be taken to improve morale and increase sales volume.

But what does a research hypothesis look like? In our appliance manufacturer example, discussions with retailers and some purchasers revealed that young, newly married, low-income household units shop many brands and many stores before making a purchase. In contrast, older, professional, high-income household units have definite store preferences but will purchase the brand stocked. In view of the payoffs the company was looking for, it would be rather important to verify these facts. Consequently, two hypotheses are as follows:

1. Young, newly married, low-income household units have weak brand loyalty and weak store preferences.
2. Old, professional, high income household units have strong store preferences and weak brand loyalty.

These statements now provide some direction for the research. They are illustrative and there may be as many as ten or fifteen. They aid in specifying the data needed to prove or disprove the hypothesis. Hypotheses are usually stated in a positive way; however, they may also be stated in question form.

In practice, it is difficult to distinguish this research from the gathering of background information. If there are separate background and exploratory studies, they can be contrasted in this way: (1) the background study would deal broadly with the environment of the problem; whereas (2) the exploratory phase is more intensive and more limited in scope, as it bores into the specified hypotheses.

If possible, the researcher personally conducts all or a major portion of this study. The task is not easily delegated to others, for the re-

80

searcher best comprehends the problem, can probe for the information sought, and can recognize a hypothetical solution when encountered.

3.3.2 Sources of Information

Ideas are likely to come from other persons; however, secondary data should also be utilized. Some of the principal sources of ideas are discussed below.

Internal sources within the concern conducting the study are generally the most important and are an excellent starting point. Executives within the company generally have familiarity with the problems and are a fruitful source of ideas. Salespeople as well as advertising, merchandising, and laboratory personnel may also have key facts. Specialists or professional persons concerned with the product and its customers, including advertising agencies, product designers, and technical persons, may be excellent sources. Competitors may be surprisingly willing to talk.

Of course, depending upon the nature of the problem customers may be an excellent source. They can give considerable information on their experience with brands, attitudes toward different brands, factors in a product purchase, and how they use the product. The proximity of retailer to the user makes them very knowledgeable concerning the users' needs, merchandising requirements, service needs, and users' attitudes.

3.3.3 Planning and Conducting the Exploration

We have discussed the most common sources of information. Before approaching them, however, one needs an orderly procedure. The researcher needs statements of immediately apparent hypotheses and the information needed to determine their validity. A list of relevant sources as well as a timetable for contacting them should be drawn up.

The position of the researcher at this state is comparable to that of a prospector hunting for gold. The researcher must hunt for pay dirt—someone's idea that reveals a solution to the marketing problem or information that points to one of the already conceived hypotheses as valid.

While thus groping, the researcher cannot follow a standardized schedule of questions. Nevertheless, when there are numerous interviews, one needs means for recording certain information to be developed in all interviews. Since the interview must be left flexible, the researcher needs to develop a form that will have designated spaces for information received during all interviews and space to write in other miscellaneous data learned in the interviews.

Group sessions of consumers are often being used now for so-called "focus interviews." In an unstructured situation where they can discuss their views freely, the conversation "snowballs" as the consumers talk under the guidance of a moderator. Ideas on both problems and on solutions may surface that are valuable to the marketer. This sort of unstructured interviewing will be discussed in Chapters 9 and 10.

Pertinent Data

The word "pertinent" is important, although it may seem obvious because logical people would not bother gathering anything that was not pertinent. Yet many studies are burdened and delayed by gathering information that has little relevance to their stated objectives. Sheer curiosity or a vaguely defined problem often leads to gathering irrelevant information. Also, businesspeople tend to think that when they are going to the expense of making a study, they should use the opportunity to find out other things that might prove useful even though unrelated to the particular problem being studied. This tendency should be resisted, because the extraneous data often have no vital usefulness in themselves and may add considerably to the cost and the work of the study. Pertinent data may be grouped under the three classifications discussed below.

Payoffs. What evidence will prove or disprove an hypothesis or show which is the best solution or course of action? Hopefully, agreement was reached on this during the exploratory research. However, researchers often have second thoughts at this stage with regard to the payoff that is to be measured, for they may find the original definition of the payoff (or payoffs where a single type of result will not suffice) is not "operational" and must be restated before it can be measured or analyzed.

The type of payoff resulting from a course of action that actually can be measured may differ from the decision maker's concept of the payoff. This is illustrated with the following fictitious case:

> A manufacturer of processed foods stimulates the sale of its products by means of coupons, with which the consumer can buy the product at a reduced price. The marketing manager raised this question, "Which is the best means of distributing coupons: (1) circulating them directly to the household, as by mail; (2) circulating them in an advertisement, as in a magazine; or (3) inserting them in packages of our various products?" When the decision maker was pressed to define what he meant by "best," he said, "I mean the most profitable means."

> Coupon redemption, however, does not in itself directly result in profits, so this could not be a variable to be related to the circulation and redemption of coupons. Of course, the direct result of coupons is to produce sales, but "sales" may be given various definitions: (1) the units sold with the coupon; (2) the total units sold at the time of coupon redemption with or without the coupon; (3) subsequent sales of the product. To be meaningful in terms of the decision maker's purpose, the concept of "sales" also may be limited only to purchases by those consumers who had not previously been habitual buyers of the particular brand and thus represented real additions to the clientele. These, then, represent direct payoffs and presumably measurable ones from the courses of action under test.

The example above is not meant to imply that only a result directly attributable to the hypothesis under test should be measured in a study. In the case above, if the decision maker really needs to have some type of profit results that can be connected with the various means of circulating coupons, this probably could have been derived through analysis of search and cost data coupled with the sales data that were related to the various forms of coupon distribution. This would introduce some very complex questions to be answered before such indirect payoffs could be defined. Our intention is not to deny the possible desirability of such payoff measurements but to point out that first of all the direct results of the hypothesis need to be measured.

Some studies are made in behalf of noncommercial sponsors or conducted for academic purposes, perhaps as a basis for a thesis. Although no commercial payoff is sought in the conclusions to be reached by such studies, it is equally important in such studies that the nature of the payoff or results be sharply and appropriately defined. Failure to do so can culminate in frustration when the researcher attempts to draw conclusions toward the end of his study. The payoff is the key variable in any conclusive research.

Interrelated factors. A research project surely does not seek to learn merely whether a payoff varies, but also why or when it varies. The payoff must be connected with some event(s) or conditions, if any conclusions are to be drawn or course of action to be recommended. Therefore, the researcher needs to anticipate relationships between the payoff variable and some other specified variables, that is, their interrelationship. Factors that are suspected of being interrelated, therefore, must be identified and defined in order to explain variations in the payoff variable. Some intimations that indicated such probable covariation should have been found in the exploratory study. That phase of the study, however, would not attempt to have measured in definite terms the extent of that covariation or how much of the variation in the payoff variable should be attributed to a particular factor or combination of factors.

The number of factors to be measured and related to changes in the payoff variable may range from one to many. A neat and simple design could be determined if only one variable were to be studied. Even so, the necessity still exists of assuring that other variables that might affect the payoff could be held constant. The difficulties of achieving this in the case of marketing phenomena will be discussed in Chapter 4. Most marketing studies must comprehend and measure the changes or levels of a number of factors.

Description. Some descriptive data are needed in conclusive research studies. The decision maker will want an ample description of the sources of the information. Also, the circumstances attending the measurement of the behavior or other phenomena studied should be described.

3.4 Deciding Whether to Proceed

We have reached step 7 in our decision model of Table 3–1. The decision maker has chosen one or a few of the alternative hypotheses to be considered in the final choice. His or her condition relative to the decision is some "state of doubt." This is not a final determination to conduct conclusive research but only a decision to proceed further with the planning of the research.

3.4.1 Goals and Decision Criteria

If the decision maker and researcher have worked closely in the formulation of the research-problem definition, there is a high probability they have a meeting of the minds and selected the most useful area for research. As a check, however, we should reexamine our goals and speculate on how the findings might contribute to their achievement. In our appliance example, the problem faced by the decision maker was what mix of retail outlets should the corporation service to attain and maintain a balanced retail distribution system in the future? What does the decision maker need to answer this question? These more operational goals might appear as follows:

1. To be able to measure consumer preference for different retail types in the purchase of appliances.
2. To be able to evaluate present distribution market by market in terms of consumer preference for retail types.
3. To be able to forecast market by market the mix of retail outlets consumers will patronize.

At this point the decision maker begins to develop a list of how the findings might contribute to the achievement of these goals. These might appear as follows:

1. If purchasers with different brand loyalty and store preference behavior fall into different socioeconomic groups, the importance of retail type in distribution can be evaluated for different segments of the market.
2. If purchasers who exhibit high store preference can be classified by socioeconomic group and retail type, present distribution can be evaluated market by market to determine if there is the correct mix of retail types to optimally participate in the market.
3. If purchasers fall into distinct socioeconomic groups, we can forecast sales by retail type, market by market, through examining the socioeconomic composition of the market.

In Section 3.1.1 we suggested that research studies often lead to other problems requiring decisions. In our example, a number of advertising

84

questions were raised as a result of the review of goals and decisions criteria. These are as follow:

1. If brand loyalty is weakening in favor of store preference, more effort should be directed to retailer relations and cooperative advertising in the retailers name than in national-brand advertising.
2. If store preference is weakening in favor of brand loyalty, retailer demands can be sacrificed in favor of national-brand advertising.
3. Advertising messages may be developed to appeal to different socioeconomic groups, depending upon their purchase behavior.

These are only a few of the ways in which this study will serve the decision maker to achieve his goals. It is mandatory that an effort be made to determine the payoff for the decision maker. On more than one occasion this exercise has shown that the study will not or will only partially solve the decision maker's problem.

3.5 Summary

In this chapter we have examined every phase of preliminary and exploratory research; let us now recapitulate. We discussed the three types of symptomatic situations (overt difficulties, latent difficulties, and unnoticed opportunities) that lead to the need to make decisions. We also noted the role of information and performance analyses as an aid in problem discovery. This led to the conduct of preliminary research for purposes of clarifying and defining the decision and research problems.

The need for background information was established and we indicated its possible scope and data sources for purposes of defining the research problem. Exploratory research to uncover hypothetical solutions comprised the second type of research. We detailed sources of information and indicated the sorts of information that might be produced in the exploration.

This led us to specify the data needed to aid the decision maker in solving his problem. We discussed the importance of payoff, interrelated factors, and descriptive data to ensure that if a study is conducted, the findings would provide a solution.

We concluded the chapter by examining the need to determine if conclusive research should be conducted. We speculated on the goals and decision criteria we might use to determine if the researcher should proceed with planning a conclusive research project. If such an analysis favors continuation of the research planning process, the next consideration is that of planning the research design—the content of Chapter 4.

4 Alternative Research Designs

In Chapter 4 we examine the first three steps in the research planning sequence: (1) anticipate data analysis and processing, (2) select either an experimental, quasi-experimental, simulation, or descriptive design, and (3) write exact statements of data to be sought. Such questions as the following are addressed:

What is research design? What does it include?

How many things must I consider in planning my research? Where do I start?

How can I be sure I collect the right data?

How many ways can I demonstrate how the data provide answers?

What is an experiment?

Does all research have to be experimental?

What alternatives to the experiment exist?

How do I know which design to use?

THE SOLUTION TO A PROBLEM may become evident in the exploratory study, and the researcher may decide that no further study appears to be desirable. In that event the person making the study will prepare the findings, a subject treated in Chapter 14, and submit them to management or the sponsor. If the solution is obscure or the risks involved are large, the undertaking of "conclusive research" to yield valid and reliable conclusions may be justified.

4.1 Nature and Function of Design

design → Conclusive research should begin with a clear and adequate research design, which is "a series of advanced decisions that, taken together, comprise a master plan or model for the conduct of the investigation."[1] *

series of advanced decisions The main characteristics of a research design may be summed up in two words: anticipation and specification. The researcher anticipates the needs and the circumstances of the proposed study, and specifies in advance what to obtain and to do, in broad rather than detailed form.

The degree of detail in research design will be inferred from the functions that it is intended to perform. These are:

1. Statement of the evidence needed to solve the problem.
2. Anticipation of what will be done with the data to produce answers to the problem.
3. Statement of the basic scheme whereby the answers will be revealed or validated.
4. Specification of the evidence—where it will be obtained and how.
5. A guide for the calculation and approval of the feasibility and cost of the project.
6. Provision of the blueprint or plan to guide the ensuing work.

4.1.1 What the Research Design Includes

Specification of the research design has already commenced as the background and exploratory studies, in addition to crystallizing the problem, also reveal a number of important by-products. The researcher will have considered the evidence needed and its availability. He or she will have already begun to formulate ideas on the approach to be used to validate the conclusions.

The researcher will also gain guidance in this phase from personal experiences as well as from the experiences of colleagues. The reports of other organizations having researched similar problems are also available and provide a rich storehouse of guidance. Nevertheless, this is no time for settling for vague notions of how the study will proceed. Following a logical train of thought is mandatory for accuracy and efficiency in research.

---

[1] Robert Ferber, Sidney Cohen, and David J. Luck, "The Design of Research Investigations," *Marketing Research Series, No. 1* (Chicago: American Marketing Association, Inc., 1958), p. 5.

It is in the selection of the research design that the researcher abides by the criteria of scientific method specified in Chapter 1. Insofar as possible it is necessary to at least attempt to observe the requisites of:

1. An orderly investigation of a defined problem.
2. The collection of adequate and representative evidence of exact and correct measurement.
3. The application of logical reasoning for drawing conclusions from the evidence which are relevant to the problem.
4. Demonstration of the validity of the findings through repeated or replicated investigation.
5. The development of principles which may be confidently applied in the future, under similar conditions.

As we shall see, the market researcher is not always able to select from designs which observe all the requisites they use in ideal goals toward which all strive.

The researcher is often pressured to begin gathering data prematurely. If a sequence of steps already has been prescribed, they promote orderliness and serve to ensure that all the needed steps are taken in the proper order. A planning sequence such as that described in Table 4–1 will enhance efficiency in the conduct of any research project. The answers to the questions, through taking the steps suggested, are necessary to draft the complete research design.

TABLE 4–1. Planning the Research Design Sequence

Questions Faced	*Steps To Take or Choices*
1. Have we correctly determined the data needed to measure the outcome of the alternative solutions?	1. Anticipate data analysis and processing.
2. What research design should be used?	2. Select experimental, quasi-experimental, or descriptive, simulation design.
3. What specific data are needed for that design?	3. Write exact statements of data to be sought.
4. From whom are such data available?	4. Search and examine relevant secondary data.
5. How should primary data be obtained?	5. Determine remaining data gaps.
a. What are the types of data?	6. Define the population from which primary data may be sought.
b. What general collection methods shall be used?	7. Determine the facts, opinions, and motives needed.
c. How should the sources be contacted?	8. Plan for obtaining data by survey, observational, or mechanical methods.

TABLE 4–1. (Cont.)

Questions Faced	Steps To Take or Choices
d. How may the data be secured from the sources?	9. If using a survey, decide whether to contact respondents by telephone, by mail, or in person.
e. Shall there be a complete count of the population or a sample drawn from it? How chosen?	10. Consider the questions and forms needed to elicit and record the data.
f. How will the field work be conducted?	11. Decide on the coverage of the population: a. Choose between a complete enumeration or sampling. b. If sampling, decide whether to select from the whole population or restricted portions of it. c. Decide how to select sample members.
	12. Map and schedule the field work.
	13. Plan the personnel requirements of the field study.
	14. Consider editing and tabulating requirements.
6. How will the data be interpreted and presented?	15. Anticipate possible interpretation of the data.
7. Can the study be afforded, and is it approved?	16. Consider the way the findings may be presented.
8. Is the design really workable and well directed toward the problem solution?	17. Determine and budget costs and submit research proposal.
	18. Pretest the design.

4.2 Anticipating Data Analysis and Processing

In Chapter 3 we gave considerable attention to the determination of the evidence needed to reach conclusions. In doing so we began to formulate ideas concerning how we are going to use the data to reach conclusions that satisfy the decision maker. It is now necessary to examine this in more detail through visualizing the expected data. A helpful first step is to put data in writing to allow precise consideration of it. A second step is to construct dummy tables for review to determine if the data will suffice to reach conclusions. A third step is to consider what techniques will be used to demonstrate the payoff.

For example, the high rate of failure among packaged food items sold in grocery supermarkets gave rise to a study to determine if measurement of consumer attributes at the end of five weeks could be used to predict supermarket management's decision to continue or discontinue new products normally made at the end of thirteen weeks.[2] Following earlier adoption process studies, six variables—awareness of product name, knowledge of product type, intent to purchase (strong and weak), and information-seeking activity (strong and weak)—were selected as the consumer attributes for measurement. The data needs were specified as shown in Table 4–2. In addition to the orderly planning of the research, this exercise is useful in the determination of the exact data needed if questionnaires are to be used.

TABLE 4–2. Data Needs for Consumer Attributes Predictor Study

Data Needs

Source:	1. Store management in stores in which new products are introduced.
	2. Housewives in market area of stores in which new products are introduced.
Timing:	1. Store management decision on new products selected at end of thirteen weeks.
	2. Information from equal groups of randomly selected housewives at the end of first, second, third, fourth, and fifth weeks after products selected are introduced.
Specific data:	1. Store management's decision to continue or discontinue the new products selected.
	2. Measure of housewives:
	a. Awareness of product name.
	b. Knowledge of product type.
	c. Weak intent to purchase.
	d. Strong intent to purchase.
	e. Weak information seeking activity.
	f. Strong information seeking activity.

Assuming that measurements of the six variables, expressed in percentages of the sample answering in the affirmative, are acquired, how can they be used for prediction purposes? Dummy tables were established similar to that in Table 4–3. Such tables were constructed at the end of each week.

In order to assess the adequacy of the data if they were collected, the researcher in this case had to decide what technique would be used to interpret the data. In our example, the research must demonstrate that the measurements of the six variables at the end of five weeks accurately discriminate between continued and discontinued products at the end of

---

[2] Patrick Dunne, "Using Adoption Process Variables as a Predictor of Product Continuance or Discontinuance" (doctoral thesis, Michigan State University, 1972).

TABLE 4–3. Hypothetical Fifth-Week Levels of the Six Predictor Variables (percentage of consumer sample possessing indicated attributes)

				Interest		Information Seeking	
		Awareness	Knowledge	Weak	Strong	Weak	Strong
Continued products at end of thirteen weeks	A	50	50	26	14	18	2
	D	50	50	24	12	20	4
	F	36	36	18	12	16	8
	G	44	40	20	6	18	8
	Mean rating	45	44	22	11	18	5.5
Discontinued products at end of thirteen weeks	B	40	40	16	6	10	0
	C	32	32	14	10	8	4
	E	32	32	14	6	8	0
	Mean rating	34.67	34.67	14.67	7.33	8.67	1.33

thirteen weeks. In this case discriminant analysis was used.[3] Although it is not our purpose at this point to dwell on the details of this technique, it may be described as follows. In this case we are trying to explain the positioning of our test products into a classification of continued or discontinued by examining six independent variables. Discriminant analysis combines the independent variables into a linear equation that properly weights the independent variables for their discriminatory power. The value of the equation is a point score for each product. A discriminant score is determined, and if the point score exceeds the discriminant score, the product is classified as continued, and if below it is discontinued.

From the hypothetical results, the work involved in reaching them can be estimated. The method of processing the data can be considered. When more complex equipment is needed, such as a computer, a very large task is involved in anticipating its operations, the programming, and staff required. This leads to another set of determinations regarding the form of the recorded observations or responses that would be the most efficient inputs to the data processing.

An additional benefit, and by no means secondary, that results from anticipatory findings is that it does give indications as to the basic design to be used in demonstrating and validating answers to the problems under consideration. As indicated in step 2 of our planning sequence in

---

[3]For a description of discriminant analysis, see Maurice G. Kendall, *A Course in Multivariate Analysis* (London: Charles Griffin and Co. Ltd., 1965), pp. 144–70; or Philip Kotler, *Marketing Decision Making: A Model Building Approach* (New York: Holt, Rinehart and Winston, 1971), pp. 602–5, or Chap. 11.

Table 4–1, the design alternatives are experimental, quasi-experimental, and descriptive.

Before turning our attention to these designs, an explanation of terminology is offered. The term "design" as developed at the beginning of this chapter refers to the entire planning sequence for a research project. The word, in practice, also refers to a specific design for validating answers to problems, and in this chapter we are using the word in the latter sense.

4.3   Experimental Designs

when effects on payoff can be reliably isolated — exp. design can be applied.

An *experiment* may be defined as the actual trial of a proposed course of action or other hypotheses under consideration, so conducted that its effects can be observed (measured) objectively and distinguished from the effects of extraneous variables. When the effects on the payoff can be reliably isolated, the experimental design can be applied.

For example, an experiment in the biological sciences might be used in seeking the cure for a disease that is epidemic in some region. A proposed drug (the hypothesis) that might cure the illness (the problem) is administered to a group of people suffering from the malady, the test group. Another group, identical to the first group in all pertinent respects, also suffering from the same illness, does not receive the drug and serves as the control group. The difference in rate of recovery between the test group and the control group is attributed to the effects of the drug.

An experimental design is the ideal and should be used whenever possible. Because of its value, we shall examine more carefully some elements of a valid experiment.

4.3.1   Essential Nature of Valid Experiments

The following are statements of elements of an experiment and symbols we shall use to refer to these different aspects.

1. The hypothesis (for example, a course of action) or proposed treatment is put into effect. We are going to term this the "experimental variable" and represent it symbolically by X.
2. Observations are made of the experimental variable's effects, which we shall denote with the symbol O. What is measured should be the sort of effects or payoffs that are relevant to the decision maker's goals (or in noncommercial research, to the investigator's purpose).
3. The phenomena observed take place in a population (almost always just a sample of that population) that fully typifies the population and environment within which the experimental variable would be applied, if it subsequently were adopted. We will designate samples from such a population as A, B, and the like.

We can illustrate this with an example. A marketer is considering erecting special displays of his product in cooperating stores. Installing a display would cost $10 for each display, and he wants advance knowledge of its effects. He plans these steps: select a few typical stores as a sample (A); observe the sales of his product in these stores for four weeks without the display, by measurements at the beginning and end of this period (O_1); install the displays—the hypothesized course of action—in the store (X) and keep them there for another four weeks; then make similar observations to measure the sales over the second four weeks (O_2). In further discussion we shall simply place these events in a line, like this:

$$A \quad O_1 \quad X \quad O_2$$

The results of this trial produce a result that we shall symbolize as Y.

$$Y = O_2 - O_1$$

Substituting assumed dollar figures, let us say that the pretest sales were $90 in the average of these stores and the results during the test (sometimes termed "posttest") were $135.

$$Y = \$135 - \$90 = \$45$$

The investigator might assert that display X produced an increment of $45 of sales. Suppose that the investigator is considering another display but does not know what one to select. In this case we could test two alternative displays, labeled X_1 and X_2, in two samples of stores, labeled sample A and sample B, for four measurements in total.

Symbolically this design is:

$$A \quad O_1 \quad X_1 \quad O_3$$
$$B \quad O_2 \quad X_2 \quad O_4$$

Now one can attribute the sales effects of both experimental variables (the two displays) and also compare their relative effects.

$$Y_{x1} = O_3 - O_1 = \$135 - \$90 = \$45$$
$$Y_{x2} = O_4 - O_2 = \$125 - \$75 = \underline{\$50}$$

The results, as is evident, measure the effects of trying both X_1 and X_2 and also suggest that X_2 is the better payoff.

The reader probably has detected a serious flaw in this reasoning, because there is no evidence of what would have happened in the absence of these experimental variables. Perhaps sales would have increased anyway, and the effects of the displays might have been nil. And so we introduced a third sample of stores, *C*, and omit the displays in them. The symbolic representation of this design may be represented as follows:

$$A \quad O_1 \quad X_1 \quad O_4$$
$$B \quad O_2 \quad X_2 \quad O_5$$
$$C \quad O_3 \quad - \quad O_6$$

Now if such a test is made, the results might look like this:

$$Y_{x1} = \$135 - \$90 = \$45$$
$$Y_{x2} = \$125 - \$75 = \$50$$
$$Y_o = \$115 - \$85 = \$30$$

The calculations are much different: the two displays produced net gains of only $15 and $20. The decision maker, taking into consideration the $10 cost of the displays, is more likely now to rule against both of them. The third sample, in which the proposed course of action was absent, is the *control* against which the trial's effects are netted out.

What essential conditions must be met for a design to qualify as an experiment? Ideally, the experimenter would be able to hold constant the extraneous variables, those other than that under test. Even in our biological example of testing a new drug, there is no way to ensure that the *test* and *control* groups have identical conditions of health. They may be common in that they all suffer from the same malady and could be selected so as to be comparable in terms of age and sex, but beyond this the numbers of variables upon which they may differ is endless. In addition, there is no assurance that the environment of both groups is common during the test.

Biological studies cannot always meet the ideal. Social research, of which marketing is a category, confronts even more vagaries and dynamics of human behavior. Consequently, we waive deliberate manipulation or control of extraneous variables as a requirement. However, in social science research there has developed in recent years the use of *laboratory experiments* that approximate the designs used in biological sciences, and these will be discussed later.

We may expect certain other characteristics in a study, if it is to qualify as an experiment. First are the three general requirements:

1. The variable under test (the treatment or solution hypothesized as being causal) can be applied deliberately and its nature specified.
2. The results, or payoff, ensuing from its application can be identified and measured in terms relevant to the given problem.
3. The extraneous variables in the environment, which plausibly could affect the results materially, can be identified.

Beyond these basic characteristics are other qualifications raised by the central question: Will the test produce *valid* results? A helpful distinction used by Seymour Banks[4] divides validity into two types: internal and external.

Internal validity means that no other plausible cause of the observed results should exist except those tested. For example, changing attitudes and knowledge of people involved throughout the test could affect results. In a before and after experimental treatment, the actual means of measurement in the initial test may condition the subjects in ways that naturally change them, apart from any effect of the experimental variable. The actual variation in the way measurements are taken, especially when a human judgment factor on the part of the person collecting data is involved, may distort results. Care should always be exercised to ensure that whenever separate groups are used for different treatments or controls they are identical in all pertinent characteristics.

External validity relates to this question: Can the conclusions of the experiment properly be projected to the real-world problem of the decision maker or scientist? A study may qualify as a "good" experiment because it has all the internal validity requirements, yet be invalid externally. Here are some of the ways Banks mentions in which an experiment might be externally invalid.

The population that served as subjects of the test may be unlike the population in which the findings would be applied, or the environment at the time of the test may differ from the environment of the real world at the time the decision is put into effect. Likewise, the treatment in the test may differ from that which would be utilized in the actual application, or the measurements taken in a four-week test may not be projectible to an application of say twelve months.

The doubts of external validity increase with the extent to which human nature is involved as variables. The possibility of invalid sources may seem to discourage the use of experiments. We are going to see, however, that alternative designs exist that, used with due caution, may render experiments widely usable in marketing.

4.3.2 Alternative Experimental Designs

Excluding from consideration the fully controlled experiment, we still have several designs that retain scientific qualities that justify classifying them as experiments. We shall discuss *laboratory experiments, field experiments,* distinguished by the timing of measurements or method of sequencing treatments, and *after-the-fact experiments.*

---

[4]Seymour Banks, *Experimentation in Marketing* (New York: McGraw-Hill Book Company, 1965), pp. 26–27. Banks credits the categorization to D. L. Campbell. For specific examples, see Kenneth P. Uhl, "Field Experimentation: Some Problems, Pitfalls and Perspectives," cited in Gerald Albaum and M. Venkatesan, *Scientific Marketing Research* (New York: The Free Press, 1971), pp. 295–307. Also see C. J. Davis, *Experimental Marketing* (New York: American Management Association, Inc., 1970), Chap. 2.

Development of
a Project

In an attempt to replicate the ideal, laboratory experiments have been used to better understand marketing phenomena. The Institute for Research in the Behavioral Economic and Management Sciences of the Purdue University Herman C. Krannert Graduate School of Industrial Administration has been a leader in the development of laboratory experiments on marketing phenomena.[5]

An interesting laboratory experiment was developed to answer two questions concerning consumers' attitudes toward package size and price.[6] Using a sample of 200 housewives in a suburb of San Diego, researchers conducted an experiment to determine answers to the following two questions: (1) Is price relevant in determining which package size is purchased? If so, can the relations be quantified? (2) If housewives were provided with value information, such as cents per pound as well as the basic prices, would this affect their purchasing behavior? Two products, detergents and soft drinks, were selected for the experiment. To simulate an actual purchase environment, all housewives were told they would receive either $4.50 worth of goods or cash at the end of the experiment. They were shown a display of popular brands of detergents and asked which one they normally purchased. They were then shown samples of all the available sizes, with prices clearly marked, on the normally purchased brand and asked which size would be their first choice. This question was repeated five times for five different sets of prices. The prices given to the various sizes were as follows:

P_0 = prices that represent as nearly as possible existing prices for the brands selected

P_1 = prices of P_0 reduced by 2 percent

P_2 = prices in which the cost in cents per pound were constant on all package sizes

P_3 = prices in which the cents per pound ratio increased with size

P_4 = prices in which the cents per pound ratio decreased with size faster than in the P_0 situation

Questioning then switched to the soft drinks, and then it returned to the detergents. This time cents per pound information, using the same prices as before, was given on all packages sizes and a choice as to size

[5] For a description of this Institute, see Philip C. Burger, Charles W. King, and Edgar A. Pessemier, "A Large Scale Systems View of Consumer Behavior Research," *Proceedings of the 1966 Symposium on Consumer Behavior* (Austin, Tex. University of Texas, 1968), pp. 229–60; also C. Pessemier, P. Burger, R. Leach, and D. Legert, "Using Laboratory Brand Preference Scales to Predict Consumer Brand Purchases," *Management Science*, February, 1971.

[6] C. W. J. Granger and A. Billson, "Consumers' Attitudes Toward Package Size and Price," *Journal of Marketing Research*, August, 1972, pp. 239–48.

was made for each of the five different prices. The percentage of choices of four sizes was then tabulated for the two sets of conditions under which choices had to be made. Although we are not concerned at this time with the actual method of interpretation and specific results, we note that the addition of the cents per pound information considerably changed choice patterns.

According to some authors,[7] laboratory experiments provide a higher level of internal validity as the respondents can be carefully controlled and/or manipulated. External validity, however, suffers in that the laboratory may not accurately depict the real-world environment. The cost, however, of laboratory experimentation is generally much less than field experimental designs.

Field Experiments

Although laboratory experiments are becoming more widely used, the field experimental design is by far the more common approach. There are many variations to field experiments, and we shall examine them in this section.

First, we shall examine three designs that can be characterized by the time at which measurements are taken. These are sometimes referred to as *informal experimentation*,[8] since there is no assurance that the extraneous variables that might affect the results have been held constant. In other words, they suffer from internal validity. Then we shall examine two types of *formal experiments*,[9] where we recognize that we cannot control all extraneous variables but recognize differences and attempt to offset differences or at least measure their influences on the results.

Design 1—pretest–posttest design. The first type of design is one in which both pretest and posttest measurements were taken. The subjects to be tested are first observed (which if they are people, usually involves interviews) and measured (pretest measurement). Then the experimental treatment is introduced. After the treatment is introduced, the subjects are measured again on the same characteristics that were observed previously (posttest measurement). An experiment must have both a control unit or group (the pretest group) and a test unit or group (the posttest group).

Envision a situation in which we wish to determine consumers' reaction to the universal product code X. In the pretest we select stores B without the UPC and measure attitudes about importance of price information over a period of time O_2 and O_4. In the posttest we select stores A with UPC and measure attitudes about price information over a similar period of time O_1 and O_3. Symbolically, this is represented as:

---

[7] See K. K. Cox and B. M. Enis, *Experimentation for Marketing Decision* (Scranton, Pa.: International Textbook Co., 1969), pp. 106–8.

[8] Ibid., pp. 17–21.

[9] Ibid.

$$A \quad O_1 \quad X \quad O_3$$
$$B \quad O_2 \qquad O_4$$

Interpretation involves arriving at a result by observing differences between the control and the test:

$$Y_x = (O_3 - O_1) - (O_4 - O_2)$$

In those cases in which more than one treatment should be tested, our example in Section 4.4.1 follows:

$$A \quad O_1 \quad X_1 \quad O_4$$
$$B \quad O_2 \quad X_2 \quad O_5$$
$$C \quad O_3 \quad - \quad O_6$$

In this case the formula for interpretation is expanded to:

$$Yx_1 = (O_4 - O_1) - (O_6 - O_3)$$
$$Yx_2 = (O_5 - O_2) - (O_6 - O_3)$$

This design features the ability to compare relative effects of two treatments, which is $Yx_1 - Yx_2$. Encompassing three or more tested treatments would still entail only simple arithmetic.

Design 2 — four-group design. Imagine a situation in which the pretest group was exposed to a number of concepts about a radically new way of performing a certain task. The posttest introduces a new product capable of performing the task. The pretest may have so conditioned the posttest group, even if they are different respondents, that their responses to the posttest are greatly distorted.

In situations where it is suspected that being subjected to the pretest measurements may bias the subjects sufficiently to distort the posttest observations (a problem of internal validity), a *four-group design* may be employed.[10] Symbolically the design is

$$A \quad O_1 \quad X \quad O_3$$
$$B \quad O_2 \qquad O_4$$
$$C \qquad X \quad O_5$$
$$D \qquad\qquad O_6$$

---

[10] The four-group design has been credited to R. L. Solomon. See his article "An Extension of Control Group Design," *Psychological Bulletin,* March, 1949, p. 140.

The added groups, *C* and *D*, are *not* given a pretest measurement. Interpretation is similar to design 1.

$$Yx = (O_3 - O_1) - (O_4 - O_2)$$

Groups *C* and *D* demonstrate what the results would be without the effect of the pretest measurement and permit this distortion to be adjusted in the interpretation as follows: $(O_5 - O_3)$ to adjust the test and $(O_6 - O_4)$ to adjust the control.

Design 3 — posttest-only design. Another design of this general type is the *posttest-only design,* wherein no measurement is applied before the tested treatment:

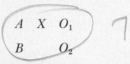

$$A \quad X \quad O_1$$
$$B \qquad O_2$$

This may seem unscientific because of a fixed notion that every experiment should show the change before and after the treatment. Yet pretest measurement may not contribute to the decision's validity. This might be the case if the decision makers need to know only the *relative* difference between the two groups *after* the proposed treatment was applied to one of them. The *absolute* change in the groups may be an aspect of indifference to them; they only want to know (relative to the control group) if results are better — and how much better — when the hypothesis is tried out.

Let us point out, though, that the pretest measurement serves another purpose: it ascertains that groups *A* and *B* were comparable at the start. The posttest-only design runs a hazard that *A* and *B* were different before the test, in significant aspects, so that the posttest difference attributed to the experimental variable was illusory. The methods of choosing the two groups in this design must avoid this hazard. If this is feasible, the posttest-only design may have much advantage in efficiency. Interpretation in this design is the simplest of all:

$$Y_x = (\bullet_1 - \bullet_2)$$

Throughout our discussion, we have been concerned about the similarity between the control and the test group. We have also been concerned about the timing of our measurements. In every case there is no assurance that our control and test groups are comparable nor that they are exposed to the same extraneous variables throughout the period of the test. Any number of variables other than the treatment under test, such as price, advertising, competitors' activities, attitude of subjects, may influence the results. Furthermore, there is no way of measuring the effects of errors resulting from the failure of being able to completely control the extraneous variables.

In an effort to offset the effects of extraneous variables, designs are used in which all the treatments on each subject are tested—one at a time in some sequence. As a result of rotating the treatments, it is hoped the extraneous variables will offset each other and "washout." These designs are known as *formal experiments* because the error resulting from differences in the groups can be measured.[11]

Design 4—Latin-squares design. As an example of rotation of experimental treatments, suppose that the marketer in the case of the displays has four alternative displays in mind. She or he also believes that there are no four drug stores sufficiently alike in the test city for comparability between their test results. (Using stores in various cities would cause worse distortion of the results.) Therefore, it is decided to rotate the displays between the stores, with a two-week period in each and a week's lapse between each test to reduce any carryover effect from a particular display. A Latin-squares design (design 4) should be used. As a diagram, this test would form a square because there would be as many test units as treatments. With four stores and four displays, we have a *4 × 4 design*, which is depicted in Table 4–4.

TABLE 4–4. Time Periods of Tests

Stores	Sept. 3–16	Sept. 23– Oct. 7	Oct. 14–27	Nov. 5–18
A	1	2	3	4
B	4	3	1	2
C	3	4	2	1
D	2	1	4	3

In this table, the numbers refer to the four treatments (the displays), which we previously would have indicated as X_1, X_2, and so forth, but here would obscure the three features of this design.[12] These features are: (1) each treatment is tested once in each store, (2) each is tested once in each time period, and (3) the order of testing runs both ways (for example, 1 to 2 and 2 to 1) an equal number of times. Thus the effects of varying store characteristics and of sequence in which the displays appear are canceled out.

Another source of bias remains. If the sales volume during the four intervals (apart from the effect of the displays) varies widely, the period with the heaviest normal sales would have undue weighting in the derived results. A control, *E*, would need to be added to the design—a store or group of stores fairly typifying *A*, *B*, *C*, and *D*—whose sales dur-

---

[11] Cox and Enis, *Experimentation for Marketing Decision*, pp. 17–21.

[12] Our diagram also omits the *O* to indicate when the observations would be made. Presumably, five measurements would be made: before the test of Sept. 3–16; after that test but before the test of Sept. 23–Oct. 7; after the Sept. 23–Oct. 7 test and before the Oct. 14–27 test; after the Oct. 14–27 test and before the Nov. 5–18 test; and the final measurement after the Nov. 5–18 test.

ing these periods would serve as a norm for adjusting the apparent sales resulting from the displays in the test stores.

Statistically, this design permits the measurement of error resulting from two noninteracting variables: difference in test stores and difference in time on the result, as well as the effect of the treatment on the result.

Statistical interpretation becomes complex with a Latin-squares design, because we then deal not only with the effects of the treatments, each of which has been tested several times and thus requires an equal number of calculations for each trial, but we also need to determine the effect of variances relative to the several different units or samples that were subjected to the tests. In design 4 this was the vertical dimension, or "column" effect, that would be determined by summing the data in each vertical column. We also need to compute variances due to the sequencing of the treatments, which in design 4 was the horizontal, or "row" effect (that is, differences in sums of horizontal rows). In short, we must determine three effects: treatments, rows, and columns. Then we adjust the treatment effect by removing any row and column effects.

We will merely indicate here the type of computations involved in a Latin-squares design; in Chapter 12 some of these measurements will be explained and the complete process may be found in other sources. These computations employ (1) the total sum of the values in all squares in the design matrix, and (2) the sums of the squares of the treatments, the columns, and the rows. A correction factor is applied also; the "degrees of freedom" in the rows, columns, and treatments must be ascertained and applied. Therefore, we encounter complexity and the desirability of a computer, but the richness and refinement of the statistical results should wholly justify the effort.

Design 5 — factorial design. Another use of rotated test units is known as *factorial design*. This might appear diagrammatically to resemble the Latin-squares type, but its purpose is quite different. Recall that in the Latin-squares example only one type of variable was considered, the displays, and that was in four discrete units (and not in degrees of some characteristic). To explain the factorial design, let us consider another sort of example. A coffee marketer is pondering the use of two promotional devices: (1) local television spot advertising, and (2) price reductions. He has reasons for believing that in his competitive markets, local television advertising alone is not very effective without also offering consumers a simultaneous price attraction to buy his brand. Conversely, a price cut without television advertising is also ineffective. He is in doubt regarding how much advertising to exert (expressed as a percentage of normal sales volume in a market area) and how much price cut to offer simultaneously.

Table 4–5 shows what the allocation of such price versus advertising tests for the coffee marketer might be like. Each of the letters represents a different test market, with the time variable being the same for all of them. It is not necessary to have a square matrix, as this is. For instance, if four price reductions and three advertising levels were to be analyzed,

TABLE 4–5. Local Advertising Expenditure as Percentage of Normal Sales

Price Off:	0.6%	1.0%	1.4%
3 cents	A	B	C
4 cents	D	E	F
5 cents	G	H	I

it would be a 4×3 design. In this example, the decision maker is only interested in the relative changes within each of the nine markets, not a comparison between markets of the absolute results, so no control is needed. Since this is a before-and-after comparison, it calls for a pretest observation of the sales volume in each market.

Factorial analysis can encompass more than two types of variables. An example cited by Banks[13] is a four-variable design involving four different advertising media, employed by the Ford Motor Company. This involves four combinations of four variables, requiring sixteen areas of test units for simultaneous measurements. The assignment of these combinations of treatments is illustrated in Table 4–6 in a 2×8 matrix. The Ford experiment was planned to devote a full model year to the test, preceded by a six-month pretest period of sales measurement and followed by an eighteen-month period to monitor the lingering effects of the advertising after its discontinuance. A rotating Latin-squares design, which would have reduced the number of markets involved, could scarcely be considered in view of the long intervals and probable carry-over effects of advertising.

TABLE 4–6. Design 5 Example

	No Radio		Radio		No Radio		Radio	
	No TV	TV	No TV	TV	No TV	TV	No TV	TV
No outdoor	1	2	3	4	5	6	7	8
Outdoor	9	10	11	12	13	14	15	16

With a factorial design, design 5, we also encounter some complex computations. We usually would want to determine the interaction of the variables on each other, which gets us into variance analysis and into netting out the remaining "main effects" of each variable. To determine the interactions, we become involved in computing standard deviations and interaction mean squares. Again, rather than venture beyond the scope of this book, we urge the interested reader to consult a statistics

---

[13] Banks, *Experimentation in Marketing*, p. 150. Used with express permission of the publisher and of the Ford Motor Company.

work. In pointing out what is involved in reaching such interpretations, we indicate the sophistication of experimental design and analysis.

Complex equations are often not justified; for instance, in the design 5 example the choice of the best combination of price-off and advertising weight among the nine tested alternatives could be read off the table, picking the highest sales result. If the decision maker or researcher instead wishes to project an optimal combination and to gain deeper insights into the price–advertising relationship, a complex factor analysis can bring these out of the data. In other words, the ability to conduct factorial designs provides invaluable insights into the interactions of the variables and into the selection of the optimal combinations. The benefits to management in complex, cost, and repetitive conditions should become a strong inducement to greater use of such experiments.

Some Other Considerations

When contemplating the selection and planning of an experiment, aspects important to the researcher include the various types that might be appropriate and the richness and complexity of the analysis that might be performed on the statistical findings. We have been dealing with these subjects. We are going to enumerate quickly some of the other important decisions to be considered in experimental design, which will suggest the extent and importance of thorough planning:

1. Determining the number and identity of variables to be tested. The answers to this basic determination may not be at all evident and may require a very good preliminary study.
2. Selecting the range of values within which these variables would occur and being sensitive to the supposed causal factor(s). It would be sheer waste to exert or measure factors within ranges that would provide no information toward the problem solution.
3. Determining the number of groups or blocks of units that are needed in the tests, in the pretests (if any), and as controls. An industrial product manufacturer conducted a costly six-month experiment with three levels of three types of promotions, using a 3 × 3 matrix that involved nine sales districts. It also utilized nine control areas, one for each test area. Only after the study was over, was it recognized that so many control areas were unnecessary; probably two or three would have typified the other nine well enough to serve as controls—with large savings on cost.[14]
4. Determining the character and interrelations of the data and their method of measurement, which tend to be even more crucial than determination of the experimental technique. Time and effort in planning should be carefully gauged to put due emphasis on the decision.

[14] Incidentally, measurements during the test and posttest period indicated such slight effects from the tested factors that the experiment was inconclusive. Perhaps trial experiments on a small scale would have shown that the tests either were not worth conducting or that higher intensities of the promotions should have been applied.

5. Determining the point at which internal validity may be increased only at the cost of lower external validity. In seeking to gain the former, the experimental model may become too unlike the real world or the subjects in the test may become biased, which would spoil the external validity. A proper balance between these qualities may be a nice question.

4.4 · Quasi-experimental Designs

This section includes a number of types of research designs which are in common use today. These are less rigorous and less specific and have somewhat informal requirements, and they have received less attention in the marketing research literature as distinct designs. This, in turn, has meant that the nomenclature for these designs is looser and unstandardized, so that one must invent or adapt labels to designate them. Despite these conditions, the designs are used to a greater extent in marketing studies—and in other areas of social science—than are pure experimental designs. Since the experimental method provides the research design in which one can have the greatest confidence, as much as possible of the precision found in true experiments should be retained. Each of the designs discussed here has retained some experimental qualities. We are going to consider two categories: after-the-fact and historical designs.

4.4.1 After-the-Fact Designs

We have chosen to call these *after-the-fact designs*. They have also been referred to as ex post facto designs.[15] In these designs the test and control group are selected after the fact. They are particularly useful when it is impossible to determine ahead of time who has received a treatment and who has not. For example, when attempting to measure the effect of advertising on sales, surveys can be conducted to determine actual purchase of a product and exposure to the product advertisement. The respondents are then broken into four cells: exposure–purchase; no exposure–purchase; exposure–no purchase; no exposure–no purchase. Those in the cell exposure–purchase are the test group, and those in the cell no exposure–purchase are the control group. The design looks like a valid experiment. There is, however, one significant difference. In a valid experiment the test and control groups are randomly selected and are assumed to be homogeneous. In this case the test and control groups may be very different, and the result—purchase of the product—may be attributed to something other than exposure to the advertising. In order to offset this disadvantage, attempts have been made to match the two groups on significant variables. Although a sound approach, the process requires very large total samples in order to have significant numbers in each cell after they are matched.

---

[15] See Hans Zeisel, "Look of Causal Analysis," cited in *Current Controversies in Marketing Research,* by Leo Bogart (Chicago: Markham Publishing Company, 1969), pp. 104–16.

This type of design is widely used in practice and can be very complex. In a study[16] designed to identify market segments in the household durable goods market, 295 recent purchasers were questioned on twelve independent socioeconomic variables and seven independent variables relating to knowledge of brands and stores and brand and store shopping behavior. After classification, respondents were placed in a 2×2 matrix identified as: high shoppers and low knowers; low shoppers and high knowers. Differences in socioeconomic characteristics for each group were sought to identify the different shopping behavior. The results showed that there are different market segments that can be identified on the basis of objective socioeconomic characteristics. The implications for brand advertising and market coverage by types of outlets are very significant.

4.4.2 Historical Designs

Historical designs employ data recorded in the past that reveal behavior and conditions that existed at some point in time. They resemble experiments in that the data being collected on the behavior of one or more variables were actual, and, therefore, any data on the nonexperimental variables or environment represented actual existence. They differ from experiments in several vital respects: (1) they are not current tests staged by the investigator with any control or manipulation possible on his part, (2) the data are obtained from secondary sources and were not originally obtained under the direction of the investigator and possibly for conflicting purposes, and (3) the investigator must be content with whatever happened to be gathered and is made available, rather than being able to designate objectives and data needs as well as determining their precision.

There are two types of historical approaches: (1) statistical and (2) case studies. One finds frequent offhand interpretations of statistics that have no formal or systematic design and are not the fruit of research. Many very systematic and admirable studies, on the other hand, are based wholly on historical statistics. Most forecasting studies by necessity are based on past data, because it would be most impracticable to try to gather current data embracing as wide a population as needed, and a collection and analysis of data over time is essential. A population forecasting study, for instance, must use already existing "vital statistics" on birth, death rates, and other demographic factors and must, from trend analyses, extrapolate relationships over many years. Only a historical design would be practicable or valid.

Time-series studies are probably the type of statistical study used most frequently. Excluding purely descriptive studies, we find in this category: (1) designs that project future conditions from series of data on past intervals, or (2) designs that seek to unearth associative relationships be-

[16] Stanley Sibley, "The Identification of Behavioral Knowledgeable and Demographic Market Segments of Purchasers of Household Durables" (doctoral thesis, Michigan State University, 1973).

tween one or more variables and to determine the effects of these relationships.

More can be accomplished when both approaches to time-series study are used. The researcher will do well to find the variable(s) that have apparent "causal" impact and then to apply their anticipated changes to projections of the dependent variable. In the type (2) time-series study, the investigator cannot say with confidence that a variance in one or more variables has caused the changes ascribed in the other variable.

If they show a consistent covariance, however, he may supply this relationship to his forecasting.

Let us take a particular example, a systematic analysis of advertising. Two series of historical data are presented in Table 4–7, which represent advertising and personal consumption expenditures each year from 1935 through 1975 (excluding the years 1936 to 1938, when no consumption data are available). As is apparent, a very strong tendency exists for advertising and personal consumption expenditures to rise in something of a consistent interrelationship. Among the thirty-eight year-to-year changes shown, in only three did advertising decline when consumption expenditures rose, and one of the three instances was a presumably abnormal war year, 1942.

These data give us grounds for anticipating that if one of these variables falls or rises, the other will, too, and vice versa. We can compute also an average ratio of the change of one variable against the change of the other. If the study's design assured that measurements were accurate and fully representative of the purported variables, those limited interpretations might be valid. But they do *not* admit the conclusions that increased advertising *causes* consumer expenditures to rise or vice versa, or the correlation may be spurious in that neither has much effect on the other.

A more rigorous design would be desirable to identify and measure the precise relationship here. This would have to encompass all variables that would be reasonably expected to affect the dependent variable materially. (Notice that we did not stipulate whether advertising or expenditures might occur first, and being in doubt, both casual directions should be analyzed.) Our design would entail scrutiny of the validity and representation of each data series and the writing of a regression formula to fathom possible multiple correlations. In using such a formula, you cannot prove cause and effect with an historical design, because you must stage an experiment isolating the suspected casual variable for proof. Even when a covariation is found to be consistent over a long period, other variables that might have been a partial or major cause still are not represented in the time series. This does not preclude the usefulness of such a statistical design for forecasting purposes, but it does limit confidence in cause-and-effect inferences.

Most of the conclusions we draw or principles we learn are not drawn from statistics, but rather from a few examples or cases. The maxim about experience being the best teacher may be untrue. Most learning by either personal or vicarious cases of experience lacks design, accurate

TABLE 4–7. Advertising and Personal Consumption Expenditures in the United States, 1935–1975

Year	Advertising Expenditures (millions of dollars)[a]	Personal Consumption Expenditures (billions of dollars)[a]
1935	1,690	56.3
1939	1,980	61.7
1940	2,088	71.9
1941	2,236	74.6
1942	2,156	82.0
1943	2,496	91.3
1944	2,724	98.5
1945	2,875	121.7
1946	3,364	147.1
1947	4,260	165.4
1948	4,864	178.3
1949	5,202	181.2
1950	5,710	191.0
1951	6,426	209.8
1952	7,156	219.8
1953	7,755	232.6
1954	8,164	238.0
1955	9,194	254.4
1956	9,905	269.9
1957	10,311	284.4
1958	10,302	290.1
1959	11,255	311.6
1960	11,932	325.2
1961	11,845	335.2
1962	12,381	355.1
1963	13,107	373.8
1964	14,155	401.2
1965	15,259	433.1
1966	16,670	465.9
1967	16,866	492.1
1968	18,127	535.8
1969	19,482	577.5
1970	19,600	616.8
1971	20,500	668.2
1972	22,500	733.0
1973	25,120	808.5
1974	26,780	885.9
1975	28,390	973.2

[a] Data are given in current dollars for the various years.

Source: Statistical Abstract of the United States *(Washington, D.C.: Government Printing Office, various years' issues, 1936 to 1975);* Advertising Age, *September 15, 1975, p. 1.*

measurement, or rigorous logic, and it hardly is trustworthy. Historical study, using past cases, can nevertheless have adequate validity when properly conducted.

A marketing researcher is very likely to take advantage of studying past experiences, when their recency or availability can provide enough evidence to determine what took place, under what conditions, and with what outcome. An example of a historical case approach is an analysis by Lee Adler of the time involved in product development.[17] Adler acquired from many past periodicals and other sources the following data on forty-two new products in consumer and industrial goods fields:

1. Product type, brand name, and manufacturer.
2. Date when its development began.
3. Date of test of initial marketing.
4. Date when large-scale marketing began.
5. Elapsed time since beginning of development.
6. Description of special factors affecting development.

As an experienced researcher, Adler drew guarded and limited interpretations from these historical data, which indicated that the development stage tends to involve far more time than marketers usually allot to it. With no criticism of this valid inference from the data, this study may be cited as exemplifying some difficulties entailed with the historical approach, to wit: (1) By drawing upon articles from twenty publications, dating as far back as seventeen years, there was little or no opportunity to scrutinize the authenticity of the stated "facts." (2) Most likely the various authors or reporters had different definitions of such terms as "test marketing" and "product development." (3) Details on particular factors affecting the length of development time evidently were meager or lacking, which a marketing decision maker would need, if he were to apply the findings to a specific proposed product. (4) It would be difficult, indeed, to determine whether the forty-two products chosen were representative of new consumer or industrial products.

A case study approach, used historically, usually differs from the one above. Valid historical case studies usually have to be conducted internally, inside the firm where the episode took place. "Facts" provided by persons who were concerned with the case tend to be colored or rationalized in their recall, so written records are very desirable. Limited records and personnel turnover dog the researcher who attempts to put together cases that occurred some time back.

If these remarks about the historical case approach seem very discouraging, we wish to counter this by stating that this can be a very fruitful design type. It is used frequently in studies of marketing personnel, fashions, the causes of products' success or failure on the market, and the location of stores or facilities. If those who participate in plans

---

[17] Lee Adler, "Time Lag in New Product Development," *Journal of Marketing*, January, 1966, pp. 17–21.

and programs that are likely to be analyzed someday in case studies would currently record ample information about their actions and reasoning, profitable and valid case studies would be made feasible when future major decisions instigate some marketing research relating to them. In such a farsighted organization, marketing research really could make experience the "great teacher."

4.4.3 Survey Research Designs

Survey research designs is a broad category into which most designs for conclusive marketing research fall. It is an appropriate term, because it describes the chief characteristic of the approach: these designs reach conclusions on the basis of evidence collected through various means of questioning and/or observation that does not measure the type of results or payoff sought in the particular decision of problem. Instead, they produce evidence that indirectly implies the results or payoff.

Experiments were described as executing demonstrations of proposed hypotheses whose results could be measured directly in terms of the kind of results or payoffs that would be desired when the full-scale course of action was chosen and put into effect. The types of designs now discussed do not execute some scaled-down demonstration of the proposed hypothesis. The evidence they produce is presumed to be related to the acceptance or rejection of the hypothesis, a sort of proxy for actual payoff, and by such indirect inferences the researcher reaches conclusions on what the results of the actual action would be.

The survey method is used most often where questionnaire-type surveys are used. A manufacturer of catsup, when surveying the buying public's opinions, obtained widespread complaint about the difficulty of getting the catsup out of the bottle. This led to the inference that a wide-mouth bottle, which actually permitted the catsup to flow much more freely, would be popular. Not content with jumping to conclusions on so little evidence, the manufacturer had some bottles designed and selected the one that enabled the easiest pouring to be the probable solution or hypothesis regarding this problem. He then packed catsup in a small quantity of such wide-mouth bottles and placed one of these new bottles and the conventional narrow-necked bottle with consumers. After they had had opportunity to use both bottles, they again were surveyed to learn which bottle they preferred. The new wide-mouth bottle received acclaim to the extent that the manufacturer inferred that catsup would sell better in the new bottle than in the old narrow-necked type of bottle. The inference drawn was, of course, from indirect evidence, for what the people had said was that they preferred the new-type bottle, which is another matter from actually buying the new bottle. Acting on this interpretation of the data, the manufacturer began to pack his catsup in the new wide-mouth bottle (but continued also to offer the narrow-necked bottle) and to place it on sale over a wide portion of the country. The results were quite contrary to expectations, as only a small minority bought the wide-necked bottle, which had to be withdrawn as unprofitable. The apparent reason for the failure was that the wide-mouth bottle was a shorter, squat bottle and appeared to hold less quantity than the taller, narrow-necked bottle. (More recently this firm reintroduced the wide-mouthed bottle, so perhaps the solution to inducing its purchase has been discovered.)

Much advertising research is of the survey type. Assumptions are made that before advertising can generate sales it must be seen, understood, and retained. Consequently, audience measurement and recall studies are conducted to partially evaluate advertising. In attempting to understand purchase motivation, field surveys are conducted, which gather data on purchase behavior and consumer behavioral traits. The two sets of data are analyzed for purposes of grouping different types of purchase behavior with different behavioral traits. Causality is then inferred from the consumer behavior traits to the purchase behavior. Unfortunately, too frequently the motivational explanations depend on the orientation of the analyst examining the different groups.

In another case this type of design was used to infer probable behavior from changes in attitudes that result from exposure to the proposed course of action. Preferences, comparative ratings of competitive products, and images are some of the attitudes that may be measured. Indirectly, from responses indicating attitudes, the behavioral results of a specific action may be inferred.

Exemplifying this type of research design was a study conducted for an automobile manufacturer. The question was the nature and intensity of the effects of certain advertising appeals under consideration. The make of car had been handicapped with a rather poor reputation and a lower share of the market than a car of its advanced features and length of time in the industry should hold. The alternative advertising messages, therefore, were tested on their ability to change the image of the car and—which was considered more vital—the image of the sort of owners that the public associated with this make. To this end, alternative advertising messages were shown to automobile owners. Then they were asked to rate this car (on a scale) for the extent to which they would associate this make with specified types of owners (for example, a school teacher, an aviator, and so forth) and with specified qualities. These were compared with the images given by another set of owners who did not read the message. The degree to which reading each advertisement moved the favorable associations upward—and unfavorable associations downward—was inferred as the power of that advertisement to obtain a stronger desire for this make.

This is, of course, an indirect inference that the attitude changes will produce more buyers. It involved some assumptions that may be critical, including the following: (1) that the images supposed by the researchers to be favorable to wanting that make actually were favorable in the interviewees' minds, (2) that their given ratings truly reflected their beliefs, and (3) that these attitudes were held so strongly that they would motivate buying behavior. The last point is a question in all attitudinal measurements, and the study's design should provide means of measuring the intensity of opinions.

4.5 Simulation[18]

Simulation, a relatively new technique for solving marketing problems, is neither an experimental or quasi-experimental design. A simulation may be described as an imitation of a genuine or real-world situation that it represents. Sometimes, when the real world cannot feasibly be given an experimental treatment, there may be an alternative of replicating it with an acceptably close resemblance. Our explanation, if not comprehensible at this point, will be clarified with an example.

Simulations should not be confused with analytical models. Such models incorporate only a few of the components of a situation, with which they seek to optimize results. This result may be optimal for the model but not optimal for the system as a whole if all components are considered. A simulation model, on the other hand, is more comprehensive in terms of components and it does not seek to optimize a single result. Because of the tying together of functional relationships among the components, it can address a number of alternatives and simply generates anticipated results. The decision maker must select the desired alternative.

The term *simulation* can be applied to almost any attempt to replicate a real-world situation. In practice, however, varying degrees of sophistication may be found in simulation. Three such degrees can be identified.

Symbolic simulation implies the use of block flow charts to trace the component flows in an identified system. For example, in a logistics simulation this would involve tracing the physical product and communication flows and diagramming them. For a marketing-mix simulation, all aspects of the marketing effort are identified and these flows to the ultimate buyer diagrammed. Once diagramming is complete, costs may be assigned to each block and some historical revenue result also applied to the end point. A major limitation of this kind of simulation is that each alternative to be tested requires a new symbolization. Nevertheless, this format does enable one to visualize and actually compare alternative courses of action.

Static simulation is considerably more complicated. In this case all identifiable components of the system are identified and replicated. This could include all internal controllable components as well as external uncontrollable components such as the environment, including market characteristics, such as customer mix, product mix purchased, number of competitors, and so on. Both costs and functional relationships between controllable and uncontrollable components are then built into the simulation. A change in any variable will generate a different result. Once again, the decision maker has the option of selecting his best result.

Dynamic simulation is the ultimate in simulation technique. It differs

---

[18] For an expanded treatment, see Donald J. Bowersox, *Logistical Management* (New York: Macmillan Publishing Co., Inc., 1974), pp. 389–499.

111

from static simulation only in that it incorporates a feedback loop which changes the outcome of alternating schemes through time. For example, a decision to introduce a new warehouse in time period 1 will have a profound affect on the consideration of other alternatives simulated in time periods 2 through n. That is, if an alternative was considered in time period 2 without incorporating the multiple influence of all decisions in time period 1, the results may be drastically different. Of course, incorporating the feedback of past decisions' possibilities complicates the establishment of functional relationships between the components.

Simulation is a powerful tool and given our capacity to process large amounts of data will probably become a much more important decision-making tool. For example, the Long Range Environmental Planning Simulator (LREPS) system diagrammed in Figure 4-1 incorporates three groups of variables, described as follows:

(1) target variables, (2) environment variables, and (3) controllable variables. The major target variables are customer service and total cost. Environmental variables are grouped into major categories of demographics, technologies, and acts of nature. Each of these categories is broken down into variables that are interactive with the model itself; that is, demographic variables defined in terms of cost-of-living indices, real-estate-value indices, and demand determinants.[19]

The major controllable variables are order characteristics, product mix, customer mix, facility structure, inventory policy, transportation, communication structure, and marketing overlap. The output capabilities of this simulator are many, but three problems it has been applied to are:[20]

1. Analysis of cost—customer service trade-offs on a distribution system redesign.
2. Analysis of inventory and location for a single market area.
3. Analysis of (a) the number or sequencing of warehouse locations, (b) inventory cost related to performance delays for an eight-location structure, and (c) market-area adjustment to postpone timing of warehouse additions.

4.6 Descriptive Studies

We should also recognize the existence of many studies whose results are descriptive, not conclusive. Most governmental and academic marketing studies probably fall within this category. For example, the United States Bureau of Mines gathers and publishes annual data on the output of various minerals and of fuel and power sources, which is research—but descriptive in nature. A professor or doctoral student makes a study of

---

[19] Ibid., pp. 398–99.
[20] Ibid., pp. 402–8.

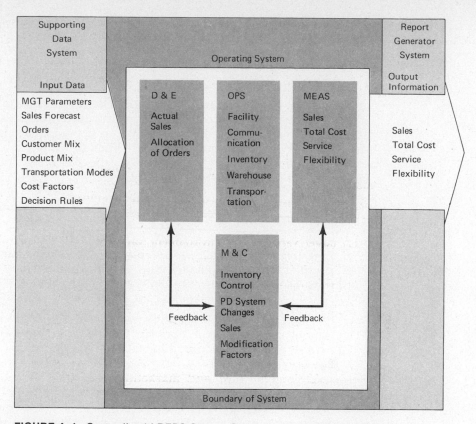

FIGURE 4-1. Generalized LREPS System Concept—Physical Distribution Model

Source: D. J. Bowersox, Logistical Management *(New York: Macmillan Publishing Co., Inc., 1974), p. 399.*

"Food Brokers: Their Nature and Functions, 1976." These are examples of research projects which obviously need to be descriptive.

Descriptive studies draw no conclusions about any hypothetical courses of action, so they have no payoffs and, therefore, cannot be categorized in relationship to experiments, quasi-experiments or simulations. The goals of descriptive studies specify the character and classifications of the findings sought. If they are to be very useful, these goals should anticipate the data requirements of the various decision makers and researchers who will seek to use them. Manifestly, these needs will be widely diverse and vary greatly between fields of knowledge. An analyst of bank markets and marketing methods for personal loans will want data of a quite different character from the media director of an advertising agency.

Therefore, we cannot sensibly classify types of descriptive studies or provide brief descriptions of their designs. In general, however, efficient gathering, accuracy, clear definitions of the scope, and breakdowns that will be useful should be comprehended in designs of descriptive studies.

113

4.7 Evaluating the Choice of Designs

After reviewing the options available, you are probably wondering how one selects the design to use. The decision maker is aware that an experimental design is the best; however, there are few instances in marketing in which *valid* experiments are used. The first level of decision is whether to use an experimental design or one of the other types suggested. The reasons are many and have to be weighed against the advantages and disadvantages of each. Although each problem requires special consideration in design selection, the following combination of virtues would provide the greatest advantage:

1. Exerts a stimulus in the test situation that is substantially like the hypothesis being considered, for which it would proxy (internal validity).
2. Produces and measures the sort of effects that have real comparability to, or foreshadow the payoff desired from, the hypothesis to be chosen (external validity).
3. Can be executed in a time period that is consistent with the competitive pressures surrounding the decision (time).
4. Can be executed in a manner that is consistent with the competitive pressures surrounding the decision (secrecy).
5. Can be executed at a cost that does not exceed the probable loss if the wrong decision was made (cost).

With the checklist above in mind, the experimental versus other types of design can be rated as in Table 4-8. We recognize that the characteristics above can be achieved only in degree, and we rate the designs as high or low on each of the characteristics.

The selection of experimental versus nonexperimental should always be made on how important the presence of the five characteristics are to the research. Given the cost of conducting research today there is no virtue in using a research design that is supposedly *more scientific* if precise causal relationships, error measurement, or small degrees of error are not important.

If the researcher opts for experimental, he or she then must select a research design from one of the many experimental designs discussed. As

TABLE 4-8. Evaluation of Research Designs for Five Characteristics

	Experimental	Quasi-experimental	Simulation
Internal validity	High	Low	High
External validity	High	Low	Low
Time	High	Low	Low
Secrecy	Low	High	High
Cost	High	Low	High

each of the formal and informal designs was discussed, we alluded to the presence or absence of the five characteristics. The researcher will have to pick that design which fits his or her needs. For example, if external validity is only of minimum importance but secrecy is very important, she or he may sacrifice external validity and use a laboratory rather than a field experiment. Or if relative measure rather than absolute measure is the desired result, a posttest-only design is less expensive than the other experimental designs.

If the researcher selects a quasi-experimental design or simulation, she or he has a wider choice of options. Again, she or he should strive to fit the design choice to the problem at hand. For in one respect each research study calls for some creativity in constructing a design for that particular study. The cataloging of designs in this chapter is not meant to imply that the researcher goes to a file drawer and selects an appropriate design. These are only representative of the kinds of designs that have been used, and ingenuity and creativity are called for in each marketing research study.

Once a design is selected, the precise statements of data needs arrived at earlier should then be checked once again to ensure that the collection of the specified data will, within the design, provide a solution.

4.8 Summary

In this chapter we have examined the series of advanced decisions that comprise the master plan for the conduct of "conclusive research." In doing so we have developed a planning sequence for the research design. We started with the anticipation of data analysis and processing, suggesting the value of writing precise statements of data needs, the construction of dummy tables, and a consideration of the techniques that will be used to demonstrate the payoff.

The specific approaches available to validate the hypothesis were examined. Experimental designs were stressed as the ideal, and laboratory, field, informal, and formal designs were described and evaluated against the requirements for external and internal validity.

Laboratory experiments offer a high level of internal validity at low cost, at the sacrifice of some external validity. Field experiments are generally more costly and have capacity for a high level of external validity with some reduction in internal validity.

Since the ideal, experimental design, is not often used because of time–cost considerations, after-the-fact, historical, and survey research designs were described. After-the-fact designs, although not strictly experiments, are used when it is impossible ahead of time to determine who has received a treatment and who has not.

Historical designs may be uniquely appropriate where a time span over the past is desirable or where their lower cost is an overriding factor. They may be time-series studies, associative relationship studies, or case studies. Survey research designs have poorer scientific quality than experiments and some historical designs but are widely used, nevertheless. Some are good at predicting the outcome of hypotheses, but some may have to draw such far-fetched inferences that it would be wiser to forgo research.

Simulation was discussed as a technique that replicates a real-world situation and allows the decision maker to experiment with a number of "what-if" alternatives. Descriptive studies also were mentioned as another category of design, but they are too various to specify any design structure for them.

Evaluating the choice of design, experimental or nonexperimental, should be based on the need for internal and external validity, time, secrecy, and cost, and the capacity of different designs to provide these requirements.

5 Plans and Proposals

We move to a level of greater detail in Chapter 5. It concerns a series of questions, whose answers would enable decision of the final question stated below:

What is a research plan? What should it contain?

What are the kinds of data it might call for? The sources of those data? The ways of reaching those sources? What are their advantages?

What is a research proposal? Is that different from a plan?

Who is it written for? What do they need to know?

What are the steps in authorizing a research study to go ahead?

What approach might be used in making that decision? What would need to be known for making it? What role would the researcher play in the decision? The decision maker?

If the proposal is given a go-ahead, what planning steps would remain?

WE NOW HAVE PROCEEDED, in the development of a possible research project, to the point of determining the data that are needed. The main concept that would structure such decisions, the design, was dealt with in Chapter 4. To some degree the nature of those data would be anticipated while envisioning the possible design. If you will refer back to Table 4–1 as a guide to progress in our discussion, you will find that this brings the work through the second step.

We are far short of a complete research plan, as indicated by the sixteen remaining steps in Table 4–1. Efficiently making those remaining decisions depends on the researcher's familiarity with the alternative methods available. When those decisions are made, they would be incorporated in a written plan, which in turn becomes the basis of estimating the projects cost and time, as well as its decision inputs. These estimates would be used in deciding whether or not to proceed with the project. If approved, its methods should be given a pretest to assure how they would work out.

The subjects mentioned in the last paragraph form this chapter's content, which is divided into these sections:

1. Summarizing subjects in the research plan. Most of them will be given extensive treatment in later chapters on techniques.
2. Chief alternatives in (a) types of information, (b) its sources, and (c) methods of communicating with those sources. This is a convenient point to bring these together in brief overview.
3. Research proposals then are described with regard to their functions and content.
4. The critical decision on whether or not to proceed with the proposed study next arises. This was mentioned when we dealt with the roles played by decision maker and researcher, in Chapter 2, where we mentioned some of the relevant factors. Here we consider a concrete decision.
5. If the project is approved, the work must be scheduled and some controls provided to meet that schedule.
6. Also we point out the precaution of pretesting the methods.

5.1 Content of the Research Plan

Research work must be conducted in accordance with plans, to be efficient, and those plans must be determined and written in advance of the work. The full details would be part of the working papers and unlikely to be a formal document. They should be specific and fully describe what is to be done in each of the phases that we will mention only briefly below, as they will be given coverage starting in Chapter 6.

Some early planning steps already have been covered at this point: (1) defining the problem, (2) establishing the alternative solutions or hypotheses to be studied, (3) considering alternative designs, (4) comparing them for their ability to provide suitable payoff data with efficient use of resources, and (5) selecting the most suitable research design. We will enumerate what else should be in the plan, which the remainder of the text will cover in detail.

1. *Secondary data.* When the needed data are available from secondary sources, either within or outside the organization, that can be a fine economy. Sources of existing data should be practically exhausted before seeking original data, so our technique chapters will begin with secondary data as the subject of Chapter 6.

2. *Primary data needs.* New problems typically call for fresh data unavailable in secondary sources, and so the data gaps need to be assessed. Then the researcher needs to decide what sorts of primary data are wanted, which we deal with in Section 5.2.

3. *Coverage.* An entire type of population may be covered as data sources, but very rarely. Instead, we usually take a sample, which needs careful definition and systematic selection. Sampling is so complicated that we devote both Chapters 7 and 8 to it.

4. *Collection instruments.* Most studies that gather primary data utilize surveys, asking the data through questionnaires, but there also may be forms needed for observations. Both types of collection instruments are discussed in Chapter 9.

5. *Field collection.* Methods used to gather information from the sample population may be critical sources of error and of cost overruns. We discuss this for each of the chief communication methods in Chapter 10.

6. *Data processing.* This is a tedious and time-consuming stage of the work when done manually. With computers used, as is now customary with large quantities of data and complex analyses, this is a very exacting stage. With either method the researcher needs to have realistic anticipations early in the project so that data processing will go smoothly and be well coordinated with analytical needs. We discuss this subject in Chapter 11.

7. *Analysis and interpretation.* These phases tightly interrelate and also should be integrated with the planning of data processing. Interpreting data and directing analysis so that it yields maximum meaning to enable pertinent conclusions are perhaps the most intricate phases of research. It is highly important to anticipate them in the research plan, as you will appreciate when studying them in Chapters 12 and 13.

8. *Presentation of findings.* The success of applied research materializes at the point where its findings are communicated or presented to the decision makers. Its anticipation is vital from the beginning of planning a project. Methods of presenting findings are discussed in Chapter 14.

Above are the eight stages of research that should be conceived in a project's plan, partially because they are the basis of the time and costs estimates. We shall expand on the aspect of data, sources, and communi-

8 stages of research that should be conceived in a project's plan.

cation alternatives in the next section and then take up the research proposal in Section 5.3.

5.2 Information and Communication Alternatives

An overview of the general options in methods of gathering data will give you perspective for subjects lying ahead. Also, this gives you some insight into the selection tasks that researchers have in formulating a research proposal. Three aspects are covered here: (1) kinds of data; (2) their sources, when original data are to be collected; and (3) ways of communicating with sources. These three types of determination are quite interconnected.

5.2.1 Types of Data

A simple classification of data is in three types: facts, opinions, and attitudes. Actually, the research planning must consider a great variety of subtypes of data within these, but the following may be sufficient for our purposes.

(1) *Facts*, of course, are information on what actually exists and seem to constitute the data most often wanted. Here are four types of facts much utilized in making marketing decisions:

1. Objects that are readily and exactly measurable (for example, the number of taverns in Tampa serving Schlitz beer or the amount of freight carried within the United States by airlines last year).

2. Buyer behavior in making purchases and in uses of goods and services.

3. Demographic data that describe characteristics of people, which are heavily used as Wells remarked:

Age, income, education and other indications of position in life space have so much influence on so many kinds of consumer behavior that users of a product or brand, viewers of a TV program, or readers of a magazine are virtually certain to differ from the rest of the population on one or more of the common demographic dimensions. Marketing researchers collect demographics as a matter of routine, and marketers feel comfortable using them.[1]

4. Other means of describing buyers and consumers has been on the basis of their life styles or psychographics. Life styles, of course, refer to modes of living that affect the products wanted and purchased, to media for reaching potential buyers, and to other marketing factors.

---

[1] William D. Wells, "Psychographics: A Critical Review," *Journal of Marketing Research*, May, 1975, p. 196.

When speaking of "facts" one should be aware that many measurements that purportedly are factual are indeed quite erroneous, a major problem for marketing researchers.

2. *Opinions* include perceptions of people or their judgments of facts and their significance, within the viewer's mind. If Mrs. A believes that Brand B coffee is darker or stronger than Brand C, that is her opinion.

3. *Attitudes* also relate to people's views, but they are learned predispositions or mental readiness to act in a certain manner. While an attitude continues, it exerts a general and consistent influence over a person's behavior toward some object, person, or group.

Information on all three of these categories may be needed in order to identify and measure the motives or causal factors that would lead to a solution. If one could reach the solution on the basis solely of facts that may be accurately measured, that would be splendid, but marketing problems usually involve subjective human elements.

5.2.2 Sources

Often we are seeking information from some organization and there is little concern about identifying the person who should supply it. Marketing information more often is from and about an individual or family, and determining who is the right person is a more troublesome matter. Specific techniques of such identification will be taken up under sampling, and here we shall only compare approaching persons singly, in panels, or in groups.

Traditionally, subjects participating in marketing studies have been selected singly. Mostly this is at home, but it might be at work, in transit, or in a central location such as a laboratory—the last-named being increasingly used. Advantages of contacting singly include getting the peculiar cross section that is appropriate for a study. Also each individual may respond without being affected by others present. This is, however, the least efficient approach.

Panels are large numbers of persons who already have consented to serve as survey subjects. Since they already are identified and willing, their responses may be obtained reliably. Also, the agency that operates a panel would have demographic facts on each individual which enables a well-tailored sample to be picked. With such prearrangement, these people may be contacted cheaply by mail, if that is an appropriate means of communication for the data wanted. Often there is no panel of the types of respondents wanted, or there is a need for a large sample concentrated in a locality, for which a panel would not suffice. Some of the other drawbacks as well as advantages of panels will be brought up later.

Groups are numbers of persons brought together to serve as research subjects. Typically this is done ad hoc or for a single occasion. Formal question-and-answer techniques may be used on groups, as in the "program analyzer" technique of registering opinions of advertising shown to an audience. A more popular use at this time is in "focus groups," which are described as follows:

The *focus group interview,* where a group of people (generally eight to twelve) are led through an open, in-depth discussion by a group moderator. The moderator's objective is to focus the discussion on the relevant subject areas in a nondirective manner.[2]

These groups thus are not asked formal lists of questions, but they enter into discussions that evolve under the steering of the moderator. For example, they might be shown a new product, as was done with Levi's for Feet with groups of young men, about which discussion develops in a natural and informal manner. This must be taped-recorded, being unstructured and oral. As the article just quoted says, they "provide a basis in depth for the development of additional research, and they may be useful as a source of new and fresh ideas for new products and services, advertising themes, packaging evaluations, and the like." The ease of setting up focus groups poses a danger of their being used for conclusive research for which they are unreliable due to the varying nature of the stimuli, the interactions of the participants, and the small samples.

5.2.3 Communication Methods

Our overview turns to the means of communicating with the appropriate sources to obtain needed primary data. The chief methods are given first, followed with more detail on surveys.

Methods of communicating (or sensing) to acquire data may be put in three categories: (1) mechanical, (2) observations, and (3) surveys.

1. *Mechanical.* Within this type we would include electronic means, which occasionally can be used to record marketing behavior. The tape recorder, which may be used to record interviews, is one example. Others include devices that record happenings: the movie camera, which records human actions; the eyecamera, which takes motion pictures of eye motions while reading; the audimeter, which records the use of radio or television sets; and various electric devices for counting traffic. As new mechanical marvels are invented to replace fallible human observation or questioning, the future will very probably bring an increasing use of machines to record marketing behavior. At present the types of data that may be recorded mechanically are very limited, and so this is the least-used method.

2. *Observational.* In simple terms, observation is the method in which what is taking place is seen and recorded. It is a widely used technique with many valuable applications, which include the following: obtaining sales records or counts indicating consumer choice, recording the stations listened to on radio and television sets, seeing the actual products in consumers' pantries, counting the wearers of various styles of clothing, counting the volume of con-

---

[2]Keith K. Cox, James B. Higginbotham, and John Burton, "Applications of Focus Group Interviews in Marketing," *Journal of Marketing,* January, 1976, p. 77.

sumer traffic (walking or riding), and watching what these people do. We should also note that the observational method is more objective than the survey method. In addition, if the observational method is used while an inquiry survey is being conducted, a number of conditions may be *observed;* this obviates the need for asking questions about them.

The observing is usually done by a person or observer, although we have mentioned some mechanical means of counting or of recording actions. Provided that the observer perceives accurately what happens and records it correctly, this method obtains factual information. Only overt behavior (that which may be seen or may be recorded mechanically) can be learned by observation.

3. *Surveys.* In this method, questions are asked or stimuli are presented in order to elicit information or reactions from the subjects who are communicated with, who are usually called *respondents*. A standardized and printed questionnaire normally is used, although there can be informal questionning with little or no structuring (as in focus groups). We are placing surveys into four types: (1) personal, (2) telephone, (3) mail, and (4) diary. While the fourth type does involve communication by mail, it has distinct characteristics.

Each of these communication methods has its special advantages, and more than one may be used in a single study for different purposes.

Personal interview surveys are the most costly, but they also tend to be the most capable of obtaining information that may be critical, such as knowledge that respondents may not readily recall or consider rather private, intentions, demographic characteristics, attitudes, opinions, and life-style. From a decision standpoint, the main advantages of conducting a survey by using personal interviews are the following:

1. The relatively short period of time required.
2. The many different types of information that can be obtained.
3. The relatively large amount of information that can be collected for each type of information provided.
4. The degree with which results can be projected to the relevant universe.

The main disadvantages of personal interviews are (1) the relatively high cost per completed interview, and (2) the relative difficulty of administering a survey using personal interviews.

The cost of obtaining information by way of the personal interview is usually high when compared with other methods. For example, in terms of cost per completed interview, personal interviews typically cost two or three times as much as telephone interviews and ten to twenty times as much as using mail questionnaires. The time required to complete a survey using personal interviews normally ranges from two to six weeks. This method is difficult to administer because the person in charge of the survey has relatively limited control over the interviewers.

Telephone interviews are the second survey means, which have these advantages:

1. The costs involved are lower than for personal interviews.
2. Telephone interviews can be completed very quickly.
3. Different types of information can be obtained.
4. It is easy to administer a telephone interview survey.
5. The results can be projected to a high degree to the relevant universe.

Telephone interviews' disadvantages are that the costs involved are higher than using mail questionnaires and that a relatively limited amount of data can be obtained for each type of information. With the right techniques, however, suprisingly long telephone interviews can be conducted. We are deferring methods of carrying out surveys until Chapters 9 and 10. The results of telephone surveys are projectible to the whole population being studied, if those people have telephones.

Mail surveys differ in several ways, including their use of a self-administered questionnaire that is completed by the respondent without direct help from an interviewer.

The mail questionnaire usually has the lowest cost per respondent of any method of obtaining respondent information. In addition, a mail survey is extremely easy to administer. You simply prepare a questionnaire, purchase a mailing list, mail the questionnaires, and tabulate the results as the completed questionnaires come back. These advantages make mail surveys very popular.

The time period required for a mail survey ranges from three to eight weeks. The main reason for this is that mail questionnaires must be mailed to the respondent, the respondent must complete the questionnaire, and then the respondent must return the questionnaire by mail. In many instances, even if the questionnaire is sent back by return mail, it can take a week or longer to obtain a response.

Low return rates have plagued users of mail surveys. If only 20 percent of the addresses return completed questionnaires, for instance, the sample may be badly misrepresentative. Excellent return rates, from 70 to 90 percent or more, are not unusual today in surveys administered by experts. Although these are still atypical, it is apparent that mail survey use is not precluded by low return rates. Another serious question is whether there is accurate two-way communication between the respondent and the researcher in the absence of personal contact. We shall describe methods of dealing with these problems in Chapters 9 and 10.

A diary also uses the mail largely, which may be supplemented with personal communications between respondents and the research organization. A diary is a self-administered collection form that is designed so that the respondents can easily and accurately record their behavior with regard to activities that are considered to be important from a marketing viewpoint. There are three basic types of diaries: purchase diaries, use diaries, and media exposure diaries.

A purchase diary provides information on purchase patterns of consumer buying. A use diary provides information about the consumption of products or services in terms of the frequency of consumption, the average amount consumed each time, and the total amount of products consumed in a given period of time. A media exposure diary provides information about which programs television viewers watch. Media exposure diaries can also be used to measure radio listening habits and magazine readership. Diaries enable the researcher to obtain an extremely large amount of detailed information about each type of information provided, especially about behavior. Also, the results of surveys using diaries can be projected to a high degree to the relevant universe.

disadvantage of diaries: The disadvantages of using diaries are the high cost per respondent, the long time period required, the limited types of information that can be obtained, and the difficulty of administering a survey using diaries.

Diary information is usually collected so that the results can be projected to the relevant universe with a high degree of confidence. However, the steps necessary to assure the projectibility through selection of the respondents involve costly field work in setting up the sample. Other costs would be incentives and encouragement to interest respondents in keeping their diaries faithfully over a rather long and tedious period, as well as a massive data-processing job when those returns come in. Despite those costs and the limitations in what people are willing to record, diaries are an important survey method of which many consumer goods manufacturers and advertising agencies make valuable use. Those users rarely attempt to operate their own diaries, in view of the efforts required, and purchase diary information from syndicated data agencies. Some of the agencies providing use and purchase information include Market Facts, Marketing Research Corporation of America (M.R.C.A.), and National Family Opinion (N.F.O.). Media exposure data, through diaries, may be purchased from such agencies as Advertising Research Bureau, Hooper, Nielsen, and Videodex.

Among the four survey methods just discussed, apparently telephone interviewing is fast ascending in use. Its speed, low cost, flexibility, and sample coverage all are attractive characteristics when modern telephone equipment and managerial techniques are utilized, as we will discuss under field methodology. Personal interviewing has a number of deterrents, including cost, difficulty of finding respondents, and growing fear of strangers. Group interviews and meeting consumers in central places such as shopping centers are means of alleviating some of these handicaps. As all four methods have unique advantages for certain situations, however, the marketing researcher should be thoroughly acquainted with each.

5.3 Research Proposals

Every study that is contemplated, requiring substantial funds and time, needs to be justified. The facts and expectations that may justify it need to be stated in written form, and this is the project *proposal*. This document should not be confused with the *research plan*, of which we spoke in

Section 5.1, for that is a detailed record of what is to be done, its costs, and its schedule (an aspect we shall discuss at the end of the chapter). The plan might be a rather thick file and is not a concise document—which is what the proposal should be.

Outside research agencies necessarily prepare a research proposal for submission to a client, possibly with a bid for the assignment. While there is not this necessity for an internal marketing research department, a written proposal is desirable to form a basis for discussion with the decision makers, and its preparation helps to define the concepts of the study. Let us take up an internal proposal first.

Formal planning is just as desirable in a marketing research department as any other activity in modern corporations. It helps to achieve organizational discipline, provides a means for determining priorities among projects, and tends to assure that the right work is executed. Since substantial projects would have to be submitted to higher levels for approval of funds, a formal proposal is needed for this. With that approval at stake, writing a proposal justifies considerable thought and pains in its preparation.

The writing of a proposal probably would wait until some discussion has taken place between the decision maker and the marketing researcher. Then a proposal would be written by the latter which might have the following content:

1. Background of the problem and the project, including department or executives sponsoring the study
2. Statement of the problem: its nature, significant effects or risks, and its payoffs
3. Data objectives
   a. The questions that are to be answered
   b. The study's data inputs
4. Research design
   a. Method, scope, and sources (briefly)
   b. How the data will be interpreted; conclusions to be reached
5. Requirements
   a. Funds and time required
   b. Desired scheduling

Many proposals may be prepared over time by an internal marketing research department, so a standardized form would be helpful. In Figure 5–1 is shown a brief proposal form that has been used in the very active marketing research operation of General Mills, Inc. This form includes most of the items that we listed above. It also provides a definite channel for approvals, specifies who should approve, and requires their signatures. Notice that each proposal must be approved on both sides of the "dialogue": (1) by the executive requesting the study, and (2) by a research supervisor or executive. Apparently, every General Mills study must pass this procedure, but you will notice that those costing under $1,500 can be approved at the product manager level, whereas those in-

Project Number _____

MARKETING RESEARCH PROJECT PROPOSAL AND EXPENDITURE APPROVAL

cc: Dir Mktg Res   Originator - (2)
    Dir Cons Res
    Interview Supv.

Requested By: _____

Title: _____   Product(S):

Date: _____   Control #:

- -

1. Problem and Background

2. Decision Involved

3. Method and Design

4. Criteria for Interpretation

- -

5. Mktg Res Budget: $_____ Est Proj Exp $\pm$ $500: $_____ Balance $_____

6. Individual who must finally approve recommended action: _____

7. Report to be delivered by ___/___/___ if authorized by ___/___/___ and test materials shipped by ___/___/___.

_____ Time & Cost (Supplier/Proj Dir) Commitments were Confirmed by	Proposal Submitted By _____ (Mktg Res Mgr)	Proposal Authorized by* _____ (Attach MR#2 & See Below)

ROUTE TO:

RECOMMEND APPROVAL OF RESEARCH EXPENDITURE

_____

	Initials	Date	Remarks (Attach note if more space is needed)
Product Manager	_____	___/___/___	
Marketing Manager	_____	___/___/___	
Director of Marketing	_____	___/___/___	
_____	_____	___/___/___	

Research Expenditure Approved By** _____ Date _____

- -

	When Project Expense Amounts to:	**Research Expenditure Must be Approved by--	*Problem & Design Must be Authorized by--
Coord of Mktg Budget	$1,499 or less	Product Manager	M-R Dir-GP/Corp
	$1,500 to $9,999	Marketing Manager	M-R Dir-GP/Corp
	$10,000 to $24,000	Dir of Marketing	M-R Dir-GP-Corp
Originator-Mktg Res Dept	over $25,000	VP Adv & Mktg Serv/ Gen'l Mgr.	Director of Mktg Res

FIGURE 5–1. Project Proposal Form

Source: Lawrence D. Gibson, "Use of Marketing Research Contractors," in Robert Ferber (ed.), Handbook of Marketing Research *(New York: McGraw-Hill Book Company, 1974), pp. 1–135.*

volving over $25,000 go to the highest marketing and research administrators.

Research proposals assume even greater importance when prepared by outside agencies for clients.[3] Frequently, such proposals are a means whereby several competing agencies may be judged in deciding which will be awarded a project. Proposal writing has been brought to a fine art among experienced research firms. Their proposals necessarily include types of information that would be inappropriate in an internal proposal. These would include the following:

1. Qualifications of the agency
   a. Its experience in the particular type of problem, industry, or techniques
   b. Professional staff who would conduct the project: their special qualifications
2. Precise description of the work to be performed
   a. Validation of interviews' authenticity
   b. Other verification procedures
3. The findings and their reporting
   a. Exactly what information or recommendations
   b. Written reports: format, content, number of copies
   c. Personal presentations (if any)
   d. Limitations on how client may use the findings
4. Specific scheduling: progress reports to be made, if any
5. Financial
   a. Fee and its basis (added fees for options)
   b. Time and method of payment
6. Security
   a. Pledge of confidentiality
   b. Who will retain working papers

Also, the external proposal would include some vital portions that we described in the internal proposal, including: background of the problem and its definition, data objectives, and design of the proposed work.

If the client wants a long and involved proposal, as government agencies often do when taking bids for research contracts, that is what would be submitted. Executives typically want concise proposals, perhaps as brief as Figure 5–1. Amplifying details always could be put in an appendix or be available in marketing research files.

5.4 Deciding Whether to Proceed

One of the most critical matters to decide, regarding proposed research work, is whether or not it is worthwhile in terms of the time and funds

---

[3] The extent to which external research organizations prepare such formal proposals is indicated in a recent study. It found that 88 percent of research agencies and 84 percent of advertising agencies have formal procedures for clients' approval of such proposals. Dik W. Twedt, "Authorization, Control, and Evaluation of Marketing Research Projects," *Journal of Marketing Research*, February, 1975, p. 87.

3 approaches to deciding whether to proceed or not?

required. In Chapter 2 we broached this matter and gave three approaches to deciding it:

1. An *intuitive* approach based on one's feelings about the risks associated with the decision and the extent to which the proposed study would reduce them.
2. A *judgmental* approach that explicitly recognizes and weighs the factors involved. This would be a deliberate study of the benefits expected versus the costs.
3. A *probabilistic* method, utilizing what is known as Bayesian analysis, which may be quite familiar to the reader. Essentially the decision maker quantifies his or her expectations, which permits calculating the benefits of acquiring the expected data.

In discussing the probabilistic approach, we will follow an example. It is one that we met earlier, of Company B's considering whether or not to market its toys in Canada. Two critical questions faced were:

1. What is the magnitude of the Canadian toy market, in the segment in which Company B would compete, in annual sales dollars?
2. What share of market would Company B be likely to capture?

The marketing manager felt that in his initial state of knowledge he faced a serious degree of uncertainty on both questions. Regarding the first question, though, the marketing research manager estimated that it would cost only $1,100 to acquire good information with which to project the market segment size. This cost was so small relative to the venture that they could safely approve that with an intuitive approach.

The second question of predicting market share would be difficult to research. The marketing research manager suggests conducting a market test, as a small experiment (but lacking controls that an experimental design should have), in a typical Canadian city of moderate size. Its cost is estimated at $70,000, a sum that would justify a sophisticated decision method. Let us describe how a probabilistic method could proceed.

A few Bayesian terms should be introduced, with which we shall refer to the decision maker's state of knowledge at three stages:

3 states of knowledge

1. The *prior* analysis stage, which is where that decision maker now stands in our discussion, with only his initial extent of knowledge.
2. The *posterior* analysis stage, which occurs after the action has been taken (on which he now is deciding), when there may be feedback about its results.
3. An intermediate stage between these, if the decision maker decides to acquire more information to be in a safer state of knowledge before making the decision. This is the *preposterior* stage.

*prior
posterior
intermediate*

As marketing research has just proposed a possible study costing $70,000, our example is at the preposterior stage. The marketing manager and research manager are going to make a joint assessment of that study, which is a sort of "value analysis." Their question is essentially this: Would possession of the information acquired through the proposed project decrease the decision risks sufficiently to offset the study's costs? Bear in mind that throughout this analysis they would be conjuring with probabilities, which are more or less educated guesses.

The marketing manager enters this decision with a definite go/no go criterion for entering the Canadian market: a net profit of $320,000 must be earned for the venture to be considered successful. Below that, the decision would be "no go." And on the basis of cost accounting and the new data on the Canadian market, Company B would have to conquer a 14 percent share of market to reach the minimum profit. The marketing manager admittedly is ignorant about what share Company E actually would achieve, but he knows that their share in the United States is 15 percent and doubts that quite that level would be attained in Canada.

Urged by the marketing researcher, the marketing manager considers various shares of market, from 9 to 18 percent, and his subjective probabilities of their attainment. These four levels (or states of nature, S) are now set forth together with estimated profits or loss and subjective probabilities of each S occurring:

(1) Alternative Market Shares, S (%)	(2) Annual Sales (millions of dollars)	(3) Payoffs: Net Profit or (Loss) (millions of dollars)	(4) Subjective Probabilities of Occurrence	(5) Column (3) × Column (4) (dollars)
18	12.0	1.0	0.15	150,000
15	10.0	0.475	0.45	213,750
12	8.0	0.0	0.30	0
9	6.0	(0.3)	0.10	(30,000)
			1.00	333,750

The bottom figure in column (5) represents the weighted payoff expected if the subjective probabilities hold true, and it is technically known as the *expected monetary value* (EMV).[4]

In using the estimates above in judging the market test proposal, we are going to collapse the four S levels into two to simplify the exposition, which does not appreciably affect the calculations. In S_1 is the state of nature above the 14 percent market-share decision criterion, and in S_2 are the two other levels as follows:

---

[4] Expected monetary value (EMV) is not the only criterion that the decision maker might adopt, although it is the most obvious one. Optional criteria arise because of variations in handling risk factors, which are ignored in the EMV criterion. Two other criteria might be that of the "maximin rule" (which calls for choosing the action that would maximize the minimum outcome, a very conservative criterion) and that of the "maximax rule" that would maximize the maximum gain. Discussion of these would run far outside our scope, and the classical discussions are found in R. D. Luce and H. Raiffa, *Games and Decisions* (New York: John Wiley & Sons, Inc., 1957).

Action	S_1: Market Share $\geq$ 14% Probability	Payoff	S_2: Market Share $<$ 14% Probability	Payoff
A_1 Market in Canada	0.6	$606,250	0.4	($75,000)
A_2 Do not market in Canada	0.6	0	0.4	0

$$\text{EMV} = 0.6(606{,}250) + 0.4(-75{,}000) = \$333{,}750$$

Obviously, the marketing manager is skating on thin ice in terms of decision risk, if he proceeds to market in Canada. The EMV is not significantly higher than the decision criterion of a 14 percent market share or $320,000 minimum profit.

The marketing researcher has the task of evaluating the probable accuracy of the proposed market test in Canada. This can be based on some personal experience and knowledge of market test results in the United States, where those firms proceeded to market the new products on the basis of those tests and could use actual sales feedback to validate the tests' results. Those posterior analyses found about an 80 percent accuracy of test data, predicting the market shares actually realized. Therefore, the marketing manager can be told that there would be an 80 percent accuracy of Canadian market share prediction (0.8 probability), which is far better than the manager's belief that his estimate has about a 0.6 accuracy.

Using these new probabilities with the proposed information, we compute the *revised expected monetary value* (EMV'):

$$\text{EMV}' = 0.8(606{,}250) + 0.2(-75{,}000) = \$470{,}000$$

We then calculate the profitability increase, or value of the additional information, by subtraction of EMV from EMV':

$$\text{EMV}' - \text{EMV} = \$470{,}000 - \$333{,}750 = \$136{,}250$$

Since the market test would cost $70,000 but increase the probable payoff or EMV by $136,250, it appears profitable to conduct it. This would assume that the cost of delay for the test would not be an appreciable loss and also that the marketing research department does not have some alternative studies under consideration with larger payoffs.

Now that you have read a simplified example of a probabilistic approach to the value analysis of proposed research, here are some sobering thoughts. The precision implied by these figures can be misleading, because they are based on estimates or guesswork. Both the decision maker and the marketing researcher are making subjective judgments, no better than their information and ability to use some objectivity in its interpretation, so there is a large element of hazard. Consider that if one later made a posterior analysis, if and when market introduction in Canada took place, the actuality might vary radically from the marketing manager's prior estimate. Let us say that it turned out to be only a 9 percent market share and a $300,000 loss. A market test that provided perfect information (an accurate forecast) would predict exactly that. Nevertheless, a number of authors have described the probabilistic method of research value analysis without noting the serious fallacy of using the decision maker's prior EMV as the basis for judging the value of the research.[5] It is, rather, apparent that research predicting a $300,000 loss and saving a firm from a disastrous move would be worth more than the $136,250 profit increase indicated by the probabilistic method.

The marketing researcher would not have a crystal ball that would foretell the findings of a proposed study, such as the Canadian market test, so the ideal basis of value analysis in unavailable. Have we then merely undergone an academic exercise in a probabilistic or Bayesian approach? As far as your authors can ascertain, such an abstruse decision method is rarely used. This is also indicated by a recent survey of large corporations' marketing research practices, which found barely 1 percent evaluating the profitability of marketing research *after* a decision has been executed, or posterior analysis.[6] If posterior analysis of research value is so rare in applied marketing, the more theoretical preposterior analysis must be extremely rare.

Reasons may be advanced, nevertheless, for conducting such probabilistic analysis in deciding on major research projects: (1) a very competent marketing executive may be able to make prior predictions that are much more dependable than our illustration and thus serve as fairly valid guides; (2) attempting this should promote sharper thinking and a richer dialogue between executives and marketing researchers; and (3) doing this may encourage more posterior analyses.

Where a probabilistic approach does not seem justified in terms of the effort and possible errors involved, a careful judgment approach may be substituted. Marketing researchers can discern, with time and diligence, the variables both in decisions and in research validity and costs that affect the cost/benefit relationship. This can produce a decision model that can, in turn, be tested in studies that lead to measurable payoffs. Perhaps this is the more practical route to obtaining better means of prejudging whether proposed marketing research is justifiable. Since the number of desirable studies normally exceeds the funds available, such a model also would apply to setting priorities among alternative studies.

5.5 Scheduling and Control

Planning is highly important if research is to be efficient and is to produce relevant and timely information for decisions. When we speak of

---

[5] For example, Donald S. Tull and Del I. Hawkins, *Marketing Research* (New York: Macmillan Publishing Co., Inc., 1976) pp. 77–78.

[6] Twedt, op. cit., p. 88.

planning relative to time, of course we are talking about scheduling. Almost all business decisions have a time constraint on them, and any research done to aid in the decision must respect this constraint. The scheduling phase has other purposes. It aids in costing the project and in determining whether time and other resources are available. It is a planning document, which enables the researchers to marshal personnel and other needs at times when needed. It is necessary to coordinate personnel and work and in controlling execution to assume timely completion.

What is involved in scheduling marketing research projects may be appreciated with an example, which we have in Table 5–1. This schedules a survey with field personal interviewing. Its initiation evidently is at just about the point where we stand in this book, because the preliminary work through a general project design seems to have been completed. Beyond lie all the research tasks that we are going to be discussing in the remainder of the book. Creation of this schedule should have started with the final date when the decision makers want a presentation of the findings. Then all the considerable tasks should be listed in their proper sequence and realistic time assigned to each. This leads to a counting back from the due date, which is May 28 in Table 5–1. If it then turns out that the work cannot be initiated by January 22, the schedule would have to be condensed by speeding up some task or reducing the scope. This record can also serve as a means of control, since each task that is under way can be monitored with regard to when it starts and when it should finish.

The written time schedule well may be supplemented with a diagram or planning network that shows the interrelations of the various tasks. Such a well-known scheduling and controlling method is the *critical path method* (CPM). Related to this is the *program evaluation and review technique* (generally known by the acronym PERT), which we will describe shortly. To this end, a chart, or *network,* of a CPM for the consumer field study is presented in Figure 5–2.

The planning network, in our illustration, is formed of circles, or *nodes,* which represent the beginning and completion of activities, from the initiation of the project (number 1) to its termination (number 35). The various nodes are sequenced, left to right, in order of their planned chronological completion. The solid lines connecting them indicate the tasks to be done or, when dashed, information that must be transmitted before a job on another route can be completed. Required times would be specified for each activity. The route that would require the most time, on which the others must wait, is designated as the critical path. The *critical path* is that series of activities that would require the most time among those being carried on simultaneously. In the early weeks of our illustration in Figure 5–2, the questionnaire's development is expected to take the most time and is the critical path. The sampling work calls for fewer days and would have some slack time, while the interviewer selection and training has more slack and would not even start for a week after the other work is initiated. Toward the end, data processing is the critical phase.

TABLE 5–1. Survey Time Schedule

Tasks in Project	Number of Days Required	Days Left Until Completion	Dates Start	End
1. Initiate work	0	126	—	—
2. Design pretest sampling plan	5	121	Jan. 22	Jan. 27
3. Gather pretest sample data	4	117	Jan. 27	Feb. 1
4. Draft pretest questionnaire	10	116	Jan. 22	Feb. 1
5. Designate pretest sample	5	112	Feb. 1	Feb. 17
6. Select pretest interviewers	5	110	Feb. 2	Feb. 7
7. Final pretest questionnaire	8	108	Feb. 1	Feb. 9
8. Reproduce pretest question-naires and forms	6	102	Feb. 9	Feb. 15
9. Prepare pretest training manual	10	100	Feb. 7	Feb. 17
10. Train interviewers for pretest	2	98	Feb. 17	Feb. 19
11. Pretest field interviewing	7	91	Feb. 19	Feb. 26
12. Tabulate field returns	3	88	Feb. 26	Mar. 1
13. Evaluate interviewers' performance	3	86	Mar. 1	Mar. 4
14. Evaluate pretest sample	2	85	Mar. 1	Mar. 3
15. Evaluate pretest questionnaire	4	84	Mar. 1	Mar. 5
16. Final sampling design and data	6	80	Mar. 3	Mar. 9
17. Select interviewers	7	78	Mar. 4	Mar. 11
18. Designate sample locations	4	75	Mar. 10	Mar. 14
19. Draft final questionnaire	10	74	Mar. 5	Mar. 15
20. Reproduce questionnaires and forms	2	72	Mar. 15	Mar. 17
21. Prepare field training manual	10	68	Mar. 11	Mar. 21
22. Train interviewers	5	63	Mar. 21	Mar. 26
23. Field interviewing	21	42	Mar. 26	Apr. 16
24. Write and debug computer program	7	41	Apr. 10	Apr. 17
25. Edit questionnaires	7	35	Apr. 16	Apr. 23
26. Keypunch returned data	12	29	Apr. 18	Apr. 30
27. Validate interviews and sample	8	27	Apr. 23	May 1
28. Verify code punching	5	24	Apr. 30	May 4
29. Evaluate interviewers' performance	4	23	May 1	May 5
30. Run data on computer (Interspersed with analysis)	10	18	Apr. 30	May 10
31. Analyze computer printouts	11	11	May 6	May 17
32. Write report	5	5	May 17	May 22
33. Reproduce report	3	3	May 22	May 25
34. Distribute report	1	2	May 25	May 26
35. Presentation of findings	3	0	May 25	May 28

Source: *Adapted from Mathew Hauck, "Planning Field Operations," in Robert Ferber (ed.),* Handbook of Marketing Research *(New York: McGraw-Hill Book Company, 1974), pp. 2–148.*

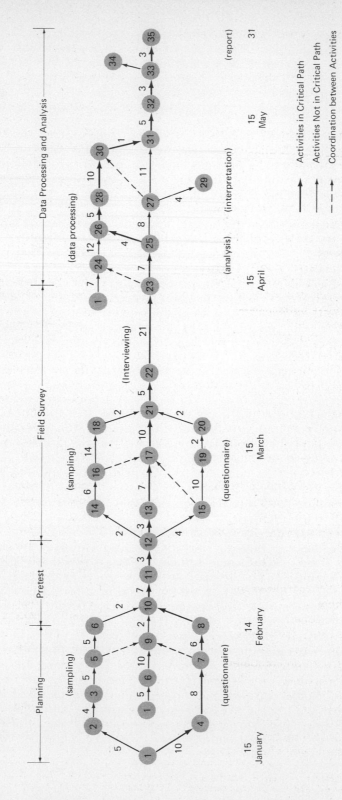

FIGURE 5–2. Planning Network for a Consumer Field Study

The numbers in circles indicate completion of each task, numbered as they are in Table 5–1, with the same time schedule. Between tasks are shown the number of days planned for executing the task.

The critical path method has numerous benefits, including (1) a charted coordination of interrelated jobs, (2) a basis of scheduling the expected occurrence of each task and of judging the likelihood of meeting deadlines, (3) the anticipation of bottlenecks and the focusing of attention on the work most likely to cause delays, and (4) the placing of responsibility among groups or departments for meeting time commitments.

The time involved in each research task is often impossible to predict with any precision. It may be wise to augment the CPM with a PERT, because a combination of these methods tends to provide more precise planning and evaluation than the CPM alone offers. The essence of PERT is making three time estimates for each activity: (1) the most likely time estimate, (2) an "optimistic" estimate of the quickest time that can be expected, and (3) a "pessimistic" estimate. There is a formula for calculating an average of these three periods and a related one for calculating the degree of uncertainty of the estimations, thus translating them into an analysis of risk situations.

Also, there should be a "resource summary" that specifies the total resources (personnel, funds, facilities) needed for each of the activities shown on the CPM chart. This enables determination of whether there are ample resources or perhaps shortages. If there is a shortage for some activity, particularly if it is on the critical path, resources might be transferred from another concurrent activity or, lacking this, one or more of the activities at that phase may have to be provided with longer time.

The determination of cost can be a very laborious matter. However, the existence of a critical path analysis can be very useful. As the CPM divides the task into activities and the resource summary should detail the number of man days required as well as the facilities needed, the costing of personnel and facilities is relatively easy. Costs to be incurred for activities such as computer usage, field work, and publication are costed on the basis of standards usually established within the company. By developing costs directly from the CPM, the researcher can achieve both cost and time control.

Another tool for planning and control in marketing research, as in all organizations, is a budget. Since budgeting techniques are well known and explained in other courses, their discussion would not be worthwhile here. Keeping control of costs, to ensure meeting budgets while also completing the planned work, is an important companion activity, although often ignored. Well-operated marketing research firms do maintain close watch on costs, especially the time spent by individuals on various projects or idle, because personnel costs are the bulk of their expenditures. Assigning costs to projects may be tedious as well as difficult, particularly the time of professional-level researchers in corporations' departments whose time is divided among many purposes.

There should be other and more detailed schedules and controls on individual major tasks. We are going to encounter a number of them in dealing with sampling, data-gathering procedures, data processing, and other phases. How valuable such records may be might be recognized in such incidents as the research manager of Company B conferring with its marketing manager about a value analysis of doing a market test in Canada. Reliable bases of estimating time and costs of alternative research designs require possession of control records, which we have discussed.

5.6 Pretesting

A so-called "law" has been bandied about lately, to the effect that "If anything can go wrong, it probably will!" More than a few people who direct marketing studies would attest that as being substantially true. That need not often be the case, however, with good management. If all the steps covered so far in this book were executed properly, many or most pitfalls would be avoided. Something more is needed, though, than the preliminary work and planning that has been prescribed, because so often something must be attempted in a study that is novel and untried (at least within the particular researcher's experience). Indeed, all original studies have something new about them, by definition.

There is only one way to be fairly sure about something novel: try it out. And so we recommend pretesting a study's methods. Pretests are particularly used for methods of gathering data. Questionnaires, interviewer instructions, and interviewers' capabilities always should be pretested, because so much can go wrong in this phase. How respondents would interpret and respond to questions is a treacherous aspect. This should be determined in pretest personal interviews, although later mail or telephone would be used, since the test should be made face to face. Pretesting also may determine whether a sampling method is feasible and foreshadow the quality of sample obtainable.

An aspect often ignored, for pretesting, is the analysis and interpretation of data. Although the research will have no actual data until near the end of the study (unless the pretest gathers sufficient data for a trial analysis), one can set up dummy tables and hypothesize data on which analytical techniques may be performed. This preview of what can be done with the anticipated data may often show that plans should be altered, in that other data, classifications, and so on, would be needed to satisfy the decision needs.

5.7 Summary

This chapter concludes a series of advanced decisions that comprise the overall planning and preliminary work underlying the conduct of a marketing research project. It followed two chapters concerned with defining problems and decisions, specifying data needs, and determining the research design to apply.

That led to the research plan itself, whose content was first described in Chapter 5. Then the major alternatives that might be adopted were

*I got to
do something
about my
reputation.*

identified, for three dimensions of original research: types of data, sources, and communication methods. These would be major considerations in developing a study's plan.

In good organizations, any proposal to conduct research must be well documented and submitted for approval. A research proposal is therefore needed. It is most needed by outside research agencies as they seek approval of potential clients for projects they might conduct, but the proposal has a number of benefits in any sort of organization. Ability to describe proposed research concisely, in such a plan, also is excellent experience for college students.

Whether the study should proceed—at least as proposed—remains as a key question. We discussed some of the risk elements and factors to consider in a value analysis of information that research might contribute. An example was carried through, for a hypothetical toy manufacturer, using probabilistic or Bayesian analysis. Despite the inherent unreliability of so subjective an approach, its benefits to better decision making were stated. And finally, if the proposal was approved, there would be much effort needed in scheduling its various activities. The schedule promotes the ability to control the work, but another step needed to enhance a project is pretesting. Its discussion closed this chapter and Part II.

CASE 3

POPULAR FINANCE CORPORATION[7]

won co.

You met with officers of Popular Finance Corporation at a quarterly operations review meeting in Chicago. The company made loans of $50 to $500 on signature only, or with automobile or household goods as collateral. It had offices across the nation.

Participating in the meeting were the following:

President: A. J. Almond

Vice-President Sales: M. A. Howe

Vice-President Operations: L. T. Boyd

Regional Managers:

East: F. A. Andersen

West: C. M. Gray

South: W. Brown

North: C. C. Green

You were attending the meeting as a representative of the advertising agency that handled Popular Finance's advertising and also conducted its marketing research.

The first part of the meeting was conducted by Mr. Boyd, who analyzed

---

[7] Names in this case are fictitious.

the operating results of the four regions and of several individual loan offices. Mr. Almond then turned the meeting over to Mr. Howe.

HOWE:

sponsorship of prof football.

I'd like to start off by telling about the fine results we're getting from our sponsorship of professional sports broadcasts. Here for the New York Area is a chart showing in blue the loan volume of our New York City offices, month by month, starting with December, 1973, and continuing through last month. Notice, of course, that there is a great fluctuation from month to month. Now here in black, we have charted the total outstanding loan volume of all small-loan companies, as reported by the Finance Clearing Association.

Now notice that back in 1974 and 1976 our loan volume curve fluctuated much more widely than did the industry curve; also, it was quite a bit lower. Look now at these dotted lines going through the two curves. They represent a thirteen-month moving average. You can see clearly that our thirteen-month moving average took a definite upturn starting in the autumn of 1977 when we first put most of our advertising budget into the sports broadcast sponsorship. The industry line went up slightly, and as you can see, we have been gaining a greater share of the market, until we are now about 10 percent.

Bringing these curves up to date, you will recall that from January through March, for good and sufficient reasons, we eliminated all advertising in this market. See that loan volume fell drastically while the outstanding volume for the other companies held up, but after we reapplied advertising in April, our volume went up slowly and then in June went up pretty fast while the industry was tapering off. In September, our outstanding loan curve crossed that of the industry, indicating that we have finally exceeded a 10 percent share.

Prob? judgment w/out study

I think this very well confirms our judgment that most small-loan borrowers are sports fans and that sponsorship of sports broadcasts is without question the most effective advertising for us to use.

ALMOND:

What about the results of the television sponsorship of football broadcasts you've started in the Houston area?

HOWE:

Well, in Houston we have a real promotion going on now. Professional football in that Astrodome down there is very popular, and their Astros draw big crowds. A major local TV station in Houston puts on its "game of the day" announced by Buck Borin, the former great All-American. They broadcast all the Astros' away games and select other highlight games every Sunday that the Astros play in Houston. They also broadcast the league's national championships and Superbowl games. We sponsor the first half of each of these games in the Houston area. We have a very good promotional stunt running at the same time, a contest in which there are prizes every week during the entire football season. First prize is a twenty-six-inch-screen Zenith color television set; the second prize, a Mixmaster or Remington electric shaver; the third prize, a wristwatch; and the next twenty-five prizes are free tickets for the entire family to attend any theater.

ALMOND: Say, that looks good.

BROWN: It is good, A. J., and there's sure a lot of interest in this contest.

HOWE: The big downtown and drive-in theaters are cooperating completely. They distribute an entry blank to every person entering the theater throughout the football season. Each entry must be mailed to Popular Finance in care of the Houston television station so we are sure that our name and sponsorship in the contest gets notice.

ANDERSEN: Why not have people mail it directly to their nearest Popular Finance office?

GREEN: Better yet, why not have them personally bring the application blank into our offices?

HOWE: But that might cut down on the entries. And we have to have an impartial set of judges for the contest, which the TV people furnish without charge. Besides distributing entry blanks in theaters, we also distribute them in our offices; everyone who comes in can get an entry blank at the counter.

BROWN: Did you tell them about the television spots?

HOWE: Oh, this TV station does a lot of spot promotional work to build up viewing for the station, and it builds these spots around its biggest programs. Usually they put on six spots a day, but for the next three weeks they'll put on twelve spots per day, and every spot will mention our broadcast and contest.

ALMOND: But, will they mention our name?

HOWE: Absolutely, they refer to this as Popular Finance's contest. Now look, here is a display poster advertising the contest, showing a picture of Buck Borin and featuring the prizes. We've distributed over 250 of these in Houston—downtown and in shopping centers.

BOYD: Do you advertise the contest on your game commercials?

HOWE: Yes, and in addition, like I just said, we're now getting twelve spots per day, further calling attention to our contest and mentioning our name. Best of all, we get these twelve spots free and also the prizes are donated free, because it's good advertising for those manufacturers to have their product mentioned.

BOYD: Gentlemen, you may be fooling yourselves. Brown, what is your increase in new accounts for last month versus the previous year?

BROWN: Well, new loans were down almost 10 percent.

BOYD: What about renewals and loans to former customers?

BROWN: Renewals are down 5 percent and loans to former customers are off slightly. Here's the reason for that: You see—

BOYD: Now isn't this just wonderful. Here we spend our effort and money on bringing to the people of Houston the cultural benefits of Buck Borin, and what happens to our volume of outstanding loans? It goes down. We put on a fancy-pants contest and spend our advertising money advertising Remington Razors and Zenith TV sets. What good does that do us? By all the standards we set in our business for measuring the efficiency of a loan office, the offices in the Houston area go down. You get so enthusiastic about your gimmicks and posters and your spot announcements that you completely forget what you are in business for. And instead of getting more business from this folderol, we're actually losing money out of the operation. How much does this program cost anyway?

HOWE: $30,000 for our share of the football broadcast, but remember that we're getting a great deal of publicity along with it.

BOYD: $30,000! Now isn't that wonderful! And are you really enjoying yourselves with all this nonsense while the home offices twiddles thumbs for some good results down there?

BROWN: You've got to remember—

BOYD: How could anybody in his right mind devote perfectly good commercial time on a high-priced football broadcast to a contest like this instead of trying to sell the service that we're in business to sell?

BROWN: We don't advertise the contest.

BOYD: You don't advertise the contest? You've been telling me that you do.

HOWE: The free spots by the station advertise the contest, but we use the regular videotapes from our agency for the commercials during the game.

BOYD: Well even at that, what are you getting out of the whole thing? Has this improved your office traffic?

BROWN: We don't know, but—

BOYD: How many people have entered the contest? Did those who entered take out loans with us?

BROWN: We had the application blanks out on front of the counter first, but then moved them to the back of the counter so the girl could personally hand one to each person and explain the rules. You see, in addition to the other prizes, if a present borrower happens to win, he gets one installment of his loan paid free in addition to his other prize. We also ask each person to have his friends put his name on applications so that if anybody wins and the name of a friend who is a borrower is on the application, that borrower will get an extra month's payment free.

BOYD: I haven't yet heard an answer to my question.

BROWN: Well, since the TV station handles all the application blanks, we don't know whether people who enter the contest take out loans. The contest entries average some 500 a week. I agree, L. T., that the results don't look good yet, but remember that the pro football season is just four weeks old and advertising would have a cumulative effect, building up gradually. We're sure this

2:45

thing will begin to percolate, since it takes more time for the advertising to work on the better income people. After all, 20,000 contest application blanks are being distributed each week.

BOYD: Nonsense! You know as well as I that this company's policy is to strive for direct-action advertising. This whole thing seems miserably handled—

BROWN: And another thing, even though our Houston business is down, maybe our competitor's is, too. Of course, we have no clearing house there like in New York.

ALMOND: It does look like you fellows forgot what business you're in. How about canceling this program; do we have a cancellation clause?

HOWE: But then we would be in a tight spot for advertising. At least on television we couldn't buy good time now for the rest of the autumn. And we've used this same Houston station in the past with what seemed very good success. So it must be reaching the right people, and look how successful sports broadcasts have been in New York.

ALMOND: Well, boys, this is very interesting, but what's the answer?

You said nothing during this conversation, but listened intently. You now break in to suggest that you make an analysis that you can present later in the meeting. You have about thirty minutes to collect your thoughts and prepare a lucid analysis of the Houston problem.

Discussion

1. What is the problem? *want to increase sales / debate @ advertising*
2. What steps should be taken in making the decision?
3. What types of research might be profitable?

CASE 4

AMERICAN MOTORS CORPORATION

It would be correct to state that American Motors Corporation (AMC) was the nation's fourth largest manufacturer of automobiles with sales revenue of over $650,000,000 in 1967. Any implication of these facts that AMC was then a healthy enterprise, though, would be very misleading. Rather, AMC had obtained less than 3 percent of automobile sales, its lowest unit volume in ten years, and sustained a crippling deficit of $76,000,000 in 1967. The company was being chronically overwhelmed by "The Big Three" of the industry (General Motors, Ford, and Chrysler).

A new top management team was brought in to save the company, which managed to halt the slide in sales volume in early 1968. They recognized that this alone could not solve AMC's plight, and they faced the grim task of establishing what would have to be accomplished for AMC to become a viable contender.

Objectives and Requirements

The management determined that there were only limited possibilities of squeezing out further economies in AMC's operations and that the fundamental requirement for survival would be expanding sales and thus cash flow. The target volume would be a 5 percent share of the total automobile market, which they forecasted as being 10 million units sold domestically. For AMC this would be a volume of 500,000 units, in contrast with the 238,000 units sold in 1967. Increasing sales by over 250,000 units against the powerful Big Three was a challenge indeed.

target market → Management also determined to target its efforts on the 25- to 34-year age group, for several reasons: (1) its predicted growth rate of 27 percent in the five years, (2) its high rate of car ownership, (3) a need to reposition AMC's consumer image as more youthful, and (4) the fact that younger buyers would be easier to conquer from other firms.

From 1968 into 1971, AMC attempted to attract a larger market share by introducing new products, models intended mainly to appeal to their young target-market segment. Two new models were introduced each year, one of them at midyear. Nearly all were below-standard-size cars, as these had grown to account for 55 percent of industry sales and were most favored by young owners. They included such sporty cars as the Javelin, the AMX, and the SC Rambler, as well as the Gremlin—AMC's first subcompact. These strenuous new product efforts raised sales by 30 percent from 1968 to 1971. This was very short of the sales gains needed to reach a 5 percent market share. Modest profits had been earned in 1968, 1969, and 1971, but a large loss in 1970 kept the company in a poor financial status.

Accomplishing any substantial increase in market share was going to be difficult, to put it mildly. Only five times in the past ten years had any of the motor corporations boosted percent of industry by as much as 5 percent over the previous year. This increase was accomplished by members of the Big Three by offering new cars. AMC had been unable to increase its modest market share by even this percentage. As 65 percent of the owners of below-standard-size cars were proving to be "loyal" to their present make (that is, repurchasing from the same company), AMC could hope to make conquests only among the disloyal minority. Apparently, it must find some dramatic and potent differential advantage outside the offering of new cars or features on them because that strategy had failed for four years.

Situation Analysis

This situation naturally had AMC executives in profound thought in 1971. Its gravity was brought home in recent surveys that Marketing Research had

143

made of owners of cars of all makes, which revealed that relative to AMC the majority of owners:

customer attitudes of AMC CARS:

1. Believed that AMC cars were poorly constructed compared with competitors'.
2. Believed that AMC cars yielded a lower resale value when traded.
3. Felt that AMC dealers' facilities and services were inadequate for their needs.
4. Had a low awareness of AMC makes.
5. Showed a general lack of purchase consideration, with less than 4 percent even shopping AMC dealers.

Now it was necessary to conceive of radical steps that AMC might take to recreate its image. To produce a set of alternative actions, brainstorming sessions were held in which AMC marketers came up with whatever ideas popped into their minds. These were culled down to a list of nine that merited a harder look. Products changes were ruled out, in view of the consumer attitudes given above.

Consumer Research

The timely next step was to conduct consumer research that would guide the decision on narrowing the alternative actions to those worthy of entering final consideration. Marketing Research carried out a qualitative form of consumer interviewing to probe what basically was bothering the consumer about U.S. automobiles. Small group sessions of automobile owners were held. The discussion director would open them by focusing on a provocative statement about cars, which led to the group members pitching into a warm discussion. From the taped conversations, three points emerged as the essence of consumers' attitudes:

what consumers wanted

1. Consumers mostly wanted a reliable and trouble-free automobile.
2. From the manufacturer they wanted tangible assurance and support of the owner's position (versus the dealer's), such as:
   a. An unconditional guarantee
   b. Better servicing
   c. Loaner cars
   d. A means of resolving disputes quickly
3. Underlying this was a basic mistrust of U.S. automobile makers.

With this basic information before them, AMC marketing specialists worked up a cohesive concept of a program that might well reach the company's marketing objective. The program would package these features:

1. A car with improved product quality.
2. A twelve-month, 12,000-miles unconditional guarantee.
3. Better predelivery service, to assure the car being delivered in good condition.

College of Notre Dame
Alma Mater

Sister Rosemarie Julie Gavin

Peter S. Michaelides

4. A loaner car for the customer to use in the event he had to leave his car at the dealer's for overnight service.

5. A direct line with which the consumer could communicate with the factory.

Then creative work was needed to express the program's concept in a manner that would be clear, believable, and attractive to consumers. Three concepts emerged that seemed almost equally effective, so that all should be tested for consumer reaction:

Concepts for consumers:

1. *The Buyer Protection Plan,* described in terms of "insurance" against money loss through car malfunction, inconvenience when overnight service was needed, and disputes over who pays for warranty service.
2. *The Guaranteed Car,* which would stress the degree to which AMC would stand behind the car and service it.
3. *American Motors Is On Your Side,* emphasizing AMC's determination to give better product and service than competitors.

These three concepts were to be presented to consumers in several thousand standardized formal interviews. Quantitatively, the sample size would yield statistical significance in the results. Most vital was designing the study to win management confidence and willingness to base a very risky decision on its findings. This meant that the obtained evidence must unequivocally measure the degree to which the program (with the selected concept) would reach AMC's desired payoff: its corporate objectives.

Discussion

1. What were the precise AMC objectives toward which the survey would be directed in its measurements?
2. What information objectives would be consistent with those decision objectives? That is, what data should be obtained to meet management's need? *marketing research*
3. What would be a suitable survey design? Justify it in terms of the situation and objectives.

CASE 5

COTTONWOOD STATION, INC. (A)

A half century ago there was a stop on the interurban railway running south from Edwardsville, Illinois, named Cottonwood Station. This name recently was revived by Dr. Merrill Ottwein for his real estate developments in the vicinity of the old interurban stop, and the name of the corporation he founded was Cottonwood Station, Incorporated.

In the late 1960s Dr. Ottwein had sold his flourishing veterinary practice and turned to other activities, of which the outstanding was land development. He had developed, on a tract of land about 2 miles south of Edwardsville, Lakewood subdivision. This was a charming subdivision designed for high-class homes, and all of its lots had been sold in 1971 despite their premium prices. At that time Dr. Ottwein and his colleagues were proceeding with an addition to Lakewood, including another small lake, and with different sorts of utilization of the large area of over 800 acres that had been brought together under Cottonwood Station, Inc. One venture was intended for economy-priced housing, for there was an obvious scarcity of new housing in that price bracket in the area. It would be located in rolling terrain at the far eastern end of the property, the opposite from Lakewood, and it was given the name Cottonwood Village.

Initial Development Stages *of Cottonwood Village*

Land planning for Cottonwood Village had begun some time earlier, and a small lake was being filled a short distance north of the site. This was an area on the west side of a circling road around the eastern acreage, at the entrance to which would be a reception center that also could serve to control privacy. As landscape planning was very important in the developer's personal value system, shrubs and trees were being grown in a nursery area for later transplanting to the Village. Underground utilities and other site requirements were planned or under way, but the major step would be selecting and procuring the housing units.

An exhaustive effort was made to determine the ideal available type of housing. The Cottonwood people estimated that truly economy housing should cost somewhat under $10,000 for a two-bedroom unit. On-site construction, even of precut houses, soon was found to be infeasible for such a figure. Modular units seemed desirable, but no manufacturer could be found in the Midwest who would be able to make and deliver units within the necessary time—and the costs were too high. All possibilities except mobile homes were eliminated, and the products of all leading and reputable manufacturers were given thorough comparison before one manufacturer in southern Michigan was determined to offer the quality, price level, and attractiveness needed.

Sites for the units and for other installations were mapped out and their preparation started. The circling road through the property was blacktopped, signs and lighting erected, and development was proceeding well when the first mobile homes were delivered in August, 1971. Soon four units, which had various options of size and luxury features, had been placed at the reception center and were ready for exhibit. Advertising was published in two area newspapers, radio commercials broadcast, literature ready and mailed, and Cottonwood Village was open for prospective customers.

Mobil homes → 4 options

Situation of the Problem

The first visitors during the opening on a Sunday near the end of September comprised a variety of age levels, economic levels, place of residence, and other aspects. It had been expected that young married people would be the most interested, but in the early showings the salesmen could discern no predominant type. Sales were quite slow and when the first one was closed, it was with an elderly retired couple. There was no indication of whether the advertising had been effective, and the fact that people were coming from towns where there had not been advertising added mystery.

Dr. Ottwein knew well from his own experience that a proper and strong marketing campaign was essential in attaining sales in real estate. At this point he recognized that he had insufficient marketing information for making vital decisions on the campaign to sell Cottonwood Village. Therefore, he turned to marketing professionals for counsel. They naturally had to become well apprised of the nature of Cottonwood Village and its situation, a background that we now will summarize. The Village was connected by a short paved road with a state highway running into Edwardsville, a county-seat city of around 12,000 population, and southward into Collinsville, which had a population of 18,000. At the southwestern limits of Edwardsville was the new campus of Southern Illinois University, whose enrollment was about 13,000. Only a handful of less than 2 percent of the students were housed on the campus, which had been intended mainly to be a commuting university, but a larger number lived in mobile home parks and other dwellings in the immediate area. Edwardsville was in the metropolitan area of St. Louis but not a suburban or bedroom community, as one would expect from its nearness, because most of the suburban sprawl had moved into Missouri rather than into Illinois.

Within that county (Madison) was a large industrial population of over 200,000, and there were many executive and professional employees of those industries who moved into the hilly land around Edwardsville and Collinsville, 7 to 20 miles from their work. The Village was less than 2 miles from Interstate 270, on which the northern metropolitan area of St. Louis and many industries could be reached in fifteen to thirty-five minutes. Also by Interstate highway downtown St. Louis could be driven to in twenty to twenty-five minutes. So there seemed to be a wide area from which Cottonwood might draw residents.

The units in Cottonwood Village were indeed mobile homes, but Dr. Ottwein had improved them after arrival in several ways. A conspicuous change was the application of Masonite-type panelling on their exteriors, giving them a wooden appearance and avoiding the garish whites and bright colors of normal mobile homes. When placed on their sites, the wheels were removed and the grading of dirt and the shrubbery concealed the usual open space at the bottom, which also avoided the mobile home look. An important departure from the usual dreary mobile homes court was placing the units at various angles in clusters. Thus, while the oblong boxiness of the unit could not be avoided, in other respects the Village appeared more like a community of houses than a congested mobile homes park. This was enhanced by pro-

appearance

147

wide range area to draw residents

viding parking areas for the automobiles, so there were no driveways running alongside the units.

The units were available in two-bedroom or three-bedroom models, with or without furniture, and with options of air conditioning, porches, and patios. Prices with furniture for two-bedroom homes ranged from $9,000 to $11,500 and those for three-bedroom homes from $9,700 to $12,200. The land, however, was leased from Cottonwood Station, Inc., which charged a space rental that included water, sewers, trash pickup, and care of lawn and landscaping. An example of average costs was the following:

features

Purchase price	$10,000
Percent down payment	20%
Amount of loan	$8,090
Years to repay	12
Monthly payment on loan	$86.90
Space rental	$65.00
Estimated insurance and taxes	$20.00
Total living costs	$171.90

For this price Dr. Ottwein believed that he was offering a very unusual combination of features perhaps unique for such low-cost home ownership and unmatched by any mobile home park in the Midwest. These features were cited:

The Environment

1. Mobile homes arranged in clusters of three to five, not in rows.
2. Natural wood exteriors (twenty-year guarantee) in subdued woodland colors (dark green, brown, tan).
3. Natural landscaping, trees left undisturbed, utilities underground, 25-acre private natural park. Patios and decks at each site.
4. Small lake for fishing and ice skating.
5. Mobile homes tied down with cables to concrete piers, not set on wheels on concrete pads. Wheels are stored for owners.
6. Paved roads and sidewalks.
7. Twenty to thirty minutes to downtown area of major city.

Mobile Modular Homes

8. Everything electric—no combustible fuels.
9. House-type furniture (rather than mobile home furniture). Basset and other name brands.
10. Forty-two-gallon water heater (many mobile homes have 30-gallon heaters).
11. Attached storm windows and extra insulation. (Ceilings and floors 6

inches, walls 3 inches; the Mobile Home Manufacturers' Association standard is 3 inches and 1½ inches, respectively).

12. One-quarter-inch natural wood paneling throughout interior.

13. Carpeting throughout interior (except bathroom).

14. House-type exterior doors with wood interior doors on all cabinets and closets.

15. Two-door refrigerator and freezer, 30-inch electric range and oven.

Services

16. Security provided (guard, entrance control, and lighting at control points).

17. Storage area and building away from living area.

18. Gardening area for residents' use.

19. Car wash facility on premises.

20. Lawn and yard care provided by management.

21. Adjacent shopping and laundry.

22. Restrictions on noxious or offensive use of facilities.

23. Buy-back provision. Owner has right to sell, but management agrees to buy back at agreed-upon depreciated value.

The unusual pattern in which the homes would be arranged and of the streets and parking area cannot be appreciated without viewing an actual map. Figure 1 is a map of approximately half of the original Cottonwood Village area. The tiny diagram at its bottom shows options that could be added to a unit.

The unusual character of Cottonwood Village added to his own limited experience in marketing real estate contributed to the complexity of Dr. Ottwein's decision outlook. A problem that we have not yet mentioned was that many of the features listed were still quite optional and could be omitted, if not justified. For instance, an ordinary-sized water heater could be offered or the car wash, laundry, or storage facilities could be excluded. A number of variables in the Cottonwood Village market mix needed decisions—in product, price, and promotion, and in the basic question of markets.

Discussion

1. What marketing questions facing Dr. Ottwein do you consider to be of some possible importance?

2. What do you consider to be the four most critical marketing decisions?

3. Assume that Cottonwood Station, Inc., would have less than $2,000 for any sort of marketing research, which would be insufficient to provide a factual basis for determining all their critical problems. For which two or three major decisions do you believe that research would have the greatest payoff? Why?

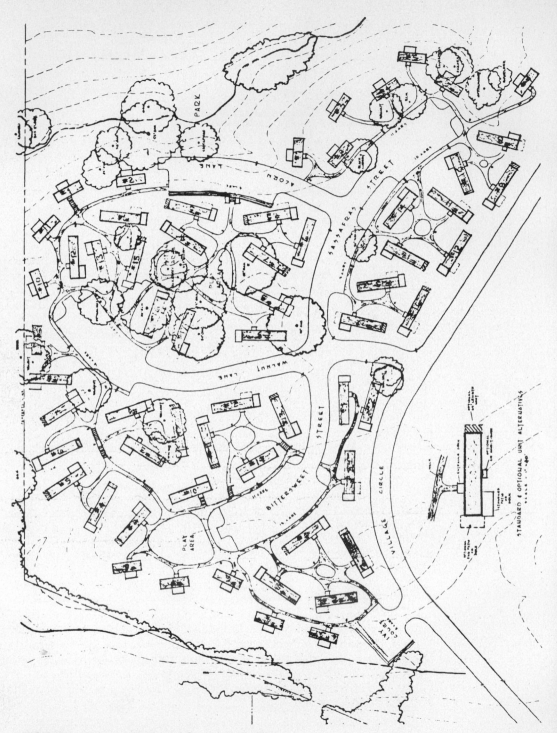

FIGURE 1. Map of a Portion of Cottonwood Village

Source: Courtesy of Cottonwood Station, Inc.

150

COCA-COLA USA (B)

The division of The Coca-Cola Company that produced and marketed the syrups for Coca-Cola, or "Coke,"[8] and other soft drinks in the United States was named Coca-Cola USA. In January, 1972, the manager of the division's Marketing Research Department, in Atlanta, was considering a request from the division's Fountain Division to launch an evaluation of the sales and profit potential of selling a new formulation of syrup in outlets of the BurgerRoyal chain.[9]

The Coca-Cola Fountain Division was engaged in marketing syrups for carbonated beverages, chiefly Coca-Cola, to operators of fountains and vending machines. Its sales representatives had encountered problems in attempting to sell syrups for the new and growing segment of the carbonated beverage industry, commonly referred to as Frozen Carbonated Beverages, through the BurgerRoyal outlets. For brevity we shall refer to these as FCB and as BR, respectively.

BR was a prospering firm in the fast-food-service industry whose outlets concentrated on hamburgers called "BurgerRoyals." A few other types of hot sandwiches, soft ice-cream, and French fries comprised the food items. Beverages included coffee, milk, iced tea in season, milk shakes, a noncarbonated orange drink, and carbonated soft drinks in three flavors (cola, lemon-lime, and root beer). Carbonated beverage sales at retail averaged around $60 per $1,000 of sales and were quite profitable. BR had been launched in Kansas City, still its headquarters, and spread west to the Rockies and mainly to the Southwest and Southeast—with an eventuality of becoming national. During 1972 BR would average around 620 units in operation, and units would average $7,000 per sales per month.

BR was possibly the first fast-service food chain to serve frozen carbonated beverages, although they were being adopted widely. BR had developed and patented its own machines to mix and serve FCB, which were considered to be superior equipment. BR also had researched syrups, for which there were special requirements in FCB machines, and had its own produced secretly by a private supplier.

The top management of BR allowed district managers some flexibility in choice of suppliers, and their Oklahoma City district (alone) chose to buy Coca-Cola syrup and sell cola drinks under that trademark. The Oklahoma City manager recently had informed the sales representative of the Fountain Division that higher executives were starting to pressure him to stop buying Coca-Cola syrup and begin using BR's own brand. He was reluctant, as that district had carried Coca-Cola from its beginning, but he also was concerned by the cost differential of $1.80 net per gallon of Coca-Cola syrup versus $1.55 for the BR private brand.

---

[8] Coca-Cola and Coke are registered trademarks of The Coca-Cola Company.
[9] The name "BurgerRoyal" and the data given in this case are fictitious.

151

The potentials of FCB syrup sales had been recognized by Coca-Cola USA, and its research laboratories had been striving to find an ideal formulation for FCB dispensers. That product had been discovered by the laboratories lately, but its marketing program was just under way. Careful testing indicated that it would produce carbonated drinks fully as palatable as any syrup then in use for FCB and would yield substantially *more cups per gallon* of syrup. The present syrups being sold by the Fountain Division yielded about 80 cups per gallon. The laboratory technicians estimated that the new FCB syrup would yield 15 to 20 percent more cups per gallon and most likely above the midpoint of that range.

The Fountain Division of the Coca-Cola Company representatives found that their new syrup was of real interest to the BR puchasing officials at Kansas City, but only for Coke. It appeared that once BR could be induced to adopt this new syrup for Coke, there would be excellent chances of also selling them root beer and lemon-lime syrups. If BR bought the new syrup, they would retail it as Coca-Cola. They said they would buy it only with proof that the syrup yield for Coca-Cola was so much higher than their own product that it would clearly offset the price difference.

The people at the Coca-Cola Company stressed to BR that the attractiveness of their brand, the world's largest seller, ought to increase carbonated beverage sales at BR outlets. The BR people countered that their Oklahoma City district was selling little more cola under that brand name than the rest of the units with BR's own supply. However, the Oklahoma City units had merely used the Coke name with no specific promotion of it. The Fountain Division hoped that cooperative point-of-sale merchandising would increase the success of Coke at BR outlets.

Discussions between the two companies had reached a stage where BR agreed to have a test conducted to demonstrate whether or not Coca-Cola would be more profitable than BR's own FCB syrup. Further, BR had asked that such a test be conducted in two of its comparable districts with one logically being continuation of Coke in the Oklahoma City area for the duration of the test. The Wichita area was a logical choice, too. Both districts could differentiate between BR units in the main city and those outlying in the district, which numbered as follows:

Oklahoma City—forty units; eighteen in Oklahoma City and others around Oklahoma.

Wichita—thirty units; fourteen in Wichita and balance around central and Western Kansas.

Both the average monthly total sales and the carbonated beverage sales per $1,000 sales volume in the units within those districts were about equivalent to the averages for the entire BR system. The average price per cup may be computed at 10 cents, the BR price for small servings, and about 60 percent of FCB sales were of cola flavor. Cost of syrup per cup roughly may be calculated as 2 cents.

The Coca-Cola USA marketing research manager had his analysts prepare careful cost estimates of a test encompassing all seventy of the units in the

Wichita and Oklahoma City districts. This could include testing of the new syrup over a six months' interval that would include both a base and a test period, as well as advertising in one city. Thus the comparative yield of Coca-Cola's syrup, the attraction of its brand name, and effects of advertising might be measured. Altogether such a test would cost around $15,000 inclusive of all overhead items and equipment.

In judging whether or not a project is economically justified, the marketing research manager used a standard that the project must be likely to yield profit to Coca-Cola USA equal to three times its expected costs. (The rate of profit on the syrup was estimated as 10 percent of sales.) This profit must be captured within one year after findings are implemented by management. In our particular case, there is an obvious first consideration: the test's results must so clearly favor adoption of Coca-Cola USA's syrups, in profitability, that BR would adopt them for the entire chain or enough of its outlets to give sufficient payout to Coca-Cola USA.

Discussion

1. On the basis of a payout analysis of anticipated results and of costs of the proposed project, should the marketing research manager authorize it? Support your answer with calculations.

2. What specific design would you use for the test? This would include specifying the areas to be used for testing and for control, what would be tested in them, and the periods of phases of the test.

3. What would be your forecast regarding how much more yield would be produced using the new Coca-Cola FCB syrup than using the BR syrup? (*Note:* Assume that BR syrup has the same yield as the old Coca-Cola syrup.) Calculate this with a Bayesian (subjective probability) approach, making up your own distribution of probabilities of how much the new syrup's yield would surpass the BR syrup. Use the categories shown in column (1), write your own probabilities in column (2), and compute the weighted probability in column (3).

(1) Alternative Yield Increases with New Syrup (%)	(2) Subjective Probabilities of Occurrence	(3) Weighted Probabilities: (1) × (2)
Less than 15		
16		
17		
18		
19		
20		
More than 20		
	1.00	

FORD MOTOR COMPANY

Several years ago, product planners in a division of the Ford Motor Company were deciding the dimensions of a new model then under planning, among other vital considerations. This question recurred annually, of course, but it seemed more serious than usual because they perceived that rival manufacturers that competed with this model were getting the cars' interiors too cramped. Those cars were popular, but it was possible that they were becoming too uncomfortable, so that a car that trended toward roomier dimensions might have an attractive differential. However, making such a move would involve a risky trade-off, for it would mean a squarer or less streamlined contour. The influence of exterior appearance on consumers' car-buying decisions was well established.

Marketing research personnel were requested to design and conduct a consumer study that would provide guidance in planning the car's internal dimensions. They created the research design that will be described, with some assistance from one of the outside agencies often used by the company.

Method

The problem was defined and the approach summarized in this statement written by the marketing researchers:

> This study provides those responsible for design with concrete expressions of the degree of consumer dissatisfaction with specific dimensions and elements of the interior package. The approach is to place the consumer in each of two cars so that her or his responses may be compared with the actual dimensions of the cars and the optimum design be indicated. Also, the intensity of criticism points up the areas of design most needful of improvement.

The general method involved placing two comparable cars of different makes side by side in a parking lot (either in a shopping center or in a downtown lot). Adults who happened by would be invited to take this test and first screened on whether they were from a car-owning household and possessed drivers' licenses. Then they would be directed to enter the left front door of the first car and adjust the front seat to a comfortable position. After moving to the right side of the front, the subject was asked to get out and then enter the rear right door (if a four-door model) or the rear seat (if a two-door). After getting out on the left side, the subject was then asked to observe the car from the front, side, and rear externally. A similar procedure was followed with the second car, as follows:

At each position within the car as well as the outside perspectives, the subject was asked questions about his or her opinion of the dimensions. A

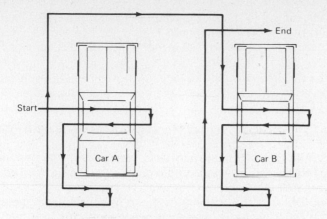

sample question was: What about the distance of the steering wheel: is it too close, about right, or too far from you? Questions like this were asked on each of thirty interior aspects as well as the three exterior viewpoints. All had three response categories, one at each extreme and the other in the middle. After the person had done this in both cars came the wrapup question: Suppose that you were going to buy a new car now that would be in the price class of these cars: which of these two would you buy? Interviewers were also to record any comments mentioned by the subjects, and these were sought in the probing at the interview's end.

Controls

The marketing researchers wanted to avoid bias, which they proposed to do by use of a number of control procedures:

1. The interviewers would be experienced personnel of the research agency and would not know who was sponsoring the study.
2. The cars would be perfectly matched pairs of the three makes (A, B, and C). They would be the same color, have the same equipment, and be in the same price class of Ford and the other two major automobile manufacturers. Both four-door and two-door models would be used, in this way:

Four-Door Sedans	Two-Door Hardtops
A versus B	A versus B
A versus C	A versus C
B versus C	B versus C

3. There would be six locations for this central place testing in a single metropolitan area, both suburban and downtown. The sample would be roughly balanced with the population in six sections of the metropolitan area.
4. Each pair of cars would be shown for two days at one location and

then moved to another location for two more days. Interviewing would run from Monday through Saturday for two weeks. Thus each pair of cars would rotate so that equal exposure was obtained in each location.

5. The two interviewers at a location would have the subjects alternate between which car was first entered (for example, A then B, B then A).

6. The interviewers also were rotated each two days among locations, in a reverse order from the cars so that one pair of interviewers would not be with the same pair of cars twice.

7. The pairing of interviewers was changed during the second week to create a fresh viewpoint in the pairs.

After the data from the one metropolitan area was processed, the Marketing Research Department could decide whether or not the test should be repeated in any other cities.

Discussion

1. Consider the type of design for the proposed research project. Would you say that it was a simulation, an experiment, or what? What aspects of the design are your reasons for classifying it as that type?

2. What conclusions apparently could be drawn validly from this study's data outputs? What do you believe the Ford Motor Company would have liked most to know about the effects of car dimensions? Would the described study have told them that reliably?

CASE 8

MILES LABORATORIES, INC. (B)

In the case of Miles Laboratories, Inc. (A), we followed a new product in its early stages of market plan development. The product was a chewable antacid tablet, which at that point had no name. Since that point the choice of a brand name had narrowed to two candidates: "Alka-2" and "Acid-aid." Hereafter we shall refer to it as Alka-2.

The first case traced the development process through two phases: (1) judging the placement of the concept in the competitive environment, and (2) screening the concept to improve it and to determine its consumer acceptability. The concept had received "go" decisions at the end of each of these phases. These three additional stages had been completed since then:

Phase 3: Feasibility. This included the preparation of a detailed product profile. On this basis, its feasibility was analyzed relative to medical, legal,

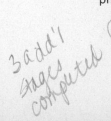
3 add'l
stages
completed

product development, and manufacturing aspects by the Miles departments responsible for those functions.

(4) *Phase 4: Strategy development.* The marketing strategy was devised,
creating an overall structure for the more detailed planning that would follow. Included in this were explicit definitions of the consumer segments
that should be attracted to the product and the health symptoms to which
the product would cater.

(5) *Phase 5: Advertising development and testing.* The desired positioning
of the product in consumers' minds was translated into alternative advertising renditions. These were successively tested with consumers to measure such effects as brand memorability, copy points recalled, believabil-
ity, and others, until the final advertisements culminated with the highest
test scores. Data on these final consumer responses were then fed into the
same mathematical market model as used before (SPRINTER) as a basis
for another go/no go decision. Again the product passed the decision.

decisions reached

Principal decisions had been reached as to (1) the competitive position of
Alka-2, (2) its consumer positioning, and (3) translation of that positioning
into advertisements that would communicate it to prospective buyers. However, there was no proof yet that these aspects of the marketing plan would
succeed, and other critical questions had not yet been researched. Now the
New Product Manager's development process called for some research that
would: (1) be *predictive* of the sales results that the product would be likely
to obtain and also (2) be *diagnostic,* to indicate which aspects in the marketing mix would enhance and which would hinder Alka-2's sales performance.

It would be premature to introduce Alka-2 on either a national or a regional basis on the basis of such flimsy evidence, encouraging though it was.
An investment of around $25,000,000 would be risked in placing it on the na-
tional market and a substantial fraction of that in a regional trial of its ability
to sell profitably. There were, however, three optional forms of smaller-scale
trials with the public that might serve for both prediction and diagnosis.
These now are described.

3 optional forms of smaller scale trials:
① simulation mrkt
② controlled market
③ traditional market test

(1) *Simulation.* In this approach the new product would not actually be
placed on sale in stores and be advertised through the media. Rather, those
situations would be simulated with consumers in a laboratory arrangement.
Two suppliers of marketing research were offering this method to Miles,
which had confidence in both. We will describe the COMP service offered by
one of these, the firm of Elrick & Lavidge, Inc.

COMP, an acronym for "comprehensive sales predictions and evaluation
system," was proposed to furnish Miles these results:

COMP. to furnish these results

1. Predict the market shares that Alka-2 probably would obtain.
2. Analyze competitive strengths and weaknesses versus Alka-2's.
3. Assess sales effects on Alka-Seltzer's share of market.
4. Test the appeal of the two names under consideration: Acid-aid and
   Alka-2.

The COMP research used a central testing facility in one of the largest
shopping centers near Chicago. It had three main stages:

[handwritten: 3 main stages of comp.]

1. Invite shoppers to participate in a product test and screen them regarding their qualifications. This phase determined whether they used antacids, their usage patterns, their awareness of the existing brands, and their brand attitudes.

2. The qualified women and men then were given a quantity of trading stamps and cash to reward their participation. Next they were exposed to a series of TV commercials for the leading brands and the test product. Each subject then was led into a simulated store, whose shelves displayed the test and competitive products at their normal prices. If these persons wished to buy some, they might. If they did not buy the test product, they were given a wrapped gift that later they would find was the test product. If they did buy it, they were given a different kind of product.

3. After enough days had elapsed to use the test product, the subjects were contacted by mail to learn their usage and to again measure their attitudes toward the various brands.

[handwritten: 2nd optional form of smaller scale trial]

②*Controlled market test.* This would comprise an actual sales experiment, held in one or more cities under the direction of a marketing research firm that had selected the particular cities for testing new products and marketing campaigns. Several research agencies were available for such a test, including A.S.I. and Market Facts, Inc. Here are some features of the latter firm's service that it calls "Marketest," a controlled distribution and product sales auditing service:[10]

[handwritten: features of Market Facts Research agency]

Offers complete distribution services with its own trucks, warehouse facilities and staff of audit specialists.

Operates in supermarkets, drugstores, mass merchandisers and home improvement centers in seven representative medium-sized Metropolitan areas.

Warehouses the test product, distributes it to the stores, stocks and prices it, services the shelves and displays, bills the stores, audits the brands in the product class and accurately forecasts national sales for the new brand.

As these agencies had contractual cooperation with major chains in the cities where they held their controlled tests, they could obtain almost instant distribution of a new product. They also had benchmark data on past performance of products earlier tested, as well as an abundance of demographic data, for each of the test cities. These would enable national projections from the sales obtained in a test city. The client manufacturer would prepare and conduct its own advertising and sales promotion in the test cities. It would not have any personal selling efforts. There were consumer panels in the test cities that might be utilized for mail surveys to track the purchases and repurchases of the test products as well as consumer satisfactions. Or similar data could be obtained by telephone interviewing services in the test cities.

---

[10] Quoted from *Improving The Cost, Speed and Accuracy of Test Marketing* (Chicago: Market Facts, Inc., undated).

3rd optional form of smaller scale Trial

③ *Traditional market test.* These were complete experiments with new products' sales in test areas, the method universally used before the advent of controlled market tests and simulations. Like the controlled form, it involved audits of actual sales in the selected markets with the conduct of a normal advertising campaign. Unlike controlled tests, the manufacturer's sales organization carried out sales efforts, obtained distribution, and performed point-of-sale promotional work. The extent of distribution and speed of attaining it therefore would vary with the salesforce's success.

Thus the traditional market test method was a complete replica of an introductory campaign for the new product. Marketing research agencies would be available to audit the rates of sales and extent of distribution at retail. Also, mail panels and telephone interviewing services could be retained to monitor consumer buying and attitudes toward the test product and competitors.

The New Products Manager at Miles had to choose among these three methods of marketing research to obtain data for another go/no go decision for Alka-2. The factors in this decision could be placed in three groups: time, cost, and degree of risk reduction in terms of the questions each would answer and its reliability.

Time. The three alternative methods compared as follows:

Simulation: three months from authorization to report of the findings.

Controlled Market test: seven to eight months. This assumes actual retail selling in two test markets for a period of six months, which was the minimum time required to stabilize sales volume as basis for a sales-level prediction. As this would be the period from the research agency's receiving the test product for distribution, shipping time might be additional.

Traditional market test: ten to eleven months, also providing for a minimum sales period of six months. At least this long would be needed because of the sell-in period and mobilization of the salesforce.

Cost. Estimates are given below, for the same periods as mentioned above. For the first two methods are cited quotations from the marketing research agencies.

Simulation: $30,000 for a sample of approximately 600 consumers.

Controlled market test: $700,000 for two medium-sized cities.

Traditional market test: $1,200,000 for the wholesale trading areas of two medium-sized cities.

Information provided.

Simulation: consumer preferences for and images of the attributes of the test product and its competitors. Market-share projections for the new brand, when the client furnishes estimates of the public's brand awareness and of the percentage of outlets that would carry it. A unique feature of this method would be comparison of effects of the alternative brand names (Alka-2 and Acid-aid) by exposing each to half the sample.

Controlled market test: actual retail sales in *two* cities with normal means of exposing consumers to advertising and to sales promotion inducements to try the new product. Guaranteed distribution to all major outlets. Very extensive familiarity with these cities, by the agency, and experience in them to serve as benchmarks. Facilities ready to track repurchase and consumer acceptance and attitude change.

Traditional market test: beyond the foregoing, this test shows the effectiveness of the salesforce and problems that it would encounter in a normal product introduction. Interest and support of wholesalers and retailers would also be tested. Miles would, however, have relatively few benchmark data on the selected city (or cities) on which to base projections.

Discussion

1. What do you observe to be the chief advantages and drawbacks to each of these three methods?
2. If you were the New Product Manager and had been given the information above by Marketing Research, which of the three methods would you want to choose for the *next* step in developing this product? Why?
3. What would you say that you would find most valuable in the information the method would offer? For what possible faults in the method would you be alert?

CASE 9

BUSINESS TEMPO PUBLICATIONS[11]

Charlie Granger pondered the situation. Charlie, a recent MBA, had been hired a week earlier as Research Associate for the Genuine Research Company with primary responsibilities in the area of research proposal preparation. After a week's orientation he had been called upon by his boss, Dr. Charles Evanston, to develop a research proposal for *Business Tempo,* a state-oriented monthly business publication. In formalizing his request, Dr. Evanston had prepared the following memorandum:

---

[11]This case was prepared by Assistant Professor Donald A. Fuller of Florida Technological University as a basis for classroom discussion and not to illustrate either effective or ineffective handling of an administration situation. Presented at a Case Workshop and distributed by the Intercollegiate Case Clearinghouse, Soldiers Field, Boston, Mass. 02163. All rights reserved to the contributor.

MEMORANDUM

TO: Charles C. Granger
         Research Associate

FROM: Dr. Charles Evanston
         Vice-President

DATE: July 14, 19xx

SUBJECT: Business Tempo Research Proposal

Charlie,
   As you know, I have been actively prospecting the <u>Business Tempo</u> account. Since you have not been involved so far in the conversations, I am including this brief scenario to aid you in the development of an in-depth proposal to conduct a subscriber study for <u>Business Tempo</u>. As usual, I must be out of town all of next week to complete the Hastings condominium study in Atlanta, so you'll have to play this thing by ear based on what I've included in this memo. I have promised <u>Business Tempo's</u> General Manager a proposal by Wednesday the 23rd. Since I'll need two days to review the proposal and suggest revisions, I'll need your draft by Monday the 21st. That gives you exactly a week to get the proposal together. Of course, Charlie, this account is an important one for the company and the usual bonus of 10 percent off the top is yours if we land the job.
   Our principal contact at Tempo Publications is Ed North, who is General Manager. Ed is extremely concerned about Tempo's continuing downward trend in paid subscriptions. Since 1969, the history of average twelve-month paid subscriptions has been as follows (ABC Audit Report):

                December 31, 1969   38,400
                             1970   39,100
                             1971   39,200
                             1972   38,700
                             1973   38,100
                             1974   37,700
                             1975   37,100
                             1976   36,500

Ed's concern is also shared by the Publisher, Mr. James Morgan, and the Editor, Mr. Bill Barron.
   Presently, <u>Business Tempo</u> publishes a wide variety of business and economic news focusing primarily on the state rather than the national situation. The publication features high-quality graphics and reproduction and prides itself on being "the"

161

source of business and economic information in the state. In
addition to the regular publication schedule, Business Tempo
publishes an expanded annual market edition which contains in-
depth reporting on the various market regions in the state. These
expanded editions are keyed around an executive mail-away
program designed to stimulate interest in the state for
development and investment purposes.

In discussions with both the Editor and Publisher it is clear
that they feel they have no direct competition within the state.
They define their editorial objective as ". . . putting together
a package of information that will attract, as readers, the
maximum number of members of the state's business community." In
reaching this objective, they feel that the inclusion of timely
marketing information and information on business trends within
the state is critical. In short, they want Business Tempo to
become a source magazine that is regularly talked about within
the state's business circles. Out-of-state subscriptions
represent a secondary market for the publication.

Last year, a local ad agency completed a demographic study of
subscribers (see Attachment 1). The overall purpose of this study
was to provide more information to potential advertisers
concerning markets reached. This was the first research effort
ever conducted by Business Tempo, and results of the last
question (rating of editorial content) raised the issue of
conducting further research concerning editorial content and
format as a means of developing direction for the publication.

In my conversations to date, I have stressed their lack of hard
information concerning what current subscribers think of
Business Tempo in terms of content and format. Obviously, the
demo study was not designed with this in mind. What they need now
is essentially a product assessment. What they don't know is who
reads what, who likes what sections or departments, overall
impressions and image, what subscribers think of the quality of
information presented, as well as reaction to possible changes in
coverage (addition of sports, politics, cultural areas, etc.). I
think a realistic product assessment along these lines can give
them some insight into the subscription problem.

At yesterday's meeting with Ed, Mr. Morgan, and Mr. Barron, we
reached an agreement that Genuine Research would develop a
research proposal for a subscriber study that focuses on the
following areas:

1. Readership of the various sections and departments of
   Business Tempo.[12]
2. Subscriber interest in the various sections and departments
   of Business Tempo.

---

[12] This business monthly, like many others, has regular sections and departments, as
well as "special stories," in each issue.

Sex:	
Male	95.0
Female	5.0
Age:	
Under 25 years	2.0
25–34	18.7
35–44	23.1
45–54	29.9
55–64	10.9
65 or older	15.4
Education:	
Less than high school	5.0
High school only	10.1
Some college	23.1
4-year degree	38.7
Master's	14.2
Professional (Ph.D., M.D.)	8.9
Marital status:	
Married	78.5
Single	21.5
Annual personal income:	
Under $10,000	1.1
$10–$19,999	17.0
$20–$20,999	25.1
$30–$39,999	21.2
$40–$49,999	10.1
$50,000 and above	25.5
Residence status:	
Northern area of state	41.9
Southern area of state	42.8
Out of state	15.3
Occupational area:	
Professional	15.4
Banking/financial	17.8
Construction	12.5
Distribution	10.7
Sales	19.1
Real estate	10.7
Other	13.8
Value of principal residence:	
Under $30,000	10.9
$30–$49,999	25.8
$50–$69,999	19.9
$70,000 and above	43.4
Rating of *Business Tempo* as a business information source:	
Excellent	12.0
Good	51.6
Fair	26.6
Poor	9.8

3. Development of some type of image of <u>Business Tempo</u>.
4. Determination of what subscribers think of the quality of information presented in <u>Business Tempo</u> (accuracy, etc).
5. Determination of any overt weaknesses in the publication.
6. Assessment of subscriber reaction to expanded editorial coverage away from traditional business areas into cultural areas, politics, etc.

Also, Mr. Morgan mentioned that a ballpark budget would be in the $5,000 to $10,000 range.

Please refer to my memoranda of December 28, 19xx, and February 1, 19xx, concerning proposal format and costing procedures (see Attachments 2 and 3). It is critical that I have your draft no later than 8:00 a.m., on the 21st.

Good luck !

ATTACHMENT 2. Memorandum

TO: All Research Associates

FROM: Dr. Charles Evanston
           Vice–President Field Research

DATE: December 28, 19XX

SUBJECT: Outline for Survey Research Proposals

In order to achieve a consistency of presentation to all potential clients, it is the policy of the firm to include the following topics in all survey research proposals:

   I. Research objectives
  II. Methodology
 III. Questionnaire design (including Exhibit I, Draft Questionnaire)
  IV. Analysis of results (specific data tables to be presented)
   V. Format of final report (including details of graphic presentation)
  VI. Time schedule
 VII. Cost estimates (to include options for at least two alternative sample sizes)

Within each of these areas your personal creativity is encouraged. All proposals must be presented to me for personal approval prior to final typing and presentation to the client.

ATTACHMENT 3. Memorandum

TO: All Research Associates

FROM: Dr. Charles Evanston
          Vice-President Field Research

DATE: February 1, 19XX

SUBJECT: Standard Costing Rates and Procedures

The following cost rates or procedures must be used when developing cost estimates for our clients. Any departure from these
guidelines must receive written prior approval from this office.

Cost Area	Rates or Procedures
Labor	
Professional staff	$35.00 per hour
Clerical personnel	6.25 per hour
Field workers (all on subcontract basis)	6.25 per hour
Printing	Consult local printer individually on each job.
Postage	Assume first-class rates on outbound questionnaire packages. Use prepaid post office box rate for returns.
Transportation	Tourist air fare if over 350 miles or 15 cents per mile by auto.
Computer costs	Consult local computer-service firms for an estimate on a case-by-case basis.
Copying costs	Assume $0.05 per copy on in-house equipment. Any extensive graphics will be subcontracted and billed to client at our cost plus 10 percent.
Office supplies	Estimate at 1 percent of total labor cost.
Selling expenses	Markup 10 percent using total project cost as base.

All telephone and personal interview work should be costed at this rate based on
your estimate of the probable number of completed interviews per hour.

PART **three** **Specifying and Gathering Data**

THE MOST LABORIOUS and time-consuming stages in a research study typically are those of gathering the data. That would not be true, however, when the needed information already has been gathered by others and has been published or is immediately available from the source that acquired them. If such secondary, or available, data would satisfy a study's needs to any degree, the advantage is obvious. Therefore, we shall take up the matter of secondary data at the outset of Part III.

The problems studied in applied marketing research tend to be unique either in kind or in essentiality of being current. These characteristics of a study entail the gathering of fresh data. A data-collection project involves three main phases: determining what to sample and how to administer the sampling; designing forms or instruments for eliciting or recording data (most often questionnaires); and the collection activities in the field. These are interrelated but will be taken up in that order. Two chapters will be devoted to sampling, not because it is more vital than the other two phases, but owing to its complexity.

Alternative methods are described at each step of data gathering. Like an adept research director, you should acquaint yourself with the virtues of each and consider the circumstances in which each would be a superior choice.

6 Utilizing Secondary Data

Chapter 6 deals primarily with the fourth step in our planning sequence from Table 4-1, "search and examine relevant secondary data." Before incurring the costly collection of primary data, every effort should be made to capitalize on others' collection of primary data. This chapter addresses such questions as:

What is meant by secondary data? Why must we review whatever secondary data are available?

Where do I start to look for secondary data?

How do I go about a systematic search for relevant secondary data?

How can secondary data be evaluated for accuracy?

As INDICATED IN CHAPTER 4, sound marketing research depends upon the existence of facts or data directly related to the problem studied. The kinds of facts or data used in marketing research are many and varied. One useful classification divides marketing data into: (1) primary data, and (2) secondary data. *Primary data* may be described as those data that have been observed and recorded by the researchers for the first time, to their knowledge. *Secondary data* may be described as those data that have been compiled by some agency other than the user.

Unfortunately, it is not always easy to differentiate secondary data from primary data. If a company subscribing to one of the syndicated data services requests special information that is not ordinarily tabulated but is available in the data collected by the services, is the company seeking secondary or primary data? In all probability, the data would be classed as secondary because the effort required to compile them and the cost involved would in no way approach the cost and effort of data sought from the original source. Fortunately, there are few cases of this sort. Historical usage warrants calling secondary data that material that can be obtained in usable form with relative ease and minor cost from a source other than the original one. Another point worth noting is that the word "secondary" refers to the source rather than to the accuracy or importance of the data.

If data are available that can be secured rapidly and at low cost, there is no sense in spending the time and effort to acquire primary data. Such considerations as availability of experienced personnel and access to the source of data materially affect the decision to collect primary data. Hence, it is self-evident that knowledge of secondary data is a great asset for the researcher. Besides knowing the chief sources, one should also know efficient methods of ferreting out information in libraries and elsewhere. These matters are covered in some detail in this chapter. The tasks in obtaining primary data are more complex and will require several chapters. The greater space devoted to the collection of primary data should not suggest that competence in gathering secondary data is less essential for the marketing researcher.

6.1 Uses of Secondary Data

Even when primary data are the principal basis of solution, doing research without using any secondary data is most unlikely. The majority of marketing decisions do not warrant the time or cost involved in collecting primary data. Even when it is necessary or desirable to obtain original information in a research project, secondary data are still useful in the total research effort. The following list presents some uses of secondary data.

1. A prerequisite to the conduct of marketing research is an adequate understanding of the problem situation. This understanding typi-

cally is based to a large extent on secondary data. Part of this would be supplied from internal sources through the marketing intelligence system, but special efforts to gather secondary data from other sources commonly are needed—on situation aspects both internal and external to the firm.

2. Further use of secondary data often is in the exploratory search for hypothetical solutions to the problem, suggested or inspired by others' publications and data.

3. In carrying out conclusive research to verify the expected effect of hypotheses under consideration, several uses may be made of secondary data. One is examining the methods employed in studies of a similar nature for guidance in a project design to gather primary data. It may be helpful, too, to employ the same classifications used in previous studies to obtain data extensively; there also may be important use of secondary data as correlates in the analysis stage.

4. Secondary data are essential in planning the sample from which primary information is to be obtained. They may be used to describe the target population that is to be sampled, as parameters and guides in the actual sample selection process, and as bases for validating the obtained sample. These uses of secondary data will become apparent in Chapters 7 and 8.

The many kinds of secondary marketing data may be grouped into two general kinds: (1) *internal data,* which are found within the organization for which the research is being done; and (2) *external data,* which are obtained from outside sources. These two types of secondary data and some of the chief sources for each are discussed further in Sections 6.2 and 6.3.

6.2 Internal Sources

A business organization that has a substantial marketing information system (MIS) would routinely gather and report most of the internal data useful in solving marketing problems. With anticipation of the types and categories of data needed repetitively, the company should make them available to the marketing research staff.

In fact, marketing research as a prime user of the system should influence the kinds of internal data the company collects on a continuous basis. The extent of information collected in the MIS will vary from company to company, but certain minimal data should be available on a regular basis.

The following list of internal data has been suggested:[1]

---

[1] Thomas C. Kelley, Jr., "The Marketing–Accounting Partnership in Business," *Journal of Marketing,* July, 1966, pp. 9–11.

Customer billing. Both correct and prompt customer billing is important from a customer-relations point of view and is vital in keeping marketing management informed as to the current status of sales.

Sales activity. Accurate and immediate reporting of sales activity is essential, including appropriate summaries by product line, geographic or sales area, and customer. Sales data can be in units or dollars or both. Ideally, meaningful comparisons to quota and previous forecasts for the period, as well as past history (where pertinent), should be incorporated into such reporting.

Information by selling activity. Reports as to profit or loss in terms of various selling activities should also include appropriate summaries by product line, by geographic or sales area, and by customer if feasible. Such reporting should make special provision for close scrutiny of sales discounts and selling expenses, while setting forth appropriate comparisons to budgeted figures and past performance, where pertinent.

Stock availability. The marketing manager who has available accurate product-inventory data by location is able to provide useful service to his customers, and at the same time he or she can keep company production managers informed as to pending requirements.

Product costs. In order to establish realistic prices on either new or existing products, the accounting costs must be known. The marketing manager must be able to work closely with the accounting department so that they can communicate to engineering personnel the limits within which changes in specifications may be made.

When the information listed is analyzed on a product, customer, and/or area base, one can examine changes between areas, products, and customers over time. Standards or norms may be established for evaluating different parts of the marketing program. For example, a declining sales volume for one product may appear to be caused by poor organization of the field selling force, but an analysis of commissions paid by products may indicate unbalanced selling effort, prompted by excessive commissions on some products and not enough on others. There are various and obvious ways that internal data may contribute to research studies.

Most of the basic data are under the jurisdiction of the accounting department, but coordination is needed between their recording procedures and needs of marketing administration—which often diverge from what seems most efficient in the accountants' views. For example, sales revenue records should reflect the managerial units—areas, customers, or product classes—used by the sales department. If the sales managers need to direct their organization according to a particular territorial configuration, then accounting records should be classified on a similar basis. Marketing cost analysis can be fully as profitable as production cost analysis, and so marketing revenue and cost data should be matched, as far as separable costs permit, by the accountants.

Other types of internal data that are not supplied through the accounting records include price lists, customer correspondence, and service records. These data are frequently neglected, although they can be compiled and reported or at least filed in a manner facilitating retrieval when useful. Public utility firms often keep files of customer complaints that are analyzed periodically. When one type of complaint is repeated frequently, the company makes a study of the cause and remedies the situation. Marketing management also may obtain important clues to product deficiencies through service records, which otherwise would require large expenditures to get the same information through collection of customer views as primary data. These are only a few illustrations of ways that company records may be fruitful sources of secondary data.

6.3 External Sources

One may approach the gathering of external secondary data by directly looking for the actual publication or compilation in which the data may be found. It is necessary to know where such information may be found.

6.3.1 Libraries

Normally we go to a library unless a logical source is closer. Most public libraries contain a large amount of business information or can provide the leads through which other sources of data may be traced. That information may be inadequate or hard to find unless the library has a separate division for business subjects and is staffed with specialized librarians. Recent squeezes on library finances have forced some to abandon or curtail their business collections and reference services. A number of cities still have very helpful business divisions in their municipal library systems, as in Cleveland and Brooklyn. These are logical places to start.

Most universities have schools of business and have special divisions or rooms in their libraries to serve these schools. Although maintained primarily for students and faculty, outside persons who need certain information may be accorded the privileges of these libraries.

Various institutions and large concerns maintain libraries with excellent collections in their fields of activity. These may be found in leading research institutions, banks, insurance companies, utilities, and manufacturing concerns. Their addresses and descriptions of their collections may be found in a directory[2] and, although not usually available to the general public, permission can be obtained to use them.

6.3.2 Literature

A great volume of literature (as distinguished from statistics) is published on the various subjects with which the marketing researcher may

---

[2] *Special Libraries and Information Centers in the United States and Canada* (Detroit: Gale Publishing Co., 1974).

be concerned. Even a librarian has difficulty in keeping abreast of all the new writings and the accumulated writings of the past; when research is undertaken in some area of marketing in a particular industry, a sizable task is involved in canvassing these materials. Some help, nevertheless, can be found in the following suggestions.

Guides to Marketing Literature

Guides or indexes to business literature provide an excellent starting point for seeking data on a given subject.[3] The following guides are available in many libraries:

> *Business Periodicals Index*
> *Public Affairs Information Service*
> *Monthly Catalog of United States Government Publications*
> *Monthly Checklist of State Publications*
> *Sources of Business Information*
> *Data Sources for Business and Market Analysis*
> *Marketing Information Guide*
> *New York Times Index*
> *Wall Street Journal Index*
> *Cumulative Book Index*
> *Encyclopedia of Business Information Sources*
> *Business Reference Sources: An Annotated Guide for Harvard Business School Students*

The *Business Periodicals Index* and the *Public Affairs Information Service* are the most general guides on business subjects available. The *Business Periodicals Index* is limited to business subjects, whereas the *Public Affairs Information Service* covers all social sciences, including commerce and economics.

These indexes are issued monthly and list new writings by topics. Both current periodical literature and books published on different business subjects are indexed. The user should note well the periodicals covered because of their differences and because many trade and professional services are not covered by either of these indexes. The illustrated page from the *Business Periodicals Index* in Figure 6–1 indicates the extent to which this index covers current literature on a topic. The *Monthly Catalog*, from which a page is reproduced in Figure 6–2, is an excellent guide to current federal government publications. The catalog is classified by government departments issuing the publication and includes all

---

[3] An excellent compilation of data sources may be found in: C. R. Goeldner and Laura M. Disks, "Business Facts: Where To Find Them," *MSU Business Topics*, Summer, 1976, pp. 23–36.

MARKET segmentation

Age and education as key correlates of store selection for female shoppers. D. N. Bellenger and others. tabs J Retailing 52:71-8 Wint '76-'77

Bank selection decisions and market segmentation. W. T. Anderson, jr. and others. J Mkt 40; 40-5 Ja '76; Discussion. 40:89-91 O '76; 41:85-7 Ja '77

Concepts for newspaper targeting explored. E. Wilken. Ed & Pub 109:16 N 20 '76

Consumer segmentation via latent class analysis. P. E. Green and others. bibl tabs J Consumer Res 3:170-4 D '76

Empirical study of time on market using multidimensional segmentation of housing markets. J. Belkin and others. tabs Am Real Estate & Urb Econ Assn J 4:57-75 Fall '76

How Colgate brand manager applied psychos to market and media for Irish Spring. il tab Media Decisions 11:70-1+ D '76

How Monsanto's Sam Dowdy markets agrichemicals. Media Decisions 11:66-9+ N '76

Identifying relevant psychographic segments: how specifying product functions can help. M. E. Goldberg. bibl tab J Consumer Res 3: 163-9 D '76

Ma Bell to fight competition with bigger marketing outlay. L. J. Haugh. il Adv Age 47:1+ D 13 '76

Segmentation of audiences. R. U. Brown. Ed & Pub 109:32 N 27 '76

MARKET share

Billion-dollar farm co-ops nobody knows. tab Bus W p54-8+ F 7 '77

Can American Motors survive its huge losses? Bus W p42-3 D 20 '76

Impacts of market-share pattern on marketing firm costs. R. Raikes and A. Heubrock. tab Am J Agric Econ 58:693-702 N '76

Measuring sales effects of some marketing mix variables and their interactions. V. K. Prasad and L. W. Ring. bibl tabs map J Mkt Res 13 391-6 N '76

Research and market share: a reappraisal of the Schumpeter hypothesis. J. B. Rosenberg. bibl tabs J Ind Econ 25:101-12 D '76

MARKET statistics

Profiles of top 100 markets in US: population, income, growth trends. maps Adv Age 47:23-94 D 13 '76

Who's big in local TV? analysis of top markets reveals range of leaders. M. Christopher. Adv Age 47:115 D 13 '76

MARKET structure

Banking market structure, risk, and the pattern of local interest rates in the United States, 1893-1911. J. A. James. bibl tabs R Econ & Stat 58:453-62 N '76

Concentration and firm stability in commercial banking. A. A. Heggestad and S. A. Rhoades. bibl tabs R Econ & Stat 58:443-52 N '76

Influence of market structure on industry advertising intensity. B. C. Brush. bibl tabs J Ind Econ 25:55-67 S '76

See also

Monopsonies

Would you want your son to marry a marketing lady? R. N. Farmer. J Mkt 41:15-18 Ja '77

See also

Education market

Price cutting

Product management

Tobacco industry

also subhead Marketing under the following subjects

Distributors, Industrial

Furniture industry

Grocery trade

Liquor industry

Public utilities

Real estate business

Savings and loan associations

Switching systems (communications)

Wine and wine making

Data processing

Industry information exchange: short-cut to market data. N. H. Stone and S. Press. Bus Q 41:53-8 Wint '76

Unique tool for marketers: PIMS. P. Smith. Duns R 108:95-6+ O '76; Same cond. Mgt R 66:32-4 Ja '77

International aspects

Penetrating international markets: key considerations for smaller firms. D. W. Hackett. J Small Bus Mgt 15:10-16 Ja '77

Quick route to overseas sales [Conval International] Ind W 191:37 N 15 '76

Laws and regulations

Marketing and the US Supreme Court, 1968-1974. R. O. Werner. J Mkt 41:32-43 Ja '77

Mathematical models

Analytical approach to marketing decisions in health-care organizations. Y. Wind and L. K. Spitz. bibl tabs Op Res 24:973-90 S '76

General model for understanding channel member behavior. R. A. Robicheaux and A. I. El-Ansary. J Retailing 52:13-30+ Wint '76-'77

Japanese demand for US coal: a market-share model. N. N. Reddy. bibl tabs Q R Econ & Bus 16:51-60 Aut '76

Measuring sales effects of some marketing mix variables and their interactions. V. K. Prasad and L. W. Ring. bibl tabs map J Mkt Res 13:391-6 N '76

MARKETING, Foreign. See Export-import trade

—Promotion

MARKETING channels

Fit products and channels to your markets. R. E. Weigand. Harvard Bus R 55:95-105 Ja '77

General model for understanding channel member behavior. R. A. Robicheaux and A. I. El-Ansary. J Retailing 52:13-30+ Wint '76-'77

Sources of power: their impact on intrachannel conflict. R. F. Lusch. bibl tabs J Mkt Res 13:382-90 N '76

MARKETING departments

Marketing controller: financial support to the marketing function. S. Trebuss. Can Bus R 3:30-3 Aut '76

MARKETING managers

FIGURE 6–1. Part of a Sample Page, *Business Periodicals Index*

Source: Courtesy of H. W. Wilson Co.

the material issued by the department in the past month. This index is not cumulative.

The *Monthly Checklist of State Publications,* available from the Superintendent of Documents, records all state documents and publications received by the Library of Congress.

77-3137

C 56.251/6:972/v.1-3

United States. Bureau of the Census.

Census of retail trade. [Washington], U.S. Dept. of Commerce, [Social and Economic Statistics Administration], Bureau of the Census; for sale by the Supt. of Docs., U.S. Govt. Print. Off.

20402

ill. 29 cm.

Quinquennial.

$8.50 (v.1) $16.00 (v.2, pt.1) $19.00 (v.2, pt.2) $18.00 (v.2, pt.3) $15.00 (v.3, pt.1) $15.00 (v.3, pt.2) $15.00 (v.3, pt.3)

1972-

"RC."

Chiefly statistics.

Prepared by Business Division.

3 vols. (105 pts.) in 7 vols.

Class note: To ascertain the part of the class following the colon, use year (e.g. 972) and the numerical designation associated with each title contained in the contents note.

CONTENTS: v.1. Summary and subject statistics.—v.2, pt.1. Area statistics, U.S. summary, Alabama-Indiana.—v.2, pt.2. Area statistics, Iowa-North Carolina.—v.2, pt.3. Area statistics, North Dakota-Wyoming.—v.3, pt.1. Major retail center statistics, Alabama-Indiana.—v.3, pt.2. Major retail center statistics, Iowa-North Carolina.—v.3, pt.3. Major retail center statistics, North Dakota-Wisconsin.

Item 132

S/N 003-024-01180-8 (v.1) : S/N 003-024-01181-6 (v.2, pt.1) : S/N 003-024-01182-4 (v.2, pt.2) : S/N 003-024-01183-2 (v.2, pt.3) : S/N 003-024-01184-1 (v.3, pt.1) : S/N 003-024-01185-9 (v.3, pt.2) : S/N 003-024-01186-7 (v.3, pt.3)

Supersedes: Census of business, retail trade

1. Retail trade — United States — Statistics — Yearbooks.

2. Retail trade — United States — Finance — Statistics —

20402

ill. 29 cm.

Quinquennial.

$12.00 (v.1) $18.00 (v.2, pt. 1) $19.00 (v.2, pt.2) $18.00 (v.2, pt. 3)

1972-

"SC."

Chiefly statistics.

Prepared by Business Division.

2 vols. (60 pts.) in 4 vols.

Class note: To ascertain the part of the class following the colon, use year (e.g. 972) and the numerical designation associated with each title contained in the contents note.

CONTENTS: v.1. Summary and subject statistics.—v.2, pt.1. Area statistics, U.S. summary, Alabama-Indiana.—v.2, pt.2. Area statistics, Iowa-North Carolina.—v.2, pt.3. Area statistics, North Dakota-Wyoming.

Item 132

S/N 003-0240-01187-5 (v.1) : S/N 003-024-01188-3 (v.2, pt.1) : S/N 003-01189-1 (v.2, pt.2) Printed as 003-024-01190-5 in error in publication : S/N 003-024-01190-5 (v.2, pt.3)

Supersedes: Census of business, selected services industries

1. Service industries — United States — Statistics — Yearbooks. 2. Service industries — United States — Finance — Statistics — Yearbooks. I. Title.

OCLC 2698282   76-600020

INTERNATIONAL COMMERCE BUREAU
Commerce Dept.
Washington, DC 20230

77-3139

C 57.102:In 8/3

United States. Bureau of International Commerce.

International marketing information series. — April 1976

FIGURE 6-2. Part of a Sample Page, *Monthly Catalog of United States Government Publications*

Sources of Business Information, by E. T. Coman,[4] *Data Sources for Business and Market Analysis,* by Natalie D. Frank,[5] and the monthly *Marketing Information Guide*[6] provide more specialized listings of marketing information. If one expects that the data will be found in newspapers, the *New York Times Index* and the *Wall Street Journal Index* list all items in these newspapers (which would include any important business news in the nation). For books alone, the annual *Cumulative Book Index* offers more compact reference and broader coverage than the periodical indexes.

A number of more specialized guides to marketing literature are found in the Bibliography Series published from time to time by the American Marketing Association. One such item is R. J. Holloway, *A Basic Bibliography on Experiments in Marketing* (Chicago: American Marketing Association, 1968). The *Journal of Marketing* in its section "Marketing Abstracts" offers an excellent list of materials recently published on studies in progress, and its book reviews describe current books of interest to the marketing researcher. The *Journal of Marketing Research* offers similar leads on more technical research subjects.

Two additional general guides are the *Encyclopedia of Business Information Sources* (2nd edition published in 1970 by Gale Research Company) and the *Business Reference Sources: An Annotated Guide for Harvard Business School Students.*

Leads toward printed material may also be obtained from the bibliographies in textbooks and technical books on marketing. In the absence of bibliographies, footnote references may be helpful. A particularly rich source of such references, in addition to condensed "how-to-do-it" information, is found in handbooks. Particularly inclusive and up-to-date is the *Handbook of Modern Marketing.*[7]

Periodicals

A very high proportion of the literature about marketing research and information used in marketing studies will also be found in periodicals. The various periodicals that may be helpful can be placed in three groups set out below.

Business periodicals. The periodicals dealing with business number many hundred, but the principal ones dealing with marketing are:

---

[4] E. T. Coman, *Sources of Business Information,* rev. ed. (Berkeley, Calif.: University of California Press, 1964).

[5] Natalie D. Frank, *Data Sources for Business and Market Analysis,* 2nd ed. (Metuchen, N.J.: Scarecrow Press, 1969).

[6] Until the end of 1971 a U.S. Department of Commerce publication, it subsequently has been published by Trade Market Information Guide, Inc., 1028 Connecticut Avenue N.W., Washington, D.C.

[7] Victor P. Buell ed., *Handbook of Modern Marketing* (New York: McGraw-Hill Book Company, 1970).

Advertising Age

Industrial Marketing

Marketing Communications

Sales and Marketing Management

Stores

In addition to these, a number of trade magazines deal with only one function or field of marketing, such as *Purchasing, Dry Goods Economist, Distribution and Warehousing, Chain Store Age, Discount Merchandiser, Men's Wear,* and *Merchandising Week.* Useful material also may be found in the periodicals that deal with business in general, such as *Fortune, Business Week,* and *Harvard Business Review.*

Researchers should be aware of special issues of some periodicals that are unusual data sources. *Advertising Age* is an example with its issue (usually in late April) on "Market Research Studies," which lists market analysis articles from both United States and Canadian sources on national, regional, and local markets. That periodical also has an August issue on leading companies' advertising strategies and expenditures.

Professional journals. These are the magazines in which members of professions publish articles on the advancement of their field or information of interest in their study areas. They are excellent for keeping in touch with current thought and new techniques. The journals of several fields in which the marketing researcher may be interested are:

International Journal of Opinion and Attitude Research

Journal of Advertising Research

Journal of the American Statistical Association

Journal of Applied Psychology

Journal of Consulting Psychology

Journal of Consumer Research

Journal of Marketing

Journal of Marketing Research

Journal of Retailing

Journal of Social Psychology

Psychometrika

Public Opinion Quarterly

Review of Economics and Statistics

Another outstanding source of advertising data is the *Standard Directory of Advertisers,* which annually serves as a guide to advertising programs of 17,000 corporations.[8]

Valuable information often is published in the professional journals of other fields, including economics, management, operations research, and

---

[8] *Standard Directory of Advertisers* (Skokie, Ill.: National Register Publishing Co., Inc., 1972 and other years).

cost accounting, but those listed above probably are closest to the interests of marketing research, especially the *Journal of Marketing* and the *Journal of Marketing Research*.

Government periodicals. The periodicals of federal and state government agencies tend to feature the reporting of statistics rather than articles; hence, they will be discussed in the following section under statistical sources. Frequently, however, they carry articles analyzing the current situation and trends or making special analyses, for example, the articles in the *Survey of Current Business*.

Miscellaneous. Valuable material may be obtained by examining publications found in specialized libraries. For example, most university libraries have graduate student theses, some of which are indexed by *Dissertation Abstracts*, which gives a brief summary of the material covered in the dissertation. If the researcher wishes to inquire further, most doctoral dissertations are available on microfilm from University Microfilms, Ann Arbor, Michigan.

Directories also often give important information. For specific types of businesses there are national directories, such as *Thomas' Register of American Manufacturers, Thomas' Wholesale Grocery and Kindred Trades Register, MacRae's Blue Book,* and *Sweet's Catalog Service*. For cities and towns there are, of course, the city directories.

6.3.3 Statistics

The marketing researcher is likely to make more frequent use of statistics than of the information found in other literature. Sometimes the needed figures are scattered through various studies and then, of course, are difficult to find. Fortunately, the most important and widely used statistics are maintained in continuous series and reported regularly in certain sources. The discussion will be confined to the latter.

Guides to Marketing Statistics

Unlike guides to the literature, indexing services give limited aid in hunting statistics. A few guides may help. One of these is the *Marketing Information Guide*,[9] to which we have referred previously. The *Checklist of Reports Issued by the Agricultural Marketing Service* is a good index of statistical data available from the Department of Agriculture. Another is *Guidelists for Marketing Research and Economic Forecasting Research,* which lists sources of indexes on all phases of the economy.[10] Other excellent sources are the *Monthly Bulletin of Statistics* issued by the United Nations as a supplement to the *United Nations Statistical Yearbook,* and the *Statistical Reporter,* issued monthly by the U.S. Office of the President, Office

---

[9] See footnote 6.
[10] Robert N. Carpenter, *Guidelists for Marketing Research and Economic Forecasting Research,* Study No. 73 (New York: American Management Association, 1966).

of Management and Budget, and covering numerous statistical sources, new reporting plans, and changes in federal statistical programs. The publication *Measuring Markets: A Guide to the Use of Federal and State Statistical Data* published in 1974 by the U.S. Department of Commerce is an excellent source document for federal and state statistics.

Periodicals

Several periodicals of the federal government are foremost among those that report current marketing statistics. The two that give the broadest range of data are the *Federal Reserve Bulletin* and the *Survey of Current Business*. Both are published monthly (and the Survey has weekly and annual supplements), and to some extent they overlap. The types of data covered in them can be judged from Figure 6–3, which produces a part of the index to monthly business statistics in the *Survey of Current Business*.

Although the statistics noted above are published only as national figures, they may provide a valuable array of data. Besides the *Survey*, the Department of Commerce issues dozens of monthly reports on production, sales, stocks, and other aspects of certain commodities and certain types of trade. Other federal departments publish current data that help the marketing researcher, such as the *Monthly Labor Review*, which gives details on consumer and wholesale prices, payrolls, employment, and other data compiled by the Department of Labor. The Department of Agriculture provides valuable facts on agricultural markets in *The Agricultural Situation* and other monthly or weekly reports, while the Department of Commerce is an even vaster source of marketing data. The latter agency has field offices in major cities, whose specialists can advise on available data from both Commerce and other federal agencies.

If you want data on regional conditions, many may be found in the monthly bulletins or special studies by the Federal Reserve Banks for their twelve reserve districts. Also, data on individual states or cities are published in the business reviews of numerous universities' business and economic research bureaus.[11] Finally, because marketing analysts may need to use financial statistics in various ways, we should mention the guide to these by Robert Morris Associates.[12]

The Census

As a census is a practically complete enumeration of important facts about the nation, to which individuals are required by law to report, the

---

[11] There is an index to all publications by the various university bureaus, which began with a cumulative number in 1951 covering their publications to that time and which is now supplemented with annual indexes. A recent number is *Bibliography of 1970 Publications of University—Bureaus of Business and Economic Research* (Boulder, Colo.: Business Research Division, University of Colorado, 1971).

[12] *Sources of Composite Financial Data: A Bibliography,* 3rd ed. (Philadelphia: Robert Morris Associates, 1971, free).

SECTIONS

General:

Business indicators	1–7
Commodity prices	7–9
Construction and real estate	9, 10
Domestic trade	10–12
Labor force, employment, and earnings	12–16
Finance	16–21
Foreign trade of the United States	21–23
Transportation and communications	23, 24

Industry:

Chemicals and allied products	24, 25
Electric power and gas	25, 26
Food and kindred products; tobacco	26–30
Leather and products	30
Lumber and products	31
Metals and manufactures	31–34
Petroleum, coal, and products	34, 36
Pulp, paper, and paper products	36, 37
Rubber and rubber products	37
Stone, clay, and glass products	38
Textile products	38–40
Transportation equipment	40

INDIVIDUAL SERIES

Advertising	10, 11, 16
Aerospace vehicles	40
Agricultural loans	16
Air carrier operations	23
Aircraft and parts	4, 6, 7, 40
Alcohol, denatured and ethyl	25
Alcoholic beverages	11, 26
Aluminum	33
Apparel	1, 3, 4, 8, 9, 11–15, 40
Asphalt and tar products	35, 36
Automobiles, etc.	1, 3–9, 11, 12, 19, 22, 23, 40
Balance of international payments	2, 3
Banking	16, 17
Barley	27
Battery shipments	34
Beef and veal	28
Beverages	4, 8, 11, 22, 23, 26
Blast furnaces, steel works, etc	5–7
Bonds, outstanding, issued, prices, sales, yields	18, 20
Brass and bronze	33
Brick	
Broker's balances	

Earnings, weekly and hourly	14, 15
Eating and drinking places	11, 12
Eggs and poultry	3, 7, 28, 29
Electric power	4, 8, 25, 26
Electrical machinery and equipment	4–8, 13–15, 19, 22, 23, 34
Employment estimates	12–15
Employment Service activities	16
Expenditures, U.S. Government	18
Explosives	25
Exports (see also individual commodities)	1, 2, 21–23
Express operations	23
Failures, industrial and commercial	7
Farm income, marketings, and prices	2, 3, 7, 8
Farm wages	15
Fats and oils	8, 22, 23, 29, 30
Federal Government finance	18
Federal Reserve banks, condition of	16
Federal Reserve member banks	17
Fertilizers	8, 25
Fire losses	10
Fish oils and fish	29
Flooring, hardwood	31
Flour, wheat	28, 29
Food products	1, 4–8, 11–15, 19, 22, 23, 26–30
Foreclosures, real estate	10
Foreign trade (see also individual commod.)	21–23
Foundry equipment	34
Freight cars (equipment)	4, 40
Fruits and vegetables	7, 8
Fuel oil	35, 36
Fuels	4, 8, 22, 23, 34–36
Furnaces	34
Furniture	4, 8, 11–15
Gas, output, prices, sales, revenues	4, 8, 26
Gasoline	1, 35
Glass and products	38
Glycerin	25
Gold	19
Grains and products	7, 8, 22, 27, 28
Grocery stores	11, 12
Gross national product	1
Gross private domestic investment	1
Gypsum and products	9, 38
Hardware stores	11
Heating equipment	9, 34
Hides and skins	8, 30
Highways and roads	9, 10
Hogs	28
Home electronic equipment	34
Home Loan banks, outstanding advances	10
Home mortgages	10
Hosiery	40
Hotels	24
Hours of work per week	14
Housefurnishings	1, 4, 8, 11, 12
Household appliances, radios, and television sets	4, 8, 11, 34

National defense expenditures	1, 18
National income and product	1, 2
National parks, visits	24
Newsprint	23, 37
New York Stock Exchange, selected data	20, 21
Nonferrous metals	4, 9, 19, 22, 23, 33
Noninstallment credit	17
Oats	27
Oil burners	34
Oils and fats	8, 22, 23, 29, 30
Orders, new and unfilled, manufactures'	6, 7
Ordnance	13–15
Paint and paint materials	8, 25
Paper and products and pulp	4–6, 9, 13–15, 19, 23, 36, 37
Parity ratio	7
Passports issued	24
Personal consumption expenditures	1
Personal income	2, 3
Personal outlays	2
Petroleum and products	4–6, 8, 11, 13–15, 19, 22, 23, 35, 36
Pig iron	32
Plant and equipment expenditures	2, 20
Plastics and resin materials	25
Population	12
Pork	28
Poultry and eggs	3, 7, 28, 29
Prices (see also individual commodities)	7–9
Printing and publishing	4, 13–15
Profits, corporate	2, 19
Public utilities	2–4, 8, 9, 13, 19–21
Pullman Company	24
Pulp and pulpwood	36
Purchasing power of the dollar	9
Radiators and convectors	34
Radio and television	4, 10, 11, 34
Railroads	2, 15, 16, 19, 20, 21, 24, 40
Railways (local) and bus lines	23
Rayon and acetate	39
Real estate	10, 17, 18
Receipts, U.S. Government	18
Recreation	8
Refrigerators and home freezers	34
Rent (housing)	
Retail trade	5, 8, 11–15, 17, 18
Rice	27
Roofing and siding, asphalt	36
Rubber and products (incl. plastics)	4–6, 9, 13–15, 23, 37
Saving, personal	2
Savings deposits	17
Securities issued	19, 20
Security markets	
Services	
Sheep	

FIGURE 6–3. Part of Index to Current Business Statistics, *Survey of Current Business.*

data that it reveals are the most basic and fruitful statistical source. Actually, there is not just one but seven regular censuses, five of which are most useful to the market researcher. The years for which they were last taken are Census of Agriculture (1974), Census of Business (1972), Census of Housing (1970), Census of Manufactures (1972), and Census of Population (1970). The censuses of business and of manufactures are usually taken every five years, the census of agriculture every five years (ending in 4 and 9) and the census of population and of housing every ten years (ending in 0.) In addition to these five censuses, the Census of Mineral Industries and the Census of Government are also taken. These have more limited application in marketing research, but in specific instances they may be of value.

In addition to the full census, the Bureau of the Census is continually making various sample surveys, estimates, and special studies. The results of these are published in many monthly, annual, or special reports, and the researcher may become familiar with these by obtaining the Bureau's quarterly *Catalog of Publications.*

The coverage of the various censuses is so extensive that no attempt will be made to describe the contents. The reader should examine the

181

Bureau of the Census publications and familiarize himself with the types of information that they contain.

Statistical Compilations

Access to statistics is greatly facilitated by a number of publications that assemble a wide variety of statistics within a single volume. The standard work of this type is the annual *Statistical Abstract of the United States,* another publication of the Bureau of the Census. The vast array of data in this volume includes not only selections from the various censuses, but also data collected by other agencies, including many outside the government. Another excellent compilation is the *Conference Board Record,* providing an interpretation of current statistics.

The County and City Data Book, a compilation of statistics derived from various censuses and government departments, provides a wide range of types of data on a city and county basis. Some of the 144 captions in this compilation are reproduced in Figure 6–4.

County Business Patterns annually provides basic manufacturing data between the Censuses of Manufactures. The information is compiled from an analysis of tax returns filed under the Old Age and Survivors Insurance Program and gives data on a geographic and type of business basis, broken down to individual counties.

Another helpful statistical compilation is the *Handbook of Basic Economic Statistics* available monthly or quarterly from the Economic Statistics Bureau of Washington, D.C. The handbook offers in one volume more than 1,800 of the basic economic series issued separately by the different government agencies.

Every two years, the Department of Commerce publishes *Business Statistics,* a supplement to the *Survey of Current Business.* This supplement makes available in one volume monthly or quarterly data on all 2,600 statistical indicators for the preceding four-year period and annual averages from 1929 to the year preceding the edition.

Market Guides

These are statistical compilations, of course, but are classified separately here because of their being particularly designed as market guides. The three following annual guides are among the better ones:

Sales and Marketing Management's "Annual Survey of Buying Power." This presents highly useful data regarding markets for consumers' goods. Included are recent population estimates, sales of five types of retail stores, individual incomes, and an index of market potential for states, counties, and cities.

Editor & Publisher's "Market Guide." This contains market maps that show trading areas and gives a variety of facts about each marketing center.

Rand McNally's *Commercial Atlas and Marketing Guide.* Although pri-

Table 2. COUNTIES
(Minus (—) denotes decrease)

Population, 1970

Codes			County	Land area	Population, 1970													
SMSA	SEA	State and county			Total		Per square mile	Change, 1960-1970		Female	Urban	Race				Age			Median age
					U.S. rank[1]	Total		Total[1]	Net migration			White	Negro			Under 5 years	18 years and over	65 years and over	
													Total	Change 1960-1970					
				1	2	3	4	5	6	7	8	9	10	11	12	13	14	15
			MICHIGAN—Con.	Sq. mi.				Per cent	Per cent	Per cent	Per cent	Per cent		Per cent	Per cent	Per cent	Per cent	Years

Retail trade, 1967

County	Establishments		Sales				Sales for all establishments by kind of business									Establishments with payroll	
	Total	With payroll	All establishments			Establishments with payroll	Food Stores	Automotive dealers	General merchandise stores	Eating and drinking places	Gasoline service stations	Furniture, home furnishings and equipment stores	Building materials, hardware, farm equipment dealers	Apparel and accessory stores	Drug stores and proprietary stores	Payroll, entire year	Paid employees, week incl. Mar. 12
			Proprietors	Total[1]	Change, 1963-1967												
	132	133	134	135	136	137	138	139	140	141	142	143	144	145	146	147	148
MICHIGAN—Con.		Per cent		$1,000	Per cent	Per cent	Per cent	Per cent	Per cent	Per cent	Per cent	Per cent	Per cent	Per cent	Per cent	$1,000	

Selected services, 1967

County	Establishments		Receipts			Receipts, all establishments			Establishments with payroll	
	Total	With payroll	All establishments		Establishments with payroll	Hotels, motels, camps	Automotive repair and services	Amusement, recreation, incl. motion pictures	Payroll, entire year	Paid employees, week incl. Mar. 12
			Total[1]	Change, 1963-1967						
	149	150	151	152	153	154	155	156	157	158
MICHIGAN—Con.		Per cent	$1,000	Per cent	Per cent	Per cent	Per cent	Per cent	$1,000	

Wholesale trade, 1967

County	Establishments	Sales		Paid employees, week incl. Mar. 12	Payroll, entire year
		Total	Merchant wholesalers		
	159	160	161	162	163
MICHIGAN—Con.		$1,000	Per cent	Per cent	$1,000

183

FIGURE 6–4. Table Captions, *County and City Data Book*

Source: County and City Data Book (Washington, D.C.: Government Printing Office, 1972).

marily an atlas, this large book also presents a great deal of market information in the form of special maps, statistics, and market indexes.

Maps

One may not think of maps under the heading of "statistics," yet maps are the medium through which the researcher may learn essential quantitative facts of location and distance in studying markets, planning surveys, and other phases of research. Several of the marketing guides previously mentioned contain detailed maps well suited to the researcher's needs. They are accompanied, as any map must be for usefulness, by data on various economic characteristics. Of particular value are the National Retail and Wholesale Marketing Maps, which incorporate data from the 1972 Census of Business and are released by the Department of Commerce.

The reader should be reminded that the foregoing description of different types of marketing literature and statistics is only suggestive. Nor should he or she expect to find all the publications listed in any single library. Further, considerable information exists that is found in special libraries, and this requires examination of additional sources.

6.3.4 Trade Associations

For data relating to a particular industry, its trade association, if one exists, may be an excellent source. The members of some trade associations cooperate in the exchange of information; however, the association usually encounters difficulties when anything beyond the most cursory sort of marketing data is sought by the association. The trade association may have basic information that is not available in libraries, and it should not be overlooked. There are thousands of trade associations, and a comprehensive list of them may be found in *Encyclopedia of Associations*.[13] For data on particular cities, nearly every commercial town has its association or chamber of commerce. Many of them collect current data on their cities or are very helpful on inquiries, although sometimes they are unduly optimistic regarding local prospects. Illustrative of the type of marketing information to be had from associations is the average age of automobiles in use, available from the Automobile Manufacturers Association. In the field of advertising, the Advertising Research Foundation, an agency supported by advertising associations, serves as the sponsor of numerous studies in related fields.

6.3.5 Publishers

The leading publishers of general magazines and newspapers as well as the television networks have been highly enterprising in collecting data or conducting marketing research. Although primarily intended to serve

[13] *Encyclopedia of Associations,* 9th ed. (Detroit: Gale Research Co., 1975).

their advertisers, much of this research is of general value in marketing research. To mention only a few of these publishers, we may cite the research departments of the New York Times Company, the *Farm Journal,* the McCall Corporation, Meredith Publishing Company, Time, Inc. (publishers of *Time*), and the *Milwaukee Journal.*

In this connection, other advertising media should not be neglected. The radio and television networks have collected substantial marketing data on the composition of their listening and viewing audiences. The widespread ownership of radio and television sets makes these data descriptive of markets in general.

6.3.6 State Governments

State governments should not be neglected as a source of marketing data. Often different government departments have information that rarely finds its way into public or private libraries. For example, information concerning miles of paved highway and traffic volume from state highway departments, retail sales tax data, gasoline sales, alcoholic beverage consumption, and many other types of reasonably current data can be secured from this source.

6.3.7 Private Sources

Frequently, one needs types of data available from private services that make a business of collecting such facts and charging for them. As these charges are considerable in some cases, the adequacy and value of these data must be appraised before deciding to purchase the service.

A few examples of companies that sell useful marketing data are Dun and Bradstreet, Inc. (information about specific concerns and credit ratings); F. W. Dodge Corporation (statistics and details on contemplated and actual construction); A. C. Nielsen Company; Market Research Corp. of America (sales or purchases of branded commodities); R. L. Polk Company (auto registrations, mailing lists); A. C. Nielsen Company (radio listenership and TV viewing data); and Daniel Starch and Staff (magazine and newspaper readership data).

In Figure 6–5 a sample of the data collected by the American Market Research Bureau and known as the Target Group Index is shown. These data are collected periodically from 20,000 adults and covers over 400 product categories. It covers purchase by brand, intensity of use, readership and TV viewing habits, buying style, self-concept, and demographics.

6.4 Obtaining Secondary Data

The experienced researcher will devise a special procedure for each study undertaken, one that will cover the most probable and appropriate data sources efficiently. The novice cannot very well determine such a

186

TARGET GROUP INDEX	ALL USERS A '000	B DOWN	C ACROSS	D INDEX	SOLE USERS A '000	B DOWN	C ACROSS	D INDEX	PRIMARY USERS A '000	B DOWN	C ACROSS	D INDEX	SECONDARY USERS A '000	B DOWN	C ACROSS	D INDEX	NON-USERS A '000	B DOWN	C ACROSS	D INDEX
ALL ADULTS	3077	100.0	2.3	100	798	100.0	0.6	100	1076	100.0	0.8	100	1203	100.0	0.9	100	104703	100.0	77.0	100
MEN	1894	61.6	2.9	130	501	62.8	0.8	133	640	59.5	1.0	126	753	62.6	1.2	132	56628	54.3	80.5	115
WOMEN	1183	38.4	1.6	73	296	37.2	0.4	70	436	40.5	0.6	77	450	37.4	0.6	71	47875	45.7	66.7	87
ADULTS 18-24	596	19.4	2.4	107	63	7.9	0.3	44	180	16.7	0.7	92	352	29.3	1.4	162	19969	18.4	78.3	102
25 - 34	723	23.5	2.4	107	145	18.2	0.6	101	255	23.7	0.9	111	322	26.8	1.1	125	22795	21.7	85.6	111
35 - 44	636	20.7	2.4	107	245	37.8	0.9	146	219	20.4	0.7	89	280	24.1	0.8	90	25565	21.3	85.6	107
55	675	21.9	2.2	98	207	25.9	0.7	116	268	24.0	0.9	111	201	16.7	0.7	75	27263	21.8	75.0	97
65 OR OVER	247	8.0	1.2	55	91	11.5	0.5	78	97	9.0	0.5	61	59	4.9	0.3	34	11352	10.8	57.0	74
NORTH EAST	1024	33.3	3.5	156	236	29.6	0.8	140	426	39.6	1.5	185	360	29.7	1.2	140	20712	19.8	71.3	93
NORTH CENTRAL	696	22.6	1.9	85	168	21.0	0.5	79	219	20.4	0.6	77	310	25.7	0.8	97	26774	27.5	79.6	103
SOUTH	1286	41.8	2.7	117	365	45.7	0.8	120	417	38.3	0.9	110	504	41.8	1.0	116	36173	34.5	75.2	98
WEST	71	2.3	0.3	14	27	3.4	0.1	14	14	1.3	0.1	8	30	2.5	0.1	15	19044	18.2	84.0	109
NEW ENGLAND	438	14.2	7.8	345	116	14.6	2.1	352	170	15.8	3.0	384	151	12.6	2.7	305	4115	3.9	73.3	95
MID ATLANTIC	612	19.9	2.0	89	147	18.5	0.6	101	255	23.7	0.8	129	95	17.4	0.6	95	17555	16.6	76.3	99
EAST CENTRAL	349	11.4	1.8	77	101	12.7	0.5	78	95	8.8	0.5	69	154	12.8	0.8	90	12216	13.6	82.3	107
WEST CENTRAL	370	12.0	1.8	77	71	8.9	0.4	57	132	12.3	0.6	79	168	13.9	0.5	80	16551	15.6	82.7	107
SOUTH EAST	1127	36.6	3.6	160	352	41.6	0.7	161	366	34.0	1.0	148	450	55.7	0.5	156	28650	21.2	61.7	94
SOUTH WEST	133	4.3	1.3	58	8	2.9	*	18	6	4.0	0.3	4	54	4.8	0.4	54	22850	12.0	61.6	109
PACIFIC	47	1.5	0.2	10	23	2.9	0.1	14	5	0.5	*	4	18	1.5	0.1	18	17052	16.3	63.6	109
COUNTY SIZE A	1109	36.0	2.4	107	127	22.2	0.4	352	394	36.7	0.9	109	538	44.7	1.2	133	34962	33.4	76.5	95
B	626	20.4	2.4	105	167	26.2	0.4	101	341	31.0	1.0	124	386	21.6	0.7	85	27806	26.6	80.2	104
C	966	31.4	2.7	118	339	42.5	0.5	160	301	28.0	0.8	106	386	27.1	0.4	102	27004	25.9	75.1	99
D	376	12.2	0.9	40	56	7.1	0.3	149	41	3.8	0.2	26	79	6.6	0.4	46	14044	14.2	75.4	99
SMSA CENTRAL CITY	1077	35.0	2.5	112	220	27.5	0.5	88	447	41.6	1.1	133	410	34.1	1.0	109	32266	30.8	76.0	99
SMSA SUBURBAN	1016	33.0	2.2	99	224	26.6	0.5	89	366	34.0	0.8	103	437	36.3	1.0	108	36134	34.7	74.3	103
NON SMSA	983	32.0	2.0	91	364	45.7	0.8	129	263	24.4	0.5	69	356	29.6	0.7	84	36296	34.7	75.7	98
GRADUATED COLLEGE	447	14.2	2.7	112	143	17.7	0.8	38	151	14.1	0.8	103	304	25.3	1.4	105	16475	15.7	80.9	116
ATTENDED COLLEGE	626	20.4	2.2	116	101	12.6	0.4	72	193	17.9	0.8	102	333	27.7	1.4	158	20283	19.4	85.0	110
GRADUATED HIGH SCHOOL	1168	37.9	2.3	103	291	36.4	0.6	99	517	48.1	1.0	130	360	29.9	0.7	81	39845	79.2	79.2	103
DID NOT GRADUATE HIGH SCHOOL	786	25.5	1.8	80	364	45.7	0.8	143	214	19.9	0.5	63	207	17.2	0.5	54	26099	26.8	64.9	84
EMPLOYED FULL TIME	1639	54.8	2.8	126	451	56.6	0.7	119	591	54.9	0.9	116	797	66.2	1.2	139	56915	54.4	80.1	114
PART TIME	357	11.6	3.3	143	123	15.1	1.4	163	127	11.8	0.6	151	210	9.0	1.0	220	8852	7.8	77.2	100
NOT EMPLOYED	881	28.6	1.1	64	228	28.3	0.4	163	357	33.2	0.6	74	299	24.8	0.5	56	59935	37.8	65.1	85
PROFESSIONAL/ MANAGERIAL	769	25.0	3.3	144	143	17.7	0.6	102	285	26.5	1.2	153	343	20.5	1.5	165	21430	20.5	90.9	118
CLERICAL/SALES	561	18.2	3.5	154	125	15.1	0.8	126	127	11.8	1.0	118	313	26.0	1.0	220	13438	12.8	83.5	108
CRAFTSMEN/FOREMEN	626	20.4	2.7	121	173	21.7	0.7	135	144	17.0	0.8	120	246	7.8	1.1	113	8745	8.4	91.6	119
OTHER EMPLOYED	604	19.6	2.3	102	235	29.4	0.6	153	216	20.1	0.8	105	154	12.8	0.6	67	21547	20.6	82.6	107
W/D INCOME 25,000 OR MORE	106	3.5	2.4	107	5	0.7	0.1	21	46	4.5	1.1	139	53	4.4	1.2	137	3655	3.7	87.6	114
15,000 - 24,999	562	18.2	3.0	104	301	9.0	0.3	51	280	26.1	1.2	148	469	17.4	0.3	99	21150	20.6	86.3	115
10,000 - 14,999	1342	16.7	1.8	135	300	37.8	0.7	131	401	37.3	1.0	130	91	40.7	0.6	141	23232	20.4	82.4	107
8,000 - 9,999	265	26.7	2.0	78	173	12.5	0.7	112	77	7.1	0.5	63	246	7.6	0.6	68	16192	12.9	82.6	106
5,000 - 9,999	615	20.0	2.4	107	146	22.7	0.7	116	144	16.0	0.8	97	91	9.3	0.7	111	10952	12.6	91.6	119
LESS THAN 5,000	334	10.9	1.2	53	146	18.3	0.5	89	76	7.1	0.3	35	112	9.3	0.4	45	16074	15.4	57.6	75
WHITE	2813	91.4	2.3	102	709	88.9	0.6	126	998	92.8	0.8	104	1106	91.9	0.9	103	96511	92.6	79.6	103
BLACK	285	9.2	2.0	87	80	11.1	0.6	126	52	4.8	0.4	125	156	7.9	0.3	185	6362	6.1	53.3	69
OTHER	29	0.9	1.1	50	3	0.0	0.2	117	26	2.4	0.9	127	4	0.3	0.0	239	1650	1.7	71.7	93
SINGLE	551	17.9	3.2	142	30	3.8	0.2	30	158	14.7	0.9	116	363	30.1	2.1	239	12309	11.8	72.0	94
MARRIED	2376	77.2	2.3	102	708	88.8	0.7	117	877	81.5	0.9	107	791	65.7	0.8	87	83369	80.1	81.3	106
WIDOWED/DIVORCED/ SEPARATED	150	4.9	1.0	42	59	7.4	0.4	64	41	3.8	0.3	33	49	4.1	0.3	36	8525	8.1	54.2	70

FIGURE 6-5. Sample Page, Target Group Index

SAMPLE PAGE	ALL USERS				SOLE USERS				PRIMARY USERS				SECONDARY USERS				NON-USERS			
TARGET GROUP INDEX	A '000	B % DOWN	C % ACROSS	D INDEX	A '000	B % DOWN	C % ACROSS	D INDEX	A '000	B % DOWN	C % ACROSS	D INDEX	A '000	B % DOWN	C % ACROSS	D INDEX	A '000	B % DOWN	C % ACROSS	D INDEX
HOUSEHOLD OF 1 OR 2 PERSONS	923	30.0	1.9	83	274	34.3	0.6	95	293	27.2	0.6	75	356	29.6	0.7	82	35591	34.0	72.2	94
3 OR 4 PERSONS	1303	42.3	2.4	106	308	38.6	0.6	97	464	43.1	0.9	108	531	44.1	1.0	110	43832	41.9	80.7	105
5 OR MORE PERSONS	652	27.7	2.6	116	236	27.1	0.7	114	319	29.6	1.0	125	316	26.5	0.7	110	25280	24.1	78.1	101
NO CHILDREN IN HOUSEHOLD	1364	44.3	2.1	93	330	41.4	0.5	87	457	42.5	0.7	89	577	47.9	0.9	100	47675	45.0	72.5	94
CHILDREN UNDER 2 YEARS	265	8.6	2.9	96	49	6.2	0.4	69	103	9.6	0.8	107	113	9.4	0.9	105	9736	9.3	80.1	104
2-5 YEARS	655	21.3	2.5	111	167	21.0	0.6	109	247	22.9	0.9	120	241	20.0	0.9	104	21642	20.7	82.9	108
6-11 YEARS	792	25.7	2.5	103	303	38.0	0.7	152	250	23.2	0.7	93	239	19.9	0.7	79	27471	26.2	80.8	105
12-17 YEARS	921	29.9	2.5	110	245	30.7	0.7	113	327	30.4	0.9	112	349	29.0	0.9	107	29406	28.1	79.7	104
MEN 16-34	838	27.2	3.4	149	129	16.2	0.5	89	302	28.0	1.2	153	407	33.8	1.6	165	22219	21.2	89.4	116
35-49	520	16.9	3.1	136	165	23.2	1.1	169	142	13.0	1.0	109	190	15.8	1.1	129	15300	14.6	91.7	119
50 OR OVER	536	17.4	2.4	104	107	23.4	1.8	140	194	18.0	1.0	108	155	12.9	0.7	77	19301	18.4	85.1	110
WOMEN 16-34	460	15.6	1.8	81	76	9.5	0.3	49	156	14.7	1.2	76	246	20.4	0.6	106	19785	14.0	75.2	98
35-49	316	10.3	1.9	78	110	13.7	0.4	105	99	10.0	0.6	76	99	8.3	0.6	99	13357	16.9	74.4	97
50 OR OVER	367	12.6	1.4	62	111	14.0	0.4	69	170	15.6	0.6	78	105	8.7	0.4	43	14633	14.2	53.7	70
MEN - M/D INCOME 15,000 OR MORE	467	15.2	4.1	130	59	7.5	0.4	64	206	19.2	1.3	164	203	16.7	1.3	143	14695	14.0	92.6	120
10,000 - 14,999	772	25.1	4.0	175	203	25.5	0.8	176	352	20.2	1.1	140	352	16.3	1.1	204	17876	17.1	91.6	119
LESS THAN 10,000	655	21.3	2.3	100	238	29.9	0.8	141	217	20.2	0.8	95	200	16.6	0.7	78	22656	23.2	84.1	109
WOMEN - M/D INCOME 15,000 OR MORE	201	6.5	1.6	71	18	2.2	0.1	24	122	11.5	1.0	123	62	5.1	1.0	56	10298	7.6	82.5	107
10,000 - 14,999	420	13.7	2.1	95	90	11.3	0.3	65	185	17.2	0.9	119	137	11.4	1.1	77	14356	13.8	73.2	95
LESS THAN 10,000	562	18.2	1.6	73	161	22.6	0.5	78	129	12.0	0.3	41	252	20.9	1.2	72	23222	22.2	56.5	76
AFFECTIONATE	870	28.3	2.3	100	174	21.8	0.5	77	315	29.3	0.8	103	361	31.7	1.0	112	30612	21.2	79.4	103
AMICABLE	665	21.6	2.6	113	80	10.0	0.3	52	289	26.9	1.1	141	296	24.6	1.1	129	20576	14.7	79.3	103
AWKWARD	929	30.2	2.5	112	224	28.0	0.6	104	315	29.4	0.9	109	390	32.4	1.2	121	28037	26.9	76.7	100
BRAVE	1577	51.2	2.6	113	351	44.0	0.6	97	512	47.6	1.0	105	714	59.3	1.2	131	50456	43.2	81.6	106
BROADMINDED	1294	42.1	2.7	116	259	32.5	0.5	91	494	44.9	1.0	124	541	44.9	1.1	126	31668	37.1	80.1	104
CREATIVE	868	28.2	2.9	127	199	25.0	0.7	112	279	26.0	0.9	117	369	32.3	1.3	146	24111	23.0	79.9	104
DOMINATING	1195	38.6	2.8	122	244	30.6	0.6	96	457	42.5	1.1	133	494	41.5	1.1	129	36444	34.8	84.0	109
EFFICIENT	774	25.2	2.0	99	216	27.1	0.6	106	250	23.2	0.7	91	309	25.6	0.9	105	27932	26.7	80.7	105
EGOCENTRIC	1395	45.5	2.0	89	421	52.6	0.6	104	522	48.5	0.7	95	452	37.6	0.7	74	50661	48.1	73.1	95
FRANK	1035	33.6	2.5	112	228	28.6	0.6	105	374	34.7	0.9	115	434	36.0	1.1	120	31268	38.7	78.6	102
FUNNY	793	25.6	3.0	133	160	20.0	0.6	103	350	32.5	1.3	167	283	23.5	1.1	125	20648	19.7	78.1	101
INTELLIGENT	647	21.0	2.4	107	96	12.0	0.4	64	457	45.4	0.9	121	273	22.5	1.0	121	23900	22.3	80.4	104
KIND	1407	45.6	2.4	107	377	47.2	0.5	104	483	45.4	0.9	110	622	51.6	1.0	114	47540	45.4	77.1	100
REFINED	1265	41.1	2.3	102	289	36.2	0.5	119	453	44.2	0.8	103	493	40.7	1.0	102	42564	40.7	78.0	100
RESERVED	660	21.4	2.5	111	132	16.6	0.5	88	272	25.3	1.0	131	255	21.2	1.1	110	19031	16.9	75.6	98
SELF-ASSURED	810	26.3	2.7	121	311	39.0	0.4	70	265	24.6	0.9	113	424	35.2	1.4	162	23078	22.6	80.6	105
SOCIABLE	1320	42.0	2.5	113	295	37.0	0.7	97	447	40.0	1.1	109	576	46.0	1.1	125	40059	34.3	77.3	100
STUBBORN	1356	44.1	2.6	115	249	53.2	0.7	61	412	47.5	1.0	124	536	49.5	1.0	92	42413	40.5	81.5	106
TENSE	1126	36.5	2.3	104	352	44.2	0.7	119	333	36.3	0.8	103	422	35.1	0.8	76	36636	37.1	76.8	104
TRUSTWORTHY	1413	42.2	2.4	107	423	53.0	0.5	91	661	63.3	1.0	123	609	67.2	1.0	116	63034	62.2	74.6	103
BRAND LOYAL	1121	36.4	2.4	105	311	36.9	0.7	112	457	39.5	0.9	123	354	35.2	0.9	85	23567	36.7	77.6	101
CAUTIOUS	1162	42.0	2.2	97	339	42.5	0.6	100	409	39.5	0.7	100	417	34.7	0.6	68	42569	40.4	76.3	102
CONFORMISTS	676	21.8	2.2	82	267	33.5	0.6	97	305	28.0	0.7	94	301	25.6	0.6	78	34365	40.5	72.6	94
ECOLOGISTS	903	32.0	2.3	96	335	41.8	0.6	119	336	31.5	0.7	103	305	25.8	0.7	77	34172	37.1	75.2	96
ECONOMY MINDED	1136	37.0	2.4	104	330	41.4	0.7	116	410	38.1	0.8	107	397	33.0	0.8	93	36556	36.9	74.6	103
EXPERIMENTERS	1274	41.4	2.1	101	372	46.7	0.7	104	506	47.2	0.7	123	394	32.7	0.6	73	44477	36.7	72.5	94
IMPULSIVE	670	21.8	2.3	102	165	20.7	0.6	96	260	24.1	0.7	100	246	20.4	0.7	97	23000	22.3	79.4	104
PERSUASIBLE	783	25.5	2.0	94	224	28.0	0.6	95	284	26.3	0.7	114	276	22.9	0.7	76	30665	29.3	76.8	100
PLANNERS	1331	43.3	2.3	102	371	46.5	0.6	109	476	44.2	0.8	104	465	40.3	0.8	95	46478	44.4	80.4	104
STYLE-CONSCIOUS	843	27.4	2.4	106	224	28.1	0.6	108	293	27.2	0.8	105	326	27.1	0.9	105	27103	25.9	79.8	100

FIGURE 6-5. Continued

plan, and should follow some general system in the search. The follow-ing simple and obvious plan should be of help to those who fail to find the data they need or who waste precious time because they lack a sys-tematic approach.

1. Internal data should be sought first. These are usually close at hand and can be acquired with less expenditure of time than ex-ternal data. Also, data found internally frequently make a search for external data unnecessary.

2. When internal sources are exhausted, a good library is the logical starting point for external data. Unless one understands the topics and terms involved, an encyclopedia should be consulted (prefera-bly the *Americana* or the *Britannica* or, if concerned with a social science, the *Encyclopedia of the Social Sciences)*. Here are both brief authoritative articles on important subjects and suggested readings.

3. Now, clear as to what is being sought, the indexes to literature or statistics can be used intelligently. If more interested in recent ma-terial, one starts with the recent monthly volumes of the indexes, then turns to the annual volumes for previous years. They classify references by topic, but one should look for a topic under various terms. If the indexes do not suggest the material, consult the bibli-ographies in technical books and textbooks and the cumulative in-dexes to past numbers in various periodicals.

4. Next, one needs to know whether the library has each of these ref-erences, and the card catalog will indicate this. Its collection may list every book by author, subject, and title, although periodicals may be given by title only.

5. Although the local library may not have all the material needed, it still may possibly be borrowed from a library that does have the material if the local library is able to make use of interlibrary loan arrangements. Another possibility is to have the other library pho-tostat the pertinent pages, if this service is offered. Of course, one must first discover what other library has the material; the local li-brary can learn this through the *Union Catalog* maintained by the Congressional Library in Washington, D.C., which has a listing of the collection of libraries all over the nation.

6. Besides libraries, one may start contacting other likely sources, among them the sources mentioned in this chapter. A wise proce-dure is to start a list of the various trade associations, governmental agencies, and other possible sources, noting their priority and keeping a record of correspondence with them.

7. The sources of material unearthed in one investigation may have continuing value in the future. This value, however, will be real-ized only by keeping permanent records of past searches. The indi-vidual index cards prepared while the material is sought should be kept permanently and will become an expanding and invaluable reference file.

6.5 Scrutinizing Secondary Data

When seeking out and using secondary data, one should realize that she or he is depending upon others for the validity of any information that may be applicable to one's study. One should not accept secondary data without first critically appraising them. To avoid neglecting some phase of this scrutiny, we offer the following factors to be considered.

6.5.1 Character of the Collecting or Sponsoring Organization

The quality of the information varies greatly with the caliber and reputation of the agency that collected it. For instance, sometimes data are collected by one organization, in an approved manner, in behalf of a sponsoring agency whose biased interpretations have hidden the real meaning of the findings. Here the character of both organizations must be considered.

The reputation of the research agency for thorough and honest work must be determined, as well as its resources and ability in relationship to the particular study. General reputation is important, but when the research has been merely a sideline to the real functions of the organization, it is the ability in research that is pertinent. The sponsoring organization may have had some hidden motive and may have biased its interpretation to "prove something." This is an all-too-common situation and, of course, discredits many or all of the data.

6.5.2 Objectives of the Original Study

A past study may have had quite different purposes from one's own problem under study and yet have produced data that ostensibly seem appropriate as secondary data for the new study. Before utilizing such readymade findings, the researcher should inquire whether the purpose of their collection might have destroyed their pertinence.

Let us cite an example of this. A large-scale study had been made of automobile dealers with the primary purpose of learning what those dealers were offering as trade-ins to prospective buyers of new cars. One distinctly secondary bit of information recorded was whether or not the salesperson offered a demonstration ride to someone posing as a buyer. When the sponsor of the study learned through these data that very few salespeople were offering such rides—particularly his make's dealers—it was a cause for deep concern and the launching of a large study into this matter. That manufacturer had been quite misled, however, by the data in the first study, which, although accurate, reflected only what a salesperson tended to do when confronted with a shopper who stated precisely the car he wanted and began dickering for price. That was the logical technique for the earlier study, in view of its purposes, but the

189

result was deceptive when viewed to be representative of automobile salespersons' behavior with all sorts of prospects.

6.5.3 Methods Employed

Lack of bias and having proper objectives will not ensure accurate facts if poor methods are followed in selecting the sample, obtaining the data, or interpreting the facts. In a study to determine the best locations to open new branch banks, the researchers relied heavily on population projections in different parts of the city made by the city planning commission. Under closer scrutiny, the researchers found that the commission arrived at these projections by subdividing on maps the usable land area and multiplying each area by the national average-sized family. Such projections were overstated and had little value for the problem at hand. When the methodology was discovered, new projections were made by systematically canvassing every real estate developer in the area about his future plans. The difference between the two projections was very great.

Methodological faults may stem from limited resources or the limited experience of the collecting agency. One should check all phases of the techniques employed. Reputable organizations either append a full-description of their methods to the report of the data, or else they willingly explain them on request.

6.5.4 Classifications and Definitions

Government data rarely are in classifications wanted by the researcher. For example, the Bureau of the Census uses classifications of counties or other political units that are difficult to regroup to reflect economic areas. In one study, which relied entirely on secondary data, mostly government data, the information available for the 3,071 counties had to be regrouped to parallel the thirty-two sales districts of the company.

One might think that such terms as *family, consuming unit, department store, employed,* and *income* are well understood. Too often, however, their definitions vary so widely as to render the data unusable for a particular study. This is why considerable effort has been made to get universal acceptance for a standard classification of consumer characteristics. In any case, the researcher must understand the classifications used before accepting data for his own purposes.

6.5.5 Timeliness

Marketing is dynamic. Although some conditions may not change materially over many years, others change very rapidly and substantially. The population of the nation changes only gradually, but that of a certain town may change more rapidly. For example, in one suburban township the population dropped 43 percent in a short period of time. This was a result of several annexations to the adjacent city, and although it does

190

not affect the overall economic area, it does drastically limit the governmental unit as a potential purchasing unit. As a result of these annexations, the assessed valuation in the area has been sharply cut and the tax revenues to the unit drastically reduced. As a potential buyer of goods and services, the potential purchasing power of this governmental unit has been cut almost in half. Some marketing "facts" lose their validity rapidly, therefore, and are of little value within months after their collection. The censuses of the federal government also suffer from "data obsolescence," particularly those taken on a ten-year cycle, such as the Census of Population and the Census of Housing. Marked changes take place before the new census is available.

The researcher may have found all the facts needed, in which case one should be congratulated. The possibilities of securing secondary data should be exhausted before going out into the field to obtain primary data, expending unnecessary effort and time.

7 Sampling Process and Selection

Chapter 7 is the first of two chapters on sampling and brings us to step number 11 of Table 4-1. It is the first point in the book where statistical aspects are dealt with extensively and concerns a universal problem in data gathering, about which one may ask:

What is sampling? Why do we call it a "universal" task?

What does one try to accomplish in sampling?

Basically, what do you do in sampling? What are the chief difficulties faced?

What are the techniques in selecting samples, broadly speaking? The specific techniques? What are their pros and cons?

After a sample has been gathered, how can one tell whether it is a proper sample?

SAMPLING IS INVOLVED in practically all the information to which we are exposed. We are accustomed to reaching conclusions about phenomena on the basis of a sample from that phenomena. For example, in a restaurant we take a few sips from a bottle of wine before accepting it; we test the temperature of a swimming pool by dipping our toe into the water before diving in; and we test-drive a new automobile at the dealer's as an indication of the performance we could expect if we purchased it. We are also exposed (by means of television, radio, newspapers) on a daily basis to projections of public opinion on various issues based on estimates from a small portion of the population.

Sampling is necessary because complete counts or observations of phenomena, in any classification of objects or events, are rarely possible or justifiable. We are limited to sampling by such factors as the time we have available to collect the information and the possibility of using up the entire object. However, when we base some of our personal generalizations on inadequate samples, they are likely to be in error. An example is a person who visits Toronto twice, happening to encounter hot, humid weather both times, and then states that its climate is "generally poor."

As has been pointed out elsewhere, sound research demands systematized procedures that adhere to certain scientific rules. When applied to sampling, such procedures must take into account the difficulties and dangers inherent in depending on samples to provide sufficiently accurate descriptions of the larger classifications that they are assumed to represent.

Practitioners obviously must be well grounded in sampling, which is a necessary tool in measuring marketing phenomena. As decisions tend to be based on information acquired from samples, business decision makers need a substantial grasp of sampling theory to appraise the reliability and appropriateness of sample information.

7.1 Reasons for Sampling

In gathering information a decision has to be made concerning whether the information sought should be acquired from every member of the group from which we are seeking the information, or from a small portion of that group. There are instances when taking a census, which is an enumeration of the entire group involved, is both practical and possible. If we are seeking information from industrial clients and the number of firms within the industry is relatively few, information gathering may warrant the conducting a census. In most instances, however, complete counts are rarely practical. Therefore, we must rely on samples in gathering information. There are several reasons why a researcher might select a sampling method rather than taking a census.

First, decision makers usually have a time frame in which to make a decision based on available information. A delay in a decision until a complete count or measure of each element of the population of interest may take so long that by the time the complete census is completed the

193

information may be useless and may result in a lost business opportunity. Therefore, information based on sample results takes less time to complete than one based on a complete enumeration.

Another consideration in deciding to use a sample is the cost of gathering the information. Depending on the information-gathering methods used, research expenditures include such factors as selecting, training, and supervising interviewers; the production costs of the questionnaires; the cost of mailing or telephone services; and so on. Information collected from a census could therefore potentially be prohibitively costly, as costs tend to increase with the amount of information sought. From a managerial point of view, the economic efficiency would be increased by utilizing a sample.

The use of sampling techniques is also warranted in situations in which the measuring of a particular element from a group would destroy the elements or render them useless after examination. A classic example of such a situation is the testing of photographic film. The manufacturer uses a destructive test, exposing the film, in testing the quality of the product. Since they would have no film left to sell, if all were tested, a representative sample of each batch is used during a particular production run.

Sampling is also desirable in cases where a complete enumeration of the population may not justifiably increase the accuracy of the information. For example, the Bureau of Labor Statistics of the U.S. Department of Labor uses a sample of grocery stores throughout the country to determine the estimated retail food prices for use in the Consumer Price Index. Given the alternative sampling techniques available, it is unlikely that the inclusion of all grocery stores in an enumeration of prices would significantly affect the outcome of the estimated retail food prices by city. One justification for utilizing a sample is that food prices do not vary by more than a few cents from one grocery store to another within a city. Therefore, even if the research funds and time were available to conduct a census, it is doubtful that the additional accuracy would be necessary for decision-making purposes.

Finally, the use of a sample is justified in situations where there is the physical impossibility of obtaining information from the entire population. Assume that we are interested in the processing and marketing of rainbow trout. To determine how much fish is available for our venture, we must know how much fish is available overall. But because of the nature of this population—births, migration, and deaths of this species—complete enumeration is not possible. However, the sampling of particular stream areas could be made and the outcome projected to the entire population that the business would eventually be concerned with.

7.2 Objectives of Sampling

In applied research, sampling is to be viewed as just one phase of the project that, in combination with the other phases, is intended to obtain the appropriate data as efficiently as possible. The scope and nature of the sample and sampling procedures and the resource expenditure that the particular problem(s) justifies are also important considerations. We should approach sampling, then, not by being concerned with alternative procedures but rather by determining what the decision maker requires — that is, the research and data objectives.

objectives of sampling needs →

needs for samples.

(1) One need is for the data to be representative of the appropriately defined population. This may mean selecting a cross section that contains certain characteristics in the same proportion as they exist in the population (for example, if income levels are significant to the problem and if 15.4 percent of the sample should be under a certain level). An appropriate target population may instead mean something else. Perhaps the decision maker wants the average income in the sample to conform to the actual average income of the population; or, he or she may prefer a "typical" range of incomes that lie in some range from the norm of income (for example, family incomes between $7,000 and $15,000 that comprise most of the population). In this case, precision in the relatively infrequent extremes may be unimportant. Indeed, the decision maker may be interested exclusively in particular segments, or more in one segment than in others. These varying needs, of course, would substantially alter the sampling methods.

(2) A second need is for the sample to be sufficiently accurate so as to provide stable results. If two samplings, using the same procedures and size of samples, obtained widely different findings, they would be so unstable that relying on the results of either would be of doubtful value. Stability depends in part on conforming to some correct procedures but depends more on the size of sample. Obviously, a sample of 1,000 is more likely to provide stable results than one of only 200 members. Attaining the confidence limits desired by the decision maker is a guiding objective.

(3) A third need is to obtain as precisely as possible the kinds and the degree of detail of information that the problem requires. This objective may seem quite obvious, but a tendency exists for instructions on sampling to ignore this factor. The specific way in which the actual procedure is designed, rather than the general sampling methods chosen, determines whether the maximum richness of findings is yielded in the gathered data.

(4) A fourth objective is that of using research resources as efficiently as time requirements permit. While adequately high standards of sampling should be sought, one should not overspend on sampling to obtain precision beyond that really needed or warranted by the risks and magnitudes involved in the particular decisions. Data that arrive too late for perceptive analysis and application to the problem have little value, no matter how excellent the sampling is. With respect to time, we should also recognize that a perishability or obsolescence factor may be important. Sometimes only fresh, recently collected data are useful, in which case large samples or complex sampling methods must be foregone, because they require too much time and the data become stale.

7.3 Elements and Concepts

The following terms will be used in our discussion, and some of them have certain meanings relative to sampling that should be kept in mind.

Population. Sometimes termed "universe," this is the totality of all phenomena having characteristics in common. The particular characteristics are a matter of definition, conforming to the interests of a specific study. The population might be very large and have a broad range of characteristics—for example, "all persons in the New England region who have had formal education beyond the sixth grade." Populations may also be quite narrow and conform to a complex and multiple number of qualifications. The term "population" does not denote only human beings. Interest might be in populations of dwellings, domesticated cats, establishments, selling interviews with certain types of customers, destinations of vehicles, or overdue accounts.

Parameter. This is a value or statement that describes a true characteristic of an entire population. Numerically, it might be expressed as an average, a range, or some other statistical measurement. It is the value that would be obtained if the entire population were covered in a given measurement, such as in a Bureau of the Census enumeration.

Statistic. The statistic is the value obtained from a sample of the population. It gives an estimate of what the populations parameter may be (with regard to a given characteristic). Probabilities are very high that the estimate departs somewhat from the parameter. This may result from *sampling error,* which is a risk inherent in the sampling method and in the fact that only a portion of the population has been included. It may result also from *nonsampling* error, because of failure to adhere to the sampling specifications, wrong measurements, being given wrong information by the respondents, and so on.

Precision. This is the opposite of error. It has been well described as "how closely we can produce from a sample the results which would be obtained if we should take a complete count or a census, using the same methods of measurement, questionnaire, interviewing procedure, type of enumerators, supervision, etc."[1] Precision results from two qualities in a sample: (1) its *representativeness,* which is how accurate a cross section of the population is likely to be obtained with the sampling method; and (2) its *stability,* which relates mainly to the sample size and proportion of the population included; for example, if a sample contained 40 percent of a population of 12,500 or 5,000 members, its results would be much more stable than samples containing only 1 percent or 125 members.

Confidence limits. Some degree of sampling error should be expected in any statistic drawn from a sample. Some slight deviation from the pa-

---

[1] M. H. Hansen, W. H. Hurwitz, and W. G. Madow, *Sample Survey Methods and Theory* (New York: John Wiley & Sons, Inc., 1953), p. 10.

[Handwritten marginal notes:]

"universe" totality of all phenomena having characteristics in common

value or statement that describes a true characteristic of an entire pop. "average" "range" measure of a pop.

value obtained from a sample of the pop.

$\bar{X} = \dfrac{\sum_{i=1}^{n} X_i}{n}$

precision $= \sqrt{|X - M|}$

rameter is highly probable. On the other hand, there might be a large deviation, although the probability of this occurring is rather small. One who is interpreting a statistic taken from a sample will want to know how accurate it is likely to be, or, in other words, what are the confidence limits? This needs to be expressed in terms both of a margin of sampling error and the probability of a parameter lying within that range of error (or we might put it: the probability that its estimate lies within certain ranges from the parameter). For example, a survey of the homes in a certain city found that 8.8 percent of them had Nabisco Shredded Wheat on hand. Projecting this sample statistic to the whole city, the analyst is told, one may expect that the parameter for the city is within ± 0.6 percentage point, with a probability of 95 percent. So she concludes that roughly between 8.2 and 9.4 percent of the city's homes have Nabisco Shredded Wheat, with a confidence that chances are nineteen out of twenty that the actual population parameter lies in that range.

These definitions of terms will suffice to launch our discussion. Some other, special ones will be given as we proceed.

7.4 The Essential Process

A number of tasks and decisions are involved in sampling, and our understanding of specific methods and principles is facilitated when we can orient these within the total sampling process. Therefore, we introduce an overview of the various phases of sampling, which are diagrammed and summarized in Table 7–1. Only a brief comment will be given for these phases here. The detailed treatment of these will come later.

Steps 1 and 2. The primary and very crucial step in sampling is defining the population[2] that is to be sampled, which will be called the *target population*. An adequate study design statement would have to spell out fully the sources from which the data are intended to be gathered (or, in observational studies, to be measured). The importance of then amplifying this definition and making it very complete can hardly be understated. Usually this definition must be given to a number of field interviewers or observers, who in turn will need to make quick determinations of whether a particular individual encountered is, or is not, qualified to be a member of the target population. Therefore, characteristics (attributes) of the target populaton must be described in terms of specifications that are readily determinable in the field. Sometimes field interviewers must ask questions of individuals to find out whether they qualify as part of the target population. These questions would be incor-

---

[2] The study might, in fact, be seeking information from more than one population, and one should make sure whether he is to sample a single population. Take, for instance, a study of classroom furniture preferences in "educational institutions." This would embrace both the elementary–secondary schools and the college–university world of higher education. The characteristics of these two types of institutions differ substantially, and one should not treat them as one educational population for which a single sampling procedure would be correct. Each would need a separate sampling plan.

how to collect data:

TABLE 7–1. Principal Steps in the Sampling Process

Questions Faced	Steps To Take
I. Definitions What are the characteristics of desired sources of information? Who or what should be represented in the sample?	1. Obtain these stipulations from the research design. 2. Define population from which this sample is to be drawn. 3. Establish a "frame" of the population in lists, maps, or working descriptions.
II. Sample design How will the sample be selected? How large a sample is needed to satisfy the requirements of the problem or decision under study?	4. Determine whether a nonprobability or a probability method will be used in selecting sample units. 5. Determine required confidence limits, the confidence coefficient, and prescribe the maximum acceptable sampling error in this decision and situation. 6. Compute size and composition of sample to meet these requirements.
III. Gather data from or about the sample Which specific members of the population will be in the sample?	7. Instruct the field staff as to identifying and selecting the actual members in the sample. 8. Pretest sampling plan. 9. Select sample and obtain data.
IV. Appraise sample results Does the obtained sample meet the specifications?	10. Compute standard errors and determine statistical significance. 11. If reliable, independent data are available, compare with sample results.

porated in the questionnaire (if one is used in the study). Some characteristics are visible and would simply be observed by a trained interviewer.

Step 3. The *frame* is, in a sense, the boundaries that circumscribe the population. Often these boundaries are geographic, which would be the case if one wanted to cover the population of the "Seattle area." Mapped and distinguishable features would need to be specified, obviously, for the sample to be taken from the desired area.

A frame also might be a listing of all members of a relevant population. For example, the names in a city directory, a city tax role, or the names of all the students enrolled at a specific university. Sometimes the population consists of the names on documents located within filing cabinets, and then the frame is the stipulation of the locations of the documents. The requirement of a frame is absent from sampling in physical sciences and some other fields where location or boundaries are not significant. However, in marketing studies the frame is essential.

A listing of every element or unit of the population would constitute a perfect sampling frame. In reality, though, most sampling frames are found to be far from perfect, owing to omissions, incomplete data, and outdated information. For example, suppose that a study involved conducting a survey of the residents of the Orlando, Florida, area by telephone. At first glance the most obvious frame for this case would involve the use of the telephone directory. Upon consideration, though, it would be a far-from-accurate frame, because many residents of Orlando would not subscribe to telephone service at the time for one reason or another, and there are many unlisted numbers. Our survey would suffer from these inaccuracies in the population's frame. These inaccuracies lead to *frame errors*. Unfortunately, some frame error is probably unavoidable in most marketing studies.

Step 4. There are two basic alternative approaches to sample selection and several alternative ways of employing each, from which the researcher must choose the most appropriate for the situation. Getting a representative sample by efficient means is the chief problem in the whole process. Alternative approaches will be discussed at length beginning in Section 7.6. Basically, however, we are concerned with practical sampling, and efficiency demands that we use efficient selection methods and also avoid taking overly large samples, which are unjustified by the level of precision needed in the decision. The decision maker must specify his or her required precision, a matter to which we will return in Section 8.1.

Steps 5 and 6. With the consideration of the sample selection method determined in step 4, one decides the desirable sample size. This is the subject of Chapter 8.

Steps 7 and 8. These are preparatory to executing the selection of the ultimate sample members. The importance of instructions, which draw upon the determinations made back in steps 2 and 3, is obvious. Step 8, the pretest, is a preliminary or shakedown trial of the whole data-gathering process, of which sampling is one aspect. Benefits of the pretest to sampling include (1) experience that indicates how readily the sampling can be administered in the field and reveals any misunderstandings and errors of the field staff; (2) foreshadowing of the range of characteristics of the population relative to the sought data, which may also provide significant stratification criteria; (3) indication of the homogeneity, distribution, and multiplicity of the population(s) samples, which might call for revision of sampling plans; and (4) partial indication of the stability likely in a sample. If the pretest is conducted in only a few clustered portions of the population, however, little or no dependable evidence may be yielded with respect to any except the first-mentioned benefit.

Steps 9, 10, and 11. Because the observations or interviews are conducted in the field, the critical problem arises of assuring that the sampling plan has faithful adherence, even though one faces the practical certainty that part of the target population will be missed. When the data are in, the researchers naturally are curious to learn whether they appear to have gotten a satisfactory sample, which is the subject that we shall treat in Section 7.10.

7.5 Sampling Conditions in Marketing

[handwritten margin note: problems of marketing researchers when they collect data]

Understanding general theories of sampling and of a sample's statistical significance is important if one is to understand the more specific subject of sampling marketing phenomena. In the practical marketing context, sampling methods that might otherwise be theoretically ideal may be quite impractical. In applied studies, too, sampling ideals must be balanced against other considerations: the degree of precision that the decision really demands, cost and time considerations, and the frequent likelihood that nonsampling errors pose a greater threat than sampling errors.

The qualifications that we have just cited do not diminish the pervasive effects of basic sampling principles, but we are going to describe numerous departures from the simpler approaches in response to conditions in marketing. First some of these conditions will be posed, and then methods often employed in marketing studies will be presented.

As our interest is particularly in the application of sampling theory in marketing, let us begin by indicating some of the ways in which marketing circumstances tend to differ from the postulates underlying general sampling theory. Some of the respects in which marketing conditions frequently or normally differ from those presumed in sampling theory are these:

1. An atomistic or highly diffused population is assumed in general theory, but marketing populations tend to be somewhat clustered. In any city, you will note a very uneven distribution of its population by either home or job location. Its gasoline stations are distributed in a different pattern and highly clustered along certain thoroughfares and near certain intersections. Out of, say, 105 gasoline stations, perhaps the thirty that pump over 50 percent of the gasoline are located in a more peculiar pattern. If the interest is battery sales, one may find, for example, that such sales are more concentrated in certain suburban stations than in downtown ones.

2. Populations of infinite or extremely large size—the assumption in general theory—tend not to be of concern in most marketing studies. Marketing studies concern finite or relatively small sizes of population that introduce special considerations in sampling.

3. Marketing managers very frequently are dealing with a population with which they have had previous sampling experience or about which they can obtain useful advance knowledge. This enables them to utilize simplifying procedures that would be inadvisable when dealing with the totally unknown population that general theory often considers.

4. We would assume in general theory that when our procedure would choose or seek a specific member of the population, it would be readily identified and observed. When we are dealing with a particular population of people, as in most marketing problems, these are mobile and often unavailable sample units, which complicates the procedures and disturbs the representativeness of the sample. A related marketing problem is the refusal of people to cooperate in providing the requested data, which either produces voids in some segments of the desired sample or entails obtaining equivalent substitute members.

5. Scientific sampling principles are sometimes knowingly violated, with probable sacrifice of sample precision, to avoid more serious nonsampling errors. For example, a particular field study may require such highly competent interviewing personnel that not enough interviewers could be found to conduct as massive a survey as probability theory would dictate necessary. In complicated studies, the quality of field work demanded may require small samples to keep the costs within permissible bounds—or it may preclude conducting field work in remote places although scientific selection would choose them.

These conditions are mentioned to bring realism into our views of sampling, not to discourage the thorough study of scientific sampling. Because of the losses that may be incurred when making business decisions based on data provided by a poor sample, marketing researchers should employ the generally accepted principles and methods of sampling insofar as conditions and practical considerations allow. In view of this, our discussion will blend the ideal with the practical.

The extent to which scientific principles are adhered to in sampling for marketing studies relates also to the aims, the time, and the financial resources of the research sponsors. High degrees of precision and fidelity to sampling principles tend to characterize academic research projects and many governmental projects that are not under time pressures. Applied studies which facilitate business decisions often face serious time perishability, in which late results have little value. The executive typically does not require very high statistical confidence limits, accepting often only a two-to-one probability level, and corporate budgets rarely lavish large sums on a single project when there are many decisions competing for research dollars and staff time. A marketing researcher should be versatile in sampling, capable of obtaining samples that give highly precise results, yet also doing more "quick and dirty" sampling that still yields findings of tolerable dependability for the purposes.

The several practical techniques that we shall discuss, however, should not be considered to be careless shortcuts. Rather they are efforts to obtain more efficiency (in time, funds, and use of expert personnel) through the use of controls, through taking a series of steps that limit error hazards, or through ingenuity in mathematical reasoning.

7.6 Basic Selection Approaches

The two qualities most desired in a sample (besides that of providing the appropriate findings), as we have noted, are its representativeness and its stability. Representativeness is of great concern, so we shall discuss in this section the manner of selecting the units to be included in the sample. In Chapter 8 we shall address the aspect of stability and the ramifications of choosing an appropriate sample size.

Sample units may be selected in a variety of ways. In practice, the method selected will depend on the objectives of the study, the available financial resources, time limitations, the nature of the population, and the expertise of the researcher. A useful way of classifying the sampling methods is shown in Figure 7–1.

The methods fall into two general types: probability selection methods, and nonprobability methods. As we will soon see, various methods of selection might be employed under each of these types. However, let us momentarily consider them only broadly.

Probability methods are those in which the sample units or members are chosen at random. This should not be confused with *opportunistic sampling* (sometimes called convenience sampling), which refers to the method where field interviewers or observers exert some influence in the selection of the sample units. Opportunistic sampling would probably contain a quite unrepresentative cross section of the target population. Random sampling rigorously adheres to a precisely specified system that permits no arbitrary or biased selection. Randomness selects the sample units by chance, but it gives every member of the population an equal chance of being selected. When this is strictly adhered to, the laws of probability apply. This has important advantages, as will be explained later.

In contrast to probability methods, *nonprobability methods* are those that purposefully or accidentally select the specific members of the sample in a nonrandom manner. A sample can be selected "accidentally" when the sampling units are selected "conveniently." In this case there is no attempt to select a representative sample. On the other hand, by the deliberate choice of the sample members according to a plan, the intention is to obtain a proper cross section of the population. In practice, certain criteria are designated for specific proportions of the population units to be included in the total sample. This avoids chance with respect to particular characteristics for which criteria were prescribed. However, it does not avoid hazards with respect to other characteristics of the obtained sample, for which no probabilities of selection can be stated. In general, probability methods are more scientific and more efficient in obtaining accurate samples, but we shall see that in some situations nonprobability methods are more practical and preferable.

202

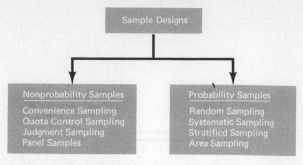

Figure 7–1. Classification of Sampling Methods

7.7 Nonprobability Methods of Selection

Let us now discuss some nonprobability sample selection methods that are useful in obtaining marketing studies' samples. Nonprobability selection can be (1) opportunistic, or (2) purposive. Opportunistic choice is done at sheer convenience. As previously stated, there is no specific "method" of choosing the sampling units. On the other hand, in purposive sampling selection the sampler designates deliberately the population units or their characteristics—not by mere whim, but by a specific method that is intended to obtain a true cross section of the population.

7.7.1 Convenience Sampling

In *convenience sampling selection,* as the name implies, the sampler chooses the sampling units on the basis of "convenience" or "accessibility." This form of sample selection is commonly used in the "man on the street" form of interviewing; and, at times, associates may be interviewed simply because they are accessible. An example of convenience sampling in testing a potential new product would simply be the adding of the new product in the appropriate section of the store and observing how well it moves in relation to other products in the same category.

It should be noted that this method of sampling should only be used for special situations in marketing research. The problem with convenience samples is that we have no exact way of determining the representativeness of the chosen sample. Generally, the "convenient" units' characteristics differ significantly from the less "convenient" units' characteristics, thereby injecting bias of unknown magnitude in the estimate. Therefore, a convenience sample is not recommended if it is used to estimate values of the target population for descriptive or causal research studies. However, this method may be used with exploratory designs when all that is needed is an approximation of the desired phenomena, and there is the constraint of obtaining this approximate estimate quickly and inexpensively. A convenience sample may also be of value in the pretest phase of the study, in which the questionnaire is pretested to help ensure question comprehension and to detect errors that so easily creep into questionnaire designs. The operation of a convenience sample in this case is best illustrated by a recent pretesting incident:

> A study was conducted on children's responses to television commercials. Immediately after exposure to the stimulus presentation, subjects were to be interviewed concerning their recall and understanding of particular commercial content.
>
> The questionnaire was pretested to ascertain whether the questions were clear and simple enough to be readily understood by children. Difficulty in arranging for children to view the commercials at convenient times (for them, their parents, and the experimenter), which was the time constraint for those conducting the experiment, called for a convenience sample— only six children, three first graders and three sixth graders, to pretest the questionnaire. They were selected because of their accessibility at the time of the pretest.
>
> The pretest indicated that in general the questionnaire was clear and simple enough for the children. However, it did uncover means to keep the interviewing procedure flexible so that changes could be instituted, depending upon the interviewing situation. Without the pretesting on a convenience sample, there would have been no opportunity to test for comprehension or potential trouble areas in the interviewing procedures.

7.7.2 Quota Control Sampling — *used only @ final phase of selecting the units in the sample.*

✱ utilizes some specific parameters & nos.

In the commonly used method of *quota control sampling*, one utilizes known parameters that describe the population. The sample planner prescribes that the field workers select a sample that conforms to these parameters. Each field worker is assigned quotas of the number of units (usually persons) to include according to one or more characteristics, for which they are to qualify an individual before interviewing her or him.

For example, you might be sampling the adults of the Baton Rouge metropolitan area and basing quotas on data about its residents. Perhaps you have decided that three characteristics closely associated with your survey's objectives are persons' sex, age, and race. You also have Census of Population data available that indicate the following percentages of Baton Rouge's over-twenty populations in cross-analysis of these three characteristics. For the first two age brackets, you are given the following percentages of that city's total adult population:

Age (years)	White Male	White Female	Nonwhite Male	Nonwhite Female
20–24	6.16	6.65	2.25	2.73
25–29	4.85	4.86	1.34	1.67
Total of age 20 and over	35.48	38.44	11.58	14.50

If the total sample was desired to be 800 persons, that simply would be broken down according to those percentages. We would specify in the age 20–24 group the following numbers: male, white—49; female, white—53; male, nonwhite—18; female, nonwhite—22. In this manner aggregate quotas are determined.

advantage

The quota control method has the advantage that the sample will conform to the chosen parameters of the population, if the field workers—or whoever does the actual selection—faithfully fill the quotas correctly. On the surface, at least, this may seem safer than trusting to chance, as in probability selection.

Quota control has potential weaknesses, however, that may destroy the validity of a sample thus obtained. Here are several:

weaknesses of quota control sampling

1. The field workers must be scrupulous and precisely fill their quotas with exactly the numbers of persons with the prescribed characteristics. An interviewer, who has completed all but one of her quota and is searching for a hard-to-find person, is likely to cheat a bit by substituting others. It is difficult to verify that the quotas are filled accurately.

2. The population may not be listed by the relevant characteristics, and they might be hard to identify. Age, for instance, would have to be asked and might be reported unreliably.

3. The data that are available may be obsolete and incorrectly report the current parameters of the population (for example, the 1970 Census data used above). Often data are unavailable in the analyses required, especially for small areas.

4. Even when the sample does conform to the characteristics used in the quotas, the sample may be distorted on other factors of importance in the study. An interviewer could canvass her assigned areas of Baton Rouge only in the daytime, but fulfill the quota. This would miss most of the employed males and females, if the survey was conducted at homes, and those found at home would scarcely be a good cross section.

Despite its faults, however, quota control sampling is widely used in marketing studies—indeed, some observers say that it is more widely used in commercial studies than random selection. Sometimes this is because of the work and time involved in selecting good probability samples. In the absence of an up-to-date directory or listing a good sample demands actual inspection of the sample areas before making interview assignments. Quota controls tend to be used in election forecast polls, for there is not time to complete probability selected assignments.

7.7.3 Judgment Sampling — *that which is done deliberately.*

sampling done deliberately

Quota control sampling is used only at the final phase of selecting the units in the sample. Judgment sampling is that which is done deliberately and not in conformance with any imposed quota. When used with multiphase procedures restricting the area, judgment may be used during the final phase or the intermediate stages of narrowing the total population down to subareas.

The term "judgment" has been used to label two quite different sorts of deliberate choice. One might be called *sampling by opinion*. Someone who is well acquainted with the population decides which members in his or her *judgment* would constitute a proper cross section representing the parameters of pertinence to the research. This method might be used in a study of sales personnel for a corporation, in which the researcher wishes to make certain analysis of top-grade, medium-grade, and low-grade salespeople. Having specified the qualities that are important in the study, the expert (perhaps the sales manager) indicates the people who, in his or her knowledge, would be representative of each of the three strata. This obviously is not a scientific method; in the absence of more certain evidence, such a judgment method might have to be used.

The other form of judgment selection might be termed a *statistical judgment*. In this method, the criteria for selection are specified and data on these factors are scrutinized to find population members that meet these specifications. The choice is deliberate (purposive), not a random manner, which involves the probabilities of drawing a chance selection that does not conform to the specifications.

A number of situations may be cited when this sort of judgment might be used logically. If a member of a panel drops out, the supervisor of the panel might take that member's attributes and seek another person with similar attributes—to be chosen deliberately. When drawing a sample of firms in an industry, such as truck lines, one might set up data describing the types of companies that would provide a proper cross section (for example, by location of its lines, number of vehicles, age of firm, credit rating, and so forth). Then one could search a trucking industry directory and choose companies that are considered to meet these criteria. A third example is the choice of subareas in an area sampling method. Suppose that eighty nonmetropolitan counties are to be chosen that would be representative of all significant types of agriculture. Data on all such counties (as in the Census of Agriculture) could be assembled, after specifying the criteria, and deliberate choice could be made to comprise a "miniature agricultural America."

This form of judgment sampling can be valid only when adequate data are available to describe the whole population's parameters and similar data to describe each member or subarea. Also, the sampler must be able to restrain any personal whim or prejudice and base selection solely on the data. With these conditions present, one can draw a representative sample by this method. It has an appealing efficiency, despite the considerable effort often entailed in preparing proper statistical criteria and in matching them, because it avoids the chances in random selection of drawing misrepresentative sample. It has the same drawback as quota control selection, in that the laws of probability cannot be applied, for the chances of inclusion in the sample are indeterminable.

A *panel* is a semipermanent sample whose members may be included repetitively for successive studies or sometimes for a number of waves of data gathering in a single study. An established panel offers a source for data or opinion reporting that affords important advantages. Panel members have agreed in advance to furnish requested information, and so communication with them ordinarily is by mail to hold down expenses.

There are a number of large national panels that are employed mainly for marketing data. Two of the pioneering leaders in this field were Market Research Corporation of America and the National Family Opinion, Inc. To give you some appreciation of what a national panel comprises, here are some facts about the Consumer Mail Panels (CMP) division of Market Facts, Inc.:

> The panel has approximately 70,000 names on file for households in the United States, with certain selection data on each of them. Of these households, 45,000 are placed in its "current balanced panel" utilized in mail surveys.

> The sample is balanced to parallel census data with respect to the population proportion in each of nine U.S. geographic regions. Within each region the sample makeup is apportioned to Census data for household income, population density, degree of urbanization, and panel member's age.

> The entire sample is divided into panels of 1,000 members each, drawn from the 45,000 in the active panel in a manner to be representative of the nation. Market Facts can use these groups of 1,000 as building blocks to provide the number of households desired by a client. The firm also can draw samples of unique characteristics for which its computer can identify panel members from recorded data—for example, frequent air travelers or buyers of denture cleaners.

> It is stated that CMP panels draw response rates of 90 percent and over for ordinary questionnaires and between 70 and 80 percent on complex questionnaires.

The ability to select and quickly contact such well-balanced samples and to obtain such relatively high response rates by mail is very attractive to research clients. It is evident why panels are being increasingly utilized. Nevertheless, there are many limitations in gathering data by mail.

From the standpoint of sampling, the method of selection is by quota control, a purposive selection. Panel members are recruited for membership, not drawn at random. For the CMP panel that we have been describing, recruiting is conducted through the following means:

1. Through selected direct mailing, using directories and lists.
2. Through current panel members, who are asked about their friends and anyone that they may know in other cities than their own, who might wish to join a panel.

3. In conjunction with personal interview studies being conducted by this agency, new members may be recruited by leaving a recruitment folder and application. If the applicant voluntarily returns the questionnaire, she may be considered as a candidate for the panel.

4. When some quota cells are proving difficult to fill, the personal interviewing staff may conduct special screening interviews to find new members with the needed characteristics.

Thus a deliberate procedure is followed to find or to screen individuals who are interested in cooperating in the panel. The incentive for cooperating, by the way, is to earn "points" that are cumulated toward earning premiums chosen from a catalog, similar to trading stamps.

advantages of panels →

The chief advantages of panels, besides cost and time saving, are sampling efficiencies. Since the panel composition is known in advance, for instance, they are in a sense prevalidated. In the event that a very high response ratio is not forthcoming, of course, the makeup of the responding portion needs to be compared with the quota benchmarks to validate the cross section. Another major advantage is the use of such a fixed sample for measuring change, in that the repeated reporting from identical sources eliminates the possible error in a changing makeup which is a hazard of noncomparability when sources are chosen anew for successive measurements. It is possible with panels, also, to trace shifts of behavior over time on the part of individual members.

Panels have disadvantages too, which may at times cause serious problems. These should be carefully scrutinized as possibly serious sample distortions:

disadvantages of panels

1. The panel may not represent accurately the whole market—or whatever it is supposed to represent. As Market Facts, Inc., recognizes in a brochure on its CMP: "No panel is a truly representative sample of the population because of the lack of willingness of about four out of five households to join and participate in a regular controlled panel facility.[3]

2. Members of a panel may become conditioned sooner or later by becoming "professional" in their behavior and observations and thus atypical of the population they are intended to represent. In recognition of this danger, the CMP panel, for instance, adds approximately 30 percent newly recruited members annually. It moves other members from active into reserve groups, and vice versa, so that in a given year only a minority is retained in the panel from the previous year.

3. Members do drop out of panels voluntarily and need replacement. The panel organization should constantly be seeking practically identical substitutes for them and for those deliberately removed, but it is not always done with equivalent replacements.

The dangers inherent in panels should not rule out their use when a

---

[3] *The Controlled Mail Panel* (Chicago: Market Facts, Inc., 1971), p. 12.

panel is well managed and its biases in samples and distorted responses are taken into account. The superiority of a panel in its efficiencies, possible depth of analysis, and disclosure of trends and flows over time tend to overshadow its shortcomings. The figures obtained from a panel, one should realize, may not be very representative in an absolute sense of being applicable to the size of the whole population. When used in a relative sense, however, they may be quite valid—and the decision maker in many or most problems is more interested in relatives than absolutes.

7.8 Probability Sampling

This section will present and explain the four inherently different approaches to probability sampling. But first we shall note some concepts that are basic to an understanding of this subject.

How does probability work in sampling? The reader may have learned this long ago, yet a momentary review may be helpful. The concept is best communicated with an illustration.

Let us say that a manufacturer of sports clothing who previously sold mainly to college women was planning to enter into the college men's field. The height of these men would be an important type of data to him, and being under the impression that height has been increasing, he would seek current figures. Let us assume that he sent his researcher to some universities to obtain such facts and that one of the universities offered her the use of recent physical examination reports on all (2,000) male students currently enrolled. The researcher took only a sample of these, but if she had included all of them in the enumeration, the parameters would have been those shown in Figure 7–2. In this chart the heights have been rounded to the nearest inch, which was sufficiently accurate for his purposes.

Through the midpoints of these vertical bars in Figure 7–2, a curved line has been drawn. As will be observed later, the distribution indicated by this curve approximates the "normal curve of error." The frequencies in the categories on either side of the midpoint of the curve descend rather evenly, and the arithmetic mean (which is 5 feet 10.2 inches) falls in the central and most numerous category.

The researcher is going to draw a probabilty (random) sample. If she drew a sample of only one, and since all members of the population would have an equal chance of being selected, she might have drawn the shortest man (5 feet 1.8 inches) or, at the other extreme, a giant of 6 feet 8.1 inches. The category with the highest probability of being chosen is in the middle group of 5 feet 10 inches. However, chances are 89 out of 100 that she would not draw the single individual from that group.

The size of sample that she elected to draw was 200 men. She could, in this case, draw the shortest 200, which would yield the quite unrepresentative mean value of 5 feet 6.8 inches. As an equal possibility (since she is selecting by chance), she could draw the 200 tallest (mean of 6 feet 4.5 inches). In Figure 7–3 we have plotted the number of possible sample means, at the indicated mean heights, that she would tend to

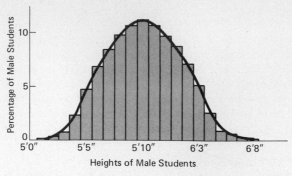

FIGURE 7–2. Distribution of Male Students' Heights in a University

Source: Based on measurements by Department of Physical Education for Men, Southern Illinois University, 1967.

draw at random. Since this is circumscribed between the values of 5 feet 6.8 inches and 6 feet 4.5 inches, a line drawn between these points would be a more peaked curve than the one in Figure 7–2. Nonetheless, it has two vital similarities: (1) its modal point also is at the population's parameter of an arithmetic mean of 5 feet 10.2 inches, and (2) it is the same type of curve.

Random selection has the important characteristic of tending to yield estimates of the population's characteristics that group around its true mean value, with a distribution of probabilities that conforms to the actual distribution of the particular characteristic over the population. And this probability operates according to the law of probability, which permits the sampling error to be estimated mathematically. The advantage of this will become more evident later, for now we shall discuss methods of probability selection.

7.8.1 Random Sampling

ea. possible sample combo. has an equally prob. of occurrence + ea item in the pop has an equal chance of being included in the sample.

In our example it would be quite easy to draw a sample from the whole population, the entire 2,000 physical examination reports. There are several methods of probability selection that the researcher might use to select the 200.

One way would be to write all 2,000 names on cards, since the forms would be too bulky. The researcher could shuffle these and take the top card; then very thoroughly reshuffle them and again take the top card; and so on, 198 more times. This would be time consuming, so she might prefer another way.

One other method, the use of random numbers, involves the very minimum of possible bias with respect to the population members designated. Random numbers are those that have been chosen entirely without human intervention, so every number has a chance of appearing equal to every other and their order of appearance is completely jumbled, with no period-

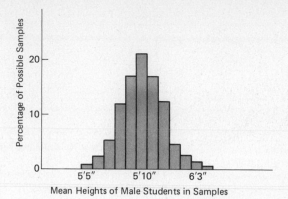

FIGURE 7-3. Distribution of Possible Sample Means of Samples of 200 Men, Drawn from the Population of Male Students in Figure 7-2

ical occurrence. Such numbers may be obtained from several published tables; a portion of one appears in Table 7-2. These numbers are grouped in fives solely for convenience and were selected individually by an electronic roulette wheel.

In our example of sampling college men's heights, the desired sample size calls for choosing 200 units out of a population of 2,000. This researcher would want 200 random numbers under 2,001 and, therefore, up to four digits. Any four-digit number above 2,000 would be ignored. Therefore, if she chose to begin with the first number in the table—although she might alter the starting point from this—she would scan and circle the four-digits groups that fall in the desired interval. Thus, she would obtain from the "population" of physical examination forms the 1950th, 1746th, 288th, 1029th, 1653rd, 1521st, and each other successive number of 2,000 or less, until she had found 2**. (See Table 7-3.)

With an *atomistic* population that is completely dispersed in location and in characteristics, simple random sampling is the logical method. This is particularly true of the infinite populations with which physical scientists so often deal.

 In principle this is the scientific ideal, because all members of the population would have an equal chance of selection. This approach may be used

TABLE 7-2. Table of Random Numbers (partial)

19502	37174	69979	20288	55210	29773	74287	75251
65344	67415	21818	59313	93278	81757	05686	73156
07082	85046	31853	38452	51474	66499	68107	23621
94049	91345	42836	09191	08007	45449		

Source: *Adapted from Rand Corporation,* A Million Random Digits *(Glencoe, Ill.: The Free Press, 1955), p. 2.*

211

TABLE 7–3. Four-Digit Groups Selected in Table of Random Numbers

19502	37174	69979	20288	55210	29773	74287	75251
65344	67415	21818	59313	93278	81757	05686	73156
07082	85046	31853	38452	51474	66499	68107	23621
94049	91345	42836	09191	08007	45449		

Source: *Rand Corporation,* A Million Random Digits *(Glencoe, Ill.: The Free Press, 1955., p. 2.*

in marketing studies when the entire population is listed and the sample might be chosen readily by some randomizing method.

Consider a type of population often sampled in marketing: households. For an example, suppose that the households in the city of Orlando, Florida, are to be sampled. This selection method requires first an up-to-date listing, for it would be ridiculous to locate and map all its approximately 45,000 homes and then sample them. If there is a satisfactory directory, splendid; but if the study requires personal visits at the homes, which by such a selection procedure would be scattered throughout the city's area of some 30 square miles, this method would be very costly. If such problems render probability sampling impractical within one city, the enormity of the job when the whole state of Florida or the whole nation is to be sampled is obvious.

Unless the population may be plucked from a file drawer or readily reached after selection from a list or a ready-made mapping of all units' locations, this theoretically ideal method is quite impractical. Even then, another objection arises: random treatment of the population risks the possibility of drawing a very unrepresentative sample (for example, getting only the tallest men in our illustration of sampling men's heights). The probabilities of such a misfortune are very small. Nevertheless, it would be preferable to avoid them. In sampling the finite and relatively fixed location types of populations that we tend to deal with in marketing research, we can turn to approaches that reduce this risk.

7.8.2 Systematic Sampling

A desirable method for selecting a random sample, if a list of the target population exists, is to use a systematic sample. This method involves selecting every n^{th} unit from the target population list after the beginning unit is chosen at random. In our example of sampling the height of college men, an ordinal selection method should be the easiest. The researcher knows that she needs every tenth of these 2,000 reports. This is derived as follows: With 2,000 students in the population *(N)* and a sample *(n)* of 200 to be chosen, the sampling fraction is n/N. For our example; $n/N = 1/10$. This indicates that 1 unit out of 10 will be selected to be included in the sample. The sampling interval is the inverse of the sampling fraction; 10 for our case. This means that after randomly selecting a starting point, every tenth unit will be chosen. To be consistently random, the researcher might choose a number between 1 and 10 from a random-number table to

212

indicate where she should start. If it turned out to be 4, she would take the fourth, fourteenth, twenty-fourth, and so forth. This presupposes that heights, in these reports, happen to be distributed randomly, or are organized in an orderly way such as a listing of the students heights from 5 feet 1.8 inches to 6 feet 8.1 inches. If this were not the case and extreme values recurred with a regular systematic frequency, the results could be seriously misleading.

However, the systematic sampling method can produce a more representative sample than a simple random sample. In our example, we are guaranteed representation from the shortest height segment to the tallest height segment. A simple random sample might not have included the shortest or the tallest members of the population. Thus, we can generalize as to the degree to which this sampling method will be more representative than a simple random sample. The representativeness of a systematic sample depends upon those items close on the list being similar to each other, and items diverse from each other are spread out on the list.

7.8.3 Stratified Sampling — *pop. divided into relatively homogeneous grps or strata + a sample is drawn from ea. grp to produce an overall sample*

Rather than have sample members selected initially from the entire population, the stratified sampling approach restricts the selection of the sample members. The restriction is accomplished by placing all members of the population into groups according to some characteristic that is common among them. Then, specified numbers of units are chosen from each of the groups, or strata, by random means. For instance, consider Figure 7–4, in which a population of families was classified by numbers of persons in each family. We could proceed at random to choose given numbers of families that had one person, two persons, and so forth.

usually performed when there is a large variation w/in the pop. on which to stratify the pop.

The number chosen in each stratum might be proportional to its share of the total population. Thus, if a sample of 400 families is to be chosen, there would be 60 families (15 percent of 400) from the first stratum, 112 from the second (28 percent of 400), and so on. If these families are selected from random within each stratum, this method provides that each has an equal chance of inclusion as fully as with simple random sampling. It might be more logical, however, to select disproportionate shares within each stratum, a matter that will be deferred to Section 7.9.1.

We could not execute stratified selection unless the population members can be identified with regard to the characteristics (hereafter referred to as the "criteria") with which they have been stratified. If the number of persons in *each* household were known, we could classify them into strata and select them by strata. A listing of families by number of persons, however, is not always available. Therefore, it might not be possible to use this particular criterion as the basis of stratification.

The stratification selection method is often practicable in sampling establishments, because some of their characteristics often appear in direc-

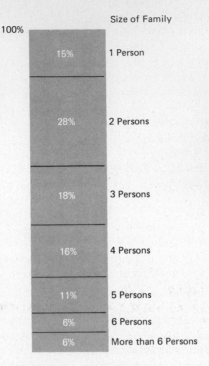

Size of Family

100%

15%	1 Person
28%	2 Persons
18%	3 Persons
16%	4 Persons
11%	5 Persons
6%	6 Persons
6%	More than 6 Persons

FIGURE 7–4. Hypothetical Family Size Distribution

tories. A survey of manufacturers in the Detroit area, for example, could use the Michigan Manufacturers Directory, because it gives the number of employees in each listed plant, which may be highly related to the desired data. This brings us to a second important requirement: that the basis of stratification be associated with the problem or characteristics that are being researched. If one were studying the merchandising of high-price carpeting, directories of department, furniture, and floor covering outlets, which might state the number of employees in each, may be used. However, the number of employees has no relationship to the quality of merchandise featured in a store (for example, discount outlets would range from very many to rather few employees), so such criteria would be irrelevant.

Stratified selection tends to be more efficient than simple random sampling. In forcing the sample in each stratum to be proportional to its portion of the whole population, the risk of under- or oversampling the strata is avoided. This markedly reduces the potential sampling error. Information on the composition of the whole population should be currently accurate, or else the allocations in each stratum will themselves be in error and the sample will be biased. Furthermore, if the criteria used to stratify the population are not associated with what the study is going to measure, they do not improve the probability of drawing a represen-

214

tative sample with respect to the data sought. Stratifying should not be done for its own sake, but it should be done when a real correlation between criteria and sought data seems likely.

7.8.4 Area Sampling

Another basis of restricting the population is clustering units into selected groups. In this form of sampling, the clusters are made up of individual units which constitute mutually exclusive and exhaustive categories or subsets. From these clusters, the researcher randomly selects those subsets to be included in the sample. Provided that the sort of phenomena sampled have fixed and known locations, they may be grouped by identifiable geographic areas, and the sample drawn is known as *area sampling.* And providing further that the number located in each area is known, the number of units to be taken from each area can be specified and made proportional to the share of the total population located in each. (Again, disproportional allocation may be used but will be considered later.) If all the areas are included in the sampling, this is a true probability sample.

Note that this approach is another form of stratification, one based on locations as the criteria of selection. Like the previously described form, it offers the advantage of controlling variability in the sample, as it assures that the geographical distribution is a proper cross section of population.

For area sampling one obviously needs a map embracing the population that is divided into smaller areas and also relevant data about those areas. The U.S. Census is conducted by areas, for which maps and certain data are published in the decennial census volumes. An example is the map of Stillwater provided by the Census of Housing, 1970, which is shown in Figure 7–5. Although this map includes only the city itself, a map of its surrounding area (Comanche County) showing the areas, known as tracts, according to which census figures are tabulated and published is also available.

We may proceed to allocate the desired sample among the total population, that is, the whole city of Stillwater. If the total sample size is to be 400 households, each of the nine tracts could be allocated a share of the sample proportional to its number of households. Thus, tract number six, which is located at the southwestern corner of the city and contained 16.9 percent of the city's households according to the 1970 Census of Housing, would be allocated sixty-nine households in our survey.

A second phase of selection now is needed to choose the particular households that would comprise the sample. In this phase we could map or list the 1,663 households in tract number six, from which we are to choose the sixty-nine households. The selection could be by the systematic method, in which we would take every twenty-fourth home, starting at some randomly selected point. We also could number all the 1,663 households and then choose sixty-nine households as designated in a

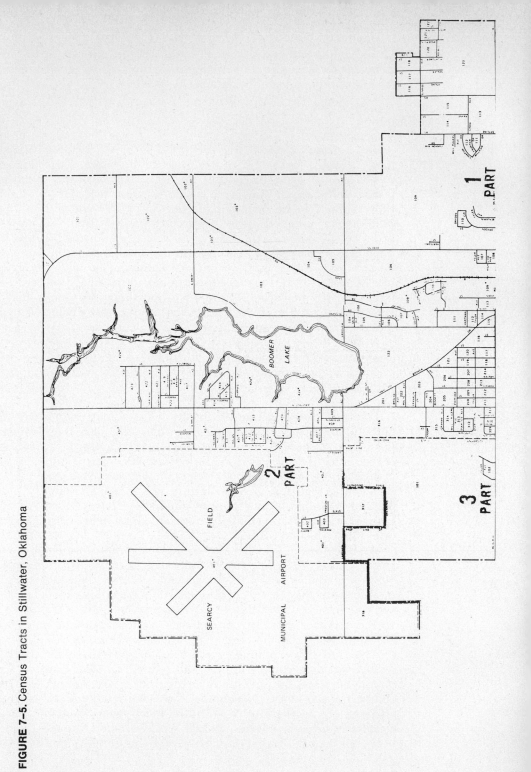

FIGURE 7–5. Census Tracts in Stillwater, Oklahoma

216

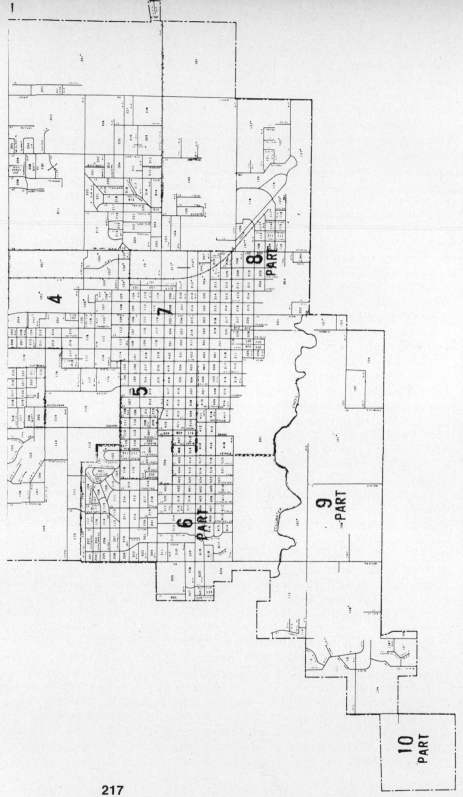

Source: Bureau of the Census, U.S. Census of Housing: 1970, Block Statistics Series HC (3), No. 193, Selected Areas in Oklahoma (Washington, D.C.: Government Printing Office, 1971).

217

table of random numbers, similar to the method illustrated in determining male students' heights. Both these methods would be simplified, if the current city directory for Stillwater is sufficiently up to date, for it would give addresses by block, thereby providing a ready-made listing for either systematic or random-number selection.

Two practical objections may be made to the method just described. One is a scientific one, in that even a relatively stable city has frequent building of new homes or razing of old ones and movement of families. For accuracy, the sampled area should be inspected to be sure that the allocation of the sample is currently the same as the distribution of the population. Another objection is that our sample in this example would be completely scattered throughout the city, which would entail much effort and time for the person canvassing in such a completely diffused pattern. Such an inefficiency should be avoided if this is possible without warping the representativeness of the sample.

The inefficiency of a scatter sample can be avoided by the use of another form of area sampling, in which the area covered is restricted to chosen portions of the whole area while the balance are eliminated. This differs from the stratification and area methods given above, wherein the restrictions served only to control the distribution of the sample selection.

This adds at least one more phase to the area selection procedure. If we were going to sample tract number six, we could cut down the coverage area greatly by picking out certain blocks in that tract and placing our subsample of sixty-nine households only in these blocks. Suppose that we decided to restrict the area in this tract to eight blocks. With random numbers we might choose blocks numbered 101, 120, 214, 221, 316, 506, 521, and 615. As all the blocks were assigned numbers, this could readily be done. Figure 7–6 shows tract number six and its block numbers.

These eight blocks together had 134 households in the 1970 Census. Assuming that we used its data, rather than a more recent city directory, a proportional allocation of households to those eight blocks, respectively, would be: 24, 11, 4, 7, 6, 7, 6, and 4. One method for choosing the sample units again could be systematic, taking every other household in each block. Alternatively, we might number all the households and choose the indicated number of homes in each block with random numbers. To be safe, one should also inspect each of the eight blocks to have a current count before making the selection. To aid the field worker in identifying the households, this inspection could list the addresses of all the sixty-nine households so that the chosen ones could be designated specifically and listed for the field coverage. To rely on field interviewers to adhere faithfully to taking every nth household, as directed, is risky.

You may have recognized that in the procedure above all the Census tracts in Stillwater were to be covered with respect to blocks selected from them. For a community of that size, such a coverage might not be too onerous or costly, but consider taking a city like Jacksonville, Florida, and its 194,000 housing units in the city proper, spread over an area of 800 square miles. As Jacksonville has 94 Census tracts, one might add

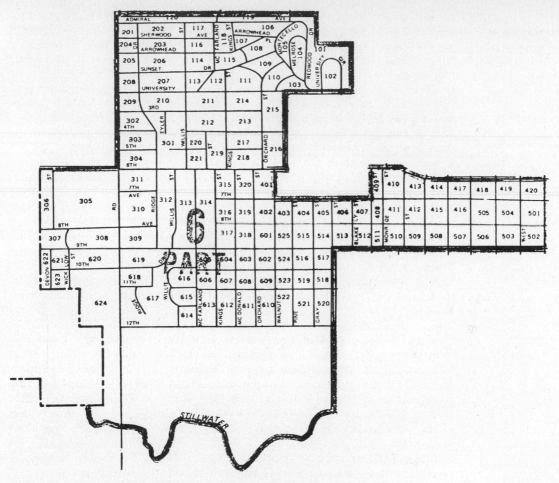

FIGURE 7–6. Census Tract Number 6 in Stillwater, Oklahoma

Source: Bureau of the Census, U.S. Census of Housing: 1970, *Block Statistics Series HC (3), No. 193, Selected Areas in Oklahoma (Washington, D.C.: Government Printing Office, 1971).*

another phase of area restriction. This would be to select only part of the tracts, eliminating the balance from coverage. Even to reduce the covered area by half, through selection of forty-seven Jacksonville tracts, would improve the efficiency of the field work substantially. Or further, one could split a number of the larger tracts so as to have a larger number to choose from—and also to include more areas that would tend to improve the representativeness. This selection of areas would be followed by selection of blocks within them, and then within the blocks would be chosen the households. All these selections could be by a random method, with the intention of obtaining a proportional cross section at each phase.

The question that now arises is: How does one decide how many of the subareas should be chosen in this area elimination method? No flat answer can be given, for this would depend on the heterogeneity existing in the population and how evenly significant characteristics are distributed around it. One can avoid the risk of taking too few areas by validating the area selections at each phase. If, for example, you had just chosen forty-seven Jacksonville Census tracts at random, you can compile data on those tracts from Census statistics on appropriate population parameters (that is, household income and/or other parameters) and determine whether or not that composite is closely comparable to the data for all of Jacksonville. If your selected areas resemble a satisfactory cross section, you can proceed to the next selection restricting phase.

We can make this validating process more concrete with an example. Returning to the city of Stillwater, remember that we made a random choice of eight blocks from tract number six. Suppose that value of the houses was a characteristic vital to your study's objectives. For all of tract number six the average value was $20,900, while in the eight selected blocks the 1970 Census data indicate an average value of $20,910.[4] This happens to squarely hit the tract's average. But if this subsample's deviation from the average value in the tract was intolerably large, a second random selection could be taken and validated. Normally one should validate by testing a number of parameters, not a single one.

We have been discussing area selection in terms of one relatively small area within the confines of a single city. Marketers usually are interested in larger areas than this—for example, all women who launder clothes at home in the United States or all dentists in California. Area restriction is a practical necessity in such studies' sampling. A national sampling can begin with all the counties in the fifty states of the nation. Beyond this breakdown, one should also delineate sections within the larger metropolitan areas and include them individually among over 3,000 county areas for selection. The reason for this is the very large concentrations in a big city, such as Los Angeles, which would be eliminated wholly if their county (for example, Los Angeles County) happened not to be chosen.

After the phase of choosing the counties and portions in metropolitan areas, these, in turn, would be subdivided into areas from which selection would be made. Then Census tracts would be selected; then blocks of small rural sections would be selected; and finally the sample units. Stratification of areas and then choice from strata should be employed to assure representativeness. For example, all counties and metropolitan sections might be stratified by educational level, by percent employed in manufacturing, or by other significant criteria. One national sample for

---

[4] In the event you are going to use Census of Housing data on value of residences, it should be noted that we have oversimplified the task. For rented housing units the Census gives monthly rental values, whereas for owned units, resale values are given. For samples combining both owned and rented, the analyst must find a means of equating rents with resale values and then convert them into the latter to provide data on one basis for sampling purposes.

a survey conducted annually divides the nation first into sixty-six cells on the basis of five criteria, which are cross-tabulated as its first phase. Each cell contains a large number of counties and metropolitan sections, and this restriction tends to improve greatly the probability of getting proper representation of these criteria and other factors that are associated with them.

There is a final phase in any form of multiphase sampling that has only been implied above: selection of the individual person (or unit) who will be included. This is a considerable problem when drawing samples from households, although it can be a serious matter when sampling business firms. (For instance, who in an office has decisive influence on choice of typewriter purchases and therefore should be interviewed in a typewriter market study?) For samples of the general population at their homes, perhaps one spokesman for each household is desired, whom interviewers should be instructed to select. Instead, the target may be a cross section of all able persons above a given age, in which case a method of rotation or the inclusion of all such persons in the selected household needs to be in the instructions. Obviously, this final phase of selection is as important to obtaining valid samples as the earlier phases.

Thus far we have described four major approaches to the probability selection: (1) simple random treatment of the population, (2) systematic sampling, (3) stratification by chosen characteristics, and (4) area selection, the geographical aspect in selecting a sample. This hardly exhausts the approaches that are used in probability selection, but they are the most commonly used sampling techniques.

7.9   Techniques for Specific Situations

A number of special procedures have been developed that increase sampling efficiency when properly employed or that apply to certain conditions. We are going to describe each briefly, although we shall not attempt to explain the mathematics relating to each of them.

7.9.1   Disproportional Sampling

We have assumed that the researcher would want to draw a sample composed of units whose members are directly in proportion of their characteristics relative to the total population. For example, if 15 percent of vacuum-cleaner owners are located in towns of under 10,000 population, proportional sampling would seek to have 15 percent of a sample's members in towns of that size category (if this characteristic is relevant to consumers' interest in a new type of vacuum cleaner). However, the following example indicates that proportional sampling may not be efficient.

Let us say that retail food stores exist in the following percentages with regard to numbers of stores and their aggregate sales volume, and within the geographical area that frames the population concerned in a study of food stores:

Types of Stores	Percentage of All Food Stores	Percentage of Retail Food Sales
Corporate chains	8	26
Voluntary group members	10	30
Large independents	12	16
Medium-sized independents	30	19
Small independents	40	9
	100	100

Perhaps the first thought is to apportion a sample to the percentage of stores in each category. In a sample of 500 stores, then, corporate chain stores would number 40, while small independents would be represented by 200 stores. On second thought, this is illogical, for the small independents hold such a small share of the sales volume and probably are relatively insignificant to the problem being investigated. And not many chain companies, store locations, types of clientele, and the like would probably be included in a subsample of a mere forty chain stores.

Therefore, disproportioned sampling seems to be indicated in this case. Perhaps the sample could be allocated on the basis of each category's share of sales. This would lead to having 130 corporate chain stores and only 45 small independents. Since this has been a deliberate manipulation of the sample apportionment and has been determined on (presumably) accurate data about the population, the obtained results can be reweighted back to their correct proportions. For instance, one item of data obtained from the disproportionate sample might have been the number of employees per store. Let us say that the aggregate number of employees found in the 130 corporate chain stores was 5,300 and in the 45 small independents was 70. These can be converted to their proper shares in proportion to the population with fractions composed of their actual proportions in the numerator and sample proportions in the denominator, like this:

Corporate chain stores: $5,300 \times 40/130 = 1,360$ employees

Small independent stores: $70 \times 200/45 = 311$ employees

This disproportional allocation is also questionable. The basic question may be: Are 130 corporate chain stores really needed to obtain a fair sample relative to the confidence interval and coefficient sought? Or would a mere 45 small independent stores suffice? Another important question brings up a sampling aspect that we have not yet mentioned: How heterogeneous are the corporate chain stores and the other strata, within the stratum, in aspects important to the study? If all corporate chain stores were alike, one store could well represent all of them—an absurd statement that emphasizes the matter of heterogeneity. If chain stores were the most heterogeneous stratum of the five, then the largest disproportionate sample might be sought from them. And if all five strata were equally heterogeneous, it might seem wisest to select 100 in each. Yet, returning to the first question raised, the problem being solved might (for example) call for a greater precision in the corporate chain stratum than in the others.

All this may seem rather confusing, and we are not going to declare that there is one correct way to allocate a sample disproportionately—either in the given case or in any other population and problem. The sample size determination should consider all three aspects: (1) the relevance of the various strata to the specific problem, (2) the desired confidence interval and coefficient, and (3) the relative degrees of heterogeneity in the subpopulations of the strata. Therefore, the determination of disproportional sample allocations is a matter for special consideration in each case.

7.9.2   Double Sampling

In determining the desirable sample size and usually in establishing the method of sample selection, the researcher must have some knowledge about the population to be sampled. Frequently, there is so little advance knowledge that it would be too risky to prepare sampling plans in such ignorance. This problem may be removed simply by taking a preliminary sample of the population, which obtains only those measurements needed to permit intelligent sampling. Thus a sort of two-phase sampling process takes place: the first phase providing information on which a more precise sample may be taken for the second sample, which is used for the intensive investigation to obtain all the data.

The first sample may be relatively large, perhaps exceeding the second sample, when the information wanted for sampling is easily obtained. Perhaps, for example, a quick telephone survey would suffice (if a large enough number of telephones) or a mere tour through areas to be sampled would provide enough information when only observable characteristics need to be recorded. One can compute the optimal allocation of field work resources between the two places or samples to determine how large the preliminary sample should be relative to that of the main investigation.[5]

An instance in which double sampling is quite desirable occurs when selecting traffic samples. This form of sampling deals with studies of any moving or transitory traffic. For example, if a study were concerned with interviewing the customers of supermarkets, and if the researcher lacked advance information of the number of customers patronizing the stores

---

[5] Such procedures are described in W. G. Cochran, *Sampling Techniques* (New York: John Wiley & Sons, Inc., 1963), pp. 328–32.

on various days at various hours, she might first have the stores sampled to obtain counts of the traffic at stipulated periods. The second sample, for the interviews, would then be based on a large preliminary determination of the population size (and perhaps observable characteristics of the customers).

7.10 Validation

The researcher is properly concerned with whether or not the gathered sample is satisfactory and wishes to "validate" it to determine whether or not the obtained sample represents an accurate cross section of the population, particularly with respect to parameters critical to his study's objectives. In part, this assurance would be enhanced by planning and supervision to assure that the field work adhered faithfully to the sampling plan.

There can be an empirical check on the characteristics of the obtained sample by comparing sample data with other reliable data, such as census benchmark data, which would be a partial check on the sample's representatives. If such classification data appear representative, then the representative character of different or original data on the population sampled depends on the logical structure of the questionnaire design and other aspects of the data-collection process. It should be emphasized, however, that available benchmark data are frequently outdated. In fact, however, the only proof of representativeness is faithful adherence to an accurate, carefully carried out, probability sample design.

The best validation of a sample is generally considered to be simply the knowledge that a good probability design has been accurately implemented. With that assurance, if in fact the sampling has been of such quality, one proceeds to compute and to use standard errors, confidence limits, and other data from the completed sample. If the initial assumptions or estimates regarding the types of frequency distributions in the various part of the population, the estimates of means, standard deviations, percentages, and so on, were reasonably accurate, then the sample should conform to the advance estimates made in the process of determining the required type and size of sample. If certain of the advance estimates were not sufficiently accurate, then the actual sample may have a higher or lower degree of reliability than desired, depending upon the differences from estimates actually determined and upon the results of different combinations of such differences. Good sample design provides a margin of error for these differences and ordinarily gives results adequate for major decision making, although it may not meet reliability requirements for certain subareas or specific detail aspects.

7.11 Summary

This discussion has had a limited objective: to provide an overview of the problems and the methods of sampling. This should enable understanding of sampling's general nature and techniques wherewith one can categorize intelligently the various methods and appreciate the work entailed and the benefits that may be gained in the various methods. Sampling is a complex subject, whose scientific execution requires mathematical knowledge and study that would be inappropriate in a comprehensive research textbook. The reader who will be engaged in sophisticated sampling must read much further about the subject.

Although adequate sampling is important to valid findings, one can place too much weight on sampling relative to the other phases in the research process. Accurate information about the best hypotheses to solve a correctly defined problem are more vital to profitable and valid research than are the niceties of scientific sampling. Most of the literature and concepts of sampling are not related to the sort of phenomena and problems encountered in marketing field studies. For example, the concept of "probability" is splendid in theory and validity, but it becomes somewhat a will-o'-the-wisp in many difficult field surveys.

Of practical necessity, then, shortcuts in sampling are used in commercial marketing surveys. Sampling sizes quite small compared to those stipulated by mathematical formulas not only are generally employed but tend to prove satisfactory for marketing decisions. The decisions of determining an appropriate sample size is dealt with in Chapter 8. Also, within the limited funds that tend to be available or justified, it may be wiser to stress high-quality work in other aspects than to skimp their quality in order to obtain very large samples.

These comments should not be derogative of the need to employ as sound sample selection methods as can be afforded. Those using data obtained from samples should always make allowance for the potential sampling error. Sampling is an essential subject to be mastered by the doer and the interpreter of marketing research.

8 Sample-Size Decisions

The size of samples is the second major determination, and Chapter 8 deals with that. It should enable you to answer such questions as these:

What is sampling error? Nonsampling error?

What conditions are prerequisite to being able to measure sampling error?

What is a confidence interval? A confidence coefficient? What do we call the principal measure of the reliability of samples? How would you calculate it?

What are the factors that affect the decision on sample size when you are measuring attributes? How should you specify them?

What is the method of solving for sample size?

What is the cost aspect of sample size?

What are the factors and method of deciding sample size when you are estimating proportions?

What is stratified sample size? How would you calculate the size of a stratified sample?

As a research investigation seeks to gather data, a vital question is whether or not the decision maker is going to be able to rely on generalizations made from the data. If the data employed as the basis of conclusions are drawn from a sample rather than a complete census of the target population, which normally is the case in marketing studies, one must know what conclusions can properly be inferred from the sample. This question may arise on two types of occasions: (1) before making the survey and measurements, when the researcher wants to specify a number of population units that are neither (a) so few as to render the risk of sampling error intolerably large, nor (b) too many, which would be inefficient; or (2) after the measurements have been made and data processed (or perhaps obtained as secondary data) when the researcher wants to judge either how large the sampling error might be and whether to accept the data's ostensible implications about the hypothesis.

Fortunately for the researcher, the science of statistics provides techniques for the determination of probable sampling error (in which interpretations may be qualified) and its effects on the needed sample size. The foundations of statistical principles are presented first, in a sense to explain why there is a justification for the use of sampling techniques. Subsequent sections tie together the statistical principles and sampling techniques designed to select the appropriate sample size.

8.1 Fundamental Conditions of Sampling:

If we are going to make general statements based on the findings of a study conducted among a sample (as opposed to an entire population), a number of conditions must be met. First, the sample must have been drawn at random.

Judgments regarding the size of sample or the statistical significance of an already measured sample may be based on mathematics employing the laws of probability. The laws are applicable, however, only when the sample selection has been at random. If the population has been stratified and then random sampling used, the laws apply—but as a special case that we shall discuss later. For the present we are considering a population in which the sample selection has been totally random.

Another necessary condition is that the relative frequency of the population's values (in the characteristic under consideration) falls in a reasonable approximation of a normal curve. One symbol μ (the Greek letter mu), stands for the arithmetic mean of the population. We are going to use that type of parameter in the following discussion, although sometimes the researcher might be concerned with some other statistical value. When a sample is drawn, the arithmetic mean of the sample measurement is, of course, only an estimate of the parameter, μ. We shall symbolize the sample mean as $\overline{X}$. The researcher desires that the difference, of $\mu \pm \overline{X}$, be small enough to provide the desired precision.

Our discussion will center around a hypothetical example as a means of reviewing the appropriate concepts. Suppose that we could obtain a hypothetical population of annual incomes of households. If we know all the incomes from the population, we could compute the population parameter average annual income. For example, let us assume that μ is \$12,200. But in most actual research situations, all members of the population cannot be measured. Instead, a sample is usually obtained and inferences about the population values are made. Now if a sample of size 100 is drawn from the population of 100,000 and the mean annual income is calculated, it might be discovered that the mean calculated from the sample values ($\overline{X}$) might be \$11,300. If another random sample of 100 individuals from the population is chosen and its mean calculated, it may be found that the average annual income mean ($\overline{X}$) is \$12,966. It is evident that although sample mean values fairly close to the true population mean were obtained, they are not identical with the true mean (μ). In fact, rarely do sample means coincide exactly with the value of the true mean. The difference between the sample mean and the true mean are due to two types of error: (1) sampling error, and (2) nonsampling error.

8.1.1 Nonsampling Error

Nonsampling error can enter into the gathered data in an insidious way. These errors include: (1) false or inaccurate reporting of the desired data, (2) poor sampling design, and/or (3) failure of field workers to follow instructions on how to select sample units. Even if we were to undertake a complete enumeration of the population, nonsampling errors might remain. These errors are not discussed in this section, for they principally stem from personnel problems such as training and supervision, and corrective action is explored in Chapter 10.

8.1.2 Sampling Error

The other error term is the *sampling error,* the error we make in selecting samples that are not representative of the population. That is, it is the difference between the sample value and the true value of the population mean. Since it is practically impossible for a smaller segment of a population to be exactly representative of the population, some degree of sampling error will be present whenever we select a sample. This holds true regardless of how careful the researcher is in randomly choosing the sample. This error, then, is a result of chance.

Sampling error can be reduced by increasing the size of the sample. In fact, it can be completely eliminated by increasing the sample to include every item in the population. Because the sampling error is the result of chance, it is subject to the laws of probability. Because of this (and as the reader should recall from elementary statistics) a sampling error will be normally distributed, and we can define its range at a given confidence level. This phenomenon is related to the concept of a sampling distribution of a statistic. And by the use of this concept, we can find a simple way of calculating the probability of selecting a sample from a population.

8.1.3 Reliability of Samples: Standard Error of the Mean

[handwritten top margin: Std. deviation of the sampling distribution of $\bar{x}$ — measure of the dispersion of a sample mean @ the pop. mean]

An important mathematical theorem known as the *central limit theorem* states that the various arithmetic means $(\bar{X})$ of a large number of random samples, each composed of the same number of units from the same population, will distribute themselves around the population's mean (μ) in a normal curve described as the sampling distribution of means. The arithmetic mean of all possible sample means of the particular sample size drawn from a population will be equal to the value of the population mean. The standard deviation of the sampling distribution of means is called the *standard error of the mean* and is defined to be :

[handwritten left: finite population:]

[handwritten: $\sigma_{\bar{x}} = \dfrac{\sigma}{\sqrt{n}}\sqrt{\dfrac{N-n}{N-1}}$]

$$\sigma_{\bar{X}} = \frac{\sigma}{\sqrt{n}}$$

[handwritten: → std. dev. of pop. / infinite population / → sample size]

where σ is the standard deviation of the population and n is the sample size.

Given the conditions set forth above, the portion under the curve, in any segment along the x axis, is indicated graphically in Figure 8–1. The degree of deviation (of the $\bar{X}$'s) from μ has the conventional or standard measure: the standard error of the mean is symbolized by $\sigma_{\bar{x}}$ in our diagram. To the negative side or left of $\bar{x}$ to the distance of $-1\sigma_{\bar{x}}$ there will be 34.14 percent of these many samples/means—and the same proportion to the positive side within $1\sigma_{\bar{x}}$ distance. If we drew one sample of that size, these combined proportions or 68.27 percent of the possible means of that sample would lie within $\pm1\sigma_{\bar{x}}$ of the true population mean (μ). If we state this another way, probability favors our obtaining a sample mean within that deviation with 68.27 chances out of 100. And there would remain 31.73 chances out of 100 of the deviation exceeding that range and lying in the "critical area."

It follows in general terms, then, that it is probable that a certain interval will inclose the true value of the population mean. This interval is termed the *confidence interval*. And the probability of a sample mean lying within the confidence interval is termed the *confidence coefficient*.

[handwritten left: the interval estimates based on specified confidence levels.]

In the example above it was stipulated that the confidence coefficient desired be 68.27 percent, and if some estimate of the frequency with which the phenomenon under investigation occurs can be imputed, one can compute the confidence interval for 1 standard deviation. The formula is simply this:

[handwritten: $\bar{X}$ = Sample mean / $\sigma_{\bar{x}}$ = Std. error of mean]

[handwritten: lower limit   upper limit]

$$\bar{X} - 1\sigma_{\bar{X}} \leq \mu \leq \bar{X} + 1\sigma_{\bar{X}}$$

[handwritten: of estimate   of estimate]

[handwritten right: → level of probability assoc w/ an interval estimate]

It can also be stated that 95.45 percent of all possible sample means lie within the intervals of $\bar{X} \pm 1.96\sigma_{\bar{x}}$ and 99.73 percent within $\bar{X} \pm 2.99\sigma_{\bar{x}}$. (It is usually customary to round off the confidence coefficients to 2 and 3, respectively.)

In the previous discussion, an assumption had been made that the standard deviation of the population (σ) was known. However, in most marketing problems involving sampling, the standard deviation of the pop-

229

[handwritten bottom: $2\sigma_{\bar{x}} = 95.4$ / $1\sigma_{\bar{x}} = 68.27$]

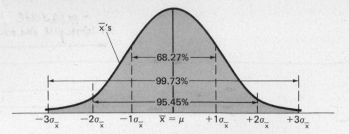

FIGURE 8–1. Sampling Distribution of the (Sample) Means

ulation is not known. If this be the case, the procedures developed previously to estimate the population mean (μ) can be followed, for we stated that a sample statistic such as a sample mean is the best estimate of its parameter. Also, $\sigma_{\bar{x}}$ must be estimated from the sample. The formula for the standard error of the mean is changed from

$$\sigma_{\bar{X}} = \sqrt{\frac{\sigma}{n}} \quad \text{to} \quad \hat{\sigma}_{\bar{X}} = \sqrt{\frac{s}{n}}$$

where

$$s = \sqrt{\frac{\Sigma\,(x - \bar{X})^2}{n - 1}} \qquad \text{(for ungrouped data)}[1]$$

and

$$s = \sqrt{\frac{\Sigma\,f\,(x - \bar{X})^2}{n - 1}} \qquad \text{(for grouped data)}[2]$$

Thus, one can estimate a population mean μ with a sample mean $\bar{X}$ and one can estimate the sampling error with the standard error of the mean $\hat{\sigma}_{\bar{x}}$ using only sample variables.

A correction factor may be applied to the estimated standard error of the mean to compensate for the size of the sample (n) in relation to the size of the population (N). The correction factor added to the formula for the estimated standard error of the mean then becomes

correction factor

$$\hat{\sigma}_{\bar{X}} = \frac{s}{\sqrt{n}}\,\sqrt{\frac{N - n}{N - 1}}$$

---

[1] A distribution of ungrouped data is one in which each class is represented by a single value.

[2] A grouped distribution is a condensation of ungrouped data in which adjacent classes of the ungrouped data are combined to form new classes in which the class now represents a range of values. In the formula above, f is the frequency of the class and x is the midpoint of the class.

230

The finite correction factor is traditionally used when the sample constitutes 5 percent or more of the population under study.

The preceding relationships can be illustrated by referring to an example:

> *Case A.* The management of the Superwonder stores, a chain of over 600 food supermarkets, is concerned with a radical redesign of their parking facilities. One of the vital facts that must be learned is the maximum number of automobiles that use the parking facilities per hour at peak hours. This can be measured readily enough by taking a traffic count at specific times, and it would be efficient to do this by using a sample of some of the 600 stores in the chain.

If the analyst estimates the standard deviation (or range within which about one third of the population would lie on either side of μ) to be 80 automobiles per hour, and if he considers a sample of 50 store locations, his calculations would be

$$\hat{\sigma}_{\bar{x}} = \frac{s}{\sqrt{n}} \qquad \hat{\sigma}_{\bar{x}} = \frac{80}{\sqrt{50}} = \frac{80}{7} = 11.4 \qquad \text{automobiles}$$

A 95 percent confidence coefficient is equal to approximately 2 standard deviations. So if this were the desired confidence coefficient, one is concerned with $2\sigma_{\bar{x}}$, which would be 2×11.4, or 22.8, automobiles. So if his study of 50 stores parking facilities found that an average of 400 automobiles per hour used the facilities in a particular period, there would be 95 chances out of 100 that the true mean of all the stores' parking facilities would range between 377.2 and 422.8 automobiles.

What does a confidence interval of ±22.8 automobiles signify? We have calculated this value in order to judge the precision of a sample estimate, in terms of its deviation from the true mean (parameter) of the population (which is unknown). If one were given the findings of 400 automobiles per hour from the survey after it had been conducted, this range could be used to judge the interpretation justifiably placed on the 400 automobiles figure.

8.1.4 Reliability of Samples: Standard Error of a Proportion

The example to which we have related involved measuring attributes such as means. Instead, a researcher may be concerned with phenomena that can be expressed as frequencies of occurrence, in percentages. The theory we discussed previously is identical to that used when dealing with population means only that a percentage frequency of occurrence is a special case of the mean attribute. The standard error of a percentage σ_p from a simple random sample is estimated by the formula

$$\text{std error} \atop \text{of a percentage} \rightarrow \hat{\sigma}_P = \sqrt{\frac{pq}{n}} \qquad {p = \text{frequency} \; ^{\#\,of\,times}_{occurs} \atop q = \text{nonoccurrence}}$$

where *p* is the frequency of occurrence of the phenomenon and *q* is the nonoccurrence of the phenomenon.

To illustrate its use, the following example is offered:

Case B. A producer of materials that are used in laboratories (of pharmaceutical companies, government agencies, and universities) has a sampling problem. One important category of his products is of two types: alpha and beta. Beta type is relatively new and is both costly and perishable, so it is important to produce it in quantities closely in line with market demand. Laboratory technology and preferences seem to have been changing rapidly in favor of beta type, so past sales records offer little basis for sales forecasting. The manufacturer's current guess is that 60 percent of the combined sales of the two products next year may be of beta type, but he is going to confirm his hypothesis by having sales representatives call on a sample of buyers to learn how much alpha and beta they intend to buy.

The decision situation in essence is as follows. The decision maker has a hypothesis about a population, and since it is being stated in quantitative terms, it is a statistical hypothesis. He or she wants to demonstrate statistically whether the hypothesis is true or false, and this will involve inferences based on samples. In our example the symbol *p* stands for the frequency of occurrences of the phenomenon. This was estimated in Case B to be 60 percent. The symbol *q* stands for its nonoccurrence, which is the complement, or 40 percent. In our example, if we consider a sample size(*n*) of 500, the calculation is

$$\hat{\sigma}_p = \sqrt{\frac{(0.60)(0.40)}{500}} = \sqrt{\frac{0.24}{500}} = \sqrt{0.00048} = 0.02191 = 2.1917\%$$

What does a confidence interval of ±2.19 percentage points signify? We have calculated this value in order to judge the precision of the sample estimate. Suppose that in Case B a sample of 500 laboratory customers has been queried and that the arithmetic mean of their replies was that 62.5 percent of their combined purchases were going to be of beta type. Our confidence interval then indicates that the actual population's average is in a range of 62.5 ± 2.19. Or we may express this as lying between 60.3 percent and 64.7 percent or: $60.3 \leqslant \mu \leqslant 64.7$. The confidence coefficient of this indicates that the sample estimate would lie within that range in 68.27 chances out of 100 (that is, the span of 1 standard deviation). If one were given the finding of 62.5 percent from the survey after it had been conducted, one would use this range to judge the interpretation one justifiably could be placed on the 62.5 percent figure.

8.2 Determining Sample Size and Efficiency When Estimating Attributes

process of selecting the sample size need into:
① specification of error that can be tolerated
② specification of confidence coefficient
③ est of std deviation

An alternative approach to using the confidence-interval calculations discussed in the preceding sections is to consider how large the survey-sample ought to be in order to obtain some desired precision in the sample estimate.

When a researcher specifies a sample size, such factors as the number of units to be included in the sample in which: (1) neither so few are selected as to render the risk of sampling error intolerably large, nor (2) too many units are included, which would raise the cost of the study to make it inefficient, must be considered. The decision maker must grapple with the trade-off of (1) increasing the sample size, which would reduce the sampling error but increase the cost, and (2) decreasing the sample size, which has the opposite effects on the sampling error and the cost. Thus, the decision maker, in conjunction with the researcher, must compromise between obtaining data with greater precision and that of lower research costs. Such a decision should not be made arbitrarily, because of the risks involved of obtaining inadequate information and/or wasting company resources. Several factors influence the size of sample selected.

8.2.1 Specification of Error That Can Be Tolerated

The first is the size of the error that would be tolerable for decision-making purposes. This involves the executive's willingness to accept risk. To illustrate, recall case A. Assume that management desired the estimate to be within ±10 automobiles per hour of the true mean. The value selected for the size of the error interval would depend upon the sensitivity of the decision outcome. In our example, if the radically new parking facilities were sensitive to the amount of customers patronizing the stores, a large size of error would be unacceptable.

8.2.2 Specification of Confidence Coefficient

A second consideration would be the degree of confidence the management wants with the results of the study. If management wants to be 100 percent confident of the results, the entire population must be studied. But as stated earlier, this is usually too impractical and costly, to say the least. Therefore, management must accept something less than 100 percent confidence. In practice, the confidence levels most often used are 99 percent, 95 percent, and 90 percent. However, other confidence levels are occasionally used in business situations. A confidence level of 95 percent is most common. That leaves a 5 percent risk of the true population statistic being outside the range of possible error specified by the confidence interval. This 5 percent risk appears to be acceptable in most marketing decisions. It will be used in our example.

233

When concerned with measuring attributes such as means, an appropriate formula for estimating the appropriate sample size is

$$\hat{\sigma}_{\bar{X}} = \frac{s}{\sqrt{n}}$$

where $\hat{\sigma}_{\bar{x}}$ is the estimate of the standard error of the mean, s the sample standard deviation, and n the size of the sample.

In our example taken from case A, let us say that the analyst wants to be 95 percent confident that the estimated sampling error in the distribution of automobiles passing through the traffic count is no larger than ±10. First, we will determine

$$1.96 \ \hat{\sigma}_{\bar{x}} = 10$$

$$\frac{10}{1.96} \cong \frac{10}{2}$$

$$\hat{\sigma}_{\bar{x}} = 5 \qquad \text{(approximately, for we rounded} \\ \text{off 1.96 to be equal to 2)}$$

In effect, the sampling error on either side of the mean for $1.96\hat{\sigma}_{\bar{x}}$, which represents the 95 percent confidence interval, must equal 10. Then $1\hat{\sigma}_{\bar{x}}$ is equal to 5. Thus, far, then, we have

$$5 = \frac{s}{\sqrt{n}}$$

There are still two unknowns in our formula, s and n.

8.2.3 Estimate of the Standard Deviation

The next step is to estimate the standard deviation of the sample, s. There are several ways by which researchers can estimate the standard deviation of the sample:

1. A pilot study may be undertaken and the standard deviation may be used from this study; or

2. If previous studies have been conducted and are considered comparable to the proposed study, then the standard deviation of previous studies may be used as the estimate; or

3. A researcher may make an educated guess as to the standard deviation. One way of accomplishing this is for the researcher to estimate what the limits of the distribution can be, that is, what the lowest and highest value for the entire range of the distribution. With this interval in mind, the standard deviation can be estimated by dividing the range by 6. Since practically all values (99.7 percent) will be included with the mean ±3 times the standard devia-

tion of the population, 1 standard deviation would be approximately found by dividing the distribution range by the value of 6.

Let us assume that in previous studies, the standard deviation has been estimated to be 85 automobiles; then

$$5 = \frac{85}{\sqrt{n}}$$

Solving for the sample size (n),

$$5 \sqrt{n} = 85$$

$$\sqrt{n} = \frac{85}{5}$$

$$\sqrt{n} = 17$$

$$n = 289$$

Thus, it would take a random sample of at least 289 of the stores' parking facilities to be 95 percent confident that the population mean is within ±10 automobiles passing through the traffic count.

Let us now assume that a survey of the 289 parking facilities was conducted and that the sample standard deviation was found to be 100 automobiles. In this case, was the sample of size 289 too large, or too small, or the correct size to sample?

$$5 = \frac{100}{\sqrt{n}}$$

$$5 \sqrt{n} = 100$$

$$\sqrt{n} = \frac{100}{5}$$

$$\sqrt{n} = 20$$

$$n = 400$$

For the precision management was seeking, the sample size of 289 was too small. It would be necessary to add an additional 111 stores' parking facilities to be sampled. Obviously, however, the researcher would not have known this fact until the data were collected. A method of determining the correct sample size from a given degree of precision is required.

8.2.4 Sequential Sampling — *doesn't make an advance determination of sample size.*

The foregoing sampling method has assumed that one sample will be drawn of a fixed size (or in double sampling, that each would have a

obtains measurements on only a single unit of the population at a time.

fixed size). The sample size would be determined prior to the drawing of the actual sample. Sequential sampling (often known as "sequential analysis") differs in that one does not make an advance determination of sample size.

In sequential sampling one usually obtains measurements on only a single unit of the population at a time. In marketing field studies, for reasons to be stated, a group of population units is measured one group at a time. The measurements of each group are cumulated with those of previously measured groups. Taking into consideration the probable sampling error, the researcher studies these cumulated results to decide whether he or she can make a decision with the size of sample thus far acquired. If the error is still too large, the study continues until the standard error is reduced to the level that management specified.

Sequential sampling may be preferable to fixed-sample-size methods when it is more efficient. A number of applications of sequential versus fixed-sample-size sampling were compared by the Statistical Research Group of Columbia University. This study "estimated that in testing hypotheses sequential sampling commonly reduces the required sample size on the average of approximately 50 percent of that required by a single sampling plan of comparable discriminating power."[3]

This study suggests that when the sequential sampling method may properly be applied, survey costs may be reduced substantially. The applicability of sequential sampling in marketing field studies seems, however, to be questionable. The problem lies in the necessity of having a randomly selected sample, or at least one that yields a truly fair cross section of the population. When one is sampling from a heterogeneous population that is distributed or scattered with no uniformity, a decent cross section is hardly likely to be obtained when only one unit is selected at a time for cumulating the measured values. Nor are small groups likely to suffice or be efficient to sample and then await calculations of their results at some central office before deciding that the study still is in the "continue sampling" zone and that field work must be resumed for another group. This is particularly true in marketing surveys in which the statistic being measured, e.g., attitudes, is in a relatively rapid state of change. In those situations, by the time the last sequential sample is measured, the results of the first samples may be outdated.

Nevertheless, some pioneering uses of sequential sampling in marketing studies have been made with apparent success. The potential efficiencies of the method are so large that there should be continued experimentation with it. If ways can be found of using it efficiently and safely in marketing studies, it should be employed more widely.

8.2.5 Cost as a Factor in the Determination of Sample Size

Another consideration in determining how many units should be selected for inclusion in the sample is the cost. Consider the previous ex-

---

[3] Statistical Research Group, Columbia University, *Sequential Analyses of Statistical Data: Applications* (New York: Columbia University Press, 1945), p. 106.

ample in case A; management wanted to be 95 percent confident of the results and they wanted the standard error in estimating the mean of the sample not to exceed 10 automobiles per hour. Recall that the original estimate of the sample size was 289 facilities. If we assume that the cost per observation was quoted at $20 (this includes the field work; the training and supervision of the observers; the coding, editing, and tabulation of the results; and the writing of the report), the total cost for the project would be $5,780 ($20 × 289). If the management of the Superwonder stores considers the cost to be above the research budget allocated for such a study, they must consider whether to (1) cancel the study, (2) select another research approach, or (3) consider the original study approach but seek alternative ways of reducing the research costs. If they elect to consider the original study approach while reducing the costs, they have several alternative decisions. One such decision may be to reduce the level of confidence from 95 percent to 90 percent. If a decision were made to accept, the sample size would then be computed by

$$\hat{\sigma}_{\bar{X}} = \frac{s}{\sqrt{n}}$$

$$\frac{10}{1.65} = \frac{85}{\sqrt{n}}$$

$$6.06 = \frac{85}{\sqrt{n}}$$

$$\sqrt{n} = \frac{85}{6.06} = 14$$

$$n \cong 196$$

It should be noted that by reducing the confidence level from 95 percent to 90 percent, management would reduce the cost from $5,780 to $3,920 (196 × $20).

Another alternative in cost reduction can be to increase the size of the allowable error from 10 automobiles per hour to 15 automobiles per hour. This decision can be made if, and only if, the sensitivity of this decision will not affect the customers' patronage as previously discussed. With the error term increased to 15 automobiles per hour and the confidence coefficient maintained at the 95 percent level, we have

$$\frac{15}{1.96} = \frac{85}{\sqrt{n}}$$

$$7.65 = \frac{85}{\sqrt{n}}$$

$$\sqrt{n} = \frac{85}{7.65} = 11.11$$

$$n \cong 123$$

This decision reduced the sample size to 123, and the cost from $5,780 to $2,460 (123 × $20).

There may be an infinite amount of combinations that could potentially modify the decision criteria for sample size selection. These possible alternatives should be considered as cost-reduction methods before the decision is made to cancel the research study.

8.3 Determining the Sample Size When Estimating Proportions

As discussed earlier, there are occasions when it is necessary to determine the sample size for a problem involving proportions. The approach in such a case differs in that it deals with the percentage of frequency of occurrence. The formula used in this case, to compute the standard deviation of a sample, is a modification of the one used for variables. The formula is

$$\hat{\sigma}_p = \sqrt{\frac{pq}{n}}$$

A procedure similar to that followed in the last section is used. To illustrate its use, recall case B: a variation of the problem might involve finding out how large the survey sample ought to be in order to obtain some desired precision in the sample estimate. With the assumption of n now unknown, an expected value of p and q is put into the equation, a confidence coefficient is selected, an allowable error is decided upon, and then n is calculated. Assume that p is estimated to be 60 percent and that the confidence level is set at 95 percent. The managers decide that the allowable error in estimating the population proportion is not to be greater than 2 percent ($p \pm 0.02$); therefore,

$$\frac{0.02}{1.96} = \sqrt{\frac{(0.60)\,(0.40)}{n}}$$

$$0.0102 = \sqrt{\frac{0.24}{n}}$$

$$\sqrt{n} = \frac{\sqrt{0.24}}{0.0102}$$

$$\sqrt{n} = \frac{0.24}{0.000104}$$

$$n = 2,308 \quad \text{(rounded)}$$

Two points are frequently overlooked in determining the sample size for a percentage frequency of occurrence. First, sample size require-

238

ments increase moderately, for a given precision, as the frequency of oc-currence approaches 50 percent and decreases as it approaches 100 per-cent or 0 percent occurrence. Table 8–1 shows the 95 percent level of confidence.

TABLE 8–1. Example of a Table Indicating Standard Errors at the 95 Percent Level of Confidence and Estimated Rate of Occurrence

					Estimated Rate of Occurrence						
Sample Size	1% or 99%	5% or 95%	10% or 90%	15% or 85%	20% or 80%	25% or 75%	30% or 70%	35% or 65%	40% or 60%	45% or 55%	50%
50	2.8	6.2	8.5	10.1	11.4	12.3	13.0	13.5	13.9	14.1	14.2
100	2.0	4.4	6.0	7.1	8.0	8.7	9.2	9.5	9.8	9.9	10.0
150	1.6	3.6	4.9	5.9	6.6	7.1	7.5	7.8	8.0	8.1	8.2
200	1.4	3.1	4.3	5.1	5.7	6.1	6.5	6.8	7.0	7.0	7.1
300	1.1	2.5	3.5	4.1	4.6	5.0	5.3	5.5	5.7	5.8	5.8
500	0.89	2.0	2.7	3.2	3.6	3.9	4.1	4.3	4.4	4.5	4.5
1,000	0.63	1.4	1.9	2.3	2.6	2.8	2.9	3.1	3.1	3.2	3.2
1,500	0.51	1.1	1.6	1.9	2.1	2.3	2.4	2.5	2.5	2.6	2.6
2,000	0.44	0.96	1.3	1.6	1.8	1.9	2.0	2.1	2.2	2.2	2.2
4,000	0.31	0.69	0.95	1.1	1.3	1.4	1.4	1.5	1.5	1.6	1.6
5,000	0.28	0.62	0.85	1.0	1.1	1.2	1.3	1.4	1.4	1.4	1.4
10,000	0.20	0.44	0.60	0.71	0.80	0.87	0.92	0.95	0.98	0.99	1.0
25,000	0.12	0.27	0.38	0.45	0.50	0.55	0.58	0.60	0.62	0.62	0.64
50,000	0.08	0.17	0.24	0.29	0.32	0.35	0.37	0.38	0.39	0.40	0.40

Although the confidence coefficient (or "level") of 95 percent is used most often, for greater assurance one may use the more stringent con-fidence coefficient of 99 percent. When this confidence requirement is stepped up from 95 to 99 percent assurance, the sample size rises roughly by half or more. To illustrate, if a simple random sample of 1,000 individuals showed that 80 percent owned a typewriter, at the 95 percent confidence interval Table 8–1 indicates that the estimated stan-dard error would be 2.6 percent. If we were to increase the confidence level to 99 percent, and wanted the standard error to remain approxi-mately 2.6 percent, the sample size would have to increase to 2,000 indi-viduals, as indicated in Table 8–2.

The sample sizes given in Table 8–1 also indicate large sample in-creases when the precision requirement is raised. Suppose, for instance, that the decision hinges on some phenomenon whose frequency of oc-currence was around 30 percent, or the reciprocal of 70 percent, and the study is to be made of a sample of 500. The decision maker asks if a larger sample would be needed if his precision requirement was ±2 per-cent rather than ±4.1 percent. The table shows that this involves increas-ing the sample almost fourfold (for example, from 500 to 2,000). The size of sample required rises at nearly the rate of the square of the added precision. In view of the substantial increases in sample sizes and accompanying costs for increasing the requirements of precision or confidence, a practical commercial executive would be reluctant to demand high levels of either unless strictly needed. Indeed, many marketing decisions would be satisfied with a low rate of confidence, such as a 60 percent level (chance of being more right than wrong), entailing relatively small samples.

In regard to our example above, we were discussing a sample size of 500 and ignoring the size of the total population from which it was drawn. That would not be a significant factor, if the population were very large relative to the sample size. But suppose that the population was only 800 total customers, which is not much larger than a sample of 500. Obviously, then, the probable error in a sample of 500 would be quite small, since it consists of most of the population. A sample of 100 of the 800 total customers also would be such a large proportion of the total population that the probable error would be less than probability theory would indicate. As a rule of thumb, such a lessening of probable sample error begins to operate when the sample comprises something over 5 percent of the population. Statisticians have investigated this tendency and developed methods of computing it. The finite correction introduced on page 230 is applied when the sample size constitutes 5 percent or more of the population under study.

8.4 Stratified Sample Size

Earlier we noted that sampling error, for a given sample size, is reduced as the sample size approaches the population size. Another condition that reduces sampling error is stratification of the population. Because allocation of the population members into strata confines each subsample's variance within the range of values in each stratum, obviously this reduces the probable error into a total sample.

In the cases we used for illustration, very likely the researcher would have some accurate advanced knowledge of certain relevant characteristics of the population. In case A, data from city or regional planning councils reports concerning the passage of automobiles in a region have been made available to management. They can stratify the stores by the average amount of traffic passing at a particular store during peak hours. Let us say that management finds a logical stratification of their stores to include the following intervals:

Stratum	Average Traffic Count per Location	Number of Stores per Location
1	1900–2100 autos	420
2	1700–1899 autos	180

TABLE 8-2. Example of a Table Indicating Standard Errors at the 99 Percent Level of Confidence and Estimated Rate of Occurrence

Sample Size	Estimated Rate of Occurrence										
	1% or 99%	5% or 95%	10% or 90%	15% or 85%	20% or 80%	25% or 75%	30% or 70%	35% or 65%	40% or 60%	45% or 55%	50%
50	4.2	9.2	12.7	15.1	17.0	18.4	19.4	20.2	20.9	21.1	21.2
100	3.0	6.5	9.0	10.7	12.0	13.0	13.7	14.3	14.7	14.9	15.0
150	2.4	5.3	7.3	8.7	9.8	10.6	11.2	11.7	12.0	12.2	12.2
200	2.1	4.6	6.7	7.6	8.4	9.2	9.7	10.1	10.4	10.6	10.6
300	1.7	3.8	5.2	6.2	6.9	7.5	7.9	8.3	8.5	8.6	
500	1.3	2.9	4.0	4.8	5.4	5.8	6.1	6.4	6.6		
1,000	0.94	2.0	2.8	3.4	3.8	4.1	4.3	4.5			
1,500	0.77	1.7	2.3	2.8	3.0	3.4	3.5				
2,000	0.67	1.5	2.0	2.4	2.7	2.9					
4,000	0.47	1.0	1.4	1.7	1.9						
5,000	0.42	0.92	1.3	1.5							
10,000	0.30	0.65	0.9								
25,000	0.19	0.41									
50,000	0.13										

Past related research had indicated that a relationship exists between passing traffic at a location and store patronage. The association was found to be that 20 percent of the traffic passing patronized the store and utilized the parking facilities.

The researcher has selected a sample of 50 and the standard deviations have been found to be:

$$\text{stratum 1:} \quad \sigma_{\bar{X}sr1} = 70$$

$$\text{stratum 2:} \quad \sigma_{\bar{X}sr2} = 95$$

Once strata have been established, what size of stratified random sample should be taken? To answer this question it is necessary to specify whether a proportional or a disproportional (optimal) stratified sample be taken. A proportional stratified sample is one in which the sample units in a given strata are allocated in proportion to the relative size of the strata. In our case, stratum 1 contains 420 stores, which represents 70 percent of the total population of 600 stores. Thus, for stratum 1 our sample would contain 35 stores drawn at random (0.70 × 50 stores in our sample). The same rationale would produce a sample of 15 stores, drawn from stratum 2. In this form of stratified sampling, only the size of the stratum is used as a guide for allocating the total sample. The researcher's calculation of the proportional sample size for each stratum employs the formula:

241

$$n_i = \frac{N_i}{N} \cdot n$$

where n_i = number of sample units from stratum i
N = total number of units in the population
N_i = total number of units in the stratum i
n = sample size desired

The standard error of the mean is

$$\sigma_{\bar{x}sr} = \sqrt{\sum_{i=1}^{k} W_i^2 \frac{\sigma_i^2}{n_i}}$$

where W_i = weight of stratum $i = N_i/N$
σ_i = standard deviation of the ith stratum
k = total number of strata

Now substituting the appropriate values in the formula,

$$\sigma_{\bar{x}sr} = \sqrt{\frac{(0.7)^2 (70)^2}{35} + \frac{(0.3)^2 (95)^2}{15}}$$

$$= \sqrt{\frac{(0.49) (4900)}{35} + \frac{(0.09) (9025)}{15}}$$

$$= \sqrt{68.6 + 54.2} = \sqrt{122.75}$$

$$= 11.079$$

As a general rule, proportional stratified sampling is a preferred method when one is interested in estimating the overall mean and the only information available to the researcher is the number of units in each stratum. Disproportionate stratified sampling is sampling in which the proportion of the units in the sample strata is not equal to the proportions of the population. Thus, the formula for the sample allocation is

$$n_i = \frac{W_i \sigma_i n}{\sum\limits_{i=1}^{k} W_i \sigma_i}$$

The disproportional stratified sample may be a more desirable method if the standard deviations of the observations in each stratum are known. Continuing the example, we now assume that the standard deviations can be estimated for each stratum. With this assumption, we can now determine the allocation of the total sample of 50 by applying the formula above:

$$n_1 = \frac{(0.7)\ (70)\ (50)}{(0.7)\ (70) + (0.3)\ (95)} = \frac{2,450}{77.5} \approx 32$$

$$n_2 = \frac{(0.3)\ (95)\ (50)}{(0.7)\ (70) + (0.3)\ (95)} = \frac{1,425}{77.5} \approx 18$$

The formula for the standard error of the mean of a disproportionate stratified sample is

$$\sigma_{\bar{x}\mathrm{sr}} = \sqrt{\frac{\left(\sum\limits_{i=1}^{k} W_i \sigma_i\right)^2}{\sum\limits_{i=1}^{k} n_i}}$$

We can now determine the standard error of the mean:

$$\sigma_{\bar{x}\mathrm{sr}} = \sqrt{\frac{[(0.7)\ (70) + (0.3)\ (95)]^2}{50}}$$

$$= \sqrt{\frac{6,006.25}{50}} = \sqrt{120.125} = 10.96$$

Recall that the standard error of the mean calculated for the simple random sample with the same specifications was 11.4. With the use of stratification, the error term was reduced to 11.08 for the proportional stratified case, and 10.96 for the disproportional case. The difference, in each case, is small insofar as our illustration is concerned, but the point is well made. One will always find that the standard error for stratified samples is smaller than for simple random samples; or, in other words, much smaller samples may be utilized when the population has been stratified before drawing the sample.

For a discussion involving the selection of appropriate sample size for other probability sampling methods, the reader is advised to consult one of the standard texts on sampling theory.[4] It should be noted that the principles discussed in this text will basically remain the same for other sampling methods, but the formulas will differ.

8.5 Sample Size in Nonprobability Sample Selection

The discussion of sample size determination has been confined to probability samples chosen at random. Sample members may also be chosen

---

[4] The reader who is interested in other sampling methods is referred to W. G. Cochran, *Sampling Techniques,* 2nd ed. (New York: John Wiley & Sons, Inc., 1963); and Leslie Kish, *Survey Sampling* (New York: John Wiley & Sons, Inc., 1965).

purposively, by deliberate selection. The methods of calculating sample size that were presented above are not applicable to purposive sampling. Probability simply does not operate when deliberate choice steps in.

While one investigation has been made to determine the accuracy of a nonprobability sample (that of a quota sample),[5] no scientific formula exists for either precalculating desirable sample sizes or interpreting the statistical significance, relative to sampling error, of data obtained in purposive selection. A researcher may deem that the method of sample selection, although purposive, is likely to obtain as proper a representation of the population as would a random selection of a given size of sample. This assumption is frequently made, and it may be correct at times, but the researchers in these instances should not blithely apply the laws of probability of their sampling and should carefully qualify any statements made relative to the statistical significance of their findings.

8.6 Summary

We have devoted two chapters to the subject of sampling, partly because of the subject's importance to sound research but even more because it can be a difficult subject to comprehend. Therefore, we first gave an overview of the stages involved in sampling to which the discussion could be oriented. Chapter 7 dealt with basic approaches regarding (1) the treatment of the population, and (2) the selecting of the sample members.

Chapter 8 considered the practical challenges faced in sample size selection. Determination of sample size led us to describe methods and certain statistical measures employed in predetermining the number of population members to be contained in the sample. Although the chapter centered around simple random sampling size selection, the discussion pointed out modifications that can be made to cope with the more specialized ways of selecting an adequate sample size.

In order to determine the adequate sample size needed, a decisional approach was offered. A process of selecting the sample size follows a well-defined progression in which the following information is needed: (1) a specification of the error that can be tolerated, (2) a specification of a confidence coefficient, and (3) an estimate of the standard deviation. With these data, the researcher can estimate the appropriate sample size using the standard error formula. But any data-gathering effort will require financial expenditures in which the more data accumulated, the higher the costs will be. Therefore, cost becomes a decision variable in our selection process. Cost-reduction methods were discussed in an effort to include "cost" as a decision criteria for sample size selection.

On the other hand, a number of samples taken in marketing research are nonprobability samples. For the sample size determination for these sampling methods, the procedures are not well determined. At best, the

---

[5] F. F. Stephan and P. J. McCarthy, *Sampling Opinions: An Analysis of Survey Procedure* (New York: John Wiley & Sons, Inc., 1958), Chap. 10.

researcher must use his or her judgment and experience for determining the appropriate sample size.

Since very little is known about the characteristics of such sampling techniques, there is no conceptual or theoretical basis for determining its sampling error. Sampling theory must be extended—theoretical constructs must be developed—to include nonprobability sampling techniques. Their increased use in marketing research demands more of scientific methodology if precision and accuracy are to be achieved.

The methods discussed in the two sampling chapters are those used in applied marketing research. Our decisional approach lets the researcher use judgment in selecting the alternative sampling designs to fit his particular situation. One must remember that complete information may be desirable, but the advantages of sampling, such as reduction in data gathering time, reduction in cost data gathering and the potential high accuracy of the results often lead to usable information for decision-making purposes.

9 Instruments for Questioning and Measurement

Chapter 9 brings us to a very demanding communications task, that of designing the forms to be used in gathering data — forms that someone else must read, understand, and respond truthfully with the desired information. This involves such questions as these:

What are some difficulties that we face in obtaining information from others?

What are the more common ways of seeking information from respondents? What are their advantages or shortcomings?

How should we go about preparing a questionnaire? What are the steps and how do they hinge on each other?

What are the kinds of questions that may be asked? What is each type good for?

What are the challenges of measurement problems? What are our alternative methods?

Don't people often slant their answers? What are some reasons and some ways of reducing such bias?

In the self-administered questionnaire, as used in mail surveys, where respondents read it themselves, what special methods are recommended?

By "INSTRUMENTS" we are referring to the tools with which information is sought and obtained. These include the forms used, the procedures to be followed, and the techniques by which desired information may be elicited. The accuracy and suitability of the obtained data depend heavily on the forms and questions used, which would be created through skill and understanding of the information needs and of the people who would be the sources. Nothing is more vital in gathering primary data.

Earlier the data objectives had been determined, relative to the defined problem and decisions served. Also, the specific populations from whom the information would be sought have been determined, in the sampling phase that you studied in Chapters 7 and 8. With that foundation, the marketing researcher should be ready to fashion the instruments for gathering the data. We shall begin that subject by considering some of the major problems faced.

9.1 Challenges of Communication

Who is not familiar with the difficulties that human beings have in communicating with one another? And who is not sometimes conscious of our problems in seeing things accurately and in recording what we believe that we have seen? These broad problems confront anyone who plans the gathering of original data. Some means of coping with them are given in the bulk of this chapter. First, let us mention some of the aspects that are challenging and crucial.

1. *Translating data objectives.* The marketing researcher may have a mutual and clear agreement with the decision maker on the problems and what is needed in terms of evidence at the point of decision. This often is not identical with what one asks or observes among the respondents who would be the sources of evidence, so the data objectives have to be transformed into the kinds of things one can ask or see that lead to the form of data inputs for the decision.

   A little example may help here. You will remember Company B in Chapter 5, which was considering marketing its toys in Canada. The marketing manager would want to know whether Canadian children would like their toys as well as the kids in the United States. The researcher knows, though, that it would be wrong to ask a child point-blank, "Do you like this toy?" Answers might be forthcoming, but not accurate reflections of how the children's attitudes would be under normal exposure to a toy. Perhaps some situation must be arranged and a series of less direct questions used.

2. *Measurability.* Observations or questions must be specific and in a form in which magnitudes and comparisons may be asserted and taken into due consideration when results are interpreted. At the minimum, information obtained from various persons or sources must be capable of being categorized in uniform ways. Ideally, all the information obtained would be in quantitative form amenable

to analytical techniques. If one could stick to objective facts, this would be readily accomplished, but the world is not like that. Some of the most relevant human phenomena are quite subjective and are difficult to classify and to measure, but this challenge must be met sufficiently to have meaningful information.

3. *Subjectivity.* The need to plumb the psyche to some depth often is essential to digging out what has to be known about people to solve a problem. This challenges researchers to find the techniques that induce people to discuss their attitudes and opinions—or at deeper levels to uncover motivations that lead to these. In doing this, the richer and deeper human information often conflicts with the measurability and accuracy of what is learned. A joke in marketing research circles several years ago when motivation research was reaching peak popularity was: "Do you want to go to a head counter or a head shrinker?" The dilemma is not that clear-cut and it is rather frequent.

4. *State of the respondent.* Whenever information is to be sought by questionning, whether informally or with the use of questionnaires, the persons to be questioned may vary widely with respect to (a) educational level, (b) prejudices and moral standards, (c) regional behavior patterns, and (d) occupational background. No matter how carefully the sample group to be questioned is screened, individual differences will be present. Whatever the variations and peculiarities that the questionnaires are to encounter, a realistic understanding of them is essential.

   Not only must the questionnaire be designed with its particular appeal in mind, but it must also be constructed so that it elicits the specific information desired from the respondents. When asked different questions, the respondent is likely to find herself in one or more of the following situations:

   a. Respondents may not understand the question; under such circumstances, answers are likely to be given that do not relate to the problem under investigation. The interviewer may not always detect this misinterpretation, as the answer may appear logical, even though another answer would have been given if the question were clearly understood.

   b. Respondents may understand the question, may wish to answer, but may not remember the necessary information. In the search for facts the respondent is frequently unable to remember, and the questionnaire must be designed to help the respondent recall information.

   c. Respondents may understand the question, have the information, yet be reluctant to give it; sometimes personal information must be obtained and the tendency may be to refuse to answer. Another aspect of the problem is that of having the respondents deliberately give incorrect information in an attempt to avoid embarrassment or to say what they think the researcher wants to hear.

      d. Respondents may understand the question, may wish to answer, but be unable to; conditions that contribute to this situation: are (1) respondents may lack facility for expressing themselves; (2) the question may be asked of the wrong people (for example, a person cannot give a useful answer regarding his brand preference for electric shavers if he does not use an electric shaver).

5. *Quantity of information.* A judgment always is involved regarding the amount of data needed related to the ability and cost of obtaining it. One aspect of this is the number and nature of subjects on which data are needed. There is a common temptation, when a firm makes the effort of a large field study, to ask respondents for information about a number of subjects of interest to the sponsor although not really pertinent to the main problem under study. This courts the danger of respondents becoming fatigued before answering all the questions and giving indifferent responses or refusing to finish. Failure to economize in the data sought also can add much to the cost and time of a project and the inundation of executives with information of little value.

    On the other hand, the quantity of information needed can be underestimated relevant to the main problems. Questioning may be too abrupt or superficial to obtain enough detail and reveal significant aspects. A frequent error is to overlook how much should be known about the respondents, because the vital factors may lie in the contrasting responses from different types of persons. With the current trend from demographic bases of classifying respondents to psychographic bases (concerned particularly with attitudes), a need arises to learn much more about them than their factual economic and social variables.

9.2 General Alternatives

Our attention in this chapter is devoted largely to procedures and options in obtaining data with questionnaires. That is not, however, the only alternative. By "questionnaire" we refer to a printed form that contains the questions to be asked as well as instructions and provisions for answers. We are going to preface the questionnaire discussion with some alternatives that may be used instead of or in conjunction with the normal survey routine, as well as to indicate the chief elements of questionnaires.

Observations may be more accurate than responses to questions, and sometimes it is easier to record what is perceived than to ask for the information. In a survey utilizing questions, some of the information may be gotten instead by observing it. Figure 9–1 was used in a simple study at service stations and utilizes both methods.

Forms used for recording observations in the field are simpler than forms containing questions. Forms recording observations have four basic functions:

CAR WASH STUDY

LOCATION #_____ INTV #_____ DATE_____

TIME: 1 [ ] 8-10 AM   3 [ ] 12-2 PM   5 [ ] 4-6 PM
          2 [ ]10-12 AM   4 [ ] 2-4 PM

APPROXIMATE AGE: 1 [ ] 16-25   2 [ ] 26-35   3 [ ] 36-50   4 [ ] 51-65

                    5 [ ] over 65

SEX: 1 [ ] Male   2 [ ] Female

CAR YEAR AND MAKE: _____
                   (Example: 1970 Buick)

Good Morning! I'm _____ from MARKETING INFORMATION SERVICE. We are interviewing customers at various service stations to find out how far people travel
to have their cars serviced.

1. How far do you live from here:
    1[ ] 1/4 mile   3[ ] 1 mile   5[ ] 3 miles
    2[ ] 1/2 mile   4[ ] 2 miles   6[ ] 4 miles
                                        7[ ] 5 or more miles

2. What is the nearest intersection to your home?

    _____ AND _____

3. Do you have your car washed at a car wash?

    1[ ] Yes   2[ ] No ─────────→ SKIP TO 6

4. How often do you have your car washed in the summer?
                          Every   Every   Every
    1[ ] Weekly   2[ ] 2 Weeks   3[ ] 3 Weeks   4[ ] Month   5[ ] Less Often

5. How often do you have your car washed in the winter?
                          Every   Every   Every
    1[ ] Weekly   2[ ] 2 Weeks   3[ ] 3 Weeks   4[ ] Month   5[ ] Less Often

6. If a car wash were to be installed here, would you use it?

    1[ ] Yes   2[ ] Maybe   3[ ] No ─────────→ CONCLUDE INTERVIEW

7. What do you like about this location for a car wash?

    [ ] Convenience   [ ] Gasoline
    [ ] Dealer/operation   [ ] All other answers

Thank you very much for your cooperation.

GALLONS OF GAS PURCHASED: Regular_____   Premium_____

PAYMENT MADE BY: 1[ ] ARCO Card   2[ ] Other Credit Card

                  3[ ] Cash

FIGURE 9–1. Car Wash Study

This form was used for a survey in service stations. It provides for both observations and responses to questions. It is shown merely as an example, for it contains vague terms and other faults.

1. Indicate specifically what is to be observed.
2. Provide a standardized procedure for recording observations.
3. Facilitate the tabulation of results.
4. Identify the place and time of the observations.

When the observer is to see and record actions as they take place (such as some form of consumer behavior or description of the clothing people are wearing), the observer may work under great pressure. In designing forms for these purposes, one should remember that the observers' prime needs are to keep their attention on the passing scene and to look at the form "out of the corner of their eyes." The various sections on the form, then, should have contrasting type and lines, and the spaces for recording should be placed close together so that the pencil need not move far. The difficulty of developing just the right form for such observational field work is exemplified by a study that merely involved counting men and women who passed and entered a particular store. The original form for these observations had to be revised three times before a suitable form design was found.

When the type of data is more subjective, it is even more important that the form be clear to the researcher. For instance, in an observational study designed to rate retail salespersons on such things as tact, sales ability, and the like, the individual observers must have a uniform understanding not only of the terms being rated but also of the subjective gradations within their meanings. In this study of retail salespersons, observers should agree on a uniform definition of tact and how to rate various expressions of it or the lack thereof.

The top and bottom sections of Figure 9–1 show a form for collecting information through observation. Notice in the top section that the day between 8:00 A.M. and 6:00 P.M. is broken up into two-hour intervals and people's ages are grouped into five areas. Notice on the bottom part of the form that plenty of space provided for the interviewer to write in the number of gallons of gas purchased. Also notice that the form provides the interviewer with an easy means of specifying whether premium or regular gas was purchased and how the respondent paid for the gasoline.

Informal interviewing is that which does not use a structured questionnaire for obtaining most of the information. These can be placed in three types: (1) focus group interviews that utilize a moderator, who guides discussion on a subject in which from six to ten people participate informally (these were described in Chapter 5), (2) personal depth interviews with a single person, and (3) projective techniques. Focus groups today are the most common form of qualitative consumer research. However, their results must be interpreted with care.[1]

Personal, in-depth interviews are nonstructured interviews with an individual. One in-depth interview may last from one to three hours. The

---

[1] A thorough analysis of focus group interviewing, from a scientific viewpoint, is presented in: Bobby J. Calder, "Focus Groups and the Nature of Qualitative Marketing Research," *Journal of Marketing Research,* August, 1977, pp. 353–62.

interviewer merely provides the topics of conversation. The respondent chooses which path the discussion takes.

The results of an in-depth interview are a direct function of the interviewer's skill and interpretation. In addition, very small sample sizes are used. The n for an entire study using in-depth interviews normally varies between six and thirty, and seldom exceeds thirty. Because of these factors, the results of a study involving in-depth interviews are not projectable to the relevant universe.

Projective techniques are a method that makes use of certain techniques from clinical psychology. The word *projective* is used because the basic procedure involves the process of trying to get an individual to project herself or himself into a hypothetical situation. The situation should be an ambiguous one, so that the respondents unconsciously project themselves in their efforts to interpret or explain it. One means is the cartoon technique, where two persons are seen to be in conversation, with the words of one printed in a balloon. The response of the other is not, with an empty balloon, and so the respondent is asked to imagine what the second person would be saying. This method can elicit such a wide variety of answers that they cannot be statistically treated and may be difficult to interpret, but they may be revealing exploratory data.

Arrangement of parts of a questionnaire offer other alternatives. In speaking of this we can point out that a questionnaire may have as many as five parts. Three of these are essential for both personal interview and mail questionnaires. These essential parts are (1) the information sought, (2) the classification information, and (3) the identification data. In mail questionnaires there should be two other parts: (4) the request for cooperation, and (5) the instructions. It is not absolutely essential for a personal interview questionnaire to have these last two elements, but many, such as that shown in Figure 9–1, do have all five elements.

The information sought usually makes up the major portion of the questionnaire (in Figure 9–1, questions 3 through 7 and the questions on "gallons of gas purchased" ask for the sought information). Classification information (demographic) describes the person (the family or firm or whatever is being studied) by various economic, social, or other characteristics that relate to the subject of the research. Classification data may be used to validate the sample as a proper cross section of the population. (In Figure 9–1, the space for age, sex, year, and make of car, and questions 1 and 2 ask for classification information.) Classification data are customarily located in the latter sections of a questionnaire, but in Figure 9–1 some of the data are provided in the beginning of the form. In instances where the interviewer is to estimate information such as age, this can be done without any interviewing problems, such as causing the respondent to be reticent about answering questions.

The identification data on this form are the location number and the interview number. These facts may be needed to verify the interview as an authentic one and to know who is responsible for the interview. The request for cooperation is the introductory statement at the beginning of the middle section of Figure 9-1. Instructions are provided by the words "Example: 1970 Buick" under the line provided for car year and make.

Questions 3 and 6 also provide instructions. Most authorities on marketing research believe that better rapport can be maintained either by not asking for demographic information until the end of the interview or by obtaining it on the basis of a personal estimate by the interviewer.

9.3 Sequence for Questionnaire Preparation

We have not yet approached the question of how to go about the preparation of a questionnaire. It is difficult to reduce such a complex task to a formula. Yet a questionnaire cannot "just grow," or it will be a helter-skelter affair. The following fourteen steps, if taken in the order given, should promote the design of a successful questionnaire.

1. Since the questionnaire is one step in the processs of organizing the data that will solve the research problem, its formulation begins in the earlier research steps. Those preliminary steps give insights into the nature of information sources and the data they might furnish. Therefore, these things have already been decided in the planning stages: the specific information needed and its sources.

2. All the information that might be furnished by these various sources should be listed, stating exactly what is to be sought. This may comprise quite a long list. Is all of it essential? If not, eliminate all items that are not essential.

3. Place yourself in the position of the people who are to give the information. Could you really furnish all this information? Could you give it in the terms specified? Which would you be most reluctant to furnish, be unlikely to tell frankly, find most difficult to answer?

4. Now you begin to understand the sequence in which these various subjects should appear on the questionnaire. You can decide which topic might be most suitable for the lead-in question, the succeeding question, and then the order of all the questions. You can recognize where qualifying questions are needed and which questions are to be omitted in the case of certain types of respondents.

5. When you have stated the topics of all the questions in the desired sequence, decide what type of question would be most suitable for each one: multiple choice, free response, and so forth. Very likely you will see that some questions need to be supplemented with illustrations or explanations.

6. The work thus far has drawn the specifications for the questions. Now comes the task of writing the actual questions. You must write these clearly to be sure that each question contains only one element (rather than two or more questions), that its relationships to any preceding questions are evident, and that any elements of bias are reduced to a minimum. This is the hardest step in the

253

whole task. Do not expect to write a satisfactory question on the first or the second try.

7. After each question, be sure to provide proper spaces for the answers. If checklists are to be used, you have another job in determining what items are to be listed. In a multiple-choice question, phrasing the alternative answers is a delicate job.

8. With the questions completed, now consider what facts will be needed to classify and understand the results properly. When you have determined the categories of classification data needed, prepare questions to ask for them. These will probably come at the end of the form.

9. The whole questionnaire now has been written—after a fashion. There probably is still a disjointed flow between questions, some clumsy or ambiguous wording, elements of bias, and other common sins of questionnaires. Subject the whole work, therefore, to a close scrutiny on all points of good design.

10. Then put yourself in the place of the respondent again. Can you answer all these questions and would you want to? Time yourself on how long it would take to obtain these answers in an interview or to write them in for a mail questionnaire. If the questionnaire seems too long, see whether anything can be omitted. A frequent error in questionnaire construction is adding a number of questions not directly related to the problem under study but representing an attempt to get the most out of the expenditure for the field work. These last-minute questions just clutter up the questionnaire. One study can do only so much, and the data sought should be no more than that needed to arrive at a solution to the problem studied.

11. Next, put yourself in the place of the interviewer. Are these questions smoothly worded and easy to ask? Is the language natural and interesting? Does it start on a cordial note? Could you easily read it and record the information given?

12. Now, be sure that the information asked for is just what you want. Reconsider the hypotheses and determine whether the information is likely to contribute to a solution to the research problem. Consider how the information is to be analyzed and cross-analyzed, and be certain that the classification questions will obtain what is needed. A return to the dummy tables discussed in Chapter 5 is helpful.

13. In preparing the questionnaire, the researcher has done all he or she can alone but would be foolish to conclude that it is now the best possible questionnaire. It probably contains faults that will not be recognized, and no "ivory tower" thinking will find those hidden faults. Rather, they are found by pretesting the questionnaire in actual interviews.

14. Finally, the form is ready for reproduction of the quantity needed. If it is a mail study or if it a very large personal interview study, the form should be printed. In smaller investigations, a cheaper and equally legible job may be done with mimeograph or

some other inexpensive process. This is not, however, a place to try strict economy by using cheap paper or crowding the form, because it is one of the small costs, and a high-quality form may substantially increase the accuracy and efficiency of interviewing. Its greater importance in mail forms has been indicated.

Preparing questionnaires or observational forms is one significant step in research that may be done properly by watching for the many pitfalls and following an orderly procedure. The neophyte in this work should be warned, though, that no questionnaire has been perfect and that an adequate one requires painstaking effort.

9.4 Questioning Methods

There are several general types of questions that may be used, depending on what information is being sought and the situation of the respondent, which we discussed in Section 9.1. Within each of these types there can be infinite variety. We are going to give just one example after a short description of these types. This begins with the broadest approach in terms of the respondent's freedom in answering and proceeds through the more specific types.

Open-ended questions. Such questions are used in qualitative interviews, in which one is trying to get a respondent to explain why a certain thing is done. After one or a few questions on the particular subject, the open end is reached, and the interviewer then starts informal interviewing to pursue the subject further. Rather than ask a fixed set of questions she formulates whatever questions are appropriate to continuing the line of questioning. The question is open-ended because the interviewer goes on into deeper questioning on the subject of the respondent's feelings. Instead of following a standardized series of questions in this depth questioning, she makes up her questions on the spot. This method of interviewing may secure more significant and complete responses than standardized questions, but the field workers must be capable of formulating the appropriate questions and of recording the varying responses.

Free response. In this type of question, the person is interrogated in a way that does not limit the possible scope of his or her responses. It is commonly employed in factual questions and sometimes in opinion or motivation questions. The two questions below are excerpts from a study on bath beads, which was of a self-administered type in which the respondent (member of a panel) filled in her own answers.[2]

Closely related are questions that confine a person to some category of response but leave it open to that person's opinion and wording. This would be called a *directed-response* question. Such a question about the

---

[2] This and subsequent examples in this section are reproduced by courtesy of Market Facts, Inc., Chicago.

4a. What was there about these bath beads marked "Use First" that you did NOT like?

_____

_____ 15 ☐☐ 16

4b. What was there about these bath beads marked "Use First" that you did like?

_____

_____ 17 ☐☐ 18

bath beads might be: "What did you think about the scent of these bath beads?"

Multiple choice. These questions list a number of answers and permit the subjects to select the answer that best approximates their own. It sometimes is called the "cafeteria" question and is suitable for either opinions or motives. Its advantages lie in enabling the person to express herself or himself, in having all the replies in similar wording, and in being easy to tabulate. Obviously, all significant degrees of answer must be offered to be a valid question.

6. How severe is the ring around the tub? ("X" ONE BOX)

Severe ring which would require cleanser to remove............ ☐ 1

Moderate ring which might or might not require a cleanser to
          remove...................................... ☐ 2   (50)

Slight ring which is easy to remove by running a washcloth
          around the tub............................. ☐ 3

Scaled response. In this increasingly popular type of question, the subjects are given a range of categories in which to express their opinions. This allows various intensities of feeling to be expressed. As this is an important technique with a number of methods, its discussion is deferred until we take up the matter of measurement. However, below is a scaled-answer question that is atypical in (1) number of intervals, (2) verbal description of the intervals, and (3) long instructions given (since this was a self-administered questionnaire).

3. I would like to know your overall opinion about these bath beads marked "Use First." Taking everything into consideration, please tell me how much you like or dislike the bath beads marked "Use First" by placing an "X" in the ONE box under the statement that best expresses your own personal opinion about this product.
You'll notice that the boxes toward the left represent a more unfavorable opinion, the boxes toward the right represent a more favorable opinion. Each set of boxes is described verbally to help you in expressing your opinion. There are no right or wrong answers -- only your personal opinion is important.

Below Average	About Average	A Little Better Than Average	A Lot Better Than Average	One Of The Best	Absolutely None Better
☐	☐ ☐	☐ ☐	☐ ☐	☐ ☐	☐ 14

256

Checklist. A checklist is a form of multiple-choice question in which the person checks one or more of the response categories, but these are not arranged in shades of meaning like the multiple choices would be. They are especially useful for factual answers. This type of question facilitates replies and tabulation, but it should not be used unless all significant categories are listed. Although an "other" space may be provided for those not listed, too often respondents do not recall such possible responses or neglect to write them in.

---

1. In the past week how many times did you, yourself, use these bath beads marked "Use First"? (CIRCLE ONE)

    1   2   3   4   5   6   7 or more   12

2. About how much product did you use each time? ("X" ONE BOX)

    1 tbsp. or less ☐ 1   4 tablespoons   ☐ 4   Just poured from box ☐ 7
    2 tablespoons   ☐ 2   5 or more tbsp. ☐ 5   13
    3 tablespoons   ☐ 3   1/3 cup   ☐ 6

Ranking questions. This is a form of opinion question in which the respondent is asked to rank comparatively the items listed. An example is the following from a questionnaire seeking data for a staff executive job description:

Rank the above roles from 1st to 7th in terms of the degree to which each job fits your actual work.

Coordinator   _____

Entrepreneur _____

Expediter   _____

Expert   _____

Forecaster   _____

Innovator   _____

Integrator   _____

These questions make tabulation simple and give a definite set of comparisons to be considered. They are not easy to answer if many items must be ranked, and they are invalid unless all the alternatives are listed. Often the respondent does not understand the terms and there is no real significance to the ranking. The researcher does not know why the person gave this order of preference. The bias of the order in which the items are listed also operates here. If more than three items are to be rank-ordered, it is better to use a type of questioning called *paired comparisons*. It is often difficult for people to choose from among more than three items. However, it is relatively easy for people to select from among two alternatives. Figure 9–2 is from part of a questionnaire that used paired comparisons. Notice that every possible pair is included. Also note that, as much as possible, each item appears first as many times as it appears second. Finally, note that if an item appears in the second pair, it does not appear in the first pair or the third pair, and so on. One disadvantage of this method is that the number of pairs can quickly become quite long.

Dichotomous questions. These questions allow only two possible answers. For instance, if a person lawfully possesses a house, there are only two alternative ways of possessing it: owning or renting it. Hence, "Do you own or rent this house?" is a dichotomous question. Much more common is the "yes-or-no" variety. These questions are easy to ask and generally easy to answer. Unfortunately, such questions are suitable mainly for simple factual questions, and they are likely to bias answers. Generally speaking, yes-or-no questions should be avoided because they do not provide much information. They can be helpful in obtaining classification data about the respondent and in guiding a respondent through a questionnaire. The two questions below seem to have been designed for those purposes.

---

4. Do you currently have a water softener in your home in working condition?

    Yes ☐ 1   No ☐ 2   (48)

5. After tub bathing without a bath additive, does a ring remain in the tub?

    Yes ☐ 1   No ☐ 2 (SKIP TO QU. 7)   (49)

In selecting the types of questions and in composing them, the researcher should anticipate some of the tasks lying ahead that will deal with the questionnaire. We shall point out three aspects of adding "ease" to those tasks.

1. *Ease of questioning.* The job of the interviewer must be considered and care taken so that she will have no difficulty in asking the questions and in following their schedule. Because she is expected to read the questions, involved expressions and tongue twisters should be avoided in a formal interview. The print should be easy to read in the rather dim light in which interviewers may have to work. Some instructions may have to be printed on the form, especially those concerning the sequence of questions; for example, "If there are no roomers living in this house, proceed to question 8." If some information is to be observed rather than asked, the spaces for this should be clearly distinguished from the questions. Instructions and checklists should be printed in a light and contrasting type from which the bolder type of the questions will stand out.

2. *Ease of recording.* Any type of questionnaire must make adequate provision for recording the information. This need is greatest in

Listed below are possible areas for improvement. These areas are grouped into pairs. *Select the area that you feel needs the most improvement* by circling the letter preceding your choice. Each area appears more than once. However, make a selection for each pair.

a. Product reliability
b. Management skills

a. Product costs
b. Distributor relations

a. Product reliability
b. Marketing

a. Operating expenses
b. Product reliability

a. Operating expenses
b. Distributor relations

a. Distributor relations
b. Management skills

a. Management skills
b. Product costs

a. Marketing
b. Product costs

a. Marketing
b. Operating expenses

a. Distributor relations
b. Product reliability

a. Product costs
b. Product reliability

a. Management skills
b. Marketing

a. Distributor relations
b. Marketing

a. Product costs
b. Operating expenses

a. Operating expenses
b. Management skills

FIGURE 9–2. Questionnaire Using Paired Comparisons

formal personal interviews when the responses must be jotted down quickly, on the spot. One good rule is: better too much than too little space for the answers. Also, the legibility of the recording is improved by having ruled lines. As far as possible, employ spaces to be checked and so avoid the need to write in answers. Always provide space for recording conditional answers (such as "don't know"); and since lists can never be complete (except in yes-and-no questions), provide space for recording unlisted answers.

3. *Ease of data processing.* Since the data on the questionnaire are to be processed after the forms are returned from the field, the design of the form should anticipate tabulation. Failure to heed the requirements of tabulation may entail delays, high costs, and limitations on the analysis when the tabulation stage is reached. Usually, the tabulation work will be done by specialists, either in an outside tabulating firm or from within the research organization. These people should be consulted at length regarding the questionnaire design, as their knowledge may save much trouble later. Tabulation is facilitated by clear and uniform answers. It also is assisted by arranging the forms so that the key data by which they are to be sorted are immediately visible. Even the way the pages of the questionnaire are folded may have a bearing on the ease of tabulation.

Increasingly, numbers are entered adjacent to the data on the questionnaires before tabulating them, since this is necessary for computers. The form should be arranged so that it will itself be the coding form, thereby avoiding the need to write the code numbers on another form. In some of the examples above, spaces in the boxes, along the right-hand margins are for insertion of the codes. The actual code numbers can be printed on the questionnaire. This is known as *precoding*. When the forms are returned to the central office, the coding involves merely circling the proper code numbers. Coding procedures are discussed more fully in Chapter 11.

9.5 Measurement Methods

Conducting a questionnaire survey is a two-way process, of course, in which the quality of the information flowing from the respondent is as important as the clarity of the questions. The researcher needs information that is not only clear and correct but can also be measured meaningfully.

Much information received is in a quantitative form when it represents facts, and numbers are readily analyzed mathematically. Some of the most significant facts and all of the attitudinal and opinion responses are, instead, expressed verbally in traditional question-and-answer procedures. In free response and open-ended questioning, the respondents' own words are probably recorded, which leads to semantic problems when researchers attempt to tell whether a number of respondents were saying the same thing and should be classified together. Unless similar answers can be summed, there can be no counting, frequency distributions, or any other statistical work performed. And unless verbal data can be transformed into statistics, only paltry findings are possible.

Checklists and multiple-choice responses partially overcome the problem, since the categories printed on the questionnaire are the terms in which the answers are couched. These responses can be counted, but that is all that can be done with them mathematically. While the frequency of responses may have some meaning to whomever is interpreting them, one can hardly impute the intensity of feeling or importance that any one category represents compared with the others. Ranking questions add a bit quantitatively, since the ranks are numbers with which there can be some computing and sharper comparisons—but whether the rankings are at equal intervals is doubtful. Thus, if a poll of 500 sportswriters, voting for first-ranking team nationally, tallied 395 for Ohio State and 97 for Southern California, it is possible that most of them believed the two teams to be very closely matched, with a hair's breadth choice between them.

By use of scaled answers, what otherwise would be qualitative information is recorded in a quantifiable form. In its simplest form, a question calling for a scaled answer is endeavoring to provide a direct measure of a respondent's opinion. A response that attempts to rank the intensity of respondents' feelings about anything will provide a basis upon which to make comparative judgments about behavior, things, ideas, and the environment in which we live. A few examples will illustrate this.

There are five types of scales:

1. Nominal scales.
2. Ordinal scales.
3. Interval scales.
4. Ratio scales.
5. Attitude measurement techniques.

A *nominal scale* is developed by assigning numbers for purposes of identification. Examples of nominal scales include Social Security numbers, credit card numbers, and bank account numbers. The normal arithmetic operations cannot be meaningfully applied to numbers on a nominal scale.

An *ordinal scale* ranks or orders items according to the degree with which the items have or do not have some attribute. Meaningful mathematical operations cannot be performed on the numbers of an ordinal scale. Letters, symbols, or words can also be used to form an ordinal scale. For example, Grade A eggs are considered better than Grade B eggs, and Grade A large eggs are "bigger and better" than Grade A medium eggs.

An *interval scale* is a scale having an arbitrary zero point with numbers placed at equally appearing intervals. A thermometer is an example of an interval scale (for example, the difference between 10°F and 20°F). All mathematical operations must be carried out with respect to the *intervals* between numbers only.

A *ratio scale* is a scale with equal-appearing intervals and a natural zero point. All the usual mathematical operations can be performed on numbers of a ratio scale.

Attitude measurement techniques are usually directed toward using the information obtained to construct some type of scale. Five of the most commonly used methods are:

1. Paired comparisons.
2. The semantic differential.
3. Thurstone scales (method of equal-appearing intervals).
4. Likert scales (the method of summated ratings).
5. The Sherif method.

Paired comparisons have been illustrated in Figure 9–2. Almost all efforts to set up a series of questions for which a quantitative scale is to be designed call for a comparative judgment to be made by the respondent. For example, the *semantic differential,* which was developed by Charles Osgood, is an excellent case in point. Respondents are asked to express their feelings about a company, product, or idea by recording their responses on a scale of adjectives (such as sweet–bitter), which are paired polar opposites. The following example illustrates this technique:

BEER

sweet	___ :	___ :	___ :	___ :	___ :	___ :	___	: bitter
light	___ :	___ :	___ :	___ :	___ :	___ :	___	: dark
modern	___ :	___ :	___ :	___ :	___ :	___ :	___	: old-fashioned

This example shows a series of differentiating alternatives set up as a scale that serves to locate the concept as a point in the semantic space. By "semantic differentiation," then, we mean the successive allocation of a concept to a point in the multidimensional semantic space by selection from among a set of given scaled semantic alternatives. The general model for this differentiating scale can be shown as:

BEER *(concept)*

(sweet)							(bitter)
Polar term x (1) : (2) : (3) : (4) : (5) : (6) : (7) :	Polar term y

in which the scale positions signify:

1. extremely x
2. quite x
3. slightly x
4. neither x nor y; equally x and y
5. slightly y
6. quite y
7. extremely y

In evaluating the usefulness in marketing research of the semantic differential as a scaling device, William A. Mindak has enumerated the following advantages:[3]

1. It provides a basis for isolating intensity of predetermined feelings.
2. Since the feelings are predetermined, it is possible to compare them over time.
3. It is reliable and repeatable.
4. Problems of question phrasing and structure are practically eliminated; however, the selection of the paired polar adjectives may present problems in terms of which of several alternative adjectives should be used.

The method of equal-appearing intervals, the *Thurstone scale*, attempts to provide a ratio scale. At least 200 statements are typed on cards and then given to judges, who place the statements on one of eleven piles, ranging from extremely negative to extremely positive. The number 6, or middle, pile is to contain only neutral statements. The method assumes that this process results in a neutral point at 6. If a statement shows a high variability of place between the judges, it is discarded.

---

[3] William A. Mindak, "Fitting the Semantic Differential to the Marketing Problem," *Journal of Marketing*, April, 1961, pp. 28–29. Reprinted from *The Journal of Marketing*, published by the American Marketing Association.

The method of summated ratings, the *Likert scale,* is usually a five-point scale ranging from strongly agree to strongly disagree. The main advantage to the method of summated ratings is that a judging group is not needed. The respondent is given a statement about a particular topic and then asked to state her or his degree of agreement or disagreement with the statement. One disadvantage of the Likert scale is that an individual's score is meaningless unless it is compared with the scores of other respondents. In the question below is a modified Likert scale.

5. Listed below are several reasons why women like yourself LIKE to use bath beads. Place an "X" in the box opposite each reason that best tells me how satisfied you are with the bath beads "Use First" in meeting each of the reasons listed.

SATISFACTION WITH BATH
BEADS "USE FIRST"

"X" ONE BOX FOR EACH REASON

LUXURY

	Completely Satisfied	Very Satisfied	Somewhat Satisfied	Mildly Satisfied	Not At All Satisfied	
High quality bath additive......................	☐ 1	☐ 2	☐ 3	☐ 4	☐ 5	(19)
Makes me feel feminine..........................	☐ 1	☐ 2	☐ 3	☐ 4	☐ 5	(20)
Makes me feel pampered..........................	☐ 1	☐ 2	☐ 3	☐ 4	☐ 5	(21)
Makes me feel glamorous	☐ 1	☐ 2	☐ 3	☐ 4	☐ 5	(22)
Gives me a feeling of luxury....................	☐ 1	☐ 2	☐ 3	☐ 4	☐ 5	(23)
It's fun to use.................................	☐ 1	☐ 2	☐ 3	☐ 4	☐ 5	(24)

One moot question about rating scales has been how many points to have on them. Perhaps five points, as in the illustration above, is the most common number of points, but some have argued for three and some for more. Research on the effects of the "rounding error" in two- or three-point and more numerous scales (due to respondents having to round their feelings to the next point up or down when categories are too few) found that "two or three scale points are in general good enough" when the researcher is interested in averages across people. However, "if the focus is on individual behavior, five- to seven-point scales should be used."[4]

Most attitude measurements assess content and direction of attitudes, but they do not provide a measure of intensity. One method for measuring intensity was developed by Sherif, Sherif, and Nebergall.[5] An example of a scale based on this method is given below, without the question.

1. This is the most important objective our division could consider.
2. This is an extremely important objective for our division.
3. This is an important objective for our division.

---

[4] Donald R. Lehmann and James Hulbert, "Are Three-Point Scales Always Good Enough?" *Journal of Marketing Research,* November, 1972, pp. 444–46.

[5] C. W. Sherif, M. Sherif, and R. E. Nebergall, *Attitude and Attitude Change* (Philadelphia: W. B. Saunders Company, 1965).

4. I guess you might call this an important objective for our division.
5. It is hard to say how important this objective is for our division.
6. I guess you might say this objective is relatively unimportant for our division.
7. This is not an important objective for our division.
8. This objective is not important for our division at all.
9. This is the least important objective our division could consider.

Analysis of responses yields three measures of an attitude: (1) the most acceptable position on an issue plus other acceptable positions (called latitude of acceptance), (2) the objectionable position on an issue, including the most objectionable position plus other objectionable positions (called latitude of rejection), and (3) positions on an issue that are neither objectionable nor acceptable (called latitude of noncommitment).

9.6.1 The Collection Instrument

The collection instrument, usually a questionnaire, can introduce bias in at least five ways:

1. Question wording.
2. Question sequence (order bias).
3. Form of the questionnaire.
4. Positional bias.
5. Method of providing for answers.

Question wording is a major source of bias. Questions should be worded so they do not "lead" the respondent, and the words should not exceed the respondent's ability to understand what is being asked. "Do you prefer cereal for breakfast?" is a leading question. If feasible, question wording should be pretested to make sure that the words and the questions are understood and are not causing bias or errors.

The order in which questions are asked can introduce bias. This type of bias is known as *order bias*. For example, if you start out by asking people personal or emotionally laden questions, the chances of obtaining truthful answers and of completing the interview are less than if you start out with rather innocuous questions. Also, the answer to a particular question can be influenced by the previous question or questions. Order bias can be controlled by rotating question order between questionnaires.

The third area of bias involving the collection instrument is the general form of the questionnaire. If you have an important questionnaire, make it look important. Make respondents feel you really want them to fill out the questionnaire by having them feel that it is urgent that they complete the form and send it in now.

Positional bias is the next type of bias. Positional bias refers to the tendency of respondents to select response alternatives because the alternatives appear in favorable locations on the questionnaire. The order in which alternative responses are presented can also influence a respondent's choice. Generally speaking, people have a tendency to select the first choice presented in a list of alternative choices.

Finally, bias can be introduced by not providing enough space in which respondents can write answers. Also, writing in answers may not be conspicuously enough requested. Related to this are failures to include popular categories in lists, because respondents may fail to recall items or ideas not listed or find it inconvenient to write them in.

9.6.2 The Respondent

The major biases introduced by respondents result from the following:

1. Deliberate falsification.
2. Incorrect responses due to faulty memory.
3. Familiarity bias.
4. Incorrect responses due to suggestibility.

A respondent may simply give an incorrect answer. Four situations contributing to this were described earlier, in Section 9.1. There are many ways to determine if the respondent is not telling the truth. One way of doing this is to repeat the question later in the interview.

Familiarity bias occurs when the person being questioned is too familiar with the subject of the questionnaire to be able to give objective answers.

Suggestibility has already been mentioned as a source of bias, and it might be caused either by the interviewer or by some implications in the questionnaire.

9.6.3 Avoiding Bias

Frequently the researcher wants bias to enter the responses, when it is desired to learn how people genuinely feel about some matter. Our concern here is with the many other situations in which the researcher wants accurate responses, which would not be forthcoming if something in the questionnaire or interview situation causes respondents to be untruthful. Also, as mentioned earlier, there are the biases residing in the respondents that lead to distortions in the information they are willing to give. With insight and understanding of the subjects to be contacted, a competent researcher can skirt or cope with these biases to a large degree.

People do have emotional hangups or other bias sources on a number of personal questions such as age or income. The age problem is sometimes solved by asking instead the year of a person's birth or high school graduation. The matter of income may be met in mail surveys by the anonymity of the respondent and in personal interviews by handing respondents a card showing income categories and a code letter for each. People seem to be more willing to speak a letter than to give an income figure.

The income misstatement problem tends to be worse in telephone interviews, since the respondent cannot see the interviewer and therefore would feel more threatened by being asked about income. A study conducted in Houston measured the extent of biases in family income responses when four approaches were tried alternatively. Our discussion is simplified by including only three, since two were similar in results. These three approaches were:

Approach 1: What was the approximate annual income for all members of your family before taxes during 1974? Was it . . .

(REPEAT UNTIL "NO." THEN CIRCLE)

more than $5,000   no. . . 1
more than $7,500   no. . . 2
more than $10,000   no. . . 3
more than $15,000   no. . . 4
more than $20,000   no. . . 5
more than $25,000   no. . . 6
             yes. . .7

Don't know/Refused X

Approach 3: What was the approximate annual income for all members of your family before taxes during 1974? Was it . . .

(REPEAT UNTIL "YES." THEN CIRCLE)

less than $5,000   yes. . . 1
less than $7,500   yes. . . 2
less than $10,000   yes. . . 3
less than $15,000   yes. . . 4
less than $20,000   yes. . . 5
less than $25,000   yes. . . 6
             no. . . 7

Don't know/Refused X

Approach 4: What was the approximate annual income for all members of your family before taxes during 1974? Was it . . .

(REPEAT UNTIL "YES." THEN CIRCLE)

more than $25,000   yes. . . 7
more than $20,000   yes. . . 6
more than $15,000   yes. . . 5
more than $10,000   yes. . . 4
more than $7,500   yes. . . 3
more than $5,000   yes. . . 2
             no. . . 1

Don't know/Refused X

The median incomes reported, for the total persons interrogated with each approach varied widely, with a $4,500 difference between approaches 1 and 4. As the current median income for the city of Houston had been independently estimated by a reliable government agency, it could be compared with the results of these approaches. Approach 3 (as well as 2, which started at a middle income level and then worked either way) both yielded estimates about $300 under the census adjusted income, which was the validating benchmark. That would be under a 2 percent error, remarkably close.[6]

Bias may arise also if respondents know, or suspect, who is sponsoring a survey, tending to slant responses favorably or unfavorably—varying with the subject matter and popularity of the supposed sponsor. Great pains must be taken to prevent any cues about these matters from getting into the questionnaires or the interview situation.

A recent example of attempting to avoid such bias may be of interest. The National Broadcasting Company was going to conduct a longitudinal panel study on factors underlying aggressive behavior among teenage boys. We will quote some things that NBC's vice-president of research and corporate planning published about their use of camouflage in this large study.

> Camouflage is the device used to minimize such bias by preventing respondents from focusing in advance on what the research wants to know. . . .
>
> To prevent our respondents—teenage boys—from concluding that we were searching for possible links between television exposure and aggressive behavior, we described the study's purpose more broadly, explaining that we were trying to find out what boys their age are really like—what they think, feel, and do.
>
> Because the teenagers realized that we wanted to know all about them and their world, we were able to ask a wide variety of questions bearing on these issues without arousing their hostility or antagonism. This made it possible to include a number of variables that would be helpful in the analyses, and also to increase the chances that the camouflage material could be made to do double duty.[7]

Concealing the purpose of a study would be unethical deceit if it would be harmful to the respondent not to understand that. Discretion and care are advisable in all communication measures taken to avoid bias. It has been shown recently, however, that even threatening questions will be given franker answers with the right questioning techniques.[8]

---

[6] William B. Locander and John P. Burton, "The Effect of Question Form on Gathering Income Data by Telephone," *Journal of Marketing Research*, May, 1976, pp. 189–92.

[7] Reprinted from William S. Rubens, "Camouflage Can Be Made To Do Double Work," *Journal of Marketing*, January, 1977, pp. 81–82.

[8] Ed Blair, Seymour Sudman, Norman M. Bradman, and Carol Stocking, "How to Ask Questions About Drinking and Sex: Response Effects in Measuring Consumer Behavior," *Journal of Marketing Research*, August, 1977, pp. 316–21.

The preceding discussion has pertained only in part to mail questionnaires, but there are some problems especially related to the design of mail questionnaires. These problems result from the lack of personal communication between those conducting the study and the respondent, and from dependence on this respondent's own willingness to fill out and return the forms.

Mail questionnaires should generally be briefer than personal interviews. When sent to the general public, they should ask fairly simple questions—although when on technical subjects and sent to interested organizations or individuals who will trouble to answer them, questions may be complex. Preaddressed envelopes with prepaid postage should be provided. Unless such precautions are observed, the rate of response may suffer. An easy-to-answer questionnaire sent by mail is shown in Figure 9–3.

Problems of misunderstanding and bias tend to be more prevalent when the respondent receives the forms by mail than when he is contacted face to face or by telephone. Intertwined with such problems are those of attracting an adequate response, a matter that relates to the subject of obtaining information from respondents. Since that subject is treated in Chapter 10, we are deferring further details to that chapter.

While discussing forms, this chapter's subject, we should also point out that mail surveys involve some elements beyond those needed in telephone and face-to-face interviewing. One is that the explanations must be more complete and leave no doubt as to what is desired. Another is the requirement of an accompanying letter stating the purpose and appealing for cooperation.

If the "cover letter" is to establish both a desire to cooperate and confidence in the character of the investigation, it should state the purpose of the study clearly and, if feasible, offer some reward or satisfaction for cooperation. Pains also should be taken to make the letter impressive and to have it convey a personal quality. The following physical characteristics are suggested to make the letter attractive:

1. Whenever costs will permit the use of an automatic typewriter that types the address and salutation to match the body of the letter, the personal quality is enhanced.

2. A hand-signed signature for a letter maximizes the personal aspect.

3. First-class postage, using stamps, for the outgoing envelope and the return envelope create a desirable impression.

4. "Personal" on the return envelope assists in establishing rapport between the signer of the letter and the respondent.

5. Some survey firms have found that when replies are to be sought from both men and women, it is more effective to differ the letters, signed by a name of the same sex as the particular respondent.

Various types of questions were then described, with examples. Measurement problems were considered with some of the useful questionnaire techniques relative to that. Next we enumerated some of the causes of bias, and some steps were discussed whereby bias may be avoided in questionnaires. Finally, we gave specific attention to mail questionnaires, and we ended with a bit of advice on pretesting.

10 Field Collection of Data

All the plans, procedures, and forms are completed when we reach Chapter 10. Now we move into the field, to the data sources, in person, by mail, or by telephone, and encounter such questions as these:

What are the major jobs to be done in the field?

What approaches and techniques tend to succeed in surveys by mail?

What methods are appropriate for telephone interviewing? What innovations are making this medium more popular?

What methods are recommended for personal interviewing? What particular challenges are there in its management?

What are some major things that may be done to minimize errors in the field? To keep control?

WHEN PRIMARY DATA ARE NEEDED, their sources are nearly always out-side the organization doing the research—that is, in the field. Planning and conducting the field work is closely connected with the two major phases covered by the preceding three chapters, sampling and the in-struments for the collection, usually questionnaires. These three phases need to be planned in conjunction, and the field work is no less critical than the two other phases. Painstaking work on sampling and question-naires can be nullified by poor field work, and no degree of subsequent analytical finesse can abstract correct conclusions from data that were er-roneously gathered in the field.

We begin this subject with a general overview of the tasks to be per-formed and of field workers' roles. Problems and techniques of the three methods of communication (mail, telephone, and personally) are then individually discussed. Discussion of a number of aspects in managing field work will complete this subject. To orient your reading to Figure 4-1, this brings us to steps 12 and 13.

10.1 Overview

By knowing the five main tasks that need to be accomplished in the field collection, which are presented first, you will be better able to compare the alternative methods and their merits for various purposes. Then let us consider the human factors of the people who gather the data in the field, which is, of course, applicable to telephone and personal inter-viewing but not to mail. We shall describe the functions of these people. Observation is dealt with first, and it is only here that we will deal with that method of data collection. Surveys, which are used more and are more complicated, are then brought into the picture in terms of inter-viewers' functions. We will concentrate on surveys in the remainder of the chapter.

10.1.1 Tasks of Field Investigation

These tasks can be summarized as five items, as we do below. They have been described here in terms of talking with respondents and asking them questions. Of course, you do not do that in mail surveys, for which the first three items might be rephrased.

1. Fulfilling the sampling plan by covering the designated areas or lo-cations and reaching the designated persons.
2. Administering the survey instrument (that is, the questionnaire or observation reporting forms) in strict accordance with instructions.
3. Recording the responses or requested information precisely as given or observed, in the terms of measurements that are called for by instructions.
4. Returning the information to the central point of editing and data processing by the requested time.
5. Completing the field work within budgeted costs.

273

Perhaps another task that might be distinguished is that of planning and supervising the work to enable these five functions to be performed adequately, mainly by the field workers. A discussion of the role of the field worker needs to differentiate between observing and interviewing. Although an interviewer may be instructed to observe some information that is to be recorded, other studies involve only making observations. The role of observer is therefore quite different from that of the interviewer.

10.1.2 Role of the Observer

By observing, we mean "perceiving" with one's visual and hearing senses, although observational studies tend to measure largely by seeing. The observer who does her or his job properly would (1) make observations at the place and times designated, (2) observe only manifest behavior and only that which is pertinent to the study's purposes or designated by the study's supervisor, and (3) record objectively and faithfully that which is perceived.

When evidence is gathered by observation, the data gathering devolves wholly on the acuity of the observer's senses and the accuracy and completeness of her or his recording. These roles thus carry a fuller responsibility than is usually borne by an interviewer. The danger entailed and the human nature of the role have been described in this way:

> One of the significant problems of the observational techniques is to ensure that the observer acts as a pure recorder rather than one who introduces his perceptual and cognitive screening into the observations. The observer himself is a respondent in that observation requires a behavioral relation between some event available and some organism that observes or responds to the event. As such, the observer is less of a camera and more of an interpreter.[1]

The complexity and inherent hazards in this role have not been as widely recognized as they deserve to be.

The observer often has to record behavior that occurs rapidly or among crowds, where there are many persons to be watched. These field conditions render the design of forms for quick recording a very important aspect. Instructions, training, and supervision obviously have great effect also on the observational function; nevertheless, interviewing is the predominant means of obtaining primary data in marketing.

10.1.3 Role of the Interviewer

Interviewing essentially is an interpersonal process in which one person (the interviewer) endeavors to elicit data or attitudinal responses from another person (the respondent). After establishing sufficient rapport, or level of understanding, with the respondent, the interviewer offers a

---

[1] Claremont Graduate School Class in Marketing Research, "Note on Direct Observation of Purchasing Behavior," *Journal of Marketing Research*, November, 1967, p. 402.

stimulus—usually a question—to obtain a response that provides the needed data. Upon receiving the response, the interviewer must interpret it in a number of ways: whether the question was understood, whether the respondent is fully and relevantly responding, what the response means. The interviewer may have to interpret and code the response into predetermined categories on the questionnaire. Or the interviewer may have been instructed to record exactly what the respondent said for interpretation later, at the editorial stage.

10.2   Mail Survey Techniques

In this form of data collection, there is no field worker, of course, since the respondent is reached by the postal service. That makes this method no less challenging, as it shifts all the functions to persons in the research organization who compile or purchase mailing lists, design and mail the questionnaires, and perform follow-up communications to attract a larger response. Much hinges on the questionnaire and its covering messages and instructions, subjects we have already discussed.

The problems peculiarly associated with mail surveys stem largely from the lack of personal communication between those conducting the study and the respondent. A related problem is dependence on the person's own willingness to fill out and return the forms. Mail studies tend to use shorter and simpler schedules of questions that provide maximum convenience for answering. The return envelope or card should be pre-addressed, with postage paid to reduce mailing effort. Unless such precautions are observed, the forms are far more likely to be put in the respondent's wastebasket than in the mailbox.

The danger of low response rates is largely avoided when the data are gathered from established survey panels. By their agreement to cooperate and the rewards they receive, panel members are likely to respond. And although they may be atypical for some purposes, well-balanced samples can be drawn from panels. One major research agency, for instance, can draw from over 61,000 households and provide a sample proportioned to recent national data on these demographic factors: income, age of panel member, population density, age of husband, household size, marital status, religious preference, occupations, education, race, and dwelling characteristics.[2] Those are the characteristics of women in the panel, it might be noted.

A major attraction of mail surveys is their cost, the least of any research medium. This fact was given by an officer of a marketing research agency that utilizes all the media, who went on to relate this about the use of a controlled mail panel:

> You can screen 20,000 households for $4,000 and then do a custom mail survey of 1,000 of these households with a four-page questionnaire for $2,000.[3]

---

[2] *Facts about CMP II* (Chicago: Market Facts, Inc., 1976).
[3] D. Frank Jones, *Marketing News,* December 17, 1976, p. 3.

To accomplish a complete survey for $6,000 is relatively economical. By double sampling in two stages and "screening" the specific types of households wanted first before sending the substantial questionnaire for the data sought to the segments wanted (for example, heavy users of one's product, young marrieds, etc.), a considerable efficiency is added. Such a panel's value is limited, of course, to studies that want to sample households.

There are a number of means whereby rather large returns can be obtained from nonpanel mail surveys. Response rates of 65 to 95 percent are reported by a number of researchers.[4] The rate of response naturally will vary with the interest and characteristics of the respondents: for instance, a 100 percent response from directors of Blue Cross Plans, cited by Kanuk and Berenson. Such rates of response compare favorably with most personal interview surveys. The head of a leading mail survey agency commented as follows:

> The Advertising Research Foundation recommends an 80 percent or better response on mail surveys, which brings the rate of nonresponse into line with the rate of substitution in well-conducted personal interview studies. In both this country and abroad, numerous mail surveys achieve better than 80 percent returns every year. However, the last few percentage points of an 80 percent response are by far the most costly to achieve, and often the researcher may feel that, for his purposes, the additional representativeness gained is not worth the additional cost.[5]

One of the chief ways to gain larger response is by follow-up efforts. In all the instances cited in the Kanuk and Berenson article, significant increases were gained—such as a survey of League of Women Voters, whose response rose from 46 to 73 percent after three reminders. The media used in the follow-up may also make a difference. In the telephone survey cited in Chapter 9, a postcard reminder raised the response rate to 69 percent, which telephone reminders bettered with a 76 percent response rate.

Moderate gains in response were found, by Kanuk and Berenson, by using a higher mailing class (for example, first class rather than third, or special delivery rather than first class). Sending a reward for response appears to gain larger increases. Again from the Kanuk and Berenson article, several surveys that compared sending a dime against no monetary reward averaged only 37 percent response with no reward, but averaged 52 percent with the dime. That gain of 15 percentage points, on average, was bettered by sending a quarter, which gained 25 points.[6] Sending more than a quarter tends to obtain still larger responses, but it is questionable whether they suffice to justify the cost.

[4] Leslie Kanuk and Conrad Berenson, "Mail Surveys and Response Rates: A Literature Survey," *Journal of Marketing Research,* November, 1975, pp. 442–48.

[5] Paul L. Erdos, "Data Collection Methods: Mail Surveys," in Robert Ferber (ed.), *Handbook of Marketing Research* (New York: McGraw-Hill Book Company, 1974), pp. 2–102.

[6] Kanuk and Berenson, op. cit., p. 447.

10.3 Telephone Survey Techniques

The use of telephones for survey communication has been rising, as mentioned earlier, for several reasons, including the speed of making contacts, the ability to make callbacks easily and at any time of day, and the willingness of people to talk on the telephone who would not open their doors to talk with a stranger. One of the main attractions, surely, is the relatively low cost compared with personal surveys.

Telephone surveys now tend to be made from a central point, often the national office of the survey agency. By renting WATS (wide-area telephone service) on a national basis, the enitre nation is callable. This also permits the continuous utilization of well-skilled interviewers, who can be supervised readily by supervisors' cutting in on interviews to monitor performance. It is a slight exaggeration, of course, to say that the "entire nation" is available by phone, since some households do not have them. Recent facts are that nearly 94 percent of U.S. households have telephones.[7] Those lacking telephones might be significant in surveying low-income individuals. As with any medium of communication, many cannot be reached because they are in transit, away from home, or lack a permanent abode. For most of the purposes of applied marketing research, though, the population having telephones is virtually complete.

More of a problem for telephone surveys is that of nonlisted numbers. The annual "RADAR" studies by Statistical Research, Inc., from 1970 through 1974 found the proportion that are nonlisted to hover around 19 percent, which would be a very significant omission.[8] This is true especially because the nonlisted are not distributed evenly; for example, nearly twice the proportion are nonwhite as white, and whereas small counties have only about 9 percent nonlisted, the five largest metropolitan areas have nearly 30 percent. This problem is solved by dialing numbers randomly (after learning from the telephone companies which exchanges have residential numbers and the range of those numbers) so that any number might happen to be dialed, whether or not listed in the directory.[9]

Interviewing methods by telephone do not differ greatly from those appropriate face to face. Rapport with the person interviewed must be developed unseen, with everything resting on the friendliness of the voice and what is said. The interviewer must be well prepared to keep the interview moving steadily, because it is much easier to lose a respondent over the phone than when in his or her presence. If long answers have to be written during the interview, there is the problem of in-

[7] U.S. Federal Communications Commission, *Statistics of Communications Common Carriers*, annual (Washington, D.C.: Government Printing Office, 1974).

[8] Gerald J. Glasser and Gale D. Metzger, "National Estimates of Nonlisted Telephone Households and Their Characteristics," *Journal of Marketing Research,* August, 1975, pp. 359–61.

[9] Mathew Hauck and Michael Cox, "Locating a Sample by Random Digit Dialing," *Public Opinion Quarterly,* Summer, 1974, pp. 253–60.

venting something to say while writing. One technique is to ask the person to repeat slowly what was said, which may last long enough to get it down.

Telephone interviewing has been revolutionized by the cathode-ray tube (CRT). The interviewer sits at a table in front of a CRT console, which has a television-like screen that displays questions, answers, and directions for conducting an interview, as in Figure 10–1. The CRT is connected with a computer that acts as the survey processor. A bank of telephone numbers, selected as random digits within the particular telephone

FIGURE 10–1. Telephone Interviewing with a CRT Console.

The next question to be asked has been displayed on the screen, inquiring the brand of cigarettes usually bought by the person being interviewed. The various answers and their code numbers also are displayed. If the response, for instance, was "Newports," the operator would record a "37" with the keyboard.

Source: Courtesy of Chilton Research Services.

exchanges for the areas being sampled, can be programmed into the survey processor. The interviewer merely signals when ready to start interviewing, and the first telephone number appears before her on the screen. When she has reached that number, each question appears successively on the screen, together with categories for answering with their code numbers. As the respondent gives an answer, the interviewer presses the proper button to record it in the computer. If the particular telephone does not answer, the number will be returned to the computer bank for later appearance; or if the desired party is to return at some time, that phone number can appear again at that time. When inconsistent or erroneous answers are given or pressed by the interviewer, the computer will reject them and so inform the interviewer. In short, a complete hands-on operation can be accomplished with the CRT and survey processor for questions, answers, and entry into data processing directly with no intervening writing, editing, coding, or card punching.

An executive of one firm offering telephone research with CRTs, Chilton Research Services, has pointed out these features of their system:[10]

> An unlimited number of surveys can be handled at a given time. . . .
>
> Rapid changes in workloads can be accommodated since the number of CRT's can be increased on relatively short notice. . . .
>
> Fast programming of questionnaires or question changes can be completed in a relatively short period of time. . . .
>
> Complex questionnaires or sample designs are simplified since the software package uses the . . . computer rather than the ingenuity of the interviewer to make decisions and follow instructions during the interview situation.
>
> Data are ready for tabulation and analysis as soon as the last interview is completed. . . .

An example given in that speech was an annual survey of 14,000 industrial executives that Chilton had conducted, requiring six weeks to finish the tabulations when using the traditional paper questionnaires in telephone interviews. This was a massive study "because we had to precode almost 5,000 items that were acceptable responses to over one-half of the questions and then to reference any of these 5,000 items to form questions later in the questionnaire."[11] When the client found that it needed the survey results within one week of the end of the interviewing, the survey was shifted to the CRT, and a data tape of the results was delivered to the client the day after interviewing was completed.

---

[10] John H. Kofron, "The Electronic Questionnaire—A Status Report," a speech delivered at 1975 AMA International Marketing Conference, April 17, 1975. Reprinted by Chilton Research Services, Radnor, Pa.

[11] Ibid.

10.4 Personal Survey Techniques

Now let us consider interviewing with a face-to-face presence of the interviewer to question the respondent. The interview may be situated on a sidewalk, at some place where people are waiting, or at a central location such as the facilities that some research firms now operate in major shopping centers. The majority of personal interviews, however, probably are made at the respondents' homes, and we will speak in terms of those. We shall divide this discussion into three parts: (1) the tasks to accomplish, (2) errors that occur in field interviewing, and (3) special techniques used in group interviews, which now are widely used.

10.4.1 Personal Interview Tasks

The tasks of the personal interviewer are summarized under two categories in the following excerpt:

> The first (major aspect) involves his function in maximizing the forces to communicate. At the same time, of course, he is attempting to reduce or eliminate the negative forces, the barriers to communication.
>
> The second major function of the interviewer is measurement, which requires him to direct and control the communication process to specific objectives. The interviewer is aware of the basic reasons for which data are being collected, although the respondent may not share this information fully. The research interviewer comes equipped with a substantial list of specific research objectives to which the interview should conform. ... It is (his) ability to so direct the communication that produces a valid interview—that is, an interview which measures the things it purports to measure.[12]

Surveys differ widely in their demands on the interviewer. When the interviewer can obtain the needed information with complete structuring (that is, employing only standardized questions that the interviewer reads verbatim), there is little reliance on the interviewer's ability "to so direct the communication that produces a valid interview," as suggested in the quotation above. In the many instances where probing or formulation of appropriate questions on the spot is needed to obtain full or appropriate information, however, great reliance is placed on the interviewer's intelligence, dependability, and grasp of the study's objectives. Interviewing usually demands skills, too, to get around respondents' reluctance, to generate a voluble and revealing discussion, or to probe for information that is hard to remember.

Business and professional interviews on matters relative to a trade, profession, or industry (for example, surveying doctors on medical matters) may place the interviewer in a more difficult role. Sometimes they

---

[12] R. L. Kahn and C. F. Cannell, *The Dynamics of Interviewing* (New York: John Wiley & Sons, Inc., 1957), p. 62.

involve technical terms and jargon and considerable understanding of the interviewee's field or profession. They may be more demanding also in that the most valuable business and professional surveys are unstructured, so that the formulation of questions devolves on the interviewer. This calls for a high level of competence and preparation of interviewers.

10.4.2 Errors in the Field

Management of the field work aims to maximize the flow of pertinent, accurate data while, in the negative aspect, minimizing the errors committed by the interviewers. The potential errors are of so many types and so capable of distorting a survey's results that our discussion will emphasize the negative side.

Deliberate Falsification

Deliberately falsifying interviews is the worst act that an interviewer may commit, too serious to be categorized among "errors." This form of deliberate cheating is fraudulent, but at one time it was rather common. Thanks to remedies that are increasingly being used (see Section 10.5), the complete faking of interviews appears to be rare in the commercial world.

Sampling Errors

A survey's sampling plan theoretically may provide for a highly representative cross section of the target population, but its precision can be destroyed by interviewers' failures to realize this plan in actual selection. We may distinguish three types of such errors.

Interviews may be attempted or held in the *wrong places*—for example, going to more convenient locations than those directed; skipping a house that was chosen by some ordinal or random sampling method in preference for calling at a neighboring home that is more attractive or where an interview seems more likely to be granted. When the interviewer is directed to prelist all the dwellings in an area prior to selecting the sample for them, she may err either by intentional omissions or by not knowing that some exist (as in multiple dwellings or garage apartments).

Another sampling error is that of interviewing the *wrong person*. Instructions may specify that a person in a certain role, within a household, office, store, or whatever is being canvassed, is the one to interview. Or perhaps the interviewer is supposed to rotate interviews between different members, such as the husband in the first house, wife in the second, and so forth but violates this with arbitrary choices. Or, unqualified persons may be interviewed—for instance, interviewing a salesperson in a retail department when its buyer was supposed to have

281

been interviewed, but proved to be unavailable at the moment. Such substitutions present likelihoods of obtaining wrong information.

The most prevalent and critical sampling failures in the field stem from nonresponses. These are of two types: (1) refusals to provide all or part of the requested information or responses, and (2) failure to reach the intended respondents because they are absent or otherwise unavailable. Both may mean serious gaps in the data gathered, and the second, or "not-at-home," problem is the worse. Its extent is suggested by an analysis of 3,000 report forms submitted by interviewers in two national studies conducted by the Survey Research Center of the University of Michigan.[13] The experience reported in "large metropolitan areas" was that 46 percent of intended interviewees were not at home on the first call and another 29 percent would not be interviewed at that time. After five calls at the designated homes to obtain interviews, approximately 5 percent had not yet been at home and another 8 percent had still not granted an interview. Another 12 percent had refused interviews. The problem is indicated to be serious, but in lower degree, in rural areas, where in the aforementioned surveys 31 percent were not at home on the first call. Ultimately, approximately 46 percent of the metropolitan area and 65 percent of the rural interviews were made. Allowing for the length of the interview sought in those studies (averaging an hour long), it remains evident that the not-at-home and refusal rates faced in any study that adheres to a strict probability sampling plan pose very serious difficulties.

Interviewing Errors

In the interpersonal process of question and answer, numerous possible errors can be made by the interviewer or person whom he or she is interrogating. Trouble may first arise in the effort to obtain proper rapport with the interviewee. If rapport is weak, the subject may be reluctant to respond or may fail to give sufficient attention to what is being asked. Confidence can be promoted with credentials. Strong rapport, on the other hand, might bias the responses, for the interviewee may come too much under the influence of the interviewer—or the latter may become so sympathetic to the interviewee that this affects the conduct of the interview or the objectivity of the reporting (and perhaps draws him or her into a long, unproductive conversation).

Interviewing errors may also stem from failure to follow instructions in administering a questionnaire. The interviewee may not receive a proper explanation of the survey's nature—or may receive one in a manner that would bias responses. The wording of a question may be altered as it is asked, or inflections may be placed on it that influence the interviewee's understanding or color his or her replies. Particular trouble may arise when the subject does not understand the question as stated, so that

---

[13] Charles S. Mayer, "The Interviewer and His Environment," *Journal of Marketing Research*, November, 1964, pp. 24–31.

the interviewer must state it in other terms for her or his benefit, because the altered wording may constitute a different question. When questions are open-ended, this involves the interviewer's formulating probing questions that go beyond the printed words. Unless the probes follow instructions faithfully, the potential for bias may be substantial.

Another type of interviewing error might be categorized as "omissions." Questions may be skipped in haste or inadvertently. A "don't know" or a very superficial response may be forthcoming when the interviewer does not press firmly, has not developed a favorable rapport, or allows insufficient time for the subject to give ample thought to the matter.

Finally, erroneous responses form another interviewing problem. The alert interviewer should recognize when the response is irrelevant to the question, is not the desired type of information, or is inconsistent with a previously given response. Responses from unqualified respondents may also be placed in this category. For instance, if a survey sought opinions on air bags only from persons who had them in their automobiles, an interviewer might err by asking this of other drivers.

Recording Errors

Given a relevant and accurate response, error may arise in the way that the interviewer records it. With time and space limitations, she may record only part of a response or so abbreviate it that significant content is lost. She may substitute her own wording for the respondent's, or unconsciously filter the response through her own biases. Where the interviewer is to enter check marks, as in multiple response or checklist answers, she may record these in the wrong boxes. These hazards are multiplied when the interviewer lacks the opportunity or is not supposed to record during the interrogation and must recall and enter the responses after the interview.

10.4.3 Group Interviews

The group or focus interview was described earlier regarding its nature and suitable applications. When six or eight persons are going to be interviewed in a body and in a free-wheeling discussion rather than answering a structured questionnaire, one clearly faces quite different problems than under the contrasting situation of interviewing a person individually.

The unstructured characteristic of group interviewing makes it similar (in that respect) to informal or depth interviewing of a single person, a somewhat clinical psychological method that is not included in our coverage of techniques. This means that the interviewer is not limited to certain concretely stated questions but rather has latitude to compose and phrase questions as the interview proceeds. The interviewer must know specifically what is desired from the group and should have a printed list of those topics, but the actual questions are improvised. Not only are the questions flexible in wording but in nature, being altered when some contingency arises that makes an elaboration or shift in the group's responses desirable. It probably is evident that an interviewer who understands the problem that thoroughly and has the skill to direct the flow of conversation, without stifling it, is a very competent one. Since the group interviews are taped, the discussion leader is not burdened with trying to write down answers and can put full attention on what is being said and looking for cues to enhance the flow of information.

The way the interviewer introduces the subject to the group is crucial because they define the rules to be followed and set the tone. Wells has written a most interesting example of such opening comments:

> Today we are going to be talking about a topic that I think you will find interesting and that I'm sure you all know a lot about, and that is shortening. First I'd like to find out something about when you use shortening. . . . Then I'd like to find out something about what you think of different forms of shortening, then different brands. Finally we're going to be talking about some advertising for shortening that you may have seen, and we'll look at some shortening commercials. . . .

> First I have a couple of requests. One is that you speak up and only one person speak at a time. We're tape-recording this, and if someone speaks very softly. . . . The other thing is, please say exactly what you think. We're just as interested in negative comments as positive ones, and in fact, the negative comments are sometimes the most useful.

> One thing more. We're not making a radio commercial or a television commercial here, so don't look for the hidden camera. Say exactly what you think, because that's what we want to know.

> Now to get started, perhaps it would be best to go around the table one at a time. I'd like to know something about your families—how many children you have, how old they are, what variety they are, and what your husband does for a living.[14]

There are two extremes in terms of the interviewer's (sometimes called "moderator's") role. One is to be as *nondirective* as is feasible, letting the group largely spark itself and the conversation flow with little interference. The other is to be quite *directive,* with the moderator taking a more frequent and firmer hand in guiding what is said. The latter approach is better when certain information is desired from each group that may be omitted unless the group is steered toward it. This also economizes on time (and length of the recording tape), with the interviewer cutting off persons who talk too long or are straying from the subject. The nondirective approach offers the advantage that when people are allowed to be completely themselves, they may be more re-

---

[14] William D. Wells, "Group Interviewing," in Robert Ferber (ed.), *Handbook of Marketing Research* (New York: McGraw-Hill Book Company, 1974), pp. 2–139.

vealing, and significant information may come out that the interviewer would not have sought.

10.5 Managing the Field Work

Management of the field work aims to maximize the flow of pertinent, accurate data while, in the negative aspect, minimizing the errors committed by the interviewers. The various potential errors can be placed under the following four categories:

1. *Deliberate falsification.* Deliberately faking interviews and turning them in as genuine is the worst interviewing sin. Partially because of stronger control methods, it now seems to be uncommon.
2. *Sampling errors.* These are too common and occur in three ways: (a) interviewing in the wrong places, (b) interviewing the wrong person—although possibly in the right place, and (c) nonresponse errors through respondents' refusal to give all the information sought or (most common of all) inability to reach the intended respondents.
3. *Interviewing errors.* Numerous errors can occur in the question-and-answer process. These may be caused by (a) lack of strong rapport between interviewer and respondent, so that the latter does not cooperate; (b) failure to follow instructions in the questionnaire's administration, either because the interviewer deviates or because the respondent does not understand; and (c) omissions of questions or of information given.
4. *Recording errors.* Given an accurate and relevant response, error may arise in the way that the interviewer records it. With time and space limitations, she or he particularly has problems in recording long responses or entering new responses that are not listed on the questionnaire (and it is easier to select one of those already printed than to write a different one).

Those are some of the hazards faced in field interviewing, either personal or telephone. Now we turn to some steps to deal with these.

10.5.1 Pretesting

Errors frequently result from what the interviewer is requested to do rather than from mistakes on the part of interviewer or the person interviewed. Obscure intent and wrong order of questions, awkward expressions, leading questions, and weak stimulation of response are among many inadequacies that may lie in the questionnaire. Sampling plans may be inappropriate to field conditions, instructions may be vague, and other deficiencies may exist that are unrecognized. They should come to light when a thorough pretesting of the procedures and

285

questionnaire is conducted by the interviewers who typify those who will do the field work.

The pretest simultaneously reveals the limitations of the interviewers. Some who performed poorly may be excluded. The survey may be made less demanding when its requirements are found to be beyond general interviewer capability. A fair production pace that may be expected of the field force may be established in this step.

10.5.2 Simplifying Procedures

A number of efficiencies have been developed to simplify field work tasks. We shall note some of these survey techniques, but it should be noted that some of them may not be suitable to all surveys.

1. The interviewer may be equipped with cards or pages to be handed to interviewees, to clarify or illustrate desired responses or to introduce the interviewer and thereby help to establish rapport. Diagrams of rating scales, pictures, statements in multiple-choice questions, and desired categories of response are other examples of such handouts.

2. The self-administered interview may substitute for having the interviewer ask the questions. The interviewee may complete her answers while the interviewer waits or the latter may call back to retrieve the answers at some specified time. The latter method, the interviewer picking up the completed questionnaire, was demonstrated in an experiment by the National Opinion Research Center, to obtain virtually as high a response rate (73 percent) as questioning conducted by the interviewer in person (76 percent).[15] Among teenage respondents the interviewer pickup method obtained 89 percent response. The cost per completed return was found to be only half that of personally administered interviews.

3. Tape recording of interviews obviously enhances the fidelity of recorded responses and eases the interviewer's role. Of little advantage where simple answers to standardized questionnaires are sought, these recorders are a virtual necessity to group or highly qualitative interviews.

4. Previous appointment, usually by telephone, tends to increase the number of completed interviews per personal visit. A specific analysis of the effect of prior telephone appointments, also by the National Opinion Research Center, found that only 1.7 personal calls at a designated home were needed to obtain an interview with an appointment, versus 2.3 calls where no appointment had been made.[16]

[15] S. Sudman, A. Greeley, and L. Pinto, "The Effectiveness of Self-Administered Questionnaires," *Journal of Marketing Research*, August 1965, pp. 293–97.

[16] Seymour Sudman, "New Uses of Telephone Methods in Survey Research," *Journal of Marketing Research* May, 1966, pp. 163–67.

5. Various ways of improving the design and legibility of questionnaires may be applied to easing the work and enhancing accuracy.

10.5.3 Instructing Field Workers

The instruction of field workers should include both providing ample instructional materials and conducting training in applying those instructions. Instructions should be stated in clear and distinct terms, of course, and should cover these topics:

1. What the survey is about (without revealing sponsorship, if that would risk interviewer bias).
2. When the survey is to start and when it is to be finished, when to call on respondents.
3. How many persons are to be interviewed, where and how to select them, and what to do about persons not at home.
4. How to introduce oneself and initiate the interview.
5. How each question should be asked and which ones are contingent on the answers to other questions.
6. Methods of probing, encouraging responses, and aiding memory.
7. If any items are to be observed, what is to be noted.
8. How each questionnaire is to be studied and corrected before returning the form.
9. What to do with the completed questionnaires.
10. When and how she will be paid for her work.
11. The exact basis on which the quality of work will be appraised.

Two examples of instructions used by a major marketing research agency are shown in Figures 10–2 and 10–3.

The "call record sheet" would facilitate an interviewer's keeping records of where she has interviewed, where she failed to, and the status. The codes enable standard records of what has happened at each address and permit the interviewer to quickly identify those where she should call back. With Figure 10–3 all interviewers are given a common starting point (SP), which would help to reduce bias in selecting residences. Also, a similar direction would be followed in choosing another block when the first one does not provide sufficient interviews.

Training should be given personally to the field staff members whenever possible. Mailed instructions commonly are the only means of training interviewers in many national surveys, and this may be the only practicable medium. Where there is nothing unusual in the interviewing techniques and the interviewers are experienced in similar work, the lack of personal training may be no appreciable detriment.

Personal training may take place at sessions in central meetings or while on the job—although using both methods is preferable. Training

287

```
MARKET FACTS, INC., 100 South Wacker Drive, Chicago, Illinois 60606

                          FIELD SURVEY

                        CALL RECORD SHEET

Job No. _____

INTERVIEWER _____   FIELD STATION _____

INSTRUCTIONS FOR USE:  Circle only one code number in the appropriate attempt
                       column.  Total the columns at the bottom of the page.

CODE DEFINITIONS:      1.  No Answer                6.  Over Quota
                       2.  Respondent Not Available 7.  Terminate at Qu.# ____
                       3.  Refused To Be Screened   8.  Completed Interview
                       4.  Not Qualified                Other (Write In)
                       5.  Qualified but Refused

Big Block/Cluster # _____
```

ADDRESS	1ST ATTEMPT	2ND ATTEMPT	3RD ATTEMPT
1.	1 2 3 4 5 6 7 8 at	1 2 3 4 5 6 7 8 at	1 2 3 4 5 6 7 8 at
2.	1 2 3 4 5 6 7 8 at	1 2 3 4 5 6 7 8 at	1 2 3 4 5 6 7 8 at
3.	1 2 3 4 5 6 7 8 at	1 2 3 4 5 6 7 8 at	1 2 3 4 5 6 7 8 at
4.	1 2 3 4 5 6 7 8 at	1 2 3 4 5 6 7 8 at	1 2 3 4 5 6 7 8 at

FIGURE 10–2. Call Record Sheet for Personal Interviews

Source: Courtesy of Market Facts, Inc., Chicago.

sessions should cover every aspect of the work and give the interviewer ample understanding of the survey's objectives and how to meet contingencies.

10.5.4 Supervision

Interviewers should be under a field supervisor whose duties would include: (1) training, assisting, and overseeing; (2) mapping, and perhaps prelisting addresses for, the specific sample selection in the field; (3) hiring local interviewing help when distant from the central office; and (4) editing the questionnaires turned in before forwarding them to the central office. The supervisor should maintain regular contact with interviewers working in dispersed locations and handle correspondence and reports to the home office. In order to be familiar with interviewers' current problems, the supervisor should also do some interviewing.

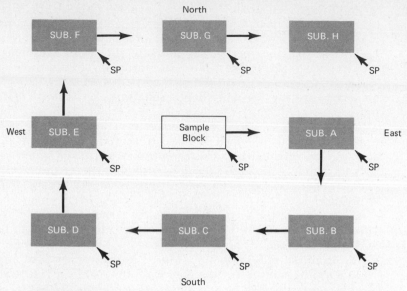

FIGURE 10–3. Diagram Instructing Interviewers for Block Substitutions
Source: Courtesy of Market Facts, Inc., Chicago.

10.5.5 Control

Good control hinges on having realistically anticipated and planned a survey, with the plan written in detail so that its execution can be followed closely. Two other steps that are instrumental in achieving control should be mentioned: scheduling and validating.

There are numerous actions to be performed in a typical field study, and they require synchronization. Some of them must be initiated far in advance of the field canvass. On this subject, let us refer back to Chapter 5. In Table 5–1 was listed such a series of actions, the time they were expected to require, and the starting dates necessary to meet the schedule. Some of those were field work tasks and others were coordinated activities. If they are charted as a critical path, as in Figure 5–2, control is more readily effected, so that all work can be completed on time. Along with scheduling would be the companion activity of budgeting, which easily gets out of hand unless time and costs are monitored closely.

Validation refers to verifying that the interviewers are submitting authentic interviews of acceptable quality. When there is no field supervision, the home office has primary responsibility in checking the field work. This check has three aspects: (1) determining that the instructions were studied and understood, (2) determining whether the reported interviews are genuine, and (3) appraising the quality of the interviewing and reporting.

Formerly, cheating was widespread among interviewers, but this type of fraud has been greatly reduced, partially through the checks that research agencies have developed as deterrents. One check consists of calling persons who were identified as interviewees on the returns, to inquire whether the interviewer actually did call. This check is more accurate when the workers have left cards to identify themselves. There has been serious abuse on the part of persons posing as interviewers to gain sales leads or for more deplorable purposes, so such identification is important.

Another type of check is to have interviewers give the persons called upon a postcard on which to indicate that the call was made. Cheating also may be revealed by a close scrutiny of returned interviews. It is not easy to fake interviews so that they resemble the genuine responses, and peculiar patterns in a particular interviewer's returns may spotlight cheating.

Evaluation of the quality of interview reporting is fully as important. Interviewers should be told in advance that their work is to be evaluated and graded. Some of the aspects that should be evaluated were indicated in the example in Section 10.5. Most interviewers will be anxious to receive a high grade so that the firm will hire them on future surveys, and their standings should be reported back to them.

10.6 Summary

One always plans the interviewing aspects of a marketing research study in such a way that the data obtained tend to be accurate. In meeting this objective, one must keep in mind the important relationship between response errors and interviewing techniques, such as adequate preparation of forms, education and training of interviewers, and effective methods of controlling the interviewing processes so that the errors may be minimized.

As indicated in Chapter 9, we do not exhaust the many details of the interviewing task. The objective has been one of providing a true understanding of the basic factors related to the data-gathering process.

CASE 10

COTTONWOOD STATION, INC. (B)

The history and characteristics of Cottonwood Station, Inc., were sketched in Case 5, Cottonwood Station, Inc. (A). Much of that case should be read as background for this case. It concluded with the founder of that real estate development firm at a stage of clarifying the problems, opportunities, and options faced in marketing the mobile home units that would be placed in the Cottonwood Village section of the firm's properties.

It was decided to launch extensive research into the identified marketing problems, for which outside assistance was obtained. Before undertaking the gathering of primary data, which would be time consuming and expensive, there was the evident need to bring together presently available data from sources in the St. Louis metropolitan area. Perhaps some decisions could proceed on the basis of those data, and unnecessary efforts might be avoided to again gather what was already available.

The principal subjects on which secondary data were desired were listed by the researchers in collaboration with Dr. Ottwein. The following list was composed:

1 Data on mobile homes parks in Madison County, Illinois (in which Cottonwood Village was located), and northern St. Louis County, Missouri. Trends should be obtained, if available.

2 Data on apartments and other rental units and on condominiums in those areas.

3 Characteristics of occupants of mobile home parks, in contrast with data on the general population.

4 National data on mobile home production, prices, design improvements, and modes of living.

5 Information on new features found in innovative and luxury mobile home parks.

6 General housing data for the entire St. Louis metropolitan area and for Madison County.

7 Types of housing, rents or values of owned residences, and occupancy rates for all census tracts in Madison County.

8 Volume of construction in the St. Louis metropolitan area, preferably broken down by counties and major cities, including data on trends and predictions, for residential buildings.

9 Mobility of the population, by age, occupation, and income levels. Data specifically on various types of homes, if available.

10 Data on trends in attitudes toward mobile home living. Perhaps only qualitative information would be available or only current data.

Discussion

1. What would you add to the list above, in data that would appear to be pertinent to Cottonwood Village's situation and available from secondary sources?

2. For each type of data given in the list above, to what specific sources would you go?

THE CAMPUS NEWS

In a prominent coeducational university that we shall call Great University, *The Campus News* is published daily except Sunday and is intended primarily for the students. It is free to students on campus; it is available at a number of convenient central points; and it is sustained in large part by revenue from the advertising.

Last March student officials of *The Campus News* approached Professor Schmidt,[17] who teaches an advanced marketing research course, to request that his class conduct a personal survey of Great University students to learn what they buy and where. Such information was often sought by potential advertisers, and it was supposed that this might be an interesting and valuable project for the marketing research students. Professor Schmidt agreed. After the class completed the preliminary phases of the research, he assigned specialized data-gathering phases to three task forces: (1) questionnaire design, (2) sample design, and (3) field investigation planning.

Residence Locations of Great University's Students, Spring Term

University City	Men	Women	Total
Dormitories	4,233	3,501	7,734
Living at home	147	105	252
Coops	206	—	206
Approved housing	1,397	89	1,486
Nonapproved housing	373	75	448
Married—off campus	584	188	772
Single—apartments	89	48	137
Married—on campus	1,598	179	1,777
Fraternity—sorority	895	572	1,467
Total	9,522	4,757	14,279

The sampling task force brought in an interim report covering the definition of the sample and some approaches to the general problem. This was discussed in class before they proceeded further. The report read as follows:

For the purpose of our survey, we have reduced the sampling universe from 14,279 to 12,144. We have eliminated all students who do not live within the boundaries of University City, and those living in nonapproved housing in University City, for the following reasons:

---

[17] Fictitious name.

1. The lack of time prohibits as extensive a survey as desirable.
2. The excluded population is beyond the scope of our immediate concern.
3. The exclusion of students living in nonapproved housing within University City was necessitated by the lack of correct available addresses. We have stratified our universe by sex, marital status, and resident location.

The following is a breakdown of the total student population to be sampled by number and percentage of each group to total universe, and the number within each group was arrived at by the use of the following formula:

$$\frac{\% \text{ of group}}{100\%} = \frac{X}{\text{total sampling universe}}$$

X is the number of interviews needed within each group.

Stratified Group	Total Within Group	Percent of Universe	Number of Interviews
Men in dormitories	4,233	34.9%	153
Men at home	147	1.2	6
Coops	206	1.6	7
Men in approved housing	1,397	11.6	50
Married men off campus	584	4.9	21
Men in fraternity houses	895	7.4	33
Women in dormitories	3,501	28.9	126
Women living at home	105	0.8	4
Women in approved housing	89	0.7	3
Married women off campus	188	1.5	7
Single women in apartments	48	0.3	2
Married women on campus	179	1.4	7
Women in sorority housing	572	4.8	20
Total	12,144	100.0%	439

The task force reported that the current year's Student Directory had been compiled and had become available. The task force found that the directory was practically complete for spring registration. They stated that certain additional tasks now lay before them. The report explained why a sample of 500 ought to prove adequate for the survey's needs, and its reasoning was acceptable.

Discussion

If you were a member of this committee, how would you answer these questions?

1. What method of sample selection would you recommend? List the steps involved.
2. How might you determine whether the proposed sample size of 500 was, or was not, proper?
3. When the survey is completed, how are the students going to know whether they have obtained a proper sample?

CASE 12

STATE FARM MUTUAL AUTOMOBILE INSURANCE COMPANY[18]

State Farm Mutual Automobile Insurance Company is one of the largest insurers of automobiles in the world. State Farm's success depends substantially on the services it renders to its policyholders, including the processing of claims on damages submitted against its policies. Several years ago, rising numbers and costs of repair claims were rendering this an increasing burden on the company and was a source of ill will with claimants. Under existing procedure, policyholders reported accidents, or other covered damages, to their State Farm agents first.

The damaged car's owner then was directed to have appraisals of costs obtained from any two of the listed garages in his area. Then the company's claims specialists would study the reasonableness of these bids, as well as determine the company's liability. After their approval, the car could be repaired. The procedure often took so long that claimants were irked, and it was expensive for the company. State Farm perceived that they could establish large claims locations, but with the added advantage of providing drive-in facilities into which driveable damaged cars with claims on State Farms policies could be brought by owners. There the company's claims personnel could inspect the car and determine whether they would approve the claim. If approved, the amount of settlement to repair the damage could be decided on the spot, which would mean one-stop service for the typical case. Then the claimant could immediately take his car to his chosen garage for repair within the approved figure.

After the State Farm Company had located and opened its first claims drive-in stations in the Chicago area, policyholders' reactions were so favorable that the company determined to establish drive-in stations in other metropolises. A top-priority area was the Metropolitan San Francisco division, with headquarters in Berkeley. To conduct the underlying research on locations, Milton Walz[19] of the central operations control staff in Bloomington, Illinois, was dispatched to devote a few weeks to arranging the San Francisco area study. One of his tasks was administering the sampling of policyholders.

The portion of the study relating to policyholders had two initial purposes:

---

[18] This case is actual and is used with permission of the company. Some of the questions at its end are hypothetical, however.

[19] Fictitious name.

(1) to map the numbers of policyholders located in various areas within the total division, and (2) to conduct a telephone survey of policyholders to test alternative locations that might be convenient to a maximum of those submitting claims.

The members of the population obviously would comprise all holders of State Farm automobile casualty policies on the date of sampling. The area concerned would be the entire Metropolitan San Francisco area, which was coterminous with the U.S. Bureau of the Census definition of that standard metropolitan statistical area and included the five counties of Alameda, Contra Costa, Marin, San Francisco, and San Mateo. The number of State Farm automobile policyholders exceeded 150,000, so large a number that their total inclusion in the study would be absurd. Therefore, sampling was indicated.

This entire population could be found in the division's policyholder records. Every policy was described on a card, whose data included the policyholder's post office, street and town address, name, telephone number, and the State Farm supervisory district of the agent. These cards were filed consecutively by policy number in drawers. These numbers were sequenced by the date when State Farm approved the insurance application. Agents frequently would cumulate applications to the end of a week before sending the batch to Berkeley, which meant that a dozen or more consecutive numbers might be clustered by a single agent's area. The file drawers each contained approximately 1,000 policy cards, in 150 drawers.

Discussion

1. Mr. Walz indicated that the universe to be studied be the company's policyholders in the San Francisco area. Would you have chosen a different universe to be studied? Why?
2. Mr. Walz decides that the sample to be selected will be drawn from the policy files. He is considering the following three methods: simple random sampling, systematic sampling, and cluster sampling. Indicate how you would select the sample for each of these methods. Which method would you recommend? Why?
3. Suppose that Mr. Walz selected a simple random sample of 800, and 725 responded in the following way: 525 indicated an interest in the new claims drive-in stations and 200 did not. Mr. Walz asks you to establish a 95 percent confidence interval for the true population proportion who are interested in the new drive-in stations.
4. If the survey was going to be conducted by personal interviews, calling at the respondents' homes, would any of Mr. Walz's sampling plans have been efficient? If not, how would you have changed it?
5. Assume now that the sample selection would manifestly be random. Mr. Walz and a colleague decided to choose a 95 percent confidence level. You are told that your estimate should have a precision of ±3 percentage points. Compute the sample size that will satisfy these requirements. (Favorable response is estimated at 60 percent.)

6. What would be the sample size if the precision requirements changed from ±3 to ±12 percentage points?
7. What would the sample size be if the confidence level is changed from 95 percent to 90 percent? Assume the same information as in question 5.

CASE 13

LOWE & HARPER DEPARTMENT STORE

Lowe & Harper Department Store was familiarly known as "Lowe's" among the people who lived in the city of Valley Springs and its vicinity. Lowe's was the major department store of that city with its main operation located downtown. Lowe's also had two suburban branches and had expanded 40 miles southward to the city of Palmer, (total population of 150,000; number of households is 43,271 in forty-one census tracts). The store in Palmer is as large as the downtown store in Valley Springs. Lowe's major merchandising policy was aimed at middle- to upper-class consumers, largely women, among whom it had a very good quality image, although it was not considered a high-fashion store. Each unit also had a basement store for selling economy grades of merchandise so that families of rather low income might also be Lowe's customers.

Discount chains had been entering Lowe's trading area with marked success, including several units of K-Mart and Zayre. Lowe's officials judged that the discounters had cut its basement store's market substantially, probably at least 20 percent. As the area's leading retailer, though, Lowe's was not accepting the discounter's incursion without countereffort. To that end, Lowe's designed its own discount merchandising strategy in its own "Lowe-Way" stores, which were ideally aimed to meet the area's tastes. The first Lowe-Way unit was opened in Palmer about eighteen months ago, and Lowe's executives waited to see results before opening others.

As the results of the first full year in Palmer were studied, adverse effects on the business of the Lowe's Palmer downstairs store were a worry. It had dropped in dollar sales by 7 percent in the face of a 11 percent growth of the Palmer retail stores. It was evident that the consumer must be researched to find the trends in department/discount store patronage and underlying motives. A regional research firm known as Market Monitors, Inc., was retained to plan and execute the survey. They were asked to find answers to these questions, particularly:

1. Could certain segments of the shopping population be distinguished as primarily department store or discount store shoppers, or were these mingled?
2. Was the Palmer loss in Lowe's volume due to switching to the Lowe-Way store, to other discounters, to other prestigious stores, or to a local drop in general purchasing?

3. What were the causal factors?

4. Did this seem to be a permanent switching away from Lowe's, or temporary one?

Planning and selecting the sample would be a critical step, both in deciding an ample but efficient size and in obtaining with precision the desired cross section. Lowe's stipulated that personal interviews be conducted. The area to be covered was framed specifically as the city of Palmer and designated outlying areas. The client requested that a "well-balanced sample be gathered with respect to demographic factors seriously affecting store patronage," but left the choice of such factors to Market Monitors.

Discussion

1. Prepare a definition of the desired population that will be both accurate and clear enough for practical use in sample planning and selection.
2. The research team assigned to this project is considering both probability and nonprobability sampling methods during their planning stage. Within each of these categories there are various methods (refer to Figure 7–1). Describe how you would select a sample from the desired population. What specific information besides that listed above is needed to guide you in drawing up your sampling plan?
3. What types of errors, if any, are likely to be observed because of the sample design you chose for this project?
4. Explain why you recommend this sample design.

CASE 14

CENTRAL CITY REPORTER (A)

The publisher and owner of *The Reporter,*[20] a newspaper serving the metropolitan area of Central City, with a population of approximately 115,000 wanted to know whether to publish complete stock-market quotations in his newspaper on a daily or on a weekly basis. Several of his friends who had been dealing in the stock market had approached him with the request that he list the complete daily stock-market quotations. They were primarily interested in the transactions conducted on the New York Exchange, even though *The Reporter* was published in a Midwestern city.

The publisher was undecided as to whether he could afford to offer detailed information about the stock market to his readers, because it is a very expensive process to set up the quotations each day and because determin-

---
[20] Fictitious name.

ing just how many stock quotations should be listed, even if done on a daily basis, is a difficult job. Some stock-market news was carried every day along with information about the commodity markets, but this was primarily limited to news stories from wire services about trading activity on the exchanges. In Sunday editions, *The Reporter* carried complete reports on the previous week's stock prices.

The publisher asked a marketing research consulting firm to look into the problem and to make recommendations. After several weeks' study, the consulting firm recommended that a telephone survey be made of the people in the metropolitan area of Central City. In view of the fact that there were two competing papers in the area, the firm felt that it would be desirable to determine what features were liked in each of the papers and what readers felt they should have in addition to the features now carried by all three newspapers. These papers were *The Reporter, The Star,* and *The University News.* The objectives of the survey were (1) to determine to what extent the people in Central City were aware that *The Reporter* carried complete stock-market quotations on Sundays, and (2) to determine the extent to which the people in Central City were aware of the use of color advertisements in *The Star.* Both objectives were to be investigated with reference to selected characteristics of those interviewed: newspaper readership, length of residence in the area, age, education, sex, and ownership of common stock. The data were to be obtained by means of a probability sample of residential telephones in the community.

The sample members were selected with the aid of a table of random numbers. Using this table, six-digit numbers were chosen, moving horizontally from left to right on the pages. The first three digits designated the page number in the Central City telephone directory, the fourth digit, the column on the page (the directory has three columns of names to a page), and the last two digits, the line number in the column. If the line number corresponded with the telephone number of a private residence, it was included in the sample; if not, the six-digit number was discarded.

Using this procedure 488 names and telephone numbers were selected, a number felt sufficient to yield about 400 completed interviews. This number of completed interviews would yield estimates of any attributes for the sample as a whole within 5 percentage points of the true value with at least 95 percent confidence, which would seem to provide ample reliability for the purposes of the study. Interviewers were to be trained in telephone interviewing and were asked to speak with an adult eighteen years of age or more. Women were employed to do the interviewing and were instructed to introduce themselves as representing the consulting firm that was making a study of the extent to which people were aware of selected features in the local newspapers. The interviewer was then to go through the questions on the questionnaire, completing them in the order shown. A copy of that form appears in Figure 1.

Calls were interspersed at different times of the day and on different days of the week, so that all types of people could be reached. To avoid interviewing too high a proportion of women, interviewers were instructed to alternate between sexes, a procedure that worked well.

If any question arose regarding the sponsorship of the survey, the inter-

Newspaper Feature Study
Midwest Research Associates, Inc.

Hello, This is Mrs._____of Midwest Research Associates. We are making a study of people's awareness of features of our local newspapers. I want to emphasize that we are not selling anything. I just want to ask you a few questions. For example,....

1. Have you noticed whether any of the local newspapers carry....

	No	DK	Yes	Which one(s)?	Daily or Sunday?
a. Drew Pearson's column?	—	—	⟶	____	____
b. Complete stock market quotations?	—	—	⟶	____	____

(If "daily")
   i. Of course, the_____carries some market news every day, but have you noticed whether any newspaper carries *complete* stock market prices daily or Sunday?

				Which one(s)?	Daily or Sunday?
	—		⟶	____	____
c. Color advertisements?	—	—	⟶	____	____

(If "yes")
   i. Can you tell me when you saw the most recent one?_____
   ii. What was it about?_____
_____

	No	DK	Yes	Which one(s)?	Daily or Sunday?
d. National weather map?	—	—	⟶	____	____
e. NY Times News Service?	—	—	⟶	____	____
f. Book review section?	—	—	⟶	____	____

2. a. (Ask only if "No" or "DK" to 1b) Am I correct that you said you did not know if any local newspapers had complete stock market coverage? Of course, none do, on a daily basis. However, were you aware that the *Reporter* carried stock market prices on Sundays?   ___ No   ___ Yes

   b. (Ask only if "No" or "DK" to 1c) Let me check your answer about color ads. Of course, none of the local newspapers carries such ads every day, but the *Star* does carry such ads occasionally. Were you aware of this?   ___ No   ___ Yes

3. Which local newspapers do you read?   How long (years)?
   ___Reporter_____   ___Star_____   ___University News_____   ___None

4. Finally, let me get some classifying information so that we can combine your answers with those of other people.
   a. How long have you lived in Central City?   _____years
   b. What is your approximate age?_____
   c. Highest grade of education?   ___Grade   ___H.S.   ___College   ___Post Graduate
   d. Do you own any common or preferred stock?   ___No   ___Yes
   e. Sex   ___Male   ___Female

Name_____   Date and time_____
Phone_____   Interviewer_____

FIGURE 1. Newspaper Feature Study

Source: Midwest Research Associates, Inc.

viewer referred the respondent to the marketing consulting firm. The interviewers were not told the real purpose of the survey nor the identity of the sponsor. At least three return calls were to be made in cases of no answer, although in most cases callbacks were made until an answer was obtained. No substitution of telephone numbers was permitted. The response rate was exceptionally high: 97 percent of the eligible sample was reached, and virtually all of these people were interviewed.

Discussion

1. Comment on whether the questionnaire is adequate to meet the purposes outlined. Suggest any changes in the questions or their sequence.
2. Was too much information sought in terms of the objectives discussed? Justify.

four

Analysis, Interpretation, and Application

OUR LAST PART is what the researcher should have been anticipating all along, ever since the possibility of a study arose in the dialogue begun in Chapter 2. Every step in its development impinges on the nature of the conclusions that ultimately will be drawn and their aptness to guiding the decisions that must be made.

This is the most intriguing portion of research and also is the most satisfying when the conclusions have a real payoff. The tasks it involves are partially artistic ones that depend on the skill and insight of the researcher and decision maker. Yet it must be formally planned and carefully executed for the sake of efficiency. In these phases lie perhaps the worst dangers of meandering and blundering. The needs for efficiency and for drawing a maximum of pertinent information and inferences, at this final stage, mean that good planning is imperative.

There are five broad stages in Part IV. The first three are not only interrelated but should be dealt with interactively and simultaneously: data processing, analysis, and interpretation. More space is given to analytical methods because they are not easily grasped by typical students and because they are more solely the researcher's responsibility than are data processing and interpretation. The fourth stage of presentation is given detailed treatment, as this is very critical to a study's reaching application and is a subject highly valuable to students for many purposes both inside and outside their careers. In "follow-through" we conclude with some remaining tasks of importance in completing the research tasks.

Chapter 15 adds a sort of "dessert" to our main courses. It discusses market analysis and sales forecasting methods, to leave you with a taste of some applications—in the areas most common in business.

11 Data Processing

Chapter 11 presents the alternative ways of processing data. This typically is done, in modern organizations, by specialists, but the researcher should make a number of decisions for which he should be able to answer such questions as these:

What are the steps through which data processing proceeds?

What first needs to be done with the crude fragments of data, in the form in which they come from the field? In what shape must they be for data-processing readiness?

What are the main methods of data processing? What are the requirements and benefits of each?

How should the researcher decide which method to choose?

AMONG THE THREE PHASES of reaching conclusions (analysis, data processing, and interpretation), the first that we shall discuss is that of data processing. Large tasks face the analyst in pulling together the bits of data, categorizing them, and performing various manipulations whenever a project involves the assembling of primary data. As secondary data arrive already processed, any additional work to process the desired values from them is seldom extensive. With primary data typically involved, a researcher must understand how to plan and use data processing. This chapter introduces this research aspect and some alternative methods from which ideal procedures may be chosen for a particular project.

11.1 General Tasks and Approaches

Data processing's total task in carrying out the analytical program is to convert crude fragments of observations and responses into orderly statistics for interpretation. We shall amplify this general description by briefly stating seven stages of data processing:

1. *Data preparation.* There are three preparation stages necessary in either manual or computer processing: editing, classifying, and coding. An additional stage with computers is card punching.

2. *Programming.* Every data-processing job, whatever the method used, needs preplanning that specifically lays out directions to the persons doing tabulating (manually) or to the machinery (with computers). This describes specifically the particular operations to take place, with what equipment, by whom, and so forth.

3. *Sorting.* All the bits of data have to be classified together with the other bits that are of the same nature, by being sorted into groups.

4. *Counting.* When the preparatory work has been done, the individual observations can be counted and accumulated in subtotals of the prescribed classifications.

5. *Summarizing.* The various subtotals and totals are brought together and summarized in tables that will exhibit the data in an informative manner.

6. *Computations.* When computers are employed, various calculations may be performed with the data during the tabulation operations. When other methods are utilized, the computations are performed as separate stages subsequent to the preparation of tables.

7. *Control.* Means for making proper checks of the accuracy of the data processing are practically essential. This includes examination of the coding and, if machines are used, the card punching and programs. Also, a base total of the number of questionnaires or other data forms being processed should be determined before the processing begins, thereby providing a total with which to verify

whether each data breakdown, or analysis, totals to exactly this base figure.

These basic functions and their sequence can serve as a point of reference during our discussion of this subject.

It is not our intention in this chapter to provide you with details on how to process data, since this discussion is not directed to technicians in that field. Many readers already will have had courses on computers, which have become almost standard in business school curricula. Another reason for not going deeply into data-processing methods is that a marketing researcher would not require in-depth knowledge. The researcher should be well acquainted with (1) how to use data-processing facilities efficiently, and (2) how to make correct decisions on the particular approach to take for any given project. In this general introduction we give the following four primary approaches, and we shall return to them in Section 11.4.

1. Use manual or personal methods of data processing.
2. Utilize data-processing-service experts, if available, who probably would use computers as their tools.
3. Utilize packaged analysis routines (or programs), chosen on the basis of personal knowledge.
4. Develop computer software, or modify existing software, specifically developed for specialized or recurring routines.

Before we can consider intelligently the choice among these four approaches, we need to understand the preparatory steps, especially the alternative data-processing methods.

11.2 Preparatory Steps

Data are rarely received in a form ready to enter processing, and getting them ready may be a substantial job. Most of it must be done personally or manually, and this may mean major costs of personnel and consumption of time. As in other tasks done by human beings, the error possibilities are considerable. And so the preparatory work needs to be well organized and supervised in each phase.

11.2.1 Editing

Editing comprises inspecting, correcting, and modifying the information found on each questionnaire received to be sure that the information is stated correctly, adequately, and on a basis common to all similar categories of reply. The first editing would take place in the field, where the interviewer or observer should carefully examine the entries made during an interview or observed episode to make them as clear, specific, and correct as possible.

When the returns arrive at a central office, an editor can make a more complete and exacting scrutiny and correction of the returns from the field. The work calls for a keen eye, thorough knowledge of the information sought in the survey, and speed combined with accurate observation. The best procedure is to have a single person specialize in all the editing for a given study, and when more than one editor is needed, for efficiency each should work through complete questionnaires.

A number of faults may call for editorial correction, of which the following are fairly common:

1. *Fictitious interviews.* Such cheating becomes apparent to experienced editors, who would reject such returns.
2. *Erroneous information.* Unfortunately, most errors are not evident, but factual errors may be recognized. If the rest of the information on the return indicates the right fact, sometimes the editor can make such a correction.
3. *Inconsistencies.* A watchful editor may note responses to two questions that could not possibly both be true. Again, one can sometimes surmise from other information which answer is correct, but the assumption is risky.
4. *Inadequate answers.* The response shown on the form may not be complete, or it may be ambiguous. Frequently, the rest of an incomplete answer can be surmised. Ambiguous or indefinite answers pose puzzles, and the editor must judge whether one can clarify them with any confidence.
5. *Irrelevant answers.* Information may be given that does not concern the purpose of a question, perhaps because the respondent misunderstood what was being asked. Another form of irrelevance occurs when respondents who were not qualified to answer a question (which the interviewer should have known from any screening questions) do answer it. Irrelevancies, of course, should be eliminated.

Inconsistencies need not all be detected manually at the editorial stage when the returns are to be *processed by computer.* Computers can determine, for example, when code numbers beyond the assigned range have been punched erroneously. (For instance, since sex would call for using only two code numbers, for example 0 and 1, the computer would reject a "2" punch for sex.) Also, computers can screen out responses to questions that some type of respondent was not supposed to answer. (If men were not supposed to answer certain questions, for instance, the computer would reject punched responses of those that did.) They can also be programmed to detect and reject inconsistencies among answers.

In addition to correcting the mistakes or possibly filling in the gaps in the responses, the editor often converts the original responses or forms of expression into uniform ones. Like answers to be grouped together need to be in a common form, so they need to be changed to a uniform basis. The editor needs to have the specific classifications used.

11.2.2 Determining Classifications

Data cannot be processed or analyzed until they have been classified into homogeneous categories—as well as in proper numerical intervals. This task of determining relevant classifications preferably was largely decided during the design stage. Again, when questionnaires were prepared, uniform categories for both statistics and qualitative responses would have been placed on the form, provided that significant categories could be anticipated. To that extent, classification work at the present stage is avoided.

Very often the researcher cannot safely anticipate what sort of responses would be forthcoming, particularly when employing free responses or open-ended questions. The determination of classifications for these responses must await the point of editing. They may also be, where categories were printed on the questionnaires, answers written in that fell outside the provided categories that need classification. Deciding classifications intelligently calls for full understanding of the purposes of the project and of the problems encountered in gathering data in the field.

The editor should examine the returns to find which categories of replies justify separate classifications. Questionnaires should be drawn from the returns in a random manner, taking normally 10 to 20 percent of the returns. These are then examined, with the editor seeking types of responses that have a common meaning in relationship to the study's objectives, as well as casting about for the best vocabulary to describe each category succinctly. Certain types of responses may appear frequently among the first portion scanned, so these would be given new classifications. The remainder would be lumped together as miscellaneous or, in census terminology, "not elsewhere classified."

Computers can assist in identifying when additional classifications are needed. When printouts from the first run of the data show an excessive frequency of responses falling under the miscellaneous code, the researcher may explore the questionnaires or source documents to determine which types of responses were numerous. When new and additional code numbers are assigned to these, it requires punching a new batch of cards to include them, and that is work that could have been avoided by alertness in the original design or personal editing.

11.2.3 Coding

For computer processing, answers that are given verbally in responses *must* be translated into codes. A code may be in letters (A, B, and so forth), as letters may be processed, but numbers are usually preferred. Manual data processing does not require such compact codes, but they

307

avoid writing effort when indicating on questionnaires the categories into which the particular responses are to be placed.

Coding may be done at either of two times. *Precoding* is determining the codes at the time of designing questionnaires, and therefore code numbers can be printed on them. This greatly reduces the task of later data preparation and also tends to reduce coding errors. Where there is *not* precoding, which is justifiable when the categories of responses could not be anticipated, this must be done after the editing.

To understand how to determine codes, one first should be acquainted with computer punch cards. Everyone probably has written data on punch cards at least when registering for classes, but perhaps not all readers know about their layouts. Therefore, in Figure 11–1 we show a punch card that indicates where numbers and other characters would be punched on the card. Before determining the code numbers, specific columns must be assigned to each question or data classification.

Where the information to be processed electronically is on questionnaires, the "source document," the researcher usually wants all the information to be put on the punch cards. This would mean that every bit of information on the questionnaire should be converted to a code, and so card columns need to be designated to provide for it. If eighty columns do not suffice, two or more punch cards may be used, tying together those for each return by means of an identifying code number.

As an example of codes, consider the portion of an actual commercial questionnaire shown in Figure 11–2. On that form the numbers along the right margin tell what columns on the punch card are assigned to each question's data. Question 1 is "self-coded" in that the indicated number of times is itself the code to be punched on the card, taking one column. Question 2 also has single-digit code numbers, which have been

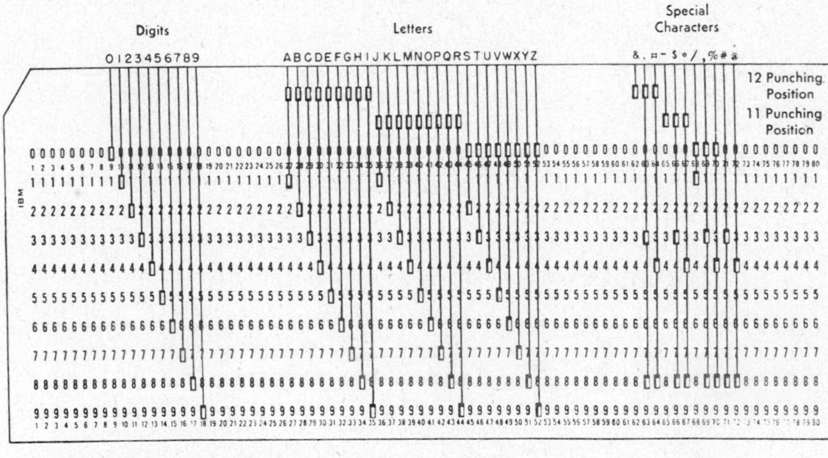

FIGURE 11–1. IBM Punch Card.

On this card are shown various punching positions used to indicate digits, letters, or special characters.

Source: Courtesy of International Business Machine Corporation.

1. In the past week how many times did you, yourself, use these bath beads marked
    "Use Second?" *(Circle one.)* 1   2   3   4   5   6   7 or more   12

2. About how much product did you use each time? ("X" ONE BOX)

1 tbsp. or less	☐ 1	4 tablespoons	☐ 4	Just poured from box ☐ 7	
2 tablespoons	☐ 2	5 or more tbsp.	☐ 5		13
3 tablespoons	☐ 3	1/3 cup	☐ 6		

3. I would like to know your overall opinion about these bath beads marked "Use
    Second." Taking everything into consideration, please tell me how much you like or
    dislike the bath beads marked "Use Second" by placing an "X" in the ONE box
    under the statement that best expresses your own personal opinion about this
    product.

    You'll notice that the boxes toward the left represent a more *unfavorable* opinion, the
    boxes toward the *right* represent a more *favorable* opinion. Each set of boxes are
    described verbally to help you in expressing your opinion. There are no right or wrong
    answers — only your personal opinion is important.

Below Average	About Average	A Little Better Than Average	A Lot Better Than Average	One Of The Best	Absolutely None Better	
☐	☐ ☐	☐ ☐	☐ ☐	☐ ☐	☐	14

4a. What was there about these bath beads marked "Use Second" that you did *NOT*
     like?

_____

_____

15 ☐☐ 16

4b. What was there about these bath beads marked "Use Second" that you did like?

_____

_____

17 ☐☐ 18

FIGURE 11–2. Questionnaire with Precoding and Boxes for Entering Codes

Source: Courtesy of Market Facts, Inc., Chicago.

given alongside each category of response. Question 3 differs in that the
editor should write in the appropriate code numbers, which presumably
range from "1" in the extreme "below-average" category to a "0" for the
higher category in the rating scale. Again, with no more than ten categories, a single punch card column suffices. There is much more editorial work involved in questions 4a and 4b, because the freely stated reasons for liking or not liking the bath beads would have to be placed in
uniform categories and these assigned code numbers. Anticipating that
the number of significant reason types might run above ten, two columns are assigned to each of questions 4a and 4b. If there were, say,
twenty-two categories to be coded, the code numbers would run from 01
to 22.

11.3 Data-Processing Methods

The various methods of processing data can be placed into two types: manual and electronic. The latter category is largely computers, but we are going to mention a few other types of equipment that may be used in data-processing systems.

11.3.1 Manual Methods

Tallying is completely by hand, entering the responses in appropriate categories on worksheets such as the one shown in Figure 11–3, which has tallied hypothetical replies to question 4b of Figure 11–2. In this simple method, the "sorting" is done individually for each observation by selecting the line on which to tally it. Tallying tends to be done more accurately by having two persons work on it, one calling off the responses while the other tallies.

The *sort-and-count method* is exactly that: first sort all questionnaires or data forms into piles, one for each answer category; then count each pile. This avoids the tallying danger of making entries on the wrong line and can be speedier, provided that it is easy to read and sort the entries for all questions and categories.

Keysort, a copyrighted name of Litton Industries, is a method using a standard card that can be sorted and counted with simple equipment manually. The data may be entered on the card itself in the field, if not

4b.	What was liked about bath beads "Use Second"									
	Made skin soft & smooth	⊤ℋℋ	⊤ℋℋ	⊤ℋℋ	⊤ℋℋ	⊤ℋℋ	⊤ℋℋ	⊤ℋℋ	⊤ℋℋ	|||	43
	Had pleasant scent	⊤ℋℋ	⊤ℋℋ	⊤ℋℋ	|||					19
	Mixed quickly with water	⊤ℋℋ	⊤ℋℋ	|||						13
	Gave a luxury feeling	⊤ℋℋ	⊤ℋℋ	⊤ℋℋ	⊤ℋℋ	||||				24
	Tub easy to clean after	⊤ℋℋ	⊤ℋℋ	⊤ℋℋ	⊤ℋℋ	⊤ℋℋ	⊤ℋℋ	⊤ℋℋ	||		37
	Not harsh to skin	⊤ℋℋ	⊤ℋℋ	||||						14
	Helped soap to lather	⊤ℋℋ	⊤ℋℋ	⊤ℋℋ	⊤ℋℋ	⊤ℋℋ	⊤ℋℋ	|||			33
	Fun to use	⊤ℋℋ	⊤ℋℋ	⊤ℋℋ							16
	Other answers	⊤ℋℋ	⊤ℋℋ	⊤ℋℋ	⊤ℋℋ						20
	No answer or d.k.	⊤ℋℋ	|||							8
											227

FIGURE 11–3. Form for Hand Tabulation, with Tallies

310

too numerous for the space, or may be transcribed from the source document. Along the edges of these cards are rows of holes that may be designated as fields and given code numbers. Then, at appropriate places for the observed data, the margin is punched to make a notch. When all the cards are notched and assembled so that the holes are in line, a long rod is inserted through the hole representing the data category being counted. When raised with this needle, the cards punched at the hold will fall; then they are counted. Two or more holes can be sorted simultaneously be inserting additional needles. Keysort is a quicker and more accurate method, once the holes are notched, and provides a compact method of filing the data when they are likely to be of future interest.

11.3.2 Electronic Methods

Mark-sensing is a basic data-input device available for computers, done with pencil marks rather than with holes punched in cards. Mark-sensing should be familiar to all college students, because machine-graded examinations are scored with pencil marks written in appropriate spaces on the answer form. The heavy, special pencils used make marks that electric current will pass through and thereby register what was entered on the sheet or source document. The machine that processes these documents can cumulate and print the total score and may also be used to print out all the answers or data given on the document.

On many occasions the ease of recording data for mechanical processing with a pencil is much more efficient than punching cards. For example, suppose that a firm's sales personnel were to observe retailers' stocks and displays when calling on them as part of a marketing study. Obviously, salespeople cannot carry around a card-punch machine. They can readily, however, make the appropriate entries on a mark-sensing form on the spot.

Often the mark-sensing card also contains card-punch columns, so the document could also be punched later. Mark-sensing alone could suffice for a marketing study's data processing, if nothing was wanted beyond totals in each scored category. Since totals will rarely suffice, however, it is very useful that mark-sensed forms can be run through automatic card-punching equipment. Thus they can become computer inputs and complex analytical operations are available.

Optical scanning is a newer technical development that may replace mark-sensing for data recorded in the field, although it has greater equipment requirements. It has the advantages, for recording purposes, of not requiring a special type of pencil, reading a higher density, and permitting more to be entered on the source document (for example, a questionnaire). It may have other uses for some research purposes, since it now can read typewriter or carefully blocked hand-printed letters.

Computer hardware is the first aspect of computers that we shall discuss. While computers offer enormous data-processing potentialities to the marketing researcher, their use requires some understanding. Our descriptions of the hardware, or equipment, nevertheless is brief and includes only the basic units of a computer system. This is about all the detail on computers that marketing researchers typically require.

The computers used for marketing data usually are of digital types, which process information represented by means of coded characters. Basic to their operation is the concept of "binary digits"—which may be in only two states, represented by either a "0" or "1." These two states make it easy to manufacture hardware components in their terms and naturally lend themselves to special numbering systems.

The overall system of a computer is shown in Figure 11–4. We shall briefly explain the nature of the basic units of equipment.

1. *Input* is the first step, wherein the data are fed into the central processing unit. The equipment that performs the inputs generally can also take the outputs and so tends to be referred to as input/output, or I/O units. A modern "card read punch" holds up to 3,100 cards in its file feed and can "read" them into the computer at a rate of over 1,000 per minute. Information can be read into the computer also on magnetic tapes, which can contain millions of information characters on a standard reel whose entirety can be fed into the computer in as little as three minutes. A more advanced development is the "drum and disc" type of memory unit to provide inputs. Input can also come directly from on-line typewriter-like keyboards or direct sensors.

2. The *central processing unit* (CPU) is the heart of the computer. The CPU contains the main trunk lines upon which all information flows to and from the machine, controlling the sequence of operations. Integral with the CPU is the arithmetic unit, which provides all of the fundamental operations of arithmetic and the logical capability to compare whether two numbers are equal or unequal. The operator communicates with the computer's CPU with a "printer-keyboard."

3. The *storage* or *memory* within the computer is an array of tiny rings or cores that may be in two states, either magnetized or not, which

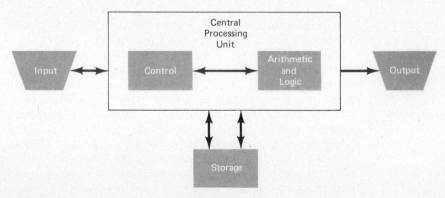

FIGURE 11–4. Schematic of a Computer System

may have values of 1 or 0. Thus, the computer stores binary information that may be related either to decimal or alphabetic code equivalents. Through series of pulses, the molecules in the cores are oriented and reoriented and thus the information in each core can be changed instantly. The size of a memory may be nearly 16,000,000 bytes, with access time as rapid as 50 nanoseconds (50 millionths of a second). In addition to the main memory, one may also have additional large storage of information in blocks as large as billions of characters.

4. *Outputs* of data or results from the CPU, as we indicated, may be on cards, tapes, or drum-and-disc-type memory units. Instead (or also), one typically wants the final results or solutions to be printed, which is done by the line printer. It can prepare various types of reports or tabulations or even mailing lists with speeds ranging up to 2,000 lines per minute and can prepare multiple copies or printing masters for further reproduction and distribution of information. Output can also be made available to on-line CRT terminals or as audio response, graphical plots, or direct control signals.

The operator of the system has available a console printer-keyboard and can control and communicate with the computer. That would be a "hands-on" operation, which is seldom used except for difficulties. More typically, a program is inputed into the CPU that automatically controls it to carry out the instructions of the job without intervention.

Computer software refers to the methods wherewith information is prepared and systematized for a computer and managed internally within its electronic subsystems. Software involves essentially systems; instructions to computers, or "programs"; and the languages in which they are written, which the computer "understands." Desirable additional elements are flow charts or decision tables, which provide definite procedures to follow in programming; and program documentation, in which the program is written in such detail that further communication between the programmer and the user of the data is unnecessary. There is no need for us to go into technical detail about these, but we are going to discuss one software element that is relevant to all marketing researchers: application packages.

Application packages are also referred to as "packaged programs," which is a fair description of them. They provide complete printed instructions on how to carry out a series of operations (that is, the programs) on computers in order to produce certain outputs. As they save the complex and time-consuming tasks of writing programs, which would require very competent programming specialists, these application packages tend to be quite advantageous to researchers. Computer manufacturers and service bureaus have created a variety of programs that are included in applications packages, which are published in manuals giving full instructions.

Two packages that have proven most useful for research applications of computers are now described, and the manuals containing them are cited.

1. *Biomedic* (BMD) was formerly the most widely used package for the purposes relevant to marketing research. It was developed for biological and medical sciences and appears to be of declining use for marketing data work. Its manual does provide a separate program for most analytical methods and is updated from time to time.[1]

2. *Statistical Package for the Social Sciences* (SPSS) offers an integrated *system* of computer programs that goes beyond BMD by including complete data-handling and file management routines. It, therefore, fills in the gaps between the separate programs and offers users computer flexibility in handling data. The number of programs that it offers now compares favorably with BMD, and it is by far the most widely used in social science research, including, of course, marketing. A rather brief primer is available for learning about the program's use and also a manual, which is a thick volume supplying a complete description of the SPSS system and all its programs.[2]

The SPSS was developed through the efforts of the University of Chicago and Stanford University, but later this service became available only through the former institution. In addition to manuals, which enable any organization using SPSS to prepare their own programs on tapes, the already prepared tapes are available from the National Opinion Research Center, University of Chicago.

The SPSS was designed for use on Control Data Corporation (CDC) computers. One can use SPSS programs on line as well as in batch operation. This provides a completely interactive mode of usage, as contrasted with running each program in its entirety before seeing any results and having those delivered typically hours later. In on-line usage, the user simply calls a certain telephone number from his terminal, then instructs the remotely located computer to load the desired program. One can thereby interactively run just what is wanted, interspersed with asking questions of it and getting the computer's answers on one's console before deciding what the computers next step should be. On-line service is available from computers located at Northwestern University (in its Vogelback Computing Center). Recently, CDC has acquired rights to this, for which a manual is available.[3]

Tape source data are also available for purchase on machine-readable tapes for a large variety of frequently used marketing and economic data. Through this very convenient method, reams of data can be purchased as direct inputs into whatever analytical programs the researcher wants to run on computers. Most notable are tapes prepared by the Bureau of the Census, which contain a vast amount of data from various censuses. These may be obtained from the Bureau in Washington. Com-

---

[1] *Biomedic Computer Programs* (Los Angeles: University of California Press, 1973).

[2] William R. Klecka, Norman H. Nie, and C. Hadlai Hull, *SPSS Primer,* and Norman H. Nie, C. Hadlai Hull, Jean G. Jackson, Karin Steinbrenner, and Dale H. Bent, *Statistical Package for the Social Sciences,* 2nd ed. (New York: McGraw-Hill Book Company, 1975).

[3] *SPSS/On Line* (Minneapolis, Minn.: Cybernet Services, Data Service Corporation, Control Data Corporation, P.O. Box 0, 1976).

plete data from *Sales Management* magazine's annual buying power surveys also are available on computer tapes. Dun & Bradstreet and a number of research agencies also provide taped data. A number of university-related research centers have taped data available on opinion and sociological subjects, including:

Institute for Social Research, Box 1248, University of Michigan, Ann Arbor, Mich.

Louis Harris Political Data Center, University of North Carolina, Chapel Hill, N.C.

National Opinion Research Center, University of Chicago, Chicago, Ill.

Roper Public Opinion Center, Williams College, Williamstown, Mass.

The ever-increasing number and variety of packaged programs and prepared data tapes are easing considerably the use of computers in marketing studies.

11.4 Deciding the Data-Processing Approach

With knowledge such as that presented in some brevity above, the marketing researcher approaches the decision on how to do the data processing. You will recall that we listed four general approaches to this question in Section 11.1. Now let us give specific attention to the factors that one should consider with regard to each of these approaches.

1. *Use manual or personal methods of data processing.* The manual methods have these advantages:
   a. Only simple worksheets are needed—no mechanical equipment.
   b. The set-up time to prepare for tabulation is quite short.
   c. The method is simple enough for any moderately intelligent clerk, without technical training.
   d. Because categories of analysis are kept in their original verbal descriptions during tabulation, there is no confusing numerical language of code numbers.
   e. When tabulating is done from the original forms, they undergo an additional editing, since the clerk may notice errors or the need to establish additional classifications for certain recurring answers not already individually classified.

   This approach is most appropriate for projects that have simple manipulative requirements in statistical analysis, that are small in scale of data treated, and that are unlikely to recur frequently. Many ad hoc marketing research projects are that simple or small-scale, particularly exploratory studies. Relevant to the technical advantages given above and to other factors, manual methods may be said to have these assets:

a. No time, clarity, or accuracy is lost in the researcher's communicating his or her desires to computer personnel (who may be located distantly) and onto computer instructions, or in interpreting their responses.

b. It has relatively low costs, when analytical needs are simple, and rapid response to changes in analytical plans.

c. The whole direction of the processing lies entirely within the researcher's knowledge and skill without outside scrutiny or constraints.

d. It demands practically nothing more than understanding clerical mechanics and the time to carry them out.

The most serious objections to manual processing usually are (1) its very low limits on the cross-analysis and manipulation of data, and (2) the time required for large quantities of data. Error potentialities and staffing clerical needs may be other obstacles.

2. *Utilize data-processing-service experts.* This is the most efficient choice where suitable experts are available and where the marketing researcher lacks expertise in data processing. The researcher may be a novice in this area, who later can direct the processing, but permanent reliance on a processing service is logical when there is a data-processing section within one's own company that has the requisite capabilities. There are also data-processing agencies in major cities that can provide economical advice and computer facilities that medium-sized companies cannot afford. When outside experts participate in the decision on the use of manual versus computer methods, they are very likely to opt for the latter, which are easier to explain and minimize the expert's time. Despite the added external costs and scheduling complications that may be involved in going outside for such service, better expertise and computational abilities often make this second alternative very attractive.

3. *Utilize packaged analysis routines or programs.* Researchers who exercise this third option presumably have familiarized themselves with data processing through trial of the second option or other means of education, providing knowledge of available software systems and how to use them. When one faces problems with great manipulative complexity or involving large volumes of data, packaged programs are particularly logical. Yet even problems that are modest, in scale or complexity can economically utilize the standard software of packaged programs when they are ones that recur periodically. One drawback is restriction to the available routines, but this is seldom a real difficulty in view of the variety now available. Perhaps a greater drawback is the time and effort invested in learning what is available, when it is appropriate, its input-format requirements, and what the output means. Many researchers cannot afford the time to learn all of this and be able to actually apply the programs to a computer. However, the situation is quite different when there are computer personnel in one's organization. Then it is more analogous to what one needs to know to drive a car, for the researcher needs to know only the inputs, assumptions,

limitations, and implications of the output. She or he can turn the rest of the job over to the computer people.

4. *Do own development of computer software.* This is logical in special cases where the packaged programs (approach 3) are deemed inadequate in view of the unique characteristics of the problem and analyses needed. It might be adopted also by a researcher who delights in designing computer programs despite the inefficiency. One quite legitimate use of this fourth approach is in developing small preparatory programs needed to massage the raw data into the shape required by standard statistical packages. In the case of truly unique problems of data manipulation, someone must write a special computer program, and some marketing researchers could do it.

Generally, regarding choices among these four alternatives, we would conclude:

1. The trend will continue toward electronic rather than manual processing, particularly as more and more small and simple computers are produced, but there may always be situations in which manual methods are faster and cheaper.
2. The third alternative will be the predominant choice as available software becomes more capable and general, because the most rapidly growing types of marketing problems fit this approach.

11.5   Steps toward Efficiency

Bear in mind that data processing can get very expensive and time consuming. Here is perhaps the stage most needing careful planning and control. Many steps may be taken to make it efficient, of which we are suggesting a few.

An important principle is to begin planning data processing as early as feasible. In a conclusive study, there should be early, if preliminary, determination of the types of findings desired, the data necessary, and the analytical requirements. This foreshadows data-processing needs. When pretests are run of the techniques, they can be evaluated for their repercussions on data processing. Often it would pay to process small-scale results from pretests on computers to check out packaged programs and permit examination of outputs. High importance should be placed on designing data forms, even for pretests, to provide for data-processing requirements. Editing needs, codes, and the entire data preparation should be practiced on pretest data.

It also is desirable to bring in any expert, from an outside agency or an internal data-processing department, whose advice may prevent much difficulty and cost later. The classification, codes, and the coding provisions on questionnaires should be given close scrutiny. The entire series of analytical steps, which will utilize techniques such as those found in Chapters 12 and 13, should be laid out so that their processing requirements may be anticipated. This also gives the researcher an opportunity to consider what data runs should have priority. Many of the analytical steps might better be deferred until the first printouts provide some clues for interpretations and suggest what would be fruitful further analyses.

Precoding is particularly desirable from the data-processing standpoint, and one benefit of pilot studies is to indicate response categories that should have codes. The ability of operators to punch cards directly from the original questionnaires (or whatever source document is used) is desirable both to save time and to avoid errors. Collecting the data in a form usable for a packaged program would be efficient and may be done if the likely program is considered when determining what to collect and the design of the collection instrument. Finally, we suggest that in large organizations one person should be appointed to serve as liaison between marketing research and the data-processing department or agency, whose depth of understanding and ability to communicate with both sides could considerably enhance efficiency.

11.6 Summary

Data processing has been discussed from the standpoint of the marketing researcher who does not need technical depth but rather practical knowledge on planning and choosing methods. This field was described as consisting of seven functions, divided between preparatory steps and several phases of the ensuing process. Four approaches to choosing the data-processing method were then listed.

The three stages of preparatory work (editing, classifying, and coding) were given detailed discussion. Then we took up manual methods of processing, again three in number (tally, sort and count, and Keysort), but briefly, since they are simple and are not the most used. More attention was given to describing electronic methods: mark-sensing and optical scanning, which tend to be precursors to computers, and computers. How computer hardware operates was explained generally, but we went into detail on one element of computer software: application packages. Availability of data on tapes was also described.

The decisive stage was then discussed, with advantages and disadvantages of each of the four approaches. Situations in which each might be most logical were described, too. Finally, we pointed out a number of steps that would enhance efficiency in data processing.

12 Data Analysis: Preliminary Considerations and Univariate Analysis

Chapter 12 introduces us to analytical methods and the more basic tools, which are the ones you are most likely to use often. You should be able to answer these questions after its study:

What is the meaning of statistical analysis? Its functions?

Beyond the basic and initial quantitative steps and values, what are the three major divisions of analytical methods? What do the names we give them signify?

What would be the first steps taken with raw data?

What are frequency distributions? The several types of central values? What can these analyses tell us?

What are the measures and calculation of dispersion?

What are the considerations in choosing methods of statistical analysis?

What are the methods of univariate analysis? How does one calculate them? What is the benefit of using them?

HAVING GATHERED THE DATA from primary or secondary sources, the researcher proceeds toward the drawing of conclusions by logical inference. At this stage those data are only hundreds or thousands of individual responses or observations, incapable of interpretation until converted into significant statistical information. Statistical analysis, thus, is essential, and is the subject of this chapter and Chapter 13.

Our approach to the subject is from the viewpoint of a researcher who would specify the analytical methods that are to be applied to the data, not that of a technical statistician who would conduct the calculations (and presumably have more complete insight into the deeper complexities of statistics). We offer, then, a sort of guide to the use of analytical methods, which includes (1) a charting of the sequential relationships between the stages and principal methods, (2) a description of each method and its formula (without a technical explanation), and (3) an example of the sort of result produced, with some indication of its functions in bringing to light the quantitative meaning of the data. For the reader who needs to know more about analytical methods, we provide footnotes indicating detailed sources.

12.1 Some Problems of Understanding

This is a note directed to a rather typical reader who approaches any discussion of mathematics or statistics with a feeling of dread, which inhibits comprehension of what is said. Acceptance of our statements here may reduce such apprehensions so that they will not interfere with increasing one's research ability with regard to analytical tools.

The following statements are true:

1. Sheer unfamiliarity with mathematical language presents a serious obstacle that disappears as one employs it.
2. Mathematical expressions are simply an alternative to verbal ones that are much more efficient in being able to say quickly in numbers and nonverbal symbols what would require many words.
3. Mathematical expressions are clear and specific, avoiding the ambiguities and nuances that obscure our verbal communication.
4. Numbers and formulas are abstractions and thus should offer no inherent confusions. Our troubles arise when we necessarily attach qualities to the numbers and try to interpret the qualitative significance of the data, that is, ask the question: What do the figures signify with regard to the real world?
5. If you regard quantitative analytical methods as possible keys to unlock the meaning of data and expand your interpretive powers, you will welcome their assistance and adopt a positive attitude toward them.

With a functional viewpoint and intention of systematizing problem solving through research, the employment of analytical methods involves two basic questions: (1) What meanings should be obtained from the

320

321

Data Analysis:
Preliminary
Considerations
and Univariate
Analysis

data with reference to the specific problems to be solved? (2) Which statistical tools are most useful in revealing those meanings and are feasible with the particular data that have been gathered? In becoming facile in answering these questions, you will acquire a valuable skill for either research or executive capabilities. Intelligent planning of statistical analysis pays dividends in several ways. We have mentioned that this stage should be anticipated from the outset of a project as an integral phase of the problem-solving system, but many of these planning decisions are not feasible until the actual data are in hand. We deal with systematic planning after our overview of the analytical tools.

12.2 Nature and Functions of Statistical Analysis

As our subject should be defined before its discussion, we offer this definition for *statistical analysis:* The refinement and manipulation of data that prepares them for the application of logical inference. Statistical analytical methods may be used in valid ways or in specious ways. This depends both on the honesty of the researcher in selecting the appropriate formulas and data inputs and on his or her understanding of the formulas and their outputs.

We are going to take up each analytical method in the approximate sequence that would be used for the mass of data assembled from field or secondary sources. There are three chief phases:

1. Bringing the raw data into measured order.
2. Summarizing the data.
3. Applying analytical methods to manipulate the data so that their interrelationships and quantitative meaning become evident.

The first two stages should offer no difficulty whatever in understanding. It is the third stage that can become highly complex and abstruse, but not necessarily so if you understand each step along the way — to the limited depth that our viewpoint requires. You will find this clarified by Figure 12–1, which orients the various analytical stages and methods.[1] The numbering in each box on the diagram relates the chart to the number of the section that discusses the particular item. As we progress in our discussion, the appropriate terminology will be defined.

12.3 Bringing the Data into Order

Raw data, as they are received from the field in primary data collection, are in no condition for interpretation. Such data constitute bits of infor-

---

[1] Figure 12–1 displays the analytical method classifications with which we deal in Chapters 12 and 13, as a simple guide for your reading. We recommend, for those with more extensive interest or applications, a very adequate and practical monograph on quantitative analytical methods and their usage. It is: Frank M. Andrews, *A Guide for Selecting Statistical Techniques for Analyzing Social Science Data* (Ann Arbor, Mich.: Survey Research Center, Institute for Social Research, The University of Michigan, 1974).

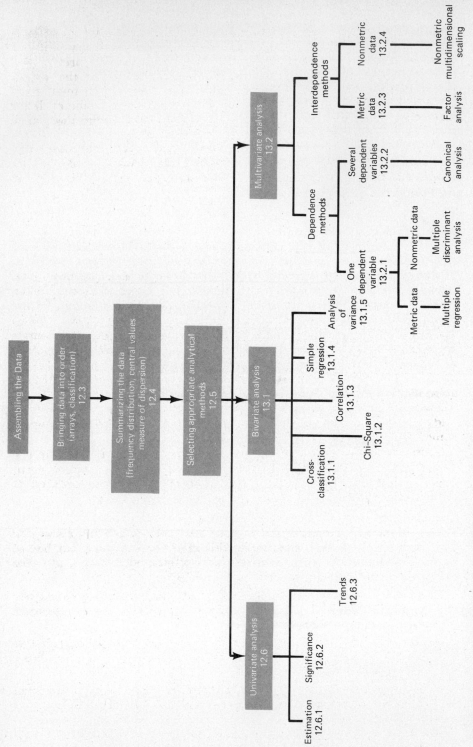

FIGURE 12–1. Classification Chart of Quantitative Analytical Methods

The indicated methods are discussed in this chapter under the section heading numbers given with each.

323

Data Analysis:
Preliminary
Considerations
and Univariate
Analysis

mation recorded on many individual forms, and substantial work must be done on them. The decisions made about these preparatory steps are based on assumptions involving general logic about the interpretive process and about the supposed nature of the data relative to the appropriate analysis. Therefore, logic and statistical procedures are involved in this first stage, although the researcher has not yet dug into the evidence and ascertained much about the directions of analysis beyond those anticipatory decisions embodied in the research design.

During this first stage, there would also be qualitative steps under way that would edit the incoming data, establish classifications, and appraise validity, as discussed in Chapter 11. The statistical step in bringing the data into order is that of classification.

Classification

array-organizing raw data in systematic order

ascending low-high

descending high-low

The primitive form in which data can be brought into quantitative order is in an *array* that lists all of them in numerical sequence. When there are only a few observations, setting up an array may not be too tedious, but usually this would be inefficient with a sizable array of data such as is usually obtained in a marketing study. For example, if an analyst were to receive 42,563 returns from the field, it would be ridiculous to construct an array of the data and to study them one by one and try to infer any meaning from them. The statistical nature of the data is more likely to be observable when they are *classified* into a relatively small number of groupings. However, what classifications are "meaningful" and appropriate for a particular purpose and nature of the evidence is something to be determined for each case individually.

Classification is possible only when it has been anticipated before the data collection, so that the factors on which breakdowns may be made are already determined. The four types of bases most frequently used in marketing studies are:[2]

4 types of bases. most frequently used in mktg studies!

1. *Quantitative*—classifying by a numerical measure. With respect to data on incomes, for example, this might include age, number of years employed, number of years of formal education, and other numerical characteristics.

2. *Qualitative*—classifying by some attribute that is not expressed numerically. Such classifications might be by type of occupations, race, or employment status.

3. *Chronological*—classifying according to the time events occur. If our study included data for 1977, 1978, and other years, this basis would be feasible.

4. *Geographical*—classifying by location. This might be a classification by state, by region, by urban versus rural, or by size of town.

---

[2] Adapted from F. E. Croxton and D. J. Cowden, *Applied General Statistics*, 2nd ed. (Englewood Cliffs, N.J.: Prentice-Hall, Inc., 1955), pp. 3–5.

What general type and specific classification bases would be likely to reveal, in our gathered data, the meaning significant to our problem? The analyst presumably is sufficiently conversant with the data and the study's objectives to render logical judgments on this. Having exercised that logic, he or she proceeds to the statistical work of establishing appropriate classifications.

A few principles that should be followed in setting classifications are as follows:

1. *Convenient number of categories.* The number of categories should be substantial enough so that differences in the data can be revealed, yet not so few as to hide important information. At the initial stages of data analysis, class intervals should be rather narrow so that significant tendencies in the data are not lost within the intervals.

2. *Similar responses within categories* (intraclass homogeneity). Responses classified in a particular category should be similar with respect to the characteristic being studied.

3. *Differences of responses between categories* (interclass heterogeneity). Given the characteristic under study, the differences in responses between categories should be dissimilar enough to reveal substantial differences between the responses.

4. *Mutual exclusive categories.* Categories should not be overlapping. They should be constructed so that any response can be placed in only one category.

5. *Exhaustive categories.* The construction of categories should provide that all responses be included in a category. This may include categories, where appropriate, of "Don't know" and "No answer" as responses.

6. *Avoid open-ended class intervals.* Open-ended class intervals should not be used, because lack of specified interval limits obscures the extremes of distribution and precludes computing the average value of the observations in such intervals.

7. *Class interval of the same width.* Class intervals should be of the same width, where possible, rather than of varying widths. Disregard of this principle may lead to situations where the intervals lack a consistent spread. However, the unequal breadth of categories may be acceptable when categories apparently contain relatively small proportions of the total response characteristic, and finer categories may be uninformative.

8. *Midpoints of class intervals.* If the respondents are likely to have broadly estimated the answers they gave, stating them in round numbers, the class intervals should be designed so that major round numbers fall at the midpoints of the class intervals. For instance, income earners may be prone to report their incomes to the nearest hundred dollars. An income category of "$4,000 to $4,099" would conceal the fact that those classified in this bracket had

tended to give their lower limit; thus, "$3,950 to $4,049" would be a better interval to use, because it places the central tendency in its middle.

12.4   Summarizing the Data

Although brought into order, the data need to be combined into condensed displays or expression before they can be analyzed or compared with the data drawn from other samples or situations.

12.4.1   Frequency Distribution

Having established tentatively suitable classifications for the data, we then place individual observations in those categories and count them. (We say tentatively because the initial categories may prove to have been too fine and may have to be combined, or if the initial categories are too broad, finer categories must be set and the data reallocated and recounted.) If the data collected will also be compared with data about the population such as census data, to assess its randomness and representativeness, the categories developed must be checked so that such a comparison can be made without interpolating. (This check should be made even before designing the questionnaire to avoid comparison problems during the analysis.) The result is a frequency distribution, which would appear as shown in Table 12–1.

This tabulation offers a rather definite notion of how income is distributed among income levels for Florida engineers. Table 12–1 shows three different forms of presenting the data: (1) the absolute frequency with which the respondents fall into a category; (2) the relative frequency, in which we indicate the percentage of the respondents in each category; and (3) the cumulative frequency, which indicates the percentage of respondents whose income levels are as much as, or less than, the level of a given category.

Our violations—having two open-ended categories and one category of less than $5,000 interval ($8,000–$9,999)—are somewhat unfortunate, but then the numbers falling within the lower income levels are obviously smaller and less representative of the distribution. Our interpretation is still hindered by the difficulty of gauging these odd numbers in a cross-comparison. The matter is greatly clarified if we compute the relative numbers (frequency) in each category on the base of 100, in other words, if we state them as percentages. This is evident in the relative frequency column of Table 12–1. This simplification is needed not merely to compare the various categories within this one frequency distribution, but perhaps we want to compare this distribution with similar data for the previous year, which would probably have a different total and therefore would lack ready comparability unless both frequency distributions were percentaged.

325

TABLE 12–1. 1973 Annual Income of Engineers in the State of Florida

Annual Income Level (dollars)	Absolute Frequency	Relative Frequency (percent)	Cumulative Frequency (percent)
Under 7,999 *Under 8000*	2 *100×2/853*	0.2	0.2
8,000–9,999 *8000–10 000*	7 *7/853×100*	0.8	1.0
10,000–14,999 *10000–15000*	75 *75/853×100*	8.8	9.8
15,000–19,999 *15000–20000*	224	26.3	36.1
20,000–24,999 *20000–25000*	209	24.5	60.6
Over 25,000 *25000–*	336	39.4	100.0
	853	100.0	

open intervals

shows relative importance of those intervals

Source: *Unpublished research of Ronald S. Rubin, Florida Technological University, 1973.*

The frequency distribution discussed above involved a single variable. When two or more variables are involved, we are concerned with the development of two-way or *n*-way frequency distributions. Frequency distributions involving more than one variable are known as *cross-classifications* or *cross-tabulations* and are discussed in Chapter 13.

12.4.2 Central Values *= average — figure rep. of an array or freq. distrib. of data.*

A single figure representative of an array or frequency distribution of data is usually wanted because one cannot look at data in the various forms in which they are compiled and obtain any specific inference from them. Analysts usually must compare magnitudes of different sets of data, which has even less practical value unless they can have each set of data condensed into a single figure. What they need is a measure of central value, or an average.

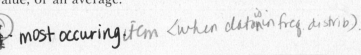

Mode *— most occurring item (when data in freq. distrib).*

The *mode* is the central value or item that occurs most often. It is most easily determined when data are categorized in a frequency distribution because the mode is that category containing the greatest number of observations. Referring to the frequency distribution of grouped data of annual income levels in Table 12–2, we observe that the *modal class* is $15,000 to $19,999 income.

The following formula demonstrates how a mode may be approximated in mathematical terms for grouped data:

$$Mo = L_{Mo} + \frac{d_1}{d_1 + d_2} \ (i)$$

*read this
study diff between these*

326

327

Data Analysis:
Preliminary
Considerations
and Univariate
Analysis

where Mo = mode

L_{Mo} = lower limit of the modal class

d_1 = difference between the frequency of the modal class and the frequency of the class immediately preceding it in the distribution

d_2 = difference between the frequency of the modal class and the frequency of the class immediately following it in the distribution

i = size of the interval of the modal class

Using the data from Table 12-2, the mode would be

$$\text{Mo} = 15,000 + \frac{132}{132 + 198}\,(4,999)$$

$$= 15,000 + \frac{659,868}{330}$$

$$= 15,000 + 1,999.60$$

$$= \$16,999.60$$

To find a crude mode from grouped data, one may use the midpoint of the modal class. In our case this would be $17,500.

Some of the more important characteristics of the mode are:

1. It is easy and quick to compute.
2. It can be located in an open-ended distribution.
3. The mode may not exist in a frequency distribution, for some values may not be identical or there may be more than one mode. A distribution with two peaks, called *bimodal*, would not indicate a central tendency.
4. The mode is not affected by extreme values in the distribution.
5. It may be very representative of a distribution if the observations are clustered at one value or in one class.

Median

The *median* tends to be the average most typical of all values in a distribution, because it is the item that lies precisely halfway between the highest and the lowest values. It is necessary to arrange the data into an ascending or decending order before one can select the median value. For ungrouped data with an odd number of observations, the median value would be easy to select. For an even number of observations, the median would be the value halfway between the two central values.

When constructing a frequency distribution of grouped data, the actual values of the observations are lost as a result of the development of class intervals. However, it is possible to approximate the median value from grouped data. The formula for computing the median value is given as

$$\text{Md} = L_{\text{Md}} + \frac{N/2 - \text{CF}}{f_{\text{Md}}} \, (i)$$

where Md = Median
L_{Md} = lower limit of the median class
N = total number of frequencies in the distribution
CF = cumulative frequencies for the class immediately below the class containing the median
f_{Md} = frequency of the median class
i = size of the interval of the median class

We can illustrate this approximation process by referring to our previous example from Table 12–2. The first step is to compute a cumulative frequency column for the data (this is the last column of Table 12–2). With this information we can proceed to locate the median class (that is, the class in our example which contains the midpoint between the 1650th and the 1651st respondent in the total sample of 3300). Applying the formula above, we find that

$$\text{Md} = 10,000 + \frac{\dfrac{3,300}{2} - 1,221}{429} \, (2,499)$$

$$= 10,000 + \frac{429}{429} \, (2,499)$$

$$= 10,000 + 2,499$$

$$= \$12,499$$

Some of the important characteristics of the median are:

1. It can be computed from open-ended distributions, for its value is located in the median class interval and that interval would not be the open-ended interval.
2. It is not influenced by extreme values. Therefore, if a distribution is highly skewed, the median is a better choice than the mean.
3. It is not affected by the value of the observations, but by the number of observations. Therefore, extreme values, whether high or low, will not distort this measure of central tendency.
4. If the class intervals are of unequal size, the median is recommended as the measure of central tendency because it is much easier to compute than the mean.
5. *easy to define + easy to understand*

unreliable
than the
mean for
statistical
inference
purposes

TABLE 12–2. Grouped Total Annual Income of a Sample of Residents of Phoenix, Arizona, 1976

Income (dollars)	Number (f)	Cumulative Frequency
Under 3,000	231	231
3,000–4,999	264	495
5,000–7,999	396	891
8,000–9,999	330	1,221
10,000–12,499	429	1,650
12,500–14,999	396	2,046
15,000–19,999	528 (modal class)	2,574
20,000–24,999	330	2,904
25,000 and over	396	3,300
	3,300	

[handwritten: 528 - 396 = 132]
[handwritten: 4,999 = 15,000–19,999]
[handwritten: 528 - 330 = 198]

Source: *Adapted from* Inside Phoenix 1976, *Phoenix Newspapers, Inc., Phoenix, Ariz., 1976.*

[handwritten margin notes: most frequently used — only one that can be computed from unordered data]

Mean *[handwritten: are — sums of values of observations ÷ no. of items observed]*

Usually one wants what the term "average" means to most of us: the arithmetic mean, which is found by dividing the sums of the values of the observations by the number of items observed. If data were grouped into a frequency distribution, the midpoint of each category would be multiplied by the number of observations in that category, each resultant category would be summed, and the total would be divided by the total number of observations. The general formula is

$$\bar{X} = \frac{\Sigma\, fx}{\Sigma\, f}$$

[handwritten: — grpd data]

where $\bar{X}$ = arithmetic mean
x = midpoint of each class
f = frequencies in each class
Σ = sum of the values.

[handwritten left margin: $(x-\mu)(x-\mu)^2$]

If the frequencies and the midpoints are large, an alternative method, called the *coded method*, reduces the size of the values to be calculated.[3]

---

[3] The formula for the coded method is

$$\bar{X} = \bar{X}_a + \frac{\Sigma\, fd}{N}\ (i)$$

where $\bar{X}_a$ = assumed mean placed at the midpoint of any class
f = frequencies in a class
d = deviations form $\bar{X}_a$ to the middle of each class in class-interval units
N = total number of frequencies in the distribution
i = size of the class interval

329

In discussing classification considerations previously, it was pointed out that open-ended categories should be avoided if possible. If open-ended categories are used, it is impossible to compute the arithmetic mean from such a distribution (since there is no "limit" to the class, we cannot assign a midpoint value).

The arithmetic mean, which is the most frequently used central value, is the only one that can be computed from unordered data. More important, it is desirable with sample data, as it can be projected to indicate the total population.

Some of the important characteristics of the mean are:

1. Its value is affected by the value of every observation; therefore, a change in the value of any observation will change the value of the mean.
2. If we have highly skewed distributions, the mean value may be distorted too much by a relatively few extreme values. Therefore, in this situation, the mean can lose its representative characteristic.
3. It possesses a feature that the sum of differences between data observations and the mean will be zero. Mathematically, then, it is a measure of centrality.
4. Its mathematical properties prove to be important when sample data are being used to make inferences about populations, and in utilizing statistical tests. As we will see in subsequent sections, the mean is suitable in analyzing interval data.
5. It cannot be computed from open-ended categories (this point has been discussed earlier).

12.4.3 Measures of Dispersion

In preceding sections it was pointed out that measures of central tendency could be computed as a single number used to represent the central value of a distribution. However, nothing has been said about the spread or scatter of the observations. Several measures of dispersion have been developed to compare the "spread" of two sets of data and the representativeness of their averages. For example, if there is a large amount of "spread" among the observations, the average value used to summarize the observations may not be at all representative of the data being studied.

Certain measures of dispersion have become extremely useful in marketing: the range, the variance and standard deviation, and the coefficient of variation.

Range

The *range* is the simplest measure of dispersion. It is the difference between the highest and lowest values in the array or distribution. It emphasizes only the extreme values of observations. Therefore, typical values will probably be ignored and this measure may give a distorted picture of the

331

Data Analysis:
Preliminary
Considerations
and Univariate
Analysis

distribution. However, the range does provide one with some indication, no matter how crude, of the breadth of observation values.

Variance and Standard Deviation

The variance and standard deviation are based on deviations from the mean. The *variance* is defined as the average of the squared deviations of the observation values from the mean of the distribution. The square root of the variance is called the *standard deviation*. Since the variance is a rather difficult measure to interpret, the standard deviation is the most frequently encountered measure of dispersion.

The appropriate general formula for calculating the standard deviation is

$$\sigma = \sqrt{\frac{\Sigma \, (x - \mu)^2}{N}}$$

where σ = standard deviation[4]
x = values of the observations
μ = mean of the observations
N = total number of observations

Table 12–3 shows the calculation of the standard deviation for weekly salaries of ten salesmen of the Magna Electric Corporation.[5]

Now that the standard deviation has been computed to be $82.31, how is it interpreted? First, it is often used to analyze its relationship to the mean of a normal distribution. As we saw in Figure 8–1, when a large number of observation values are analyzed, they often distribute themselves about their arithmetic mean in a symmetrical way. The standard deviation is an important measure because of its relationship with the mean within the symmetrical distribution.

One relationship is in terms of the percent of observations within 1 standard deviation below and above the mean. Therefore, in a normal distribution, about 68 percent of the observations lie within the μ (mean) and ±1 standard deviation. And, one sixth of the remaining salesmen earn more than 1 standard deviation from the mean, and one sixth earn less than one standard deviation from the mean. These properties make the standard deviation an extremely valuable tool in sampling, correlation, and other analytical areas, which are discussed in subsequent sections and chapters.

Another analytical use of the standard deviation is when one needs to compare two samples with comparable means. The standard deviation is used as the common denominator in comparing the representativeness of the two means. An assumption usually made is that the two means are

---

[4] The symbols used in this formula are appropriate when the data represent all the values in a population. If the standard deviation is being computed from sample data, different symbols are used, to maintain a distinction between the population and the sample.

[5] Fictitious name.

TABLE 12-3. Computation of the Standard Deviation (Ungrouped Data)

Salesmen	Weekly Salaries of Salesmen, x (dollars)	(x − μ)	(x − μ)²
A	185	−156.5	24,492.25
B	260	−81.5	6,642.25
C	300	−41.5	1,722.25
D	325	−16.5	272.25
E	330	−11.5	132.25
F	335	−6.5	42.25
G	350	+8.5	72.25
H	400	+58.5	3,422.25
I	450	+108.5	11,772.25
J	480	+138.5	19,182.25
		0	67,752.50

$$\mu = \frac{\Sigma x}{N} \qquad \sigma = \sqrt{\frac{\Sigma(x - \mu)^2}{N}}$$

$$= \frac{3,415}{10} \qquad = \sqrt{\frac{67,752.50}{10}}$$

$$= \$341.50 \qquad = \sqrt{6,775.25}$$

$$\qquad\qquad\qquad = \$82.31$$

about equal. With the standard deviation as the comparable measurement of variability, the smaller standard deviation of the two indicates that that distribution is more homogeneous.

Some of the more important characteristics of the standard deviation are:

1. A change in any of the observations values will change the standard deviation value.
2. Like the mean, it can lose its representativeness as a result of highly skewed distributions.
3. Like the mean, the standard deviation cannot be computed from open-ended categories.

Coefficient of Variation

If there is a need to compare the dispersions of more than one distribution, then a measure of relative dispersion called the *coefficient of variation* can be used. The formula is

333

Data Analysis:
Preliminary
Considerations
and Univariate
Analysis

$$\text{C.V.} = \frac{\sigma}{\mu}(100) \quad \text{or} \quad \text{C.V.} = \frac{s}{\overline{X}}(100)$$

where C.V. = coefficient of variation

σ = standard deviation of the population

μ = mean of the population

s = standard deviation of the sample

$\overline{X}$ = mean of the sample

If we desire to compare the dispersions of two distributions, say one with a standard deviation of $1,000 and the other with a standard deviation of $500, can we conclude that the first distribution has twice the variability of the second distribution? Or that the first distribution is more widely dispersed than that of the second? Therefore, what is needed for comparative purposes is the degree of relative dispersion, of which the coefficient of variation is the most popular measure.

Thus, for illustrative purposes, if the mean annual salary for the first distribution is $15,000, the coefficient of variation is

$$\text{C.V.} = \frac{\$1,000}{\$15,000}(100) = 6.6\%$$

Let us assume that the mean annual salary of the second distribution is $17,000. The coefficient of variation for this distribution is

$$\text{C.V.} = \frac{\$500}{\$17,000}(100) = 2.9\%$$

This indicates that the income distribution of the second distribution is more homogeneous than that of the first distribution. This may be stated another way. The standard deviation is 6.6 percent of the mean for the first distribution of annual salaries and 2.9 percent of the mean of the second distribution.

The stages of ordering and of summarizing the data are normal procedure in preparing the data for analysis. There are a number of alternative analysis procedures from which selection is made relative primarily to what one is trying to measure and secondarily to the character of the data. We now turn our discussion to the selection of the appropriate analytical methods.

12.5 Selecting Appropriate Analytical Methods

Some marketing research studies are concluded at the summarizing stage, but most involve additional analysis of the data. Therefore, the researcher must determine the appropriate analytical techniques available for use to bring out its quantitative meaning.

This section is designed to examine the basic considerations that dictate the researcher's selection of an analytical technique. The field of data analysis is vast, in the sense that there are a large number of analytical techniques available. Therefore, it seems useful to develop a classification scheme representing the more common considerations by which a researcher chooses an appropriate analytical technique.

One useful classification of these considerations is based upon the following:

1. *The scale by which variables are measured* (metric versus nonmetric). When data are qualitative and not measured with numbers, except when some synthetic numbering system is applied, they are called *nonmetric*. As an example, a *nominal scale* assigns words, such as "favorable" or "unfavorable," to categorize a response.

    Another nonmetric scale is the *ordinal scale.* Some responses in a beverage taste test might be a ranking of alternatives as to sweetness. Here the respondent assigns an order of preference using ordinal values—first, second, third, and so on. These rankings indicate the order of preference but not the degree of the respondents preference (there is no meaningful interval between the rankings).

    On the other hand, the following fact is *metric,* given in numbers: The airline distance from New York to Atlanta is 748 miles. This fact is an example of a *ratio scale*, which has characteristics of equal intervals, each described with a number, and a true zero point. Unfortunately, most behavioral data obtained in marketing cannot be measured by this scale.

    The *interval scale* is similar to the ratio scale with regard to equal intervals, but there is no true zero point. The zero point is set arbitrarily by the researcher. Therefore, the numbers associated with the intervals on the scale can be added and subtracted to obtain averages, but arithmetic operations are not permitted on the measurements themselves. A classic example of the use of an interval scale is that of the thermometer. We cannot say that 80°F is twice as hot as 40°F, but we can describe the distance between 80°F and 40°F as the same as the distance between 100°F and 60°F.

    The researcher must be cautious when selecting statistical techniques to choose methods which utilize the characteristics of one's measurement scale. A summary of the techniques of statistical analysis appropriate to the type of measurement scale is given in Table 12–4.

2. *Parametric versus nonparametric* data. When data are parametric, they are distributed around their mean or central value in a symmetrical fashion similar to the normal curve of probability. You will recall our discussion of this curve with regard to sampling, in which the curve depicting the data's frequency distribution rises symmetrically from the extreme values to a peak at the central value. When phenomena are parametric, one may use probabilistic tests of statistical significance regarding any samples drawn from

TABLE 12–4. Statistical Analysis Appropriate to the Level of Measurement Scale

Type of Scale	Appropriate Average	Appropriate Measure of Dispersion	Appropriate Measurement of Correlation	Test of Significance
Nominal	Mode	None	Contingency coefficient	Chi-square test
Ordinal	Median	Percentile	Rank correlation	Sign test
Interval	Arithmetic mean	Standard deviation	Coefficient of correlation	t test or F test
Ratio	Geometric mean	Coefficient of variation	All of the above	All of the above

Source: *Adapted from Sidney Siegel,* Nonparametric Statistics for the Behavioral Sciences *(New York: McGraw-Hill Book Company, 1956), p. 30.*

such a population—an important advantage in interpretation. Nonparametric data obviously are the converse: their distribution is in some fashion that does not substantially conform with the normal curve of probability. And by this token, whether or not samples of such data are statistically significant must be judged by tests other than the stronger tests based on probability. A large category of marketing data that inherently cannot be parametric are those with unequal or unmeasurable scale intervals between categories. An example is ranking responses, which might be used in the beverage reactions case above, where one cannot interpret the intervals between a first, second, or third ranking.

3. *Number of variables to be analyzed.* The number of variables to be analyzed together may range from one to several, and we categorize this aspect into three groupings of analytical methods that deal with:

   a. *Univariate,* in which a single variable is being analyzed alone.

   b. *Bivariate,* where some association is being measured between two variables simultaneously.

   c. *Multivariate,* where simultaneous relationships between three or more variables are measured.

4. *Dependence versus interdependence.* Related to the number of variables to be analyzed is the relationship between variables. For our purposes, the term "relationship" is to mean that changes in two (or more) variables are associated with each other. In analyzing associative relationships, two types of variables are considered: *criterion* and *predictor variables* (often referred to respectively as dependent and independent variables). The predictor variable presumably exerts an influence or explains the level of the criterion variable (the variable to be estimated). A distinction may be involved in analytical decisions between an occasion when (a) one has a single variable that is being tested for its dependence on other (independent) vari-

335

ables, as against an occasion when (b) "the researcher is investigating the interrelationships, and therefore the interdependence, among all the variables. . . ."[6]

The discussion above highlighted some of the more important considerations in the selection of an analytical technique. Since the field of data analysis is so large, it seems useful to approach our selection of methods from the simple cases involving single-variable data and progress to the more complex situations of multivariate data. However, it must be noted that the selection of the various analytical methods available differ, depending upon the interaction of the considerations above. For example, techniques will differ depending on the number of variables studied and on the types of scales by which the variables are measured. The decision criteria discussed will be enumerated in our discussion of the major types of analytical techniques. Figure 12–1 summarizes our classification framework and indicates the direction of our discussion.

The next section examines the analytical techniques found under the classification of univariate analysis. We shall describe analyses that may be performed with a single type of variable to bring out its quantitative meaning, to discern how it performs in a number of situations, and to test the statistical significance of its reported values. We leave to Chapter 13 an overview discussion of the bivariate and multivariate techniques.

12.6 Univariate Analysis

We begin with some fairly simple statistical analyses that implement the inferential process. These often suffice to solve the problem or to guide the decision maker's choices, but more sophisticated analyses tend to be necessary when one seeks to penetrate to the underlying causes.

12.6.1 Estimation

Point Estimation

In many marketing situations, an investigator may need to know a particular population value (parameter) for decision-making purposes. He may need to know the average sales per store, or the average consumption per month for a given product or service, or the average income of a particular community, and so on. In most instances, the population parameter will be unknown. Therefore, our main concern may be to estimate, from a sample, the population parameter.

---

[6] J. N. Sheth, "The Multivariate Revolution in Marketing Research," *Journal of Marketing,* January, 1971, p. 15. This article has been useful as a source for this chapter on multivariate techniques, including the classification scheme displayed in Figure 12–1. A commentary on this article that expands on the techniques given by Sheth is found in T. C. Kinnear and J. R. Taylor, "Multivariate Methods in Marketing Research: A Further Attempt at Classification," *Journal of Marketing,* October, 1971, pp. 56–59.

337

Data Analysis:
Preliminary
Considerations
and Univariate
Analysis

The procedure for estimating a population parameter can be illustrated best by an example. Suppose that a chain of specialty shops is interested in establishing another shop in a new shopping mall. Their shops are usually located in communities that have average incomes above the national average. Therefore, before a decision can be made as to whether their new shop can be situated in this new mall, management must find the average income of the community and compare it with the national average.

It will probably be too costly to try to find the income of each family in the community and then compute the population parameter average income. Therefore, a researcher would choose a sample, collect data on family incomes from those in the sample, and calculate a relevant statistic (estimate) representative of the population parameter average income.

A single number (point) estimate is usually the simplest to calculate. But only by chance will this point estimate be the same as the true population parameter. If, for example, the specialty shop's management conducted a survey of a sample of members of the prospective community and found that the mean family income was $20,000, this would be a point estimate of the population mean.

If the management wanted to know the aggregate total annual income for the community, they need only to multiply the mean figure by the total amount of families in the community. The aggregate estimate projected from the sample could then be used as an estimate of the total purchasing power of the community, a relevant statistic in deciding a store location.

However, other statistical estimators of central tendency could have been used, such as the median or the mode. Suppose for the moment that the researcher calculated the median to be $15,000; they could expect half of the families to have incomes over $15,000 and half to be less. The mode indicated a value of $11,000; more families had incomes at this level. These three values each indicate an estimate of the true population parameter average income. But which one is more representative of the population parameter of average income.

The question posed suggests that some criteria must be used to determine the most appropriate estimator for the given situation. Let us, then, discuss the criteria statisticians developed, such that when we have an estimator that satisfies these criteria, it will be a "good" estimator:[7]

1. *Unbiasedness.* When the expected value, $E[x]$, of a statistic used as an estimator is equal to the population parameter, that estimator is, then, unbiased.
2. *Consistency.* When an estimator approaches the population parameter as the sample size increases, the estimator is, then, a consistent estimator of the population parameter.
3. *Efficiency.* If we could find an estimator with a variance smaller than

[7] Alexander Mood and Franklin Graybill, *Introduction Theory of Statistics*, 2nd ed. (New York: McGraw-Hill Book Company, 1963), pp. 167–78.

the variance of another estimator, given the same sample size, we could say that estimator is an efficient estimator.

4. *Sufficiency.* A statistic is a sufficient estimator if it utilizes all the information that a sample contains about the parameter. That is, we can find no other estimator that would add additional information about the parameter.

Each criterion is an important characteristic which an estimator should possess if possible. However, few estimators possess all these properties. Therefore, how can estimators with these desirable properties be found? The question posed suggests that methods are needed for determining "good" estimators.

If we have a particular statistic and would like to use it as an estimator, we can attempt to find the desirable properties it possesses. For example, if we consider a unimodal symmetrical population, the sample median is an unbiased and consistent estimator of the population mean. On the other hand, the mean of the sample not only possesses the properties above, but is a more efficient estimator than the sample median.

It turns out that there are a number of ways of finding "good" estimators: the method of maximum likelihood, the method of moments, the method of least squares, and the method of Bayes. It is beyond the scope of this text to elaborate on each of these methods. However, descriptions of these methods can be found in Mood and Graybill.[8]

The preceding paragraphs have dealt with some desirable properties of point estimators. In most of the discussion to follow, the estimators will be the sample means that fulfill the criteria above in the particular situations where they will be used in our examples of statistical analysis. But remember, other statistics are useful when situations exist where other methods of estimating central tendency may be better than the mean.

Interval Estimates

At times, it may be more useful to have a range of values within which the true population exists rather than a point estimation. An alternative way of estimating the population mean is to say that the mean is between two values, the confidence interval. From our previous example of average income levels, say, the average family income in the prospective community is between \$17,000 and \$23,000:

$$\$17{,}000 < \mu < \$23{,}000$$

Recall From Chapter 8 that the interval is given by

$$\bar{X} - C.L.\hat{\sigma}_{\bar{X}} \leq \mu \leq \bar{X} + C.L.\hat{\sigma}_{\bar{X}}$$

where C.L. refers to the confidence level. Through the use of probability theory, we can calculate the probability that the true population mean

---

[8] Ibid., pp. 178–92, 340–43.

339
Data Analysis:
Preliminary
Considerations
and Univariate
Analysis

lies between the sample estimate (mean) plus and minus the standard error of the sampling distribution.

To illustrate, suppose that the decision maker selects the 68 percent confidence level. With the mean $(\bar{X})$ found to be \$20,000, and the standard error calculated from the sample standard deviation \$3,000 ($\sigma_{\bar{x}}$ = \$3,000), the decision maker can now say that there is a 68 percent chance that the true population parameter (mean) lies between the interval \$17,000 and \$23,000.

Dispersion in Estimation

A single value was provided that would partially describe an entire frequency distribution, in the measures of central tendency. When making logical interpretations about such an average, however, the analyst may want to know how confidently he might assert that it really describes the phenomenon. The old joke about the statistician who drowned in a river *averaging* three feet depth is relevant. Are the individual values clustered around that average or scattered widely from it? We have already commented that the researcher may be interested in a measure of "scatter" (1) between points, or ranges, and (2) around a point, or deviation.

Measures of dispersion are needed to form a judgment about the reliability of the estimated average value. For example, if there is a large amount of spread among the values from the average value, the average value used to summarize the data may not be all that representative of the data being studied. Methods for computing the most common of these measures have been presented in Section 12.4.3.

In some analytical situations, the strategy of statistical inference is based upon the relationship among the mean, the standard deviation, and the laws of probability. It is hoped that the discussion introduced in this chapter would lead to better understanding of the importance of the use of the measure of dispersion.

12.6.2 Significance

Estimates take on significance only with comparisons, and the interpreter must bear in mind that the figure was based on a sample — except in the unusual cases where a complete population has been enumerated. He or she needs some measurement of how confidently any average figure can be taken as an accurate description of the population that it purports to represent. This degree of confidence, as you recall from our sampling discussion, is related to the size of sample taken and to the *dispersion* of the data from the mean or central value.

Testing Significance of a Sample Mean and a Population Mean

The first of the tests of hypotheses concerns a sample mean and a population mean or hypothetical mean. For an example, the specialty-chain-store case is continued to illustrate the discussion. Suppose that the regional planning council of the particular community in which the specialty chain is considering locating their new store released a report that the average family income of the community's citizens is $24,000. Since income level is an important aspect in the decision of locating one of their stores, the researcher has been assigned to verify the council's claim. The researcher takes a sample of 200 residents, with the result that the sample mean income is equal to $17,000. Approaching this with a null hypothesis, the researcher states that the mean income of the sample residents is the same as the income level of the total population as reported by the council.

To confirm the statement above, the researcher must examine the probability of obtaining a sample mean of $17,000 if the population mean is really $24,000. This brings up the subject of hypothesis testing in terms of the statistical significance of the difference between the sample mean and the population mean (council's stated income level). The null hypothesis and the alternative hypothesis, are:

$$H_1 : \mu = \$24,000$$

$$H_1 : \mu < \$24,000$$

You should recall our discussion of confidence limits, or the significance of difference, in Chapter 8. That should be brought to bear in this situation. The researcher here, let us say, wishes to employ a 95 percent confidence coefficient, leaving only a 5 percent critical probability that he or she will want to reject the null hypothesis if the probability of obtaining a sample mean of $17,000 by chance is less than 5 percent when the true mean is, in fact, $24,000.[9]

In this case, notice that one is concerned only with a deviation in one direction, often called a *one-tailed test* because the rejection area lies only to one side of the arithmetic mean. For this purpose one would not utilize -1.96 standard deviations to achieve 95 percent confidence, but only -1.64 standard deviations. The research data also provided a standard deviation of the sample of $5,000.

The procedure in this situation is to apply a Z test to the data.[10] The Z test is stated:

$$Z = \frac{\bar{X} - \mu}{\hat{\sigma}_{\bar{x}}}$$

where Z = number of standard deviations for the desired level of confidence

---

[9] The situation in essence is as follows. The decision maker has a hypothesis about a population, and since it is being stated in quantitative terms, it is a statistical hypothesis. He or she wants to demonstrate statistically whether the hypothesis is true or false, and this will involve inferences based on samples. A sample error may result in an erroneous inference, which may be the result of either of these types of error:

Type I error: The hypothesis is actually true, but the sample data indicate that it is false.
Type II error: The sample data indicate that the hypothesis is true, but actually it is false.

[10] The Z statistic is appropriate if (1) the sample comes from a normal population, and (2) sample is large enough for the central limit theorem to be operative ($n > 30$).

341

Data Analysis:
Preliminary
Considerations
and Univariate
Analysis

$\bar{X} =$ mean of the sample

$\mu =$ mean of the population or hypothetical mean

$\hat{\sigma}_{\bar{x}} =$ estimate for the standard error of the mean

and

$$\hat{\sigma}_{\bar{x}} = \frac{s}{\sqrt{n-1}}$$

where $s =$ standard deviation of the sample

$n =$ number in the sample

Therefore, the unbiased estimate of the standard error of the mean is

$$\hat{\sigma}_{\bar{x}} = \frac{\$5,000}{\sqrt{200-1}} = \frac{5,000}{14.1} = \$354.61$$

and

$$Z = \frac{\$17,000 - \$24,000}{\$354.61} = (-19.74)$$

This value can be compared with the critical value of the Z statistic. Since the value of the computed Z statistic (-19.74) is larger than -1.64, one would reject the null hypothesis because the $\$17,000$ income level lies more than 1.64 standard errors away from the population mean of $\$24,000$. The researcher must conclude that the true population mean is not $\$24,000$. A difference this large (calculated as $Z = -19.74$ and the critical value as $Z = -1.64$) is not a random fluctuation in the sample data.

It is left to the management of the specialty chain to translate the researcher's conclusion into the decision process as to the accuracy of the planning council's report.

Testing for Significance of Differences in Two Means

A second type of hypothesis test concerns testing for significance of differences in two means. As an example, consider the hypothetical case of the Ultrafab Company, which manufactures a type of production machinery. The design of a machine that they have been making and selling will be termed Model A, and a new design has just come out that is Model B. Despite their designers' belief that Model B will produce more efficiently than Model A, Ultrafab's management wants this to be proven in actual usage by companies to whom they supply machinery. Therefore, it was arranged to have several customers try Model B and Model A under precisely similar conditions to determine how many units each model would produce in 1 hour, excluding any rejected for not meeting specifications. This was conducted in seven customers' plants, although later one trial of Model A had to be discarded as not being comparable, which left Ultrafab with six trials of Model A to compare with seven of Model B.

The result of the experiment was that the arithmetic mean of Model A trials was 183 units per hour versus Model B's mean of 190 units per hour. The Ultrafab management was unwilling to accept the hypothesis that Model B was superior to Model A until that difference was proven to be statistically significant. Let us, therefore, test the null hypothesis that Model B is not superior to Model A in production rate.

In considering the difference between the means of two small samples, we see that the standard deviations employed above are not suitable. Instead, small samples require the use of the Student t values, which are given in prepared tables of the "critical value of t" (Table of Appendix C). A preliminary decision must be the level of significance that will be used, which, let us say, is the 0.05 level—or a 95 percent confidence level. The formula for solving this problem is

$$t = \frac{X_1 - X_2}{\sqrt{\dfrac{\Sigma \ (X_1 - \bar{X}_1)^2 + \Sigma \ (X_2 - \bar{X}_2)^2 \ (n_1 + n_2)}{n_1 + n_2 - 2}}}$$

This computation involves the arithmetic means of each of the compared samples of machine trials, X_1 and X_2, and the number of observations in each sample, n_1 and n_2. The number of degrees of freedom is also included with the denominator of $n_1 + n_2 - 2$.

The results of the thirteen trials of the machines and calculations to solve the formula are shown in Table 12–5.

Substituting these calculations into the formula, we have

$$t = \frac{183 - 190}{\sqrt{\dfrac{128 + 88 \ (6 + 7)}{6 + 7 - 2}}} = -2.843$$

If we refer to a table of the distribution of t values, we find that when there are eleven degrees of freedom and a 0.05 level of significance, our t value is 2.201. This means that our computed value of t for our sample must lie within the range +2.201 to −2.201. As our t value of −2.843 lies outside that range, we conclude that confidence *is* justified that Model B produces more units than Model A, and thus we demonstrate that we would not commit a Type II error of interpretation in accepting that implication. We should advise the Ultrafab people that the results of these machine trials are significant in terms of their statistical confidence requirements.

TABLE 12–5. Results of the Thirteen Trials To Solve the Formula

Trial Number	Model A Number of Units Made X_1	$X_1 - X_1$	$(X_1 - X_1)^2$	Trial Number	Model B Number of Units Made X_2	$X_2 - X_2$	$(X_2 - X_2)^2$
1	176	−7	49	7	185	−5	25
2	180	−3	9	8	187	−3	9
3	181	−2	4	9	187	−3	9
4	184	+1	1	10	190	0	0
5	187	+4	16	11	192	+2	4
6	190	+7	49	12	194	+4	16
			128	13	195	+5	25
	$X_1 = 183$				$X_2 = 190$		88

Determining Significance of Differences in Nonintervally Scaled Measurements

When a researcher collects data that are either ordinally or nominally scaled, the statistical significance tests discussed in the preceding subsection are not applicable. This precludes the use of the mean and standard deviation as measures of central tendency and dispersion, respectively. Therefore, when a researcher is interested in hypotheses concerning the form of a population frequency or that involving comparing populations, nonparametric statistical methods must be applied instead of parametric methods (as was previously discussed).

There are a number of nonparametric methods, and their application depends upon the level of measurement (nominal versus ordinal), the number of samples (one, two, or multiple samples), and whether the samples are independent or related in some way. (For an independent sample, the response or observation does not depend on another response or observation. In a dependent sample, given two sets of observations, the observations are made on the same respondent, once before the introduction of a variable and once again after. The sample is now related.)

Since it is beyond the scope of this text to present all the tests, their formulas and calculations, our discussion will be confined to discussing when and how to use those most commonly applied to marketing research. For those interested, however, the Appendix at the end of this chapter discusses additional nonintervally scaled measures of significance. Several sources are also available which present this information in detail.[11]

[11] Those interested in nonparametric tests should consult one of the following books on the subject: W. J. Conover, *Practical Nonparametric Methods* (New York: John Wiley & Sons, Inc., 1971); D. A. S. Fraser, *Nonparametric Methods in Statistics* (New York: John Wiley & Sons, Inc., 1957); William Hayes, *Statistics* (New York: Holt, Rinehart and Winston, 1963), pp. 578–697; or Sidney Siegel, *Nonparametric Statistics for the Behavioral Sciences* (New York: McGraw-Hill Book Company, 1956).

Chi-square one-sample test. At times research is undertaken in which the researcher is interested in the number of observations or responses that occur in various categories. If the data are nominally scaled, a *chi-square* analysis is an appropriate test. The technique is that of the goodness of fit, in which the researcher tests whether a significant difference exists between the observed number of responses in each category and the expected number for each category (which is based on the null hypothesis).

Consider as a hypothetical illustration a soft drink bottler, who has recently developed a new drink which quenches one's thirst after participating in strenuous exercise (such as athletes after competition). This bottler is considering bottling this product in four different sizes: 7 ounces, 12 ounces, 16 ounces, and 32 ounces. From the bottler's past sales records of their other soft drinks, 10 percent purchased the 7-ounce bottle, 35 percent purchased the 12-ounce bottle, 25 percent purchased the 16-ounce bottle, and 30 percent purchased the 32-ounce bottle. The bottler is interested if this consumption pattern exists for the new soft drink. If there is a change in the consumption pattern, this would necessitate a change in the percentage of bottling sizes. The bottler decides to conduct a test market to determine the purchasing pattern of the various bottle sizes for the new drink.

After a two-week market test, the data gathered indicated that 15,980 bottles of the new drink were sold and the distribution of sales by size was as follows:

7 oz	12 oz	16 oz	32 oz
1,698	5,683	3,945	4,654

The bottler asks: Do the figures from the test market indicate a change in the consumption pattern for the new drink? In this one-sample case, the chi-square test is appropriate. This means that we test whether a significant difference exists between the observed number of bottles of various sizes purchased and the expected number based on past sales data (in other words, based on H_0). Thus, the expected frequencies can be deduced from the null hypothesis in the following manner. The null hypothesis would state that the consumption of sales by bottle size would follow the sales pattern indicated above. Thus the expected sales would be: $15,980 \times 0.10 = 1,598$ for the 7-ounce bottle; $15,980 \times 0.35 = 5,593$ for the 12-ounce bottle; $15,980 \times 0.25 = 3,995$ for the 16-ounce bottle; and $15,980 \times 0.30 = 4,794$ for the 32-ounce bottle.

The test statistic is

$$\chi^2 = \sum_{i=1}^{n} \frac{(O_i - E_i)^2}{E_i}$$

where O_i = observed number of cases in the ith category

345

Data Analysis:
Preliminary
Considerations
and Univariate
Analysis

E_i = expected number of cases in the ith category

n = number of categories

The appropriate statistic is computed as:

$$\chi^2 = \frac{(1,698 - 1,598)^2}{1,598} + \frac{(5,683 - 5,593)^2}{5,593} + \frac{(3,945 - 3,995)^2}{3,995}$$

$$+ \frac{(4,654 - 4,794)^2}{4,794} = 12.43$$

The sampling distribution of χ^2 under H_0 follows the chi-square distribution with $(n - 1)$ degrees of freedom. Suppose that the researcher has chosen a significance level of $\alpha = 0.05$. The table value of chi-square (Appendix D) for 3 degrees of freedom and the $\alpha = 0.05$ is 7.81. Since the calculated χ^2 (12.43) exceeds the critical value at the α level of significance, the null hypothesis is rejected. Therefore, the market-test results indicate that sales of the new soft drink for various bottle sizes follow a different consumption pattern.

Median test. One of the simplest of the order methods is a procedure for testing whether two independent groups differ on the basis of deviations from the median. This test will determine if two random samples have been drawn from populations with the same median (the null hypothesis).

The different sample groups are combined into a single distribution and the grand median for the sample is obtained. Then each value in each group is compared with the grand median. If the particular value is above the grand median, the observation is assigned to a "plus" category. If the value is below the grand median, it is assigned to a "minus" category. Under the null hypothesis, the probability that observations will fall in each of the categories should be the same for each and every population.

To illustrate its application, suppose that a bank wanted to determine if there was a difference in the satisfaction of services between the bank's two types of customers: regular accounts and commercial accounts. The bank marketing department developed a questionnaire about its services using Likert-type statements, which are ordinally scaled. The questionnaire was mailed to a random sample of both groups of customers. Upon returning the questionnaire to the bank, the scores were recorded as shown in Table 12–6.

The test statistic is calculated by the following formula:

$$\chi^2 = \frac{n \left(\mid ad - bc \mid - \dfrac{n}{2} \right)^2}{(a + b)\,(c + d)\,(a + c)\,(b + d)}$$

Calculated χ^2 for the service scores is

$$\chi^2 = \frac{30 \left(\mid (8)(8) - (5)(5) \mid - \frac{30}{2} \right)^2}{(13)(13)(13)(13)}$$

$$= \frac{30 \, (\mid 64 - 25 \mid - 3)^2}{28,561}$$

$$= \frac{17,280}{28,561}$$

$$= 0.61$$

TABLE 12–6. Scores of Regular and Commercial Accounts with Respect to Services Rendered by the Bank

Regular Accounts	Commercial Accounts	Ranking of Entire Raw Scores Regular	Commercial
19	48	27	21
70	52	12	19
77	69	7	13
14	13	29	30
83	73	3	9
87	15	2	28
68	50	14	20
72	61	10	17
76	21	8	26
90	47	1	22
26	80	25	5
66	36	15	24
60	78	18	6
81	71	4	11
46	65	23	16

Table 12–7 indicates those scores that fall above and below the grand median.

TABLE 12–7. Scores of Customers Compared to the Grand Median

	Regular Account	Commercial Account	Total
Above grand median	8	5	13
	(a)	(b)	(a + b)
Below grand median	5	8	13
	(c)	(d)	(c + d)
Total	13	13	26
	(a + c)	(b + d)	(a + b + c + d) = n

The critical value from a chi-square table (Appendix D) for 1 degree of freedom $[(r-1)(c-1)=1]$ and a specified $\alpha = 0.05$ is 3.84. Therefore, the null hypothesis is not rejected. The results indicate that there does not appear to be a difference in service satisfaction with regard to a change in the bank's service between regular and commercial customers.

12.6.3 Trends

When studying a particular variable, the interest is often in what may happen to that factor in the future. If data on that variable are possessed that cover some span of time to show historical trends, such a *time series* can be the base for a trajectory into the future. A time series is composed of the values of some phenomenon that existed at several times in the past, preferably at equal intervals and including more than ten observations. Obviously, one must be assured that similar measuring methods and definitions were used throughout the series. For instance, food store sales in 1960 are not comparable with those of 1977, either in the mix and breadth of merchandise sold by the stores or in the real value of a dollar.

Following are United States annual disposable income data in a time series adjusted for the changing value of the dollar, on the basis of its 1972 value:

Year	Annual Disposable Income (billions of dollars)	Year	Annual Disposable Income (billions of dollars)
1961	500.6	1969	712.3
1962	521.6	1970	741.6
1963	539.6	1971	769.0
1964	577.3	1972	801.3
1965	612.4	1973	854.7
1966	643.6	1974	840.8
1967	669.8	1975	855.5
1968		1976	905.8 (est.)

Data of this type could have been useful, for example, to a researcher who was conducting, in 1976, a study whose findings would be contingent on the probable consumption of cookies and crackers to the year 1980. She has sound reason to believe that cookie and cracker consumption is related to future incomes, which is a logical interpretation. Let us consider what she might do in determining probable future incomes.

There is clearly a linear trend in these income data (and there would have been a curvilinear trend if we had not deflated them for the inflationary factor that operated over this period), as we see when they are charted in Figure 12–2. The researcher might draw freehand a trend

347

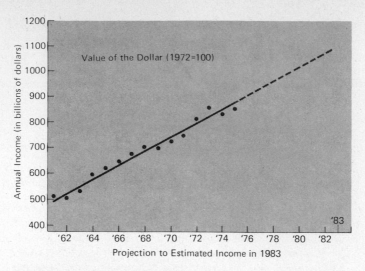

FIGURE 12–2. Annual Disposable Income in the United States, at a Constant Value of the Dollar (1972 = 100)

Source: U.S. Department of Commerce, Survey of Current Business, *various issues.*

line through these data and extend it onward to 1980, which would be a crude type of statistical interpretation, relevant to his logical inference. She would be more precise and on safer grounds, however, if she calculated the trend.

The preferable method of computing the trend line for the observed data would be the *least-squares* method. This would be that line from which the sum of the squares of the observed deviations would be minimized. If the nature of the observations indicates that a straight line would adequately describe their trend, one would compute an arithmetic straight line. This could be done by the *long* method, in which our computations would work from the origin, or by the alternative, *coded* method, which would work both ways from the middle observation. See Table 12–8 for the computation of the least-squares method.

Frequently, the most suitable trend line is not straight but is a curve, typically a parabola. A different formula, of course, is applicable in this case. Where cyclical or seasonal influences impose recurring fluctuations on the data, still other and more complicated formulas should be employed, if our interest is in the secular (long-run) trends to remove such fluctuations. Usually such fluctuations can be ironed out, however, more simply with a *moving average.* For instance, if there were recurring fluctuations in our income data, perhaps a four-year moving average (1961–1964, 1971–1974, and the like) would suffice to remove their obscuring of the secular income trend.

Another way to represent a time series is to use *index numbers.* By taking one year as the base date with a value of 100, relative changes from that point are computed for other observations over time. Thus, another

348

TABLE 12–8. Least-Squares Trend Computations of Personal Disposable Income, 1961–1975, in Billions of 1972 Dollars

Year, X	Income, Y	x	x^2	xy	Trend Value, Y_t
1961	$ 500.6	−7	49	−3,504.2	$499.3
1962	521.6	−6	36	−3,129.6	526.4
1963	539.2	−5	25	−2,696.0	553.5
1964	577.3	−4	16	−2,309.2	580.6
1965	612.4	−3	9	−1,837.2	607.7
1966	643.6	−2	4	−1,287.2	634.8
1967	669.8	−1	1	−669.8	661.9
1968	695.0	0	0	0.0	689.0
1969	712.3	+1	1	+712.3	716.1
1970	741.6	+2	4	+1,483.2	743.2
1971	769.0	+3	9	+2,307.0	770.3
1972	801.3	+4	16	+3,205.2	797.4
1973	854.7	+5	25	+4,273.5	824.5
1974	840.8	+6	36	+5,044.8	851.6
1975	855.5	+7	49	+5,988.5	878.7
	$10,334.9		280	7,581.3	

$Y_t = a + bx$

where Y_t = trend value for a given time period

     a = value of Y_t when $x = 0$

     b = slope of the line, or the increase or decrease in Y_t for each change in the time period

     x = coded time period selected

$$a = \frac{Y}{N} = \frac{10{,}334.9}{15} = 689.0 \quad \text{where } N = \text{number of years}$$

$$b = \frac{xy}{x^2} = \frac{7{,}581.3}{280} = 27.1$$

$$Y_t = 689 + 27.1x$$

period whose value was 4 percent higher than the base period would become 104. This not only simplifies changes over time but also between different time series.

Index numbers facilitate comparison of items expressed in different absolute measurements, such as in dollars, feet, and pounds, by converting the different measurements to relative values. For example, with per capita income and consumer price levels both shown as indexes based on a given year, say 1967, we can compare their levels in 1972. Thus, if the CPI for a particular year was 125.5, and if per capita income index stood at 148.6, we readily see then that income had risen faster than prices. This comparison would have been a complicated one using the absolute numbers.

Management, with a need for detailed and specialized indexes for planning and decision making, may choose from a wealth of published index-number series. Many time series of data useful in marketing problems are published periodically, both as aggregate and as index numbers, some of which were described in Chapter 6.

12.7 Summary

This chapter sought to highlight the basic considerations that are involved in choosing a method by which to summarize and analyze data. The primary concern has been with four major steps: (1) bringing the data into order, (2) summarizing the data, (3) considering factors involved in the choice of an analysis method, and (4) analyzing univariate data.

Throughout our discussion we pointed out the relevant factors that must be taken into consideration when choosing from the many available statistical techniques. This chapter provides the necessary background for our discussion of bivariate and multivariate techniques in Chapter 13.

Appendix: Nonintervally Scaled Measures of Significance–Kolmogorov-Smirnov Test and the McNemar Test

In chapter 12, two commonly used nonintervally scaled measures of significance have been discussed. Let us now consider two additional tests to demonstrate methods of significance testing with nominally and ordinally scaled data.

Kolmogorov-Smirnov one-sample test. The Komogorov-Smirnov one-sample test is similar to the chi-square test of goodness of fit. That is, it is concerned with the degree of agreement between the distribution of observed values and some specified theoretical distribution (expected frequencies). But Kolmogorov–Smirnov test is chosen because the researcher wants to compare the distribution on an *ordinal scale*.

Briefly, consider an example of a paint manufacturer who is interested in developing a new color, Jungle Green. The company is interested in testing four different shades of this color: very light, light, bright, and dark. Each color differs slightly in shade from the others, so the four shades can be discerned from the darkest to the lightest in color. Each respondent is shown four prints of the different color shades and asked for his or her preference. If color shade is unimportant, the photographs of each shade should be chosen equally often except for random differences. If color shade is important, the respondents should consistently prefer one of the extreme shades.

Since shade represents a natural ordering, the Kolmogorov–Smirnov test is applied to test the preference hypothesis. The test involves speci-

350

351

Data Analysis:
Preliminary
Considerations
and Univariate
Analysis

fying the cumulative frequency distribution that would occur under the null hypothesis (theoretical distribution), and comparing that with the observed cumulative frequency distribution. Reference to the sampling distribution, then, indicates whether such a divergence between the two distributions is likely to be due to chance or if the observed magnitude truly occurred as the result of a preference.

Suppose, for example, that a sample of 200 homeowners were shown the four shades with the following results: 80 preferred the "very light" shade, 60 preferred the "light" shade, 40 preferred the "bright" shade, and 20 preferred the "dark" shade. The manufacturer asks: "Do these results indicate a preference?" If they do, the manufacturer would produce only those shades preferred by the homeowners. Table 12–9 shows the appropriate data in tabular form.

TABLE 12–9. Homeowners Preference for the Shade of Jungle Green Paint

	Rank of Shade Chosen			
	Very Light	Light	Bright	Dark
f = number of homeowners choosing that rank	80	60	40	20
$F_0(X)$ = theoretical cumulative distribution of choices under H_0	0.25	0.50	0.75	1.00
$S_n(X)$ = cumulative distribution of observed choices	0.40	0.70	0.90	1.00
$F_0(X) - S_n(X)$	0.15	0.20	0.15	0.00

The Kolmogorov-Smirnov D test focuses on the largest absolute values of the deviations among observed and theoretical proportions:

$$D = \text{maximum} |F_0(X) - S_n(X)|$$

where $F_0(X)$ = specified cumulative frequency distribution under H_0 for any value x, and is the proportion of cases expected to have scores equal to or less than x

$S_n(X)$ = observed cumulative frequency distribution of a random sample of N observations, where X is any possible score

If the researcher chooses an $\alpha = 0.05$, the critical value of D for large samples is given by $1.36/\sqrt{n}$, where n is the sample size. For our example, the critical value is 0.096. Inspection of the bottom row of Table 12–9 quickly reveals that the D for these data is 0.20. The calculated D exceeds the critical value, and thus the null hypothesis of no preference among shades is rejected. The results show significant preferences among the color shades of Jungle Green.

McNemar test for the significance of changes. The McNemar test is applicable for analyzing research designs of those of a before-and-after situation, and the data are measured nominally. In this case, the samples are related, in which the individual is used as his or her own control. Thus this technique might be used to test the effectiveness of a particular treatment, say, mailed coupons, and the individual's purchase rate for the particular product. The null hypothesis would be that for those individuals who change their purchase rate, the probability that any individuals will change their purchase rate from low to high is equal to the probability that they will change their purchase rate from high to low, which is equal to one half. To test the null hypothesis, we examine the cases of change.

A study of a change in the purchase rate among a sample of individuals who received the coupons generated the results given in Table 12–10.

TABLE 12–10. Individual's Purchase Rate Change Before and After the Mail Coupon Campaign

	After Campaign		
Before Campaign	*High Purchase Rate*	*Low Purchase Rate*	*Total*
Low purchase rate	70 (A)	180 (B)	210
High purchase rate	80 (C)	30 (D)	150
Total	110	250	260

Notice that those cases which show changes before and after the campaign appear in cells *A* and *D*. An individual is placed in cell *A* if he or she changed from a low-purchase to a high-purchase rate. He or she is placed in cell *D* if changed from a low to a low purchase rate. If no change is observed, he or she is placed in either cell *B* or *C*.

The researcher wishes to know if the mailed coupon campaign was a success. The null hypothesis would be stated that the campaign was not successful. To test the null hypothesis, it is necessary to examine the cases of change in cells *A* and *D*.

The McNemar test involves calculating the χ^2 value according to the formula

$$\chi^2 = \frac{(|A - D| - 1)^2}{A + D}$$

This expression directs one to subtract 1 from the absolute value of the difference between *A* and *D* before squaring. This correction is nec-

353

Data Analysis:
Preliminary
Considerations
and Univariate
Analysis

essary because chi-square is a continuous distribution which is used to approximate a discrete distribution.

The calculated χ^2 turns out to be

$$\chi^2 = \frac{(|70 - 30| - 1)^2}{100}$$

$$= 15.21$$

For $\alpha = 0.05$, the critical value of χ^2 is 3.84 (from the chi-square distribution table found in Appendix D) for 1 degree of freedom [degrees of freedom are found by $(r - 1)(c - 1) = 1$, where r is the number of rows and c is the number of columns]. Thus, the null hypothesis is rejected, for the calculated χ^2 exceeds the critical value of χ^2 from the table. The mail coupon campaign was successful in increasing the purchase rate of the product under study.

13 Data Analysis: Bivariate and Multivariate Analysis

Our explanations of analytical methods continue in Chapter 13. Several of the more advanced, but very useful, types of analysis will be presented with some deliberation, for they are complicated. You should emerge with answers to questions such as these:

What exactly does "bivariate analysis" mean?

What are the methods of, and the interpretations made possible by, cross-tabulations?

What purpose is served by the chi-square technique? How is it calculated?

What is the central value of correlation? Its meaning? How can you measure correlation when your data are nonparametric?

Regression analysis is a tool for accomplishing what? What measurements are used in regression?

How would you test for differences among more than two groups of data? How would you determine relationships between sets of independent variables?

IN CHAPTER 12 WE DISCUSSED some of the important considerations in the selection of appropriate analytical methods. Its purpose was to convey an appreciation of the complexity of the selection process, while indicating a classification system that would simplify the process. After a general discussion of these considerations, we turned our attention to the problem of univariate analysis. Specifically, we attempted to give the reader an overview of those statistical techniques that have been most applicable in marketing research. This chapter will introduce the use of analytical methods applicable to bivariate and multivariate variables.

13.1 Bivariate Analysis

The amount of information that can be gleaned by analyzing the behavior of just one variable is obviously meager. The answers to marketing problems usually involve the seeking of causes, not merely how a critical variable behaves or would be projected into the future should past trends continue. Beyond the simplest form of analysis, univariate, is the analysis of two variables, termed *bivariate*. One of the two variables is the sort of output or behavior that is under study or being sought; an example might be an airline's passenger traffic between cities A and B that it is seeking to stimulate. This output would be related to (dependent on) some other variable and so is termed the *dependent variable*. The other variable (termed the *independent variable*) might be selected from anything suspected of being related to traffic volume, such as the number of flights, extent of promotional effort, special fares, or particular services.

The forms of bivariate analysis that are most useful fall into five categories: cross-classification, chi-square, correlation, regression, and analysis of variance.

13.1.1 Cross-Classification

Beginning the statistical work in a relatively easy fashion, we can cross-tabulate different factors against one another. This involves the simultaneous influence of variables in two or more informational categories. For instance, let us take up the question of dependency of household incomes and educational level, whose frequency distribution by income categories and educational level is given in Table 13–1.

The analyst is trying to explain why incomes differ, and conceives that it may be related to each income earner's educational level. When figures in Table 13–1 are studied, one has a distinct impression that a strong relationship exists between income and educational level attained.

To facilitate comparison of the data, one should show percentages rather than frequencies, for it will indicate more clearly the relative size of two or more values. The simplicity of calculating percentages has led to its wide applicability throughout society and as a statistical tool in marketing research. Unfortunately, its extensive use has led, at times,

TABLE 13–1. Head of the Household's Income Level and Educational Level Attained

Education of Head of Household	Income Level (dollars)								
	Under 5,000	5,000– 7,999	8,000– 9,999	10,000– 12,499	12,500– 14,999	15,000– 19,999	20,000– 24,999	25,000 and over	Total
Grade school or less	232	136	61	48	40	46	16	13	592
1–3 years of high school	145	99	46	80	51	61	26	33	541
Graduated high school	196	217	137	187	217	220	164	139	1477
1–3 years of college	116	81	91	139	148	220	122	132	1049
Graduated college	29	56	34	43	74	137	117	178	668
Graduate studies	7	31	11	38	40	76	85	165	453
Total	725	620	380	535	570	760	530	660	4780

whether inadvertently or intentionally, to deception, distortion, and mis-interpretation. Therefore, when one examines a percentage, two basic questions should always be asked: (1) In which direction should the percentage be computed? (2) How do you interpret the percentage of differences?

In a two-way frequency distribution, the question arises as to which base to use for 100 percent, and Table 13–1 might be percentaged in either dimension. Tables 13–2 and 13–3 are equivalent to Table 13–1, but are based on percentages calculated in different directions, vertically in Table 13–2 and horizontally in Table 13–3.

Each table conveys quite different information. Table 13–2 suggests that educational level is affected by income. Table 13–3, on the other hand, conveys that income is affected by educational level attained. We

TABLE 13–2. Family Income by Educational Level Attained (percent)

Education of Head of Household	Income Level (dollars)							
	Under 5,000	5,000– 7,999	8,000– 9,999	10,000– 12,499	12,500– 14,999	15,000– 19,999	20,000– 24,999	25,000 and over
Grade school or less	32	22	16	9	7	6	3	2
1–3 years of high school	20	16	12	15	9	8	5	5
Graduated high school	27	35	36	35	38	29	31	21
1–3 years of college	16	13	24	26	26	29	23	20
Graduated college	4	9	9	8	13	18	22	27
Graduated studies	1	5	3	7	7	10	16	25
Total	100	100	100	100	100	100	100	100

TABLE 13–3. Educational Level Attained by Family Income (percent)

Education of Head of Household	Income Level (dollars)								
	Under 5,000	5,000–7,999	8,000–9,999	10,000–12,499	12,500–14,999	15,000–19,999	20,000–24,999	25,000 and over	Total
Grade school or less	39	23	10	8	7	8	3	2	100
1–3 years of high school	27	18	9	15	9	11	5	6	100
Graduated high school	13	15	9	13	15	15	11	9	100
1–3 years of college	11	8	9	13	14	21	12	12	100
Graduated college	4	8	5	6	11	21	18	27	100
Graduate studies	2	7	2	8	9	17	19	36	100

hardly surmise that educational level of the head of the household would depend on income but rather intend to analyze variables on which income may be dependent. Conventionally, the rule to apply in determining which direction to use to compute percentages is to calculate percentages in the direction of the causal factor. In other words, calculate percentages across the dependent variable.

In our example, educational level attained is considered the cause (independent variable) and income level the effect (dependent variable). However, situations might arise when the direction of causation may not be easily determined. In such cases, the general guidelines discussed above should be followed. But for purposes of analysis, the analyst could consider computing percentages in each direction, which may give useful information. On the other hand, given the problem definition, the analyst could consider one of the variables as the dependent variable and calculate the appropriate percentage.

Cross-tabulations of other factors, such as sex, race, industry, and occupation might also be suspected of having significant influence on income and could be cross-tabulated. Another dimension could be added to our tabulation, too, by breaking down each educational level by sex, race, or some other relevant factor. The addition of another factor may uncover a relationship not immediately discernible: or it may modify a conclusion drawn on the basis of the two-variable tabulation.

This brings us to the second problem usually encountered when using percentages; the misinterpretation of the measurement of percentage differences. Percentages can be used in three ways to measure differences: absolute difference, relative difference, and percentage of possible difference. Since the three concepts differ, there is the chance of misrepresentation. Therefore, each method is explored using an example.

Suppose that an advertiser was interested in the awareness of his company, and knowledge of its message to inform the public about the company. In the past, they have been advertising in magazines and they now want to extend their magazine advertising by including a new publication. The company wants to know if the advertising in the new publication is getting the company's story across to the public. They run a control test of recall before the advertising, and again after it has run over a period of months, with the results shown in Table 13–4.

Examining Table 13–4, we see that subscribers to the new magazine increased their awareness of the company more than did nonsubscribers in terms of absolute differences. The *absolute difference method* indicates that the level increased 20 percent (75 − 55) for the subscribers and 15 percent (45 − 30) for the nonsubscribers. This method is often used because of its simplicity of calculation, but it suffers from possible misinterpretation, since the researcher must make a distinction between percent and percentage points.

Another method of comparison of percentage differences often applied is the *relative difference method.* This method shows a 36.4 percent increase for subscribers (75 − 55)/55 × 100 = 36.4 percent, whereas the nonsubscribers increased by (45 − 30)/30 × 100 = 50 percent. But this method is often misleading, because it exaggerates the impression of a slight increase from a very small base.

A third method, often regarded as a better way to interpret the data than either of the other methods discussed, is the *percentage of possible differences.* The principal rationale for using this method can be found in the "ceiling effect." When causal relationships are involved, the objective is generally to convert unfavorable behavior to favorable behavior. If one begins with a higher proportion of favorable behavior, then, one will find greater difficulty getting significant increases in favorable behavior. The percentage-of-possible-differences method shows that the maximum number of percentage points the subscribers could have increased was (100 − 55) = 45 percentage points. The increase observed was (75 − 55) = 20 percentage points. Therefore, the subscribers show 20/45 × 100 = 44.4 percent of the possible difference; and the nonsubscribers show only 15/70 × 100 = 21.4 percent of the maximum possible change.

Since the results of these three methods conflict, an explanation of the principal arguments for the use of each must be offered to avoid misunderstandings of their interpretation.

13.1.2 Chi-Square

In addition to estimation and tests of statistical significance of the kind we have discussed in Chapter 12, an important part of data analysis is to determine if an association exists between two variables. An analytical technique used for determining the degree of association in cross-tabulated data is the chi-square test.

One is very often working with nonmetric data; and the chi-square technique can be used to determine whether or not there is an association, statistically, between the data or sets of data and some other data or standard with which it is to be compared.

In scientific fashion one begins by testing the null hypothesis that there is no relationship between the variables; that is, the two variables are not contingent upon one another. After the chi-square value for the

TABLE 13–4. Individual's Knowledge of Company by Exposure to the Magazine Advertising (percent)

	Before Ad Appears in New Magazine	After Ad Appears in New Magazine
Subscribers to the new magazine	55	75
Nonsubscribers to the new magazine	30	45

data has been computed, it is then compared with a standard table of the critical value of chi-square, which may be found in Appendix D or in handbooks of statistical tables. If the particular sample's chi-square value exceeds the critical value found in the table, the null hypothesis is rejected and the inference is that the difference between our sample and chance expectations is too large to be attributed to random error—that the variables are not independent and a significant relationship does exist.

In one study an experiment was run to determine whether children at different levels of cognitive development (measured by school grade) were capable of recalling the brand name from a breakfast cereal commercial.[1] In this case, the marketing-oriented element was "name of the cereal." The children were shown the commercial and then were asked questions related to their ability to recall information from the message. A random sample of children, representing different stages of cognitive development, provided the data in Table 13–5.

TABLE 13–5. Recall of Specific Element of Commercial by Stage of Cognitive Development

Recall of Product	Stage of Cognitive Development			
	First Grade: Stage II	Third Grade: Stage III	Sixth Grade: Stage IV	Total
Name of cereal	5 (10.5)	12 (11.5)	16 (11)	33
Cereal (in general)	17 (11.5)	12 (12.5)	7 (12)	36
Total Responses	22	24	23	69

Source: *Adapted from Ronald S. Rubin, "The Effects of Cognitive Development on Children's Responses to Television Advertising,"* Journal of Business Research, *October, 1974, p. 413.*

The null hypothesis is that there will be no difference in children's ability to recall the specific element from the commercial, regardless of

---

[1] Ronald S. Rubin, "The Effects of Cognitive Development on Children's Responses to Television Advertising," *Journal of Business Research*, October, 1974, pp. 408–19.

stage of cognitive development. Suppose that a significance level of $\alpha = 0.05$ (or 95 percent probability of positive significance) was chosen for the test. The computation of the χ^2 statistic involves computing an expected frequency for each cell, squaring each variance (squared differences between the observed and expected frequencies for each cell), and then dividing that by the values of the expected frequency and summing over the values. The formula is

$$\chi^2 = \sum_{i=1}^{n} \frac{(f_{oi} - f_{ei})^2}{f_{ei}}$$

where f_{oi} = observed frequency
f_{ei} = expected frequency, computed for the ith cell by multiplying the row total in which the cell appears times the column total in which the cell appears and dividing by the total number of observations in the entire table (To illustrate, for the cell represented by the intersection of the categories "first grade" and "name of cereal,"

$$f_{ei} = \frac{33 \times 22}{69} = 10.5$$

The other expected frequencies are calculated in a similar manner and are shown in parentheses in Table 13-5.

The calculated value of χ^2 is

$$\chi^2 = \frac{(5 - 10.5)^2}{10.5} + \frac{(12 - 11.5)^2}{11.5} + \frac{(16 - 11)^2}{11} + \frac{(17 - 11.5)^2}{11.5}$$

$$+ \frac{(12 - 12.5)^2}{12.5} + \frac{(7 - 12)^2}{12}$$

$$= 9.90$$

The shape of the χ^2 distribution, it should be recalled, varies with the number of degrees of freedom that is found by $(r - 1)(c - 1)$, where r is the number of rows and c is the number of columns. Entering the prepared critical value table (Appendix D), for 2 degrees of freedom at the 0.05 level, we read the critical value to be 5.99. Since the computed χ^2 value is larger than this critical value, we conclude that a child's stage of cognitive development and his ability to recall specific information are not independent; a significant relationship does exist. However, notice that this test informs us only that there is a significant relationship between the two variables. It does not tell us the degree or the strength of this relationship. The degree of its relationship can be determined from the computation of a contingency coefficient, which will be discussed in a subsequent section.

Although there are no assumptions made as to the shape of the data distribution for this nonparametric technique, there are restrictions on its application. As a rule of thumb, if the degrees of freedom is greater than 1, not more than 20 percent of the cells should have expected frequencies of less than 5. If this requirement cannot be met, the researcher should attempt to combine cells, until it conforms to this rule, but only if the combination would not render the data meaningless.

13.1.3 Correlation

Correlation is the measurement of the degree to which changes in one variable (the dependent one) are associated with changes in another. Cross-tabulation only provided an indication of such a relationship, but a specific value needs to be calculated to make exact comparisons of how different factors covary with the one being studied. Such covariance may be portrayed graphically, as in Figure 13–1, which provides a visual relationship of two variables. Notice that this contains individual data from an array, not grouped data. When the dependent variable is related to a single independent variable, as in this case, we call this measurement *simple correlation*. Later we shall discuss the more complex measurement of multiple correlation.

The usefulness of being able to summarize magnitudes by computing averages will be recalled, and likewise some summary value is needed to express the degree of association between two variables. That type of central value is called the *correlation coefficient*. It is based on the difference between the observed values of each variable and its arithmetic mean. The means of the two variables shown in Figure 13–1 are desig-

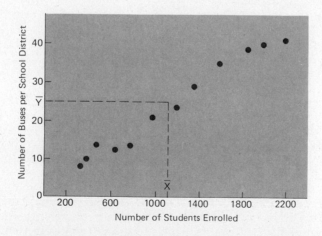

FIGURE 13–1. Graphic Correlation

On this scatter chart are plotted the number of students enrolled and number of school buses operated in twelve rural consolidated school districts (the figures being assumed). Each dot represents one school district. As the dots are clustered along a diagonal axis, it is apparent that substantial correlation exists between the two variables.

361

nated on their axes as $\bar{X}$ and $\bar{Y}$, and the point where they coincide is also indicated. The correlation coefficient, then, is measured in terms of the distances of the observations, on both the *X* and *Y* scales, from that point.

The data depicted in Figure 13–1 are assumed for purposes of illustration, and this is a case of a school bus manufacturer, the Bonnie Bus Company, seeking some reliable yardstick for market analysis. The analyst suspects that there may be a close relationship between the numbers of students in a rural consolidated school district and the number of school buses owned. If that relationship is found, it would be very convenient, because one can easily obtain data on districts' enrollments, but not actual buses owned. A sample has been obtained from a dozen school districts to which the company already sells that has both types of data, and in Figure 13–1 this dependent variable (buses) has been plotted on the vertical axis, with the independent variable on the horizontal axis.

In Figure 13–1 the number of school buses' values *(Y)* and the district's student enrollment values *(X)* tend to deviate from their mean in the same direction, along a northeast to southwest vector. That indicates positive correlation. Had they fallen along a straight line, or in perfect covariation with one another, they would be given a + 1.0 correlation coefficient. A perfect covariation along the perpendicular, northwest to southeast vector, would be a −1.0 correlation coefficent. Complete scatter with no covariation would be 0.0.

In the algebraic formula, the symbol for correlation is *r*, and that of *x* against *y* is written r_{xy}. This is computed with the standard deviations, that of the covariance being divided by the square root of the product of the variances of each variable as follows:

$$ r = \frac{\Sigma\ xy}{\sqrt{(\Sigma\ x^2)\ (\Sigma\ y^2)}} $$

where x = deviation of each case from the mean $\bar{X}$
          y = deviation of each case from the mean $\bar{Y}$
   $\Sigma\ xy$ = value of covariation
      x^2 = square of each x deviation
      y^2 = square of each y deviation

However, the need to compute means and deviations makes the formula somewhat cumbersome and time consuming. Statisticians have devised a much more efficient formula, which computes the coefficient directly from various summaries of values (instead of means and deviations). There are a number of versions of this efficient formula. Presented here is one of the more popular:

$$ r = \frac{N\ \Sigma\ XY - (\Sigma\ X)\ (\Sigma\ Y)}{\sqrt{[N\ \Sigma\ X^2 - (\Sigma\ X)^2]\ [N\ \Sigma\ Y^2 - (\Sigma\ Y)^2]}} $$

Illustrated in Table 13–6 are the data from Figure 13–1 for computation for the Pearson r.

Computing r,

$$r = \frac{(12)(394,215) - (13,370)\,(278)}{\sqrt{[(12)(19,339,400) - (13,370)^2]\,[(12)\,(8,100) - (278)^2]}}$$

$$= 0.9837$$

The values in Figure 13–1 display a high degree of correlation of $+$ 0.9837. The analyst should also be interested in the *coefficient of determination,* which is the square of the coefficient of correlation, or r^2. This indicates the proportion of variance, in the dependent variable, that is associated with (or determined by) the independent variable. In our example $r^2 = 0.9676$. This means that nearly 97 percent of the variation in school buses may be explained in terms of student enrollments. That would be a phenomenally high covariation that hardly ever is found among market analysis variables.

A final word of caution is needed, however, for there are many variables that may vary together for unknown reasons. In such a situation, a researcher may assume a causal relationship between two variables just because they are associated in a statistical sense. Note that statistical correlation does not in any way demonstrate causation. One could probably find a close relationship between camera sales and television sets, but one is not the cause and the other the effect. Preferably, changes in each of these variables are probably a result of a change in a consumer's in-

TABLE 13–6. Correlation between Number of Buses per School District and Number of Students Enrolled

Number of Students, X	Number of Buses, Y	XY	X²	Y²
325	7	2,275	105,625	49
375	10	3,750	140,625	100
450	13	5,850	202,500	169
620	12	7,440	384,400	144
775	13	10,075	600,625	169
950	21	19,950	902,500	441
1,150	23	26,450	1,322,500	529
1,300	28	36,400	1,690,000	784
1,525	35	53,375	2,325,625	1,225
1,800	37	66,600	3,240,000	1,369
1,950	39	76,050	3,802,500	1,521
2,150	40	86,000	4,622,500	1,600
13,370	278	394,215	19,339,400	8,100

come level. A relationship such as the one above is known as *spurious correlation*. Therefore, one must first determine if a logical relationship may exist between variables, which in turn would support a further analysis.

Nonparametric Measures of Correlation

The correlation method discussed above cannot be used when measurements are either nominally or ordinally scaled. Therefore, nonparametric techniques must be applied.

Correlation of Nominally Scaled Data

The *contingency coefficient, C,* is a measure of the extent of association between two sets of attributes. To compute *C,* the observations of the two attributes are arranged into a contingency table of frequencies. The degree of association is calculated by using the following formula:

$$C = \sqrt{\frac{\chi^2}{N + \chi^2}}$$

where χ^2 is computed by the method presented in Section 13.1.2, and N is the total size of the sample.

Let us return to our example from Section 13.1.2 and compute C for the data as follows:

$$C = \sqrt{\frac{9.9}{69 + 9.9}} = 0.354$$

We therefore determine that the correlation, expressed by the contingency coefficient, is $C = 0.354$. Does this value indicate a strong or weak association? We must compare the calculated value against its limits.

The relative ease of computation of C may seem to make it a widely applicable measure of association. However, as Siegel points out, it has several limitations or deficiencies.[2] When there is a lack of any association between variables, the coefficient will be zero, but it cannot attain unity (for a perfectly correlated situation). The upper limit for the contingency coefficient is a function of the number of categories. For instance, the upper limit of C for a 2×2 table is 0.707, for a 3×3 table it is 0.816, and for a 10×10 table it is 0.949. Consequently, two contingency coefficients are not comparable unless comparisons are made with tables of the same size. In examining our example, we cannot calculate its upper limit, for the number of categories are not the same for each variable (the number of rows does not equal the number of columns). It may, however, lie between 0.707 and 0.816. If we accept this crude range of its approximate limits, the calculated value thereby suggests

---

[2] Sidney Siegel, *Nonparametric Statistics for the Behavioral Sciences* (New York: McGraw-Hill Book Company, 1956), p. 201.

that there is, at best, a moderate association between the variables. Another limitation is that C is not directly comparable to any other measure of correlation, such as the Pearson r.

However, in spite of these limitations, the contingency coefficient is often used to indicate a degree of association between two sets of scores to which none of the other measures of association is applicable (because of the freedom from statistical assumptions and requirements).

Rank Correlation Coefficient

When the data are ordinally scaled, and a degree of association between two ordinally scaled variables is sought, the Spearman's rank correlation coefficient, r_s (sometimes called rho), can be applied.[3] To illustrate its use, let us consider the following example. Suppose that a researcher was interested in the effect of an individual's social-status striving upon his purchase behavior. The researcher wants to find the degree of correlation between these two variables. A scale designed to measure social-status striving was developed around the Likert scale. Social-status striving was indicated by agreement with such statements as, "It is valuable to trace your family tree," "People should not marry below their social class," and so forth. The use of the Likert scale to determine attitudes is qualitative in nature. On the other hand, purchase behavior (sales) is measured with a ratio scale. The study was conducted with ten individuals and the Likert scores for each individual were paired with their actual purchases. The scores are then transformed into rankings. The results are illustrated in Table 13–7, where X and Y are ranked, and the differences between the rankings are computed.

To measure the extent of rank correlation, we use the following statistic:

$$r_s = 1 - \frac{6 \sum_{i=1}^{n} d_i^2}{N\,(N^2 - 1)}$$

where N is the number of pairs of ranks and d is the difference between the two rankings, $Y - X$. Applying the preceding formula to our illustration, we compute

$$r_s = 1 - \frac{(6)\,(50)}{(10)\,(100 - 1)}$$

$$= 1 - \frac{300}{990}$$

$$= 1 - 0.303$$

$$= 0.697$$

---

[3] Another ordinally scaled measure of correlation is the Kendall rank correlation coefficient, τ (tau). See Siegel, op. cit., pp. 213–29.

TABLE 13-7. Ranks of Sales and Attitude Needed to Compute a Rank Correlation Coefficient

Individual	Rank of Sales, Y	Rank Attitude of Social Striving, X	Difference, (d)	Difference Squared, d²
1	6	5	+1	1
2	2	4	−2	4
3	1	2	−1	1
4	7	10	−3	9
5	4	3	+1	1
6	3	1	+2	4
7	9	6	+3	9
8	5	9	−4	16
9	8	7	+1	1
10	10	8	+2	4
				$\Sigma\,d^2 = 50$

Thus, there is a relatively high degree of correlation between actual purchasing behavior and social-status striving attitude.

Now, we can test the significance of the obtained value. The null hypothesis is that the two variables are not associated, $r_s = 0$. That is, we may wish to test the H_0 that the two variables are not associated in the population and that the observed value of r_s differs from zero only by chance. When the number of sample-paired observations are equal to or greater than ten, a t statistic can be computed according to the following formula:

$$t = r_s \sqrt{\frac{n-2}{1-r_s^2}}$$

$$= 0.697 \sqrt{\frac{10-2}{1-(0.697)^2}} = 2.749$$

which is then referred to a t table (see Appendix C) for degrees of freedom $= n - 2$, 8 df. The critical value of t for $\alpha = 0.05$ and 8 df is 2.306. We would reject H_0 at $\alpha = 0.05$, concluding that social-status strivings and purchase behavior are associated in the population of which ten individuals were a sample.

13.1.4 Regression Analysis

Regression analysis is another tool of simple correlation, through which one can predict one variable (dependent) on the basis of another (independent) variable. It also guides the analyst toward uncovering causal relationships between variables.

Figure 13-2 again shows the observations plotted in Figure 13-1, but a diagonal line has been drawn through their midst. It is called the *line of regression* and indicates the functional relationship between two variables. It is the slope of the linear relationship and may be termed the *slope parameter*. It is computed with the *estimating equation,* which is simply the linear formula $y = a + bx$. To use this equation, one must determine the values of a (the point where the line intercepts the y axis) and b (the slope of the line) by simultaneous equations. That is, one computes simultaneously two different equations containing the same values.

$$\Sigma\, y = \quad Na + b\, \Sigma\, x \qquad\qquad (1)$$

$$\Sigma\, xy = \quad a\, \Sigma\, x + b\, \Sigma\, X^2 \qquad (2)$$

However, our preference is to avoid the use of these equations because they require the time-consuming computations of means and deviations from the means. Instead, we shall apply a simplified version to determine the values of a and b:

$$b = \frac{N\, \Sigma\, XY - (\Sigma\, X)\, (\Sigma\, Y)}{N\, \Sigma\, X^2 - (\Sigma\, X)^2}$$

$$a = \frac{\Sigma\, Y - b\, \Sigma\, X}{N}$$

This pair of formulas uses the information obtained from summing various columns of numbers (as in Section 13.1.3), correlation analysis. We already know these values from Table 13-6 ($\Sigma\, X$, $\Sigma\, Y$, $\Sigma\, XY$, $\Sigma\, X^2$) and can easily calculate $(\Sigma\, X)^2$. The computation becomes

$$b = \frac{(12)\,(394{,}215) - (13{,}370)\,(278)}{(12)\,(19{,}339{,}400) - 178{,}756{,}900}$$

$$= 0.019$$

$$a = \frac{278 - (0.019)\,(13{,}370)}{12}$$

$$= 1.997 \quad \text{(rounded to 2.0)}$$

For the data in Figure 13–2, our estimating equation turns out to be

$$Y_c = 2.0 + 0.019X$$

Having this equation, we can substitute any known value of X into it and thereby determine an estimate of the corresponding value of Y. Suppose that the researcher with Bonnie Bus Company has information that a certain school district, in a territory that Bonnie is just entering, has 2,000 pupils. He or she would substitute this value into the independent factor (X) in the formula as follows:

$$Y_c = 2.0 + 0.019 \times 2{,}000$$

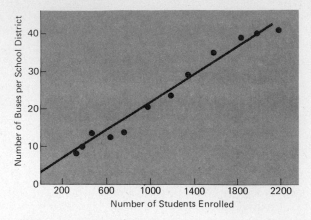

FIGURE 13–2. Regression

On the same observations as graphed in Figure 13–1, a line of regression is drawn. This line was computed with the estimating equation of the relationship between the dependent-variable dimension (number of school buses) and the independent-variable dimension (number of students).

Therefore, $Y = 40$, so it is estimated that this district should have forty school buses.

We must realize that the correlation and regression measurements that we have been discussing are linear and are computed with linear formulas. Generally speaking, these are straight-line relationships, although one form of curvilinear relationship can be obtained by substituting the logarithmic values for Y and X into the equation.

Statistical significance must be taken into consideration when the foregoing measurements are interpreted, when, as usual, they are based on data from samples. With regard to interpretations from the *estimating equation*, the measurement of the probable margin of sampling error is called the *standard error of estimate*. We shall illustrate this through the estimate of school buses by the Bonnie Bus Company. The analyst had estimated that a school district would have forty buses but wants to know "how good" that estimate probably is. To determine this with the standard error of estimate, he or she would compute for the twelve school districts in the sample the number of buses that would be computed for them by the estimating equation. He or she already has the schools' actual numbers of buses which is also needed for the computation. The formula can be described verbally as: The square root of this fraction is equal to the sum of the squares of the deviations of the actual values from the line of deviation, divided by the total number of items in the sample, less the number of rows and columns (which gives the "degrees of freedom").

That formula would be given the following algebraic expression to find s_{yx}, which is the symbol for the standard error of estimate:

$$s_{yx} = \sqrt{\frac{\Sigma\, Y^2 - a\,(\Sigma\, Y) - b\,(\Sigma\, XY)}{N - 2}}$$

Substituting the data from our school bus example:

$$s_{yx} = \sqrt{\frac{8,100 - (2)\,(278) - (0.019)\,(394,215)}{12 - 2}}$$

$$= 2.3$$

This means that the probability of any estimate based on the computed line of deviation (estimating equation) would lie within $\pm$ 2.3 buses of the actual value, with chances of 68 out of 100. In other words, the probabilty of the actual number of buses for the particular district with 2,000 students is 40 ± 2.3, a range of from 37.7 to 42.3 buses. This is a considerable standard error, because our sample of twelve observations is so small.

13.1.5 Analysis of Variance

In Chapter 12 we discussed the test of significance of difference between a sample mean and a hypothetical mean, and between two sample means. However, the researcher may wish to test for differences among more than *two* groups of data. Therefore, the tests explained in Chapter 12 will not be applicable when more than two means are involved in the analysis. In such situations the most commonly used procedure for testing the significance of the differences among several means simultaneously is the *analysis of variance (ANOVA)*. Since rigorous proofs would be quite mathematical, we shall forgo them in favor of a description of what is involved.

As an illustration, suppose that an experiment was conducted in which the researcher was interested in the effect that three different advertising themes have on an individual's perception. A pupilometer is used to measure a person's change in perception (measure of interest in a theme). Each of the experimental groups consists of people chosen at random and independently, and the researcher assigns them at random to each experimental treatment.

The first question the researcher may ask is: "Are the advertising themes really different?" In other words, are the sample means (measure of interest) different because of the different advertising themes? Or may these differences in the means be attributed to chance fluctuations? The null hypothesis of "no difference" in the population means is H_0: $\mu_1 = \mu_2 = \mu_3$. The test of this hypothesis requires a measure of the degree to which the sample means differ, and we therefore calculate their variance.

The equality tested is usually called the *partition sum of squares,* for the ANOVA test calls for the experimentally different samples to be partitioned into two distinct parts. And the values termed *sum of squared deviations* are calculated rather than the sample variances themselves.

The meaning of this partition of the sum of squared deviations (also called *sum of squares*) into two parts is the essence of the ANOVA test. An individual's score in any sample can differ from another's. These observed differences can be attributed to two sources. First, some individuals are in different treatment (experiment) groups, and their differences could be due to different treatments. The measure termed *sum of squares between groups* reflects the contribution of different treatments to intergroup differences. Secondly, individuals in the same treatment groups can differ because of chance variation or individual differences, for each individual within the group receives exactly the same experimental treatment. The *sum of squares within groups* reflects the intragroup difference.

We now have our standard for comparison. The explanation above suggests that the measure of the difference *between* the different groups relative to the differences that exist *within* each group would determine the equality or inequality of the means. If the null hypothesis were true, we should expect the variance among the sampling groups to be equal, except for possible sampling error. On the other hand, if the null hypothesis were not true, we should expect the variance *between* the groups to be higher than the variance *within* the groups. This relationship of the variance between and the variance within is expressed as an *F* ratio, computed by dividing the treatment mean square (that is, the between-group sum of squares divided by its degrees of freedom) by the within-group mean square (that is, the within-group sum of squares divided by its degrees of freedom).

To interpret this *F* ratio, if the computed *F* ratio is greater than the theoretical *F* ratio from the *F* table (Appendix E), the null hypothesis is rejected, which means that the differences among the means are significant. If the computed *F* ratio is less than the critical *F* value, the null hypothesis is accepted, which means that the differences among the means is not significant.

To illustrate this procedure, let us reconsider the advertising example above. The researcher selects a random sample of eighteen people for the experiment, of which six were shown a direct promise-of-benefit theme (advertisement A), six were shown a provocative theme (advertisement B), and six were shown a command theme (advertisement C). Results of this experiment are shown in Table 13–8. The mean of each test group is given, as well as the grand mean of all eighteen scores, denoted by $\bar{\bar{X}}$.

The ANOVA procedure begins by calculating the total sum of squares by squaring the deviations of each value from the grand mean and summing these squared values. The formula is given by

$$\text{SS}_\text{T} \text{ (total sum of squares)} = \sum_j \sum_i (X_{ij} - \bar{\bar{X}})^2$$

where X_{ij} is the score in the *i*th row and the *j*th column:

$$\text{SS}_\text{T} = (2 - 4.55)^2 + (4 - 4.55)^2 + \cdots + (8 - 4.55)^2$$
$$= 78.4$$

The next step is to calculate the between-group sum of squares. The difference between each group mean and the grand mean, squared, and summing the squared deviations and multiplying the squared deviations by the number of items making up each mean results in the between-group sum of squares:

$$SS_B \text{ (between-group sum of squares)}$$
$$= n_i \Sigma (\bar{X}_j - \bar{\bar{X}})^2$$
$$= 6 [(3.33 - 4.55)^2 + (6 - 4.55)^2 + (4.33 - 4.55)^2]$$
$$= 21.8$$

Finally, one calculates the within-group sum of squares, which is found by computing the difference between each observation and its own mean, squaring each of these deviations, and summing over the entire sample:

$$SS_W \text{ (within-group sum of squares)}$$
$$= \sum_{i=1}^{n} \sum_{j=1}^{m} (X_{ij} - \bar{X}_j)^2$$
$$= (2 - 3.33)^2 + (4 - 3.33)^2 + \cdots + (8 - 6)^2 + (6 - 6)^2 + \cdots$$
$$+ (5 - 4.33)^2 + (8 - 4.33)^2$$
$$= 56.6$$

It can be shown that $SS_T = SS_B + SS_W$.

The final step is to compute the F ratio, but we must first compute the estimate of the variation between groups, known as the between-group (treatment) mean square (BMS), and the within-group (error) mean square (WMS) as follows:

$$BMS = \frac{SS_B}{n-1} = \frac{21.8}{3-1} = 10.9$$

where n is the number of treatments and

$$WMS = \frac{SS_W}{N-n} = \frac{56.6}{18-3} = 3.77$$

where N is the total number of observations.
Our F value is the ratio of these two variances:

$$F = \frac{BMS}{WMS} = \frac{10.9}{3.77} = 2.89$$

TABLE 13-8. Pupilometer Scores for the Test Advertisements

	Advertisement A	Advertisement B	Advertisement C
	2	8	5
	4	6	7
	3	5	3
	5	7	2
	4	6	1
	2	4	8
Total	20	36	26

$$\text{Mean } \bar{X}_A = 3.33 \qquad \bar{X}_B = 6 \qquad \bar{X}_C = 4.33$$

Grand mean

$$\bar{X} = \frac{\sum\limits_{j=1}^{3} \sum\limits_{i=1}^{n_j} X_{ij}}{N} = 4.55$$

To determine whether the calculated F value is significant, one compares it with the F value found in an F table for 2 df (numerator) and 15 df (denominator) for the desired level of significance. In our illustration, we will assume a 0.05 level. The F-table value is 3.68 (Appendix E). Therefore, we cannot reject the null hypothesis, and we can conclude that the three means from the three test groups are equal. Thus, the different advertisements tested did not elicit a difference in perception. Table 13–9 is the analysis-of-variance table for the example cited.

After examining the results, the researcher hypothesizes that another variable may be interacting with that of the advertising theme and so decides to assemble additional information. Suppose that he or she uses the same three advertising themes but conducts the experiments in six different cities, three rural and three urban. In this case the difference in the cities could reflect a difference in perception of the experimental

TABLE 13-9. Analysis-of-Variance Table of Advertisement Treatment Versus Perception

Source of Variation	Sum of Squares		Degrees of Freedom		Mean Square	F Ratio
Between group	21.8	÷	2	=	10.9	2.89
Within group	56.6	÷	15	=	3.77	
Total	78.4		18			

themes. The rationale to seek this additional information lies in the belief that urban residents hold different attitudes and perceptions than those in rural areas. Therefore, their perceptions of advertising themes could be different, especially if the advertisements reflect ecological issues.

In the previous example, the city influence is masked in the error term. If this influence is great, the error term could be large and the resulting F ratio would be small. Therefore, the ANOVA procedure can also "block" the city influence from the error term, for further examination. This design now has two null hypotheses:

$$H_0: \mu_1 = \mu_2 = \mu_3 \quad \text{for the treatments}$$
$$H_0: \mu_1 = \mu_2 = \mu_3 \quad \text{for the blocks}$$

The data in Table 13–10 are basically the same as those of Table 13–8, except that the data in Table 13–10 have been rearranged by city.

TABLE 13–10. Pupilometer Scores for the Test Advertisements Blocked by City

	Treatment			Block	
City	Advertisement A	Advertisement B	Advertisement C	Total	Mean
1	2	8	5	15	5
2	4	6	7	17	5.66
3	3	5	3	11	3.66
4	5	7	2	14	4.66
5	4	6	1	11	3.66
6	2	4	8	14	4.66
Total	20	36	26		
Mean	$\bar{X}_A = 3.33$	$\bar{X}_B = 6$	$\bar{X}_C = 4.33$		
Grand mean		$\bar{\bar{X}} = 4.55$			

A new equation for the blocked data is introduced:

$$SS_{BL} = m \sum_{i=1}^{n} (\bar{X}_{BL} - \bar{\bar{X}})^2$$

$$= 3[(5 - 4.55)^2 + (5.66 - 4.55)^2 + \ldots$$

$$+ (4.66 - 4.55)^2$$

$$= 9.13$$

A new error term SS_W is calculated:

$$SS_W = \sum_{i=1}^{n} \sum_{j=1}^{m} (X_{ij} - \bar{X}_{BL} - \bar{X}_j + \bar{\bar{X}})^2$$

$$= (2 - 5 - 3.33 + 4.55)^2 + \cdots + (8 - 5 - 6 + 4.55)^2 + \cdots$$

$$+ (8 - 4.66 - 4.33 + 4.55)^2$$

$$= 47.5$$

The formulas for SS_B and SS_T remain the same as in the previous example. Table 13-11 is the analysis-of-variance table for our illustration.

TABLE 13–11. Analysis-of-Variance Table of Advertisement Treatment Versus Perception by City

Source of Variation	Sum of Squares		Degrees of Freedom		Mean Square	F Ratio
Block (city)	9.13	÷	5	=	1.83	0.38
Treatment (between group)	21.8	÷	2	=	10.9	2.29
Error (within group)	47.5	÷	10	=	4.75	
Total	78.43		17			

There are now two *F* ratios to test, one corresponding to cities and the other to the advertising treatments. The degrees of freedom for this example are found as follows:

df for the blocks = number of blocks − 1

df for the treatments = number of treatments − 1

df for the error term = (number of blocks − 1) multiplied by the (number of treatments − 1)

total df = (number of blocks multiplied by the number of treatments) − 1

The calculated *F* for the block mean sum of square is 0.38. The critical *F* for $\alpha = 0.05$ and $df_1 = 5$ (df_1 of the numerator) and $df_2 = 18$ (df_2 of the denominator) is 2.77. The calculated *F* for the treatment effect is 2.29. The critical *F* value for $\alpha = 0.05$ and $df_1 = 2$ and $df_2 = 10$ is 4.10. Since both calculated *F* values are less than the critical *F* values from the table, again the evidence is not sufficient to reject the null hypothesis. Neither the advertising themes nor the factor of different cities affect the perception of the individuals. In this example, interest was focused on two distinct experimental factors: the advertisement themes and the cities from which the samples were drawn. Either or both of these factors might have influenced the perception scores. Regardless of the results obtained, the main advantage of ANOVA is that it enables the researcher to take into account the interaction of two variables simultaneously.

13.2 Multivariate Analysis

To this point we have considered only analytical methods treating a single variable or a pair of variables. The frequent inadequacy of these methods in uncovering cause-and-effect relationships in marketing problems is suggested in these words of J. N. Sheth: "The marketplace is a complex phenomenon. A multitude of factors intervene between the marketing activities of companies and market responses."[4] To put it slightly differently, a single factor is seldom the predominant cause of any marketing behavior, so the researcher may be unable to find statistical leads to causation in bivariate analysis that examines the relationships of independent variables to the dependent variable under study. Multivariate analysis includes those methods that simultaneously analyze the behavior of more than two variables. Their formulas necessarily are more complex than those we have described, too complex to explain in these pages. We suggest below occasions when each method applies and how each tool contributes to the analysis.

Reference to Figure 12–1 is desirable for reorientation to the plan of this section. It expresses some questions that the analyst much answer in order to choose a multivariate analysis that is appropriate:

Is one to measure the dependence of certain variables on others, or are all to be treated as independent of each other?

If dependent, is only one variable considered dependent or more than one?

Are the data employed metric or nonmetric?

Five multivariate methods are described here that may be suitable under particular situations, which are indicated by answers to those questions. These were selected as some of the more common multivariate analyses, but others may be found in the references provided.

13.2.1 Analysis of One Dependent Variable

Where one has only a single dependent variable that is metric and whose fluctuations are to be measured against a number of independent variables, we have an extension of the bivariate methods of correlation and regression.

In *multiple correlation,* we expand the equation to obtain the *coefficient of multiple correlation (R)* by taking two or more factors into it. These would

---

[4] J. N. Sheth, "The Multivariate Revolution in Marketing Research," *Journal of Marketing,* January, 1971, p. 13.

be factors suspected of influencing the behavior of the dependent variable *(Y)*. For the Bonnie Bus Company example, they might be: numbers of students *(X)* and area of the school district in square miles *(Z)*. Therefore, we would compute $R_{y.xz}$—and if that proved to be higher than the +0.983 computed for r_{yx} (in this case exceedingly unlikely!), we would decide that there is a higher association of buses with this combination of factors than with enrollments alone.

The *coefficient of determination, R^2*, is the proportion of the variation in *Y* explained by all the *X*'s. For instance, if $R^2 = 0.96$, the independent variables, *X* and *Z* in this case, are responsible for 0.96 percent of the observed variation in *Y*. If $R^2 = 1$, the regression equation contains every variable that has an influence on *Y*. When an R^2 in excess of 0.75 occurs, we can state that the regression equation may be viewed as a fairly good model for predicting purposes. Referring to our example of $R^2 = 0.96$, it appears that other factors which have been excluded from the regression equation would be influential in determining *Y*, bus requirements. Otherwise, 0.04 percent of the bus requirements would not be unexplained. Nevertheless, the equation representing $R^2 = 0.96$ appears to be a reasonable predictor of bus requirements.

Multiple correlation is more tedious than our illustration may imply, for there may be numerous factors suspected of correlation, and they are likely to have varying degrees of influence. That would call for testing various weightings of the factors. The *coefficient of partial correlation* $(r_{Y1.2})$ is a useful measure in this case. This measure shows the proportion of variation in one variable explained holding all others constant. The coefficient of partial correlation squared, then, is a relative measure of which variable adds to the knowledge of *Y* after the other predictor variables have been held constant (that is, the remaining variables are taken into account but are held constant). There may be times when the addition of variables will not always add information for predicting purposes.

Complex correlation procedures today are readily performed with computers, which would also be used to determine a companion measurement, *multiple regression*. We can compute a predicting equation analogous to the one developed for simple linear regression analysis given by

$$Y_c = \hat{a} + \hat{b}_1 X_1 + \hat{b}_2 X_2$$

As in bivariate analysis, estimating equations can be tested to find the one that most accurately predicts the dependent (unknown) variable. Additional terms are entered into the formula to represent the other independent variable and possible weights are placed on variables. Again statistical significance should be computed to determine the effect of probable sampling error on permissible confidence in the estimates.

When we depart from metric values, measured on quantitative scales of numbers, into nonmetric data, it becomes impossible to calculate the quantitative associations between variables that have been discussed. The problem is often faced, though, when one has descriptions of the attributes of sample members and needs to establish some formula with which he can predict the categories into which individuals would fall. That is, the analyst is seeking a method by which one can discriminate efficiently between the members of various groups, a process that is logically termed *discriminant analysis. Multiple* discriminant analysis indicates that several independent variables are being appraised for their ability to differentiate between members of the sample in a simultaneous analysis.

The result of a discriminate analysis is that the discriminate equation can be used to predict which class a new observation will belong to. The analysis involves a transformation of scores on individuals from a set of independent predictor variables. For each individual's scores, Y_i is the linear function of the predictor variables, where

$$Y_i = c_1X_1 + c_2X_2$$

and Y_i = discriminant value of the *i*th element of the population

X_i = explanatory variable

c_1 = weighted parameter specifying the relationship between X_i and Y_i

Given the linear discriminant equation, a classification boundary between the two groups, Y_c (critical value, the boundary between the two groups), can be identified. To classify an individual, if Y_i (discriminant value of the *i*th element of the population) is greater than Y_c, the individual belongs in one group. If $Y_i < Y_c$, the individual goes in the other group.

An instance where this would be useful would be a study to find what characterizes innovative automobile buyers (who quickly adopt new styles) and differentiates them from noninnovators.[5] One might gather information about automobile buyers' characteristics as well as whether they bought quite innovative or conventional designs of cars. One then conducts multiple discriminant analysis by computing a *linear discriminant function* that will discriminate between innovative and noninnovative buyers. In this method "Weights are assigned to the variables such that the ratio of the difference between the means of the two groups to the standard deviation within groups is maximized."[6] Also determined is the importance of the independent variables, relative to each other, in contributing to the total difference in the different groups' point scores (for example, between totals of innovators and of noninnovators).

---

[5] For specific methodology in multiple discriminant analysis, see T. S. Robertson and J. N. Kennedy, "Prediction of Consumer Innovators: Application of Multiple Discriminant Analysis," *Journal of Marketing Research*, February, 1968, pp. 64–69. This was reprinted in D. A. Aaker, ed., *Multivariate Analysis in Marketing: Theory and Application* (Belmont, Calif.: Wadsworth Publishing Company. Inc., 1971). The Aaker work offers excellent explanations and examples of many methods of multivariate analysis.

[6] T. S. Robertson and J. N. Kennedy, *Journal of Marketing Research*, February, 1968, p. 67.

13.2.2 Analysis of Several Dependent Variables

On somewhat rare occasions the analyst is faced with determining the relationships of several or a set of dependent variables—not a single one—to a set of independent variables, a composite association. The statistical method for such analysis is known as *canonical analysis*. This procedure can be utilized with either metric or nonmetric data.

In canonical analysis one works with composites, utilizing a composite of the dependent variables and another composite of the independent variables. For example, brand loyalty, the dependent set of variables, can be measured by such variables as quantity purchased, intention to purchase, time interval between purchases, and dollars spent. This set of variables representing brand loyalty can be determined by another set of independent variables consisting of the product's attributes, such as size, color, package design, price, shape, convenience, economy, dependability, status, and so on. One seeks to maximize the degree of simple correlation between the dependent and independent composite variables. The objective, to slightly paraphrase an article by Green, Halbert, and Robinson,[7] is to seek two sets of weighting coefficients such that if linear combinations of each set are formed and correlated in a simple linear correlation, that particular set of composite variables would be more highly correlated than would be any alternative sets. This is accomplished by a method of deriving weights for each set of variables that would maximally correlate their weighted sums. Insofar as the interpretation of the resulting linear combinations, one examines the weights within each equation.

13.2.3 Independent Variables with Metric Data

In the preceding methods of multivariate analysis the purpose usually was to predict one unknown variable, the dependent one, or to explain it on the basis of other variables. The methods now to be considered are for investigating the interrelationships among all the relevant variables, with none being dependent. It is a situation in which all the variables are treated as independent, and the interest is in analyzing their interdependence.

A general and frequently used independence analysis is that of *factor analysis*. Factor analysis seeks to resolve a large set of measured variables in terms of relatively few new categories, known as *factors*. These are linear combinations of the data. The results of factor analysis can be applied in these ways: (1) to reveal the underlying or latent factors that determine the relationship between the observed data; (2) to make evident relationships between data that had been obscure before such analysis; and (3) to provide a classification scheme when data scored on various rating scales have to be grouped, perhaps to reveal some unusual clusters of the data.

---

[7] P. E. Green, M. H. Halbert, and P. J. Robinson, "Canonical Analysis: An Exposition and Illustrative Application," *Journal of Marketing Research,* February, 1966, pp. 32–39.

As the factors are linear combinations of data for which a line could be drawn for graphed data to represent its dimension, the coordinate distance of each observation or variable is measured to obtain the *factor loadings*, which represent the degree of correlation between the particular variable and factor. The loadings are derived by the same principle of least squares as is used in regression analysis. The factor loadings are then placed in a matrix of correlations between the variable and the factors. A summary of this indicates the proportion of the total variation represented by those factors. There are various types of matrixes that may be used and procedures for "rotation" of the initial results that may bring to light relationships not previously seen and clarify the common factors underlying the data. Factor analysis is a complicated tool whose use depends highly on the judgment of the analyst and is too technical to be illustrated here. It can be very useful when faced with a mass of data that are defying analysis, and guidance can be obtained from clearly written sources.[8]

13.2.4   Independent Variables with Nonmetric Data

Where the information being analyzed is nonmetric, usually expressed on rating scales whereby people express how similar or different they perceive objects to be, other approaches are needed in analysis. Again we are concerned with studying the interdependence between responses, all variables being treated as independent.

Discriminant analysis has become a popular tool for analyzing nonmetric multidimensionally scaled data. In this method the observations (the responses as to perceived similarities or dissimilarities) are placed or mapped in a multidimensional space. In multidimensional scaling, a spatial representation or map of product attributes is prepared. The responses of attribute opinions are plotted in the product spaces, expressed in any of the several forms of data appropriate for discriminant analysis. The procedure, as explained by R. M. Johnson, includes (1) obtaining each respondent's opinions of where each product, brand, or whatever is being evaluated stands in the product space; and (2) locating each respondent's ideal point in the product space for such a product.[9]

The results of such analysis (which may be expressed either graphically or numerically) indicate market clusters or segments and their sizes, as well as where competing brands or products stand relative to such clusters. Such analyses can yield valuable objectives for determination of marketing strategies. Let us describe two illustrative cases.

A published example, under its common designation "market structure analysis," dealt with a certain category of machine tools—numerically controlled machining centers.[10] In conducting this study, the re-

---

[8] For an introduction to factor analysis, see Aaker, op. cit., pp. 209–11. The method is illustrated in that book with a chapter by W. D. Wells and J. N. Sheth from Robert Ferber (ed.), *Handbook of Market Research (New York: McGraw-Hill Book Company, 1971).*

[9] R. M. Johnson, "Market Segmentation—A Strategic Management Tool," *Journal of Marketing Research,* February, 1971, pp. 13–18.

[10] *Market Structure Analysis* (Chicago: Market Facts, Inc., undated).

search firm first questioned respondents who exercised major buying influence on machine tool purchases among industrial companies that use such equipment. These respondents described the product attributes of each brand of machining centers that they considered relevant to decisions regarding their possible purchase. When this information had been gathered, a multiple discriminant analysis program was used to isolate a combination of attributes that discriminated most among groups and among competitive brands of the product. That is, it brought out the critical motivations for selecting one brand over another. In this particular case, the discriminating factors were placed in two sets, according to the two major categories of purchasing attributes for such a product: the first discriminant category related to "performance" and the second related to "economics." Specific attributes in the first category included "rate of production," "speed of machine turnaround" and others; the second category included "initial cost," "elimination of accessory tooling," and others.

Analysis of scaled responses, which would provide quantitative inputs, would be aggregated to obtain average responses. These should be in terms both of the degree of importance placed on each critical attribute and of how a respondent scores each competing brand on those attributes. As we have two major categories or dimensions into which the attributes were grouped, the scores can be mapped on paper in two-dimensional space. In Figure 13–3 we depict the positioning of seven brands of machining centers with regard to the performance category on the horizontal axis and economy on the vertical axis.

We cannot interpret the positions of the competing brands until we

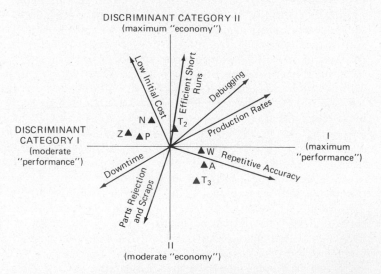

FIGURE 13–3. Positioning of Several Manufacturers' Machining Centers' in Industrial Buyers' Responses—Example of Discriminant Analysis

Source: Courtesy of Market Facts, Inc., Chicago.

know the *ideal* product attributes as the respondents saw them. They could hardly be expected to share identical perceptions on desirable product attributes, but rather would tend to fall into clusters or segments. The respondents were asked, independent of rating the brands, to scale the ideal machining center on various factors of performance and economy. These can also be plotted on a two-dimensional graph and related to the standing of the relative brands, the same positions as in Figure 13–3. Further, the research determined the quantitative buying potential of each respondent company. The answers relative to attributes tended to cluster into five segments. These segments, with their relative size, are shown in Figure 13–4, in addition to the respondents' perceptions of the seven brands.

To interpret Figure 13–4, consider it from the standpoint of the manufacturer of brands T_2 and T_3. Brand T_2 is very advantageously perceived for suiting cluster 1, the largest potential segment. It also is nearest to the ideals of cluster 2. Brand T_3 is not well off, as an appeal to cluster 3, because of its low ratings on economy attributes. Neither of its products is likely to be attractive to clusters 4 and 5, which comprise 36 percent of the market.

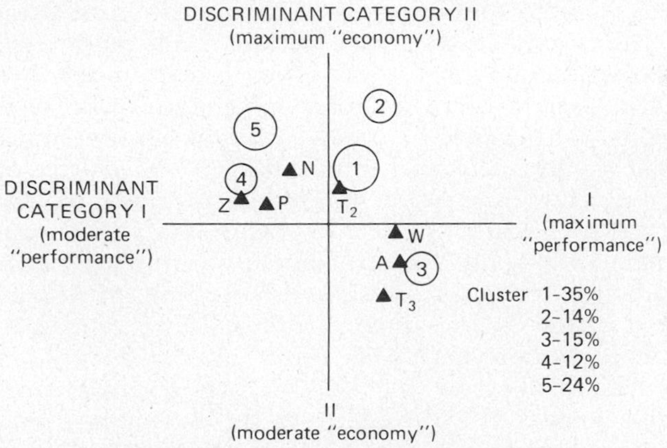

FIGURE 13–4. Market Structure for Machining Centers, in Terms of "Ideal" Attributes, from the Viewpoint of Industrial Buyers

Source: Courtesy of Market Facts, Inc., Chicago.

The market structure analysis method just described may offer sufficient guidance for marketing decisions if all the critical factors may be placed accurately in two categories and dimensions. However, the market segmentation task typically is more sophisticated than this, with a greater number of dimensions significant to the marketing decisions. Let us describe a study of a consumer packaged good whose design took many buying motive factors into analysis. We shall describe its general characteristics and the technical factor analysis that was explained in its publication.[11]

The particular qualitative market analysis had the advantage of using a consumer panel, for which a rich variety of data was available on members' purchasing behavior relative to the product class, demographic characteristics, and measures of their attitudes related to their general life-style. In addition to the great variety of factor data obtained on these people (housewives), the study began in an opposite direction from typical past consumer research designs; it began by measuring various independent consumer variables, as well as purchasing behavior, and then it grouped the respondents into segments with those results.

This study was interested in two types of the consumer product and in two brands within each type. The analysis began with data on purchases of the two product types, which were the dependent variables in its equation. For independent variables it used data—also on *each* respondent—including 151 measures of attitudes, opinions, and interests and a number of demographic factors. Using factor analysis, the 151 attitudinal factors were condensed into 26 factors that had major effect on the covariance. Then canonical correlation analysis was the method used to determine relationships between the product-type variables and the independent variables. After that assessment, the canonical analysis was carried further to develop a classification system of the consumers that defined "the number, nature, size, and consumption characteristics of customer segments with respect to the product under investigation."[12]

The foregoing analysis led to categorization of the housewives in two dimensions: (1) negative or positive outlook on life, and (2) stage of life cycle. They were then segmented into a 3×3 matrix on those dimensions, producing nine segments that were given names ranging from "young independents" to "old low achievers." Then the consumption data obtained on those panel members was applied to their segments to calculate what percentage of unit volume was contributed by each segment. For Brand A, for instance, almost 70 percent of its volume came from "old high achievers." The results, as in the market structure analysis described earlier, targeted the markets and also provided the marketer with profiles in great depth on the buying and attitudinal characteristics of consumers in general and the patrons of each competing brand.

13.3 Planning Requirements for Efficient Analysis

Major methods for bringing meaning out of gathered data have now been viewed. They offer a powerful kit of tools—but only to one who is skilled in using them efficiently. In other words, they should be geared with the rest of the project as a *system*. In a broad sense, that means that

---

[11] Ronald E. Frank and Charles E. Strain, "A Segmentation Research Design Using Consumer Panel Data," *Journal of Marketing Research*, November, 1972, pp. 385–90.

[12] Ibid., p. 387.

the analytical treatment of the data needs to be interlocked with all steps of marketing research. More narrowly, statistical analysis is integrally related to two concurrent phases: data processing and logical interpretation. Before leaving this phase, let us expound some ideas about proper planning.

Here are suggestions on systematic planning of quantitative analysis:

1. Be sure that the decision model expresses sharply the kinds of results on which the decision should be based. If the analyst is told only to compare the results of exposure to Advertisement A with that of Advertisement B, she is in no position to plan analytical methods. The needs can come into focus if she is told that (a) the purpose is to forecast changes in preferences for certain brands following exposure to A or B, or that (b) the purpose is to identify segments or commonalties among persons who have certain attitude shifts after one of those exposures, or some other purpose.

2. Evaluate what analytical methods are feasible with the particular parameters and descriptions that the data plans would obtain. Then consider whether those methods would produce the statistical measurements required by the decision model. Some examples of mistakes to avoid are:

   a. Obtaining in a survey (nominal or ordinal) nonmetric responses that are incapable of converting to metric data to satisfy decision needs. Often respondents honestly can give only nonmetric answers, in which case it is better to be realistic at the outset about the limited analytical procedures.

   b. Employing intervals in the classifications on survey forms that are too broad or have some other fault that precludes a sufficiently fine analysis.

   c. Permitting incompatible categories to be used in successive studies or in data from different sources that need to be compared or combined.

3. Have clear statements of the precision or sampling error limits that will be required, and consider whether this precludes using some statistical tools because they would yield unreliable results.

4. Write examples of the forms of data that the contemplated analytical methods would yield, in the course of early project planning. Such a test should clarify whether or not an appropriate series of analyses has been planned.

5. As the analysis stage approaches, write a sequence of statistical steps that probably will be followed to obtain the desired values. Simple measurements of central values, distributions, or gross changes would be planned first. Further steps would be contingent on what these early analyses show. One's original plans for sophisticated analysis might be abridged, if this preliminary study finds that crucial subsamples or cells would be too small. On the contrary, unexpected relationships might come out that would call for greater analysis than planned.

6. Be familiar with the outputs and limitations of each analytical

method, as well as its data requirements, to enable quick and accurate decisions on analytical steps as the picture unfolds.

13.4 Summary

Modern analytical methods hold potential power for making timely and correct decisions or solving problems of great complexity, but only for the analyst who has anticipated their use. On the negative side, inefficient data analysis can cause heavy cost and delays that are partially due to failures to synchronize statistical analysis with data processing and inference. Information can become useless, regardless of the analytical competence of the researcher, if it is not communicated and utilized by marketing managers. Therefore, once the data have been analyzed, one must prepare to draw conclusions and report as effectively as possible the information gathered for decision-making purposes. In Chapter 14 we will be concerned with the final phases of the research process: interpretation, effective communication and reporting, and the follow-through—a review of the efficiency of the research project.

14 Interpretation, Presentation, and Follow-Through

In Chapter 14 we complete the research process. In the three phases covered here, these are some key questions:

What do the statistical findings mean?

What are some means of improving one's abilities to make accurate interpretations?

What are the ways of reporting a study's results? Is this really a critical phase?

What is a good format for packaging finds in a report?

What principles would enhance my writing of reports?

What are the appropriate ways of showing findings graphically?

What are some good tips on making effective presentations?

After a project is reported, is anything left for the researcher to do regarding it?

THE CLIMAX OF THE RESEARCH PROCESS is approached as one prepares to draw conclusions and report findings. The whole investigation culminates and reaches fruition in drawing inferences that lead to conclusions as to the course of action (or problem solution). This phase calls for a high degree of interpretive skill, both quantitative (dealt with in Chapters 12 and 13) and logical.

The purpose of this chapter, then, is threefold: The first concern is a discussion of the inductive and deductive thought processes which lead to the logical interpretation of data. Then the emphasis is on a number of principles that should aid considerably in reaching valid interpretations. Although the technical research work ends with the interpretation of the data into findings relevant to the problem, the researcher's tasks have not ended. Several steps remain that would be important to the utilization of the findings and to the future of the researcher and his organization. The first of these steps is the preparation and transmittal of a clear, accurate, and convincing report of the findings, which is a demanding task with high potential payoff. The second step is to appraise the effectiveness and benefits of the findings in relationship to the cost and design of the research, a task that may take some time to accomplish. A third step is to project future problems, decisions, and research needs that imaginative study of the completed project can yield. A fourth step involves relating the completed project to the larger marketing information system.

14.1 Nature of Interpretation

Interpretation, in our usage of this word, means *to bring out the meaning of data*—or, one might say, to convert mere data into information. We have discussed the quantitative or analytical phase, and now we come to what tends to be the more crucial phase: the logical interpretation that infers relevant meanings from the data. As stated earlier, the interpreter alternates between these two activities as this work proceeds.

The work of reaching the final set of interpretations typically goes through numerous steps. In actuality, any study involves a number of questions and determinations at each step, which relate to various data and potentially significant implications and cross-relationships. If one counted all the logical and statistical steps taken in even a moderately complex study, this would aggregate a large number. If the nature and succession of interpretive steps were unplanned, the work would be helter-skelter, intolerably time consuming, and ultimately unproductive. Planning is very important in this phase of research.

Logical thought has two general phases, which we all practice whether or not consciously: induction and deduction. *Induction* is pulling together the implications of various relevant items of evidence in order to form a general proposition. *Deduction* is reasoning from relevant general propositions to a significant meaning with regard to a specific case in point (see Figure 14–1). These phases may be distinguished better with an ex-

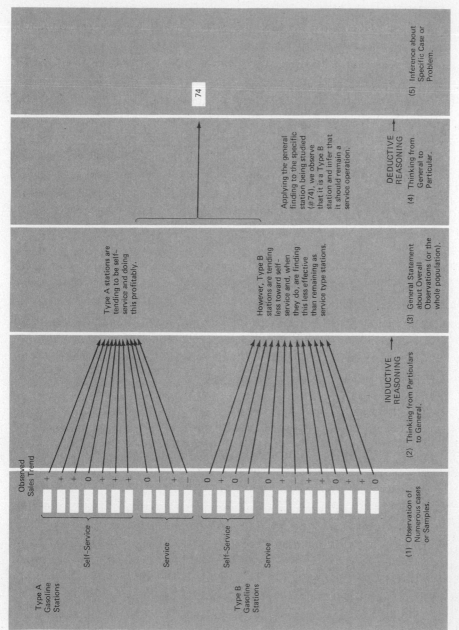

Observed
Sales Trend

Type A
Gasoline
Stations

Self-Service

+ + + 0 + + +

Service

0 | + |

Type B
Gasoline
Stations

Self-Service

0 + 0 |

Service

0 + | + + 0 + + 0

Type A stations are
tending to be self-
service and doing
this profitably.

However, Type B
stations are tending
less toward self-
service and, when
they do, are finding
this less effective
than remaining as
service type stations.

Applying the general
finding to the specific
station being studied
(#74), we observe
that it is a Type B
station and infer that
it should remain a
service operation.

74

INDUCTIVE
REASONING

DEDUCTIVE
REASONING

(1) Observation of
Numerous cases
or Samples.

(2) Thinking from Particulars
to General.

(3) General Statement
about Overall
Observations (or the
whole population).

(4) Thinking from
General to
Particular.

(5) Inference about
Specific Case or
Problem.

FIGURE 14–1. Diagram of Inductive and Deductive Reasoning

ample, so let us cite three hypothetical steps in the logic of Delta brand's marketing manager:

Induction: Delta's share of market, for that type of consumer product, has slipped from 16 percent to 13 percent over the recent period while its share of new tryers has slipped from 18 percent to 10 percent.

Deduction: Delta falls into a general class of brands, in past marketing experience, that may have certain deficiencies in their programs that result in attracting fewer new users. These should be checked into.

Induction: Investigation of this matter finds that Delta has done about as much to attract new users as its competitors in various methods, except offering price inducements.

Deduction: (and so forth)

From these two basic thought dimensions evolve numerous methods of inferences, of which a few will be noted as we discuss this subject.

14.2   The Interpretive Process

As we pointed out in Chapters 12 and 13, the subject of statistical analysis should be subservient to logical interpretation, or inference. However complex or formidable analytical tools may seem, they are selected at each step in the unfolding interpretation in response to a logically inferred need. Although proper statistical processes clarify quantitative relationships, the *qualitiative* meaning of the data relative to the decision and its situation is more fundamental in leading to conclusions.

Looking back, you may recall that the logical and mental processes were primary in determining a study's design and the specifications and classifications of data that were to be acquired to fulfill that design. Throughout the research process one question has been outstanding: What does it *mean?* This single broad question devolves into very many questions that probe the meaning of many items of information and their interrelations, as the interpretive process moves forward. *System* should be the keynote of this process, for a disorganized or unplanned approach to the received data will lead to chaotic groping toward shaky conclusions.

14.2.1   Planning the Interpretations

When the project was designed initially, as we described in Chapter 4, the planning of the interpretation process began. The whole project design should have been conceived in anticipation of the interpretations. The more fully and foresightedly one determines the design, the better he is prepared with a plan of interpretations. For instance, the specified types of data and the units in which they are measured are decisions that should have been made with a view toward how they would enter into the interpretations.

Now that we have reached the stage of drawing conclusions, the model of the problem or decision (which was the framework of the research design) should serve as a blueprint for the type of sequence of interpretations. If the design was a rigorous experiment, it would have explicitly stated the inferential and statistical operations that are now to take place. In marketing and other social sciences, as we explained earlier, one cannot so strictly structure hypothesized cause-and-effect relationships or test them under closely controlled conditions. With serious limitations on the predetermination of the interpretation process at the design stage, preparing a thoughtful schedule of the logical and statistical work would need to occur just before the interpretations begin, rather than at earlier stages.

It would be misleading to suggest that the decision model, at least in its earlier forms, can provide a complete, ready-made guidance of interpretation. Adhering to such a prefabricated plan would be unlikely to attain an ample and accurate analysis. Consider these reasons why the course of interpretations should be freshly determined as this process begins and should possibly be modified as the work proceeds.

1. The analyst is not likely to fully anticipate the character, magnitudes, and implications of the data. Until one has seen the gathered data, one is uncertain of what they hold in store relative to the problems under study. Proper and adequate analysis is contingent on the data themselves.

2. It is very difficult to be imaginative and realistic about the nature of the interpretation process, even for a straightforward analysis. As one digs into the data and as some statistical values are calculated, the analysis becomes involved and takes unexpected directions. It would be wasteful to specify too fully in advance all the statistical work. Rather, one must await the results of the early interpretive steps that should suggest what further work would be profitable.

3. In a more philosophical vein, let us admit that any investigator tends to approach a problem with some preconceptions and biases, however objective he or she tries to be. When one confronts the evidence, he or she should be as open-minded as possible and in a state of readiness to view the findings with minimum prejudice. Therefore, despite there being somewhat of an interpretation plan implicit in the problem model, he should take a fresh view of the findings and look for hitherto unexpected meanings and relationships within the data.

It is necessary that the analyst maintain an open-minded attitude and suspend judgment until the final phases of the analysis. Ideally, researchers should sit at a console and put their program and data into a computer, which almost instantly feeds back to them the answer, and after interpreting this result, the researcher feeds in another calculation stemming from that result—and so on through many calculations until the problem is solved.

Another element that demands flexibility in the interpretive process is that *insight* into the suspected meaning of data often does not dawn on the analyst or decision maker until he or she studies the data in depth. We should also point out that insight is a personal and invaluable capability that is born of experience and rarely gained from books and formal education. That typically rare quality of understanding "what the figures mean" is, to use an old phrase, what separates the men from the boys in data interpretation. Consider the following actual exchange regarding survey data obtained in a study of housewives' attitudes toward gas and electric kitchen ranges conducted for a utility company that sells both gas and electricity. The researcher was discussing some data with a merchandising manager for the utility company.

Researcher: Look at these replies to the question, "If you were buying an electric range completely equipped with all modern features, what would its price probably be? For a gas range also completely equipped with all modern features, what would its price probably be?" The average price given for electric was $238 and for gas ranges was $205. I'd say that is an advantage for gas.

Merchandise Manager: I wouldn't say that at all. It seems to me what that shows is that most women just cannot conceive of a gas range that has all the features of a modern electric range. So that is a mark against gas.

Further probing of this attitude found that the merchandising manager's intuition (or experience?) was right.

Now that some general aspects of interpretation have been discussed, we are going to present a sequence of steps that this process might follow up to the point where it would enter complex interpretations unique to a particular study.

1. The first interpretive step is to appraise the validity of the data being received. If they are secondary data, the reputation and methods of the gathering agency should have been scrutinized. If primary data have been gathered, the apparent authenticity and accuracy of responses should be considered, as well as the character of the sample and quality of field work. All the premises underlying proper sampling that were given in Chapters 7 and 8 should be examined.

2. Classification of data, to the extent not incorporated in questionnaires, is a qualitative determination, aside from its statistical implications. The type of classification base is one decision—whether quantitative, qualitative, chronological, geographical, or other, and specific category definitions are then decided.

3. Editing of the returned data is primarily a qualitative task, whose nature was described as a prelude to data processing.

4. With the information now entering data processing, the analyst will usually ask for simple descriptive measurements: mean or

median values, frequency distributions, and percentaging of them.

5. At this point it is also logical to call for appropriate indications of statistical confidence, such as standard deviation, or F or t values, to be able to judge how far one can safely go in drawing inferences that are justifiable (not rendered questionable by sheer statistical error). Before that can be done, however, a qualitative judgment has to be made as to the confidence limits permissible in view of the specific problem being solved. A scientific study would tend to call for 95 percent or 99 percent confidence, but many business decisions would demand lesser confidence limits.

6. Now that preliminary interpretations have been made, the qualitative analysis begins in stipulating what sorts of values will be needed in order to execute the logic appropriate to solving the problem. If only a superficial picture of a situation is needed, perhaps all the pertinent statistical analysis is done and the analyst can proceed to summarize what he perceives as significant.

7. The type of conclusion desired may be that of predicting the future state or value of a key variable. Perhaps its direction of change seems so dependable that a mere projection of it from a past time series would be sufficient. Then both the statistical work and inference would be simple.

8. Predicting the future of a variable in an important decision normally justifies a more sophisticated inferential method. The analyst desires to project that variable on the basis of associated independent variables. In this event, she or he may use historical patterns of interrelated change, or regression analysis, to provide the basis of prediction. One may begin merely with scatter diagrams of past behavior of these variables to "eyeball" their past covariation as well as cross-tabulations. After that screening, one might go to computations of simple correlation and then to regression equations, if one seems to be finding single independent variables that account for a preponderance of covariation. One may also make a more scientific effort by having correlation of combinations of independent factors measured to have still more covariation accounted for in the basis of forecasting.

9. The foregoing step was one of finding past association, which might have been spurious and unreliable for forecasting. Logical thinking of course should probe behind any measure of correlation to judge whether any true cause-and-effect relationship exists there. Many spurious correlations (such as the inverse association between birth rates and number of elevators per capita) could be mentioned to underline the importance of this inferential step. For quantitative verification of such inferences, the analyst may call for measurements of intercorrelations between variables that would clue her or him to the existence of more underlying variables that have not been tested.

10. The analyst may instead—or also—be intent on probing the struc-

ture underlying the surface behavior to determine why such behavior occurs, to find the ultimate causes. Such reasoning tends to need more complex measurements in such methods as canonical or factorial analysis than does mere forecasting. In marketing the objective of inferences often is to uncover diverse market segments, for which the analyst might want cluster analysis.

The steps above provide simply a crude itinerary of a sequence of inferential reasoning. At each point the question should be raised: What is the probable statistical error inherent in these figures, and would that nullify the differences that I would infer between certain key figures? Recognize that at every step the first concern is the qualitative inference to be made, which would be followed by choice of analytical method to reveal the quantitative values, and that would be accomplished with data processing—leading to inferences regarding what its outputs mean—and then the process is repeated until the ultimate values and inferences become possible and conclusions are reached.

14.2.2 Disciplined Interpretation

Our perceptions can be distorted and limited very easily, and our thinking processes can take wrong turns too readily. There is no truth in the adage that "figures speak for themselves." People state what the figures mean (when they have the figures to interpret and regardless of the statistical refinements lavished on the data), and dangerous errors are often committed. Firm discipline over one's mental processes and the ability to work as dispassionately as possible are necessary.

Let us make this plea for sound logic more concrete and helpful. Our discussion of interpretation, for this purpose, concludes with several maxims that every researcher would do well to heed.

Produce honest and sober interpretations. One does not need dishonest intentions to violate this principle. Often a proper interpretation of findings would conclude that all is well and nothing needs radical change, but this seems dull and perhaps implies that the study has not been fruitful. To gain attention and to be exciting, one may dramatize and exaggerate or distort some aspects, a temptation to be firmly resisted.

Keep objectives and simple principles in the forefront. Data should be drawn on only as they fit the research purposes and should be presented with economy in detail. Any complex analyses should proceed from the simpler, more fundamental aspects and should not be done just to be or to appear to be sophisticated. Complexities will not be dazzling and confusing when thus approached.

Beware of the limitations of small samples. One may be tempted to "blow up" results obtained from a sample into generalities describing a large population. For example, a study on public relations reported that a certain practice was more common among banks than manufacturers, stating that 60 percent of the banks did this, as against 54 percent of the manufacturers. This was based on samples of sixty-two manufacturers and five banks. What might have been the conclusions, if one more bank were included? Less flagrantly, many studies may be noted to project subsamples without recognition of sampling error.

Give fair weight to all evidence. Anyone may have a bias toward reaching a particular conclusion. One can too readily highlight the facts favoring one of the alternative answers. Sometimes a number of aspects are favorable to one solution or course of action and a few are unfavorable. Yet a single factor might be crucial and nullify the propriety of recommending that conclusion. An example was a major corporation that studied the desirability of buying a small concern existing in another field, a concern whose product might be expanded to a national market. The corporation overlooked the aspect that all firms in that other field were small and local in their marketing. When the major company entered that product line, they found themselves frustrated by the undercover "wheeling and dealing," which local firms could get away with but a major and conspicuous company could not.

Give due attention to infrequent significant answers. When seeking opinions or ideas, one may miss the significance of some answers because they are found in very few of the responses obtained in a survey. It is easy to overlook these few flecks of gold among a mass of shallow responses.

Recognize averages as merely tendencies. When arrays of data have been boiled down into averages and the analyst studies only these, he or she can forget that these averages do not represent homogenous cases. Quite the contrary, there may be a vast dispersion among the data that have been averaged, and to draw conclusions that relate to the atypical few that are described by the averages would be quite wrong.

Distinguish between opinion and fact. By the time the findings have become expressed in numbers and summarized, we may tend to be impressed by numbers as being facts. The persons providing the data, instead, may have been responding from dim memory or giving outright guesses. A wise course is to review the whole data-gathering process and to reconsider the reliability of data before proceeding to interpret them.

Look for causes and do not confuse them with effects. We have just been discussing the problem of finding causes and not assuming that associated factors are causal. This is a trap, particularly when there are no data available over a period of time that would permit dynamics to be examined. A danger always exists that the superficial aspects have been measured and little is known about causes, so that the researcher dwells on the former and misleads the decision makers.

A related problem, when finding that factors are correlated, is to assume too hastily that one of them is the cause. Examples are found in some studies of television and radio commercials, which measure both a person's exposure to the commercial and the brand he buys. Close correlations between brand usage and favorable attitudes toward the commercials advertising the brand can lead to the conclusion that liking the commercials is a vital factor in winning sales. However, consider the reverse proposition: that when one likes brand X, she might have a favorable bias toward any advertising of brand X. The reverse inference is just as plausible as the first one, and without other data to support it, the first inference seems unwarranted. A third danger in causal inference is this: having found two factors to be well correlated, the researcher ignores any other factors and misses the true or more basic causal factor. There may be an autocorrelation caused by other factors, and this sort of situation should always be suspected.

The ability to reach valid interpretations has been treated in some detail because of its importance as the focal point from which inferences lead to conclusions. Good planning and anticipation pay off well in this stage, for interpretation can otherwise become snarled and wasteful. The technical research work ends with the interpretation of the data into the findings. The researcher's task now turns to the transmittal of a clear, accurate, and convincing report of the findings.

14.3   Role of the Report

Consider that the goal of a marketing study, in the commercial world, is the guidance of those with a marketing problem to solve — the researcher's clients, if one operates as an independent professional, or the marketing executives of the concern that employs him or her. Only if the report gives the client an understanding of the data and conclusions, establishes conviction that its conclusions are correct, and obtains appropriate action is the effort and outlay for the research justified. The successful report breathes life into the statistical and logical findings and wins the acceptance of those who will translate the findings into action.

The report serves three chief functions. First, it is the means whereby the data, analyses, and findings are placed in an organized and permanent form. As it is the only systematic record of the research, it serves as an essential reference for future research along related lines.

Second, the quality of the research work is likely to be judged mainly by the report. The key decision-making persons whom the research serves seldom have much personal contact with a researcher within their firm and still less with an outside research agency. Since the report is their index of the researcher's skill and performance, the time, thought, and effort spent on it is vital to his or her future.

Third, and most important, the effectiveness of the report may determine the action taken. Properly organized and lucid reports lead to appropriate action or policies — the goal of all commercial or administrative research. In urgent situations, too, convincing reports may inspire decision makers to promptness. The ability of the project findings to induce correct action or perceptions is the main criterion of its success, and that hinges greatly on the report.

As findings may be presented orally or in writing, the term "report" refers to either form of presentation. It is preferable to have the opportunity of presenting findings personally to permit oral discussion and questions to be raised for clarification, in addition to the more essential written report. We will be speaking of the written and oral form for the ability to communicate well in both speech and writing can hardly be underestimated in its essentiality for the researcher's success. Many sound research projects have had no effect because their results were badly presented. Good communicators are rare in our age, even among university-trained young people, and this is a most valuable skill for any career.

14.3.1   Types of Reports

One of the essentials, if you are going to write an effective report, is to plan its contents well. Each report is a tailor-made job that is adapted to the character of the problem, the information contained therein, and to the thought modes and preferences of those who will be utilizing the report. In a broad way, however, we may distinguish several types of reports that would require differing general formats.

There may be *progress reports*, submitted when administrators want intermediate statements on progress of a project under way, but these are mere memoranda. The findings may be reported in any or all of these forms:

1. *Basic report.* This is the first report prepared on the project's findings, written by the researcher for his or her own use, composed of working papers and preliminary drafts. It provides the basis for the final report and then becomes a record for the files. Unfortunately, the need to consider this a report is often overlooked, so that no standard arrangement for such reports is determined and no orderly file—or even retention—of them is provided. Unless this is done, this basic and complete record of the work and findings is unavailable in the future when its methodology or data are needed for reference or to aid other studies.

2. *Reports for publication.* Often such reports are prepared from research findings for articles in trade and professional journals, popular magazines, bulletins, or monographs. Publications and their audiences vary, so no one description can cover this category of report. If his report or article is to be accepted, it is very important that the writer of the report determine the character and interests of the audience to be reached as well as the publisher's policies, and to write appropriately. Normally these are relatively condensed reports, for publishers do not want to waste words nor will readers tolerate too much verbosity. Only in very technical periodicals or special monographs would much detail on procedures be included.

3. *Technical reports.* These reports usually are intended for scientific or

technically trained persons. They would be interested typically in specific descriptions of the entire procedures employed, which usually would follow the introduction of the problem and hypotheses researched. They also are interested in the logical and statistical details that led to the conclusions, so they may be given these step by step in progression toward the interpretations. Tests of statistical significance tend to be desired by such readers. When the stage of conclusions is reached, then, the technical reader has had the whole development of the underlying data and reasoning. These reports may also have complicated technical appendixes on the methodology and complete bibliographies to provide the reader with further sources or substantiation.

4. *Reports for executives.* These are reports intended for decision makers. These are the busy people who want primarily, the "meat" of a research project, its major conclusions and recommendations. They do not want the voluminous details that are suitable for the technical report, and methodological information would better be put in an appendix where they can refer to it if they wish.

In the balance of this chapter we will be dealing with reports for executives. Some of the principles would apply to any written report, and bear in mind that reports may be arranged and written in many styles. What we discuss are suggestions only; the style used should be adapted to the reader and the subject.

14.3.2 Contents of the Report for Executives

The character of an executive report must be determined from the characteristics called for by the persons concerned; sometimes flashy, dramatic reports are called for. But many, perhaps most, executives are more conservative and want a plain, straightforward report. Brevity and ease of reading are important to such an audience, of course, but the statements made should be complete, explicit, and supported with data and/or reasoning.

A generally useful outline of the report for executives runs as follows:

Letter of transmittal accompanying the report
  I. Title page
 II. Table of contents
III. Executive synopsis
 IV. Introduction
  V. Methodology
 VI. Findings
VII. Limitations
VIII. Conclusions (drawn from the data) and recommendations (stemming from the conclusions)
 IX. Appendix
  X. Bibliography (if pertinent)

This outline shows the conventional and logical arrangement of the steps in report preparation. Each section should incorporate the following information.

Letter of transmittal.   The letter of transmittal indicates to whom the report is directed, the reasons for doing the work, and the official authorization for the research.

Title page.   The title page should be simple and dignified. The title page should show the subject of the report, for whom and by whom it was prepared, and the dates of completion and submittal.

Ordinarily, the title page appears first, but some report writers prefer to put the letter of transmittal first to show that they are submitting the report to the person named in the letter.

Table of contents.   If the report is lengthy, inclusion of a guide to its contents would be desirable. The table of contents is an outline of the order of appearance of the numerous divisions of the report, with page numbers. Also, if the report includes a number of tables, charts, figures, and/or illustrations, a separate table for each category would immediately follow the table of contents. These additional tables may be constructed either as a continuation of the table of contents or as separate tables on individual pages.

Executive synopsis.   To many executives, the synopsis is the heart of the report and cannot be underestimated. It enables an executive to quickly grasp the import of the research. Many busy executives may read only the synopsis. When time permits or when particular findings are pertinent, he or she can turn to the body of the report and more carefully study that particular portion, which should be referenced or tabbed so that it can be found quickly. The synopsis precedes detailed reasoning or evidence. It concisely summarizes all the essential parts of the report, which include all the major facts as well as major findings and conclusions. In summary, the synopsis is a report in miniature, written such that comprehension of the material is not sacrificed. It should be noted that the synopsis can only be prepared after the full report is written, then inserted in the appropriate place.

Introduction.   The introduction serves to orient the reader to the detailed discussion of the problem at hand. Usually included in this section are the reasons for doing the work, the scope of the work, the formulation of the problem(s) to be studied, the objectives to be achieved, and the hypotheses upon which the research is based. A historical background may be included in this section if it is relevant to an understanding of the problem. In most instances material from the research proposal may be utilized in the introductory section.

Methodology.   A description of the procedures employed to achieve the objectives follows the introductory section. This section is difficult for the report writer to communicate, for he must remember that most executives are not deeply interested in research methodology, nor do they typically understand the technical language. However, the writer needs to convey to the executives some essentials of the research methodology, thus enabling the reader to understand "why" a particular method was employed rather of another. The description should include a discussion of whether the design was exploratory, descriptive, conclusive, or experimental; the various sources of data canvassed and utilized; the sampling setup; the type of questionnaire used and the reasons for its form; and the number and types of research workers used, such as interviewers, supervisors, and staff. A statement of unique methods for handling any special problems is also essential in good report preparation and should be included in this section.

At the very minimum, the writer should state why a particular method or procedure was chosen, and its perceived advantages over alternative procedures.

Findings.   The discussion of findings will normally be the longest section of the report. If the problem is to be solved, the data gathered must be examined as they relate to the objectives of the study. Usually such data are voluminous in their raw form. If they are to be interpreted, they must first be organized such that their meaning can be conveyed to the reader. This task is achieved through the use of the various analytical and statistical techniques. To facilitate the reader's understanding of the significance of the results, it may be quite helpful to discuss, in general terms, the method utilized in the analysis. The presentation of the findings is accomplished by a number of devices. Tables, charts, and graphs are frequently used to explain relationships of the data analyzed. Whenever they are used, they should be explained with sufficient clarity to aid the reader to understand their meaning. However, detailed repetition in the body of the report of the material presented in the tables, charts, or graphs only wastes time and space. One should remember to incorporate in this section only material that helps the reader understand the conclusions and recommendations.

The completeness with which the results are reported is related to the reader and to the purposes the report is meant to serve. The degree of detail in which the results are reported is influenced by the audience. Generally, the results should be explained in sufficient detail to enable the reader to have an adequate understanding of the work. A portion of the very detailed information may be put into an appendix for further study by those who consider it relevant.

Limitations.   Problems may arise during the research which are of sufficient importance to warrant discussion in a separate section of the report. The researcher should state such limitations to provide the reader with insight into special conditions pertaining to the work. An illustrative list of limitations might include a time constraint for completing the work, the degree the results can be generalized to a larger population, the potential effects of nonresponse error, or the potential effects of substituting a sampling unit in the field because of not-at-home elements. In writing this section, one should not overemphasize the limitations so much that you destroy confidence in the work. The limitations should be reported within their proper prospective, indicating the accuracy of the interpretation of the results.

Conclusions and recommendations. The conclusions are drawn by inference, either inductive or deductive, from the findings. The conclusions verify or deny the premises or hypotheses upon which the investigation has been conducted. Care should be taken to state a conclusion for each objective or problem delimited in the proposal or statement of the research objectives. Conclusions should flow logically from the findings. But since drawing conclusions involves the human process of interpretation, faulty conclusions may result. A review of the interpretive process at the beginning of this chapter should help one avoid this inherent problem.

The recommendations concerning the action to be taken follow the conclusions. Where recommendations involve policy decisions, some researchers prefer to report only conclusions and leave recommendations to those at the policymaking level of management. The researcher is often in the best position to determine recommendations, and, if asked to do so, should state them as completely as possible, including who should do what, where, when, and why. But making recommendations not only depends on the nature of the decision to be made, but also on the researcher's knowledge of the total situation of the problem. In many instances the researcher does not have this "total picture" of the situation.

Whether this researcher recommends action or not, it is within his or her authority to make recommendations on plans for further investigation of this or allied problems. The researcher is probably the most competent person to determine what additional inquiry may be profitably undertaken.

Appendix. The appendix provides materials supplementary to those given in the body of the report. Generally, the appendix material contains detailed and/or expanded information such as detailed computations from which the tables in the report are generated, a copy of the questionnaire used in gathering the data, interviewer instructions, detailed statistical tables, calculations used to support the sample size chosen and so on.

Bibliography. If pertinent, the bibliography is usually the final section of the report presentation. It contains detailed information on references or source materials found in various forms of communications, such as proceedings of conferences, books, pamphlets, and periodicals.

14.4 Principles of Report Preparation

Reports may be composed of words, numbers, and graphics; virtually all have the first two of those elements, and many reinforce or clarify them with charts or pictures of some sort. A report writer should have skill in using each of these media and should be aware that they are tools for conveying a particular meaning to the reader. One must have a complete grasp of the investigation and be able to use his or her means of communication (words, symbols, illustrations) to bring out that understanding to others. We will divide this section into three parts: one to deal with each of those three media.

If the report writer can learn about the tastes and thought modes of the audience, he or she may cater to them and thus make the presentation more effective. The key executives, sometimes the single key executive, might be one of these special types: (1) a person of strong interests or bias that would be instrumental in accepting or rejecting the findings, in which case the writer uses care to begin with aspects that would be most interesting to him or her and to avoid expressions and tactics that would be off-putting; (2) a hesitant decision maker, who needs strong stimuli to become actively concerned and willing to make decisions on the matter, in which case a colorful and vivid presentation may be needed; (3) the very analytical type, who wants complete data and full pages of discussion for careful deliberation; or (4) the dynamic or synthetic thinker, who wants to waste no time in getting to the meat of the matter, with economy of words and figures. Unless certain that the chief decision makers are one of these special types, one should write a rather plain and straightforward report. Our discussion will have such a normal report in mind.

14.4.1 Principles of Report Writing

The ideas on good report writing presented in this section have been condensed from a number of authoritative sources on this subject. A complete and detailed discussion can be found in several well-known texts devoted entirely to the subject. Those who need to develop competence in effective report writing may find the following procedural outline useful.

The fundamental medium of communicating research findings is words. Regardless of what statistics and graphs the report may show, there should be verbal statement of every finding, as only words are the precise and universal communication mode. The report writer must have a complete grasp of the investigation and then be able to use various means of communications (words, symbols, illustrations) to bring that understanding to others. If one fails in this, much of the time, effort, and money spent on the research has been wasted. Good English, of course, is imperative for making good impressions, but that is just the minimum requirement. As important as correctness, skillful use of language is vital in presenting ideas effectively and making their meaning clear. Such mastery is rarely possessed by university students or indeed by many in businesses or government. It is not acquired easily and comes from reading others' effective writing and practicing report preparation. Patience is needed, for it may take many report-writing jobs to become reasonably proficient.

We have already presented a detailed outline of the logical order for a report. Here are some specific pointers in making written reports suitable for executives.

Make it easy to follow. The logical structure of the material, especially in the body of the report, should be self-evident and the topics easy to find. Have explicit headlines to indicate every different subject; often subheadings for subtopics should be used in addition to major headings. Most novice writers seem unaware of the advantages of using headings to label each major aspect. Paragraphs, incidentally, should be kept short and deal with only one point.

Make it clear. Clarity in writing is a quality of communication that good writers develop only after considerable experience. Few people can write so clearly that they cannot be misunderstood. An excellent check on a report's clarity is to have two or three people unfamiliar with the study read the report. Any vagueness that their critical reading reveals ought to be corrected, because vagueness can produce wrong decisions and substantial losses. Some excellent writers report that they frequently restate an idea five or six times before it is acceptable. Do not feel discouraged about needing time to write; for clarity, not speed, is the aim of a good report writer.

Use good sentence structure. Well-constructed sentences are a mark of skill in writing, and to write such sentences you must first know what you want to say. Sentences should be short. Long, involved sentences are difficult to read, even though they may be grammatically correct. Sentences should flow pleasantly. Poorly constructed sentences lead to confusion, whereas well-constructed sentences make the reader think clearly.

Use nontechnical language. As Britt expressed it: "The readers of your reports are busy people; and very few of them can balance a research report, a cup of coffee, and a dictionary at one time."[1] Replace technical terms, such as "linear equations" and "unimodal," with descriptive explanations. Aim the report at the experience level of the reader. If it is necessary to use technical terms, a brief description and/or explanation should be included in the report. A section of the appendix may be utilized for such technical explanations.

Make it brief. Britt emphasizes that "Many a researcher seems to have a greater feeling of accomplishment if he has a written report of over 100 pages instead of only 10 pages."[2] The report should be long enough to cover the objectives of the study. Highlight major points by stressing the big issues and taking them up first. Omit detail unless it is really needed to comprehend significant points. Write concisely and to the point. Value clarity rather than impressing the reader with your expertise and vocabulary.

Stress practical action. The nontechnical person of affairs may feel

---

[1] S. H. Britt, "The Writing of Readable Research Reports," *Journal of Marketing Research,* May, 1971, p. 265.
[2] Ibid., p. 265.

that the statements of researchers or technicians are true theoretically under idealized conditions but not in reality. This usually results from not fully appreciating the evidence that has been presented. Use analogies, specific examples, or comparisons drawn from experiences familiar to the reader. These show that the researcher has taken a realistic point of view.

Vary typography. Variations in type sizes and skillful use of white space may attract attention to major and minor parts or ideas in the report, as well as facilitating reading. Use capitalization or "false" caps (capitalizing the initial letter in each word) to emphasize central ideas. Use quotation marks, italics, or underlining to further fortify key words or ideas. Dots, exclamation marks, and lead lines will direct attention to significant parts of a page. Overuse of such devices, however, may cheapen the appearance of a report or delude the reader into superficial consideration of it. Contrasting colors may be used but tend to be distracting and are not worth the effort.

To illustrate variations in typography, we are going to exerpt from an actual report to a client. The client was the Chicago Transit Authority (CTA), which, in preparing to buy several hundred new buses, decided to determine its riders' preferences regarding alternative features in those buses, as well as attitudinal information of riders toward the CTA. Figure 14–2 shows two segments from the report. Some of our principles are well exemplified in the CTA report. Notice the use of capitals, underlining, and dots for emphasis and variety. Indentations also bring variety and guide attention. The wording is clear and adequate but not complicated. Numbers are expressed largely by numerals rather than in words. An attractive written report such as this one is within any literate person's ability as long as he clearly thinks through the findings he wants to communicate, and writes with care.

Use visual devices in the report. Visual devices may be used, including graphs, pictures, or maps, to give the report a dynamic quality and emphasis. Such devices need to be selected sparingly and used to supplement, not replace, the written text. Section 14.4.3 will discuss principles of graphical presentation.

14.4.2 Principles of Tabular Presentation

Proper handling of statistical material is essential in good report writing. Part of the statistics mentioned in a report can be incorporated in its statements, particularly where they are relatively brief and are described in the context. In Figure 14–2 most of the statistics are contained in the verbal statements, and the breakdown of seat-color preferences at the end of our excerpt is run into the text. Where series of statistics must be presented or analyzed, however, they can be effectively presented only as separate exhibits. Large statistical exhibits should be placed in tables separate from the reading matter but adjacent to the discussion of the particular data shown.

Figure 14–3 illustrates good rules for tabular presentation. It shows data

A. AGE

1. Frequency of Use

There appear to be three reasonably distinct usage patterns among age-groups:

- The young (under 26 years), among whom about six out of ten use CTA nearly every day.

- The middle-aged (26–55 years), among whom slightly more than half use CTA nearly every day and about 15 percent use it two or three times a week.

- The old (over 55 years), among whom somewhat more than four out of ten use CTA every day and nearly three out of ten use it two or three times a week.

There is no pattern of use among age groups at lower levels of frequency, except among older respondents; fewer (about 13 percent) are very infrequent riders (less than once every two weeks) than among the other age groups where from 16 percent to 22 percent rarely use CTA.

2. Mode

B. OTHER FINDINGS

Several interesting findings, in addition to understanding the bus riders' preferences, emerged from the study.

- People, on the whole, very much want and like the idea of making changes in the interiors of CTA buses. This is true regardless of age, sex, income, race or the frequency with which CTA is used.

- The younger the person, however, the more likely he is to want changes made. The older the person, the less likely he is to want these changes, although even among persons age 56 and over the vast majority prefer the new bus features.

Some examples of the difference age makes are as follows:

- In choosing the color seat preferred, the older one is the more likely he is to want to stick with the present green color.

	Age of Respondent				
Preferred	17 or under	18 to 25	26 to 35	36 to 55	56 or older
	%	%	%	%	%
Orange	33.3	35.8	35.8	30.9	21.2
Brown	47.6	39.8	40.6	33.0	29.8
Green	16.7	17.0	17.6	28.3	39.4

FIGURE 14.2. Two Portions of the Text of Summary Research Report to a Client, the Chicago Transit Authority

Source: Courtesy of Market Facts, Inc., Chicago.

403

arranged in chronological columns; all figures refer to the same units (millions of dollars), and the data are accompanied by footnotes and references to sources. The various features, as found in Figure 14–3, are related to the text by written symbols, which indicate the principle involved (for example, symbols 9a and 9b refer to principle 9 in the following list of ten important principles for tabular presentation).

1. *Title.* This should be written after the table is finished so that it may be a proper description. It should be brief—verbs and articles omitted—yet self-explanatory, clearly stating the nature, classification, and time reference of the information given (1a).
2. *Number.* Tables are numbered to show their position in a series, using arabic numbers (2a).
3. *Arrangement of items.* Items should be arranged using whatever scheme brings out the most significant aspect of the data. When the data related to political divisions and location are important, arrangement may be geographical. When data relate to time, arrangement may be by appropriate period—years, months, and so forth. When order of magnitude is most important, data are arranged in that order, and this arrangement is most general (3a).

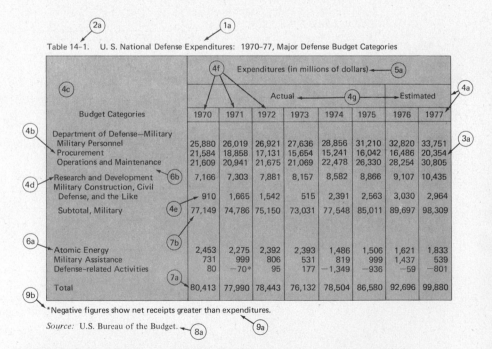

Table 14–1.   U. S. National Defense Expenditures: 1970–77, Major Defense Budget Categories

Budget Categories	1970	1971	1972	1973	1974	1975	1976	1977
Department of Defense—Military								
Military Personnel	25,880	26,019	26,921	27,636	28,856	31,210	32,820	33,751
Procurement	21,584	18,858	17,131	15,654	15,241	16,042	16,486	20,354
Operations and Maintenance	21,609	20,941	21,675	21,069	22,478	26,330	28,254	30,805
Research and Development	7,166	7,303	7,881	8,157	8,582	8,866	9,107	10,435
Military Construction, Civil Defense, and the Like	910	1,665	1,542	515	2,391	2,563	3,030	2,964
Subtotal, Military	77,149	74,786	75,150	73,031	77,548	85,011	89,697	98,309
Atomic Energy	2,453	2,275	2,392	2,393	1,486	1,506	1,621	1,833
Military Assistance	731	999	806	531	819	999	1,437	539
Defense-related Activities	80	−70*	95	177	−1,349	−936	−59	−801
Total	80,413	77,990	78,443	76,132	78,504	86,580	92,696	99,880

*Negative figures show net receipts greater than expenditures.

Source: U.S. Bureau of the Budget.

FIGURE 14–3. Tabular Arrangement of Data

This table illustrates certain of the suggestions on tabular arrangements discussed in the accompanying text. The circled figures are keyed to the points in the discussion.

Source: U.S. Bureau of the Budget.

Alphabetical arrangement is used when locating the item in the list is important. Other bases may be used; for example, items may be arranged by numerical designation, such as sales territories 1, 2, and so forth, or by such categories as class expenditures.

4. *Captions and stubs. Captions* are the designations placed over the vertical columns (4a); *stubs* are those at the left, opposite the horizontal lines of figures (4b). They should be brief and descriptive. A heading over the stubs should describe them as a whole (4c). Where subclasses are shown with their subtotals, the stubs for the subclasses are shown with their subtotals, the stubs for the subclasses are indented opposite the subtotals (4d). If more than one line is required for a stub, place the figures opposite the first line (4e). If one of the captions is "miscellaneous," it should be at the right-hand side. Chronological columns may read from the latest time toward the more remote or vice versa (4f), but the arrangement should be followed consistently. The chronology should be in definite order. A *master caption* can be placed above two or more adjacent columnar captions when it describes something these columns have in common (4g).

5. *Units of measurement.* Units of measurement should be stated in the caption unless they are self-evident (5a).

6. *Ruling, spaces, and leaders.* Rather than ruling the tables across or vertically, white spaces are often used to set figures apart. Skipping lines between different sections of the data (6a) or between every three to five lines (6b) also aids the eye. Vertical ruling is needed when complicated captions are used. Horizontal rulings are used after the captions and below the figures. Frequently, a helpful procedure is to draw a line under the total (when at the top) or above the total line when it is at the bottom. Using leaders (.....) in a stub assists the eye and helps smooth over uneven entries.

7. *Totals.* Totals should in most cases be shown at the bottom (7a), although the top may be preferred when special emphasis is to be given to certain categories. Whichever method is chosen, it should be employed consistently in all tables. When averages are shown, they usually stand at the bottom or just to the right of the column. Subtotals may be shown for each separate classification composed of two or more significant subclassifications (7b). If the totals are at the bottom of the table, subtotals follow the items subtotaled. When the total is at the top, subtotals precede them.

8. *Sources of the data.* Unless they are primary data, sources of data should be cited in order that the source may be referred to if necessary. Place the citation below the table at the left (8a).

9. *Footnotes.* Footnotes are given to explain anything that cannot be incorporated in the table, including certain qualifications on the data or methods of computation (9a). They follow the table but precede the source. They should be indicated by symbols (9b) or

letters, not by numbers, which might be mistaken for part of the table.

10. *Emphasis.* Emphasis is obtained by contrasting type faces among the figures, stubs, and possibly captions. Use of light and heavy lines or of double lines also gives emphasis or directs the eye.

14.4.3 Principles of Graphic Presentation

Throughout this chapter we have stressed the need for "telling the story" in such a way that proper emphasis is given to the important parts of the report. Graphic materials serve to drive the point home. Since graphics are fundamentally a visual aid to understanding tabular and expository materials, they are to be used sparingly. Whatever the graphic devices selected, the researcher must be constantly on guard to make sure that they present a complete picture of one central point or idea. Figure 14–4 illustrates the various features that should be included in the construction of an effective chart.

Although a number of varieties of graphic materials are available, suggestions for their use are discussed only under the headings of line diagrams, bar charts, pictographs, pie charts, and map charts or cartograms. The device used will, of course, be determined by purpose, type of research subject, type of presentation, and audience.

Line or curve diagrams. Ideally, these diagrams are used to show continuous functions, such as growth or rate of change, as illustrated in

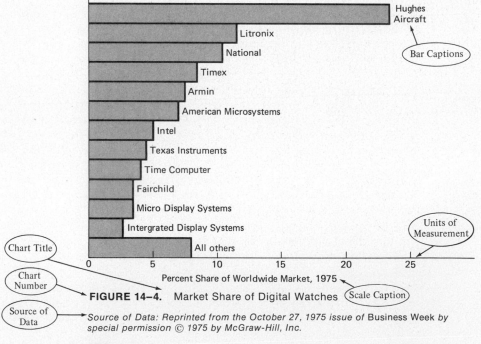

FIGURE 14–4. Market Share of Digital Watches

Source of Data: Reprinted from the October 27, 1975 issue of Business Week by special permission © 1975 by McGraw-Hill, Inc.

406

Figure 14–5. In practice, however, line diagrams generally show only growth between points on the diagram. For example, a ten-year sales' record showing total annual sales would be diagrammed as a line connecting the total annual sales data but would not show the amplitude of changes that took place during each year.

The line diagram is a very commonly used type of chart and gives a definite feeling of change. It allows several series of data to be shown in one chart and their changes to be compared relative to one another. Certain rules apply when constructing line diagrams:

1. Choose the scale with care, for distorting the scale, either horizontally or vertically, changes the angle of the lines. If the series of data employs different units of measurement (such as dollars spent on advertising and number of packages sold) or on different scales (such as total dollar sales and advertising expenditures), one scale should be given at the right of the chart and the other at the left. When only one scale is used and the chart is not too wide, the scale is shown only at the left side.

2. Coordinate lines usually must be drawn horizontally across the chart to guide the eye to the scale, but there should be as few of these lines as possible. Sometimes it suffices to have just one coordinate line, drawn above the curves to lend dimension without conflicting with the data portrayed.

3. The lines used should emphasize the curve and make it stand out

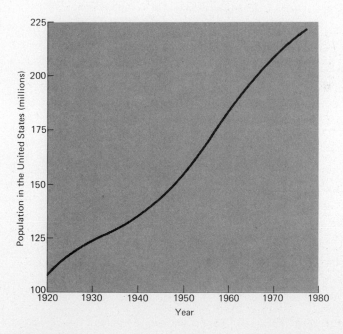

FIGURE 14–5.   Curve Diagram: Increase in U.S. Population, 1920–1975

Source: Bureau of the Census, Current Population Reports.

from the border and coordinate lines. The border, in turn, should be heavier than the coordinates. When two or more curves are shown, each should be clearly distinguishable and identified, either by labeling it on the chart or by using a legend. Too many curves plotted on a single chart become confusing; usually four is the maximum for effectiveness.

4. Always show a base line for zero, the bottom border of the chart. Sometimes the curves would be so far above the base line of zero, if the same scale is maintained vertically all the way down, that the chart would be grotesquely long; in this case zero should be shown at the base line and the vertical scale broken with a zigzag in the border just above zero.

Bar charts. This type of chart seems to be even more popular than the line diagram. The bar chart consists of bars running either vertically or horizontally, with an individual bar drawn from each observation, as in Figure 14–6. These individual bars emphasize the separateness of each observation and its magnitude. Comparisons of individual items can be made more easily in the bar chart than in the line diagram. The vertical bars are more appropriate for data that are classified quantitatively or chronologically as in Figure 14–6. Where the classification is qualitative or geographic, the horizontal chart is preferable, as in Figure 14–7.

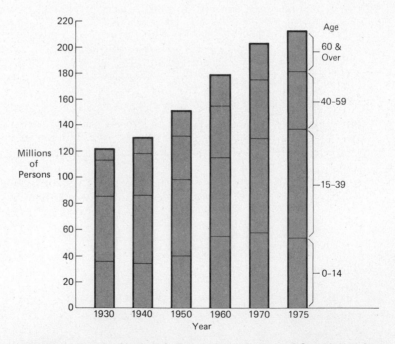

FIGURE 14–6. Bar Chart: U.S. Population, 45 Years of Growth and Change

Source: "U.S. Population: 200 Years of Growth and Change," Road Maps of Industry, No. 1887 (New York: The National Industrial Conference Board, Inc., 1976).

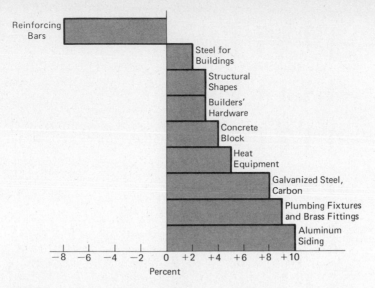

FIGURE 14-7. Bilateral Bar Chart. Percentage Changes in the Wholesale Price Index for Selected Construction Materials, 1975–1976.

Source: Adapted from the U.S. Department of Commerce, U.S. Industrial Outlook 1977, p. 17.

A bar chart may be used to depict continuity of data or to show rate of change, but a line diagram is preferable to emphasize rate and direction of change.

When two or more series of data are to be shown in bar charts, one useful type is a *component bar chart,* of which Figure 14–6 is an example. With distinctive shadings or colors, the components making up the total are shown as divisions of a vertical bar for each interval. This has a disadvantage, though, in that only the component at the bottom has a constant base line and has a readily evident amount of change. The 60 and over component in Figure 14–6 is difficult to judge. An alternative, if change in each factor is to be emphasized and the total omitted, is to have bars for each factor and group them together for each time period.

Still another modification of the bar chart can be used to show both positive and negative quantities or changes. This is the *bilateral bar chart,* in which bars may run to either side of the base line, which we see in Figure 14–7. These bars should run horizontally to make negative values as visible as the positive.

Other charts. Another graphic form is the *pictograph,* which uses tiny pictures or symbols to represent the idea or subject and show the length of bars (see Figure 14–8). This device tends to make the chart more popular and to give it reality in the reader's mind. They are more appropriate for bar-type charts than for the curves in a line chart, where the pictures usually cannot be large enough to be identified. The little

409

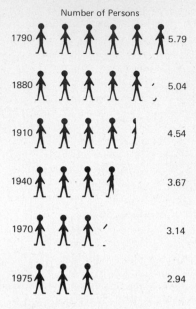

Number of Persons

1790   5.79

1880   5.04

1910   4.54

1940   3.67

1970   3.14

1975   2.94

FIGURE 14–8. Pictograph: Average Household Size

Source: "U.S. Population: 200 Years of Growth and Change,"
Road Maps of Industry, No. 1887 (New York: The National
Industrial Conference Board, Inc., 1976).

pictures tend to be more difficult to read than a bar chart, but the picto-gram is not intended for detailed study and precise measurement.

The *pie chart* is another well-known method of presenting data. Here a circle represents the whole quantity and is divided into slices whose areas are commensurate with the various proportions that each com-ponent is of the whole. For example, if one were interested in a profile of the American traveler, and it was estimated that 39 percent travel to visit friends and relatives, one could portray the nation's "purpose of trip" as a circle or pie with a slice for "visit friends and relatives" that represents 39 percent of the circle's area (see Figure 14–9). In arriving at the appropriate proportion of the pie, one must calculate the propor-tion of degrees in a circle. Since there are 360 degrees in a circle, 3.6 de-grees would represent 1 percent of the circle. Therefore, in our illus-trated example, the 39 percent would represent 140 degrees of the circle ($3.6 \times 39 = 140.4$). The remainder of the slices of the circle are calcu-lated in the same manner. It is advisable to note that one should include the units of value within each slice, or if the slices are too narrow, the units and captions should appear near the slice with an arrow pointing to the appropriate slice. Also, a good rule to follow is to begin slicing the pie from 12 o'clock position and work your way around clockwise with the sections positioned in decreasing order of magnitude. Where there is only one "pie" shown, cut into relatively few slices, the divisions may be shown strikingly. Pie charts become difficult to interpret, however, when they are cut into many pieces and when several are shown alongside one another. Pie charts may be appropriate in showing the division of a whole, but for other purposes they are markedly inferior to curve diagrams or bar charts. The pie chart is one of several types of "area" diagrams in which the area of the figures represents the relative quantities. The areas may be geometrical figures or pictures. They are so inferior to the types of charts just described that they will not be discussed.

Maps or *cartograms* are useful to show data where the geographical location is important or the physical area of the territory is significant. Maps may be shaded in various ways to show relative values, as in Figure 14–10. They may be used for political subdivisions (states, counties, and the like), for sales areas, or for showing the distribution of elements within an area, such as economic classes in a city. If shadings are properly graduated, relative densities, such as population, may be shown with maps. Maps have their uses, but they are not suitable means for comparing quantitative data accurately, because the areas of the various units are not related to the data shown.

To resolve this problem, a *distortion map* may be used, as in Figure 14–11, in which the areas assigned each unit are proportionate to the magnitude of its data. The reader may be familiar with maps of this type, which might, for example, show New York as the largest area because it is highest in the statistics being depicted. Even the distortion map does not lend itself to ready comparison of the various areas shown, however, and maps are a poor means of facilitating comparison of data. For instance, Nevada

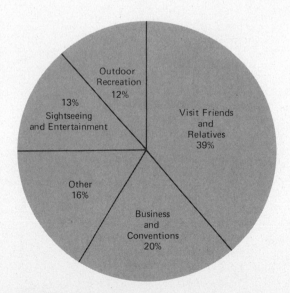

FIGURE 14–9. Pie Chart: Profile of the U.S. Traveler in 1972 by Purpose of Trip

Source: "Domestic Travel and Tourism," Road Maps of Industry No. 1741 *(New York: The National Industrial Conference Board, Inc., 1974).*

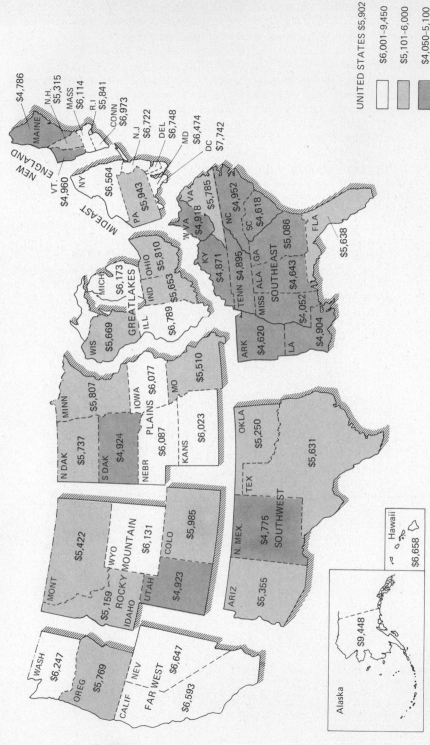

FIGURE 14-10. Statistical Map: Per Capita Personal Income, 1975

Source: U.S. Department of Commerce, Bureau of Economic Analysis, Survey of Current Business, August, 1976, p. 28.

has an area that is 91 times that of Rhode Island, but the latter has a population that is approximately double Nevada's. No shadings can so contrast that the small area of Rhode Island overshadows Nevada on a population map.

14.5 Personal Presentations

Most research reports are probably submitted to the executives or clients only as written reports. Where major decisions are involved, however, communicating with key decision makers in writing alone might be unfortunate. Despite the care with which the report is prepared and reproduced, it may not challenge the executive's interest, may receive only a cursory reading, or may be misinterpreted. Furthermore, the report cannot, of course, answer new questions that arise in the minds of its readers. When a number of persons are involved, their separate reading of the report does not bring them together to discuss and reach a mutual conclusion.

Whenever they can, researchers should present the findings in person at a meeting of the executives who are concerned. There one may

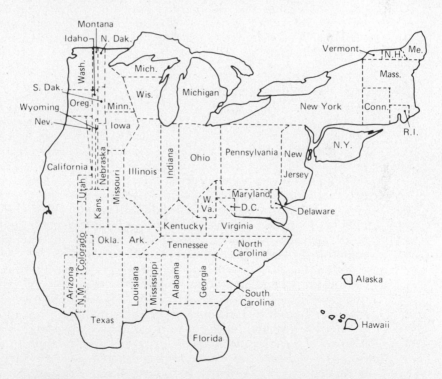

FIGURE 14–11. Distortion Map: Each State in Proportion to Its 1970 Population

Source: Louis E. Boone and David L. Kurtz, Contemporary Marketing *(Hinsdale, Ill.: The Dryden Press, 1974), p. 94.*

use his skills in exposition, may learn directly the reactions, may answer questions, and may counter any opposition or skepticism that arises. This does not mean that the personal presentation replaces the written report. All the interested persons ought to receive the latter. The report may be distributed before the meeting to permit some orientation beforehand, but usually this is unwise, since these persons might misinterpret the report before it can be explained to them. The report should be in the hands of those present at the meeting, however, and referred to throughout the presentation so that the executives will be both familiar with it and interested in it.

Like any other meeting, the research presentation ought to be completely planned in advance. Generally, it should be held where ventilation, lighting, and seating are good, and where such distractions as ringing telephones will not intrude. Adequate time should be allowed for a full discussion. A high executive should be asked to sponsor the meeting and invite the others to it, for its importance is likely to be judged by his rank.

The first step in developing an effective presentation is to know your audience. You must know who plans to attend, and what information they already know and do not know about the subject to be presented. You must know what they are capable of understanding without elaborate explanations and definitions. You must know what areas you will have to stress, and anticipate what questions they may raise. This audience analysis requires much forethought, but it is necessary for effective communication.

14.5.1 Selection of the Delivery Technique

Selection of the delivery technique is the next critical step in the development of a report presentation. There are four basic forms of delivery: (1) impromptu, (2) speaking from memory, (3) reading from a script (report), and (4) extemporaneous. The first two methods are not recommended for presentations of research to executives. Impromptu delivery becomes too risky where accuracy is a vital part of the presentation.

Speaking from memory has its disadvantages, too; one may have a memory lapse and fail to convey important information; and the presentation may be inflexible, without the capability of changing direction smoothly if the audience interrupts the presentation.

Often, an adequate presentation involves no more than sitting at a conference table and reading the report page by page, answering any questions that come up along the way. When delivering a talk in this manner, there is no danger of forgetting anything. Even though the talk is completely written out, you must practice its presentation. During the delivery it is important to look up from time to time to maintain eye contact. Audience involvement may be reduced considerably if your movements are restricted to simply reading the report. Such a situation demands that the speaker develop even more than the usual facial expressions, gestures, and voice variations to maintain audience interest.

On the other hand, extemporaneous delivery is also carefully planned and rehearsed. Its preparation includes the planning and organizing steps described in Section 14.3. But the outline preparation is the final step; the presentation is not written out in script form. The outline, which is used as a guide, should include any vital facts and figures that must be presented accurately.

Prior to the presentation, the delivery should be rehearsed several times until it can be presented smoothly. Advantages of extemporaneous delivery include the ease with which one can maintain eye contact with the audience. One has only the need to glance occasionally at the outline to guide the direction of the talk. The constant eye contact facilitates audience interest in what is being communicated. Also, one has greater flexibility in the delivery, in that if the audience seems to be having difficulty understanding a particular portion of the talk, one has the opportunity to rephrase the thought in a different way for better understanding.

14.5.2 Considerations in the Use of Visual Aids

Closely related to the selection of a delivery technique is the consideration of using visual aids to enhance the presentation. One authoritative source cited reasons for the effective use of visual aids as follows:[3]

1. *People are visually minded.* We are visually oriented from birth. People grow up surrounded by the visual influences of television, movies, books, school blackboards and projectors, road signs, advertising signs—all kinds of visual stimulation. People expect visuals in meetings, and visuals help the speaker control the meeting and maintain the group's attention.

2. *Retention is increased.* Speeches may motivate, but what about retention? When relying on verbalization alone to communicate, an estimated 90 percent of a message is misinterpreted or forgotten entirely; that is, we retain only 10 percent of what we hear! But by adding appropriate visual aids to verbalization retention is increased to approximately 50 percent.

3. *Visualization encourages organization.* Visualizing forces a speaker to organize his thoughts in an orderly fashion that will lead to a conclusion. In so doing, he will learn to simplify and condense his message into a concise, understandable story, which saves both time and expense.

4. *Misunderstandings are less likely to occur.* Seeing and hearing the message simultaneously, meeting participants can understand the speaker's intent more easily and quickly, and misinformation can be effectively avoided.

---

[3] *Bright Ideas in Overhead Projection: A Guide to More Effective Meetings* (St. Paul, Minn.: Visual Products Division, 3M Company, undated), pp. 6–7. Some of the material which appears on page 415 is used with permission of Minnesota Mining and Manufacturing Company.

When selecting the appropriate visual aids, several points should be considered:

1. The visual should be created to reinforce, to highlight, or to simplify the presenter's ideas.
2. The visualized information should be easy to comprehend. It should not be cluttered with too much material, that is, "busy." The audience should be able to grasp the idea without devoting too much time to gazing at the visual. To help accomplish this, it is best to display only one idea or concept at a time.
3. The visual should be large enough for the entire audience to see easily. Therefore, in selecting the appropriate visual technique, the size and the location of the audience and the various capabilities and availability of all the visual display equipment must be taken into consideration.
4. A decision has to be made concerning the selection of the most effective visual presentation technique. The most widely used include:
    a. *Write-on technique.* The speaker has the opportunity to include additional information during his presentation by simply writing directly on the surface of the medium used.
    b. *Pointer technique.* This technique simply involves pointing to the idea with a pen, pencil, or other indicator.
    c. *Revelation technique.* With the use of certain media the ideas or concepts described can be covered up, and as the speaker makes a point, a section of the covered-up material will be revealed. This eliminates the problem of the audience jumping ahead of the commentary.
    d. *On-and-off technique.* With a flick of the projector switch you can turn your audience's attention to the projected material on the screen. After the point is made, the projector can be turned off.
    e. *Overlay technique.* This technique can be used only with an overhead projector. By using different layers of transparencies, each adding additional information, complicated ideas can be simplified by building the concept as you add the additional overlay of material.

Before a decision can be made as to the visual presentation technique to utilize, one must take into consideration the availability, the appropriateness, and most effective technique, given the situation.

14.5.3 Types of Visual Delivery Techniques

We shall now discuss briefly a number of types of visual delivery techniques. Visual presentations of at least some features of a report may be blown up on large sheets so that there is something before a meeting at all times. A *flip chart* with individual pages bound together at the top may be used effectively. Information written on the pages can be covered with a strip and revealed as the speaker makes his point. With this piece of delivery equipment one can also start with blank pages and write on information as the talk progresses. A third effective presentation method using the flip chart is the use of a pointer to attract attention. One problem associated with the flip chart is that it is difficult to return to earlier exhibits.

Other forms of display boards include the use of chalk boards, magnetic boards, and feltboards. The chalkboard allows the presenter to write on information and direct attention through use of a pointer. The other two delivery methods offer some of the same advantages but are less flexible in the variety of presentation techniques.

Anything that can be photographed can be reproduced on a transparent slide. With the advent of remote control, and magazine-loaded projectors, the speaker can provide a very polished presentation. With the flick of the on–off switch of the projector, audience's attention can be directed to the projected material. The use of a pointer will also focus attention to major points on the screen.

The use of the overhead projector utilizing transparencies gives the presenter still more versatility. All the previously discussed presentation techniques can be utilized with this delivery method.

Other delivery methods, such as film and videotape, can be used effectively, depending on the particular situation. If, for example, motion was needed for an effective presentation, these two techniques would deliver a high impact because of their ability to capture action and achieve dramatic situations not yet possible in other media. The use of videotape rates especially high in immediacy and impact. For example, a report orally presented at company headquarters can be taped and delivered to other divisions or branches of the parent company with the impact of face-to-face communications.

Similar factors govern the use of slides or films in presentation meetings. Time and cost factors may determine whether to use them. If plans are being made for personal presentations to a number of audiences, films or slides may be less costly as well as easier to handle than charts.

A fairly new mass medium that has come into prominence is the use of *video magnification.* With the use of closed-circuit television, a speaker can be projected on a screen many times larger than life. Imagine a large auditorium holding several hundred people. Through the benefits of modern audio equipment, every audience member will be able to hear each word. However, it is likely that many people in the audience will not be able to see the presentation very clearly. At times, mannerisms and facial expressions may not be discernible, and they may be necessary to a thorough understanding of the presentation. Also, those persons who are farthest from the podium may find it difficult to concentrate and maintain their attention when the speaker is too far away to see clearly. For this reason, visuals are now being displayed on large screens. This delivery method can add immeasurably to the success of a large conference presentation.

Because personal presentations, like advertisements, are intended to be convincing, they should stress some important key theme that will be appealing. At the outset this should be "headlined" to arouse the audience's interest in the same manner that a newspaper headline arouses interest in a story. The presentation should communicate the action and follow-up in practical terms, based on three basic steps: (1) the problem, (2) the need for action, and (3) the benefits to be derived by following the recommendations. The degree of dramatics and extent of visual materials, of course, depends on the tastes and sophistication of the key members of the audience. Dignity and restraint should nearly always characterize research reports, but many researchers by nature tend to err in that direction rather than putting verve and color into written and personal communications that may prove critical in reception and acceptance.

14.6   Follow-Through

When a study's findings have been prepared and submitted to the decision makers, the marketing researcher might consider that the task is finished. With the demands of other problems and decision makers for new research projects, there may be strong temptation to take that view. The far-sighted researcher, however, recognizes that tasks remain that are of importance to the firm and to its research program. There are several such additional steps, and they will occupy the balance of this chapter.

A concept stressed recurringly through this book has been of *efficiency* in research. The researcher should follow through beyond the mere reporting of findings, which might be likened somewhat to a golfer's *follow-through* of his swing after impact with the ball. Good research follow-through adds efficiency to the specific project and to the total research effort, just as a golfer's follow-through adds distance to a drive.

While the records are still at hand and the experiences of conducting the study are still distinctly remembered, the principal researcher should make a careful review of what happened. Errors of many sorts may have occurred, and expectations may not have been realized. The next project undertaken may steer clear of inefficiencies and weaknesses that afflicted the just completed one, but this will happen only if there is a disciplined effort to review what has taken place—and these lessons are remembered.

Reviews like this should be routine, carried out for every completed project. If they are to be done regularly, there should be the systematic approach of establishing a checklist of aspects to be scrutinized. These might be grouped under the four questions below, each of which will be discussed subsequently.

1. Was the conduct of the study kept under sufficient control as it proceeded, so that its plans were accomplished?

2. Were the obtained data valid and reliable?
3. Were the findings logical and appropriate to the decisions faced?
4. Were the decision makers perceptive, and did they accept the findings? What actions were determined that appear to have been based on the findings? Were any actions taken that were contrary to the findings?

These questions relate to how successful the project was in attaining its objectives. Their answers may be difficult to obtain, especially to the last group, but they are clearly important to increasing the benefits of the research program.

14.6.1 Control

Three aspects of the conduct of research work all need good control: costs, completion by target date, and quality of work performed. If there has been adequate control, all three aspects should have been satisfied in accordance with the initial plans. Now that the project is completed, the management of marketing research should audit the performance and ascertain if these plans were indeed fulfilled. If they were not, it should be determined whether (1) controls, including reporting of progress and corrective action, may have been weak or neglected, or (2) planning may have lacked realism and failed to anticipate limitations on research staff abilities or conditions that would be faced. The cause for failure to meet objectives may be found to have been extraordinary events that could not be foreseen, but with recognition of such experiences, future planning may allow for them.

Control of time may be the most obvious necessity, as findings delivered too late for the executives' consideration would have little value. There should have been specified dates for completion, understood by those responsible for each phase, and if any failures to meet these dates had escaped the earlier attention of research management, needs to tighten control are very evident. If a critical path method is established for every major project, it is likely to be kept on its target dates. If review of completed projects finds that they are typically falling behind schedule, future planning should allow more time for the delayed phases.

Cost control may have been combined with time control by also scheduling it specifically for each activity performed. Keeping current with respect to the costs of an individual project, however, tends to be impractical except perhaps for direct labor costs on the basis of actual versus planned time spent on phases of the project. An advantage of having research work conducted by an outside agency is that it would work for specified fees, which obviates the principal firm's need to maintain detailed cost control. Substantial work and expense inputs must be expended on any project, nevertheless, by the client or principal organization for which a study is conducted, and so it always has some problems of its own cost control. The total costs, in any case, cannot be determined until some time after a project's completion, and so the total evaluation of costs versus plans must always be a posterior judgment. Such appraisals and identification of cost overruns obviously are important in sharpening the cost estimates of future projects, and thus heightening the efficiency of the firm's marketing research. The prudent research manager will also be observing carefully the quality and types of research performance by outside agencies to improve his evaluation of proposed fees.

Quality control is still more complicated and less readily judged, particularly when the work is being conducted in the field and in outside agencies. Some efforts should be made while a study is in the field, by the sponsoring organization, to check on whether data-gathering work is proceeding according to specifications, but time and distance constraints tend to prevent such current controls. Assessment of the research work quality thus tends to take place after field work is over, and it will take place partially during the data-processing and interpretative stages, where faults often come to light. A final assessment should then take place after the whole study has been completed and reported, when this can be done more leisurely. When outside agencies have been employed, it is valuable to use a "contractor rating system" such as one proposed by C. S. Mayer, which specifies particular aspects of the work to be evaluated and weightings assigned to each.[4]

14.6.2 Validity

One may use the term *valid* with regard to the correctness of various aspects of the research project, into which error may so easily creep and distort findings. The review of a completed project should scrutinize such possibilities, which you might prefer to categorize under *quality control.* There are types of validity, however, that are not matters of control of the project work but rather concern the validity of the findings in the real world in which they are to be applied.

The responsible researchers surely would be sensitive to whether the findings seem valid as they interpret them and draft the report. If any independent data exist against which the plausibility of findings could have been checked they should have done that. Executives may have raised serious challenges to validity when the findings were presented to them. Nevertheless, there are validity problems that may have been impossible to assess until the later point in time of the follow-through that we are discussing. We refer particularly to the predictions or projections that applied research typically must make, whose validity cannot be judged until some later time. For this phase of the follow-through, researchers should watch developments over time and consider whether their data projections were accurate enough. If not, needs are pinpointed to develop greater realism or accuracy in the interpreting of

[4] C. S. Mayer, "Evaluating the Quality of Marketing Research Contractors," *Journal of Marketing Research* May, 1967, pp. 134–41.

data into the future, when their findings would become translated into action.

14.6.3 Appropriateness

Another important question to be raised in the follow-through is whether or not the reported findings were appropriate to the problem or decision to which they were supposed to be addressed. In hindsight, it may be found that the problem was misconceived in the first place and that the research should have been targeted on a somewhat different problem. Such an error may be attributable to faulty communication between decision maker and researcher or wrong interpretation by the researcher of what was wanted. If, instead, it turns out (as it so often does) that the decision maker had misjudged the nature of the problem or decision to be faced, the researcher may need to take pains on the next occasion of planning research to help in evolving a sharper and more appropriate definition of the problem.

14.6.4 Acceptability

Perhaps the most vital question to be appraised, from the viewpoint of the research program's welfare, is whether or not the important decision makers accepted the findings. An experienced marketing researcher could tell you of the frustration undergone when one's careful findings have not been accepted by the decision makers served. Sometimes the executives will overtly and pointedly reject the findings. If this takes place during a personal presentation, the researcher may at least be able to salvage beneficial insight into why the findings were being rejected. Unfortunately, the failure to accept the results tends to be more subtle, with no outright criticism and rejections, but to be evident in failure to elicit any questions and responses from executives and to produce any action consistent with their implications or recommendations. Where there is no personal meeting to present and discuss findings or where someone at a higher level than the researcher's contacts makes the real decisions, such a situation is more likely.

Sensible research directors and analysts, however, become well acquainted around their organizations and should have enough rapport with higher-level managers to obtain clear indications of the acceptability of their findings and the degree of confidence placed in them. If not, they may glean some indications from the office grapevine. (The outside research or consulting firm works under this disadvantage of lacking continuing inside contacts and often is in the dark regarding acceptance of its findings.) Where the finding's nature provides direct evidence on the course of action to be taken, the actual taking of such action clearly signals acceptance of the findings. However, other crucial factors lying outside the study's scope may have proved determining, so it is well to learn why the action was taken rather than to automatically construe some contrary decision as negating the study in the executives' views.

421

For the many studies that are exploratory or intended only to describe conditions or give feedback, on the contrary, one cannot judge a study's acceptance by any decision or action resulting and needs to use other means of inferring acceptance.

14.7 Posterior Analysis of Payouts

Anyone who is responsible for a marketing research activity should be concerned about its *payout*—the benefits to the sponsoring enterprise yielded by the expenditure on the research. As most applied marketing research is conducted for profit-making businesses, we may equate payout with profits while recognizing the governmental or not-for-profit organizations that sponsor research would seek another type of payout. There are two potent reasons for concern with payout: (1) the resources available for marketing research are scarce and need to be allocated to projects with the highest payout or return on investment; and (2) the future security and expansion of the marketing research department, which is a staff unit that might be considered expendable during a financial stringency, depends on the values that executives place on its services. Therefore, the more convincingly and authentically the marketing research manager can demonstrate the payout of expenditures, the better the chances are of obtaining more generous resources and of being effective.

While the needs of a cost/payout analysis are important, its achievement on anything but a gross "guesstimate" basis is usually very difficult. For studies whose findings cannot be connected with a particular decision opportunity, because they were not so intended, the researcher can assign only a subjective opinion of their likely value to the organization. Even here one can estimate the risk and profit potentialities to the firm of that aspect or operation that the study concerned and rank expenditures against one's ranking of those profit areas.

For most studies too, although lacking in any objective criterion of profitability or risk reduction, the observant research manager can rank them by their apparent effects on decision makers. For example, where action was taken on the problem researched that was consistent with the study—and the action appears to be successful with regard to its objective—a project would be given high rating. Where a study was commended by pleased executives, although no decision seemed to be forthcoming, the rating would be much lower—and so on. Such qualitative assessments would produce no evidence to support the value of research to the firm, but they would be some guidance whereby the research manager could make better allocations in the future or give better advice to executives when they are stipulating the projects to be conducted.

With some effort one can also find projects whose payout is fairly demonstrable. In a positive sense are those that produced action or enabled sales to be made that are of measurable profitability. The question here is how much of that profit may be attributed to marketing research, because if the same action would have been taken in the same manner

422

without the information produced by research, its payout would be nil. If profitable sales could not have been made without the research findings or the actions had some critical features uncovered through the research, there is positive evidence that it was profitable. Of course, arriving at the amount of attributable profit still would entail some guesswork.

The estimations for a cost/payout appraisal can be radically improved if pains are taken to specify expectations at a project's beginning. If prior estimates or premises for a decision are established before research is approved, a discussion that you may recall from Chapter 5, the researcher can make posterior measurements that indicate what the research has contributed. Suppose, as one relevant situation, that a marketing executive has estimated a new product's sales potential to be 250,000 units per year, with a probability of 60 percent. If a test marketing study or other research method established that there would be only about 20 percent probability of reaching that sales level and the highest probability of only a 150,000-unit sales, there would be both a large risk reduction and improved profitability by avoiding money-losing decisions. Perhaps the more accurate sales forecast would reduce plant and production costs by $75,000 and eliminate advertising to poor potential markets at another $16,000 saving. Or the information might have prevented the company from going into a losing venture that most probably would have lost $300,000 over a period of years, with capital that could be producing some estimated profit in established lines.

Very rarely do executives desire to make a Bayesian analysis of their expected value (payout) of alternative decisions and their subjective probability that given states of nature will materialize that affect that payout—and they usually lack the time. Typically, they do well when they explicitly state the alternative courses of action that they are considering. The marketing researcher may interpret whatever indications he or she can evoke from the decision maker, however, into an implied set of probabilities although only for really high risk problems. Crude as these estimates would be, they should prove worth the effort when the time comes for posterior assessment of what the research project contributed.

The research manager also needs to develop criteria for judging his cost/payout values. Suppose that his or her posterior analysis of project 76 was that it yielded $30,000 of profit or risk reduction to the firm, and its cost was $20,000. Offhand one might conclude that the project was profitable, with its estimate of a 2:3 ratio of cost to payout. Still, appraisal of other projects may find that their payouts ran three to six times their costs. Also, study of important decisions made without benefit of marketing research suggests that $20,000 would have yielded far more than a 2:3 ratio to payout if it had been invested in studies for them. The manager may decide that his or her rule would be requiring at least a 2:6 cost to anticipated payout as the criterion in allocating funds to projects thereafter. This might include some margin for error because, for example, a 2:3 prior estimate of a payout ratio might have a large margin of estimating error, which is probably larger for the payout estimate than for the cost estimate.

Decisions, decisions!—that is what a research manager faces in deciding how the limited resources made available are going to be allocated among many more problems and decisions than can possibly be researched. Some rational basis for such decisions is clearly needed, best of all one that can be expressed quantitatively with some confidence and applied to all future research requests and opportunities. If one can establish a reasonably reliable "return on investment" for the whole research operation, which now is being recommended,[5] this would be an inestimable boon to increasing the support of his activities. More significantly, it would substantially improve the *efficiency* of marketing and its enormous expenditures.

---

[5] This approach is illustrated in Dik W. Twedt, "What is the 'Return on Investment' in Marketing Research?" *Journal of Marketing,* January, 1966, pp. 62–63.

15 Market Analysis and Forecasting

Our text ends with Chapter 15. We have ended the marketing research process and now consider some applications in the related and most common subjects of market analysis and sales forecasting. The answers sought by firms in these applied areas relate to the following recurring questions:

Who are the particular types of buyers that would be logical targets for our products?

How can they be described? What uses, needs, and motives do they have for our products?

What is the total potential market, in our industry, for such products? In the segments we select for targets?

What is the market potential in particular areas?

What volume of sales should we forecast for our products during the coming year (or whatever the forecast period)?

"KNOW THY CUSTOMER" is a basic commandment for marketers. As manufacturers and merchants have become increasingly remote from individual customers, with modern large-scale operations, these customers have become legion and very difficult to know. Perhaps in terms of today's situations, that commandment should be rephrased as "Know thy market." In this chapter we shall describe a system of market studies that would have general usefulness, although manufacturers are used for examples.

15.1 Market Decisions and Studies

As an overview of the chapter's subject matter, let us first consider the series of decisions to which such research would be applied. The gravest decision for a new venture in manufacturing would probably be: What should we make? Or of a new service firm: What services should we offer? These determinations would be based partially on answers to these market analysis questions posed by Blaine Cooke:[1]

1. Does such a set of wants (that the product or service would satisfy) in fact exist?
2. On what scale does it exist?
3. What economic value will buyers attach to the satisfaction of these wants?
4. What costs are involved in providing satisfaction of these wants?
5. In what sense and to what degree are these wants unsatisfied or inadequately satisfied?

If it is decided to go ahead with the product or service, decisions must be made about its marketing that call for a foundation of market knowledge. Key questions here would include:

1. Who specifically would do the buying or influence the choice?
2. Where are they located?
3. Where and how do they buy?
4. What buyer motivations should be appealed to?

Again these are questions that competent market analysis would answer. After the product or service is placed on the market, another question will be faced repeatedly due to the need to plan ahead: What are the probable future sales, during a given coming period? As the central foundation of the firm's planning, both short- and long-range market and sales projections are vital management needs.

The questions posited above call for a series of studies that build up to a final stage of sales forecasting. You might think of this as a sub-

---

[1] Blaine Cooke, in V. P. Buell (ed.) *Handbook of Modern Marketing* (New York: McGraw-Hill Book Company, 1970), pp. 2–45.

system within the larger marketing research and management information systems. It may aptly be called a system due to its feeding into a series of planning decisions, the interconnection between its phases, and the repetitive cycle that it should follow. We consider that this field of research application has five phases and describe them concisely below.

1. *Market identification* has the purpose of finding and categorizing the specific types of buyers or sectors, within the large macrocosm of total markets, that contain sufficient potential purchasing power for the firm's products or services to be logical focuses of its efforts.
2. *Market diagnosis* is the second phase, which seeks to understand the characteristics of those markets or segments, including their buying needs, motivations, and practices.
3. *Total market potential analysis* follows to determine how large the entire potential market for the product is—or for those segments that are targeted for the particular firm, within a specified period of time.
4. *Area market potential analysis* then breaks down the total potential into those for particular geographical areas.
5. *Sales forecasts,* which would come later, estimate the dollar or unit sales of the product (and also for the firm) to be anticipated during a specific future period under given external and internal variable factors.

The first two phases are primarily qualitative in nature, but the market potential and forecasting phases are highly quantitative. Total potentials may be broken down into those for varieties or models of a product or for various market segments. Areas used in the geographic analysis of potentials typically are sales regions and districts to provide control yardsticks for operating the marketing organization as well as planning and budgeting. These analyses deal with current or very recent indicators of potentials. The firm must project the existing situation, however, into the future with its sales forecast, which completes the cycle of market analysis. Such forecasts normally are made annually, with possible interim review and modification, but the four previous phases of market analysis may not be conducted with such a periodic regularity.

15.2   Market Identification and Diagnosis

This section deals with the first two phases named above, in combination, in three uses: market targeting, market definition, and segmentation.

15.2.1   Market Targeting

The first stage is to identify the broad areas of buyer categories that represent some probable potential for buying one's product or service. For *existing* products this involves merely determining the types of buyers who are already buying that sort of product. For beer, present consumers constitute the types of individuals who represent practically all of the potential beer-consuming public—whose characteristics are already well known to any alert brewing company through consumer surveys that would be a routine procedure. Its market targeting task would be confined to monitoring changes in the sizes and consumption rates of various buyer categories and the geographic changes in numbers of consumers. For a stable product that has approximately saturated its market—beer, bed linens, stationery, and the like—market targeting is uncomplicated.

Where the product has specialty characteristics that render its market different from the usual products in its field, market targeting faces greater uncertainty. If you were studying the feasibility of importing a quality German brand of beer, not previously sold in North America, you perhaps would need to find that narrower market that is paying premium prices for European beers and also make assessments whether there is some potential among those who now buy premium-priced domestic beers. If you were introducing a low-calorie beer, there would be more novelty to this product, and its potential markets presumably are far from saturation, as well as undefined. The difficulty is still greater when one is offering something so new that it has no real counterpart existing, such as insurance policies to cover legal costs that some prominent insurance companies have announced.

In decisions on a new product, the firm should first conduct consumer or buyer research to find who has the greatest interest and probability of buying the new product or service, thus targeting the market. Notice the difference in approach to market targeting from that of existing products, where one starts by defining the product and then defines the market. With an innovation this task begins with the market and its wants and works from there to defining what sort of product (or service) would satisfy those wants. This, in turn, leads to the third stage: assessing whether the new product converges with the demands so well that these buyers truly represent a market for it.

15.2.2 Market Definition

The market that has been targeted is a vague and useless concept unless it is stated in definite terms that will be clear and suitable to identify those who compose that market. Its definition must employ words that categorize it, preferably with uniform usages that others will understand precisely. If the task of targeting the market employed primary data that a researcher gathered with surveys or observations of buyers, he or she should have used a recognized terminology to describe them. If a device was invented to arrest snoring (a great boon to mankind), it would hardly suffice to describe its market as "people who snore," since there is no means of selecting persons who have that trait and other attributes that would make them probable buyers of the device. We might be frustrated in finding such indicators of snorers, but fortunately most markets can be described in terms of standardized meanings.

Consumer markets have usually been described in demographic terms (vital statistics on the population). If the unit of consumption is families, they might be described in terms of these characteristics:

Composition of members.

Number of members.

Household head's occupation or education.

Family income.

Ethnic origin or race.

Number of wage earners.

Home ownership.

Geographic location of home.

If the unit is individuals, some of these characteristics might be used to identify them, in addition to such factors as age and sex. Demographic descriptions can serve as indicators that anyone may use and may combine with other data if standard breakdowns are used to categorize the description.

Demographic identifications have proven often to be too superficial or insignificant to describe markets with enough precision. As we shortly will find with regard to stratifying markets, the really important distinctions that signify markets may be other and more subtle characteristics. Social class, stage in life, psychological traits, and behavioral variables may be the desirable bases for defining markets, but techniques to detect such common qualities among those with the strongest buying potential for some product or service are difficult. After such criteria are identified, they must be correlated with some demographic factors, if one is going to literally delineate the markets demographically. To find replacements for demographic profiles and bases for stratification, efforts have built on psychologists' work in motivation research and in standard personality inventories. These have been blended in what now is called "psychographic research." Progress in this now-popular type of research appears to be very promising.[2]

When we turn from consumer to industrial, institutional, and governmental markets, we find the latter more readily identified. (Because they are fairly similar, we shall refer to these three types of markets as "industrial.") The number of potential buyers is much smaller than for consumer goods and services, and the reasons for possible purchase tend to be more objective and evident to sellers. The commonly short distribution channels or direct sale from manufacturer to industrial buyer, in these markets, also contributes to having a clearer knowledge of buyers and users and of the specific things they buy or need.

Definition of industrial markets is greatly facilitated by a generally used system of categorization, the Standard Industrial Classification system (SIC). This was created by the Bureau of the Census in cooperation

---

[2] William D. Wells, "Psychographics: A Critical Review," *Journal of Marketing Research,* May, 1975, pp. 196–213, is an excellent review with interesting case histories and voluminous bibliography.

with various industries, and it is periodically revised to better reflect the changes in significant lines of business.[3] For most lines of business, as well as for governmental and nonprofit enterprises, it provides a standard terminology and code number, down to four digits. The two left-hand digits indicate the major industry grouping, which are divided among nine categories, as follows:

> 01 to 09 Agriculture
> 10 to 14 Mining
> 15 to 17 Contract construction
> 19 to 39 Manufacturing
> 40 to 49 Transportation, communication, electric, gas, and sanitary
>   services
> 50 to 59 Wholesale and retail trades
> 60 to 67 Finance, insurance, and real estate
> 70 to 89 Services
> 91 to 94 Government

To illustrate the use of the SIC, let us say that you are concerned with markets for electric wiring among manufacturers of equipment. You then would look for data under the SIC designation of 36, which deals with "Electric machinery, equipment, and supplies." Actually your analysis, though, is to be limited to household electric appliances, and you would use for this the code number 363. One type of appliance of interest to you is sewing machines, which has its own code number, 3635. Most reports of industrial data adhere to the Census practice of classifying data by SIC numbers, a great boon to market analysts.

The SIC categories cannot fit perfectly all desired breakdowns of market segments for certain products. One problem is product lines that cross a number of SIC categories, with no individual designation. An example recently has been cited in the packaging industry, of which parts fall into five SIC two-digit categories: 26—paper and allied products; 28—chemicals and allied products; 32—stone, clay, and glass; 33—primary metal industries; and 34—fabricated metal products.[4]

15.2.3   Market Segmentation

Intelligent marketers would recognize that the demand for their products does not lie in merely one homogenous market, but rather is composed of various subtypes of markets that have varying characteristics and degrees of purchase potential for his product. They thus perceive their need to disaggregate that whole market into its various significant strata. That process is *market segmentation*, which may be defined as: the process by which a firm partitions its prospective customers (the market)

---

[3] Executive Office of the President, Office of Management and Budget, *Standard Industrial Classification Manual,* 1972 (Washington, D.C.: Government Printing Office, 1972).

[4] *The Marketing News,* October 15, 1972, p. 3.

into subgroups or submarkets (segments). The objective of segmentation is to group individual prospects so that their responses to marketing inputs should vary greatly *among* segments, but little *within* segments.[5] As segmentation is vital to efficient marketing, its procedures are important among the marketing researcher's techniques.

The tasks involved in market segmentation are fairly obvious: (1) identify and differentiate between the various market segments, in terms of characteristics or descriptions; (2) diagnose their relative buying interest in the product or brand; and (3) quantify their levels of buying potential. As the third step falls under the subject of quantitative methods, we defer it to Section 15.3.

The segments first must be identified in terms of whatever descriptive factors are available that can actually be tagged to possible buyers of the particular product or service. The key problem is to find those factors that will differentiate the really higher potential segments. To attempt this on a hit-or-miss basis would be very inefficient and confusing, so an orderly analytical approach is needed. One could apply factor analysis randomly to many suspected variables but only if one had indicators of buying interest relative to every variable, which would not be worthwhile. Let us describe two illustrative cases of orderly procedures.

Discriminant analysis, one approach, was illustrated in a published example, under the designation "market structure analysis," which dealt with a certain category of machine tools—numerically controlled machining centers.[6] We described the method of discriminant analysis in Section 13.2.4 and presented two diagrams of multidimensional scaling (MDS) of its results as Figures 13–3 and 13–4. We also described there another study under the category that employed factor analysis and canonical analysis.[7] You will find much in current marketing research literature on additional ingenious methods of segmenting markets, as this is an area of much interest and potential profit.[8]

15.3 Total Potential Analysis

In speaking of total potential for some product or service, we are usually referring to the total of the nation. A seller whose entire operations are confined to less total area might not be concerned with national demand, but we shall assume the latter. The alternative of *area* potentials will be taken up in Section 15.4. We are also going to be concerned primarily

---

[5] H. W. Boyd, Jr., and W. F. Massy, *Marketing Management* (New York: Harcourt Brace Jovanovich, Inc., 1972), p. 87.

[6] *Market Structure Analysis* (Chicago: Market Facts, Inc., undated).

[7] Ronald E. Frank and Charles E. Strain, "A Segmentation Research Design Using Consumer Panel Data," *Journal of Marketing Research,* November, 1972, pp. 385–90.

[8] A more recently reported technique for categorizing consumers is on the basis of their judgments regarding brands, ideal products, and product features as sets of points in a common multidimensional space. This was described by Paul E. Green, Yoram Wind, and Henry J. Claycamp, "Brand-Features Congruence Mapping," *Journal of Marketing Research,* August, 1975, pp. 306–13.

with total *market* potential. As expressed in our earlier definition, this normally is interpreted as meaning the maximum sales opportunities for *all* sellers of a product or a service. An individual seller should determine the market potential before proceeding to determine the sales potential that represents his proper share of that larger demand.

Let us recognize as our discussion begins that the concept of maximum sales opportunities is an elusive one for any product (including services) that has not yet saturated its potential demand. Prior to the introduction of the Ford Model T car in the early 1900s, the automobile manufacturers logically might have considered the total demand for their industry to be rather small, but the advent of Henry Ford's mass-produced and low-priced offering quickly transformed the potential into a very large one. A more modern example was DuPont's Teflon coating on cooking utensils, which had a discouraging sales record during its first few years on the market. However, product improvements were made and a new marketing strategy devised, and the new offering was placed in test markets that demonstrated a promisingly large market potential. With this market evidence, DuPont proceeded to make Teflon an outstanding market success.[9]

We should recognize that new products offer peculiar and harder challenges to the marketer than products that already exist. The latter already have a sales history and to some degree are amenable to historical designs of research; whereas with a new product the analyst must work more with primary data and grope among more unknowns. We shall mention distinctions in applicable methods between new and established products. Our discussion will be divided between "macro" and "micro" analysis methods, which will be differentiated below.

15.3.1 Macro Potential Analysis Methods

The macro methods begin with the large picture of the already documented demand for an entire industry or type of product and, on that basis, proceed to estimate the demand for the particular product concerned. The analyst deals with large aggregates from the beginning and disaggregates toward determining the demand (for all sellers, unless, like DuPont's Teflon, the firm is sole seller of its unique product) for the particular product. We shall describe two macro approaches that are widely useful.

Corollary products. The demand for the product concerned may be correlated with the demand for products now on the market, whose sales data are available. (This may be utilized for an existing product but is more useful in determining demand for a new product.) The new product might tend to supplant those products, or the use or ownership of products now on the market might be related to the new product. Thus, one can estimate the total demand for color television by relating it to the rate of replacement of black-and-white television. Researchers

---

[9] James Becknell, Jr., and Robert W. McIsaac, "Test Marketing Cookware Coated with 'Teflon,'" *Journal of Advertising Research,* September, 1963, pp. 2–8.

were able to make initial estimates of the demand for automatic clothes dryers through analyzing the sale of automatic washing machines— which had preceded dryers by several years. Close scrutiny is needed to be sure that some relationship between the uses of the products exists, or that owning the existing product is a reliable indicator of an effective demand for the new product.

Some time must elapse before consumers' buying inertia is overcome and regular purchase of the new product becomes established. This requires a substantial discount of the demand for existing products in estimating that of the new one. One must also allow for the popularity of competitive products and for the innovator's ability to promote the new product. Measurements based on actual sales of corollary products are crude, of course, but experience and buyers' surveys increase their accuracy.

Statistical derivation. Markets may be estimated through the use of macro statistics. This approach may be used for existing products but is more pertinent to new products, where the analyst may have no better basis of estimation. There may be data available reporting an entire industry's sales or those of a very broad product line within which one's particular product would be classified. Clues to market size may be derived from data in either the Census of Manufacturers or the Census of Business, which publish total enumeration data on sales of manufacturers or of merchants, respectively. These may be too heterogeneous for accurate guidance, but there also have been some comprehensive studies to determine expenditures of consumers or of certain industries on specific types of products.

15.3.2 Micro Potential Analysis Methods

In micro analysis, one begins with individual or sampled evidence of buyers' proclivities to purchase the product or service concerned. These are then aggregated and projected to the estimated total market potential size. Thus, it works in the direction opposite from macro analysis, toward the same objective. We shall explain two methods of accomplishing this.

Buying intention surveys. Substantial data on the probable market size can be obtained by going to consumers (or to business buyers and others who influence purchasing for industrial products). Some of the relevant data usually obtained tell (1) whether consumers have a current or prospective need for the product and, if so, how much of existing substitute products they use; (2) whether they approve of a new product's design in comparison with existing substitutes; and (3) how much potential purchasers are willing to pay for the product. One also can draw upon the merchandising sense and experience of merchants by approaching them for appraisals of the product and its likely demand. The responses are to be appraised with some skepticism, however, and should take into account the realism with which these people appear to judge their future point-of-purchase behavior. Nevertheless, such information can provide excellent insight into probable market composition and some clues about its size.

Surveys of consumer buying intentions usually must be conducted through field surveys by specialized interviewers. Since industrial-goods manufacturers frequently have direct contact with buyers through their sales forces, fairly objective data indicative of its sales potential should be obtainable, when a well-informed individual in the buying account can be reached by a capable sales representative. Airco is one industrial supplier that obtains such data through sales personnel and then combines them to calculate a total market potential. Its suggestions to its sales-force, given in Figure 15–1, are ingenious and shed light on the tasks involved.

Test markets. A far more costly, but also much more convincing, method of estimating the total potential market is by experimentation. An actual selling campaign carried on in selected test markets may be used as empirical demonstration of how much of the product will be sold. DuPont experienced a more than doubling of sales for cookware coated with Teflon. This was an impressive experiment conducted in nine cities as test markets and four cities as controls, but we are not attempting to present its technical details and conclusions here.

The best of market tests has some limitations as a conclusive indicator of total market potential. As ever, there is the question of representativeness. With products that are novelties to consumers, buying inertia may so delay trial of the product that full potential has not even been approached during the test period. There is the contrary danger that the product could be faddish, with no large permanent market. Although there are these dangers to be faced seriously, market tests provide impressive and often accurate gauges of a new product's market potential.

Simulations. Market tests that fully replicate the entire marketing mix, of the type just described, are being considerably replaced by two less costly forms of new product testing for sales prediction: (1) the "controlled" market test that shortcuts some phases, and (2) simulations. Simulations provide some surrogate and more quickly obtained indicator of sales response, stopping short of the normal consumer buying process. Both of these approaches were described in our Miles Laboratories, Inc. (B) case, Case 8. We refer you there for more details on simulations. Another term for this method is "laboratory test markets."[10]

15.4 Area Potential Analysis

In this type of analysis, the researcher finds the current relative sales fertility of different markets, that is, the best markets at that time. He

---

[10] For comparisons of this with three other techniques, see Edward M. Tauber, "Forecasting Sales Prior to Test Market," *Journal of Marketing*, January, 1977, pp. 80–84.

In many cases it will be possible to obtain the potential purchases of a customer directly from a purchasing agent, buyer, or other responsible individual within the account. At times, customer personnel might not be able to give you their anticipated total purchases of the products that you market for 1963, but they might very well be able and willing to give you the amount they have purchased in 1962. With this information, you should be able to come up with a good figure for 1963.

Potential may also be arrived at through observation made of the type of equipment at the customer's location that either consumes the products we make or could possibly be replaced by products we make.

It may be possible to relate the number of personnel involved in welding and cutting production or maintenance processes that consume our products to accounts with similar operations where the potential is known.

Relationships can also be made between the type of industry and the total number of employees working at an account which closely resembles or corresponds to a similar size plant in a similar industry where the potential is known.

In some cases, you may have a reliable estimate on the amount of one or two product lines consumed at a specific point which complement or supplement other product lines that we market.

It might be possible to arrive at a pretty good estimate of the unknown product line potentials because of their relationship with products of known potential.

Refer to government contracts and contract awards, as well as requests for bids from accounts in private industry.

Sometimes, salesmen who sell product lines that are complementary to ours can be quite helpful. For example, a machine tool man may know of an account's plan to buy a certain amount of tools which happen to be used in conjunction with one of our products or processes.

Chambers of commerce and local utilities, particularly power and light companies, are aware of new companies coming into a particular area before this information is generally available. Local banks also, at times, possess this information; and many times if you have a personal relationship with individuals at basic sources such as this, they might be able to help you get the information you need.

Dun and Bradstreet reference books and state and local directories can provide valuable information such as the number of employees at specific using points in the event that you do not possess this information. In turn, this information would give you some idea as to what type of our products might be consumed and the amount of consumption.

FIGURE 15–1. Suggestions to Salespersons for Estimating Account Potential

also may determine the *size* of these markets, the amount of the product that buyers will take. Most often, the markets under study are areas: states, cities, counties, or sales territories, or the markets may be certain classes of the population: such as farmers, homeowners, or persons at certain income levels. For industrial goods the markets are more likely to comprise various classifications of industrial buyers. Area potential analysis serves these chief purposes in manufacturing enterprises:

1. Selecting the most fertile markets in which to concentrate advertising and other promotion.
2. Allocating sales personnel and aligning their territories in accordance with sales possibilities.
3. Setting equitable sales quotas and establishing accurate yardsticks for measuring sales performance.
4. Avoiding distribution in territories that are too "thin" or avoiding costly distribution channels in areas where sales possibilities do not merit them.
5. Detecting strengths and weaknesses in the distributive organization.

435

Area *market* potential analysis seeks to find the best markets for a particular product or service. By the term "best," one might mean the market with the highest potential per capita, the highest total market, or the market with the greatest profit possibilities. (Thus, buying power per family in the suburb of Winnetka is 2.9 times that of Chicago, but its total buying power is relatively small.) One might refer to demand at the place where buyers live or where they buy. (Winnetka residents, for example, would tend to buy certain goods outside their home town in various shopping centers.) Area sales potentials for a particular firm may be derived after area market potentials have been estimated. Whichever he is seeking, the market analyst has the task of establishing a market index or guide to tell where and how much the product ought to sell currently.

Determining appropriate market areas and their boundaries is a prerequisite for estimating area market potentials and market shares. Marketers who have field salesforces must align these areas with their salesmen's territories, but usually analysis requires more and finer divisions than the number of sales territories. The particular geographic segmentation used will depend upon the particular market to be cultivated. A vast amount of statistical data has been assembled on a geographic basis and expressed in the form of trading areas. The Department of Commerce has divided the country into 216 Key Manufacturing Market Centers. It also has released national retail and wholesale marketing maps with specific data on retail trade for all standard metropolitan statistical areas and other counties that had sales of $100,000 or more.

There are five major methods of determining area market potential and market shares: (1) direct, (2) corollary-product index, (3) general buying power index, (4) arbitrary factors, and (5) multiple correlation.

15.4.1 Direct-Data Method

The direct-data method uses the actual sales figures of one's product in each market as a direct index of potential sales. Guided by sales of the whole industry selling the product, the manufacturer takes his competitors' experience into consideration and is not misguided by the strengths and weaknesses peculiar to his own sales penetration. The industry's sales become the index of potential business. From such figures, the market analyst can learn the market areas in which the best sales have been obtained by the industry, the share of business one's firm has gained, and whether its pattern of strong and weak markets parallels that of the industry.

Let us show how an imaginary firm, the Cathode Company, might use the direct-data method. Its industry trade association, say, pools the sales figures of its members. These are released by states, in totals only, to member concerns. Using these figures, the Cathode Company might make such comparisons as those in Table 15–1.

These figures show the states that represent strong and weak areas for the industry's sales and the Cathode Company's success in attaining this average. Good management seeks to capitalize on the strong areas and avoid excessive promotion in the weak. With these indexes, Cathode

TABLE 15–1. Comparison of Hypothetical Sales Data

States	Cathode Co. Sales Volume (dollars)	Cathode Co. Sales Percent of United States	Industry Sales Volume (dollars)	Industry Sales Percent of United States	Cathode Sales as Percentage of Total Industry
Connecticut	250,000	1.3	2,500,000	1.5	10.0
Maine	86,000	0.4	1,150,000	0.7	7.5
Massachusetts	980,000	5.0	5,500,000	3.4	17.8
New Hampshire	77,000	0.4	1,100,000	0.7	7.0
Rhode Island	140,000	0.7	1,900,000	1.2	7.4
Vermont	70,000	0.4	840,000	0.5	8.3
New England	1,603,000	8.2	12,990,000	8.0	12.3
United States	19,600,000	100.0	161,247,000	100.0	12.1

can formulate plans more intelligently and take remedial steps in areas where the company is not securing its share of the market.

Unfortunately, few industries make available such data on competitors' sales. In some industries, such as automobiles and motorboats, licensing or tax records serve as sources. In a relatively few industries such as the electrical appliance industry, trade associations collect and issue these statistics.

For many consumers' goods, one can use figures on consumer purchases rather than manufacturers' sales. The services that provide audits of retail store sales or the purchases of consumer panels, which we described previously, may be utilized for this analysis. Only a fraction of industry can take advantage of such data, since they are gathered only for certain types of branded goods. Several breakdowns may be available, but since the sample obtained from any particular area is small, the breakdowns have only a limited ability to pinpoint markets.

A fundamental limitation on using sales data as a determinant of potential market is the assumption that past experience is the equivalent of present sales potential. In marketing some staples this may be a proper guide, but in dynamic markets, shifting demands and the probable existence of hitherto untapped demands render this an unsafe assumption. Generally, the analyst should try to use one of the other methods.

15.4.2 Corollary-Product Method

For area market analysis, a possible index to area potential utilizes sales volumes of another product, the purchase of which is linked with the demand for one's own product to vary with that of the corollary product. Such measurement is especially possible in the case of a replacement part, such as radio tubes or auto batteries. By studying the past relationship between sales of the principal product and of the replacement part, the analyst may be able to establish the areas where high potential exists, as well as to determine the quantity of the product that ought to be sold.

This method requires both the determination of a consistent relationship between the sales of the corollary product and one's own product and the availability of sales data on the other product. Only in limited instances is the corollary-product method feasible, but it can be a very helpful market index.

15.4.3 Buying Power Indexes

As the amount of buying by the inhabitants of a locality tends to vary with their command of purchasing power, an index of the amount of buying power in various localities is a gauge of their relative potential sales. General buying power indexes have served as useful and simple yardsticks for measuring markets.

Magazine circulation has been advanced as one index. It is argued that people who buy magazines have money to spend; hence, magazine circulation is a yardstick of buying power. Certain "class" magazines may serve as special guides for relevant products—thus the circulation figures of *Sports Afield* might help the market planning of a sporting rifle manufacturer.

Total retail sales in various markets might be used as another index of their general fertility for consumer-product sales. The Census of Business provides this yardstick, giving actual rather than estimated figures of the entire retail sales of every state, county, and individual town of over 2,500 population. Annual sales estimates are provided by *Sales Management* and biennial data by Standard Rate and Data Service.

The best known of these indexes, for consumer goods, appears in *Sales Management* in an annual Buying Power Survey index. Figure 15–2 shows excerpts from that issue covering 1975 for the state of Nevada. Of most general usefulness is the "buying power index" that appears in the lower right corner. It is a ready-made general index of buying power based on a weighted average of the three factors reported: population, retail sales, and effective buying income (income after taxes). If a firm judged that its own potentials would be accurately indicated by this, it would expect that 0.313 percent of its national total should be in Nevada and 0.258 percent in its two metropolitan counties (Clark and Washoe). The index is a fine time saver.

The *Sales Management* guide now goes further by predicting future market potential in a separate volume. This is illustrated for Nevada in our Figure 15–3. The rate of increase projected for that state to 1980 is considerably above the growth projected for the nation, especially retail sales in Las Vegas. The state's effective buying-power growth-rate prediction indeed is more than double their average growth prediction for "the thirty most affluent markets." If this guide is reliable for a firm's products, there will be much more gold in Nevada!

15.4.4 Arbitrary-Factors Method

A general index's prime weakness is its failure to account for the factors uniquely affecting the demand for particular products. For the host of

NEVADA

METRO AREAS COUNTIES CITIES	Total Pop. (Thousands)	% Of U.S.	Median Age Of Pop.	18–24 Years	25–34 Years	35–49 Years	50 & Over	Households (Thousands)	Total Retail Sales ($000)	Food ($000)	Eating & Drinking Places ($000)	General Mdse. ($000)	Furnit.-Furnish.-Appl. ($000)	Automotive ($000)	Drug ($000)
LAS VEGAS	335.3	.1563	27.3	12.6	13.4	18.7	21.0	117.5	1,167,260	223,313	127,120	139,928	60,493	205,165	35,443
Clark	335.3	.1563	27.3	12.6	13.4	18.7	21.0	117.5	1,167,260	223,313	127,120	139,928	60,493	205,165	35,443
• Las Vegas	159.7	.0744	28.4	11.2	12.9	19.1	22.4	56.9	729,094	159,101	62,263	73,151	49,225	168,643	20,189
SUBURBAN TOTAL	175.6	.0819	26.4	13.8	14.1	18.3	19.6	60.6	438,166	64,212	64,857	66,777	11,268	36,522	15,254
RENO	149.6	.0697	30.9	11.9	14.9	18.3	25.6	56.5	552,086	109,549	44,556	70,175	27,396	105,618	12,173
Washoe	149.6	.0697	30.9	11.9	14.9	18.3	25.6	56.5	552,086	109,549	44,556	70,175	27,396	105,618	12,173
• Reno	85.9	.0400	32.2	13.2	14.7	17.6	28.2	34.5	444,082	76,246	33,820	56,871	23,042	100,898	9,611
SUBURBAN TOTAL	63.7	.0297	29.2	10.2	15.0	19.2	22.1	22.0	108,004	33,303	10,736	13,304	4,354	4,720	2,562
OTHER DESIGNATED COUNTIES															
Carson City	26.0	.0121	29.7	12.2	12.9	19.6	23.5	8.9	83,322	19,794	5,101	2,004	5,058	15,844	3,296
Carson City	26.0	.0121	29.7	12.2	12.9	19.6	23.5	8.9	83,322	19,794	5,101	2,004	5,058	15,844	3,296
Churchill	12.8	.0059	27.8	12.9	14.6	16.2	23.3	4.6	31,885	9,848	2,970	2,072	904	6,786	597
Elko	16.6	.0078	27.7	13.7	11.8	17.2	24.2	6.0	58,556	14,560	5,166	3,033	1,166	6,388	3,845
Humboldt	6.3	.0030	30.4	12.5	11.6	17.6	27.1	2.2	27,057	6,296	2,426	618	980	2,108	864
Mineral	7.4	.0035	28.0	13.8	13.1	16.1	24.8	2.7	13,069	3,091	674	1,821	356	1,965	252
White Pine	11.3	.0053	26.4	13.4	12.6	16.8	22.4	3.9	33,777	7,067	5,217	3,366	1,153	8,028	740
TOTAL METRO COUNTIES	484.9	.2260	28.5	12.4	13.8	18.6	22.4	174.0	1,719,346	332,862	171,676	210,103	87,889	310,783	47,616
TOTAL DESIGNATED COUNTIES	565.3	.2636	28.5	12.5	13.7	18.5	22.6	202.3	1,967,012	393,518	193,230	223,017	97,506	351,902	57,210
TOTAL STATE	602.9	.2810	28.7	12.5	13.7	18.5	22.9	216.0	2,052,106	415,342	208,399	225,171	98,151	360,552	60,414

EFFECTIVE BUYING INCOME 1975

METRO AREAS COUNTIES CITIES	Total EBI ($000)	Median Hsld. EBI	(A) $8,000–$9,999	(B) $10,000–$14,999	(C) $15,000–$24,999	(D) $25,000 & Over	Buying Power Index
LAS VEGAS	1,800,497	13,959	8.6	22.0	32.7	12.8	.1739
Clark	1,800,497	13,959	8.6	22.0	32.7	12.8	.1739
• Las Vegas	878,344	14,143	7.7	20.4	33.1	13.2	.0925
SUBURBAN TOTAL	922,153	13,791	9.5	23.3	32.2	12.4	.0814
RENO	903,957	13,971	8.1	20.4	31.8	14.1	.0837
Washoe	903,957	13,971	8.1	20.4	31.8	14.1	.0837
• Reno	540,425	13,434	8.3	19.6	30.2	13.8	.0555
SUBURBAN TOTAL	363,532	14,747	7.7	21.9	34.4	14.5	.0282
OTHER DESIGNATED COUNTIES							
Carson City	144,016	14,707	7.7	23.0	34.7	13.9	.0132
Carson City	144,016	14,707	7.7	23.0	34.7	13.9	.0132
Churchill	54,122	9,970	10.9	22.8	21.2	5.8	.0055
Elko	85,831	13,286	7.5	24.6	31.1	9.9	.0086
Humboldt	32,040	12,813	7.8	22.3	29.2	11.2	.0035
Mineral	44,054	15,101	5.3	22.9	34.0	16.4	.0035
White Pine	47,854	11,345	12.8	36.1	22.1	4.2	.0051
TOTAL METRO COUNTIES	2,704,454	13,963	8.5	21.4	32.4	13.2	.2576
TOTAL DESIGNATED COUNTIES	3,112,371	13,814	8.5	21.8	32.0	12.9	.2970
TOTAL STATE	3,310,653	13,723	8.5	22.0	31.7	12.7	.3137

FIGURE 15–2. Data in *Sales and Marketing Management's* Annual Survey of Buying Power

Excerpts from the 1976 report, indicating the types of data provided for all states in the United States and provinces in Canada.

Source: Used by permission of Sales and Marketing Management. *Copyright 1976. Further reproduction not licensed.*

products, demand for which will not follow any averaging figures, a tailor-made index is needed. To obtain such an index one must (1) isolate the important factors affecting this product's demand; (2) obtain data on these factors, suitably classified; (3) convert figures in different units to a common denominator; and (4) combine these series into one index, weighting those with the greater influence. These factors may be selected through the experience or good sense of marketers who have realistic knowledge of the demand conditions for the product. We speak of *factors* because, in the complex of markets, no single factor alone is likely to shape the demand for any product. Among the data employed, incidentally, might be one of the indexes already discussed. When blended with special factors applying to the product, such an index may give a valid yardstick for the particular product.

As a hypothetical example, a manufacturer of auto parts might find that *Sales Management's* buying power index poorly reflected the demand for its type of product and therefore constructed their own index with arbitrarily selected factors. They might utilize data from various sources,

STATE SMM METROPOLITAN AREA County	POPULATION					EFFECTIVE BUYING INCOME				RETAIL SALES				BUYING POWER INDEX	
	12/31/75 Total Pop. (Thous.)	12/31/80 Total Pop. (Thous.)	% Change 1975–1980	12/31/80 Total Households (Thous.)	% Change 1975–1980	1980 Total EBI ($000)	% Change 1975–1980	Average Household EBI 1975	1980	1980 Total Retail Sales ($000)	% Change 1975–1980	Retail Sales Per Household 1975	1980	1975	1980
NEVADA															
LAS VEGAS	335.3	384.9	14.8	144.3	22.8	2,916,600	62.0	15,323	20,212	1,870,550	60.3	9,934	12,963	.1739	.1913
Clark	335.3	384.9	14.8	144.3	22.8	2,916,600	62.0	15,323	20,212	1,870,550	60.3	9,934	12,963	.1739	.1913
RENO	149.6	176.4	17.9	71.3	26.2	1,531,816	69.5	15,999	21,484	728,166	31.9	9,771	10,213	.0837	.0897
Washoe	149.6	176.4	17.9	71.3	26.2	1,531,816	69.5	15,999	21,484	728,166	31.9	9,771	10,213	.0837	.0897
TOTAL METRO COUNTIES	484.9	561.3	15.8	215.6	23.9	4,448,416	64.5	15,543	20,633	2,598,716	51.1	9,881	12,053	.2576	.2810
TOTAL STATE	602.9	693.4	15.0	265.9	23.1	5,419,827	63.7	15,327	20,383	3,104,386	51.3	9,500	11,675	.3137	.3413

FIGURE 15–3. Projections from *Sales and Marketing Management's* Annual Survey of Buying Power

Source: Used by permission of Sales and Marketing Management. *Copyright 1976. Further reproduction not licensed.*

although our example will utilize those we have just seen from the *Sales Management* survey. Let us say that they used automotive sales (with a weight of 4 points), total population (3 points), and effective buying income (3 points). Applying those weightings to the three factors expressed as percentages of the United States totals, the following arbitrary-factors index might be computed for the Reno, Nevada area:

Factor	Unweighted Percent of Total United States	Weights	Weighted Percent
Automotive sales	0.0944	4	0.3776
Total population	0.0697	3	0.2091
Effective buying income	0.0837	3	0.2611
		10	0.8478 ÷ 10 = 0.0848

It will be noted that this yields a somewhat higher index for the Reno area than its buying power index in Figure 15–2 (0.0837).

15.4.5 Multiple-Correlation Method

Dissatisfaction with the cruder yardsticks of market potential led to the development of the multiple-correlation method, which is based on the theory that, if certain factors are truly related to the demand for the product, this has been evidenced in the past. Thus, the best combination of these factors is that which most closely correlates with past sales of the industry. The relationship that has held true in the past should hold true in the present; markets shown to be relatively high or low by this multiple index are presumed to offer those relative potentials to the manufacturer at present.

440

Up to a point, the method resembles the arbitrary-factors method, but the analyst does not arbitrarily select the factors. Instead, one experiments with all factors suspected of having a strong causal relationship to product demand. These factors may be correlated separately before combining them, but the analyst must be careful not to overlook factors with a negative correlation or factors whose influence can be recognized only when combined with other influencing factors. Since the correlation is multiple, various combinations and weightings of independent variables must be tried against the one dependent variable, the product sales. Until this long process of testing has been performed, the analyst cannot select the series for the index with any confidence.

The degree of correlation might be judged graphically by plotting each combination against the dependent variables in pairs and eliminating those which appear to have the poorer correlation. Simple graphic judgment is too imprecise to select among alternative combinations of data series, and anyway one must necessarily use a computer to do the complex and numerous calculations involved—for there may be a very large number of possibly associated factors, with many combinations and weightings to be tested. Among the various analytical methods suitable to market analysis determinations, factor analysis is particularly helpful in selecting the optimal combination of factors and their factor loadings.

Multiple correlation represents the furthest advance in market analysis, although some recently advocated new techniques or combinations of techniques may be better. Multiple correlation has these defects: (1) it is so complicated that businessmen are unlikely to understand or have faith in it; (2) the correlation found may be spurious—a mere coincidence rather than an actual cause-and-effect relationship; (3) the method assumes that the pattern of sales success realized in the past by the industry ought to be that of the future; (4) the cost and effort of the calculation may not be worth the result; and (5) the data needed may be unobtainable.

15.5   Sales Forecasting

Sales forecasting undertakes to measure the most likely level of sales during a specific period in the future. Predicting future market levels is both difficult and hazardous, but it is imperative because of the many forward commitments that every business must make. Although sales forecasting has been developing as a distinct branch of research, it is actually an extension of market analysis. Specialized business economists often are retained to do market and sales forecasting, but otherwise it is in the province of the marketing research department.

Some businesses have a routine need for long-range sales forecasting—five years or longer—others require occasional forecasts. The principles involved in making forecasts are sufficiently similar that we shall not distinguish between the long-range and short-range forecast. Utilities must design and locate their facilities to provide for demand ten years or more ahead. Frequently, manufacturers must plan their plant construction just as far in advance. Short-range forecasting is more evident on the business scene. Annual forecasts of sales in the approaching fiscal year are a first step in budgeting all the activities and variable expenditures of the firm.

Since almost all major functions of the business have a stake in the final forecasts, a number of executives may participate in the review of preliminary forecasts. When the final forecasts are established, the figures must be distributed to the responsible executives for application.

Sales forecasting has two points of departure: one uses the whole economy; the other, individual markets. The first starts with economic forecasts of the national economy, probably beginning with the estimate of the gross national product (GNP). This is a published projection of federal government forecasts, although private economists also predict GNP. The segments within the GNP forecast more directly affecting the particular business are also examined. Next, the level of the particular industry and its major product fields may be forecasted. From this, a sales forecast for the specific company may be derived when other factors peculiar to that company are considered. Finally, the forecast is broken down to the individual items produced or marketed by the company.

The second approach builds up from the individual markets and products that, taken together, compose the total sales forecast for the company. Initially, individual market areas and end uses of the product might be examined to judge what may happen within individual customer categories. Specific plans of the company, such as product-line expansions or new production facilities, are weighed into the consolidations of the individual market forecasts.

In practice, it is unwise to use either approach exclusively. The company exists in the context of the national economy, yet it may be affected by forces and actions that are not reflected in total industry data. One can make separate forecasts from each of the approaches discussed and then compromise them, but this is not essential.

Whatever methods are employed in the forecasting procedure, they require the following sequence of steps:[11]

1. Determine the purposes for which forecasts are to be used.
2. Divide the company's products into homogeneous groups.
3. Determine the factors affecting the sales of each product group and their relative importance.
4. Choose the forecasting method or methods best suited to the job.
5. Gather all the available data.
6. Analyze the data.
7. Check and cross-check the deductions resulting from the analysis.
8. Make assumptions regarding the effect of factors that cannot be measured or forecast.
9. Convert the deductions and assumptions into specific product and territorial forecasts and quotas.

---

[11] "Forecasting Sales," *Studies in Business Policy, No. 106* (New York: The National Industrial Conference Board, Inc., 1964), p. 8

10. Apply these to the company's operation.
11. Review performance and revise forecasts periodically.

15.5.1 Opinion Methods

Forecasts of sales may be determined in part by the judgment of persons who are believed to be familiar with the conditions foreshadowing future demand. The methods worthy of consideration find safety in numbers, because several persons participate in the forecasting.

Jury of executive opinion. The jury-of-executive-opinion method makes use of the opinions of executives of the company, preferably those most qualified to foresee the trend of business. The method provides a forecast quickly and easily and often is the only feasible means of forecasting, but it does have demerits. The forecasters think subjectively and may be affected by the mass psychology of businesspersons, with whom moods of optimism and pessimism are contagious. To overcome this, the executives may be provided with economic facts bearing on the general business situation. Before making their individual forecasts, they may participate in meetings to discuss the facts and conditions; at later meetings they may discuss their forecasts with each other. A tendency exists, as well, to arrive at a composite by averaging different opinions. This does not necessarily lead to more accuracy, but a carefully executed use of the *Delphi technique,* which is based primarily on this idea, is reputed to substantially enhance a forecast's validity.

Grass-roots approach. This approach calls upon each of the salespeople in the various sales districts to make a forecast for his or her district. Usually the salesperson is urged to tabulate anticipated sales for each account in the territory. The forecasts are checked by district managers and finally combined into a composite forecast at the head office. This method incorporates the influences affecting sales in each area. There are many advantages to the method: it uses the knowledge of those closest to the market, is psychologically good for the salesforce if quotas are based on the estimates, and easily lends itself to market area analysis or any other breakdown. On the other hand, salespersons have neither the temperament nor the training for making objective forecasts, as a rule are unaware of more general economic forces bearing on the forecast, and trend to underestimate if quotas are based upon the estimates. Companies using this method have found three principal means of increasing its accuracy:[12]

1. Putting past performance records in the hands of salespeople for their guidance in making estimates of future sales.
2. Giving the salespeople an official business outlook forecast for their guidance.
3. Having the regional manager discuss the forecasts with each sales-

---

[12] "Forecasting Sales," p. 24.

443

person in order to temper the latter's thinking and assay the reasons behind unusual forecasts.

The method is most valid in industries whose product is sold directly to a relatively few customers, who are thus able to give the salesforce an indication of the future demand for the product.

Surveys of buying intentions. A third opinion method of projecting future sales is on the basis of what purchasers say they expect to buy during the forthcoming year or period. Repetitive surveys, using uniform questioning and sampling procedures, provide a means of judging at least the direction and perhaps the degree of change in probable buying rates.

A number of surveys of buying intentions, both public and private, are conducted annually. Those conducted among business buyers appear to be better developed than those conducted in the consumer area. The forecasts of car loadings based on shippers' forecasts have been fairly accurate for a number of years. Among the best known of the more general surveys in industrial areas are those on new plant and equipment expenditures of the U.S. Department of Commerce and those of the McGraw-Hill magazines.

Most prominent among surveys of consumers' intentions is that conducted by the University of Michigan Survey Research Center. Its "Survey of Consumer Finances" has been particularly applicable to consumer-durable-goods forecasts. Private research firms conduct similar surveys for clients. Their results have proved reasonably accurate in most years, but forecasters should allow some margin of error in buyers' anticipations.

15.5.2 Statistical Methods

By utilizing the analysis of statistics as far as practicable, one narrows the latitude for inference and places the forecast on a more objective basis. Although one may doubt whether forecasting can ever be a true science, since every estimate of the future contains some speculation, the statistical method tends to be scientific.

The two types of statistical forecasting methods are essentially: trend and cycle analysis, and correlation methods. Although these might be used singly, it is better to employ both before arriving at the final forecast. Many companies, indeed, combine these methods with an opinion method and average the results into a composite forecast.

Trend and cycle analysis. This type of analysis describes the group of statistical forecasts that project data of the present and recent past into the future. *Trend analysis* is predicated on the assumption that a current trend will continue; hence, one may project historical series of data on the company's and industry's sales. Such projections are not mere lines drawn on a chart, but should be based on the proper statistical formulas for computing secular trends.

Cycle analysis recognizes that history tends to repeat itself in the ups and downs of business. The timing and degree of the incidence of the business cycle on various products' sales differ, and a careful study must be made for each product. A trend analysis is faulty if it does not take cyclical swings into consideration. Cyclical estimates are more likely to be accurate for long-range than for short-range forecasts. Indeed, the timing of cycles has been so erratic that the effect of this force seldom can be foretold over a short period.

Trend and cycle analysis is somewhat the counterpart of using direct sales analysis in measuring market potential, for it employs sales figures as the basis of the sales forecast.

Correlation methods. Correlation analysis is quite different. In correlation analysis the forecaster needs to find and measure the factors sensitive to coming changes in demand well in advance of the time when the product's sales are affected. That is, one seeks to find a "lead–lag" relationship in which the product's sales lag behind the indicators. Substantial progress has been made in identifying factors that have a lead relationship, at least with respect to changes in the general economy. The National Bureau of Economic Research determined that the following series of regularly published data tend to have this "lead" property:[13]

> Business failures—total liabilities (inverse correlation).
>
> Industrial common stock price index.
>
> Manufacturers' new orders—total durable goods industries.
>
> Construction contracts awarded in thirty-seven states—nonresidential and residential buildings—in square feet.
>
> Average weekly hours per manufacturing worker.
>
> New business incorporations—total number.
>
> Wholesale price index of twenty-eight basic commodities.

For individual enterprises, simple measures may provide clues to the future. A consumer-goods manufacturer may find that sales at the retail level anticipate changes in factory sales by a given number of months. Some industrial-goods manufacturers may judge future sales by an "end-use" analysis of the industries to which they sell, but this requires one to find clues to future volume in those industries. That is, it requires correlating past sales for many years with some objective characteristic of the buyers, such as number of employees or kilowatt-hours used, and then measuring the changes in the magnitude of the objective characteristic in the future. Whatever the factors found suitable, however, the objective is the same: finding factors that change in advance of and in the same direction as changes in the demand for the product.

Simple correlation is a useful tool, but sales tend to be correlated with a combination of factors. Therefore, multiple correlation formulas typi-

---

[13] Geoffrey Moore, "Measuring Recessions," *Occasional Paper, No. 61* (New York: National Bureau of Economic Research, 1958).

cally are needed, which lead to a regression formula with which future sales levels can be projected mathematically.

The hunt for factors with a lead–lag relationship to the sales of a specific product may be tedious. Usually, many indicators selected by judgment must be tried before a satisfactory one is found. A major step in sales forecasting is finding and selecting the statistical series that is pertinent as well as accurate. For many of the ideal forecasting factors, data may be nonexistent or inaccessible, while available data may not be useful. Gross national income is a significant figure for the forecaster, but this figure is determined only quarterly, which scarcely enables the analyst to detect sensitive and temporary shifts in time to alter sales forecasts properly. Retail sales data are widely deemed to be good barometers of changing demand, but indexes of total retail sales are not published until two months after the month reported; this overall delay of three months gives the figures only historical significance for short-run forecasts.

A large number of sources and types of data may be valid forecasting indicators for a number of businesses. Hence, the analyst needs to know about these data and about their virtues and limitations. The possible sources of forecasting data are many, and the analyst learns to discriminate and understand the character and significance of available series. One should then test their statistical applicability to the markets and sales that one is trying to forecast.

Input/output analysis. The concept of input/output is becoming a widely used and valuable tool. In this type of analysis the analyst should take into consideration a large number of factors, or inputs, that influence the outputs he is trying to predict. In a standard model for the entire national economy, a 90×90 matrix of columns is employed, in which the inputs are arrayed horizontally as the column headings and the outputs are labeled as the stubs. With an input/output (I/O) model, technological and other changes can be calculated for each industry arrayed across the matrix columns as inputs. Then, with the total prediction for each industry, which is a potential customer of other industries, its total can be distributed across the various industries from which it purchases. We have made only a very general statement, indeed, about the nature of I/O analysis, and one must turn to the extensive technical literature for an adequate explanation.

An example of I/O use in sales forecasting was recently reported in the refractories division of Combustion Engineering, Inc.[14] This forecast was performed in six stages, which are depicted in Figure 15–4. The top two boxes in the "hierarchy of forecasts" comprise inputs into the I/O model. From those individual industry forecasts were determined the customer class potentials and then the market forecasts of refractories consumption. Then the sales forecasts for Combustion Engineering's division were made over a long-term, and then over a short-term, period.

---

[14] Elliot D. Ranard, "Use of Input/Output Concepts in Sales Forecasting," *Journal of Marketing Research*, February, 1972, pp. 53–58.

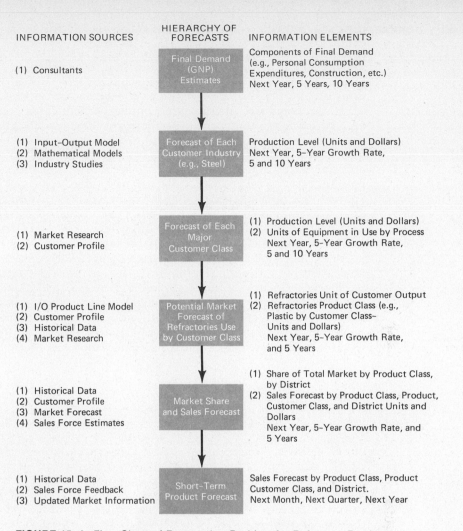

INFORMATION SOURCES	HIERARCHY OF FORECASTS	INFORMATION ELEMENTS
(1) Consultants	Final Demand (GNP) Estimates	Components of Final Demand (e.g., Personal Consumption Expenditures, Construction, etc.) Next Year, 5 Years, 10 Years
(1) Input–Output Model (2) Mathematical Models (3) Industry Studies	Forecast of Each Customer Industry (e.g., Steel)	Production Level (Units and Dollars) Next Year, 5-Year Growth Rate, 5 and 10 Years
(1) Market Research (2) Customer Profile	Forecast of Each Major Customer Class	(1) Production Level (Units and Dollars) (2) Units of Equipment in Use by Process Next Year, 5-Year Growth Rate, 5 and 10 Years
(1) I/O Product Line Model (2) Customer Profile (3) Historical Data (4) Market Research	Potential Market Forecast of Refractories Use by Customer Class	(1) Refractories Unit of Customer Output (2) Refractories Product Class (e.g., Plastic by Customer Class– Units and Dollars) Next Year, 5-Year Growth Rate, and 5 Years
(1) Historical Data (2) Customer Profile (3) Market Forecast (4) Sales Force Estimates	Market Share and Sales Forecast	(1) Share of Total Market by Product Class, by District (2) Sales Forecast by Product Class, Product, Customer Class, and District Units and Dollars Next Year, 5-Year Growth Rate, and 5 Years
(1) Historical Data (2) Sales Force Feedback (3) Updated Market Information	Short-Term Product Forecast	Sales Forecast by Product Class, Product Customer Class, and District. Next Month, Next Quarter, Next Year

FIGURE 15–4. Flow Chart of Forecasting Problem for Refractory Products

Source: Reprinted from The Journal of Marketing Research, *published by the American Marketing Association, February, 1972, p. 54.*

The chart is interesting with respect to its forecasting information sources listed at the left, as well as the forecast outputs shown at the right.

The use of I/O analysis in sales forecasting seems to be valuable largely for products sold to industrial, governmental, and institutional markets that have discrete segments and usage patterns. They also would need to have demands derived objectively from more primary demands that are predictable. For consumer products and services, the other methods described earlier are applicable. We should recognize, too, that many of the values calculated to enter in an I/O matrix are reached by utilizing one of the other statistical or opinion methods of forecasting.

15.6 Summary

Market-potential measurement is the kind of marketing research most generally done in business. This might be expected because many decisions turn on detailed knowledge of the best sales opportunities and of what sales volume to plan in forthcoming periods. This general research area of market-potential measurement may be divided into (1) qualitative market analysis, which identifies and diagnoses markets; and (2) quantitative analysis, which cannot be done accurately without a logical qualitative basis. Quantitative analysis is used to estimate current potentials and also to make sales forecasts of future demand. The potential analysis may be of the total market for an industry, product, or service— or it may compare various areas' potentials. In either case, one may be measuring "market" potential for all sellers of a particular product or the "sales" potential for an individual seller.

All estimates of market potentials, whether in current or future markets, are subject to some degree of error since they are, after all, merely intelligent estimates. Their accuracy improves as techniques are refined and data are made more dependable. Accuracy increases further when the analyst compares estimates with subsequent results and keeps adequate records of the methodology used in past efforts. In the meantime, when management uses the analyst's conclusions, it must recognize that they are affected by some degree of imprecision.

CASE 15

CENTRAL CITY REPORTER (B)

After the data in Case 14, Central City Reporter (A), had been collected and analyzed, they were put in tabular form ready for presentation in a report. Tables 1 through 16 were prepared by the technical staff and made ready for the report writer to incorporate in the final report. Refer to the questionnaire given with Case 14 so that you will be familiar with the questions that drew the responses described in these tables.

Discussion

Assuming that you are the report writer, do the two tasks described in the following assignment.

1. Prepare an outline of the various sections that you would set up for the final report.

2. Write an overall summary for a company executive to read so that he
or she will understand highlights of the report.

TABLE 1. Survey Sample

Total telephone numbers selected	488	
Noneligible numbers (disconnected, nonresidential phone, and the like)	63	
Eligible sample	425	
Interviewed		400
Refused		12
No answer		13

TABLE 2. Newspapers Read

Question 3 Local Newspapers Read	Percent of Sample
The Reporter only	29
The Star only	32
The University News only	4
The Reporter and *The Star*	25
The Reporter and *The University News*	2
The Star and *The University News*	1
All three	2
None	5
Total	100
Base	400

TABLE 3. Stock-Market Readership

Question 1B Notice of Stock-Market Quotations	Percent of Sample	
No	43	
Don't know	9	
Yes: *The Reporter*	26	
Sunday		20
Daily		5
Don't know		1
Yes: *The Star*	16	
Sunday		5
Daily		10
Don't know		1
Yes: *The Reporter* and *The Star*	3	
Sunday		1
Daily		2
Yes: Don't know which paper	3	

TABLE 4. Local Newspapers Read (percent) [a]

Question 1B Notice of Stock-Market Quotations	The Reporter only	The Star only	Both	Neither
No or don't know	35	61	48	91
Yes: *The Reporter*	56	6	24	3
Yes: *The Star*	4	31	15	3
Yes: Both	3	1	6	
Yes: Don't know which	2		7	3
Total	100	99[b]	100	100
Base	124	132	110	34

[a] Excluding *The University News.*
[b] In this table and those that follow some columns do not total 100 percent because individual percentages are rounded.

TABLE 5. Reader by Sex (percent)

Question 1B Notice of Stock-Market Quotations	Male	Female
No or don't know	48	56
Yes: *The Reporter*	29	23
Yes: *The Star*	15	17
Yes: Both	4	2
Yes: Don't know which	3	2
Total	99	100
Base	205	195

TABLE 6. Education of Readers (percent)

Question 1B Notice of Stock-Market Quotations	Grade School	High School	College or More
No or don't know	50	50	55
Yes: *The Reporter*	22	23	30
Yes: *The Star*	22	18	12
Yes: Both	4	4	2
Yes: Don't know which		5	1
Total	98	100	100
Base	50	167	178

TABLE 7. Length of Readers Residence in Area (percent)

Question 1B Notice of Stock-Market Quotations	Less Than 1 Year	1–2.9 Years	3–9.9 Years	10 or More Years
No or don't know	70	55	49	51
Yes: *The Reporter*	26	24	32	25
Yes: *The Star*	4	11	14	19

450

TABLE 7. *Continued*

Question 1B Notice of Stock-Market Quotations	Less Than 1 Year	1–2.9 Years	3–9.9 Years	10 or More Years
Yes: Both		8	1	2
Yes: Don't know which		2	4	3
Total	100	100	100	100
Base	23	62	77	237

TABLE 8. Respondents' Notice of Color Ads

Question 1C Notice of Color Ads	Percent of Sample
No	36
Don't know	6
Yes: *The Reporter*	14
Yes: *The Star*	31
Yes: *The Reporter* and *The Star*	6
Yes: Don't know which paper	7
Total	100
Base	400

TABLE 9. Notice of Color Ads Broken Down by Length of Residence in Area (percent)

Question 1C Notice of Color Ads	Less Than 1 Year	1–2.9 Years	3–9.9 Years	10 or More Years
No or don't know	61	56	45	35
Yes: *The Reporter*	13	11	18	13
Yes: *The Star*	17	23	22	37
Yes: Both		5	9	6
Yes: Don't know which	9	5	5	9
Total	100	100	99	100
Base	23	62	77	237

TABLE 10. Readership of Drew Pearson's Column (percent)

	Local Newspaper Read				
Question 1A Notice of Feature	The Reporter	The Star	The University News	None	Total
No or don't know	69	52	64	95	62
Yes: *The Reporter*	3	1	6	5	3
Yes: *The Star*	23	43	28		32

TABLE 10. *Continued*

	Local Newspaper Read				
Question 1A *Notice of Feature*	The Reporter	The Star	The University News	*None*	*Total*
Yes: *The University News*	1				a
Yes: *The Reporter* and *The Star*	1	1			a
Yes: Don't know which	3	3	3		3
Total	100	100	101	100	100
Base (mentions)	234	242	34	20	530

a Less than 0.5 percent.

TABLE 11. Notice of *New York Times* News Service (percent)

	Local Newspaper Read				
Question 1E *Notice of Feature*	The Reporter	The Star	The University News	*None*	*Total*
No or don't know	80	89	76	95	85
Yes: *The Reporter*	16	4	18		10
Yes: *The Star*	1	5			2
Yes: *The University News*			3		a
Yes: *The Reporter* and *The Star*	1	1	3	5	1
Yes: Don't know which	2	1			1
Total	100	100	100	100	99
Base	234	242	34	20	530

a Less than 0.5 percent.

TABLE 12. Readership of National Weather Map (percent)

	Local Newspaper Read				
Question 1D *Notice of Feature*	The Reporter	The Star	The University News	*None*	*Total*
No or don't know	50	42	65	95	48
Yes: *The Reporter*	20	4	12		12
Yes: *The Star*	20	46	18		31
Yes: *The Reporter* and *The Star*	5	5	3		5
Yes: Don't know which	5	3	3	5	4
Total	100	100	101	100	100
Base	234	242	34	20	530

TABLE 13. Readership of the Book Review Section (percent)

Question 1F Notice of Feature	Local Newspaper Read				
	The Reporter	The Star	The University News	None	Total
No or don't know	61	55	56	95	59
Yes: *The Reporter*	18	6	3		11
Yes: *The Star*	11	31	6		19
Yes: *The University News*	1	1	15	5	2
Yes: *The Reporter* and *The Star*	5	4	6		4
Yes: *The Star* and *The University News*	1	1	6		1
Yes: All three	1		3		1
Yes: Don't know which	3	2	6		3
Total	101	100	101	100	100
Base	234	242	34	20	530

TABLE 14. Age Breakdown of Respondents (percent)

Questions 3 and 4B Newspapers Read	Under 29	30–39	40–59	60 and Over
The Reporter only	33	30	21	37
The Star only	26	35	32	38
The University News only	11	1		
The Reporter and *The Star*	11	27	38	25
The Reporter and *The University News*	4	2	1	
The Star and *The University News*	2		1	
All three	4	1	2	
None	9	4	5	
Total	100	100	100	100
Base	122	85	126	63

TABLE 15. Education of Respondents (percent)

Questions 3 and 4C Newspapers Read	Grade School or Less	High School	College or More
The Reporter only	38	30	25
The Star only	32	34	30
The University News only			8
The Reporter and *The Star*	22	30	22
The Reporter and *The University News*			4
The Star and *The University News*		1	1
All three		1	4
None	8	4	5
Total	100	100	99
Base	50	167	178

453

TABLE 16. Stock Ownership of Respondent

Question 4D Own Common or Preferred Stock	Percent of Sample
Yes	22
No	77
No answer	1
Total	100
Base	400

CASE 16

ACETAM LABORATORIES, INC.

Acetam Laboratories is the manufacturer of a medicine tablet which is described as safe and quick to provide temporary relief from headache, muscular aches, aches and pains associated with neuralgia, discomfort of fever due to colds and flu, and minor aches and pains of arthritis. The marketing research manager was interested in finding out which medicine on the market, directly competing with Acetam, was preferred for the following medical discomforts: headache, muscular aches, neuralgia, fever due to colds, and aches due to arthritis. The research department conducted a survey in which hundreds of individuals were questioned as to their preference of a medicine that was a safe, fast pain reliever for these ailments. The following tabulation of answers was presented to the research manager for interpretation:

	Ailment				
Medicine	Cold	Headache	Muscular Aches	Neuralgia	Arthritis
Acetam	297	432	78	165	154
T-Nol	123	115	34	195	65
Day Care	359	0	0	0	0
Aspirin	304	157	237	104	377
Anacin	267	126	189	197	277
Others	68	487	390	376	335

After the results of the survey, Acetam decided to develop an advertising campaign geared to television audiences. After a three-month campaign, the marketing manager received a report based on a survey conducted by the Universal Broadcasting System (UBS). In this study, hundreds of individuals were interviewed on a number of topics, among them their preference for an over-the-counter medicine that was safe, fast pain reliever. The UBS reproduced a special report for the major medicine selected for the ailments described above. The report indicated for the Acetam Tablets that preference

454

had changed to: colds, 356; headache, 450; muscular aches, 80; neuralgia, 200; and arthritis, 300.

Discussion

1. If you were Acetam's marketing manager, how would you interpret the relative importance of *each* medicine for the stated ailments?
2. How would you represent, in terms of percents, the influence that each ailment had upon the selection of the medicine purchased?
3. How would you interpret and summarize the resurvey figures stated in the UBS report?

CASE 17

VALUE-MART DISCOUNT STORES

Value-Mart Discount Stores[15] is a regionally based chain of twenty stores. Merchandise that consumers purchase regularly is usually priced on a competitive basis. Value-Mart is contemplating purchasing a large lot of wooden folding chairs direct from the manufacturer. The manufacturer produces three different styles in the stained chairs. Because Value-Mart estimated that 20,000 of these chairs will be sold next year, the marketing research department was asked to conduct an in-store survey to see if the consumers had a preference for style of chair. If the consumers perceived a difference in style and preferred a particular style, the buyer for Value-Mart would place an order reflecting the consumers' preference.

The company decides to make the final determination on the basis of a limited sales test, where each style is introduced in independent random samples of eight stores each. The test results are as follows:

	Style of Chair		
Store	Style 1	Style 2	Style 3
A	41	50	43
B	36	35	30
C	40	57	41
D	52	53	54
E	37	62	30
F	38	49	29
G	42	55	33
H	39	48	30

---

[15] Fictitious name.

Discussion

1. What analytical technique(s) would be appropriate for analyzing the data? Run an analysis on the data. What conclusion(s) do you reach?

CASE 18

RAINBOW PAINT COMPANY

As a basis for setting up forecasts of its business volume during 1977, the marketing research manager of the Rainbow Paint Company made an inquiry into the outlook of its customers. The company manufactured a general line of exterior and interior paints and sold to three categories of buyers: contractors, industrial users, and retail building supply dealers. (There is no question about the fairness of the sampling of customers in this survey.)

The number of customers queried and their expressed outlooks for 1977 were as follows:

Type of Customer	Expect That Their Business Will:		
	Increase	Remain the Same	Decrease
Industrial	95	60	50
Contractor	130	90	90
Retailer	45	40	70

Discussion

1. When the research manager received these data he realized that he could compute the percentages either horizontally or vertically. In which dimension should they be computed? For what reason? Compute the percentages.

CASE 19

HANOVER DEPARTMENT STORE

The personnel manager of Hanover Department Store believes that her department receives an average of fifteen complaints per week about the performance of the sales personnel. The Vice-President of Personnel wants a study conducted to verify the claim. If the personnel manager's idea of the number of complaints is an understatement, something must be done to improve the manner in which the sales personnel handle the store's customers. A sample of three months yielded an average of nineteen complaints a week, with a standard deviation of three complaints.

Discussion

1. Run an analysis of the data, making the appropriate assumptions. From the standpoint of statistical significance, how strongly would you rely on your conclusion?

CASE 20

SUDSWAY COMPANY

When the Sudsway Company interviews prospective salespersons, they are given the Bromberg test. This test, named for the psychologist who devised it, measures the degree to which the candidate seems to have a propensity, and the personality, for selling. The test has been employed since 1964, and one day early in 1977 the sales manager asked that an analysis be made of how accurate the test had been in indicating selling ability. A few times earlier the test scores had been evaluated in terms of how well they predicted whether salespersons would or would not remain permanently with the company (which the scores did predict fairly well), but how well they predicted the relative effectiveness of those who did stay with Sudsway had not been tested.

This task was delegated to the marketing research supervisor. She agreed with the sales manager's view that the first year of selling would not fairly indicate a person's ability, and decided that an average of five years of selling would be a proper range, to smooth out year-to-year oscillations. Therefore, only people with at least five years of selling with Sudsway were included, and to avoid inclusion of persons with noncomparable ages, she excluded those who had been selling more than ten years.

Twelve persons in the salesforce had been hired from 1970 through 1975, and their employment records were obtained from the personnel office. The extent to which these people had attained their annual sales quota seemed a fair indicator of sales effectiveness. The data collected were as follows:

Salesperson	Average Percentage of Sales Quota Obtained 1970–1975	Score on Bromberg Test When Hired
A	87	75
B	98	90
C	110	96
D	108	92
E	93	82
F	100	84
G	103	91
H	98	87
I	101	83
J	105	90
K	96	84
L	107	92

Discussion

1. What analytic technique(s) would be appropriate for analyzing these data? Use a simple method to perform the calculations. Do you find that the Bromberg test relates well to subsequent sales effectiveness?

CASE 21

COCA-COLA USA (C)

The Coca-Cola Company was a very prosperous enterprise in September, 1962, and had enjoyed during the past ten years a sales increase from $246,000,000 to $567,000,000. Despite some diversification of products, its original Coca-Cola[16] brand still accounted for the greater part of company sales volume.

A basic tenet of the Company was that soft drinks live or die on their advertising. In the annual advertising campaigns for Coca-Cola, there was concentration on a single theme, rendered over radio and television as a sung jingle. At the time of which we speak, the current theme was "Zing—Refreshing New Feeling!" As a theme survived for only two or three years, the search was on to find a new theme that would be a fitting successor.

An extensive series of studies was under way, for which the advertising agency McCann-Erickson, Inc., was responsible. These studies were systematically designed to explore a large number of candidate jingles that had been created by the agency. This series had begun in June, 1961, and culminated within a year, and three possible jingles rated highest. They incorporated either the theme (1) "Spirit of Coke" or (2) "Things Go Better With

---

[16] "Coca-Cola" and "Coke" are registered trademarks of The Coca-Cola Company.

Coke" (TGB). There were two versions of music to accompany them, known as "musical" (soft music) and "sounds" (sound effects of pouring Coke). These were the three finalists among the jingles:

Spirit—sounds
TGB—sounds
TGB—musical

To select the most effective of these, a conclusive study was conducted from June through August of 1962. Its methodology and results are presented next.

Objective. To select the most effective of the three radio jingles emerging from earlier studies, by testing each under normal competitive conditions. "Effectiveness" was defined as the message's ability to change consumer awareness, image, and use of Coca-Cola.

Behavioral model. The scheme of how advertising operates, as visualized by the responsible advertising agency personnel, was roughly like this:

1. Advertising's ultimate result should be increased sales.
2. Nevertheless, advertising has a gradual and cumulative effect on the prospective buyer in eventually changing his attitude to the point of actually buying the brand. Therefore, actual sales response may be remote from the incidence of the advertising.
3. A consumer's progress toward actual brand adoption tends to follow these five cumulative steps:
   a. He or she becomes aware of the brand's advertising, which leads to:
   b. Becoming more aware of the brand, which leads to:
   c. An increasingly favorable image of the brand, which leads to:
   d. The brand becoming his or her favorite, which leads to:
   e. Increased purchase of the brand.

This process tends to be slow. Therefore, measurement of advertising's effects in a short test period must be sensitive to the extent to which the prospective buyers are moved through these successive stages.

Method. Two phases would be conducted, so as to reflect the problem model:

1. A marketing experiment isolating the effects of the three selected commercials in separate markets, in which sales results would be determined. As a "control" for evaluating the three test commercials, the current theme ("Zing . . . ") would be given a similar market test.
2. An interview survey of consumers in these same markets. This would be a "before-and-after" survey of the same persons to determine changes in their attitudes and consumption, in terms of the five stages listed above, in association with their exposure to the test advertising.

Some details of the research were as follows:

1. *Exposure to advertising.* Each of the three selected commercials and the current one would be broadcast in spot radio time, in a pair of cities. In all markets this would be carried on from July 9 to August 5, 1962. In each market the broadcast weight would be intensive, using over four times the normal frequency of radio commercials for Coke. In timing, 40 percent of the spots would be at heavy auto traffic periods and 50 percent at periods of heavy teenager listening. Three-fourths of the commercials would be of sixty-second length and the balance of thirty seconds.

2. *Sales measurements.* Numbers of cases of Coke sold by each bottler would be determined. These would be reported, as normally, by month, and June, July, and August sales would be analyzed. July would, of course, include twenty-three days of the advertising exposure period. Thus, pretest, test, and posttest months would be provided. Consumer purchase data also would be asked in the before and after surveys.

3. *Interview method.* Telephone interviews would be conducted by interviewers in the test and control cities, who would identify themselves only as working for Marplan. Two waves of interviews would take place: the week following July 2, and the week following August 6. All persons who were successfully interviewed in wave 1 would be called in wave 2, and the identical questionnaire used in each wave. Thus, attitudes and buying behavior after the test period could be compared with those existing before it.

4. *Interview content.* The following data were sought in the telephone interviews:

   Brand awareness. Awareness of Coca-Cola and competing brands.

   Consumption. Share of the last ten bottles consumed which was represented by Coke, and share of the "last bottle" consumed held by Coke.

   Attitudes. Brands favored and why; selected image factors.

   Advertising reactions. Which advertising preferred, message recall, media recall, likes and dislikes of advertising.

Sample. The market areas were deliberately chosen on the basis of twenty-seven competitive consumption and economic factors. Two cities were selected for each of the three commercials tested and, for the control area that broadcasted the current jingle. After considering all nonsuburban cities of 40,000 to 75,000 population (130 in all), the researchers found only seven that qualified, so an eighth, larger city was added. Each city was the location of a Coca-Cola bottler serving its surrounding area.

For each pair, one city of high per capita consumption of coke and one of low consumption was chosen. The following pairs were used:

Test jingle 1—Texarkana, Texas
                    Parkersburg, West Virginia

Test jingle 2—Tyler, Texas
Pittsfield, Massachusetts
Test jingle 3—Lake Charles, Louisiana
Sioux Falls, South Dakota
Control jingle—Spartanburg, South Carolina
Stockton, California

Per capita consumption of Coke in these cities ranged from an average of 42 bottles in the four low cities to 130 bottles in the high cities.

The interview panel for the telephone survey was composed, for the first ("before") interview, of at least 500 persons in each city, with a total sample of 4,022. In the second wave ("after"), successful interviews were made with 81 percent of these persons, for a total sample of 3,242. Numbers were selected at random from local telephone directories. Quotas assigned to interviewers required that 20 percent be with teenaged boys, 20 percent with teenaged girls, 40 percent with housewives under forty-five years who had teenaged children, and 20 percent with other housewives under forty-five years.

Findings. The changes between wave 1 and wave 2 of the surveys were analyzed with respect to five key criteria[17] involving the person's favorite brand and which brand was drunk last. The changes in each test market that were large enough to be statistically significant were as follows:

Teenagers: TGB—sounds increased in three criteria, in the person's favorite brand and in brand drunk last.

Spirit—sounds increased in three of the criteria.

TGB—musical decreased in three criteria but did increase as the person's favorite brand.

Control commercial's markets showed increase only in the brand drunk last.

Housewives: TGB—sounds increased in all five criteria, in favorite brand, and in brand drunk last.

Spirit—sounds increased only in brand drunk last.

TGB—musical increased in two criteria and in brand drunk last.

Control commercial increased in all five criteria and in brand drunk last.

Analysis was also made with the five-stage "problem model" to determine the extent to which consumers moved forward through the four steps toward actual purchase of Coke. Little difference was found between the four sets of markets, with consistent moving forward in three of the steps in each case. The only exception was in favor of TGB—sounds, for which teenagers moved forward in all four steps. Playback of particular copy points in each com-

---

[17] These five key criteria were the five steps listed in the behavioral model.

mercial was also studied, which revealed no practical differences among the four sets of markets.

Case sales in the four sets of markets were compared with sales during the same months of the previous year (1961). Similar comparison was made for sales in the neighboring bottlers' areas, which served as a control comparison of normal advertising weight using the existing commercial. The percentage sales changes for each test market and neighboring bottlers were as follows:

	June 1962 Versus 1961	July 1962 Versus 1961	August 1962 Versus 1961
TGB—music:			
Test cities	+9	+5	+4
Neighboring cities	−3	+6	+11
Spirit—sounds:			
Test cities	+8	+20	+11
Neighboring cities	+7	+8	+8
TGB—sounds:			
Test cities	+10	+24	+18
Neighboring cities	+3	+15	+10
Control (Zing . . .)			
Test cities	−16	+2	+6
Neighboring cities	+2	+15	+13

Conclusion. TGB—sounds should be chosen as the new Coke commercial. It should be researched further for various creative developments of video, artists, print, and other advertising elements.

The foregoing research findings were presented to the client in a meeting in the middle of September, 1962. At that time the agency also advocated that TGB—sounds be adopted. The client's advertising executives took the matter under consideration.

The agency received on September 30 a detailed response from the client regarding the recommendations in the research report. The essence of their crucial view was this: the client could find no mandate in the research data for their adopting "Things Go Better." Rather it was felt that other conclusions might be supported by the data and that no decision to change the theme was justified.

Discussion

1. After examining and interpreting the statistical results of the research, what conclusion would you draw?
2. What grounds do you find that might be the basis of the company's reluctance to accept the advertising agency's recommendation of TGB—sounds?

3. The 1963 marketing plans anticipated that a new jingle and its theme would be introduced no later than March. If the advertising agency wanted to maintain that no additional research was needed, what evidence could be the basis of its position?

CASE 22

MILES LABORATORIES, INC. (C)

After the relative advantages of the three methods of new product testing described in the Miles Laboratories (B) case had been considered, one was chosen as the next stage in developing the chewable antacid tablet. The choice was a simulation, and the firm of Elrick & Lavidge, Inc., was retained to do this research work. The methods of this simulation were given in that case.

The COMP test was begun in January, 1973, and its results presented to Miles Laboratories in early April. Over 1,100 subjects—men and women both—took part in the test, with usable responses. You may recall the sequence of three stages in this technique:

Phase 1. Interviewees were screened at a leading shopping center to determine whether each person was qualified as a user of antacids. If so, answers were obtained on the relative importance of various attributes of antacids. Also, attitudes toward the existing brands were obtained.

Phase 2. The person was then shown a series of commercials on the new Miles product and those being used by existing brands (see Figure 1). After that, he or she was given $1.50 and a quantity of trading stamps. Then this subject was taken into a simulated store with the new product and competing products on display at normal prices. If the subject wished, these items could be purchased. Attribute ratings of the brands were then asked for. Upon departure, a parting gift package containing the new product was presented if the product had not been purchased in the laboratory store. If it had, another gift was given (in either case the gift was wrapped to conceal its identity until later).

Phase 3. Follow-up inquiry was by mail, timed to contact the consumers when they normally would have used most of the new product. The follow-up sought data on purchases and usage. It also obtained purchase intentions and attribute ratings of the new product compared with competitive brands, with the latter data in a form comparable to ratings obtained in the second stage.

One objective was to compare the optional brand names Alka-2 and Acid-aid. For this, half of the subjects were shown and given the product with one

'' WEDDING ''

VO ANNOUNCER: Now, for the groom

with heartburn

who's been waiting at the altar

for his best man who has the ring.

For the best man with heartburn

who's waiting to find out why his rented formal came with two vests, and no pants.

For the manager of the rental company with heartburn

who's waiting to find out who got two pants and no vest.

Alka-2.

The antacid tablet that's

made to fall apart.

That's why it chews fast

gets to your heartburn fast.

Never chalky, never gritty

Alka-2.

Made to fall apart. So it chews fast, works fast.

©1973 MILES CONSUMER PRODUCTS GROUP, MILES LABORATORIES, INC., Elkhart, Indiana 46514

FIGURE 1. Storyboard for an Alka-2 Television Commercial

Reprinted with special permission

464

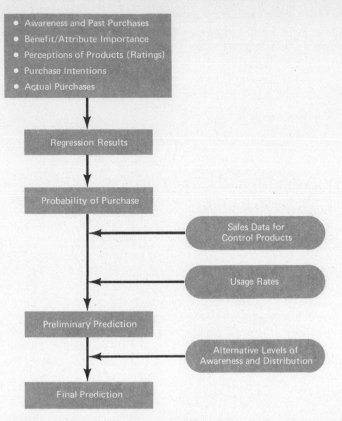

- Awareness and Past Purchases
- Benefit/Attribute Importance
- Perceptions of Products (Ratings)
- Purchase Intentions
- Actual Purchases

Regression Results

Probability of Purchase

Sales Data for Control Products

Usage Rates

Preliminary Prediction

Alternative Levels of Awareness and Distribution

Final Prediction

FIGURE 2. Steps in Development of Sales Estimates in the COMP System of Simulation

Source: Courtesy of Elrick & Lavidge, Inc.

brand name; the other half saw the other name. Alka-2 was significantly higher in ratings and was adopted.

A main purpose of the COMP test was to predict the likely share of market that Alka-2 would achieve. This was computed with a mathematical model that Elrick & Lavidge had developed, whose steps are shown in Figure 2. The firm had employed that model for numerous other new products, which validated its reliability with empirical market results of those products, after their actual market launchings. For most of them, COMP had been accurate within a range of 1 to 3 points from the market share that materialized.

The simulation's most vital benefit, in the view of the New Product Manager, was this market-share prediction. Financial requirements had set a criterion of 8 percent share of market (SOM) for Alka-2 to be acceptable. Elrick & Lavidge's report gave the grid of projected SOM for this brand that is shown in Table 1, which was computed by the method described in Figure 2.

The client company would need to supply estimates of both consumer awareness and effective distribution in order to interpret the grid in Table 1. Neither of these, of course, had yet been demonstrated for Alka-2. The company's typical experience with past consumer products had been achievement above 50 percent awareness and distribution in over two thirds of retail outlets.

TABLE 1. Grid of Expected Market Shares for New Chewable Antacid Tablet Brand[a]

Consumers' Unaided Awareness of New Brand (percent)	Effective Distribution			
	X percent	Y percent	Z percent	100 percent
30	3	3	4	5
40	5	6	8	9
50	7	7	10	13
60	9	10	12	14

[a] The data given are disguised.

Source: *Elrick & Lavidge, Inc., by special permission of Miles Laboratories, Inc.*

Another question was concerned with how much of the market share Alka-2 would attract from existing brands, with particular concern about cannibalizing a serious fraction of Alka-Seltzer's SOM. The data in Table 2 were projected from the COMP data with regard to that question. One of the brands given is Alka-Seltzer.

TABLE 2. Market Shares of Competing Brands Projected for Possible Alka-2 Brand Shares[a]

Brand	Brand Share of Total Market for Each Brand If Alka-2 Conquers the Following Market Shares (percent)			
	0 percent	4 percent	8 percent	14 percent
A	18	17	16	15
B	16	15	14	13
C	15	14	14	13
D	12	12	12	11
All others	38	38	36	34

[a] The data given are disguised.

Source: *Elrick & Lavidge, Inc., by special permission of Miles Laboratories, Inc.*

Most of the subjects actually bought one of the brands of antacids that were on display in the simulated store. Below are the proportions who bought each brand. Among those who bought Alka-2, the brand they said they used most is also shown. Again the data are disguised.

Brand	Percentage Who Bought Each Brand in Test Center	Brand "Used Most" by Those Who Bought Alka-2 in Test Center (percent)
Alka-2	30	—
A	19	26
B	17	24
C	13	17
D	11	14
Others	8	12
Nothing	20	7
	100[a]	100

[a] Adds to more than 100 percent because some people bought two brands.

At the end of the test period, after the subjects presumably had used the free package of Alka-2 at home (which over 90 percent did), they were asked their purchase intentions regarding Alka-2. Given four categories of response, their answers were distributed as follows:

Intention Toward Alka-2	Percent of Persons in Test
Definitely would buy	55
Probably would buy	18
Probably not buy	14
Definitely not buy	13
	100

A list of attributes that people had mentioned about antacids, in previous surveys, was shown to the subjects in this test to obtain their ratings of relative importance. Then, after the advertising had been seen, they were asked to score each brand (including Alka-2) on these attributes. Similar attitude information was gathered in the third stage, after they had used Alka-2. The composite standing of Alka-2 against all major competing brands (on a base score of 100) was also computed. It is these figures that we show in Table 3.

TABLE 3. Composite Ratings of Alka-2 Compared with Other Antacid Brands by Subjects in Simulation Test (Parity Score of Equal Rating = 100)

Attribute	Before Using Alka-2	After Using Alka-2
Reduces acid indigestion	93	99
Relieves heartburn	94	104
Gives fast relief	97	100
Relieves gassy, bloated feeling	93	94

TABLE 3. *Continued*

Attribute	Before Using Alka-2	After Using Alka-2
Relieves stomach ache	92	101
Tastes pleasant	100	105
Good for nausea	92	101
No bad after-taste	94	108
Relieves nervous stomach	97	99
Easy to chew, swallow	96	115
Good after too much food	92	102
Good for headache with upset stomach	99	97
Good value for money	89	112
Doesn't taste chalky	96	97
Dissolves quickly in mouth	97	116
Tastes fresh	100	110
Good after drinking too much	93	93

[a] The data are disguised.

Source: *Elrick & Lavidge, Inc., by special permission of Miles Laboratories, Inc.*

The subjects also were asked, after using Alka-2, what they most liked about it and what they disliked. The answers were approximately as follows:

Most Liked		Disliked	
Comment	Percent	Comment	Percent
Good taste	41	Crumbles	11
Works fast	27	Chalky taste	9
Dissolves quickly	26	Didn't help enough	7
Effective	19	Unpleasant taste	6
Easy to use	12	Works too slowly	2
Easy to carry	7		

With these data and finer detail that we have not presented, the New Products Manager needed to make another go/no go decision about Alka-2. If again this product had a favorable "go" decision, he also would have to decide which step should come next. The alternatives would include two of the options considered in the Miles Laboratories, Inc. (B) case, given first below:

1. Conduct a controlled market test.
2. Conduct a traditional market test.
3. Introduce the product in one region only, to be confined there until there was adequate assurance that Alka-2 would succeed and meet Miles Laboratories' objectives for products.

4. Roll out the product into national introduction, which necessarily would have to be phased into one region after another.

The fourth option would risk an investment of well above $25,000,000, little of which could be recovered if the product failed. The third option could be tried in the West Coast region, which constituted about 15 percent of the U.S. market and would take an investment of over $5,000,000.

If the decision at this point was "no go," the cycle would return to an earlier stage, where it would be restarted only after solutions were found to make the product viable.

Discussion

1. On the basis of the evidence, would you recommend that Miles Laboratories proceed further with Alka-2? Why?
2. Appraise the COMP simulation method and its findings. What do you consider to be its favorable features? What seem to be its limitations or possible faulty implications?
3. If Alka-2 is given a "go" decision at this point, which of the four options should be chosen as the next step? Give your reasoning.
4. If requested by your instructor, write a report on the management of Miles Laboratories stating the conclusions you draw from the COMP research, and justifying them.

CASE 23

COCA-COLA USA (D)

In 1972 the marketing research department of Coca-Cola USA undertook a test of its syrup for frozen carbonated beverage (hereinafter referred to as FCB) dispensing. This test employed only Coca-Cola[18] and was conducted in cooperation with a prospering fast-food service chain, BurgerRoyal Corporation[19] (to which we shall refer as BR). The BR outlets also offered two other FCB products, root beer and lemon-lime, but cola outsold them. The situation that led to this research contained three notable factors:

1. BR was using Coca-Cola syrup in only one of its districts, the Oklahoma City district, which had only 40 of BR's total of 620 units.
2. Even the Oklahoma City district was on the verge of switching from

---

[18] "Coca-Cola" and "Coke" are registered trademarks of The Coca-Cola Company. All data given in this case are disguised.

[19] Fictitious name.

Coca-Cola syrup to BR's own brand of cola, which was used in all the other BR units for FCB flavors, because of the relatively higher cost per cup of the Coca-Cola.

3. The Cola-Cola Company research laboratories had just developed a syrup for FCB dispensers whose high yield, or number of cups per gallon, seemed likely to more than compensate for the price differential. The laboratories had predicted a 15 to 20 percent yield increase over existing syrups, such as BR's own brand. The syrup could be produced in any flavor.

Cola-Cola USA agreed to conduct and pay for the $15,000 study, if BR would cooperate by handling Coke in the units participating in the test for its duration. Also, BR executives expressed an interest in handling Coke if the test proved it to be truly more profitable than their own. It was agreed that during the summer of 1972 the test would be conducted in the Oklahoma City district and in the adjoining and generally comparable Wichita district, as two market areas should corroborate the test's results.

The methods of the test are summarized below.

Timing. There was a *base period,* prior to the introduction of the Coke, from which variations during the test could be measured. The month of March was selected as the base period. April would then be a month of preparation for the test.

The *test period* would be four months long, May, June, July, and August. Over this length of time the personnel of the BR outlets should be retrained to methods of using the Coke syrup, and other test factors could take effect. It was expected that the yield of BR's own syrup would also increase during the summer, as higher operating rates in that season would mean more efficient dispenser performance for all syrups.

Areas. Four areas were delineated in the total area being researched, which are numbered and described below:

1. Wichita city: fourteen BR outlets located in the central city and suburbs.
2. Balance of Wichita district: sixteen units located in other Kansas cities, excluding northeastern Kansas (Topeka and north).
3. Oklahoma City: eighteen units located in the central city and suburbs.
4. Balance of Oklahoma: twenty-two units located in other Oklahoma cities, except the eastern one fourth of the state.

Test areas would be areas 1 and 3, in which variables under test would be introduced. *Control* areas would be areas 2 and 4.

Variables tested. In area 3 the Coca-Cola syrup would be introduced in April and then continue to be used through August. No promotional campaign would launched in Oklahoma City, however, since its outlets had been serving the regular Coca-Cola syrup for years, and the effects of a new campaign in BR outlets would not be as evident as where BR outlets would switch brands. In control area 4, BR stands would be changing to the BR syrup for cola FCB dispensing to enable comparisons with the yield in area 3 with the Coke syrup.

In area 1 the FCB Coke syrup would replace the BR syrup in April. Also a Coca-Cola USA-sponsored advertising program would be launched in May, utilizing radio and newspaper media in Wichita and linking BR stands with Coke. Point-of-purchase materials would also feature Coke at those outlets. In area 2 nothing would be changed, and use of the BR cola syrup would be continued. (*Note:* With only a few exceptions, the BR locations outside Wichita were in cities where Wichita radio and newspaper had no considerable influence).

Measurements. The following would be measured during both the base and test periods, cumulated to monthly totals:

1. Total sales of each BR unit in the four areas (all food and beverages).
2. Sales, in dollars, of all FCB beverages (cola, root beer, and lemon-lime).
3. Gallons of FCB syrup consumed at each unit.

In Wichita, the running of Coca-Cola USA's special advertising would be monitored and its costs reported by the accounting division. Coca-Cola USA special field representatives not only instructed and supervised the use of the Coke FCB syrup but also watched in each area for the occurrence of any serious distortions in the test or control areas' measurements.

Plan of analysis. Two types of operating results were to be calculated that would serve as the principal payoff variables: sales volume and yield. Dollar sales volume per $1,000 of total food and beverage sales was considered to be the proper variable, because the amount of beverages sold at any fast-food outlet was very dependent on the amount of food or total volume. As both total monthly sales at each unit and its total FCB monthly sales were obtained, the desired ratio was readily calculated.

Yield was to be expressed in terms of the number of 10-cent cups produced per gallon of syrup, as a monthly average per store. Number of cups was readily derived from dollar FCB sales, and the number of gallons of FCB syrup delivered to each outlet was available from BR's district office records.

Neither of those measurements in absolute terms would give an accurate indication of the *change* in sales or yield between March and the four test months. This was because the test areas presumably would be at different levels of FCB sales and of yields in the base month of March. Indeed, it was known in advance that Oklahoma outlets tended to sell considerably more FCB as a percentage of total sales than did Kansas outlets. This difficulty would be avoided by converting the sales and yield figures to index numbers. March figures for each of the four test or control areas would be given a value of 100 and the test period's quantity expressed relative to that (for example, if 9 percent higher than March, its index number would be 109).

The individual four summer months' sales and yield figures were desired, in order to examine trends, but they would be totaled in calculating final results. Then changes between the March base and the four-month average index number would be determined for each of the two test areas against its control area. These would serve as the chief indicators of the effects of the tested variables.

The BR decision makers would probably base their decision on how much profit, if any, they would gain through changing to Coca-Cola FCB syrup and to the Coca-Cola brand. They naturally would not divulge profit figures to the Coca-Cola USA researchers, but it could be assumed that any substantial increases in yield and/or sales volume of FCB would produce increased profits for BR. Coca-Cola USA sales executives also would use interpretations of the sales effects of the switchover to their FCB syrup relative to its higher price differential. Partially this would be for planning a sales presentation to BR on the test findings. Coca-Cola USA also would determine its potential sales volume and profit gains if the BR business was won over to its syrups. Coca-Cola USA would use a profit rate of 10 percent of sales, which takes into consideration the introductory costs of the Coca-Cola brand and syrup in BR outlets over the first year of sales.

Tables 1 and 2 present data obtained from the test.

TABLE 1. Dollar Sales of FCB per $1,000 of Total Sales by BurgerRoyal Outlets (rounded to nearest dollar)

	March	May	June	July	August	4-Month Average May–August
Wichita District						
1. Wichita City—test	50	162	177	192	175	179
2. Other Kansas—control	52	155	167	165	156	161
Oklahoma City District						
1. Oklahoma City—test	71	151	171	173	172	167
2. Other Oklahoma—control	70	146	162	163	160	158

TABLE 2. Number of Equivalent 10-Cent Cups per Gallon Obtained in Test and Control Areas (rounded to nearest whole number)

	March	May	June	July	August	4-Month Average May–August
Wichita District						
1. Wichita City—test	77	95	93	101	95	96
2. Other Kansas—control	75	80	81	80	78	80
Oklahoma City District						
1. Oklahoma City—test	70	89	90	93	93	91
2. Other Oklahoma—control	77	87	88	86	85	86

Changes in yield, defined as the number of equivalent retail cups per gallon, was considered to be fairly measured after the April changeover and the FCB Coca-Cola syrup was operating efficiently in the machines. As the yield in the control areas, not using the Coca-Cola syrup, also rose with the seasonal increase in summer FCB sales, the apparent gain in the test areas needs to be adjusted accordingly. That is, the "expected" increase in yield in

the test area due to the seasonal rise shown in the paired control area needs
to be calculated from the March base month. The difference between the actual control area yield and the expected yield then could be attributed to efficiency of the Coca-Cola syrup. One must recognize also that the data above
are for *all three flavors* of frozen carbonated beverages, although cola was
the *only* one using the new syrup and proved to constitute approximately 60
percent of the districts' FCB sales.

Discussion

1. Calculate the quantitative results of the test and report them in orderly, written form.
2. State logical inferences that you would expect the BurgerRoyal decision makers to draw from the data, together with their likely reasoning. They, of course, would consider that the Coca-Cola syrup would
   cost them $1.80, net of discounts and allowances, versus the cost of
   $1.55 per gallon of the FCB syrups they are now buying unbranded.
3. State inferences that you would expect the sales officials of Coca-Cola
   USA's Fountain Division to draw regarding the expected profitability
   of the BR syrup business, if it could be obtained. Use a net profit rate
   of 10 percent of sales.
4. Finally, from the standpoint of the Coca-Cola USA marketing research department, make a cost/benefit analysis of whether the
   project was justified. Its costs were nearly $15,000, and the standard
   for appraisal is that results should produce benefits to the company
   of three times research costs in the first year of application.

CASE 24

FLORIDA ENGINEERING SOCIETY JOURNAL*

The advertising manager of the *Florida Engineering Society Journal*
needed information about the publication's readership. Such information
would aid him in assuring advertisers that it would be advantageous to advertise in the *Journal.* There are various types of engineers practicing in Florida, and most engineers subscribe to a publication that is geared specifically
toward their field. The *Journal* is a general publication, however, not geared
toward a specific type of engineer. Therefore, data must be available to show
advertisers that the *Journal* is an effective alternative to other engineering
publications for reaching the desired markets.

The advertising manager asked a marketing research consulting firm, Market Data, Inc.,[20] to look into the problem and make recommendations. After

---

* Used with permission of the Florida Engineering Society.
[20] Fictitious name.

several weeks of study, the research consulting firm recommended that a mail survey be made of the Society's membership. In view of the fact that there were other engineering publications competing for advertising dollars, the research firm felt that it would be desirable to determine the following objectives: (1) to find out the effectiveness of advertisements appearing in the *Journal,* (2) to find out the percentage of readers concerned with material/equipment decisions and the related dollar volume, (3) to find out what types of engineers read the *Journal,* (4) to find out what types of consumer-goods advertisements would be of interest to readers should such advertisements appear in the *Journal,* and (5) to find out the readership appeal of the *Journal* in general.

The advertising manager stipulated that the entire membership of the Society was to be interviewed. Therefore, the research firm decided that a mailed questionnaire would be the least expensive and most practical method for reaching the Society's 2,500 members dispersed throughout the state of Florida.

Using this procedure, 885 members responded to the survey. After the data had been collected and analyzed, they were put in tabular form ready for presentation in a report. Tables 1 through 15 were prepared by the technical staff and made ready for the report writer to incorporate in the final report.

Discussion

Assuming that you are the report writer, do the three tasks described in the following assignment.

1. Prepare an outline of the various sections that you would set up for the final report.

TABLE 1. Survey Sample of Engineers Cross-Tabulated by Areas and Field of Engineering

	Field							
Area	Mechanical	Electrical	Chemical	Civil	Industrial	Survey	Other	Total
Industrial	27	78	5	13	12	0	8	143
Construction	20	14	1	52	2	3	1	93
Education	1	5	0	12	0	0	7	25
Government	11	11	2	86	1	2	13	126
Private practice	62	40	4	272	2	11	21	412
Other	5	24	0	10	1	1	13	54
Total	126	172	12	445	18	17	63	853

Valid responses: 853
Missing responses: 32

2. Write an overall summary for the advertising manager to read so that he will have a good idea about the major highlights of the report.
3. Develop one or more graphic aids for the presentation of data you believe would present a more complete picture of one central point than the tabular form can present.

TABLE 2. Disposition of the *Florida Engineering Society Journal*

Question Response	Response Count	Percentage
Read and discard it	301	34.2
Read and pass it on	235	26.7
Read and file it for reference	242	27.5
Read and retain certain sections (photostat, cut out, etc.)	87	9.9
Other (please specify)	16	1.8

TABLE 2A. Disposition of *Journal* If Passed On

Question Response	Response Count	Percentage
Other engineers	101	35.5
Other employees	88	30.8
Family members	7	2.4
Placed on display (reading table, etc.)	82	28.6
Other (please specify)	8	2.8

TABLE 3. Amount of *Journal* Read

Question Response	Response Count	Percentage
Cover to cover	97	11.0
Selected articles and advertisements	580	65.8
Selected articles and no advertisements	43	4.9
Thumb through it	159	18.0
Other (please specify)	2	.2

TABLE 4. *Journal* Advertisements Used for Information

Question Response	Response Count	Percentage
Yes	536	61.3
No	339	38.7

TABLE 5. Categories of Advertisements in the *Journal* Cross-Tabulated by Field of Engineering (percent) [a] (Engineers Ranked Advertisements Read)

| | Field of Engineering | | | | | | |
Category of Advertisement	Mechanical	Electrical	Chemical	Civil	Industrial	Survey	Other
Professional engineering services	44.0	48.1	25.0	45.3	83.3	50.0	54.1
Construction equipment and supplies	75.8	54.7	60.0	74.3	66.7	77.8	66.7
Electrical and/or electronic equipment	40.8	74.6	100.0	24.0	20.0	80.0	55.8
Pollution control equipment	58.1	37.6	60.0	71.4	50.0	51.7	64.3
Computer and computer services	20.9	24.5	25.0	21.5	40.0	25.0	26.4
Position and/or positions wanted	42.9	47.3	50.0	56.1	60.0	71.5	39.1
Other	42.8	33.4	0	26.4	50.0	0	12.5

[a] Only the combined percentages for rankings 1 and 2 of each category are presented.

TABLE 6. Categories of Advertisements in the *Journal* Cross-Tabulated by Area of Engineering (percent) [a] (Engineers Ranked Advertisements Read)

| | Area of Engineering | | | | | |
Category of Advertisement	Industrial	Construction	Education	Government	Private Practice	Other
Professional engineering services	40.8	38.8	66.6	46.9	48.5	55.5
Construction equipment and supplies	57.4	87.9	50.0	74.5	79.1	63.2
Electrical and/or electronic equipment	62.3	54.3	25.0	38.4	31.3	53.0
Pollution control equipment	47.7	58.9	100.0	52.1	69.7	47.4
Computer and computer services	25.6	12.0	0	20.0	25.0	20.0
Position and/or positions wanted	45.9	42.1	50.0	59.3	52.2	52.7
Other	28.6	20.0	0	33.3	22.6	42.9

[a] Only the combined percentages for rankings 1 and 2 of each category are presented.

TABLE 7. Cross Tabulation of Usable Advertising Information from Various Publications by Field of Engineering [a] (Engineers Ranked Usable Information from Publications)

Publications	Mechanical	Electrical	Chemical	Civil	Industrial	Survey	Other
Backsights and Foresights	6.3	10.0	33.3	27.3	0	66.6	44.4
Dixie Contractor	21.0	8.6	0	34.3	50.0	50.0	0
Florida Builder	36.3	35.5	33.3	34.8	50.0	50.0	36.4
Florida Contractor	57.2	45.7	0	54.3	66.7	50.0	46.2
Florida Engineering Society Journal	88.7	77.8	100.0	80.4	85.7	96.0	88.5
Overflow	38.5	22.7	60.0	56.5	50.0	50.0	75.1
Electrical South	48.5	84.9	0	9.1	66.6	0	25.0
Other publications	66.6	75.0	66.7	66.7	0	50.0	100.0

[a] Only the combined percentages for rankings 1 and 2 of each category are presented.

TABLE 8. Editorial Content and Readability of Publications Cross-Tabulated by Field of Engineering (Percentage for rankings 1 and 2 of each category)

Publications	Mechanical	Electrical	Chemical	Civil	Industrial	Survey	Other
Backsights and Foresights	14.3	6.7	0	31.3	0	70.0	0
Dixie Contractor	26.6	0	66.7	39.3	50.0	50.0	33.3
Florida Builder	26.9	41.4	33.3	28.6	50.0	50.0	45.5
Florida Contractor	57.5	59.4	25.0	50.7	33.3	50.0	46.2
Florida Engineering Society Journal	95.5	74.3	80.0	87.1	100.0	100.0	97.1
Overflow	45.4	11.8	60.0	60.0	0	50.0	66.6
Electrical South	39.3	86.0	0	10.0	50.0	0	37.5
Other publications	83.4	95.7	100.0	87.6	0	50.0	0

TABLE 9. Engineer's Responsibilities for Specifying/Recommending/Buying Materials and/or Equipment

Question Response	Response Count	Percentage
Buy materials and/or equipment	234	27.4
Specify the purchase of materials and/or equipment	348	40.8
Recommend materials and/or equipment to be purchased	153	17.9
Do not buy, specify, or recommend the purchase of materials and/or equipment	118	13.8

TABLE 10. Dollar Volume of Material and/or Equipment Purchased, Specified, or Recommended by Area of Engineering

Area of Engineering	Dollar Volume					
	0–9,999	10,000–99,999	100,000–249,999	250,000–499,999	500,000 and over	
Industrial	19	28	23	9	43	count
	16.1%	22.2%	21.5%	11.0%	12.5%	percentage
Construction	11	8	13	12	42	
	9.3%	6.3%	12.1%	14.6%	12.2%	
Education	11	9	3	0	2	
	9.3%	7.1%	2.8%	0.0%	0.6%	
Government	29	27	13	11	27	
	24.6%	21.4%	12.1%	13.4%	7.8%	
Private practice	35	46	51	45	211	
	29.7%	36.5%	47.7%	54.9%	61.2%	
Other	13	8	4	5	20	
	11.0%	6.3%	3.7%	6.1%	5.8%	

Valid responses: 778
Missing responses 107

TABLE 11. Dollar Volume of Material and/or Equipment Purchased, Specified, or Recommended by Field of Engineering

Field of Engineering	Dollar Volume					
	0–9,999	10,000–99,999	100,000–249,999	250,000–499,999	500,000 and over	
Mechanical	7	15	14	14	69	count
	6.0%	11.9%	13.1%	17.1%	19.9%	percentage
Electrical	27	24	24	15	65	
	23.1%	19.0%	22.4%	18.3%	18.8%	
Chemical	4	2	2	0	4	
	3.4%	1.6%	1.9%	0.0%	1.2%	
Civil	62	70	50	47	177	
	53.3%	55.6%	46.7%	57.3%	51.2%	
Industrial	2	4	4	1	2	
	1.7%	3.2%	3.7%	1.2%	0.6%	
Surveying	1	4	0	3	5	
	0.9%	3.2%	0.0%	3.7%	1.4%	
Other	14	7	13	2	24	
	12.0%	5.6%	12.1%	2.4%	6.9%	

Valid responses: 778
Missing responses: 107

TABLE 12. Changes Desired in the *Journal*

Categories of Responses	Number of Responses	Percent of Total Responses
No response	553	62.556
None	105	11.877
Editorial content	101	11.425
Informative news	54	6.108
Personal criticisms	44	4.977
Local chapter news	24	2.714
Miscellaneous	4	0.452

TABLE 13. Consumer Goods and Services Requested Advertised in the *Journal*

Question Response	Response Count	Percentage
Clothing	101	11.4
Hobby supplies and equipment	290	32.8
Hotels and restaurants	255	28.8
Household goods	124	14.0
Sporting goods	255	28.8
Stocks, bonds, and investment opportunities	425	48.0
Other (please specify)	127	14.14

TABLE 14. Family Income Compared to Members in Household

	Dollar Volume						
Members in Household	Under 7,999	8,000– 9,999	10,000– 14,999	15,000– 19,999	20,000– 24,999	Over 25,000	
1	0	0	10	15	9	17	count
	0.0%	0.0%	13.5%	6.8%	4.5%	5.2%	percentage
2	1	3	23	45	43	82	
	50.0%	42.9%	31.1%	20.7%	21.3%	25.0%	
3	1	2	25	104	113	162	
	50.0%	28.6%	33.8%	47.3%	55.7%	49.4%	
4	0	1	9	27	20	26	
	0.0%	14.3%	12.2%	12.3%	9.9%	7.9%	
5	0	1	2	22	11	23	
	0.0%	14.3%	2.7%	10.0%	5.4%	7.0%	
6	0	0	3	5	2	11	
	0.0%	0.0%	4.1%	2.3%	1.0%	3.4%	
7 or more	0	0	2	2	4	7	
	0.0%	0.0%	2.8%	0.9%	2.0%	1.8%	
Total	2	7	74	220	202	328	(833)

479

TABLE 15.   Marital Status Compared with Age Group

Age Group	Single	Married (No Dependents)	Married with Dependents	
Under 20	0	0	0	count
	0.0%	0.0%	0.0%	percentage
20–29	15	27	38	
	27.8%	13.9%	6.3%	
30–39	14	22	194	
	25.9%	11.3%	32.0%	
40–49	14	25	253	
	25.9%	12.9%	41.7%	
50–59	4	65	102	
	7.4%	33.5%	16.8%	
60 and over	7	55	20	
	13.0%	28.4%	3.3%	
Total	54	194	607	

CASE 25

PYRAMID BUILDING SUPPLY, INC.

The top management of Pyramid Building Supply, Inc.,[21] was concerned, in early 1977, with the selection of locations for opening new yards in 1978. Pyramid was founded in 1954 when an Augusta, Georgia, building supplies dealer decided that his existing yard in the city was too cramped and on unduly expensive property. He also decided to innovate with a cash-and-carry policy that would enable him to offer dramatic price cuts that would expand volume fast. The large new yard was located several miles outside of Augusta on a good highway, and almost immediately city and rural buyers alike were flocking to Pyramid. Thus began a building supply yard chain that had spread across six southeastern states by 1977.

With the experience of establishing sixty-seven yards, Pyramid was confident of its formula for success and determined to continue expansion. Each new outlet was a hazardous investment, though, and its location had to be chosen painstakingly. Five new yards were to be built and opened in the coming year. Three would be within the bounds of the areas now being served by Pyramid's existing outlets, in order to consolidate its territory. Two other yards were to be outside Pyramid's present areas, and the marketing research department was beginning its study of possible locations for these two areas. Much information needed to be gathered and sifted on probably fifteen to twenty alternative towns for the basis of selecting the most fertile market area.

In considering locations, obviously the nature of Pyramid's patronage was

---

[21] The name of the firm and geographical locations are disguised.

an important factor. Building contractors and tradesmen formed the greater part of volume, around 60 percent. The balance was composed of farmers, householders, and hobbyists. Lumber and building materials dominated the sales mix, with 72 percent of total dollar volume, maintaining that proportion despite expansion of merchandise lines into appliances, building hardware, garden supplies and equipment, and home entertainment equipment.

The existing total area already entered by Pyramid is indicated by the shaded area in Figure 1. Several cities lying short distances outside that area are shown on the map to facilitate orienting it to detailed maps. The firm had not determined that its expansion would be in any particular direction, and the new locations might lie in different directions. One stipulation was that the new locations ought not to lie more than 100 miles from Pyramid's present trading areas, the shaded zone.

Although the new Pyramid yards might not be adjacent to cities, the market analyst began his study with the larger ones lying within the 100-mile

FIGURE 1. Areas Presently Served by Pyramid Building Supply, Inc.

The shaded area is an approximate representation of retail trading areas within which Pyramid has existing yards. Some cities on the periphery, outside that area are indicated.

limit. Those were cities that have been designated as "metropolitan area"—inclusive of the whole county in which the principal city lies and sometimes additional counties in its urbanized area. He counted seventeen such metropolitan areas, of which seven are listed in Table 1; the other ten were:

Biloxi–Gulfport, Miss.

Danville, Va.

Fayetteville, N.C.

Florence, Ala.

Lynchburg, Va.

Meridian, Miss.

Nashville, Tenn.

Tampa–St. Petersburg, Fla.

West Palm Beach, Fla.

Wilmington, N.C.

Some of the metropolitan areas embraced two or three principal cities.

The analysis would proceed to choose not only the particular city but also pinpoint the desired location near it (as Pyramid's policy was to locate outside a city), but that level of detail was not yet considered.

As a trial effort, the analyst selected seven of the metropolitan areas and obtained data for them from Sales Management's Annual Survey of Buying Power, covering 1975. He extracted figures on three important market factors: population, income, and retail sales, with two types of income and sales data. These are given in Table 1.

In judging the potentials for a new Pyramid yard, one consideration was that any yard was expected to develop a sales volume of around $4 million

TABLE 1. Selected Data on Seven Metropolitan Areas

Metropolitan Areas	Population (thousands)	Effective Buying Income (thousands of dollars)		Sales (thousands of dollars)	
		Total	Per Household	Total Retail	Lumber–Building–Hardware
Bristol–Johnson City– Kingsport, Tenn.–Va.	401.2	1,552,237	10,218	1,014,603	100,897
Chattanooga, Tenn.	391.9	1,790,345	12,160	1,170,621	68,132
Jackson, Miss.	288.5	1,294,409	12,230	874,240	32,332
Lakeland–Winter Haven, Fla.	273.4	1,257,430	11,017	978,557	79,209
Raleigh–Durham, N.C.	481.0	2,454,283	13,497	1,330,780	69,830
Roanoke, Va.	217.2	1,034,446	12,240	689,126	30,454
Sarasota, Fla.	169.4	937,768	9,579	608,759	68,006

Source: *"Survey of Buying Power,"* Sales and Marketing Management, *July 26, 1976. Quoted with the specific permission of* Sales and Marketing Management *magazine. Further reproduction is not permitted without the written permission of Sales Management, Inc.*

within three or four years. Seldom did a yard obtain more than 20 percent of the total retail business in the trading area, in its lines, although many approached that market share where competition was not intense, and 15 percent was around average. The typical sales breakdown by merchandise lines in Pyramid stores was: lumber and building materials, 70 percent; building hardware, 10 percent; home appliances, 13 percent; garden supplies, 5 percent; miscellaneous (including new lines of home entertainment equipment), 2 percent.

Discussion

1. How can the data be used to evaluate cities or metropolitan areas as potential sites for two new Pyramid yards?
2. Among the seven metropolitan areas, what preliminary conclusions would you draw as to which two of them would be the best locations for the new Pyramid yards? How did you reach this conclusion?
3. What additional data do you need to choose a metropolitan area for a future store? Obtain those data (to the extent that they are available in a nearby library) and draw any different conclusions they point to.
4. If any of the ten other metropolitan areas in the 100-mile radius seems to you to be more attractive for this type of business, obtain similar data on it. Does this change your conclusion?
5. Not all the data given above are available for cities not located within designated Standard Metropolitan Statistical Areas in the Census or in *Sales Management*'s guide. Look into what would be available on a city or county basis, and report how that would limit the analysis.
6. Choosing a city or metropolitan area for location is obviously only a first step. Conceive of the subsequent decisions that must be made before a particular site is identified, and for each decision list types of information needed to make it fairly accurate.

Epilogue

OUR BOOK HAS DEALT with the field of marketing research as it is practiced today. You may be more concerned, though, with its practice in the future. These concluding remarks recognize that concern by identifying some new directions and suggesting new horizons that may impact heavily on the conduct of marketing research.

Three developments are chosen for particular attention: (1) environmental monitoring as a basis for marketing strategy, (2) use of marketing research in the formulation of public policy, and (3) new communication techniques.

Environmental Monitoring[1]

Exploring the uncontrollable variables that affect future decisions is increasingly a task for marketing research, particularly among business corporations as they establish operating objectives. The environments that are monitored may include the technological, social, cultural, political, legal, support, competitive, and economic.

The economic environment has been a major area of concern to marketing researchers and will continue to be. Such factors as gross national product, growth ratios, employment levels, and income and price trends are all important in marketing planning. Keeping up to date on such variables and interpreting them has been within the realm of marketing research.

Attention today, though, is being turned to other variables. *Social* and *cultural* monitoring, for instance, has revealed eroding confidence in corporations' leadership and ability to balance profit with service to the consuming public.[2] Another serious revelation is that record growth in the labor force means that perhaps 40 percent of young adults must be absorbed in jobs outside the private sector.[3] Recognizing this, much of the young public is failing to support private industry while favoring greater governmental regulation.

Monitoring of the *political* and *legal* arena is needed to anticipate new restraints and identify new market opportunities. Consider the impact of the Occupational Health and Safety Act (OSHA) in two instances: safety regulations for lawn mowers and cleanliness standards for food warehouses. For the lawn mower manufacturer, gearing up for product changes to meet safety requirements poses financial as well as production problems. The OSHA regulations on sanitary standards, on the contrary, present new market opportunities for cleaning equipment and chemicals. In both of these instances, monitoring by marketing research

---

[1] For a more detailed treatment, see T. A. Staudt, D. A. Taylor, and D. J. Bowersox, *A Managerial Introduction to Marketing*, 3rd ed. (Englewood Cliffs, N.J.: Prentice-Hall, Inc., 1976), Chap. 4.

[2] These types of questions have been asked from year to year by the Harris surveys.

[3] Seymour L. Wolfbein, "The Emerging Labor Force in the United States" (unpublished report, Temple University).

can enable the manufacturer to take timely action to prevent violations or to capture opportunity.

By *support* environment, we refer to the institutional structure supporting manufacturers' delivery to ultimate buyers, with distribution channels and provision of service requirements. Here are two examples of such changes:

1. Monitoring revealed to the household appliance industry that about 50 percent of all appliances were being sold into the builder's market rather than to ultimate consumers. This alerted the industry to study and make plans regarding ideal channels to serve this growing and predominant market sector.

2. Current data indicate a strong trend toward eating outside the home, to the extent that by 1985 perhaps two out of three meals will be eaten out. Food manufacturers traditionally have placed their resources mainly in the retail sector, which caters to food served in the home. The imperative need to monitor this trend and be ready to shift resources to the institutional market is apparent and is a task of marketing research.

The *competitive* environment is linked to the support environment and is no less dynamic. Over time a company's actual competition changes in nature, intensity, and identity of who is competing. Changes in competitive nature need to be anticipated through marketing research so that a firm's marketing mix may be adjusted promptly. An example was the shift in the middle 1970s in the automobile and appliance industries to intense price competition and the use of rebates. Intensity of competition changes, too, as witnessed in the petroleum industry with the oil shortages. Identity may change in such ways as when there is vertical integration in the distributive trades or erstwhile competitive manufacturers start to cooperate (for example, Johnson & Johnson selling private-label goods to American Hospital Supply, a customer and a competitor).

While the technological environment lies outside the province of marketing, it is vital in assessing marketing trends. Marketing research should be on the lookout for developments that spell new opportunities or threats to existing products. Consider in that regard two budding developments: (1) the state of battery technology, which may vitally affect the future of using small gasoline-powered engines on mowers; and (2) the flail mower, which may substitute for the often-dangerous rotary blades. Most of the foregoing environmental changes lie basically in other fields, but marketing research has responsibility for monitoring their marketing implications. We expect that marketing research will assume increasing responsibility for these kinds of continuous analysis.

Public Policy Formulation

We have cited business applications of marketing research mostly in our examples, which has characterized its main uses. But its application in public policy decisions is on the increase. Besides the use of marketing research by some government agencies that produce goods and services (which is similar to use by private companies), there is growing use in what have been termed (1) regulatory public policy, and (2) functional public policy.[4] Let us consider these two uses.

Regulatory Public Policy

In the case of *regulatory public policy*, we refer to the research of regulatory agencies such as the Federal Trade Commission, the Food and Drug Administration, the Department of Transportation, as well as all the state and local regulatory agencies, such as the state licensing bureaus, bureaus of consumer affairs, banking and insurance commissions, and local zoning agencies.

A number of research studies that may be termed marketing research have been conducted to review and assess the effectiveness and use of consumer involvement by the FTC to provide consumer input into business practices, consumer remedy legislation, or commission rulings.[5] These have covered such issues as the extent of consumer involvement and attitudes toward marketing, consumerism, and government regulation.

Wilkie and Gardner point out that marketing research should lead rather than lag the formulation of public policy.[6] In this respect they suggest in Table 1 a listing of research areas susceptible to marketing research. As an illustration, they suggest that corrective advertising remedies at present do not sufficiently consider the residual effects of deceptive advertising, media selection and scheduling, budget, and copy elements in their attempts to most effectively irradicate the injustice. All of these are susceptible to marketing research.

At the state levels, banking commissions generally rely on market research analysis of area potentials prior to approving branch bank locations. State bureaus of consumer affairs are continuously monitoring consumers for consumer complaints, attitudes about regulatory legislation, and identification of areas needing regulation. Recent controversies faced by public service commissions over the use of nuclear power plants or by departments of natural resources in the use of natural resources for recreational purposes usually come to the floor of state legislatures supported by marketing research derived from attitudinal information

---

[4] See William L. Wilkie and David M. Gardner, "The Role of Marketing Research in Public Policy Decision Making," *Journal of Marketing,* January, 1974, pp. 38–47, and J. R. Brent Ritchie and Roger J. LaBreque, "Marketing Research and Public Policy: A Functional Perspective," *Journal of Marketing,* July, 1975, pp. 12–19.

[5] See Priscilla Ann LaBarbera, "An Empirical Investigation of Consumer Participants in Federal Trade Commission Consumer Protection Rule Making Procedures" (unpublished doctoral dissertation, Graduate School of Business Administration, Michigan State University, 1976); and Hiram C. Barksdale, William R. Darden, and William D. Perreault, "Changes in Consumer Attitudes Toward Marketing, Consumerism and Government Regulation" (unpublished manuscript, 1975).

[6] Wilkie and Gardner, op. cit., p. 41.

TABLE 1. Topics for Future Research in Regulating Public Policy

A. Program priorities
   1. Consumer environment descriptions
   2. Models for resource allocation
   3. Social cost/benefit measurements
   4. Structural versus trade practice remedy
B. Stimulus research
   1. Advertising effects
   2. Personal selling and promotion
   3. Pricing
   4. Product quality
   5. Guarantee and warranty
C. Response research
   1. Product information
   2. Consumer education
D. Product and segment research
   1. Special markets
   2. Specific products and services

Source: *William L. Wilkie and David M. Gardner, "The Role of Marketing Research in Public Policy Decision Making,"* Journal of Marketing, *January, 1974, pp. 44.*

from affected users. Even at the local levels, zoning ordinances are developed from extensive population trend and land-use studies. In many instances, local agencies require studies of market potential prior to approving locations for restaurants, hotels, and other recreational enterprises. Sometimes they conduct the studies themselves or require them of the applying citizen.

We have mentioned only a few such examples, but a compilation of the marketing research conducted by all such agencies would only strengthen our point.

Functional Public Policy

The term *functional public policy,* proposed by Ritchie and LaBreque,[7] refers to (1) the marketing research conducted by those agencies engaged in conferring goods and services, and (2) marketing research conducted by public agencies to support their programs. Examples of the first type are the work done by the departments of natural resources in the provision of recreational facilities, public health agencies in health care services, and boards of education in the supply of educational services. Examples of the latter are studies conducted by the Department of Health, Education, and Welfare to develop useful "social indicators" to be used to evaluate programs for renewal, and those by state departments of

_____
[7] Op. cit., p. 12.

488

commerce for the purpose of luring new industries to their areas or to establish trade offices.

In almost all cases, functional public policy marketing research starts with *need identification*, a fundamental marketing principle. The delivery programs, where goods and services are supplied or where programs are seeking justification, the details are developed in terms of the identified need. If the purpose is to justify a program, the program results are compared with the researched need, and appropriate adjustments are made.

Any review of requests for proposals for such agencies as the Department of Transportation or that of Health, Education, and Welfare will attest to the use of marketing research by these agencies.

Table 2 shows the expenditures for social science research by federal agencies and departments. This is the category within which most marketing research, by other than university contractors, falls. The numbers

TABLE 2. Federal Departments and Agencies Funding Other Than University Social Science Research

	Social Science Research (millions of dollars)	
	Basic	*Applied*
Department of Commerce		
Economic Development Administration		0.354
Health, Education, and Welfare		
Alcohol, Drug Abuse, and Mental		
Health Administration	0.506	3.838
Health Resources Administration		8.199
Office of Education		2.894
Office of Human Development		7.326
Office of the Secretary	2.352	25.200
Social and Rehabilitation Service		10.400
Department of Housing and Urban Development		32.288
Department of Interior		
National Park Service	0.020	
Office of Water Resources and Technology	0.130	0.302
Law Enforcement Assistance Administration		7.373
Manpower Administration	0.263	4.535
Department of State		
Agency for International Development		3.103
Federal Energy Administration		0.466
National Science Foundation		8.114
Total	3.261	114.392

Source: *Compiled from* Federal Funds for Research, Development, and Other Scientific Activities, FY 1974–75–76 *(Washington, D.C.: National Science Foundation, 1976).*

are large, and many private marketing research agencies cultivate these opportunities as aggressively as the private sector.

New Communication Technology

Perhaps the most dramatic developments in communication devices are those that permit almost instantaneous two-way communication between a household and a central location. Foremost are the developing technology of fiber optics and that of inexpensive devices that utilize cable television systems for two-way communication, the television picture tube or a terminal acting as the display medium. Fiber optics technology is based on a glass cable that can transmit many thousands of two-way messages relatively inexpensively. Still other inexpensive devices have been developed that utilize telephone lines. The possible use of these devices ranges from participatory democracy through political referendum and in-house purchasing to simplified marketing research field inquiries. In the realm of marketing research, field work can be completed rapidly, obviating the need to drop studies because information is needed prior to a reasonable completion date. The use of consumer diaries by consumer panels could be replaced by spot checks of in-house inventories. Whatever the future of these developments holds, the cost of field research should be reduced considerably.

The foregoing may have provided some sense of change, although only a few directions have been described. Before closing we shall refer briefly to three other challenging areas:

1. *Ethical problems,* still not wholly resolved, could seriously threaten the relationship between marketing research and those it serves. On the consumers' side, one issue is confidentiality of information. There was, properly, an outcry in 1975 when it was admitted that leading research firms were using invisible ink codes on questionnaires so that the identity of mail respondents could be determined. In the face of an apparent increasing desire for privacy, such practices could destroy the ability to obtain information. Also, there have been ethical problems involved in the rivalry between marketing research agencies and in misrepresentations to research clients. Adherence to ethical codes is a requisite to health of the marketing research profession.

2. *Decision science* needs to be vastly advanced for marketing research to achieve its possible benefits to society and/or to the firms and agencies employing it. Informal and ad hoc decisions, rather than deliberate and systematic ones, are still general practice. Organizations that are now formulating their decisions and using explicit models properly are showing the way toward optimal use of data and of computers. Only as there is greater science and foresight in problem definition and decision methods can marketing research make its contributions.

490

3. The potential *societal benefits* of marketing research are enormous and very important. Yet these would be realized only as enterprises appreciate that its findings should not be keys to the manipulation of buyers but rather a bond with them. That is, marketing research, when so employed, should serve to *mutual* advantage.

With these parting thoughts, we join you in looking ahead.

Appendixes

APPENDIX A. Table of Random Numbers

46	96	85	77	27	92	86	26	45	21	89	91	71	42	64	64	58	22	75	81	74	91	48	46	18
44	19	15	32	63	55	87	77	33	29	45	00	31	34	84	05	72	90	44	27	78	22	07	62	17
34	39	80	62	24	33	81	67	28	11	34	79	26	35	34	23	09	94	00	80	55	31	63	27	91
74	97	80	30	65	07	71	30	01	84	47	45	89	70	74	13	04	90	51	27	61	34	63	87	44
22	14	61	60	86	38	33	71	13	33	72	08	16	13	50	56	48	51	29	48	30	93	45	66	29
40	03	96	40	03	47	24	60	09	21	21	18	00	05	86	52	85	40	73	73	57	68	36	33	91
52	33	76	44	56	15	47	75	78	73	78	19	87	06	98	47	48	02	62	03	42	05	32	55	02
37	59	20	40	93	17	82	24	19	90	80	87	32	74	59	84	24	49	79	17	23	75	83	42	00
11	02	55	57	48	84	74	36	22	67	19	20	15	92	53	37	13	75	54	89	56	73	23	39	07
10	33	79	26	34	54	71	33	89	74	68	48	23	17	49	18	81	05	52	85	70	05	73	11	17
67	59	28	25	47	89	11	65	65	20	42	23	96	41	64	20	30	89	87	64	37	93	36	96	35
93	50	75	20	09	18	54	34	68	02	54	87	23	05	43	36	98	29	97	93	87	08	30	92	98
24	43	23	72	80	64	34	27	23	46	15	36	10	63	21	59	69	76	02	62	31	62	47	60	34
39	91	63	18	38	27	10	78	88	84	42	32	00	97	92	00	04	94	50	05	75	82	70	80	35
74	62	19	67	54	18	28	92	33	69	98	96	74	35	72	11	68	25	08	95	31	79	11	79	54
91	03	35	60	81	16	61	97	25	14	78	21	22	05	25	47	26	37	80	39	19	06	41	02	00
42	57	66	76	72	91	03	63	48	46	44	01	33	53	62	28	80	59	55	05	02	16	13	17	54
06	36	63	06	15	03	72	38	01	58	25	37	66	48	56	19	56	41	29	28	76	49	74	39	50
92	70	96	70	89	80	87	14	25	49	25	94	62	78	26	15	41	39	48	75	64	69	61	06	38
91	08	88	53	52	13	04	82	23	00	26	36	47	44	04	08	84	80	07	44	76	51	52	41	59
68	85	97	74	47	53	90	05	90	84	87	48	25	01	11	05	45	11	43	15	60	40	31	84	59
59	54	13	09	13	80	42	29	63	03	24	64	12	43	28	10	01	65	62	07	79	83	05	59	61
39	18	32	69	33	46	58	19	34	03	59	28	97	31	02	65	47	47	70	39	74	17	30	22	65
67	43	31	09	12	60	19	57	63	78	11	80	10	97	15	70	04	89	81	78	54	84	87	83	42
61	75	37	19	56	90	75	39	03	56	49	92	72	95	27	52	87	47	12	52	54	62	43	23	13
78	10	91	11	00	63	19	63	74	58	69	03	51	38	60	36	53	56	77	06	69	03	89	91	24
93	23	71	58	09	78	08	03	07	71	79	32	25	19	61	04	40	33	12	06	78	91	97	88	95
37	55	48	82	63	89	92	59	14	72	19	17	22	51	90	20	03	64	96	60	48	01	95	44	84
62	13	11	71	17	23	29	25	13	85	33	35	07	69	25	68	57	92	57	11	84	44	01	33	66
29	89	97	47	03	13	20	86	22	45	59	98	64	53	89	64	94	81	55	87	73	81	58	46	42
16	94	85	82	89	07	17	30	29	89	89	80	98	36	25	36	53	02	49	14	34	03	52	09	20
04	93	10	59	75	12	98	84	60	93	68	16	87	60	11	50	46	56	58	45	88	72	50	46	11
95	71	43	68	97	18	85	17	13	08	00	50	77	50	46	92	45	26	97	21	48	22	23	08	32
86	05	39	14	35	48	68	18	36	57	09	62	40	28	87	08	74	79	91	08	27	12	43	32	03
59	30	60	10	41	31	00	69	63	77	01	89	94	60	19	02	70	88	72	33	38	88	20	60	86
05	45	35	40	54	03	98	96	76	27	77	84	80	08	64	60	44	34	54	24	85	20	85	77	32
71	85	17	74	66	27	85	19	55	56	51	36	48	92	32	44	40	47	10	38	22	52	42	29	96
80	20	32	80	98	00	40	92	57	51	52	83	14	55	31	99	73	23	40	07	64	54	44	99	21
13	50	78	02	73	39	66	82	01	28	67	51	75	66	33	97	47	58	42	44	88	09	28	58	06
67	92	65	41	45	36	77	96	46	21	14	39	56	36	70	15	74	43	62	69	82	30	77	28	77
72	56	73	44	26	04	62	81	15	35	79	26	99	57	28	22	25	94	80	62	95	48	98	23	86
28	86	85	64	94	11	58	78	45	36	34	45	91	38	51	10	68	36	87	81	16	77	30	19	36
69	57	40	80	44	94	60	82	94	93	98	01	48	50	57	69	60	77	69	60	74	22	05	77	17
71	20	03	30	79	25	74	17	78	34	54	45	04	77	42	59	75	78	64	99	37	03	18	03	36
89	98	55	98	22	45	12	49	82	71	57	33	28	69	50	59	15	09	25	79	39	42	84	18	70
58	74	82	81	14	02	01	05	77	94	65	57	70	39	42	48	56	84	31	59	18	70	41	74	60
50	54	73	81	91	07	81	26	25	45	49	61	22	88	41	20	00	15	59	93	51	60	65	65	63
49	33	72	90	10	20	65	28	44	63	95	86	75	78	69	24	41	65	86	10	34	10	32	00	93
11	85	01	43	65	02	85	69	56	88	34	29	64	35	48	15	70	11	77	83	01	34	82	91	04
34	22	46	41	84	74	27	02	57	77	47	93	72	02	95	63	75	74	69	69	61	34	31	92	13

Source: *Adapted with permission from* A Million Random Digits *by the Rand Corporation, Copyright, 1955, The Free Press.*

495

APPENDIX B. Cumulative Normal Distribution

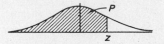

Values of P corresponding to z for the normal curve. z is the standard normal variable. The value of P for $-z$ equals one minus the value of P for $+z$, e.g., the P for -1.62 equals $1 - .9474 = .0526$.

z	.00	.01	.02	.03	.04	.05	.06	.07	.08	.09
.0	.5000	.5040	.5080	.5120	.5160	.5199	.5239	.5279	.5319	.5359
.1	.5398	.5438	.5478	.5517	.5557	.5596	.5636	.5675	.5714	.5753
.2	.5793	.5832	.5871	.5910	.5948	.5987	.6026	.6064	.6103	.6141
.3	.6179	.6217	.6255	.6293	.6331	.6368	.6406	.6443	.6480	.6517
.4	.6554	.6591	.6628	.6664	.6700	.6736	.6772	.6808	.6844	.6879
.5	.6915	.6950	.6985	.7019	.7054	.7088	.7123	.7157	.7190	.7224
.6	.7257	.7291	.7324	.7357	.7389	.7422	.7454	.7486	.7517	.7549
.7	.7580	.7611	.7642	.7673	.7704	.7734	.7764	.7794	.7823	.7852
.8	.7881	.7910	.7939	.7967	.7995	.8023	.8051	.8078	.8106	.8133
.9	.8159	.8186	.8212	.8238	.8264	.8289	.8315	.8340	.8365	.8389
1.0	.8413	.8438	.8461	.8485	.8508	.8531	.8554	.8577	.8599	.8621
1.1	.8643	.8665	.8686	.8708	.8729	.8749	.8770	.8790	.8810	.8830
1.2	.8849	.8869	.8888	.8907	.8925	.8944	.8962	.8980	.8997	.9015
1.3	.9032	.9049	.9066	.9082	.9099	.9115	.9131	.9147	.9162	.9177
1.4	.9192	.9207	.9222	.9236	.9251	.9265	.9279	.9292	.9306	.9319
1.5	.9332	.9345	.9357	.9370	.9382	.9394	.9406	.9418	.9429	.9441
1.6	.9452	.9463	.9474	.9484	.9495	.9505	.9515	.9525	.9535	.9545
1.7	.9554	.9564	.9573	.9582	.9591	.9599	.9608	.9616	.9625	.9633
1.8	.9641	.9649	.9656	.9664	.9671	.9678	.9686	.9693	.9699	.9706
1.9	.9713	.9719	.9726	.9732	.9738	.9744	.9750	.9756	.9761	.9767
2.0	.9772	.9778	.9783	.9788	.9793	.9798	.9803	.9808	.9812	.9817
2.1	.9821	.9826	.9830	.9834	.9838	.9842	.9846	.9850	.9854	.9857
2.2	.9861	.9864	.9868	.9871	.9875	.9878	.9881	.9884	.9887	.9890
2.3	.9893	.9896	.9898	.9901	.9904	.9906	.9909	.9911	.9913	.9916
2.4	.9918	.9920	.9922	.9925	.9927	.9929	.9931	.9932	.9934	.9936
2.5	.9938	.9940	.9941	.9943	.9945	.9946	.9948	.9949	.9951	.9952
2.6	.9953	.9955	.9956	.9957	.9959	.9960	.9961	.9962	.9963	.9964
2.7	.9965	.9966	.9967	.9968	.9969	.9970	.9971	.9972	.9973	.9974
2.8	.9974	.9975	.9976	.9977	.9977	.9978	.9979	.9979	.9980	.9981
2.9	.9981	.9982	.9982	.9983	.9984	.9984	.9985	.9985	.9986	.9986
3.0	.9987	.9987	.9987	.9988	.9988	.9989	.9989	.9989	.9990	.9990
3.1	.9990	.9991	.9991	.9991	.9992	.9992	.9992	.9992	.9993	.9993
3.2	.9993	.9993	.9994	.9994	.9994	.9994	.9994	.9995	.9995	.9995
3.3	.9995	.9995	.9995	.9996	.9996	.9996	.9996	.9996	.9996	.9997
3.4	.9997	.9997	.9997	.9997	.9997	.9997	.9997	.9997	.9997	.9998

Source: Paul E. Green and Donald S. Tull, Research for Marketing Decisions, 3rd ed. (Englewood Cliffs, N.J.: Prentice-Hall, Inc., 1975), p. 736. Reprinted by permission of Prentice-Hall, Inc., Englewood Cliffs, N.J.

APPENDIX C. Percentiles of the _t_ Distribution (one- and two-tailed tests)[a]

d.f.	P = .50 (.25)	.20 (.10)	.10 (.05)	.05 (.025)	.02 (.01)	.01 (.005)	.001 (.0005)
1	1.000	3.078	6.314	12.706	31.821	63.657	636.619
2	.816	1.886	2.920	4.303	6.965	9.925	31.598
3	.765	1.638	2.353	3.182	4.541	5.841	12.941
4	.741	1.533	2.132	2.776	3.747	4.604	8.610
5	.727	1.476	2.015	2.571	3.365	4.032	6.859
6	.718	1.440	1.943	2.447	3.143	3.707	5.959
7	.711	1.415	1.895	2.365	2.998	3.499	5.405
8	.706	1.397	1.860	2.306	2.896	3.355	5.041
9	.703	1.383	1.833	2.262	2.821	3.250	4.781
10	.700	1.372	1.812	2.228	2.764	3.169	4.587
11	.697	1.363	1.796	2.201	2.718	3.106	4.437
12	.695	1.356	1.782	2.179	2.681	3.055	4.318
13	.694	1.350	1.771	2.160	2.650	3.012	4.221
14	.692	1.345	1.761	2.145	2.624	2.977	4.140
15	.691	1.341	1.753	2.131	2.602	2.947	4.073
16	.690	1.337	1.746	2.120	2.583	2.921	4.015
17	.689	1.333	1.740	2.110	2.567	2.898	3.965
18	.688	1.330	1.734	2.101	2.552	2.878	3.922
19	.688	1.328	1.729	2.093	2.339	2.861	3.883
20	.687	1.325	1.725	2.086	2.528	2.845	3.850
21	.686	1.323	1.721	2.080	2.518	2.831	3.819
22	.686	1.321	1.717	2.074	2.508	2.819	3.792
23	.685	1.319	1.714	2.069	2.500	2.807	3.767
24	.685	1.318	1.711	2.064	2.492	2.797	3.745
25	.684	1.316	1.708	2.060	2.485	2.787	3.725
26	.684	1.315	1.706	2.056	2.479	2.779	3.707
27	.684	1.314	1.703	2.052	2.473	2.771	3.690
28	.683	1.313	1.701	2.048	2.467	2.763	3.674
29	.683	1.311	1.699	2.045	2.462	2.756	3.659
30	.683	1.310	1.697	2.042	2.457	2.750	3.646
40	.681	1.303	1.684	2.021	2.423	2.704	3.551
60	.679	1.296	1.671	2.000	2.390	2.660	3.460
120	.677	1.289	1.658	1.980	2.358	2.617	3.373
∞	.674	1.282	1.645	1.960	2.326	2.576	3.291

[a] The p in parentheses is for a one-tailed test.

Source: Abridged from Table IV of R. A. Fisher, Statistical Methods for Research Workers, _14th ed., (Copyright © 1970 University of Adelaide.)_

APPENDIX D. Percentiles of the χ^2 Distribution

Values of χ^2 corresponding to P

df	$\chi^2_{.005}$	$\chi^2_{.01}$	$\chi^2_{.025}$	$\chi^2_{.05}$	$\chi^2_{.10}$	$\chi^2_{.90}$	$\chi^2_{.95}$	$\chi^2_{.975}$	$\chi^2_{.99}$	$\chi^2_{.995}$
1	.000039	.00016	.00098	.0039	.0158	2.71	3.84	5.02	6.63	7.88
2	.0100	.0201	.0506	.1026	.2107	4.61	5.99	7.38	9.21	10.60
3	.0717	.115	.216	.352	.584	6.25	7.81	9.35	11.34	12.84
4	.207	.297	.484	.711	1.064	7.78	9.49	11.14	13.28	14.86
5	.412	.554	.831	1.15	1.61	9.24	11.07	12.83	15.09	16.75
6	.676	.872	1.24	1.64	2.20	10.64	12.59	14.45	16.81	18.55
7	.989	1.24	1.69	2.17	2.83	12.02	14.07	16.01	18.48	20.28
8	1.34	1.65	2.18	2.73	3.49	13.36	15.51	17.53	20.09	21.96
9	1.73	2.09	2.70	3.33	4.17	14.68	16.92	19.02	21.67	23.59
10	2.16	2.56	3.25	3.94	4.87	15.99	18.31	20.48	23.21	25.19
11	2.60	3.05	3.82	4.57	5.58	17.28	19.68	21.92	24.73	26.76
12	3.07	3.57	4.40	5.23	6.30	18.55	21.03	23.34	26.22	28.30
13	3.57	4.11	5.01	5.89	7.04	19.81	22.36	24.74	27.69	29.82
14	4.07	4.66	5.63	6.57	7.79	21.06	23.68	26.12	29.14	31.32
15	4.60	5.23	6.26	7.26	8.55	22.31	25.00	27.49	30.58	32.80
16	5.14	5.81	6.91	7.96	9.31	23.54	26.30	28.85	32.00	34.27
18	6.26	7.01	8.23	9.39	10.86	25.99	28.87	31.53	34.81	37.16
20	7.43	8.26	9.59	10.85	12.44	28.41	31.41	34.17	37.57	40.00
24	9.89	10.86	12.40	13.85	15.66	33.20	36.42	39.36	42.98	45.56
30	13.79	14.95	16.79	18.49	20.60	40.26	43.77	46.98	50.89	53.67
40	20.71	22.16	24.43	26.51	29.05	51.81	55.76	59.34	63.69	66.77
60	35.53	37.48	40.48	43.19	46.46	74.40	79.08	83.30	88.38	91.95
120	83.85	86.92	91.58	95.70	100.62	140.23	146.57	152.21	158.95	163.64

Source: Paul E. Green and Donald S. Tull, Research for Marketing Decisions, *3rd ed. (Englewood Cliffs, N.J.: Prentice-Hall, Inc., 1975), p. 760. Reprinted by permission of Prentice-Hall, Inc., Englewood Cliffs, N.J.*

APPENDIX E. Percentiles of the F Distribution

$$F_{.90}(n_1, n_2) \qquad \alpha = 0.1$$

n_1 = degrees of freedom for numerator

n_2 = degrees of freedom for denominator

$n_2 \backslash n_1$	1	2	3	4	5	6	7	8	9	10	12	15	20	24	30	40	60	120	∞
1	39.86	49.50	53.59	55.83	57.24	58.20	58.91	59.44	59.86	60.19	60.71	61.22	61.74	62.00	62.26	62.53	62.79	63.06	63.33
2	8.53	9.00	9.16	9.24	9.29	9.33	9.35	9.37	9.38	9.39	9.41	9.42	9.44	9.45	9.46	9.47	9.47	9.48	9.49
3	5.54	5.46	5.39	5.34	5.31	5.28	5.27	5.25	5.24	5.23	5.22	5.20	5.18	5.18	5.17	5.16	5.15	5.14	5.13
4	4.54	4.32	4.19	4.11	4.05	4.01	3.98	3.95	3.94	3.92	3.90	3.87	3.84	3.83	3.82	3.80	3.79	3.78	3.76
5	4.06	3.78	3.62	3.52	3.45	3.40	3.37	3.34	3.32	3.30	3.27	3.24	3.21	3.19	3.17	3.16	3.14	3.12	3.10
6	3.78	3.46	3.29	3.18	3.11	3.05	3.01	2.98	2.96	2.94	2.90	2.87	2.84	2.82	2.80	2.78	2.76	2.74	2.72
7	3.59	3.26	3.07	2.96	2.88	2.83	2.78	2.75	2.72	2.70	2.67	2.63	2.59	2.58	2.56	2.54	2.51	2.49	2.47
8	3.46	3.11	2.92	2.81	2.73	2.67	2.62	2.59	2.56	2.54	2.50	2.46	2.42	2.40	2.38	2.36	2.34	2.32	2.29
9	3.36	3.01	2.81	2.69	2.61	2.55	2.51	2.47	2.44	2.42	2.38	2.34	2.30	2.28	2.25	2.23	2.21	2.18	2.16
10	3.29	2.92	2.73	2.61	2.52	2.46	2.41	2.38	2.35	2.32	2.28	2.24	2.20	2.18	2.16	2.13	2.11	2.08	2.06
11	3.23	2.86	2.66	2.54	2.45	2.39	2.34	2.30	2.27	2.25	2.21	2.17	2.12	2.10	2.08	2.05	2.03	2.00	1.97
12	3.18	2.81	2.61	2.48	2.39	2.33	2.28	2.24	2.21	2.19	2.15	2.10	2.06	2.04	2.01	1.99	1.96	1.93	1.90
13	3.14	2.76	2.56	2.43	2.35	2.28	2.23	2.20	2.16	2.14	2.10	2.05	2.01	1.98	1.96	1.93	1.90	1.88	1.85
14	3.10	2.73	2.52	2.39	2.31	2.24	2.19	2.15	2.12	2.10	2.05	2.01	1.96	1.94	1.91	1.89	1.86	1.83	1.80
15	3.07	2.70	2.49	2.36	2.27	2.21	2.16	2.12	2.09	2.06	2.02	1.97	1.92	1.90	1.87	1.85	1.82	1.79	1.76
16	3.05	2.67	2.46	2.33	2.24	2.18	2.13	2.09	2.06	2.03	1.99	1.94	1.89	1.87	1.84	1.81	1.78	1.75	1.72
17	3.03	2.64	2.44	2.31	2.22	2.15	2.10	2.06	2.03	2.00	1.96	1.91	1.86	1.84	1.81	1.78	1.75	1.72	1.69
18	3.01	2.62	2.42	2.29	2.20	2.13	2.08	2.04	2.00	1.98	1.93	1.89	1.84	1.81	1.78	1.75	1.72	1.69	1.66
19	2.99	2.61	2.40	2.27	2.18	2.11	2.06	2.02	1.98	1.96	1.91	1.86	1.81	1.79	1.76	1.73	1.70	1.67	1.63
20	2.97	2.59	2.38	2.25	2.16	2.09	2.04	2.00	1.96	1.94	1.89	1.84	1.79	1.77	1.74	1.71	1.68	1.64	1.61
21	2.96	2.57	2.36	2.23	2.14	2.08	2.02	1.98	1.95	1.92	1.87	1.83	1.78	1.75	1.72	1.69	1.66	1.62	1.59
22	2.95	2.56	2.35	2.22	2.13	2.06	2.01	1.97	1.93	1.90	1.86	1.81	1.76	1.73	1.70	1.67	1.64	1.60	1.57
23	2.94	2.55	2.34	2.21	2.11	2.05	1.99	1.95	1.92	1.89	1.84	1.80	1.74	1.72	1.69	1.66	1.62	1.59	1.55
24	2.93	2.54	2.33	2.19	2.10	2.04	1.98	1.94	1.91	1.88	1.83	1.78	1.73	1.70	1.67	1.64	1.61	1.57	1.53
25	2.92	2.53	2.32	2.18	2.09	2.02	1.97	1.93	1.89	1.87	1.82	1.77	1.72	1.69	1.66	1.63	1.59	1.56	1.52
26	2.91	2.52	2.31	2.17	2.08	2.01	1.96	1.92	1.88	1.86	1.81	1.76	1.71	1.68	1.65	1.61	1.58	1.54	1.50
27	2.90	2.51	2.30	2.17	2.07	2.00	1.95	1.91	1.87	1.85	1.80	1.75	1.70	1.67	1.64	1.60	1.57	1.53	1.49
28	2.89	2.50	2.29	2.16	2.06	2.00	1.94	1.90	1.87	1.84	1.79	1.74	1.69	1.66	1.63	1.59	1.56	1.52	1.48
29	2.89	2.50	2.28	2.15	2.06	1.99	1.93	1.89	1.86	1.83	1.78	1.73	1.68	1.65	1.62	1.58	1.55	1.51	1.47
30	2.88	2.49	2.28	2.14	2.05	1.98	1.93	1.88	1.85	1.82	1.77	1.72	1.67	1.64	1.61	1.57	1.54	1.50	1.46
40	2.84	2.44	2.23	2.09	2.00	1.93	1.87	1.83	1.79	1.76	1.71	1.66	1.61	1.57	1.54	1.51	1.47	1.42	1.38
60	2.79	2.39	2.18	2.04	1.95	1.87	1.82	1.77	1.74	1.71	1.66	1.60	1.54	1.51	1.48	1.44	1.40	1.35	1.29
120	2.75	2.35	2.13	1.99	1.90	1.82	1.77	1.72	1.68	1.65	1.60	1.55	1.48	1.45	1.41	1.37	1.32	1.26	1.19
∞	2.71	2.30	2.08	1.94	1.85	1.77	1.72	1.67	1.63	1.60	1.55	1.49	1.42	1.38	1.34	1.30	1.24	1.17	1.00

Source: Adapted with permission from Biometrika Tables for Statisticians, Vol. 1 (2nd ed.), edited by E. S. Pearson and H. O. Hartley, Copyright 1958, Cambridge University Press.

APPENDIX E. *Continued*

$$F_{.975}(n_1, n_2)$$

α = 0.025

n_1 = degrees of freedom for numerator

n_2 = degrees of freedom for denominator

n_2 \ n_1	1	2	3	4	5	6	7	8	9	10	12	15	20	24	30	40	60	120	∞
1	647.8	799.5	864.2	899.6	921.8	937.1	948.2	956.7	963.3	968.6	976.7	984.9	993.1	997.2	1001	1006	1010	1014	1018
2	38.51	39.00	39.17	39.25	39.30	39.33	39.36	39.37	39.39	39.40	39.41	39.43	39.45	39.46	39.46	39.47	39.48	39.49	39.50
3	17.44	16.04	15.44	15.10	14.88	14.73	14.62	14.54	14.47	14.42	14.34	14.25	14.17	14.12	14.08	14.04	13.99	13.95	13.90
4	12.22	10.65	9.98	9.60	9.36	9.20	9.07	8.98	8.90	8.84	8.75	8.66	8.56	8.51	8.46	8.41	8.36	8.31	8.26
5	10.01	8.43	7.76	7.39	7.15	6.98	6.85	6.76	6.68	6.62	6.52	6.43	6.33	6.28	6.23	6.18	6.12	6.07	6.02
6	8.81	7.26	6.60	6.23	5.99	5.82	5.70	5.60	5.52	5.46	5.37	5.27	5.17	5.12	5.07	5.01	4.96	4.90	4.85
7	8.07	6.54	5.89	5.52	5.29	5.12	4.99	4.90	4.82	4.76	4.67	4.57	4.47	4.42	4.36	4.31	4.25	4.20	4.14
8	7.57	6.06	5.42	5.05	4.82	4.65	4.53	4.43	4.36	4.30	4.20	4.10	4.00	3.95	3.89	3.84	3.78	3.73	3.67
9	7.21	5.71	5.08	4.72	4.48	4.32	4.20	4.10	4.03	3.96	3.87	3.77	3.67	3.61	3.56	3.51	3.45	3.39	3.33
10	6.94	5.46	4.83	4.47	4.24	4.07	3.95	3.85	3.78	3.72	3.62	3.52	3.42	3.37	3.31	3.26	3.20	3.14	3.08
11	6.72	5.26	4.63	4.28	4.04	3.88	3.76	3.66	3.59	3.53	3.43	3.33	3.23	3.17	3.12	3.06	3.00	2.94	2.88
12	6.55	5.10	4.47	4.12	3.89	3.73	3.61	3.51	3.44	3.37	3.28	3.18	3.07	3.02	2.96	2.91	2.85	2.79	2.72
13	6.41	4.97	4.35	4.00	3.77	3.60	3.48	3.39	3.31	3.25	3.15	3.05	2.95	2.89	2.84	2.78	2.72	2.66	2.60
14	6.30	4.86	4.24	3.89	3.66	3.50	3.38	3.29	3.21	3.15	3.05	2.95	2.84	2.79	2.73	2.67	2.61	2.55	2.49
15	6.20	4.77	4.15	3.80	3.58	3.41	3.29	3.20	3.12	3.06	2.96	2.86	2.76	2.70	2.64	2.59	2.52	2.46	2.40
16	6.12	4.69	4.08	3.73	3.50	3.34	3.22	3.12	3.05	2.99	2.89	2.79	2.68	2.63	2.57	2.51	2.45	2.38	2.32
17	6.04	4.62	4.01	3.66	3.44	3.28	3.16	3.06	2.98	2.92	2.82	2.72	2.62	2.56	2.50	2.44	2.38	2.32	2.25
18	5.98	4.56	3.95	3.61	3.38	3.22	3.10	3.01	2.93	2.87	2.77	2.67	2.56	2.50	2.44	2.38	2.32	2.26	2.19
19	5.92	4.51	3.90	3.56	3.33	3.17	3.05	2.96	2.88	2.82	2.72	2.62	2.51	2.45	2.39	2.33	2.27	2.20	2.13
20	5.87	4.46	3.86	3.51	3.29	3.13	3.01	2.91	2.84	2.77	2.68	2.57	2.46	2.41	2.35	2.29	2.22	2.16	2.09
21	5.83	4.42	3.82	3.48	3.25	3.09	2.97	2.87	2.80	2.73	2.64	2.53	2.42	2.37	2.31	2.25	2.18	2.11	2.04
22	5.79	4.38	3.78	3.44	3.22	3.05	2.93	2.84	2.76	2.70	2.60	2.50	2.39	2.33	2.27	2.21	2.14	2.08	2.00
23	5.75	4.35	3.75	3.41	3.18	3.02	2.90	2.81	2.73	2.67	2.57	2.47	2.36	2.30	2.24	2.18	2.11	2.04	1.97
24	5.72	4.32	3.72	3.38	3.15	2.99	2.87	2.78	2.70	2.64	2.54	2.44	2.33	2.27	2.21	2.15	2.08	2.01	1.94
25	5.69	4.29	3.69	3.35	3.13	2.97	2.85	2.75	2.68	2.61	2.51	2.41	2.30	2.24	2.18	2.12	2.05	1.98	1.91
26	5.66	4.27	3.67	3.33	3.10	2.94	2.82	2.73	2.65	2.59	2.49	2.39	2.28	2.22	2.16	2.09	2.03	1.95	1.88
27	5.63	4.24	3.65	3.31	3.08	2.92	2.80	2.71	2.63	2.57	2.47	2.36	2.25	2.19	2.13	2.07	2.00	1.93	1.85
28	5.61	4.22	3.63	3.29	3.06	2.90	2.78	2.69	2.61	2.55	2.45	2.34	2.23	2.17	2.11	2.05	1.98	1.91	1.83
29	5.59	4.20	3.61	3.27	3.04	2.88	2.76	2.67	2.59	2.53	2.43	2.32	2.21	2.15	2.09	2.03	1.96	1.89	1.81
30	5.57	4.18	3.59	3.25	3.03	2.87	2.75	2.65	2.57	2.51	2.41	2.31	2.20	2.14	2.07	2.01	1.94	1.87	1.79
40	5.42	4.05	3.46	3.13	2.90	2.74	2.62	2.53	2.45	2.39	2.29	2.18	2.07	2.01	1.94	1.88	1.80	1.72	1.64
60	5.29	3.93	3.34	3.01	2.79	2.63	2.51	2.41	2.33	2.27	2.17	2.06	1.94	1.88	1.82	1.74	1.67	1.58	1.48
120	5.15	3.80	3.23	2.89	2.67	2.52	2.39	2.30	2.22	2.16	2.05	1.94	1.82	1.76	1.69	1.61	1.53	1.43	1.31
∞	5.02	3.69	3.12	2.79	2.57	2.41	2.29	2.19	2.11	2.05	1.94	1.83	1.71	1.64	1.57	1.48	1.39	1.27	1.00

APPENDIX E. *Continued*

$$F_{.95}(n_1, n_2) \qquad \alpha = 0.05$$

n_1 = degrees of freedom for numerator

n_2 = degrees of freedom for denominator

n_2 \ n_1	1	2	3	4	5	6	7	8	9	10	12	15	20	24	30	40	60	120	∞
1	161.4	199.5	215.7	224.6	230.2	234.0	236.8	238.9	240.5	241.9	243.9	245.9	248.0	249.1	250.1	251.1	252.2	253.3	254.3
2	18.51	19.00	19.16	19.25	19.30	19.33	19.35	19.37	19.38	19.40	19.41	19.43	19.45	19.45	19.46	19.47	19.48	19.49	19.50
3	10.13	9.55	9.28	9.12	9.01	8.94	8.89	8.85	8.81	8.79	8.74	8.70	8.66	8.64	8.62	8.59	8.57	8.55	8.53
4	7.71	6.94	6.59	6.39	6.26	6.16	6.09	6.04	6.00	5.96	5.91	5.86	5.80	5.77	5.75	5.72	5.69	5.66	5.63
5	6.61	5.79	5.41	5.19	5.05	4.95	4.88	4.82	4.77	4.74	4.68	4.62	4.56	4.53	4.50	4.46	4.43	4.40	4.36
6	5.99	5.14	4.76	4.53	4.39	4.28	4.21	4.15	4.10	4.06	4.00	3.94	3.87	3.84	3.81	3.77	3.74	3.70	3.67
7	5.59	4.74	4.35	4.12	3.97	3.87	3.79	3.73	3.68	3.64	3.57	3.51	3.44	3.41	3.38	3.34	3.30	3.27	3.23
8	5.32	4.46	4.07	3.84	3.69	3.58	3.50	3.44	3.39	3.35	3.28	3.22	3.15	3.12	3.08	3.04	3.01	2.97	2.93
9	5.12	4.26	3.86	3.63	3.48	3.37	3.29	3.23	3.18	3.14	3.07	3.01	2.94	2.90	2.86	2.83	2.79	2.75	2.71
10	4.96	4.10	3.71	3.48	3.33	3.22	3.14	3.07	3.02	2.98	2.91	2.85	2.77	2.74	2.70	2.66	2.62	2.58	2.54
11	4.84	3.98	3.59	3.36	3.20	3.09	3.01	2.95	2.90	2.85	2.79	2.72	2.65	2.61	2.57	2.53	2.49	2.45	2.40
12	4.75	3.89	3.49	3.26	3.11	3.00	2.91	2.85	2.80	2.75	2.69	2.62	2.54	2.51	2.47	2.43	2.38	2.34	2.30
13	4.67	3.81	3.41	3.18	3.03	2.92	2.83	2.77	2.71	2.67	2.60	2.53	2.46	2.42	2.38	2.34	2.30	2.25	2.21
14	4.60	3.74	3.34	3.11	2.96	2.85	2.76	2.70	2.65	2.60	2.53	2.46	2.39	2.35	2.31	2.27	2.22	2.18	2.13
15	4.54	3.68	3.29	3.06	2.90	2.79	2.71	2.64	2.59	2.54	2.48	2.40	2.33	2.29	2.25	2.20	2.16	2.11	2.07
16	4.49	3.63	3.24	3.01	2.85	2.74	2.66	2.59	2.54	2.49	2.42	2.35	2.28	2.24	2.19	2.15	2.11	2.06	2.01
17	4.45	3.59	3.20	2.96	2.81	2.70	2.61	2.55	2.49	2.45	2.38	2.31	2.23	2.19	2.15	2.10	2.06	2.01	1.96
18	4.41	3.55	3.16	2.93	2.77	2.66	2.58	2.51	2.46	2.41	2.34	2.27	2.19	2.15	2.11	2.06	2.02	1.97	1.92
19	4.38	3.52	3.13	2.90	2.74	2.63	2.54	2.48	2.42	2.38	2.31	2.23	2.16	2.11	2.07	2.03	1.98	1.93	1.88
20	4.35	3.49	3.10	2.87	2.71	2.60	2.51	2.45	2.39	2.35	2.28	2.20	2.12	2.08	2.04	1.99	1.95	1.90	1.84
21	4.32	3.47	3.07	2.84	2.68	2.57	2.49	2.42	2.37	2.32	2.25	2.18	2.10	2.05	2.01	1.96	1.92	1.87	1.81
22	4.30	3.44	3.05	2.82	2.66	2.55	2.46	2.40	2.34	2.30	2.23	2.15	2.07	2.03	1.98	1.94	1.89	1.84	1.78
23	4.28	3.42	3.03	2.80	2.64	2.53	2.44	2.37	2.32	2.27	2.20	2.13	2.05	2.01	1.96	1.91	1.86	1.81	1.76
24	4.26	3.40	3.01	2.78	2.62	2.51	2.42	2.36	2.30	2.25	2.18	2.11	2.03	1.98	1.94	1.89	1.84	1.79	1.73
25	4.24	3.39	2.99	2.76	2.60	2.49	2.40	2.34	2.28	2.24	2.16	2.09	2.01	1.96	1.92	1.87	1.82	1.77	1.71
26	4.23	3.37	2.98	2.74	2.59	2.47	2.39	2.32	2.27	2.22	2.15	2.07	1.99	1.95	1.90	1.85	1.80	1.75	1.69
27	4.21	3.35	2.96	2.73	2.57	2.46	2.37	2.31	2.25	2.20	2.13	2.06	1.97	1.93	1.88	1.84	1.79	1.73	1.67
28	4.20	3.34	2.95	2.71	2.56	2.45	2.36	2.29	2.24	2.19	2.12	2.04	1.96	1.91	1.87	1.82	1.77	1.71	1.65
29	4.18	3.33	2.93	2.70	2.55	2.43	2.35	2.28	2.22	2.18	2.10	2.03	1.94	1.90	1.85	1.81	1.75	1.70	1.64
30	4.17	3.32	2.92	2.69	2.53	2.42	2.33	2.27	2.21	2.16	2.09	2.01	1.93	1.89	1.84	1.79	1.74	1.68	1.62
40	4.08	3.23	2.84	2.61	2.45	2.34	2.25	2.18	2.12	2.08	2.00	1.92	1.84	1.79	1.74	1.69	1.64	1.58	1.51
60	4.00	3.15	2.76	2.53	2.37	2.25	2.17	2.10	2.04	1.99	1.92	1.84	1.75	1.70	1.65	1.59	1.53	1.47	1.39
120	3.92	3.07	2.68	2.45	2.29	2.17	2.09	2.02	1.96	1.91	1.83	1.75	1.66	1.61	1.55	1.50	1.43	1.35	1.25
∞	3.84	3.00	2.60	2.37	2.21	2.10	2.01	1.94	1.88	1.83	1.75	1.67	1.57	1.52	1.46	1.39	1.32	1.22	1.00

APPENDIX E. *Continued*

$$F_{.99}(n_1, n_2)$$

$$\alpha = 0.01$$

n_1 = degrees of freedom for denominator

n_2 \\ n_1	1	2	3	4	5	6	7	8	9	10	12	15	20	24	30	40	60	120	∞
1	4052	4999.5	5403	5625	5764	5859	5928	5982	6022	6056	6106	6157	6209	6235	6261	6287	6313	6339	6366
2	98.50	99.00	99.17	99.25	99.30	99.33	99.36	99.37	99.39	99.40	99.42	99.43	99.45	99.46	99.47	99.47	99.48	99.49	99.50
3	34.12	30.82	29.46	28.71	28.24	27.91	27.67	27.49	27.35	27.23	27.05	26.87	26.69	26.60	26.50	26.41	26.32	26.22	26.13
4	21.20	18.00	16.69	15.98	15.52	15.21	14.98	14.80	14.66	14.55	14.37	14.20	14.02	13.93	13.84	13.75	13.65	13.56	13.46
5	16.26	13.27	12.06	11.39	10.97	10.67	10.46	10.29	10.16	10.05	9.89	9.72	9.55	9.47	9.38	9.29	9.20	9.11	9.02
6	13.75	10.92	9.78	9.15	8.75	8.47	8.26	8.10	7.98	7.87	7.72	7.56	7.40	7.31	7.23	7.14	7.06	6.97	6.88
7	12.25	9.55	8.45	7.85	7.46	7.19	6.99	6.84	6.72	6.62	6.47	6.31	6.16	6.07	5.99	5.91	5.82	5.74	5.65
8	11.26	8.65	7.59	7.01	6.63	6.37	6.18	6.03	5.91	5.81	5.67	5.52	5.36	5.28	5.20	5.12	5.03	4.95	4.86
9	10.56	8.02	6.99	6.42	6.06	5.80	5.61	5.47	5.35	5.26	5.11	4.96	4.81	4.73	4.65	4.57	4.48	4.40	4.31
10	10.04	7.56	6.55	5.99	5.64	5.39	5.20	5.06	4.94	4.85	4.71	4.56	4.41	4.33	4.25	4.17	4.08	4.00	3.91
11	9.65	7.21	6.22	5.67	5.32	5.07	4.89	4.74	4.63	4.54	4.40	4.25	4.10	4.02	3.94	3.86	3.78	3.69	3.60
12	9.33	6.93	5.95	5.41	5.06	4.82	4.64	4.50	4.39	4.30	4.16	4.01	3.86	3.78	3.70	3.62	3.54	3.45	3.36
13	9.07	6.70	5.74	5.21	4.86	4.62	4.44	4.30	4.19	4.10	3.96	3.82	3.66	3.59	3.51	3.43	3.34	3.25	3.17
14	8.86	6.51	5.56	5.04	4.69	4.46	4.28	4.14	4.03	3.94	3.80	3.66	3.51	3.43	3.35	3.27	3.18	3.09	3.00
15	8.68	6.36	5.42	4.89	4.56	4.32	4.14	4.00	3.89	3.80	3.67	3.52	3.37	3.29	3.21	3.13	3.05	2.96	2.87
16	8.53	6.23	5.29	4.77	4.44	4.20	4.03	3.89	3.78	3.69	3.55	3.41	3.26	3.18	3.10	3.02	2.93	2.84	2.75
17	8.40	6.11	5.18	4.67	4.34	4.10	3.93	3.79	3.68	3.59	3.46	3.31	3.16	3.08	3.00	2.92	2.83	2.75	2.65
18	8.29	6.01	5.09	4.58	4.25	4.01	3.84	3.71	3.60	3.51	3.37	3.23	3.08	3.00	2.92	2.84	2.75	2.66	2.57
19	8.18	5.93	5.01	4.50	4.17	3.94	3.77	3.63	3.52	3.43	3.30	3.15	3.00	2.92	2.84	2.76	2.67	2.58	2.49
20	8.10	5.85	4.94	4.43	4.10	3.87	3.70	3.56	3.46	3.37	3.23	3.09	2.94	2.86	2.78	2.69	2.61	2.52	2.42
21	8.02	5.78	4.87	4.37	4.04	3.81	3.64	3.51	3.40	3.31	3.17	3.03	2.88	2.80	2.72	2.64	2.55	2.46	2.36
22	7.95	5.72	4.82	4.31	3.99	3.76	3.59	3.45	3.35	3.26	3.12	2.98	2.83	2.75	2.67	2.58	2.50	2.40	2.31
23	7.88	5.66	4.76	4.26	3.94	3.71	3.54	3.41	3.30	3.21	3.07	2.93	2.78	2.70	2.62	2.54	2.45	2.35	2.26
24	7.82	5.61	4.72	4.22	3.90	3.67	3.50	3.36	3.26	3.17	3.03	2.89	2.74	2.66	2.58	2.49	2.40	2.31	2.21
25	7.77	5.57	4.68	4.18	3.85	3.63	3.46	3.32	3.22	3.13	2.99	2.85	2.70	2.62	2.54	2.45	2.36	2.27	2.17
26	7.72	5.53	4.64	4.14	3.82	3.59	3.42	3.29	3.18	3.09	2.96	2.81	2.66	2.58	2.50	2.42	2.33	2.23	2.13
27	7.68	5.49	4.60	4.11	3.78	3.56	3.39	3.26	3.15	3.06	2.93	2.78	2.63	2.55	2.47	2.38	2.29	2.20	2.10
28	7.64	5.45	4.57	4.07	3.75	3.53	3.36	3.23	3.12	3.03	2.90	2.75	2.60	2.52	2.44	2.35	2.26	2.17	2.06
29	7.60	5.42	4.54	4.04	3.73	3.50	3.33	3.20	3.09	3.00	2.87	2.73	2.57	2.49	2.41	2.33	2.23	2.14	2.03
30	7.56	5.39	4.51	4.02	3.70	3.47	3.30	3.17	3.07	2.98	2.84	2.70	2.55	2.47	2.39	2.30	2.21	2.11	2.01
40	7.31	5.18	4.31	3.83	3.51	3.29	3.12	2.99	2.89	2.80	2.66	2.52	2.37	2.29	2.20	2.11	2.02	1.92	1.80
60	7.08	4.98	4.13	3.65	3.34	3.12	2.95	2.82	2.72	2.63	2.50	2.35	2.20	2.12	2.03	1.94	1.84	1.73	1.60
120	6.85	4.79	3.95	3.48	3.17	2.96	2.79	2.66	2.56	2.47	2.34	2.19	2.03	1.95	1.86	1.76	1.66	1.53	1.38
∞	6.63	4.61	3.78	3.32	3.02	2.80	2.64	2.51	2.41	2.32	2.18	2.04	1.88	1.79	1.70	1.59	1.47	1.32	1.00

n_2 = degrees of freedom for denominator

Selected Bibliography

Chapter 1

BERG, THOMAS L., *Mismarketing: Case Histories of Marketing Misfires,* Garden City, NY: Doubleday & Co., Inc., 1971.

BUZZELL, ROBERT D., "Is Marketing a Science?" *Harvard Business Review,* January/February, 1963, pp. 32–40, 166–170.

RAMOND, CHARLES, *The Art of Using Science in Marketing.* New York: Harper & Row, 1974.

RAPOPORT, ANATOL, *Science and the Goals of Man.* New York: Harper & Row, 1950.

TWEDT, DIK W., ed., *1973 Survey of Marketing Research.* Chicago: American Marketing Association, 1973. This is repeated at five year intervals.

Chapter 2

ENIS, BEN M. and CHARLES L. BROOME, *Marketing Decisions, A Bayesian Approach.* Scranton, Pa.: Intext Educational Publishers, 1971.

FERBER, ROBERT, ed., *Handbook of Marketing Research.* New York: McGraw-Hill Book Co., 1974, Section I.

GREEN, PAUL E., and DONALD S. TULL, *Research for Marketing Decisions* (3rd ed.), Englewood Cliffs, N.J.: Prentice-Hall, Inc., 1975.

JOLSON, MARVIN A. and RICHARD T. HISE, *Quantitative Techniques for Marketing Decisions.* New York: The MacMillan Company, 1973.

KOTLER, PHILIP, *Marketing Decision Making: A Model Building Approach.* New York: Holt, Rinehart & Winston, 1971.

MURDICK, ROBERT G. and JOEL E. ROSS, *Introduction to Management Information Systems.* Englewood Cliffs, N.J.: Prentice-Hall, Inc., 1977.

Chapter 3

BERGER, FRED R., *Studying Deductive Logic.* Englewood Cliffs, N.J.: Prentice-Hall, Inc., 1977.

COHEN, MORRIS R. and ERNEST NAGEL, *An Introduction to Logic.* New York: Harcourt, Brace & World, 1962.

ENNIS, ROBERT H., *Ordinary Logic.* Englewood Cliffs, N.J.: Prentice-Hall, Inc., 1969.

FOGG, C. DAVIS, "Planning Gains in Market Share," *Journal of Marketing,* July 1974, p. 35.

HULBERT, JAMES M. and NORMAN E. TOY, "A Strategic Framework for Marketing Control," *Journal of Marketing,* April 1977, pp. 12–20.

Chapter 4

ANDERSON, VIRGIL E., *Design of Experiments.* New York: M. Dekker, 1974.

BANKS, SEYMOUR, *Experimentation in Marketing.* New York: McGraw-Hill Book Co., 1965.

CAMPBELL, DONALD T. and JULIAN C. STANLEY, *Experimental and Quasi-experimental Design for Research.* Chicago: Rand McNally, 1966.

COX, K. K. and B. M. ENIS, *Experimentation for Marketing Decisions.* Scranton, Pa.: International Textbook Co., 1969.

DAVIS, C. J., *Experimental Marketing.* New York: American Management Association, Inc., 1970.

EDWARDS, ALLEN L., *Experimental Design in Psychological Research.* New York: Holt, Rinehart & Winston, 1972.

FISHER, SIR RONALD A., *The Design of Experiments* (8th ed.). New York: Harper & Row, 1971.

HEWITT, HUDY C., *Scope of Experimental Analysis.* Englewood Cliffs, N.J.: Prentice-Hall, Inc., 1973.

RAPPAPORT, ALFRED, *Information for Decision Making: Quantitative and Behavioral Dimensions* (2nd ed.). Englewood Cliffs, N.J.: Prentice-Hall, Inc., 1975.

SHANNON, ROBERT E., *Systems Simulation: The Art and Science.* Englewood Cliffs, N.J.: Prentice-Hall, Inc. 1975.

SIEGEL, SIDNEY, *Nonparametric Statistics for the Behavioral Sciences.* New York: McGraw-Hill Book Co., 1956.

Chapter 5

COX, K. K., JAMES B. HIGGINBOTHAM, and JOHN BURTON, "Applications of Focus Groups Interviews in Marketing, *Journal of Marketing,* January 1976, pp. 75–78.

FERBER, ROBERT, *Handbook of Marketing Research.* New York: McGraw-Hill Book Co., 1974, Sections I and II.

GREEN, PAUL E. and DONALD S. TULL, *Research for Marketing Decisions* (3rd ed.). Englewood Cliffs, N.J.: Prentice-Hall, Inc., 1975.

TWEDT, DIK W., "Authorization, Control, and Evaluation of Marketing Research Projects," *Journal of Marketing Research,* February 1975, pp. 85–8.

WELLS, WILLIAM D., "Psychographics: A Critical Review," *Journal of Marketing Research,* May 1975, pp. 194–99.

Chapter 6

FRANK, NATALIE D., *Data Sources for Business and Market Analysis* (2nd ed.). Metuchen, N.J.: Scarecrow Press, 1969.

Marketing Information Guide. Garden City, N.Y.: Trade Market Information Guides, Inc., Hoke Communications, Inc., monthly.

Encyclopedia of Business Information Sources (2nd ed.). Detroit: Gale Research Co., 1970.

Special Libraries and Information Centers in the United States and Canada. Detroit: Gale Research Co., 1974.

Chapter 7

COCHRAN, WILLIAM G., *Sampling Techniques* (2nd ed.). New York: John Wiley & Sons, Inc., 1963.

DEMING, W. E., *Sampling Design in Business Research.* New York: John Wiley & Sons, Inc., 1961.

DEMING, W. E., *Some Theory of Sampling.* New York: Dover Publications, Inc., 1966.

FERBER, ROBERT, *Market Research.* New York: McGraw-Hill Book Company, Inc., 1949.

FERBER, ROBERT and P. J. VERDOORN, *Research Methods in Economics and Business.* New York: Macmillan, 1962.

HANSEN, M. H., W. N. HURWITZ, and W. G. MADOW, *Sample Survey Methods and Theory,* Vols. I and II. New York: John Wiley & Sons, Inc., 1953.

KISH, LESLIE, *Survey Sampling.* New York: John Wiley & Sons, Inc., 1965.

SMITH, L. H. and D. R. WILLIAMS, *Statistical Analysis for Business.* Belmont, California: Wadsworth Publishing Company, 1971, Chapters 6 and 7.

Stephan, F. F. and P. J. McCARTHY, *Sampling Opinions: An Analysis of Survey Procedure.* New York: John Wiley & Sons, Inc., 1963.

YAMANE, TARO, *Elementary Sampling Theory.* Englewood Cliffs, N.J.: Prentice-Hall, Inc., 1967.

YATES, FRANK, *Sampling Methods for Censuses and Surveys* (3rd ed.). London: Charles Griffin & Co., Ltd., 1971.

Chapter 8*

COCHRAN, WILLIAM G., *Sampling Techniques* (2nd ed.). New York: John Wiley & Sons, 1963.

FERBER, ROBERT, *Market Research.* New York: McGraw-Hill Book Company, Inc., 1949.

FERBER, ROBERT and P. J. VERDOORN, *Research Methods in Economics and Business.* New York: Macmillan, 1962.

HANSEN, M. H., W. N. HURWITZ, and W. G. MADOW, *Sample Survey Methods and Theory,* Vols. I and II. New York: John Wiley & Sons, Inc., 1953.

KISH, LESLIE, *Survey Sampling.* New York: John Wiley & Sons, Inc., 1965.

Chapter 9

BERDIE, DOUGLAS R. and JOHN F. ANDERSON, *Questionnaires: Design and Use.* Metuchen, N.J.: Scarecrow Press, 1974.

CLARK, MALCOLM, *Perplexity and Questioning.* The Hague: Nijhoff, 1972.

FERBER, ROBERT, ed., *Handbook of Marketing Research.* New York: McGraw-Hill Book Co., 1974, Section III.

OPPENHEIM, ABRAHAM N., *Questionnaire Design and Attitude Measurement.* New York: Basic Books, 1966.

SPAETH, MARY A., *Recent Publications on Survey Research Techniques,* Journal of Marketing Research, August 1977, pp. 403–9.

WARWICK, DONALD P. and CHARLES A. LININGER, *The Sample Survey: Theory and Practice.* New York: McGraw-Hill Book Co., 1975.

Chapter 10

CONVERSE, JEAN M., *Conversations at Random: Survey Research, an Interviewer's Viewpoint.* New York: John Wiley & Sons, 1974.

FERBER, ROBERT, ed., *Handbook of Marketing Research.* New York: McGraw-Hill Book Co., 1974, Section II-B.

GARRETT, ANNETTE M., *Interviewing, Its Prin-*

*Note: The general works on sampling listed in the Selected Bibliography section in Chapter 7 offer additional discussions on sample size that are more useful for introductory reading.

ciples and Methods. New York: Family Service Association of America, 1972.

GORDEN, RAYMOND L., *Interviewing: Strategy, Techniques, and Tactics.* Homewood, Ill.: Dorsey Press, 1975.

Manual of Procedures for Hiring and Training Interviewers. Chicago: National Opinion Research Center, University of Chicago, 1967.

SMITH, JOHN M. F., *Interviewing in Market and Social Research.* London: Routledge and K. Paul, 1972.

SUDMAN, SEYMOUR, *Response Effect in Surveys.* Chicago: Aldine Publishing Co., 1974.

WEBER, DEAN and RICHARD C. BURT, *Who's Home When.* Washington: U.S. Bureau of the Census, 1973.

ed.). Englewood Cliffs, N.J.: Prentice-Hall, Inc., 1971.

HAYES, WILLIAM, *Statistics for Social Sciences* (2nd ed.). New York: Holt, Rinehart and Winston, 1973.

HUFF, DARRELL, *How to Lie with Statistics.* New York: W. W. Norton Company, 1954.

MASON, R. D., *Statistical Techniques in Business and Economics* (3rd ed.). Homewood, Illinois: Richard D. Irwin, Inc., 1974.

SIEGEL, SIDNEY, *Nonparametric Statistics for Behavioral Sciences.* New York: McGraw-Hill Book Company, 1956.

YAMANE, TARO, *Statistics, An Introductory Analysis.* New York: Harper and Row, 1964.

ZIESEL, HANS, *Say It with Figures* (5th ed. rev.). New York: Harper and Row, 1968.

Chapter 11

AWAD, ELIAS M., *Business Data Processing* (4th ed.). Englewood Cliffs, N.J.: Prentice-Hall, Inc. 1975.

AWAD, ELIAS M., *Introduction to Computers in Business.* Englewood Cliffs, N.J.: Prentice-Hall, Inc., 1977.

BOYES, RODNEY L., *Introduction to Electronic Computing and Management Approaches.* New York: John Wiley and Son, 1971.

FUORI, WILLIAM M., *Introduction to the Computer: The Tool of Business* (2nd ed.). Englewood Cliffs, N.J.: Prentice-Hall, Inc., 1977.

KATZAN, HARRY, *Computer System Organization and Programming.* Chicago: Scientific Research Associates, 1976.

NIE, NORMAN H., C. HADLEY HULL, JEAN G. JACKSON, KARIN STREINBRENNER, and DALE H. BENT, *Statistical Packages for the Social Sciences* (2nd ed.). New York: McGraw-Hill Book Co., 1975.

Chapter 12

CONOVER, W. J., *Practical Nonparametric Methods.* New York: John Wiley & Sons, 1971.

FREUND, JOHN E., *Mathematical Statistics* (2nd

Chapter 13

AAKER, D. A., ed., *Multivariate Analysis in Marketing: Theory and Application.* Belmont, California: Wadsworth Publishing Company, 1971.

ANDERSON, T. W., *Introduction to Multivariate Statistical Analysis.* New York: John Wiley & Sons, 1958.

CONOVER, W. J., *Practical Nonparametric Methods.* New York: John Wiley & Sons, 1971.

FERBER, ROBERT, *Handbook of Marketing Research.* New York: McGraw-Hill Book Company, 1974, Parts D and E.

GREEN, P. E. and F. J. CARMONE, *Multidimensional Scaling and Related Techniques in Marketing Analysis.* Allyn and Bacon, 1970.

GREEN, PAUL E. and DONALD S. TULL, *Research for Marketing Decisions* (3rd ed.). Englewood Cliffs, N.J.: Prentice-Hall, Inc., 1975.

GREEN, P. E., M. H. HALBERT, and P. J. ROBINSON, "Canonical Analysis: An Exposition and Illustrative Approach," *Journal of Marketing Research,* February 1966, pp. 32–39.

GUENTHER, WILLIAM C., *Analysis of Variance.* Englewood Cliffs, N.J.: Prentice-Hall, Inc., 1964.

HORST, PAUL, *Factor Analysis of Data Matrices.*

New York: Holt, Rinehart, and Winston, Inc., 1965.

JOHNSTON, J., *Econometric Methods* (2nd ed.). New York: McGraw-Hill Book Company, 1971.

KINNEAR, T. C. and J. R. TAYLOR, "Multivariate Methods in Marketing Research: A Further Attempt at Classification," *Journal of Marketing,* October 1971, pp. 56–59.

MASON, R. D., *Statistical Techniques in Business and Economics* (3rd ed.). Homewood, Illinois: Richard D. Irwin, 1974.

MORRISON, D. F., *Multivariate Statistical Methods.* New York: McGraw-Hill Book Company, 1967.

MORRISON, D., "On the Interpretation of Discriminant Analysis," *Journal of Marketing Research,* May 1969, pp. 156–63.

SHETH, J. N., "The Multivariate Revolution in Marketing Research," *Journal of Marketing,* January 1971, pp. 13–19.

SIEGEL, SIDNEY, *Nonparametric Statistics for the Behavioral Sciences.* New York: McGraw-Hill Book Company, 1956.

WILLIAMS, E. J., *Regressional Analysis.* New York: John Wiley & Sons, Inc., 1959.

Chapter 14

BRITT, S. H., "The Writing of Readable Research Reports," *Journal of Marketing Research,* May 1971, pp. 262–66.

BROWN, L., *Effective Business Report Writing* (3rd ed.). Englewood Cliffs, N.J: Prentice-Hall, Inc., 1973.

DAWE, J. and W. J. LORD, *Functional Business Communication* (2nd ed.). Englewood Cliffs, N.J: Prentice-Hall, Inc., 1974.

GALLAGHER, WILLIAM J., *Report Writing for Management.* Reading, Massachusetts: Addison-Wesley Publishing Company, 1969.

GRAVES, H. R. and L. S. S. HOFFMAN, *Report Writing* (4th ed.). Englewood Cliffs, N.J: Prentice-Hall, Inc., 1965.

HINSTREET, W. A. and W. M. BATY, *Business Communications.* Belmont, California: Wadsworth Publishing Company, 1969.

LESIKAR, RAYMOND V., *Report Writing for Business* (5th ed.). Homewood, Illinois: Richard D. Irwin, Inc., 1977.

MCBURNEY, JAMES H. and ERNEST J. WRAGE, *Guide to Good Speech* (3rd ed.). Englewood Cliffs, N.J: Prentice-Hall, Inc., 1965.

MARTILLA, JOHN A. and DAVIS W. CARVEY, "Four Subtle Sins in Marketing Research," *Journal of Marketing,* January 1975, pp. 8–15.

MINOR, ED, *Simplified Techniques for Preparing Visual Instructional Materials.* New York: McGraw-Hill Book Company, 1962.

ROBINSON, D. M., *Writing Reports for Management Decisions.* Columbus, Ohio: C. E. Merrill Publishing Company, 1969.

SPEAR, MARY E., *Practical Charting Techniques.* New York: McGraw-Hill Book Company, 1969.

TWEDT, D. W., "What is the Return on Investment in Marketing Research?" *Journal of Marketing,* January 1966, pp. 62–63.

Chapter 15

BOLT, GORDON J., *Market and Sales Forecasting.* New York: Halstead Press Division, 1972.

CANTOR, JEREMIAH, *Pragmatic Forecasting.* New York: American Management Association, 1971.

Editor & Publisher Market Guide. New York: Editor & Publisher, annual.

A Guide to Consumer Markets. New York: The Conference Board, 1970 and monthly supplements.

HUGHES, G. DAVID, *Demand Analysis for Marketing Decisions.* Homewood, Ill.: R. D. Irwin, Inc., 1973.

Measuring Markets: A Guide to the Use of Federal and State Statistical Data. Washington: Superintendant of Documents, U.S. Government Printing Office.

MURDICK, ROBERT G., *Sales Forecasting for Lower Costs and Higher Profits.* Englewood Cliffs, N.J.: Prentice-Hall, Inc., 1967.

PARKER, GEORGE G. C. and EDILBERTO L. SE-
GURA, "How to Get a Better Forecast," *Harvard Business Review*, March/April 1971, pp.
98–102.

PEARCE, COLIN, *Prediction Techniques for Marketing Planners*. New York: John Wiley &
Son, 1973.

SHOEMAKER, ROBERT and RICHARD STAELIN,
"The Effects of Sampling Variations on
Sales Forecasts for New Consumer Products," *Journal of Marketing Research*, May
1976, pp. 138–43.

Epilogue

DAY, GEORGE S., "The Threats to Marketing
Research," *Journal of Marketing Research*,
November 1975, pp. 462–67.

Name Index

Subject Index

513